The Revised Waite's Compendium of Natal Astrology

Born in Tunbridge Wells, Kent, at 1.50 a.m. on 2 April 1953, Alan Candlish was raised and educated in Dartford. He worked for some years in the telecommunications and electronics industries and has travelled widely. His life was radically altered in the early 1980s and led him to the intense study of Christianity, Astrology and AiKiDo, all of which he practises and teaches.

THE REVISED WAITE'S COMPENDIUM
OF NATAL ASTROLOGY

with Ephemeris for 1900–2010

and Universal Tables of Houses

Original edition by Herbert T. Waite

Revised by Colin Evans

Updated by Brian E. F. Gardener

Revised and re-presented by Alan Candlish

ARKANA

ARKANA

Published by the Penguin Group
Penguin Books Ltd, 27 Wrights Lane, London w8 5tz, England
Viking Penguin, a division of Penguin Books USA Inc.
375 Hudson Street, New York, New York 10014, USA
Penguin Books Australia Ltd, Ringwood, Victoria, Australia
Penguin Books Canada Ltd, 2801 John Street, Markham, Ontario, Canada l.3r 1b4
Penguin Books (NZ) Ltd, 182–190 Wairau Road, Auckland 10, New Zealand

Penguin Books Ltd, Registered Offices: Harmondsworth, Middlesex, England

First published 1917
Revised editions published 1953, 1967, 1971, 1981
This revised and re-presented edition published by Arkana 1990
1 3 5 7 9 10 8 6 4 2

Calculations for House Tables and Ephemeris Data provided by
Electric Ephemeris Astrological Software House, London, nw3
Typesetting of tables by Paul Sally of Informac, London
Ephemeris design by Alan Candlish, London
Symbols used in this book produced by Alan James, London

Printed in England by Clays Ltd, St Ives plc
Filmset in 10/12 pt Monophoto Ehrhardt

Contents

Contents

II. *Astrological Judgement of Planets*

III. *Aspects*

Contents

IV. *Character Delineations of the Signs of the Zodiac*

V. *The Twelve Houses of the Chart*

VIII. *Casting the Horoscope: the House Cusps*

IX. *Casting the Horoscope: Planets*

x. *The Judgement of the Horoscope*

xi. *Condensed Ephemeris*

xii. *Univeral Tables of Houses*

xiii. *Geographical and Time Data*

Contents

Preface

For over seventy years this book has been a starting point for many newcomers to astrology and has proved useful to experienced astrologers who wish to carry their 'tools' with them in a single volume. Advances in the science of astrology, which have been continuing for thousands of years and have been especially notable in this last century, have necessitated the revision of Waite's original text from time to time. For example, the introduction to planets (p. 24), written by Colin Evans in 1952, covered a subject that was not a generally accepted part of astrology thirty-five years earlier, when Herbert T. Waite originally published his book.

I apologize to those readers whose familiarity with past editions will be disrupted by the radical changes to the ephemeris, most notably the provision of tables for midnight instead of noon. However, all changes have been made with the beginner in mind, so that most of the calculations will be easier to work out now.

The accuracy of the ephemeris and tables of houses, achieved through the use of modern technology, represents the main improvement to this thoroughly revised edition, while the addition of the Koch house cusps to the tables of houses offers a wider choice of house systems. Because of the revised format of the ephemeris, *chapters* VII, VIII and IX have been largely rewritten.

Mundane astronomical details have been added, as astronomical knowledge of the planetary movements and recognition of the planets as they wander the celestial sphere is surely useful. Appendix IV gives insights into the quality of energies represented by Chiron, the 'new' comet whose discovery in 1977 caused excitement in various parts of the astrological community. Appendix V has been added to show the variety of specialist subjects one may branch out into, with recommended reading for those who have become familiar with chart erection and the language of astrology.

The geographical and time zone information (with place names updated) from the previous edition has been included, and efforts have been made to amend any errors. However, for countries not listed it is worth referring to the publications recommended on pp. 162–4.

British Summer Time data is given up to the moment of writing, but there is a possibility that it may alter in the future (see also p. 340).

The original preface by Waite is reproduced entirely as well as the relevant part of introductions by Colin Evans and Brian Gardener. On reading them one will no doubt notice the respect each author had for the previous author(s) and especially for Waite himself. I join them in that respect. Especially considering the fact that the technological facilities available to me were not available to previous authors and that virtually all their calculations were performed by hand, their task was phenomenal: one stands in awe of the sheer mental and physical effort required, which they must have performed as a labour of love.

My thanks to Al H. Morrison for providing information on Chiron and for his encouragement to me writing on the subject; to Melanie Reinhart for her assistance with Chiron, especially by zodiac signs; to Nicola Zussman, who assisted in the preparation of various parts of the book; and to all those who have assisted me with this task.

Every effort has been made to rid this edition of past errors as well as any new ones. I will be grateful to readers who point out any error that may have been overlooked.

Alan Candlish

From the Preface to the 1981 Edition

If you have read the introduction to this book written in 1952 by Colin Evans, you may understand how much regard he had for Herbert Waite's work in naming his essentially new book *The New Waite's Compendium of Natal Astrology*. For sixty-four years this book, originally conceived by Herbert Waite in his 1917 edition and rewritten in its present form by Colin Evans in 1952, has constantly withstood the test of time, and its increasing demand in these days of scientific advancement and computer technology by astrologers and students alike pays tribute to the author's excellent work.

. . .

Daylight-Saving Time tables once again presented a special problem, since sources of information are unreliable and scarce. Daylight-Saving Time from 1970 onwards has therefore been omitted,* as with so many countries now making almost annual changes both in the amount of adjustment and dates, any information prepared could only lead the student into confusion. It is better nowadays for the subject to check through friends and relatives for more reliable information. Information up to 1970, although brief, is included and for this I am indebted to Miss A. W. Elliott of the BBC and to those embassies who were able to help. The accuracy of this table nevertheless still remains suspect since it is inevitable that certain countries, in addition to those listed, observe time changes.

I would finally like to acknowledge the excellent work of Herbert

---

* British Summer Time has been reinstated in the present edition; see ephemeris, years 1970–90; and p. 340.

Waite and Colin Evans, whose contributions to astrology contained within these pages have been an inspiration to my own humble efforts.

Brian E. F. Gardener

From the Introduction to the 1953 Edition

The great value of Waite's idea and the excellence of the way he carried it out are sufficiently attested by the success and popularity of editions constantly reprinted without change over thirty years and the clamorous demand for a new edition now; although from 1917 to 1951 the book had rapidly been losing part of its practical utility by the mere fact that the condensed ephemeris was never carried beyond 1916. The publishers' intention of adding data for the subsequent years, in order to issue a more useful edition about 1948 or 1949, was frustrated because nobody could answer the anxious questionings of admirers of his work by ascertaining whether the author was still among us in this disordered post-war world, or, if so, get into communication with him.

. . .

With regard to the tables of houses, the maddening plan, commonly adopted (following Raphael's lead) in England, of giving the cusps at irregular broken intervals of minutes and seconds of sidereal time (for the sake of making the MC always an exact degree) and of giving tables for latitudes of important towns in broken degrees (odd minutes) of latitude has been abandoned. It has always led to the student having the alternatives of (*a*) calculating the correct interpolations for latitude and sidereal time between (for example) latitude 56°28′ and 57°9′, and between 1h 47m 49s and 1h 51m 38s, in order to find the Ascendant for latitude 56°53′ at sidereal time 1h 49m 15s, or (*b*) using the *nearest* latitude and time as a rough approximation. The former involves such tiresome arithmetic as finding $\frac{86}{229}$ of 0°37′, and $\frac{25}{41}$ of 0°26′. The latter involves such

5

errors, often, in the Ascendant, that it becomes worse than useless to attempt going closer than the nearest whole degree, if as close. The plan here adopted includes the selection of geographical latitudes of whole degrees only, except that an extra table is given for London (51°30′), and sidereal times at uniform regular intervals of twelve minutes (much less than the *average* interval used by Waite). This enormously simplifies the arithmetic needed for accurate interpolation: a doubly important matter in condensed tables.

An even more important criticism of the tables of houses as originally given, though one in which Herbert Waite simply did what everybody else was then doing, is that they perpetuated the deplorable error of encouraging the ordinary student to look on the 'publishers' system' of house division as if it were the one and only established, standard, universally recognized, or traditional system; or as if the house cusps given were simply records of natural or astronomical facts, as objective and non-controversial as the longitudes of the planets in an ephemeris. Today no good teacher of astrology in touch with the thought of the leading workers in this field would dream of letting even a beginner receive or retain such a fallacious impression.

The Ascendant is, indeed, a simple fact of mathematical astronomy about which there is no dispute. It is the longitude used for the cusp of the first house in all generally and widely known systems of house division employed from the earliest times, long before Christ, to the present day. The MC is similarly a simple and non-controversial fact of mathematical astronomy, and while the most ancient system of house division, still advocated and used today by a few, though not most, of the leading authorities, does not employ the MC as cusp of the tenth house, all other house systems in at all wide usage do, and always have. So, for houses 1 and 10 (and consequently for the opposite houses, 7 and 4) the usual published tables of houses may justifiably be looked on as 'standard'. When it comes, however, to the intermediate houses, 11, 12, 2, 3, and their 'opposite numbers' west of the meridian, there is no one system that has any right to be so regarded. At the very least, six entirely different systems, often giving quite different signs on these intermediate house cusps, are in current daily use for standard 'orthodox' astrology by leading astrologers of today in England and on the continent of Europe and in America. Four of these are much more ancient than, and one of them much newer than, the system of Placidus. And Placidus is the one most hotly attacked by almost all sound theoreticians on this feature of Western astrology. But it is the system which happened to be in vogue when the first Raphael, by no means a specialist authority on the subject, 'took it for granted' in compiling his tables of houses for some important cities, which became the basis of the complete tables published by the firm who acquired his copyrights; and these, filling an urgent need for published tables, to save the individual calculation of all house cusps, and making no mention that they represented one system in particular, arbitrarily selected, rather than others with better claim to be considered 'standard', led to the average student omitting any study of the house division question whatever and simply accepting the 'published tables of houses' as blindly as the ephemeris. Let those who, for what they deem sound reasons, still prefer the Placidean system by all means continue to use it; they may be right; but let it be for some better reason than that they do not know at all what system it is nor what other systems there are, but simply use 'the published tables of houses'! That is the view of all the best teachers today, and in fighting for it I have the support of the Federation of British Astrologers, and of the leading and most responsible officers in the Faculty of Astrological Studies and in the Astrological Lodge of the Theosophical Society (London).

I have therefore planned and compiled the tables of houses with a view to presenting side by side, with complete impartiality, the necessary cusps for erecting a horoscope by any of the following systems (named here in chronological order of their first known use), all in current use today for standard astrology: Equal Houses, Porphyry, Regiomontanus,* Campanus, Placidus, *and* Natural

---

* Regiomontanus himself (Johan Müller of Königsberg) is much later than Campanus but the *system* of the former is much the older, having been used centuries earlier by Ibn Ezra.

Graduation (my own system). I have also included a short chapter explaining, as simply as possible, the principles of these systems and their differences, without arguing for or against any one system.

The changes here outlined have meant that it has been impossible to use any of the pages compiled by Waite for either the ephemeris or the tables of houses. In computing these afresh, full use has been made of astronomical facts and mathematical results already computed by others, and ascertainable from their publications, which it would have been stupid, as well as heroically laborious, for an individual to attempt to calculate all over again quite independently, giving, if correctly done, precisely the same figures, with no evidence that he *had* done the work afresh! (Though I have *had* to do this for Regiomontanus, Campanus and Natural Graduation cusps.*)

. . .

Waite's delineations of the twelve character types represented by the twelve signs are so much loved and admired by some colleagues whose views I value that I have retained these. They are virtually all of his own work that I *have* retained, in what I hope that he, if, still on this plane, he comes across my new structure built on his foundation, or if, on some higher plane, he has awareness of it, will not find a too unworthy new fulfilment of his own original aims.

Colin Evans, 1952

---

* Involving almost 30,000 separate new computations.

Preface to the First Edition

As a student of astrology I always resented the fact that it was impossible to carry about with me ephemerides for sixty or seventy years, and tables of houses for most of the civilized world with which to erect the horoscopes of the sceptics I met and silence them then, there and for ever. And I felt this all the more, for as a civil engineer I am used to my trusty little pocket-book friends Molesworth and Hurst, which I always have with me, ready for any poser that may crop up in my profession.

I therefore set to work to remedy the evil and make my own astrological pocket friend and companion. It proved to be a somewhat formidable task, owing to the irregular motion of the planets; but by dint of labour and the exercise of a little ingenuity I succeeded in compiling a really useful condensed ephemeris and tables of houses sufficiently accurate for the purposes for which they were intended.

Having encountered many students who envied my possession, I decided to publish it to the astrological world; but in coming to this decision I realized that while the advanced student would be concerned only with the bare ephemeris and tables of houses, there would be many who would appreciate some explanations and instructions, and others who would make their first acquaintance with the science through this little book. I have sought, therefore, in the small space at my command to satisfy these three classes of readers. The simple rules given will enable those who have no ready access to the complete ephemeris for the year in question, and tables of houses for the place, to erect a horoscope correctly to within a very small fraction of a degree, in most cases not exceeding a minute or two of longitude.

9

Those who know anything of astrology will appreciate the usefulness of the book while realizing its limitations. I must, however, warn the beginner that although he will find herein sufficient to convince him of the truth of astrology, thus making the work of real interest and service to him, before he can hope to enter into the delights of this fascinating and useful science, wide study of the standard works and mathematical exactness are absolutely necessary. Patience, precision, well-developed reasoning powers and experience are essential if any real headway is to be made in this profound subject, and while this book is a useful auxiliary to experience and will tend to keep interest from flagging, without warning it might lead to slipshod methods and so defeat its aims, so far as the beginner is concerned. The complete ephemeris is a *sine qua non* for complete calculations, and the beginner will be well advised to bear this in mind if attempting the calculation of directions. The latter branch of astrology is not dealt with here, as it would not be in the interest of the beginner, and advanced students will know just how far they can use the condensed ephemeris for this purpose, when unable to procure a full ephemeris at the time.

Let none look upon astrology as a fatalistic creed, for so regarded it becomes a power of evil, slowly but surely robbing the student of all initiative and effort. In order to avoid the possibility of the exoteric side of the subject obtaining too great a hold on the mind, the esoteric meaning should be sought by linking the science to philosophy and religion. Astrology then becomes helpful and illuminating: its great and beautiful inner truths are then revealed, and the student realizes that astrology is nothing more nor less than Natural Religion. It gives the student firsthand proof that materialistic philosophies have no foundation in fact, and leaves him in no doubt that this world is not the illusion and the dream that idealistic philosophers would have us believe. Astrology is, in fact, the natural link between science and religion, showing that Spirit and Matter are two aspects, or manifestations, of the one universal All; that All is Law.

Every science is in its infancy, and even the great basic laws of gravitation and evolution, though demonstrable, have still to be explained as to cause, owing to the limitations of man in his present stage of evolution; but it is remarkable that material-minded people, who pride themselves on having succeeded in material matters by the application of science, should yet be blind to the fact that just as science is essential for right thought, action and progress in worldly affairs, so it must be essential for the understanding and development of the soul and the ascertainment of other matters on which they are content to speculate, but which also must be part of the law of the universe. This law, the several manifestations of the one universal Spirit, astrology, the mother of all science, seeks to explain. Like the other sciences, it is not perfect, yet, rightly understood, it guides man to an understanding of himself and warns him of the rocks ahead, just as the lighthouse warns the mariner of the hidden reef. But the mariner has to weather the gale and understand his work; so also must the student understand his science, and weather the tempest of the soul.

Herbert T. Waite

I
Essential Preliminaries

1. Astronomy, Pure and Applied. Pure astronomy is the
science that deals with the physical natures, positions, and movements of the celestial bodies. Applied astronomy, including naviga-
tion, astrology, and chronometry (the three arts from which the
study of pure astronomy later developed), makes practical use of
some of the facts studied by pure astronomy.

2. Astrology is thus an art based on a science. It uses the facts
revealed by astronomy as to the relative positions and apparent
movements of the Sun, Moon and planets (mainly) in the local sky
as indicators of influences affecting human consciousness and experience in life on Earth. It does not depend at all on the acceptance or
non-acceptance of any of the theories sometimes held about whether
such influences are actually caused by the planets, etc. with which
astrology associates them, or whether the skies simply furnish a
'clock' (as it were) to time the complex recurrences of cyclic developments in psychology and history, or whether the unity of the
universe as a self-consistent Divine Idea is what makes symbolic
analogies reliable means of prediction.

3. The Horoscope, in the sense in which the word is currently
used by people with a reputable position in astrology, is a complete
chart or diagram of the solar system in relation to a particular place
on Earth (such as the place of a person's birth) at a given moment of
time (such as the birth time), along with a full and reasoned
judgement of what is to be inferred from it as to the nature of, and
probable developments from, an event occurring at that place and
time; for example, a man's character and the general tendencies of
his life. The name horoscope may also be used for the chart or

diagram itself. It is wrong to use the word horoscope for a stock reading, or generalization, applied to everyone born with the Sun in a certain part of the zodiac without taking account of the other factors that make all the difference to an individual case, however good a purpose such readings may serve.

4. *To Cast a Horoscope,* or draw up a diagram or chart of the kind referred to above, it is necessary to know the place, date and time of birth. This includes knowing what system of time was used when that birth time was recorded (e.g. Central European Time, British Summer Time). This is one reason the *place* matters. Also, geographical latitude determines the parts of the heavens 'rising' and 'setting' at a given moment, and, thus, which parts of the star-pattern in the skies were on the eastern horizon, which overhead and so on. What in the eastern sky might denote the personality of the native, would at another place be in mid-sky, denoting the sort of public reputation he attains, and at another place would be in the west and indicate the kind of second person he gets paired with. All this will be briefly taught in the pages that follow.

5. *The Two Equinoxes* (vernal and autumnal) are the points in the heavens where, or the moments in the year when, the Sun is exactly over the Earth's own middle line, the Equator, in spring and autumn. It then shines equally on the northern and southern hemi-spheres of the Earth, and makes night the same length as day all over the world.

6. *The Two Solstices* are the points or times at which the Sun is midway between the two equinoxes, and therefore is farthest north or south from the Equator, and makes the longest night and shortest day, or the reverse, the inequality being greatest for places farthest from the Equator.

7. *The Ecliptic* is the circle among the 'fixed' stars marked out by the Sun's successive positions during the year as seen from the Earth.

8. *The Zodiac* is a belt of space round the celestial sphere having the ecliptic as its middle line, and thought of as, at least, 'wide' enough to include the paths or orbits of all planets and the Moon. It *may* be thought of as covering the whole celestial sphere,

with the ecliptic as its middle line, just as the Equator is the middle line of the Earth.

9. Quarters of the Zodiac. The zodiac begins at the spring equinox (vernal equinoctial point) where the ecliptic crosses the Equator from south to north. It is divided into four quarters at the equinoxes and solstices, each quarter showing one of the alternate processes of separation and convergence of the ecliptic and Equator. Each quarter is divided into three parts – a cardinal sign, which begins the process of separation or convergence; a fixed sign, which persists in the same process; and a mutable sign, which completes it in readiness to commence the opposite process in the next quarter. This divides the whole zodiac into twelve parts, the twelve signs.

10. Longitude on Earth (geographical longitude) is distance measured along or parallel to the Equator *on Earth*, starting from the longitude of Greenwich Observatory. The point on the Equator nearest to Greenwich is also the point on the Equator nearest to all places from the South Pole to the North Pole that have the same longitude as Greenwich, longitude 0°. Other places are so many degrees (up to 180°) east or west (from Greenwich) in longitude.

Longitude in the heavens (celestial or zodiacal longitude) is distance similarly measured along the ecliptic, starting at the beginning of the zodiac, and measured always in the same direction, up to 360°, the direction in which the Sun seems to move round the ecliptic, which may be called 'eastward'.

11. Right Ascension, or RA, is distance *in the heavens* measured along or parallel to the Equator (like longitude on Earth), but starting at the beginning of the zodiac. As the Earth rolls over on itself completely (axial rotation) in one day, this point of the celestial equator (and ecliptic) is carried round the *Earth*'s Equator from 0° geographical longitude to 180° west and then the rest of the way back to 0°.

12. Sidereal Time is measured by this apparent movement of the sky as a whole, caused by the Earth's axial rotation. As 360° of RA pass over a particular place in twenty-four sidereal hours (a sidereal day), one hour of sidereal time corresponds to 15° of RA; 1° of RA to four minutes of time.

13. True Solar Time. As the Sun moves round the entire 360° of the ecliptic in a year, it advances in the signs by (roughly) 1° per day. Noon is when the Sun is halfway between rising and setting. So when the ecliptic point in which the Sun was at noon yesterday is itself halfway between rising and setting today, it is not yet quite noon but will be when the *next* degree of the ecliptic gets there, which *now* contains the Sun. This makes a true solar day a little longer than a sidereal day, and a true solar hour a fraction longer than a sidereal hour. It also makes the sidereal time at noon about four minutes more every day – about two hours more each month.

14. Mean Time. The length of a true solar day or hour varies a little at different seasons of the year; a sundial shows true solar time. For practical convenience, our ordinary clocks show 'mean time', making a mean hour always the same length, the *average* length of a true solar hour. 'Mean noon' is the moment when it would be noon if the Sun really kept mean time instead of true solar time.

15. The Numbering of Hours of sidereal time starts from the moment when the beginning of the zodiac is midway between rising and setting. This is oh om os* (no hours, no minutes, no seconds) of ST (sidereal time) at the place concerned. The numbering of hours of mean time starts at mean midnight (twelve hours earlier than mean noon), when the Sun, if its speed were uniform so that it kept mean time, would be halfway from setting to rising again. This is oh om os of (local) mean time at the place concerned. So ST at mean noon is anything from oh to 24h, according to the day of the year.

16. Local, Standard and Greenwich Time; Zone Time. As the Sun, or any star or any point on the ecliptic, rises, sets and 'culminates' (reaches its midway point between rising and setting above the Earth, or between setting and rising below the Earth), owing to Earth's axial rotation (rolling over on itself), it is obvious

---

* In technical works the 'h', 'm', and 's' are written small and high up, like the 'degree' symbol. In this book the notation used here is preferred.

that when it is noon at one place, because the Sun is culminating, it will not yet be noon at a place farther west, but will be later than noon at a place farther east. This produces the difference in local mean time at different places.

The same is true if we are talking about a certain point of the ecliptic as rising or culminating, making a similar difference to local sidereal time according to the geographical longitude of the place. Fifteen degrees of longitude on Earth correspond to one hour of whichever kind of time (mean or sidereal) we are discussing. So when the local mean time at Philadelphia (75° W from Greenwich) is 13h 0m, or 1 p.m., the mean time at Greenwich will be 18h 0m, or 6 p.m. And when sidereal time at Philadelphia is 13h 0m, then sidereal time at Greenwich is 18h 0m.

'Standard Time' is the mean time used all over a large area, though not the real local time except for one part of that area. Thus all over England the Standard Time is Greenwich Mean Time (GMT), though the local time at Yarmouth (east coast) is nearly seven minutes more than the time at Greenwich. The modern idea is to adopt everywhere as standard time a 'zone time' that differs from GMT by an exact number of hours or half hours instead of by odd minutes and seconds.

Summer Time, or **Daylight-Saving Time,** is Standard Time (usually zone time) with an hour (sometimes two hours) added by law, to economize artificial lighting and heating by getting the working day started earlier.

17. The Planets swing round the Sun at various speeds, according to their distance from it. The Earth takes $365\frac{1}{4}$ days, which we call a year, to complete the orbit along which it travels right round the Sun. It is this orbital movement of the Earth, causing the Sun to be seen in different directions, that 'moves' the Sun from one part of the zodiac to another. The movement of planets other than Earth in the zodiac are the combined results of the Earth's own movement and the planets' movements in their respective orbits. The Moon swings round the Earth, and thus is carried round the Sun, the combination of the Moon's and the Earth's orbital movements causing the Moon's movement through the zodiac.

*18. **Direct and Retrograde Motion, Stations.*** The Sun's and Moon's changes of position in the zodiac are always direct, that is, forward, or eastward. But the relative positions of Earth and the other planets cause the planets' movements in the zodiac to be sometimes direct (forwards) and sometimes retrograde (backwards). When direct motion is just changing to retrograde, or the reverse, the planet is stationary, or in its station.

*19. **Latitude and Declination.*** Latitude *on Earth* (geographical latitude) is distance northward or southward from the Equator. Distance from a circle to any point on a sphere is measured from the nearest point on that circle along a line that is part of a circle perpendicular to the former one. All circles on a sphere perpendicular to one circle meet at two opposite points, called the poles, of that one. Thus lines perpendicular to the Equator, called meridians, pass through the poles of the Equator, which on Earth are the geographical North and South Poles. If a place has latitude 45°, this means that it is 45° (an eighth of a circle) distant from the nearest point on the Equator towards one of the poles – the North Pole, if the place has latitude 45° N – measured along *a* meridian (*the* meridian of the place).

Declination is distance from the Equator in the heavens, measured the same way. Thus if the declination of a star is the same as the latitude of my home, then the star is exactly over my home when it culminates. If not, the star passes over my meridian somewhere north or south of my home.

Latitude *in the heavens* (celestial latitude) means distance north or south from the ecliptic, measured similarly. Lines perpendicular to the ecliptic are ecliptic secondaries, and meet at the poles of the ecliptic, or ecliptic poles, which are about 23°27′ (roughly a sixteenth of a circle) away from the poles of the Equator (celestial poles in the heavens, or geographical poles on the Earth). This 23°27′ is the obliquity of the ecliptic, and the distance between ecliptic and Equator at the solstices, and maximum declination of the Sun. The orbits of the Moon and planets are tilted southwards and northwards through the plane (or level) of the ecliptic, so that the Moon or a planet is on the ecliptic (where it has 0° latitude) only twice in the time it takes to go round its orbit. The rest of the time it 'has latitude', meaning that it is some way north or south from the ecliptic.

20. Nodes are the points where a planet or the Moon crosses the ecliptic. The Moon's nodes move backwards through the zodiac at the rate of about 1° in 19 days, roughly. The Ascending Node is the one where the planet or Moon is crossing the ecliptic from south to north; the other, the Descending Node, is where the planet or Moon is crossing the ecliptic from north to south. These two nodes of the Moon are sometimes called the Dragon's Head and Tail (*Caput* and *Cauda Draconis*, in the traditional Latin).

21. The Fixed Stars are so called because the pattern they make, as seen from Earth, does not change (noticeably) in a short enough time to be observed by one generation of mankind. The 'wanderers' (original meaning of 'planets') are the Sun and Moon and the planets proper, which can easily be seen to be moving about in the star pattern, all on or near the ecliptic circle, owing to their orbital motions. Some astrologers use the fixed stars (though only the more prominent of those that are near the ecliptic) in horoscopes. But the main practice of astrology confines itself to Sun, Moon and planets, and to certain points in the heavens that take their significance from the orbits of these (such as the nodes). The Earth's daily axial rotation causes stars, as part of the entire sky pattern, to wheel round once a day, without altering their relative positions in that pattern. Those stars that are exactly on the Equator go round the circle of the Equator itself in the sidereal day; the others, round smaller circles parallel to the Equator.

22. Rising and Setting. If the star's declination added to the geographical latitude of a place on Earth makes more than 90°, the star does not rise or set; the whole circle round which it is carried in one sidereal day is either in the sky above that place or under the Earth. Otherwise the star rises and sets once a day. The same is true of any point on the ecliptic circle, and of any other point in the heavens. If we disregard the amount by which a planet or the Sun or Moon changes its place in the zodiac and in the star pattern during one day (a small amount, in any case), then the same is true for Sun,

Moon and planets. Their rising, passing over the sky, setting, passing under the Earth and rising again has nothing to do with the orbital movements that carry them from one sign of the zodiac to another, but only with the passage of sidereal time, which measures the Earth's axial rotation.

23. The Solar System consists mainly of the Sun, Moon and planets – all near enough together for light to take only a matter of minutes going from one to another. The 'fixed stars' are so unimaginably far away that the light from the nearest of them takes four years to reach us; from others, many hundreds of years.

24. Loose Use of Words. The word 'stars' is sometimes, in popular language, loosely applied to all the celestial bodies used in astrology, including Sun, Moon and planets, besides the fixed stars. The name 'planets', now restricted by astronomers to bodies that swing round the Sun, is still, for convenience, used by astrologers, in its original sense of 'wanderers', for the planets (other than Earth), *and* the Sun *and* the Moon.

25. The Horizon of a place is the circle round the sphere that divides it (as viewed from that place on Earth) into upper and lower hemispheres, separating 'above' from 'below'. All along one half of this circle are the points where different stars 'rise' (come up into the sky from below the Earth); that semicircle is the eastern horizon. The East Point is the middle point of the eastern horizon, where the Equator crosses it. Stars set on the western horizon, the other half of the same circle, whose mid-point is the West Point, where the Equator crosses it again. Stars 'culminate' above the Earth when they reach the upper (half of the) meridian, the midway line between east and west, and 'culminate' below when they cross the lower meridian (under the Earth).

26. The Zenith and Nadir are the points exactly over and under any given place on Earth, the middle points of the upper and lower hemispheres of the sky. They are therefore on the meridian. They are where it crosses the prime vertical, the line that connects east and west round the sphere exactly over and under our place on Earth and meets the Equator where they both cut the horizon, at the East and West Points. The North and South Points of the horizon are where the meridian cuts it. Verticals are lines perpendicular to the horizon, and meet at the Zenith and Nadir, the poles of the horizon circle. So 'the' meridian is both 'a' meridian (perpendicular to Equator) and a vertical (perpendicular to the horizon).

27. Ascendant and MC (Midheaven), and Their Opposite Points. The Ascendant and Descendant are the two opposite points where the ecliptic cuts the eastern and western horizons; the MC and IC (abbreviations of Latin phrases for 'midheaven' and 'deepest heaven') are where the ecliptic cuts the meridian above and below. The degree of the zodiac (as measured on the ecliptic) that is the Ascendant is different every moment for the same place, and different at the same moment for places with different geographical latitudes. MC and IC are the same for all places at the same sidereal time, but change according to the sidereal time, all round the zodiac, in a day. The Ascendant and Descendant, on the contrary, differ according to the geographical latitude of the place, as well as according to time.

28. Houses and Cusps. Houses are the twelve divisions of a chart representing different departments of life and consciousness. The cusp of each house is the chief longitude (degree of the zodiac) in that house. A planet near a cusp has more effect on affairs of that house than a planet anywhere else. Traditionally, in European astrology, the cusp is also the beginning of the house, though authorities who take this view still allow a planet a few degrees (about five) before a cusp to be reckoned as belonging to the house. Another view, adopted lately by users of some systems (see below) of house division, is that the same cusps are the 'centres' of the houses, half the house being before the cusp. Different methods of dividing the sky into houses are preferred by different authorities (see pp. 91– 100).

29. Angular Cusps, Quadrants, Kinds of Houses. 'Angular cusps', or 'angles', is the usual name for the four most important house cusps: the first and tenth, and the opposite ones, the seventh and fourth. These are the beginnings of the four quadrants of the chart. Most systems of house division use Ascendant and Descendant as cusps of first and seventh houses, and MC and

IC as cusps of tenth and fourth houses. All systems differ as to where the other (intermediate) cusps come. Some astrologers prefer one system and some another. The house after each angular house is the succedent house; that before each angular house is the cadent house. If we compare the twelve houses to the twelve signs, then angular, succedent and cadent houses may be compared to cardinal, fixed and mutable signs, respectively.

30. Elements and Polarities. The first four signs of the zodiac (all three signs of the first quarter and the cardinal sign of the next) represent the four traditional 'elements' of man's make-up and of the universe: Fire, Earth, Air, Water (in that order). The next four signs, the same elements in the same order. Similarly the last four signs. This causes each quarter of the zodiac to begin with a cardinal sign of a different element, in the order Fire, Water, Air, Earth (1st, 4th, 7th, 10th signs). Signs are alternately of the two opposing polarities, positive and negative, so that Fire and Air signs are positive, Water and Earth signs negative, with a Fire sign always opposite an Air sign, and Water always opposite Earth.

31. The Names and Symbols of the Planets, in their order outward from the Sun, with the shorthand symbol used by astrologers for each planet, are: ☿ MERCURY, ♀ VENUS, ⊕ EARTH, ♂ MARS, ♃ JUPITER, ♄ SATURN (all known to the ancients); and beyond these, ♅ URANUS, ♆ NEPTUNE, ♇ PLUTO.

32. Other Important Symbols are: ⊙ the SUN, ☽ the MOON, ☊ the ASCENDING NODE and ☋ the DESCENDING NODE (of the Moon, unless otherwise specified).

33. The Part of Fortune. The astronomical symbol ⊕ shown above for Earth is used in astrology for the 'Part of Fortune'. This is the point of the sky where the Moon would be if it were the same distance in front of or behind the Ascendant, in the zodiac, as it actually is in front of or behind the Sun. In a symbolic sense, though not quite accurately, it stands for the position of the Moon at sunrise.

34. The Names and Symbols of the Signs, their qualities and elements and polarities (+ positive and − negative), and the symbols used for them in astronomy and astrology are:

First Quarter: Spring		opposite		Third Quarter: Autumn
Cardinal ARIES (Fire) +	♈	,,	♎	(Air) + LIBRA Cardinal
March–April				*September–October*
Fixed TAURUS (Earth) −	♉	,,	♏	(Water) − SCORPIO Fixed
April–May				*October–November*
Mutable GEMINI (Air) +	♊	,,	♐	(Fire) + SAGITTARIUS Mutable
May–June				*November–December*

Second Quarter: Summer		,,		Fourth Quarter: Winter
Cardinal CANCER (Water) −	♋	,,	♑	(Earth) − CAPRICORN Cardinal
June–July				*December–January*
Fixed LEO (Fire) +	♌	,,	♒	(Air) + AQUARIUS Fixed
July–August				*January–February*
Mutable VIRGO (Earth) −	♍	,,	♓	(Water) − PISCES Mutable
August–September				*February–March*

The seasons and months named above are those in which the Sun is in each quarter or sign. It enters each sign *about* the 20th of each month. It is important to know which sign is opposite which.

35. The Zodiacal Constellations, Equinox Zodiac and Stellar Zodiac. A constellation is some fixed stars grouped by the eye into a fanciful picture. The traditional constellations round the ecliptic circle and roughly covering the width formerly attributed to the zodiac (which now is thought of as wider, since Pluto, discovered in 1931, goes farther north and south from the ecliptic than any planet known before) have the names that are given above as names of the signs. If we did not bother about the fact that the vernal equinoctial point is slowly moving backwards through the constellations, we might find it convenient to identify one sign of the zodiac with one group of stars that is seen in that sign, and to form that group of stars into a fanciful picture denoting the life-type that experience has shown to be associated with that sign of the zodiac, and then to name both sign and constellation by an allegorical name suggesting that life-type. After some centuries, however, the same sign, as defined by distance from the vernal equinoctial point, would cover a different, or partly different, group of stars. That is what has actually happened. Thus the signs no longer correspond to the constellation of the same names. A large school of Hindu astrologers and a very few European astrologers do, however, use a 'stellar' zodiac, in which the signs are made to coincide with what they believe to have been the same fixed-star positions with which they formerly coincided. So this stellar zodiac does not begin at the vernal equinox now, and its quarters and signs no longer have any special relation to the separation and convergence of ecliptic and Equator.

A table (based on computations published by Cyril Fagan, chief advocate of a stellar zodiac in Western astrology) is given after the ephemeris in this book ('The Stellar Zodiac') for those who wish to experiment by converting the zodiacal positions in the standard European equinox-zodiac into positions in the Hindu fixed-star zodiac.

II
Astrological Judgement of Planets

36. *'Good' and 'Bad' Planets.* All forces in the created universe
are in themselves good; all can be misused to make them bad.
However, one may be violent, another restrictive, and these present
difficulties to cope with. These, rightly coped with and used, may be
fruitful in great achievement. A third may be pleasant, harmonious,
easy, and seem to make any effort on our part unnecessary. This, if
we are content to drift, may make us idle and self-indulgent, with
fruitless lives. Superficially, the two former may be called 'bad' or
'unlucky', and the latter 'good' or 'lucky'. There is no fatalism in
astrology. With the very same winds, two sailing ships can be steered
from the same port to very different destinations if the captain
knows the winds and uses them with skill and with a clear idea of the
course he wishes to take. It is the same with the influences shown in
a horoscope. The so-called 'good' ones will prove really good only if
wise use is made of the opportunities they present. The so-called
'bad' ones, disastrous if we ignore them, may be the very means of
producing the greatest good if we recognize their nature and deal
with them accordingly. We are not fated to good or evil; at most,
'fated' to have certain factors to deal with, from which we can make
either good or evil; but we need to know what those factors are, and
this, to a large extent, a horoscope can show us. Mars denotes
aggressive virility and force; Neptune, the vision and imagination
that are not bound to the material world; the combination may
produce either a Crusader-Saint, with deeds of martial heroism and
experience of mystical spiritual vision, or a murderous gangster drug
addict, who escapes from reality in the fantasies of the opium dream
and returns to shoot up bank managers. Though, for brevity and

concreteness, phrases are used in what follows that might suggest good or evil fortune or character, as if fatalistically shown by the skies, yet this paragraph must always be borne in mind.

37. Benefics and Malefics. Traditionally, Venus and Jupiter are the two benefics, the 'Lesser Fortune' and the 'Greater Fortune', fortunate or 'lucky' planets; Mars and Saturn are the two malefics, the 'Lesser' and 'Greater Infortune', 'evil' or 'unlucky'; Sun, Moon and Mercury are 'variable', becoming 'good' or 'bad' according to their positions and the other planets that are combined in any way with them. Uranus, Neptune, Pluto, all of relatively recent discovery, have naturally no 'traditional' character, but each when newly known tended to be regarded as 'bad'; which by no means now describes their more fully studied effects. (Comparably, electricity, before understood at all, simply connoted the deadly thunderbolt; now it is known as a source of energy that provides heat and light, and powers a multitude of machines.)

38. The Astronomical and Astrological Significance of Each Body. *Astronomy* is the child of the oldest science in the world – astrology: it is concerned with the distribution, motions and characteristics of the heavenly bodies, the objective manifestations of the laws governing the physical universe.

Astrology is concerned with the subjective manifestations of the same physical and metaphysical laws and, chiefly, the determination of their influence over the growth of the soul of the individual. The resultant experiences, both physical and metaphysical, are dependent on the use or abuse of the divine principles: since man is a part of the whole and that there can be but One God, One Law, One Life, all that there is in life must be a manifestation of the One Universal Spirit. The main use of astrology is as a *tool for self-development* in order to enable man to know himself and thus recognize his weaknesses of body and character in order to make the most of the strength both within and beyond him. Astrology is the soul of astronomy.

NB. The solar period is the time taken for a given planet to orbit the Sun. As we are concerned with geocentric astrology, these periods are not so regular, as the planets appear sometimes to go backwards or be 'retrograde'.

SUN ☉: The source of all light, warmth and thus life in our solar system. It consists of a globe of gas with a density 1.4 times that of water, 1.4 million km in diameter,* a solar day that varies from 26 days at its equator to 37 days at its poles, burning at a temperature of 5,800°C on the surface. It is over 1.3 million times larger than Earth, by volume, and has its own orbit around the galactic centre lasting 250 million years.

For thousands of years astrologers have regarded the Sun as the giver of all life, permeating all things visible and invisible, and moulding by law our bodies and characters, just as by law it moulded the Earth on which we live. It is the great central power station through which the primal energy of the limitless universe is transmitted to us.

MERCURY ☿: The closest known planet to the Sun orbits it every 88.0 days at a velocity of 47.9 km/s, maintaining a mean distance of 57.9 million km from it. It is 4,880 km in diameter and rotates on its own axis every 58.7 days. Mercury is 'the winged messenger of the Gods', ruling communication, logic, thinking and memory.

VENUS ♀: Our closest planetary neighbour. It orbits the Sun at a mean distance of 108.2 km travelling at 35.0 km/s in a period of 224.7 days and is 12,100 km in diameter. Venus rotates on its own axis every 243 days. Astrologically ruling feelings and intuition, Venus is known as the planet of harmony, love and unity.

EARTH ⊕: The third planet from the Sun, at a mean distance of 149.6 million km, travels at a mean velocity of 30.0 km/s and is 12,756 km in diameter. It rotates on its own axis in just under 24 hours and orbits the Sun in 365.25 days. In geocentric astrology the Earth is considered the focal point, not because anyone believes that the stars and the Sun revolve around it, but simply because we live here. The zodiac used in geocentric astrology begins at 0° of Aries, which is determined by the vernal equinox. It has not a vast amount to do with the stellar zodiac used in the East other than the fact that they coincide with each other at some point once every 25,800 years or so. This is due to the precession of the equinox, which is caused by the tilt in the Earth's axis. In geocentric astrology this is explained

---

* All figures rounded to one decimal place.

through the 2,000-year (approximately) ages of the signs of the zodiac. We now seem to be on the threshold of the age of Aquarius, leaving the age of Pisces.

MOON, or Luna ☽): The satellite of Earth. It has a diameter of 3,476 km and orbits Earth at a mean distance of 384,402 km. Keeping the same face towards Earth constantly, it has a sidereal month of 27.3 solar days and a synodic month of 29.5 solar days. It travels at a velocity of 30 km/s.

The Moon is known to influence the waters of Earth and for thousands of years has been used to indicate favourable times for sowing and reaping crops.

Waite himself acknowledges that

> while holding the position of district engineer on an important railway in Brazil, administered by an English company, [he] made his first acquaintance with astrological thought through the company's contract with the suppliers of wood sleepers for the railway. The engineers, having proved by experience that their native inspectors were right in their statement that lunar conditions, affecting the rise and fall of sap in the trees, were largely responsible for the splitting, warping and short 'life' of sleepers, the contracts included lunar stipulations, based on astrological law, resulting in great saving to the company in addition to enhancing the security of the permanent way.

The Moon rules the emotions, instincts and subconscious of the individual, having much to do with imagination. Subjectively the Moon reflects the soul of the individual, as, objectively, the Moon has no light of its own, but reflects the light of the Sun.

MARS ♂: The fourth planet from the Sun, at a mean distance of 227.9 million km, and the first beyond Earth. It is 6,790 km in diameter with a solar period of 687.0 days at a mean velocity of 24.1 km/s. It rotates on its own axis in 24 hours, 37 minutes and 22.6 seconds.

Astrologically, Mars has been known as the 'Energizer', having much to do with dynamism, which, when properly expressed, produces courage, strength and endurance. A surgeon operating on the brain with a scalpel is one illustration of this energy; someone splintering your front door with an axe is expressing the same energy.

ASTEROIDS: Between Mars and Jupiter is the asteroid belt, containing a thousand or so asteroids. Some astrologers take them into account when interpreting charts. Perhaps the most popular asteroids in Britain are Vesta, Juno, Pallas and Ceres, while America, Urania, Apollo and Atlantis may be more popular in the US. They are very small and we shall not be looking at them astrologically.

JUPITER ♃: With the exception of the Sun, Jupiter is by far the largest planet known to man, having a diameter of 143,200 km. It is 778.3 million km from the Sun, has a mean orbital velocity of 13.1 km/s and a solar period of 11.9 years. It turns on its own axis in just under 10 hours.

Astrologically, Jupiter rules mercy, morality and justice. Known as the Greater Benefic, its abuses range from hypocrisy (especially religious) to tyranny and excesses of many sorts.

SATURN ♄: The second largest planet, Saturn is 120,000 km in diameter. It is 1,427 million km from the Sun, and orbits it at 9.6 km/s in 29.5 years. It turns on its own axis in approximately 10 hours and 14 minutes at its equator, and has a system of rings around it.

Astrologically, it has been known as the Greater Malefic (a term I abhor). Limitation, restriction, foundation and consolidation are its domain as well as time. Waite suggests,

> Saturn is the sternest and hardest teacher in the great school of the soul; but if the scholar be willing to learn, then will patience, faithfulness, contemplation, chastity, prudence, stability and tenacity become part of him.

CHIRON ⚷: See Appendix IV.

URANUS ♅: About half the size of Saturn but twice as far from the Sun, Uranus is 51,800 km in diameter and 2,869.6 million km from the Sun. It has a solar period of 84.0 years, travelling at 6.8 km/s. It rotates on its own axis in 10 hours and 49 minutes.

Astrologically, the planet of genius and inventiveness, Uranus has much to do with sudden change, and recent research has shown that it is vitally connected with flashes of inspiration. Having a definite influence over the nerves and magnetic conditions of the body, it is considered by some astrologers to govern the etheric body and one's ability to see it. Uranus is sometimes called 'the Magician'.

NEPTUNE ♆: The second farthest planet from the Sun, except when Pluto's eccentric orbit brings it within Neptune's orbit (see Pluto). It is 49,500 km in diameter, 4,496.6 million km from the Sun, and at a velocity of 5.4 km/s, has a solar period of 164.8 years. It rotates on its axis in 15 hours and 48 minutes.

Astrologically, 'the Dreamer' has much to do with escapism and mysticism. Governing the spiritual life, i.e. the sage, prophet, seer, which, if neglected, may lead to drug or alcohol abuse. A dreamy nature, strange experiences and states of mind, and prophecy are Neptunian products.

PLUTO ♇: Normally the most distant planet known to man, at a mean distance of 5,900 million km, Pluto has an eccentric orbit, which brought it within Neptune's orbit in 1989. Still very little is known about it physically. It may be about 3,000 km in diameter (smaller than our own Moon) or as much as 6,000 km, with a velocity of 4.7 km/s and a solar period of 247.7 years.

Astrologically, the planet of transformation, ruling both the 'underworld' and 'rebirth' in one's lifetime. Pluto transits are very powerful, raising very deep issues: sexuality, violent crime, power, paranoia and even the drainage system of one's dwelling. All these issues, and more, must be faced in order to be reborn. One cannot see, let alone live in, the light without at least acknowledging one's own darkness.

FIXED STARS: These are the stars of the constellations and are incredibly far away. Some astrologers take them into account. However, this is a rather advanced subject to be left at this point.

39. The Moon's Ascending Node (Dragon's Head) and the opposite point (Descending Node, Dragon's Tail) are by some authorities ignored; by others the former is considered a fortunate or helpful, and the latter an unfortunate or hindering, influence. Here are two examples: the Ascending Node is that which draws one forward, and the Descending Node, that which holds one back; the Ascending Node is the point of honour/honesty, and the Descending Node, dishonour/dishonesty (with oneself and hence with others). Note that there are two North Nodes, called the Mean and the True Nodes; the former is more commonly used and is the one given in the ephemeris.

40. Use of the Part of Fortune. Not used by all astrologers, but, when used, considered an indication of worldly good fortune in connection with the matters denoted by the part of the chart where it occurs.

41. The Sun as Significator denotes people in authority and important positions, the husband in a female horoscope, the father; and is a symbol of vitality, prosperity, when well-placed and not badly aspected. Esoterically, it is the physical symbol (for Earth-dwellers) of the Creative Spirit, Centre and Source of Life, Deity.

42. The Moon as Significator denotes the wife in a male horoscope, the masses or 'common people', the mother.

43. Rulership, Dignities, Debilities. Each sign of the zodiac is said to have a certain planet as its 'ruler'. This means two things: (1) the planet is 'dignified' when in that sign; that is, its influence is made stronger and more harmonious and beneficial; (2) the planet, even when in any other sign, 'represents' its own rulership sign, as it were. If a certain sign is on the cusp of the house dealing with possessions and income, and the ruling planet of that sign is in some other house and some other sign, then the matters denoted by that other house, and the characteristics indicated by that other sign, will affect the finances, just as will the characteristics denoted by the sign on the house of possessions and the influence denoted by the ruling planet of this sign. The opposite sign to a planet's rulership is the planet's 'detriment', where it is debilitated – acts undesirably, distortedly, or weakly.

44. Exaltations. Each planet also has one sign where it is traditionally 'exalted' – where its good influence is markedly emphasized. (Traditionally, it is exalted in a *particular degree* of that sign, though the exaltation degrees are now usually ignored.) The opposite sign is its 'fall', where its influence is made weak or injurious.

45. 'Strong by Sign'. Apart from, and less important than, the rulership, exaltation, detriment and fall, there are certain signs that have enough affinity with a particular planet for it to be strengthened when in them.

46. The 'New' Planets' Dignities. The three 'new' planets (♅, ♆, ♇) have no traditional rulership, but may be considered joint rulers of certain signs without deposing the traditional rulers.

47. Two Rulership Series. The Sun rules only one sign, Leo; the Moon only one, Cancer. Planets in order outward from the Sun (☿ ♀ ♂ ♃ ♄) rule signs in order from the next after Leo, forward in the zodiac (♍ ♎ ♏ ♐ ♑); and in order *towards* the Sun the remaining signs (so that ♄ ♃ ♂ ♀ ☿ rule ♒ ♓ ♈ ♉ ♊). Uranus and Neptune are accepted as joint rulers of Aquarius and Pisces respectively, and Pluto of Scorpio.

48. Table of Rulership.

Sign	Ruler	Exaltation	Strong	Detriment	Fall
♈	♂	☉	♃	♀	♄
♉	♀	☽	♃ ♄	♂ ♆	♅
♊	☿	☊	♄	♃ ⚷?	☋
♋	☽	♃	☿ ♆	♄	♂
♌	☉	♆	♂ ⚷?	♄ ♅	♆
♍	☿	☿ ⚷?	♄	♃ ♆	♀
♎	♀	♄	♃	♂	☉
♏	♂ ♇	♅	☉ ⚷?	♀	☽
♐	♃ ⚷?	☋	♀ ☉	☿	☊
♑	♄	♂	☿	☽	♃
♒	♄ ♅	♆	♀	☉	♆
♓	♃ ♆	♀	☽	☿	☿ ⚷?

NB: *A question mark in the table indicates a tentative suggestion proposed by Melanie Reinhart (see Appendix IV).*

31

49. Personal Characteristics Shown by the Planets. As every planet is in everybody's horoscope (and everybody has in his character the germs of all qualities), the following must be interpreted as meaning that the characteristics are likely to be *marked* in the case of a person in whose chart the planet mentioned is specially *prominent* by position – especially if it is rising at birth, or is the ruling planet (or joint ruler) of the sign that is on the ascendant, or is in strong aspect to the Sun or to the ruling planet of the Ascendant, or to the Moon:

SUN: pride, generosity, egoism, honour, loyalty, ardour, vitality, consciousness.

MOON: sensitivity, sentiment, maternal instinct, femininity, changeableness, subconscious, imagination, emotion.

MERCURY: quickness, sharpness, cleverness or intelligence, ready wit, flow of words, communication.

VENUS: beauty, grace, charm, artistic tastes, affection, sociability, intuition.

MARS: virility, energy, courage, initiative, impulsiveness, passion, aggression, dynamism.

JUPITER: optimism, cheer, generosity, joviality, ability at sports, strength, nobility, ceremoniousness, expansion.

SATURN: caution, taciturnity, pessimism, self-restraint, profundity, steadfastness, consolidation.

URANUS: originality, inspiration, eccentricity, individualism, 'the Magician', involving sudden or drastic change.

NEPTUNE: mysticism, vagueness, fantasy, imagination, clairvoyance, elusiveness, prophecy.

PLUTO: transformation, regeneration, the manifesting of the subconscious by way of sudden change like 'death' and 'rebirth'. Drastic alterations to predetermined ideas and ethics.

CHIRON: see Appendix IV.

III
Aspects

50. Planets in Combination. Influences denoted by different planets interact and combine, either harmoniously (beneficially) or discordantly (injuriously) – but compare Section 36 – according to their distance apart in the zodiac, which is the angle between the two lines from two planets to Earth, and therefore the manner in which the two 'rays of influence' impinge on one another when reaching us. Harmonious are the aspects equal to a zodiacal distance of 120°, or four whole signs, as they share the same element, as when two planets are in the same part of two signs of the same element (Fire, Earth, Air, Water); and half or a quarter of that angle (60°, 30°), as when two planets are two signs or one sign, apart respectively.

Discordant, difficult, or 'bad' are the aspects based on halving and quartering the zodiac; 90° (three signs) apart (same 'quality', cardinal, fixed or mutable), and opposition (six signs apart, opposite one another, 180° apart, in the same parts of opposite signs), and half of the former (45°, one and half signs apart), and one and a half times the 'square' or 90° aspect (135°, four and a half signs, apart). Traditionally regarded as 'bad' or discordant, not always so regarded by the moderns, and perhaps too difficult to interpret correctly for the beginner to be advised to notice it at all, is the aspect called 'Inconjunct', or 'Quincunx', five signs apart (150°). Of these, the aspects of two, three, four, six, whole signs are strong and important, the others relatively weak and unimportant.

The 'conjunction' is when two planets are together in the zodiac (0° apart). It is 'good' between two good planets or a neutral and a good planet; 'bad' between two bad ones or a neutral and a bad one, and mixed in its effects between a good planet and a bad one. But

33

note again that 'good' and 'bad' are really wrong descriptions (see Section 36).

51. Table of Aspects, with the shorthand symbol used for each aspect.

Name of aspect	Symbol used	Signs apart	Degrees apart	Strength of aspect	Nature of aspect
CONJUNCTION	☌	0	0	Strong	Variable
SEXTILE	✶	2	60	Strong	Harmonious
SQUARE	☐	3	90	Strong	Discordant
TRINE	△	4	120	Strong	Harmonious
OPPOSITION	☍	6	180	Strong	Discordant
SEMI-SEXTILE	⊻	1	30	Weak	Harmonious
SEMI-SQUARE	∠	$1\frac{1}{2}$	45	Weak	Discordant
SESQUI-SQUARE	⟁	$4\frac{1}{2}$	135	Weak	Discordant
INCONJUNCT	⚻	5	150	Weak	Discordant?

'New' aspects, introduced by Kepler

Name of aspect	Symbol used	Signs apart	Degrees apart	Strength of aspect	Nature of aspect
QUINTILE	Q	$2\frac{2}{5}$	72	Weak	Harmonious
SEMI-QUINTILE	⊥	$1\frac{1}{5}$	36	Very Weak	Harmonious
BIQUINTILE	⊥	$4\frac{4}{5}$	144	Very Weak	Harmonious

52. Orbs of Aspects. An aspect need not be exact; if one planet is within a certain number of degrees of being in a certain aspect to another, that aspect is considered to exist between them. The margin of inexactitude allowed is called the 'orb' of the aspect. How many degrees of orb to allow is a vexed question; as a rough and ready guide for the beginner the following orbs may be used:

Strong Aspects: about 8° (up to 10° if Sun or Moon is involved).

Weak Aspects: about 3° at most.

Very Weak Aspects: 1° or 2°.

Less in all cases if the inexactitude puts planets in signs in which they would not be if the aspect were exact. For instance, if one planet is in Aries and the other in Gemini, the aspect would be sextile if exact: but if the first is in 3° Aries and the other in 27° Taurus, this is only 6° short of the exact aspect that would exist if the second planet were in 3° Gemini; but is probably a much weaker aspect than if there were only 6° orb between one in 10° Aries and the other in 4° or 16° Gemini, that is, both in the signs that make sextile aspect to one another.

53. Mutual Reception. Two planets are in mutual reception (equivalent to a harmonious aspect, fairly strong) if each is in the other's rulership sign, or if each is in the other's exaltation sign; ♃ ♉, ♀ ♐.

54. Tendencies Indicated by Harmonious Aspects (for Conjunctions, see Section 56).

SUN OR MOON WITH A PLANET OR ONE ANOTHER

⊙ and ☿: strong in intellect, subject to signs they are in, in literary or mathematical pursuits, strong in memory with an ability for instant recall.

⊙ and ♀: affectionate, lucky, pleasure-loving, artistic.

⊙ and ♂: vitality, energy, health, gift of command, courage, initiative.

⊙ and ♃: moral, honour, charity, generosity, sympathy, ceremonious, cheery.

⊙ and ♄: prudence, honesty, faithfulness, patience, endurance, seriousness.

⊙ and ♅: genius, originality, individualism, independence of outlook and character, occultism.

⊙ and ♆: spiritual, musical, sensuous, lucky, charming, intuitive.

⊙ and ♇: dynamic, periodic transformation, perceptive.

⊙ and ☽: subconscious instincts in harmony with conscious reason; success, ambition, public recognition, good luck.

☽ and any planet: similar to ☉ and same planet, but more affecting feelings and subconscious inclinations than fundamental character and conscious or deliberate choice.

MERCURY WITH ANOTHER PLANET

☿ and ♀: artistic, poetical, musical, kind, happy.

☿ and ♂: witty, sarcastic, clever at technical things, engineering, etc.

☿ and ♃: just, philosophical, religious, potential for fame.

☿ and ♄: serious-minded, scientific, profound in study, intellectual.

☿ and ♅: inventive genius, fine original mind, aptitude for occult studies.

☿ and ♆: poetical, idealistic, gifted for imaginative literature, fiction.

☿ and ♇: penetrating observation, very strong communication, charismatic speakers and/or very good writers.

VENUS WITH ANOTHER PLANET

♀ and ♂: strong animal nature, 'great lovers', free with money, good marriage.

♀ and ♃: very fortunate, fine lovable nature, happy in marriage.

♀ and ♄: virtue, steadfast affections, fidelity, serene patience.

♀ and ♅: sudden gains and journeys, peculiar but happy love-episodes, original if eccentric artistic genius.

♀ and ♆: refined, dreamers, imaginatively artistic, idealistic love; sensuous, fascinating.

♀ and ♇: potential for highly transformative partnerships/friendships.

MARS WITH ANOTHER PLANET

♂ and ♃: generous, just, enthusiastic, free with money, great fighters.

♂ and ♄: brave endurance, persistent energy, able to command, vigorous old age.

♂ and ♅: great energy, often unpredictable in action, constructive genius or invention, inspired fighters.

♂ and ♆: magnetic, pushing, confident, fascinating, changeable.

♂ and ♇: courageous, resilient, powerful dynamism.

JUPITER WITH ANOTHER PLANET

♃ and ♄: religious, profoundly philosophical, charitable, financially fortunate, apt for political success.

♃ and ♅: sudden gains, originality, unconventionality, independent outlook in religion and philosophy, probably with occult leanings.

♃ and ♆: psychic, perhaps mediumistic, spiritual, sensuous, emotional, lucky.

♃ and ♇: enthusiastic, philosophical/religious guidance, crusading, ability to cut through unnecessary debris; spiritual/religious experience possibly leading to conversion.

SATURN WITH ANOTHER PLANET

♄ and ♅: occult gifts and interests, magnetic, aptitude for revolutionary politics.

♄ and ♆: psychic gifts, if utilized, mystical philosophy, self-control, mental concentration, gift for meditation (spiritual).

♄ and ♇: high-minded, austere, honest, reliable, determined, resilient in the face of disasters, survivors, requirement for ruthless self-examination.

URANUS, NEPTUNE AND PLUTO

♅ and ♆: exalted nature, psychic and occult, originality especially in matters of spiritual vision or imaginative fantasy.

♅ and ♇: requirement to overthrow outmoded systems, inbuilt sense of the new order.

Ψ and ♀: powerful visionary, idealist; leaders/innovators of spiritual systems; profound healing potential, fascinating individuals.

55. *Tendencies Suggested by Discordant Aspects* (for Conjunctions, see Section 56).

SUN OR MOON WITH A PLANET OR ONE ANOTHER

☽ and ☿: an uncharitable tongue, gossip. (NB: ☉ and ☿ cannot make a discordant aspect.)

☉ and ♀: love difficulties, social restrictions.

☉ and ♂: hastiness, rashness, bad-temper, accidents, operations, fevers, sensuality or lust, violence, combativeness.

☉ and ♃: extravagance, religious differences, litigation, disappointments, exaggeration, boasting.

☉ and ♄: selfish, despondent, taciturn, thwarted, oppressed with responsibilities, sluggish.

☉ and ♅: sudden disasters, eccentricity, love-sorrows, estrangements, nerve troubles.

☉ and Ψ: treachery from others, disappointments, sensuality, impracticability.

☉ and ♀: internal/external power struggles; transformation is demanded and often resisted.

☉ and ☽: psychological tensions and conflict, reason at variance with desire or instinct with will.

☽ and any planet: similar to ☉ and same planet, but affecting subconscious inclinations and instinctive reactions, and feelings, rather than conscious or deliberate choice or experience. Especially difficult with ♀ – repressed/difficult emotions may lead to depression.

MERCURY AN ANOTHER PLANET

☿ and ♀: conceited, perhaps especially with musical interests, bad taste in art.

☿ and ♂: impulsive, harsh, turbulent, self-assertive, neurotic, too subtle, sarcastic and ironic, sharp and clever.

☿ and ♃: hypocrisy, scepticism, bad judgement, litigation, grandiose lying.

☿ and ♄: worry, enmity, over-seriousness, pessimistic philosophy, political trickery.

☿ and ♅: neurotic, erratic, eccentric if clever, a rebel in intellectual matters, abrupt speech, curt and brusque.

☿ and ♆: diffuse and scattered mind and thoughts, nebulous and confused, sensuous, especially in fantasies, dishonesty or untruthfulness or theft.

☿ and ♇: demanding, communication induces stress, manipulative and point labouring.

VENUS AND ANOTHER PLANET

♀ and ♂: loose morals, oversexed, intemperate, separations.

♀ and ♃: extravagance, treachery from others, religious strife.

♀ and ♄: obstacles, frustration or sorrows, in love affairs; losses, sensuality.

♀ and ♅: dangerous or unconventional and illicit love episodes, losses, estrangements in emotional relationships, or bereavements.

♀ and ♆: sensuality, drink, drugs, deceiving or being deceived in love, the 'eternal triangle'.

♀ and ♇: requirement for the individual to change within a relationship; individual likely to want partner or relationship to change instead; power struggle within relationships with time for change; crisis partnerships.

MARS AND ANOTHER PLANET

♂ and ♃: extravagance, litigation, losses.

♂ and ♄: danger through recklessness, unwisely enthusiastic, unlucky accidents, losses, violent, sarcastic, churlish.

♂ and ♅: nerve troubles, love dangers, rash eccentric impulses, sudden accidents, partings, and bereavements, brusque manners.

♂ and Ψ: sensuality, intemperance, drugs, immorality, unhealthy imagination.

♂ and ♇: ego struggles, tendency to suppress emotions (especially anger); eruptive, can lead to physical difficulties, illness.

JUPITER AND ANOTHER PLANET

♃ and ♄: melancholy, misfortune, losses, bigotry.

♃ and ♅: sudden losses and accidents, litigation, eccentric religious views.

♃ and Ψ: superstition, credulity, sensuality, pride, intemperance.

♃ and ♇: overbearing, dictatorial; difficulties with belief systems, potential hypocrites/bigots.

SATURN AND ANOTHER PLANET

♄ and ♅: eccentricity in tastes and opinions and beliefs, unsociable individualism.

♄ and Ψ: selfish, temperamentally moody, pessimistically imaginative, self-deception, cowardice.

♄ and ♇: narrow-minded, stern/harsh, cynical (see Section 54 for resolution).

URANUS, NEPTUNE AND PLUTO

♅ and Ψ: sudden, unpredictable and eccentric, moods and fancies.

♅ and ♇: disruptive, rebellious, reckless, deep discontent; requirement to cast out useless habit/response patterns.

Ψ and ♇: unreliable, mesmerizing, false prophets, deceived/deceiving gurus; power abuse, possibly grey to black magic leanings; honesty and discrimination required in relation to spiritual values.

56. How to Interpret a Conjunction ☉ conjunct with ☽: this 'new moon' position is favourable to beginnings, new enterprises, etc.

⊙ conjunct with ♀, ♃: harmonious (see Section 54).

⊙ conjunct with ♂, ♄: discordant (see Section 55).

⊙ conjunct with ♅, ♆: mixture of the good and bad effects of discordant and harmonious aspects (see Sections 54 and 55).

☽ in conjunction with any planet: see ⊙ in conjunction with same planet, above, but affecting feelings more than fundamental character.

☿ in conjunctions: see ⊙ in same conjunctions; but specially affecting communications (speech, writing) and brainwork.

♀ or ♃ in conjunction with ♂ or ♄: mixture of the harmonious and discordant aspects (see Sections 54 and 55).

♀ or ♃ in conjunction with ♅ or ♆: mixture of harmonious and discordant aspects, the former predominating (see Sections 54 and 55).

♂ or ♄ in conjunction with ♅ or ♆: discordant (see Section 55).

♅ in conjunction with ♆: mixture of discordant and harmonious effects (see Sections 54 and 55).

NB: Any conjunction is made more definitely discordant or harmonious by discordant or harmonious aspects with a third planet.

57. Character Not Doomed. Nobody is condemned at birth by his horoscope to be immoral, dishonest, etc. Such qualities or tendencies indicated by any aspect are to be interpreted as warnings that such a fault might, with that horoscope, be too easily developed if not guarded against. The need to guard against it may result in a conspicuous freedom from it and possession or cultivation of the opposite virtue.

IV
Character Delineations of the Signs of the Zodiac

58. Waite's Signs. Sections 62–74 were written by Herbert Waite for the original edition of the *Compendium*. They are so highly thought of by eminent leaders in the teaching of astrology in England that it was decided to retain them, without change, in the present work. It is clear in this section that Waite specifies 'body types' according to the sign on the Ascendant (the rising sign). However, some physical attributes depend on the Sun sign. The Sun sign may often govern physical attributes on one side of the body (generally the left), while the rising sign governs the other side. Where Waite's notes on health in relation to the Sun sign are concerned it is worth noting that his remarks will also apply when this sign is on the cusp of the sixth house (the house of health).

59. In Judging Character from the horoscope we have to consider:

(i) The sign containing the Ascendant; the sign containing the ruling planet of the sign containing the Ascendant; planets *in* the Ascendant *sign*, or within about 10° of the Ascendant itself if in an adjoining sign. All these may be taken as depicting the type of personality that the native outwardly represents – in appearance, behaviour, relations with other people. The Ascendant sign is primary, and the other factors mentioned may be regarded as modifying it to various extents, needing experience to estimate well. Aspects to the ruling planet of the Ascendant sign and to planets in the Ascendant sign or near the Ascendant must also be taken into account.

(ii) The sign in which the Sun is placed, with the aspects to the Sun, as denoting the fundamental character or ego of the person, which may or may not be like the surface personality shown by the Ascendant, but gives his real motivation, in his reason and spiritual nature.

(iii) The sign in which the Moon is placed, with aspects to the Moon, as showing the desire-nature, the subconscious psychological tendencies, or the involuntary reactions and feelings, of the person.

(iv) The sign position and aspects of Mercury, as indicating the type of mentality and thought processes in the Earth-mind, whose organ is the brain.

Each of the following sign character-readings must, therefore, be taken as denoting the basic character (if it is the Sun sign), the emotional nature (if it is the Moon sign), the manifested personality (if it is the Ascendant sign), or a second superimposed and fainter manifested personality modifying the predominant manifested personality if it is the sign containing the Ascendant-ruler. Any of these receives additional modifications from any planets in the sign and from aspects to Sun, Moon or ruling planets.

60. Sign Characters Classified by Quality

CARDINAL SIGNS give restlessness and activity of mind and body, somewhat at the expense of thoroughness of detail as a rule. An enterprising and independent spirit is produced, inclined to constant moving about.

FIXED SIGNS denote stubbornness, fixity of purpose, self-reliance, will-power, and great determination to overcome obstacles to the ambition.

MUTABLE SIGNS give the power of dispassionate judgement, great versatility and adaptability, ability in detail work and criticism; some indecision, excess of subtlety, vacillation and pessimism may be shown, with the disposition to leave undertakings uncompleted. (*Waite*)

61. Sign Characters Classified by Element

FIRE SIGNS tend to produce more or less headstrong natures,

emotional, intuitive, exaggerative, enthusiastic, energetic, aspiring and ambitious. Usually noble aims.

AIR SIGNS incline to intellectual work, principally, giving the ability to receive a good education. The nature is humane and refined, and there is innate wisdom.

WATER SIGNS give excess of emotion and extreme sensitivity, and impressionability. The nature is naturally sociable and there is love of home comforts. (NB: Water signs usually give some psychic power, clairvoyance, etc.; especially true of Pisces. *Evans*)

EARTH SIGNS give the 'earthy', practical nature, and incline to caution, method, shrewdness and diplomacy. (*Waite*)

62. The Twelve Signs of the Zodiac. A brief description of the characteristics given by each of the twelve signs, and of the type of body produced by each sign when rising on the eastern horizon.

For the convenience of the reader the following is repeated:

The Ascendant, or the sign rising on the eastern horizon at the moment of birth, denotes the type of body and brain, the physical temperament and mental outlook.*

The Moon ☽, through the sign in which it was placed at birth, denotes the personal characteristics; the senses and the functioning of the body as a whole; the Soul.

The Sun ☉, through the sign in which its rays vitalized the Earth at the time of birth, denotes the real self, the Ego – that part of the Universal Spirit imprisoned, for purposes of tuition in constructive Love and Wisdom, in the body of flesh.

---

* Planets rising near the Ascendant very considerably alter the type of body and general appearance. The Sun and Moon also modify the type of body. Saturn near the Ascendant gives a short stature, even when a tall sign is rising. Mars generally gives red or sandy hair. Venus gives roundness to the face.

It should be clearly understood that the descriptions of types of body given in the following pages are applicable to the *rising sign*: for instance, anyone born between 21 March and 20 April would not necessarily have the sign Aries rising.

(*Waite*)

The physical body and brain (Ascendant) act as the vehicle and limiting factor for the expression of as much of the pure or real mind (☉) as the Soul (☽) reflects and modifies through the desires.

Limitations of space preclude anything like a complete treatment of any part of the judgement of a horoscope, but the following brief descriptions may be taken as showing

(i) Individual characteristics, when ☉ is in a sign;

(ii) Personal characteristics (in a general sense) when ☽ is in a sign;

(iii) Mental outlook, or 'what is bred in the bone', when the Ascendant is in a sign.

Aspects to the Sun modify the individual characteristics; aspects to the Moon modify the personal characteristics; aspects to the Ascendant and ruling planet affect the physical body and brain and mental outlook.

63. ♈ The Sign Aries ♈
the Positive House of its Ruler, ♂. ☉ in ♈ 21 March to 20 April

This sign belongs to the *fiery* element, and is of the *cardinal* quality. Aries individuals are characterized by intellectuality, self-reliance, activity, energy and impulsiveness. They are pioneers in the realms of thought and action, though they are more idealistic than practical. Always wilful and headstrong when young, most of them fail to achieve the necessary measure of caution even in mature life, and continue to go to extremes. Self-restraint, calmness, coolness and consideration for the feelings of others are not virtues of these people, as a rule, though what they lack in this respect they gain in dauntless courage, enthusiasm and zeal, either for their own work or for any cause they may take up.

Aries people love approbation, and if this is given them, they are tireless in their efforts for their employers; but they resent being driven and, if this is attempted, either throw up their posts in indignation or take revenge by means of acting and deception, for when perverting the influence of the sign, they are arch-deceivers. It may be said that it takes an Arian to deceive an Arian, as they are extremely perceptive and intuitive, being able to sense others to an extraordinary degree. When acting up to the highest in them they are prophetic and clairvoyant, and should the Moon be in Libra clairvoyance is very often produced. They usually have too much self-esteem, more especially when the Moon is also in a fiery sign, though the Moon in Capricorn renders them lacking in this respect. Interference and restriction they find hard to endure, and independence, freedom of action, and constant change and novelty seem to be the breath of life to them. Usually there are many changes of occupation during their lives.

New ideas and schemes crowd on top of one another in their brains, and they are always embarking on fresh enterprises, great or small, according to their station in life. If they can visualize the end of an enterprise, they are rarely swerved from the determination to carry it through; but it is this mental picture of a work completed in a short time that spurs them on to the finish. Thus they are not adapted for work requiring patient application over a long period, and, unless the horoscope is strong for detail, they are better fitted to create, organize and lead, rather than to personally work out their schemes in practical detail.

They are intellectual, but, as a rule, their great activity of mind and body leads to diffusion and the inability to marshal their thoughts sufficiently to show all that is in them.

Voluble and often brilliant in conversation, they do not always adhere strictly to truth, and in this, as in all they do, exaggeration and imagination can generally be discerned.

None are more alive to their own interests than Aries people, and unless the individual character is stronger than the personal, this trait results in jealousy and covetousness, often putting them back in life. There is much danger of this with the combination of ⊙ in ♈, ☽ in ♏. In this, as in all the signs, there will be found people who *use* the influence, and those who *abuse* it. The first are the pioneering and reforming leaders of men; frank, candid, intense, intellectual, aspiring; perhaps a little too 'touchy', assertive, exaggerative and venturesome. The second place self-interest above principle, are aggressive, presumptuous, too changeable, inconstant, and sensitive, yet inconsiderate of others; magnifying everything that engages their attention, as well as their own powers. They ape their superiors, ever seeking to place themselves on an equality with them, are unduly familiar and personal, and if one gives them the proverbial 'inch' they promptly take a 'yard'. These personal Arians are typical usurpers.

HEALTH Aries governs the head and brain. Though the general health is usually good and the constitution sound, Aries people are always highly strung, and their natural inclination to go to extremes often results in severe headaches, toothache, brain-fever, neuralgia, etc. Prolonged worry and the physical and mental excesses to which their nature renders them liable sometimes completely unhinge their minds.

OCCUPATION Actors, designers, herbalists, nature-cure doctors, guides and travellers, surveyors, architects, electricians, agents of all kinds, company promoters, freelance journalists, novelists, etc., are found amongst the Aries people.

TYPE OF BODY Average stature; spare, lean, but with strong body and large bones; head broad at top, narrowing down somewhat noticeably at chin; visage and neck rather long, and complexion dusky or ruddy; thick shoulders; hair light to reddish in those having the nose pinched or 'button-holed', dark in those having the ram-like face with bushy eyebrows; eyes blue to grey, sometimes light brown; quick sight; widow's peak hairline; eyebrows sometimes joined.

64. ♉ The Sign Taurus ♉
the Negative House of its Ruler, ♀. ☉ in ♉ 21 April to 20 May

This sign belongs to the *earthy* element, and is of the *fixed* quality. Taurean individuals are practical, sure, plodding, secretive, reserved, fixed in purpose, possessing as a rule more vitality of mind and body than those born under any other sign. Extremely strong-willed, they can be led but never driven. They are the manufacturers, the builders, those who make and mould things. While the Arian nature is to create the idea, the main scheme, and to lead and inspire others to put it into practical use, the Taurean nature is to handle the materials for the scheme, mould and erect them. The Arian is the architect, the Taurean the builder. Though the terms may be interpreted in their actual meaning, they are used in their broadest sense. For instance, let the Arian be the company promoter, then the Taurean is the mathematician and the financial expert.

Taureans are averse to change, not very adaptable, and the knowledge and skill they obtain is largely bought at the price of experience, as they stick to their own conservative methods long after a more flexible mentality would have lined up in the ranks of advancing science. They are usually slow to anger, but when once aroused lose all control, becoming furious and violent, though the combination of ☉ in ♉ and ☽ in ♈, ♌ or ♐ renders them quick to anger and violence. The latter combinations, while stirring the Taurean into action, also incline to bring out some of the lower Venusian tendencies, such as gambling, over-eating, and drinking, sensuality, conceit, etc.

When it is remembered that this is a fixed and earthy sign and represents the negative side of Venus, some idea of the laziness, love of sensuous and worldly pleasures, fondness for the table, obstinacy (pig-headedness), and even slovenliness, latent within the Taurean may be gleaned. If they are living principally in the personal or *desire* part of their nature, these tendencies will obtain more or less sway over them. On the other hand, the more individualized they become, the more real *will* they show, displaying wonderful powers of concentration and indomitable perseverance. Though rarely anything but practical and objective, they are then generous, kind and full of feeling for others.

Fixed 'earthly' or objective feeling being the main feature of this sign, the Taureans are either faithful and kind friends, or somewhat relentless enemies, only appeasable, if at all, through an appeal to their feelings. In their family life it will often be noticed that they seem to provoke quarrels for the sake of the pleasure it evidently affords them to 'patch it up again'. All Taureans should be very careful in their choice of a marriage partner, for they are more liable than most to err in this direction, more especially when they marry young.

The Venus influence inclines them to a love of music, and they are generally very good vocalists. Taurus also gives a gift for mathematics and finance. The Taurean is usually somewhat of a fatalist, even when professing indifference or scepticism with regard to occult subjects. If at all religious, they incline to ceremony and ritual, but the average personal Taurean evinces little interest in religious observances.

HEALTH Taurus governs the neck and the throat. The constitution is usually exceptionally strong and robust. The neck and throat being the weakest parts, Taureans are subject to sore throats, diphtheria, mumps, quinsy, tumours in the region of the throat. They are also liable to heart and kidney troubles, diabetes, etc. Laziness is fatal to their health, work their best medicine.

OCCUPATION Cashiers, financial agents, municipal accountants, collectors, stockbrokers, etc., are found among Taureans. Their great vitality and magnetism make them good masseurs, doctors, nurses. Many have good mechanical ability and succeed well either in the actual manual work connected with mechanism or as foremen. Manufacturers of paper, sweet-stuffs, chemicals, etc., are also found amongst them, as are many following agricultural pursuits. They make excellent chefs and cooks.

TYPE OF BODY Average to short stature; heavy, strong and thick-set body, especially hands and neck, inclining to stoutness; broad and full forehead, big mouth and usually thick lips with fleshy cheeks and jaw; big and prominent eyes; black or coarse sandy hair, usually wavy or curly; nose sometimes aquiline, though usually broad and full.

65. ♊ *The Sign Gemini* ♊
the Positive House of its Ruler, ☿. ☉ in ♊ 21 May to 20 June

This sign is of the *airy* element and *mutable* quality.

Gemini individuals are dual in nature, intellectual, clever, inspirational, nervous and restless. Happy, elusive, brilliant, charming, with wonderful powers of imagination, they are so contradictory in nature that one might, at times, think them stolid materialistic pessimists. This is due to their airy, mutable, and mercurial disposition, which makes them reflect every phase and change in their environment. They live mostly in the mind and have a great love of intellectual pursuits, though the knowledge they gain is more often than not the result of picking the brains of others and lightly skimming over books, never sticking for long to any one study. At times, however, they have a fit of enthusiasm and go to extremes in mental studies. They are active, positive, very adaptable and versatile, and very clever with their hands.

When acting along purely personal lines, they are cunning, acute, very clever, neither over-scrupulous nor truthful, materialistic, yet always elusive and difficult to understand.

The combination of ☉ in ♊ with ☽ in ♈, ♌ or ♐ increases the positiveness and acuteness of the nature and inclines in many ways to extremes, though giving much force and ability. There is also danger with these combinations of over-assertiveness, which is harmful to the Gemini nature, as there is not the inherent fixity and stamina behind them to enable them, if put to the test, to meet much opposition without great depletion of the nervous system. ☉ in ♊ is perhaps best combined with ☽ in either airy or earthy signs. With ☽ in watery signs the sensational tendencies need combating.

It has been said of Mercurian people that they can be 'all things to all men', and this is certainly true of Gemini subjects, their versatility being remarkable; but in this lies their greatest weakness, for so volatile is their nature that they find great difficulty in remaining long enough at any one post or undertaking to extract the maximum of success from it. In this way worry through instability of finance often comes upon them. As a rule, they lack the one-pointedness that makes for success, though they are extremely capable workers in many spheres. In affairs of the heart and friendship they are often considered false, yet they are usually honest in intention, and their fickleness is due to the fact that they can love with one side of their twin nature (their symbol is The Twins), while the other side starts to reason out sensations and criticize, thus nullifying the love impulse. They have great powers of expression and, when nervousness has been overcome, make eloquent public speakers, diplomats and actors. They delight in hearing or telling a good story or pun.

50

HEALTH Gemini governs the lungs, arms, hands, and nerves. The constitution is not very strong and the health quickly breaks up when the nerves are affected by worry, overwork, shock, etc. There is often catarrhal trouble with the nose and bronchial tubes, while pneumonia and diseases of the lungs generally need to be guarded against. Stammering and very quick speech are also associated with this sign.

OCCUPATION Their quick, keen and subtle mentality renders Gemini people excellent brokers, dealers and auctioneers, while they also excel as public speakers, reporters, journalists, barristers, book-keepers, clerks; in fact, in any mental work that combines change with the necessity of keenness of brain rather than solid, patient effort.

TYPE OF BODY Tall stature; thin, upright body; long face and features; sanguine complexion as a rule, though sometimes obscure and dark; when complexion is dark, the eyes are very handsome, usually hazel, big and piercing; hair light in first 10° of sign; after, dark, sometimes black; long arms and hands, very quick and active in movement, carriage and communication; often 'speak with their hands'.

66. ♋ *The Sign Cancer* ♋
the House of its Ruler, ☽. ☉ *in* ♋ 21 June to 21 July

This sign is of the *watery* element, and *cardinal* quality. Cancer individuals are very emotional and sensitive, intensely romantic, with vivid imagination. Like the crab, their symbol in the zodiac, they are extremely tenacious. They are nearly always political and apt to make an idol of some sensational political opportunist.

Cancer persons seem to be drawn to football or cricket matches, political meetings and similar functions where sensation is the main feature; and there they can be studied to advantage. The dignified and quiet man of business then reveals much of his nature; first, the staunch supporter of a particular *party* is seen, then one notices how his tense features and excited gestures reflect every ebb and flow of the fortunes of that party; then, completely under the sway of sensation, he shouts the names of his particular idols, admiringly, coaxingly, fiercely, according to his mood, but always in a personal way, though he has never met them in his life. All this is typical of the Cancerian's glory in movement, action and sensation, besides which it shows up his tendency to be prejudiced, to tinge with the personal element all that comes into his life, thus limiting and cramping his vision.

Where Gemini would take ideas from a novel, history or person, and from them elaborate some mental vision, Cancer would live and *feel* the part; and thus we often find Cancerians playing a role, *imagining* themselves martyrs or heroes. Similarly they are often plagiarists and copyists, reproducing the thoughts of others, while a short time spent by them in any fresh locality often results in their unconsciously 'absorbing' the manners and vocal intonation of the people they have contacted most. This liability to absorb the nature of others should warn the Cancerian to choose carefully his environment and friends. Deep down within them there is a love of all things mystical and occult, antique and curious. They appreciate home comforts, ease and luxury. Sensitivity about their families, relations and friends is a very marked feature with them. Retentiveness and tenacity are part of them, and even in the faculty of memory this will be noticed, for they can recall in exact detail minute incidents that have happened many years ago.

They are inventive and original, and many great organizers are found among them. In business and matters to do with real estate, they show much aptitude. They have a good sense of value, and their economy in small things is often taken to extremes; but in the spending of big sums their sense of proportion is sometimes somewhat lacking.

Of warm affections and sociable nature, they are really shy at bottom, and their ambitions and desires are usually more idealistic than passionate, sensual and worldly; though they are apt to be impressed by ceremony and the gaudy trappings and pompous pretensions of temporal power.

Always eloquent when at their ease, they often give proof of their gifts on the public platform. The combination of ⊙ in ♋ and ☽ in

♐ or ♍ gives much ability in this respect. They take great interest in gardening of all kinds. Music especially appeals to them, and they are often very accomplished in this direction.

HEALTH Cancer rules the breast and stomach. Giving way to excessive emotion and sensitiveness often causes Cancerians to suffer from gastric and stomach troubles. Pleurisy and all watery and inflammatory diseases are associated with this sign. Vitality is not over-strong.

OCCUPATION Cancerians love the sea and make excellent sailors and naval captains. Their strong domesticity makes women under this sign the best of housekeepers, hotel-keepers, midwives, etc., while they love to deal in liquids, making good barmaids, laundresses, etc. Dealers in all manner of second-hand articles, curios, etc., real-estate agents, builders' merchants, are also found under Cancer.

TYPE OF BODY Average to small stature; somewhat fleshy body, upper part larger than lower; round and full face, forehead usually prominent or even bulging, wide at temples; pale complexion; small blue or grey eyes; hair brown; usually short nose, slightly upturned; somewhat ungainly carriage, especially in mature life.

67. ♌ The Sign Leo ♌
the House of its Ruler, ☉*.* ☉ *in* ♌ 22 July to 21 August

This sign is of the element *fire*, and of *fixed* quality. Leo individuals are proud, passionate, ambitious, masterful, honourable, irrepressible, delighting in all that is really big in life. It has been said that they are the born commanders, rulers and kings as much in the material universe as in the realms of the heart, this being their birthright gained through loyalty and the mastery of true obedience. However this may be, Leo persons certainly rank amongst the best organizers and methodizers of the world. They are also usually capable of exercising authority.

Faith seems inherent with them, though it assumes a great variety of forms. Many are staunch upholders of ancient religious doctrines, and will tell one, with evident sincerity, 'I *know* my belief is the only one.' Others subscribing to totally different and often absurd doctrines will say the same thing. Though many people express belief, none leave one so impressed by their sincerity as do the Leo types. They are generous and warm-hearted, cheerful and sociable, and there is a sterling worth about most of them that cannot pass long unnoticed. They rarely go totally to the bad, though many have to pass through the Fire of uncontrolled desire before they realize the Divine Spark within them; for the strength, vitality and intensity of Leo when turned into sensual and dissolute channels is a terrible force, such a torrent as only Leo himself can stem. But the fall of Leo is more often due to the influence of others than inherent vice. Leo people are particularly subject to disillusionments with regard to their friends.

They generally show pride, though this varies with the type – personal or individual. The personal type is either haughty and boastful, assuming a superiority that he is far from possessing, or accomplished yet discontented or disdainful, looking down on others and showing no desire to give proof of his accomplishments; while the pride of the individual type is neither supercilious aloofness nor empty conceit, but the outward sign of a certain good opinion of himself, quite legitimate and natural.

The combination of ☉ in ♌ and ☽ in ♈, ♌ or ♐ is very good in many respects. With ☽ in ♉ or ♏ the Leo person needs much self-control to combat the lower tendencies of two very strong signs, in order to derive the best from the combination.

Getting to the root of a matter with wonderful directness, Leo people are practical and hard-headed, yet ever ready to obey the dictates of a warm heart, for they are sensitive and emotional as well as intuitive.

Unlike the first fixed sign, Taurus, Leo, though quick to take offence, as quickly forgives; and while Leo likes luxury and pleasure, sometimes too much, it is usually of a very different kind to the sensuous variety favoured by Taurus.

These people are capable of long-sustained effort and the carrying out of great schemes. They seem to do best when having authority over others, as chiefs, managers or foremen. Their will-power and self-control are usually very strong and they are faithful and trustworthy, sticking hard and fast to their principles and their work. Reverses to them are but the spur to victory. More often than not they appeal to the best in a man to obtain what is due to them, though there is the domineering spirit latent within them and some tendency to dramatic display.

HEALTH Leo governs the heart and the back. Discord, contention and excess are enemies to the normally strong Leo constitution. Under their influence the heart suffers. Affections of the ribs, side and back, pleurisy, fevers and convulsions are other illnesses to which Leo people are subject, while they are often troubled with their eyes. Rest in solitude and peace is a wonderful curative agent with them.

OCCUPATION They excel as organizers, leaders, managers or foremen. Many social welfare workers are found amongst them, especially women; organists and musicians showing preference for the really grand and inspiring in their art; artists, actors. They do not like manual labour and usually do better in a professional rather than a business career.

TYPE OF BODY Tall to average stature; big-boned and well-knit body, usually lean in young life, inclining to fullness later; somewhat narrow hips; yellow or dark flaxen hair, a lion's mane when worn long; sanguine or florid complexion; big round head; usually blue or grey, or grey-brown eyes; quick sight; commanding and brisk carriage.

68. ♍ *The Sign Virgo* ♍
the Negative House of its Ruler, ☿. ☉ *in* ♍ 22 August to 21 September

This sign is of the element *earth*, and of *mutable* quality. Virgo individuals are shrewd, discriminative, diplomatic, quietly active and reserved. They are often thought harsh and taciturn, but the fact is they conceal behind a cold and matter-of-fact exterior the peculiar nervousness of their negative, mercurial temperament. At bottom they are extremely kind and sympathetic, yet so nervous and retiring that, many times, when expected to say a word in consolation, they refrain for fear the mention of the subject should revive sorrowful remembrances in their friends; in some cases their fear is that they may appear too sympathetic and not sufficiently worldly and business-like. They, more than those born in any other sign, usually feel the need to bolster themselves up and even repress some of their finer instincts in order to keep their equilibrium. It may be said that they maintain their cool and dignified attitude and often impressive presence at the expense of an ill-deserved reputation for coldness of feeling; and thus their true nature is rarely, if ever, seen. When in authority over others, they are rather too exacting, though just to a fault.

This is said to be the sign of service, but since all life is service in some form or other, the statement that Virgo is the servant and not the master is very misleading. As a matter of fact, so industrious, scientific and adaptable is the Virgo man that very often he rises rapidly to a position of command.

They are essentially methodical and logical, and with suitable training possess the power to tabulate in clear and precise form the most involved schemes and statistics. Their mental abilities are very good, and they have the analytical type of mind; are very clever in detail work, and their mental working capacity is often extraordinary.

They delight in quoting from famous authors, and history and statistics especially appeal to them. Drugs, patent foods and the like have a strange fascination for them.

Shrewd and subtle, when too material they are amongst the sharpest and least scrupulous of businessmen. With their positive Mercurian brother, Gemini, they constitute a combination that would hoodwink the world if so inclined. But the good type of Virgo is the most conscientious, methodical, reliable and hardworking man that could be desired.

Virgo people know instinctively when a thing can be improved upon, and they generally bring about the improvement, being very inventive. They are gifted with manual dexterity and are excellent technicians, but their sphere seems to be more the office and the archive than the field of construction.

Their faults are vacillation and lack of self-confidence, often held in check by innate conscientiousness, but the best of them have, at times, to recognize a certain inclination to give way before difficulties. It is always more or less a struggle for Virgo people to make up their minds, as their nature is to discriminate; and seeing so many points that are hidden from other minds it is all the harder for them to decide on any particular line of action. It is owing to this that responsibility is sometimes a strain on them, but none could say that they are more suited to be servants than masters without a careful consideration of the horoscope as a whole. With the Moon in fixed and fiery signs, they make capable and practical leaders.

HEALTH   Virgo rules the bowels, and worry and overwork usually cause diarrhoea, flatulence and other afflictions of this part of the body. Care in diet is essential to the health of Virgo people. They are much given to worry, which reacts on their nerves. Drugs and alcohol are very harmful to them.

OCCUPATION   Virgo people do well in all business connected with food and drugs. They make splendid analytical chemists. Editors and literary critics of the solid rather than the superficial class are found amongst them. They are fitted by their tact, mental ability and business aptitude for practically any professional or business vocation.

TYPE OF BODY   Tall to average stature; well-knit and often plump body; ruddy or dark complexion; hair ginger-reddish to very dark, tighter curls than Leo (when curly); fine, but coarse beards on males; oval face, round forehead; peculiar nose, outstanding, with pronounced curves at side of nostrils, slightly upturned.

69. ♎ The Sign Libra ♎
the Positive House of its Ruler, ♀. ☉ in ♎ 22 September to 22 October

This sign is of the element *air*, and of *cardinal* quality. Libra individuals are refined, artistic, very perceptive, intuitive, lovers of pleasure, beauty and elegance, harmony and order. They seem to have the ability to mentally balance (♎ the balance), and seek to arrive at an impartial judgement on most things. They will be found to compare and criticize everything they see, and in the lower order of Libran this is carried to excess, becoming irksome to those about them. This class, though often the very best judges of style, elegance and beauty of dress, fabrics and most ornamental things, too often spend the greater part of their lives in prying into other people's affairs and 'picking them to pieces'. Their curiosity seems insatiable, and they will be found in their element at every sale, bazaar, church service, wedding or funeral of note, observing and comparing every detail of their surroundings, *always seeking to draw conclusions*; fashion, ceremony, convention, family histories and social scandal seem to be the breath of life to the personal Libran. These people show much the same dislike of contention to be noted in the better type of Libran, but while they would go out of their way to avoid a brawl where the differences of others are concerned, are very bitter and go to extremes if provoked themselves. In love and marriage their critical nature soon destroys their happiness.

The combination ⊙ in ♎ and ☽ in ♋ or ♏ needs much control to combat the undesirable traits of Libra; though a very careful study of the horoscope is necessary before it can be pronounced a wholly personal one. And the innate refinement of Libra must always be borne in mind, as it gives a certain indefinable elegance and charm to all its children, making even the moral lapses that many a Libran fails to guard against far removed from the ordinary conception of vulgarity and vice. Many 'fops', fast-livers, and gamblers are Librans, but their airy elegance, natural politeness and *bonhomie* does much to disarm their critics. Their nature is flexible and sensitive, the feelings and emotions very strong, swaying them to such a degree that association and union with others to a large extent moulds their lives.

The good type of Libra shows much sweetness and harmony of nature – justice, courtesy, kindness, generosity and charming manners being very marked.

Their mental powers are good and they are desirous of mental improvement, often becoming very accomplished. It is rarely, however, that they study anything outside their profession very deeply, being changeable and subject to many moods and fancies, unless the horoscope as a whole shows marked perseverance and will-power.

They show great interest in all occult matters.

Libra gives a gift for music, poetry and painting, and an inclination for the law and the higher professions generally.

Libra people are inclined, at times, to vacillate and delay their decisions until too late. They would do well to cultivate concentration.

HEALTH Libra rules the loins and kidneys. The constitution is usually strong, but excess in eating and especially drinking affects the kidneys and the bladder, sometimes causing stone or gravel. Pains in the loins, weakness of the lower part of the back, and humid feet are also associated with this sign. Libra people often fret and allow themselves to get into a very melancholy state. Beautiful and peaceful surroundings are their best medicine.

OCCUPATION Barristers, lawyers, musical and theatrical people generally and those having the direction and management of the artistic side of public amusements are found amongst Librans. Secretarial work is also to their liking, and they are clever as artists and decorators. In trade they are antique and art dealers, and have much to do with perfumery, fabrics, fancy stationery, etc.

Many nuns and Sisters of Mercy are Librans.

TYPE OF BODY Tall to average stature; well-formed, usually beautiful body; round face, generally lovely, with fine, soft red-and-white complexion; smooth long hair, sometimes flaxen, but often dark in latter half of sign; inclining to stoutness after youth; blue eyes as a rule, though sometimes hazel or brown, and full of feeling.

70. ♏ *The Sign Scorpio* ♏
the Negative House of its Ruler, ♂. ☉ *in* ♏ 23 October to
21 November

This sign is of the element *water*, and of *fixed* quality. Scorpio individuals are determined, tenacious, very secretive, critical, cautious, keen and shrewd. They are very magnetic and many possess a strange hypnotic power over others. It may be said that the most powerful natures, for good or for evil, belong to this sign.

There will be noticed in the higher class of Scorpions a silent watchfulness, something unfathomable, yet all-comprehensive in the eyes, a calmness and quiet intensity and determination bespeaking some wonderful force hidden within them. There is an impressive dignity about them, warning all that no liberty may be taken there. The most magnetic and emotional orators and preachers, the most capable diplomats and the greatest seers are found amongst this class; but there are all too few of them.* A deep study of the sign is necessary to form any idea of the wonderful power of the regenerated Scorpion, but it will here suffice to say that Scorpio represents the sex principle, and when it is remembered that this is a *watery*, or sensational and emotional, sign of *fixed* quality, we can imagine the debauchery and degradation of which these Martians are capable when perverting that principle; moreover, we are enabled to understand something of their dramatic nature and of that extraordinary power of attraction and attachment that any observer of human nature will have noticed in Scorpions of both sexes.

The generality of Scorpions are strong-willed, bold and self-confident, somewhat too direct in manner, showing a masterful temper on the slightest provocation, and resenting anything like a liberty from their fellows. When these people dislike anything, they are very bitter and dogmatic. Endowed with all the perceptive and critical

* Traditionally associated with the Scorpion, Scorpio is still recognized as a very deep sign by many astrologers, having three different 'levels'. The vengeful scorpion is the first. Second is the eagle, which has few predators and dwells above most other creatures; in human terms this represents a stage of 'comfortable development', which may be interpreted as 'I have made it.' However, the phoenix is associated with the highest evolution of the sign. It rises above the ashes of the 'burned eagle', admittedly a pagan image of transformation. A Christian symbol for this higher type is the dove, representing the Holy Spirit. As a source of healing and other 'miraculous' powers it is unrivalled. As Waite suggests, there are not too many of these latter types abroad; understandably, as one must know the first two levels in order to achieve the last.

qualities of Libra, they lack the elegance and relative harmlessness of the latter sign, and are often relentless and destructive in their criticisms, being capable of biting sarcasm unequalled by any other sign. Thus they make many enemies.

There is always an element of secrecy about them, and they seem to take a delight in baulking the curiosity of others; yet they will unravel the life of another, being natural detectives. More often than not there are tragic and secret love affairs in their lives, and few of them seem to escape having the works of the devil pushed right under their noses at some period of their careers.

For all their strength of character, most of them are very sensitive, fear the opinion of the world too much and dread the very thought of being ill; while they can generally be swayed through their deep emotions. Their innate fixity of purpose, excellent abilities and dislike of change nearly always result in a secure and often influential position in life; yet, although they display a desire to dominate and govern others, it is doubtful if the majority of them are ambitious beyond the point that gives a certain ease and security of circumstances. If once ambition is awakened, however, their whole energies go to the one point and great things are accomplished, their working power then becoming enormous.

Though they are given to delay matters, when once they have made up their minds, they are resistless in their determination to attain their object. They are cool, collected and resourceful; in fact, resourcefulness in word and deed is an outstanding feature of their character and they are at their best in an emergency. They make firm friends and passionate and jealous lovers, inclining to acts of violence if crossed in love, while they will brook no interference from parents or others in such matters.

They spend money freely on themselves and cannot, as a class, be considered generous, but when they have succeeded in amassing money, often do great good without courting publicity.

The mentality is subtle and acute, capable of great persistence in the unravelling of mysteries of any kind. Thus they are excellent research workers, detectives, occultists, doctors and, being also endowed with manual dexterity, make splendid surgeons. The combination of ☉ in ♏ and ☽ in ♋ inclines much to the medical profession. Many of the cleverest chess players are Scorpions, and there seems little doubt that Napoleon's great military genius was largely due to this sign rising at his birth.

The faults of the Scorpion are many, not least amongst which are pride, harshness and scepticism, and a tendency to be too exacting, selfish, dogmatic, violent and unforgiving; but the power for good within him is probably greater than that possessed by any other, since he is endowed with great magnetism, invincible will, and executive ability beyond the ordinary to carry out the work of destroying evil and constructing good.

HEALTH Scorpio governs the secret parts. The constitution is usually strong, with great powers of resisting disease. Scorpions suffer from all diseases and infections of the generative organs, discharges from the private parts, afflictions of the bladder and poisoning of the blood, pains in the groin, kidney troubles, etc.

OCCUPATION Scorpions succeed in all martial employments, such as doctor, surgeon, butcher, mechanical engineers, ironmongers, smiths, etc. They are also hypnotists and magnetic healers, occultists, chemists, inventors of all kinds, detectives, etc. They are in their element at sea and make good naval officers and sailors.

TYPE OF BODY Average to tall stature; corpulent and strong body, usually very hairy; hair rarely fine and generally coarse, thick and curling; bullet-shaped top part of head, prominent over eyes; square face, aquiline or sometimes ill-shapen 'squashed-out' type of nose, the face often reminding one of an eagle. As a rule, the higher the type, the finer the hair.

71. ♐ The Sign Sagittarius ♐
the Positive House of its Ruler, ♃. ☉ in ♐ 22 November to 20 December

This sign is of the element *fire*, and of *mutable* quality. Sagittarius individuals are optimistic, cheerful, honourable, loyal, independent, enterprising and very active. They possess a natural gift for prophecy and wonderful intuition. The higher class of Sagittarian combines a keen sense of justice with a philosophical, innately religious, kind and merciful nature; his character is reflected in his face and his bearing, giving to the eyes a marked openness, kindness and honesty of expression; to the bearing a lofty and noble dignity. They will be found amongst the most merciful judges, the most loved of religious and social workers, the greatest mystics, seers, and philosophers. People seem to gravitate to them for guidance in both spiritual and material matters, for they are Nature's teachers, philosophers and friends, the perfect arbitrators and law-givers, finding their greatest pleasure in life in showing others that All is Law, and that all pain and discord are due to the fact that this great truth has yet to be internally realized by the majority of mankind. But it is by Law that the Sagittarian comes into his heritage, and he has to learn through rebelliousness, diffusiveness and other abuses of his higher nature. Thus we find the true rebel against everything, in this sign, and even the religious hypocrite, the advertising philanthropist and the worst of the toadies to power, especially that of the orthodox clergy and the law.

In this latter stage we see the Sagittarian at his worst, the worshipper of form, enslaved by ritual, ceremony and convention. His impressionable nature is then working only through the senses; outer perception rules his life, inner perception is not yet his. And it is just this that makes him the hypocrite, for though he is honestly swayed through his senses, he is yet aware of the white flame of truth within him, there to light his way through the dark maze of conventionality and hollow ceremony; but material ambition and desire for preferment have a strong hold on him, and thus he becomes the plausible toady and hypocrite, chiefly in the domains of the Church, the law and politics, since these constitute his natural bent.

In the rebel we get the awakening of the inner self. Thomas Carlyle was typical of the class. The inherent honesty of the Sagittarian has triumphed at last, revolting against hypocrisy and the blind worship of form, power and authority; his intuition now enables him to see through the hollow sham of most things in this material world, and he becomes a dangerous enemy to the established order of things, principally to the lower Sagittarians installed in their lucrative posts in the Church and the law. But gradually he reduces his militant and rebellious activities, for he has glimpsed the Great Law working in All, and his philosophy has made him more tolerant of the weaknesses of others. And so he comes into his heritage to guide and uplift, rather than destroy and cast down.

This is a contradictory sign, in many ways similar to its opposite, Gemini, though showing its changeableness in advancing and relatively permanent states of consciousness, causing the Sagittarian to modify his views and change his profession or trade, always once, and mostly many times during his life. Sagittarians are born teachers, and no sooner do they gain knowledge than they are eagerly imparting it to others. Even the lower order of them will rarely abuse a personal trust. They like one to place implicit confidence in them, and through this characteristic and their innate honesty are probably trusted more than any other class. They are far too outspoken, causing annoyance to sensitive people and often putting themselves back in life through making their ambitions too evident. Somewhat hasty and impulsive, their fiery anger is soon aroused when their great intuition enables them to wound and cover their enemies with confusion in a very few words, for they know instinctively the weakest points of others and shoot their mental arrows straight to the vulnerable spot. Morally they know no fear, and are such great lovers of liberty, freedom of speech, and justice that, either in their own defence or in the cause of another, they will fight to the end to redress an injury, though avoiding physical violence if at all possible, as they are really peaceable and humane in nature.

Their nature seems to oblige them to seek the company of others, and they are splendid companions, showing great insight into human nature and possessing a keen sense of humour.

They have strong will-power, and work feverishly to complete a task, yet they are generally better adapted to work in partnership or co-operation with others than by themselves, though they are very independent, dislike restraint, and always seek to rule and lead others. They have splendid foresight and are born organizers, combining these qualities with dash and precision. It is typical of them to say that they like to do something big, difficult and even dangerous, but soon over and done with! For they love change and novelty.

As a class they are generous, but where money is concerned are always on their guard, and through their intense dislike of being imposed upon are often thought niggardly. Music always appeals to them, and many are very accomplished musicians, while all things artistic have a marked fascination for them and they are amongst the best judges of beauty and ornamentation.

The mentality is of a high order, fitting them for all the higher professions, philosophy and the most abstruse subjects. They have a gift for languages, good executive ability and manual dexterity. Amongst their faults are irritability, restlessness and a tendency to be too assertive, intolerant, defiant, distant and casual; while they go to extremes, often dissipate their energies on too many schemes, are a little inclined to exaggeration and lack concentration unless fairly individualized.

HEALTH Sagittarius governs the thighs and hips. This sign gives a sound and wiry constitution, but Sagittarians are always highly strung; excesses, worry or overwork cause nervous breakdowns. Fistulas, tumours and all diseases affecting the hips and thighs are associated with this sign; sciatica, rheumatism, varicose veins, too-heated blood, fevers, etc. Fresh air and exercise are absolutely essential for the well-being of Sagittarians.

OCCUPATION Military officers, civil engineers, politicians, clergymen, college professors and barristers are found among Sagittarians; also commercial travellers, advertising and advance agents, inspectors, horsedealers, bookmakers, etc.

TYPE OF BODY Above the average stature and usually tall; wiry and well-formed body; generally good looking, with very expressive and open-looking eyes; sunburnt colour of complexion; hair light brown or chestnut to dark; inclined to baldness; peculiarity about front teeth. Eyes usually blue or hazel, sometimes brown; high forehead, oval face; dignified and commanding carriage.

*

72. ♑ *The Sign Capricorn* ♑
the Negative House of its Ruler, ♄. ☉ in ♑ 21 December to
19 January

This sign is of the element *earth*, and of *cardinal* quality.

Capricorn individuals are economical, practical, persevering, shrewd, diplomatic, reserved, cautious. They are essentially plodders, and a self-made man of business who has started with nothing and created a huge store is typical of the class. The higher type of Capricorns impress one by their solidity, gravity, faithfulness, impartiality and wonderful capacity for plodding, patient and thorough industry. They are just, but one must not look to them for allowances for failings, nor the mercy of the Sagittarian for the wrong-doer. Justice, hard and stern, they give, as judges or as men of business. They expect from an employee what he was engaged to do; they ask no more, but they will accept no less. They give the exact value for money and they expect it from others. To waste time or material is a crime to them; not even the crumbs from their tables are wasted; yet, if careful, they are certainly not mean. Neatness and tidiness are born in them. One might sum them up as the most eminently sensible, practical and exact of the human type, possessing stability, endurance, calm and earnest perseverance probably unequalled by any other sign. They will be found amongst the greatest financiers and bankers, real-estate brokers, government contractors and officials, judges and scientists. Though they are brisk, there is nothing dashing or assertive about them, and their bearing is more often solid and heavy than dignified, the dominant notes being gravity and reflection, with occasional lapses into sparkling but quiet wit, gaiety and even eloquence.

The lower type of Capricorn is easily recognizable, for Saturn leaves his mark on his unwilling pupils for all to see. The sallow, discontented and gloomy face; the miserly, deceitful, surly, distant and repining nature; the humility of a Uriah Heep and the avarice of a Gaspard are the signs; and some of them are always to be seen.

The average Capricorns are self-possessed and somewhat self-centred people, very firm-willed, subtle, cautious and suspicious.

Very subject to moods, they have at times to fight hard against discontent and melancholy. Ambition is very strong with them, and it is a poor specimen of their class who does not leave this world far richer than he entered it. As a rule their lives are not altogether happy, and there is generally a lot of enmity towards them from many sources, partly through their own self-centred natures and partly because they are misunderstood by others.

They have much force of character and strong temper though nothing like the irresistible nature of the fixed signs; but when they encounter a stronger will than their own they can wait a long while and attain their object by subtle and roundabout routes. They are fitted to rule and manage, and are never happy unless exercising authority and power, no matter what their sphere in life. Usually they lead more or less public lives and have much to do with the masses, often working great good amongst them, according to their peculiar and Saturnine lights.

Though they make good friends and are sociable in their own circle, they do not take easily to strangers, and are very reserved and uncommunicative with them. They always hold people at a distance until quite sure of them, and those who offend them usually rue it and do not get the chance to repeat the offence, for they make bad enemies. The mentality is clever, subtle, acute and profound, fitting them either for entirely mental pursuits or for business organization and management, as they also possess executive ability, great tact, diplomacy, prudence and method. The combination of ☉ in ♑ and ☽ in ♌ gives many successful speculators, while ☽ in ♐ inclines to legal matters and oratory, though lessening concentration.

Capricorns make subtle and often brilliant debaters, and delight in getting the best of an argument. Like Cancer people, they are nearly always political, and are not as a rule inclined to worry about the moral aspect of the power that subjugates peoples and builds empires so long as it is orthodox and has been ordained by the powers that be; for they are fatalists and compulsionists at heart, and when in power themselves often become the greatest despots, even when they have obtained their power by fighting despotism.

They always look up to intellect, but are usually too material-

67

minded to be much affected by others, anything unconventional and unorthodox being their *bête noire*. They run in a groove mentally, and quickly bridle if anyone dares to suggest that their ideas are wrong.

They are not idealistic, and their mission seems to be to conserve what is conventional and orthodox in order that the more advanced and inspirational element of humanity may not revolutionize the world in too great a hurry. If all the world consisted of Capricorns it would be a hive of industry and order; but we should be offering up human sacrifices to wooden gods as of old and doing much as we did thousands of years ago; for Capricorn does not *create*, at most it improves, organizes, methodizes and sacrifices.

The keynotes of Capricorn seem to be ambition, duty and sacrifice. These self-centred people, strange as it may be, though they sacrifice others, will sacrifice themselves more than most, when what they consider to be their duty calls. Kind and affectionate and yearning for sympathy, Saturn yet seems to withhold something from them, for they are usually more feared than liked, more respected than loved.

Their faults are malice and revengefulness, a tendency to go to extremes to satisfy ambition, to badger and nag at others, and to be cold and inconsiderate of the feelings and wishes of others, fanatical in regard to some religious creed, toadies to the aristocracy, even when railing at them, worshippers of power.

HEALTH Capricorn rules the knees. The constitution is fairly strong, but Capricorns are usually subject to much ill-health, especially women, often becoming very despondent and melancholy. All diseases of the knees, itch, cutaneous complaints and rheumatism are associated with this sign.

OCCUPATION Managers and organizers of all huge enterprises requiring persistent and long-sustained effort, contractors, real-estate agents and brokers, lawyers, farmers and agricultural workers and dealers, researchers, landed-proprietors, etc., are found amongst Capricorns.

TYPE OF BODY Average to short stature, usually dry and bony body; face angular and long, with long chin and nose; long, small neck; narrow chest and weak or slightly deformed knees; some peculiarity of carriage; lank and thin hair and beard, usually dark; peculiarity of thumbs; dimpled or cleft chin.

73. ♒ *The Sign Aquarius* ♒
the Positive House of its Ruler, ♄. ☉ in ♒ 20 January to 18 February

This sign is of the element *air*, and of *fixed* quality. Aquarius individuals are refined, artistic, intellectual, faithful and humane. The higher type of Aquarian combines all the practical and persevering qualities of Capricorn with much intuition, very exalted ideals of life, and the natural ability to read character.

They are quiet but very intense, strong and forceful characters, impressing one with their strange magnetism and a wonderful mentality combined with a disposition delightfully open and naïve. Typical representatives of this class were Ruskin and Charles Dickens. Each showed, in his own peculiar way, a vast understanding of humanity and the splendid literary gift of the sign. The marked magnetism of Aquarians makes them in many ways as strong and forceful as Scorpions, yet the impression they give is quite unlike Scorpio, for there is an airy-mental electrifying 'something' about them that ever eludes the understanding of even the most intuitive of character-readers. This quality of theirs, and the fact that they exhibit inventiveness, idealism and the power to transcend the material and think far ahead of the times in which they live, seems conclusive proof that Uranus the Awakener is to a great extent the ruler of this sign.

In the lower types of Aquarius the Uranian influence is even more marked, for then we see the fiery and erratic temper, extreme independence, sudden fits of eccentricity and seething internal unrest, reminding one of a volcano that may erupt at any minute, perverse and threatening in its silence as it gives off the fumes of anger. These fits of strange and often unaccountable silence are a marked feature of the sign, and even in the more evolved types they will occasionally be noticed, making the Aquarian a very difficult person to understand and get on with when in these moods.

In the lower type we get the extreme egoist, false, scheming and selfish, using his mental gifts and inflexible will for ambition and personal aggrandizement only, entirely regardless of principle.

The average Aquarians are fixed, strong-willed and intellectual characters, generally reserved, quiet and thoughtful in mien, though, at times, showing a naïveté and apparent frivolousness of character which deceives others as to their true worth. Nervous and highly strung, they are very quick and active, and capable of enormous temporary resistance to fatigue, often injuring their health through incessant and prolonged application to some particular work.

Some of their peculiarities are a desire to be quite alone at times; to resent the interference or even help of others in their work unless they are in command; to be very reserved and secretive if questioned on any matter, when if left to tell their tale at their own time they would be quite frank. They are also subject to many disappointments and disillusionments with regard to other people, for they read character so quickly that the outer veneer of society does not hold them long entranced, and they seem to feel, as a consequence, a kind of mental isolation and solitude. If they become attached to others they are very faithful and seem to be able to hold their friends and lovers in a very marked manner. At the same time, they do not readily give their confidence to other people, and it is practically impossible for them to 'make friends' again if once offended or deceived, so deep is their resentment and sensitiveness. Though their friendships are usually life-long and no sacrifice is too great for those they love, they are generally undemonstrative. They are always found declaiming against snobbishness, but, to others, they often appear to ignore or be too casual or condescending to those below them in station; yet they delight to engage in humanitarian works, and freely give both their time and money.

All things intellectual and artistic appeal to them strongly, and they will be found to frequent, very much, public lectures and meetings, the opera, theatres, etc., and they make very good entertainers, impersonators, etc.

The mentality is very clear and profound, fitting them for literary and scientific pursuits. There is much originality and usually a marked gift for character impersonation, poetry, novel-writing or music, while they are capable of controlling others as managers or inspectors, more especially in any position in which they can instruct as well as direct.

Electrical work in any of its branches seems to appeal especially to them, and in the higher types the literary gift is sure to come out.

They show a horror of cruelty in any form, and are great lovers of dumb animals.

Their faults include scepticism, a tendency to be too fixed and self-opinionated, strange and sudden fits of waywardness and silence, and concentrated and lasting dislike for those who offend them. Often they make their lives sad, gloomy and lonely through their own strange and erratic temperaments, living in the mind far too much for their well-being, while some of the worst religious fanatics are found in this sign, generally inclining to form and ceremony, though sometimes evincing egotism and megalomania.

HEALTH Aquarius rules the ankles and legs. The constitution is not very strong, though wiry. Swollen legs and ankles and all diseases and weaknesses of these parts, poor circulation, cramps, pains through flatulence, spasmodic and nervous diseases are peculiar to this sign. The Moon in Aquarius, especially when badly aspected, gives trouble with the eyes. The quiet and peaceful contemplation of nature is the best medicine for those born in this sign.

OCCUPATION Railway, post office and telegraph employees, managers, engineers and surveyors, are largely recruited from Aquarians. Reformers and revolutionists in many spheres are amongst them, and they will be found much in evidence in all public companies and associations. Musicians, poets, astronomers, astrologers, literary workers, artists, secretaries, etc., are other occupations of this sign.

TYPE OF BODY Average to short stature, thick-set and usually plump and well-made; good complexion, from pearly pink-and-white to sanguine; peculiar salt and pepper hair, wiry in tight curls, flaxen or sandy when young, going darker as life advances, until whitening prematurely; somewhat long face, often very good looking; hazel or blue and magnetic eyes.

74. ♓ The Sign Pisces ♓
the Negative House of its Ruler, ♃. ☉ in ♓ 19 February to 20 March

This sign is of the element *water*, and of *mutable* quality. Pisces individuals are patient, emotional, sympathetic, honourable, generous, and hospitable. Very sensitive and impressionable, they possess subtlety and a natural power of persuasion, having a wonderful capacity for quiet and tactful persistence when dealing with others, serving as an asset against an often painful sensitivity which tends to keep them in the background in life. This excessive sensitivity is usually noticed when the Moon is in a watery or earthy sign.

The higher types of the sign impress one by their ready sympathy, broad-mindedness, patience and quietness of mien. Marked features about them are their quickness of understanding and willingness to listen to and learn from others. They show great interest in archaeology, geology and, in fact, all nature studies, and are very psychic and mediumistic characters. Occultism especially appeals to them.

As they like to combine the practical with the theoretical, they are very useful and well-informed people on a great variety of subjects, while their literary abilities are often pronounced.

In the lower types the duality of the sign is more easily seen than in the more individualized Pisceans, though in all a certain contradiction and duality of nature will be noted. The less evolved type is either a very weak and dissipated person, his own worst enemy, knocked about from pillar to post by circumstances that he seems powerless to control; or impetuous, assertive and seemingly confident, but unable to do what he professes and easily beaten in a test of strength and spirit. Deceit, hypocrisy, lying, lack of self-confidence and initiative, fretfulness, peevishness and morbid fear of reverses; a feeling that fate is against them and everyone conspiring to do them harm; alcoholism and all the vices of the senses will be found in these types; while they quickly absorb the magnetism from evil associates and are often led to their ruin. Yet this is a Jupiterian sign, and it will be noticed that the schemer and the thief amongst Pisceans often voluntarily returns what he has stolen and in many ways atones for any evil act. Similarly their enemies usually become their friends, so difficult is it to harbour resentment against them, for they have no inherent vice; while they themselves quickly forgive an injury. These personal Pisceans are great talkers and boasters, and of them it may truly be said that one 'cannot get a word in edgeways', in vivid contrast to their quiet, reserved and somewhat silent individualized brethren. They are, like the lower type of their positive brothers, the Sagittarians, much swayed by form and ceremony.

The average Pisceans are good-natured, friendly, sympathetic and benevolent people, kind and easy-going, loving beauty and refinement in everything. Somewhat timid and shy at bottom, they are nevertheless capable of taking care of themselves and show much spirit and dignity if anyone presumes to take advantage of their good nature and inoffensiveness, though they detest anything violent and vulgar. The fact that a very large number of nurses, hospital attendants and officials of charitable institutions and organizations are found amongst Pisceans is significant of their sympathetic and humane natures. They seem to be fated to have something to do with charity and nursing at some period of their lives.

They are usually best fitted to fill some post under others, and though frequently fretting under authority, know instinctively that if having to rely entirely on their own initiative they would be liable to worry, apprehension and failure. Through this they often make the fortunes of more self-confident men, remaining frequently but ill rewarded for their labours. When seeking their fortunes otherwise than in the employment of others, they should join with a suitable partner.

They are mentally ambitious, being very desirous of perfection in their studies, though somewhat lacking in concentration. Their material ambition might be said to work from point to point, as they rarely set out with a fixed idea of what they want, their careers, more often than not, being moulded by circumstances. They often follow two or more occupations at the same time, travel entering largely into their lives, while the more change and novelty they get in their employment the happier they are.

The mentality is good, method and order being much in evidence, fitting them for organization in many spheres. Their vivid imagination, excellent powers of expression, and understanding of the inner meaning of words make them capable literary workers, while their considerable adaptability and versatility open up a large and varied field for their activities. Music, singing, painting and drawing very much appeal to them, and they generally show aptitude in one or more of these accomplishments.

Their main object should be to cultivate concentration and fixity of purpose, and combat excessive sensitivity. Their faults, like those of the Sagittarians, are usually such as can easily be forgiven, but they are too ready to vacillate and be discouraged and despondent, often feeling themselves somewhat of martyrs, incline to dissipate their energies in too many schemes, and seem to wait for approbation to spur them on, being very disappointed if it is not forthcoming.

HEALTH Pisces governs the feet. The constitution is rarely strong, and there is usually much trouble with the feet through lameness and pains, swellings, and rheumatism proceeding from impure blood.

Other marked features of the sign are blotches, boils, ulcers, tumours, mucous diseases and discharges of the bowels, and colds and chills caught through the feet, often leading to consumption. Fresh air and exercise, and the avoidence of low-lying and damp localities, are essential for the health of Pisces people.

OCCUPATION Chiefs of department, organizing agents and secretaries, agents of all descriptions, literary workers, bookkeepers, librarians, nurses, sailors and naval officers, caterers, hotel-keepers, etc., are found amongst Pisceans.

TYPE OF BODY Average to short stature; fleshy and lymphatic body; short thick limbs; pale complexion; rather large face; hair ranging from light brown to dark; usually prominent and sleepy-looking eyes, often subject to styes and redness on the lids; often a peculiarity about the feet, which may be found in excess of 90 degrees to each other when standing, and may be either particularly large or small and dainty.

V

The Twelve Houses of the Chart

---

75. *The Three Kinds of Houses.* The horoscope chart is divided into twelve houses (sections), namely:

Four Angular Houses: I, IV, VII, X.
Four Succedent Houses: II, V, VIII, XI.
Four Cadent Houses: III, VI, IX, XII.*

One house of each kind (angular, succedent, cadent) make up a quadrant of the horoscope, if each house be considered to begin at its cusp. (If the other view be taken, that the cusp is the centre of the house, then a quadrant begins and ends at cusps of angular houses, and contains the second half of one angular house, the whole of one succedent and one cadent house, and the first half of another angular house.)

76. *Houses and Signs.* The houses are sometimes regarded as being so analogous to the twelve signs of the zodiac that the ruler (Mars) of the first sign (Aries) is called the 'natural ruler' of the first house, even though the sign Aries be nowhere near the first house; Venus (ruler of Taurus) the natural ruler of the second house; and so on. The so-called 'accidental ruler' of the first house is the ruler of whatever sign may be on the cusp of house I. Thus if the cusp of the second house is 25° Sagittarius, then Venus (ruler of Taurus, the second sign) is 'natural ruler', and Jupiter (ruling planet of Sagittarius) is 'accidental ruler', of the second house. But the planet that

---

* Houses are referred to by roman numerals throughout the text, but by arabic numerals in the ephemeris.

is actually *in* the house is probably the 'effective', or more important, 'ruler' of that house, if any planet *is* in the house. As ruling or most important planet of a house, therefore, consider:

(i) The planet contained in the house itself, if any; if more than one, the one nearest to the cusp, or, if one before and one after the cusp, the one after the cusp, if at least in the half-house that starts at the cusp.

(ii) If there be no planet in the house, the 'accidental ruler' (ruling planet of the sign on the cusp of the house).

77. *Influences in Houses.* The matters dealt with by a particular house, however, are subject to the combined influences inferred from the most important or ruling planet (as above), the aspects to that planet, the sign containing the accidental ruler, the aspects, house positions, and sign position of the 'natural ruler'; and the nature and aspects of any other planets that are actually in the house, and the signs *they* are in (because part of the house may be in a sign not on the cusp).

78. Subject Matter of Each House

HOUSE I. The person himself (the native); his personal appearance, the character he *shows*, his personality as manifested in life on Earth; his behaviour and manner in general, and general tendencies as to personal relations with others.

HOUSE II. Money and movable possessions; income and expenditure; financial fortunes; attitude towards these and one's own body.

HOUSE III. Brainwork, communications, going about, brethren and neighbours (including studies, speech, languages, writing, publicity, agencies, retail trade, short journeys, and relationships with brothers, sisters, cousins, etc.).

HOUSE IV. Home environment, closing years of retirement from public work, dwelling place, houses and landed property, and one of the parents (probably the mother); one's roots. First house of the unconscious.

HOUSE V. Creation, recreation, procreation; love affairs, courtship; childbirth and the begetting of children; children and the young in general; creative artistic work; amusements and pleasures; business or professional work connected with amusement and pleasure (the stage, screen, concert platform, etc.); sexual compatibility in married life; gambling or speculation.

HOUSE VI. Servants and employees; or relations with employer and work, as a subordinate employee; service and healing; sickness and recovery; which parts of the body are most likely to suffer in illness or injury.

HOUSE VII. Pairing with an equal; marriage and agreed partnerships (domestic or professional or commercial); joint undertakings, company business; war, litigation, open conflict with an opponent (as in an election or competition); one's 'opposite number', in fact.

HOUSE VIII. Death (one's own or anyone else's affecting one); inheritance of goods or money or characteristics etc.; any activities or interests concerned with death or the dead (undertaker's business, position as executor of will, mediumship for communication with the departed, etc.); 'other people's money' (position as custodian or manager of it; finances as affected by husband's or wife's or partner's affairs); bequests and legacies; by analogy, the energies involved with orgasm, sleep and transformation. The second house of the unconscious.

HOUSE IX. 'Remote exploration' in either a geographical or metaphysical sense: foreign travel, relations with foreigners, foreign interests or people; religious and philosophical outlook and experiences and interests; the law and lawyers; the Church and churchmen; predictive dreams.

HOUSE X. Fame or notoriety, reputation, public work, career, professional business and position in the world, which are reflections of one's true vocation (i.e. MC or Midheaven); the other parent (probably father).

HOUSE XI. Position in social organization – friends, acquaintances, social contacts, interests in open societies or organizations for social reform or idealistic or altruistic or philanthropic purposes.

HOUSE XII. The secret inner life; secret societies (Freemasonry, etc.); places of seclusion and restraint (hospitals, prisons, asylums, orphanages and similar institutions); life of fantasy and day-dream;

conspiracies and intrigue, secret enemies or enmities; idle dreams. Third house of the unconscious (collective unconscious?).

79. **Element Affinities of Houses.** Adventurous and creative houses, corresponding to the Fire signs of the zodiac, are the first, fifth and ninth. Materialistic houses, corresponding to the Earth signs, are the second, sixth and tenth. Mental houses, corresponding to the Air signs, are the third, seventh, eleventh. Psychic houses, corresponding to the Water signs, are the fourth, eighth, twelfth.

Planets in Houses

Subject to modifications by aspects and by the sign each planet is in, and other considerations, the following give an idea of the meaning of each planet in or ruling each house (numbers I–XII show the houses).

80. **Sun in:**

I Health, vitality, honour, courage, success.

II Financial prosperity.

III Success in writing or the like, in going about, in dealings with kindred and neighbours.

IV Good auguries for matters of residence, home life and real estate.

V Richness of love life and emotional experience, speculation; good for pleasure, children, social functions.

VI Success in employment; possibly delicate health.

VII Good for marriage, partnership or company business, popularity.

VIII Success in other things *through* marriage or partners, or inheritance.

IX Success in law or the Church, or abroad.

X Success in occupation and career, positions of responsibility.

XI Social and material success through friends and superiors.

XII Retired life and occupation, much withdrawn.

81. **Moon in:**

I Changeable, imaginative, acquisitive, journeys.

II Fluctuating 'ups and downs' in finances (aspects, good or bad, make great difference).

III Many journeys or removals: inquiring, active mind.

IV Good for real estate, inheritance and domestic life; changes.

V Many love affairs, some fickleness perhaps, tends to large family.

VI Best as employee, gain in service; sometimes not very strong vitality.

VII Success in marriage and partnership (if with good aspects to Moon), popularity, and publicity.

VIII Legacies; gain or loss (according to aspects) through deaths.

IX Much travel, or changeable outlook in matters of religion and philosophy; success in these things if well-aspected.

X Fluctuating variations of success (good, with good aspects) in profession and public life, with changes probable; popularity in profession.

XI Popularity socially, many associates, women friends.

XII Good for interests associated with hospitals, prisons, etc.; some seclusion.

82. Mercury in:

I Witty, quick-witted, good speaker, good dealer.

II Financial gain through brainwork.

III Good brain, excellent for brainworking professions.

IV Many changes of residence.

V Clever children, mental pleasures.

VI Good as employee in brainwork.

VII Marriage with mental interests shared; good for businesses (companies or partnerships) in Mercurian lines (journalism, publishing, transport, etc.).

VIII Nerviness; gain or loss through deaths.

IX Good intellect, professional abilities (especially law or Church); much travel.

X Professional career in Mercury lines (literary, publishing, commerce, transport).

XI Clever, not always reliable, friends.

XII Worries, mental distractions.

83. Venus in:

I Pleasing disposition, popular, artistic, sociable, good looks.

   II Financial success, if no bad aspects.

  III Harmony with relatives of same generation; success in studies
      and in things involving going from place to place in own
      country; perhaps in literary work, especially of artistic or
      romantic kinds.

  IV Harmonious closing years of life; good fortune in matters of
      real estate; peaceful home life.

   V Good for love, children, pleasure, artistic or musical work.

  VI Good for health and for employment.

 VII Success in marriage and partnership.

VIII Money by legacies or marriage, if not badly aspected.

  IX Gain through travel, or happiness in religion.

   X Gain through parents, happiness in career.

  XI Pleasure and profit through friendships.

 XII Charitable, or gain from charity; secret love affairs.

84. Mars in:

   I Enterprising spirit, quick temper, quick worker, energetic,
      plucky.

  II Extravagance, heavy expenses or losses, wealth needs effort to
      gain.

  III Combative mind, quarrels with kindred, perhaps literary.

  IV Troubled home life; losses in real estate.

   V Trouble through children, love affairs, pleasure, gambling; if
      with good aspects, male children.

  VI Trouble through servants or with employers; illnesses, if any,
      feverish or inflammatory – wounds, cuts, burns.

 VII Passionate or unfortunate marriage; conflict; possible loss of
      spouse.

VIII Legacies; if with bad aspects, possibilities of disputes *re* legacies
      or inheritance, or of violent manner of death; bereavements.

  IX Militant in religious and philosophical matters; litigation;
      dangers in foreign travel.

   X Masterful; warlike, or surgical, or engineering, or similar occupa-
      tions; difficulties or troubles regarding career or business, or
      parents (or one).

  XI Unpopularity, or trouble with, or death of, friends.

XII Dangers of persecution, treachery, self-undoing literal or metaphorical.

85. Jupiter in:

I Noble nature, wise, merciful, religious.

II Best indication of financial prosperity, if no bad aspects; some extravagance possible, especially with bad aspects.

III Refined mind, good for going about, and relations with kinsmen.

IV Domestic happiness, prosperity from parents, or from real estate.

V Fortunate in children and speculation, expansive in social pleasures.

VI Success as employer or employee; health good if not badly aspected.

VII Excellent for marriage and partnership.

VIII Legacies, money by marriage.

IX Success in religion, law, the Church, voyages abroad.

X Rise to affluence, fame.

XI Influential friends, social popularity.

XII Success in occultism or Freemasonry; benevolence.

86. Saturn in:

I Cautious, worldly, acquisitive, persistent.

II Economy, restricted means, gain difficult and needs hard work.

III Slow but thoughtful mind; on cold terms with relatives.

IV Unhappy or cramped home life.

V Sorrow through children; losses in speculation; frustration in love.

VI Trouble with servants or in employment; ill health if with bad aspects, especially lingering or chronic maladies, or through cold.

VII Late, not always happy, marriage, or with discrepancy in age or social rank.

VIII If with bad aspects, many losses by death; slow death.

IX Troubles through, or frustration in, travel or religion; if with good aspects, very serious philosophical mind.

X Slow rise in life; if with bad aspects, risks of ultimate downfall.

XI Friends faithful and few, or (with bad aspects) lost through death.

XII Morbid introspection or fantasies; risks through treachery.

87. Uranus in:

I Strong will, independence, originality, although restless and highly strung.

II Speculation, financial independence.

III Inventiveness, exaggeration, contradiction of ideas.

IV Domestic instability, enforced changes.

V Creative originality, sudden infatuations.

VI Unusual career; unusual health symptoms.

VII Competitive nature; sudden attachments in love, erratic romances, jealousy.

VIII Unexpected financial gains through legacy, sudden accidents.

IX Unorthodox philosophical outlook; unexpected journeys.

X Versatile; seeks freedom; powerful position through advancement.

XI Sudden friendships and attachments; high ideals.

XII Intuitive nature.

88. Neptune in:

I Visionary, idealistic, receptive, imaginative, changeable.

II Financial compunctions, indifferent to money.

III Impressionable, intuitive.

IV Strong parental ties, seclusion in latter years.

V Pleasure-seeking, though easily bored.

VI Lack of effort; sensitive to environment.

VII Sacrificial demands in marriage.

VIII Sensitivity, financial disappointments.

IX Mystical, idealistic, inconclusive.

X Artistic occupation, impractical, high inspirations.

XI Demanding nature with friends.

XII Charitable, sympathetic, contemplative.

89. Pluto in:

I Sense of adventure, good potentialities, courage, stable, learns by experience.

  II Sensational and unusual activities.

 III Versatile, original, revolutionary.

 IV Many changes in home and environment.

  V Impulsive creative urge.

 VI Resourceful career in help to others.

 VII Co-operative, self-sufficient, secretive.

VIII Desire for truth, shrewd, philosophical.

 IX Quest for knowledge, love of travel.

  X Independence, self-assertive, quest for power.

 XI Prefers company of others, influential.

XII Mystical interest, suppressed emotions.

VI

The Rival Systems of House Division

NB: *You cannot fully understand this chapter without having read pp. 5–8 (Introduction) and mastered pp. 12–23 especially paragraphs 5, 6, 10, 11, 12, 19, 22, 25, 26, 27, 28.*

90. Placidus. The system most widely used at the present day is that of Placidus, seventeenth century, generally adopted in England in the eighteenth century, and now (quite mistakenly) supposed, by those no better informed, to be the standard traditional system, simply because tables of houses based on it, but not mentioning this fact or containing any hint that it is merely one system of many, were published over a century ago, and have since been imitated and continued, and enable students to copy the houses from them without any inquiry as to what they mean. The ordinary tables of houses on sale are really tables of the 'Houses According to Placidus'.

91. Placidus System Applied to 0° Aries or Libra. Ascendant and MC are used as cusps of houses I and X. If the Ascendant happens to be 0° of Aries, it will be the MC six sidereal hours later, the Descendant six hours after that, the IC six hours later still, and the Ascendant again after another six hours, completing the twenty-four hours. From eastern horizon (where it is Ascendant) to the meridian over the Earth (where it is MC) and from there to western horizon (where it is Descendant) are the two diurnal semi-arcs of this degree; and under the Earth are its two nocturnal semi-arcs. This degree, and also 0° of Libra, takes thus an equal period of six hours to go through each semi-arc, which corresponds to one quadrant of the horoscope chart. So Placidus makes 0° of Aries or Libra each cusp in turn, in reverse numerical order, namely, cusps I, XII,

XI, X, IX, VIII, VII, VI, V, IV, III, II, and I again at equal intervals of two hours sidereal time.

92. *Applied to Other Degrees and Signs.* But at the geographical latitude of London, for instance, o° of Gemini, as a random example, takes nearly eight hours going through each diurnal semi-arc (or backwards through the two quadrants from I to X and from X to VII), and only about four hours going through each of the other two semi-arcs (or quadrants of the chart), under the Earth. So, for London, Placidus makes o° Gemini cusp I at sidereal time 20h 0m, XII at 22h 37m, XI at 1h 14m, X at 3h 51m, taking about 2h 37m from cusp to cusp above the Earth, and then at the shorter interval of about 1h 24m (all these times are only approximate) he makes it reach in turn each of the remaining cusps below the Earth. This system is therefore based on *artificially equalized* subdivisions of the *naturally unequal* amounts of time a degree of the zodiac spends in each quadrant. Taking each degree in turn, after the time when it is Ascendant at a given place has been calculated, as well as the time when it is MC (the same at all places), it is easy, by this system, to make a complete table of houses for that place. But without such a complete table it would be far too difficult for most people to calculate what are the twelve cusps at a given moment. So this is a good 'publisher's system' for tables of houses!

93. *Notes on Placidus.* This is the only system that is not geometrical: does not divide the entire celestial sphere into areas, equal or unequal, by lines meeting at any two opposite points (which would be poles of whatever primary circle might be used as basis of a system of house division. No such primary circle is the basis of the Placidus system). All other systems are geometrical, and divide the whole sphere into areas bounded by lines perpendicular to, and meeting at the poles of, one primary circle. As some degrees of the zodiac are never Ascendant or Descendant (cusps I and VII) at geographical latitudes greater than 66°33′, those degrees, at such places, have no time-interval from cusp I to cusp X to divide (and similarly in the other three quadrants), so cannot be given any house position, and if not exactly MC or IC (cusp X or IV), have to be left out of the horoscope, along with any planet, or even the Sun or

Moon, happening to be in those degrees. A well-known New York lady, author and lecturer, has no Jupiter in her horoscope by this system, for that reason, having been born at latitude 70° N. in Greenland.

94. *The Equal House System* simply uses Ascendant as cusp I and then divides the whole zodiac into twelve equal parts for the twelve houses, by putting the same degree of the next sign on the next cusp (II), the same degree of the sign after that on cusp III, and so on all round. As the MC is usually more or less than 90° (or three signs) from the Ascendant, the MC by this system, is not usually cusp X or any other cusp, but is by modern users of the system considered an important point in the sky and marked wherever it comes, which may be in *any* house above the horizon. Then perhaps the Equal House cusp X is judged as indicating the career to which the native's personality inclines him, while the MC in another part of the chart may show the career into which worldly conditions force him. This system (but with no use of the MC at all in olden days) is the most ancient of all.

95. *The Porphyry System* (the second oldest of all, still in use) simply divides into three equal parts that section of the zodiac, whether less or more than 90°, that is contained in each quadrant, after allotting the MC to cusp X and the Ascendant to cusp I, so that if there be 45° of the zodiac between MC and Ascendant, and 135° between Ascendant and IC, the degrees between cusps will be 15° between each pair of cusps from X to I, and 45° between each pair from I to IV.

96. *The Natural Graduation System*, discovered or invented, and introduced by Colin Evans some years ago, and still not widely accepted, aims at improving on the Porphyry system by abolishing the arbitrary method of making artificially equal subdivisions of naturally unequal quadrants. Dividing the horoscope chart into twenty-four half-houses (because the middle point of each quadrant is halfway between one cusp and another, and it is a disputed question whether the cusp is the beginning or the centre of a house), this system assumes that these (or any smaller fractions into which we might divide houses) are *gradually* and *continuously*

increasing, as measured in degrees of the zodiac, in both directions, from a minimum at the middle of a quadrant holding less than 90° of the zodiac, to a maximum at the middle of each neighbouring quadrant, which holds more than 90°. If the second half-house from the middle of a quadrant is (say) one and a half times as 'big' (in the zodiac) as the one nearest the middle of that quadrant, then the one that is third from the middle of the quadrant will be one and a half times as great as the one second from the middle; and so on till the maximum is reached at the middle of the next quadrant. Joining these half-houses two-and-two gives the houses.

97. *Campanus and Regiomontanus* are the names associated with the other two systems in common use. The Campanus system, which dates from the thirteenth century, is now the most favoured in Britain by those who reject Placidus; the Regiomontanus system (dating from Ibn Ezra in the eleventh century, but made more widely known by Regiomontanus in the fourteenth century) is more used on the Continent but was the one used by the greatest British astrologers before the general adoption of Placidus. Both these systems reflect the idea that as we look eastward for the first house, midway between east and west in the upper sky for the tenth, west for the seventh, and so on, the primary circle to which house boundaries should be perpendicular must be the line that runs east and west from our place on Earth, the prime vertical. After all (it may be argued), the Ascendant and the MC are on the horizon and the meridian, which are perpendicular to the prime vertical, and meet at its poles, which are the North and South Points of the horizon. So Campanus and Regiomontanus make all the other cusps also points on lines perpendicular to the prime vertical and meeting at the North and South Points of the horizon. The difference between these two systems is that Campanus sets these lines equally wide apart, thus dividing the prime vertical itself into twelve equal parts between the twelve cusps, while Regiomontanus spaces them unequally, so as to divide the *Equator* equally. (Horizon and meridian are the only two lines perpendicular to the prime vertical that can divide *both* it *and* the Equator equally at the same time.)

98. *The Kochian System.* The Kochian system is a method

of house division, devised by the German astrologer Koch, based on the individual calculation of the cusps of intermediate houses for the place of birth. It is one of the methods that trisects the diurnal semi-arc by time division. This method produces a grid that has no valid application in polar regions, and tables of houses are available only to 60° of latitude; even so, it rapidly gained support among astrologers after its introduction in 1962. It has been remarked (by Genuit) that 'One wonders why, over hundreds of years, nobody has hit on this correct and obvious idea.' The method is sometimes called the GOH system (derived from the German *Geburtsortes Hausertabellen*) and sometimes the Birthplace system.

It is reportedly the most widely used system in the United States and is used by some of the leading lights in the field of astrological/ in-depth psychology in many places throughout the world. I have no experience using the Kochian system, as the Natural Graduation system is adequate, progressions and transits to a cusp invariably show up within 1° of that given cusp.

99. Other Systems. There are other systems, but none that the beginner need bother with for purely practical purposes. The tables of houses given in the present book provide for the use of any or all of the systems mentioned here, leaving the choice to the student. Those who feel they do not yet know enough of the subject to make a well-guided choice are advised to start with the Equal House system, as being the simplest of all, but to experiment soon with Natural Graduation and either Regiomontanus or Campanus, or both. If under a teacher, you should use the system that teacher advises till you outgrow tuition.

100. When Systems are the Same. At geographical latitude 0° (i.e. at places on the Equator) there is no difference between the systems of Placidus, Regiomontanus and Campanus, and relatively little difference between Equal House, Porphyry and Natural Graduation, or between these three and the other three. At 6h and 18h the Ascendant is the same at all geographical latitudes, and exactly 90° from the MC. There is then no difference at all (whatever the geographical latitude) between the Equal House, Porphyry and Natural Graduation systems, and less difference than at other times between Placidus, Campanus and Regiomontanus, or between these and the other three systems.

101. **When Planets 'Have Latitude'.** Any planet is on the ecliptic only at two moments in the whole time taken for its orbital journey round the Sun (from about three months for Mercury to about 250 years for Pluto). At all other times the planet 'has latitude'. Boundary lines of houses or parts of houses in the Equal House, Porphyry and Natural Graduation systems, being perpendicular to the ecliptic, the zodiac's middle line, are also boundary lines of signs or degrees or other fractions of the zodiac. So even if a planet has much latitude, its place in the zodiac gives its real house position (house position of the planet's bodily location in the heavens) in these three systems. But the boundary lines of houses or any parts of houses in the Regiomontanus, Campanus and Placidus systems slant obliquely across the ecliptic and across lines perpendicular to it, and therefore slope away from one degree or sign of the zodiac into another as they extend northward or southward from the ecliptic. Hence when a planet has latitude (when it is not exactly on the ecliptic) the house position of the actual body of the planet is different from the house position of the point on the ecliptic that has the same zodiacal longitude. However, users of these systems still represent the planets in a chart by the zodiacal degrees the planets occupy, as if the planets were on the ecliptic. This is called the 'zodiacal position' of each planet. The house position of the planet's true bodily place in the heavens is called its mundane position and, when these systems of house division are used, needs very elaborate mathematical calculation to determine. It is employed only in some advanced techniques of timing predicted events. In the Equal House, Porphyry and Natural Graduation systems there is no distinction between zodiacal and mundane positions of planets.

102. **Difficulty of Choice.** On theoretical grounds good cases can be made out for all systems, though there are specially serious difficulties about Placidus. The test of practical use seems to give excellent results for each system in the hands of the best astrologers who use it. So there, for the moment, this controversial question must be left.

103. Cusps as Centres or as House Boundaries. At the present day, users of the Equal House, Placidus and Regiomontanus systems generally regard the cusp as the beginning of the house, though allowing planets a few degrees before it (up to perhaps 5° of the zodiac so long as that is only a small fraction of a whole house) to be considered as belonging to the house. This is the traditional view in European astrology (not in Indian). Users of the Natural Graduation, Porphyry and Campanus systems now mostly regard the half-house before a cusp as belonging to the same house as that cusp, so that the cusp becomes the 'centre' of the house. Some of the exponents of these systems take pains to mark on the chart not only the twelve cusps (as most important points in the twelve houses) but also the twelve 'midcusps', or points in between the cusps where half-houses beginning at cusps end, and half-houses that end at cusps begin, thus showing the actual beginning and end (as well as centre) of each house, according to the theory that the cusp is the centre of the house. Other (perhaps most) users of these systems, while regarding the cusp as centre of the house, do not think it important to mark the exact point where they consider the house begins, because house influence any really considerable distance from the cusp seems to be rather weak, and, such as it is, to spread a good deal over both the adjoining houses. Space in this book has made it quite impossible to provide for the 'midcusps' or half-house boundaries in the tables of houses, but after the tables of houses will be found a page of special tables by which those willing to take a little more trouble (hardly any for Natural Graduation, rather more for Regiomontanus and Placidus, most for Campanus) can find cusps in degrees and minutes by *all* systems except Koch, and midcusps for Natural Graduation and Campanus.*

---

* Colin Evans introduced the overlap theory, which suggests that the half-house before a cusp is an area of overlapping between two houses, while the half-house after the cusp belongs exclusively to that house. I endorse this theory also. *A.C.*

VII

Casting the Horoscope:
Finding the Sidereal Time of Birth

104. Information Needed

DATE OF BIRTH. This is the year, month and day of month.

MOMENT OF BIRTH. This is the hour and minute and (for great exactitude, hardly ever obtainable) second of time; for most practical purposes, the hour and approximate minute as nearly as known.

PLACE OF BIRTH. This means the geographical latitude and longitude, or longitude equivalent, of birthplace, and the Standard Time area or zone of birthplace.

105. Notes on Date and Time.
There is seldom any difficulty about date (except that a Russian birth may possibly involve a doubt whether it is an old-style or a new-style date – see p. 334–6).

Fortunately, *very great* exactitude about time seldom makes any appreciable difference to the reading of a natal, or birth, horoscope, though in special cases it may (and it does, for some advanced methods of predicting future events or tendencies with correct dates of their likely occurrence, where even a few seconds difference can matter greatly). 'Fortunately' is said because really exact birth time is so seldom obtainable. Opinions differ as to the values of various methods of 'rectification' (theoretical calculation of birth time, by astrological methods, more exactly than the time is recorded), but all of them are too difficult for the beginner to tackle, besides being more or less disputable as to which methods are valid. So the horoscope must be treated as more or less exact according to how closely birth time can be found out by making inquiries of relatives, etc. Accurate birth times are now more frequently given than in the past. This is no doubt due to the availability of digital watches as well as a revived interest in astrology. However it leads to the question of what the exact moment of birth is. Is it emergence from the womb, cutting the umbilical cord or the first breath/scream? The last is the most important, especially to those with an interest in either the Natural Graduation or Kochian systems. This is because the first breath is an outwardly visible and audible action heralding the incarnation of Spirit into Matter.

106. Note on Place. Standard Time area or zone means whether the birthplace is in a country that uses (or did at date of birth) GMT, or Paris mean time, or Dublin mean time, or Indian Standard Time, or American 'Eastern' or 'Mountain' time, etc. Particulars of standard zone times for different countries, and in some cases for before and after certain dates when a country changed its Standard Time, are given near the end of this book. When possible, and when it seems necessary, make inquiries as to the kind of time meant in the reported time of birth. Often the official standard or zone time was used on railways, etc., from the official date, but ignored by ordinary people in their private lives, who continued for some years to use the same kind of time as before the official adoption of railway time.

The geographical latitude is needed because it alters the Ascendant and other house cusps, and so means using a different page of the tables of houses given in this book. The geographical longitude or longitude equivalent is wanted because when Greenwich sidereal time at the moment of birth has been found as explained below, this has to be turned into local sidereal time of birth by adding or subtracting the longitude equivalent. This is one hour for every $15°$ of longitude, and 4 minutes for every extra $1°$ of longitude, one minute for every $15'$ of longitude, and four seconds of time for every $1'$ of longitude. Or it may be found from the table on p. 328. This longitude equivalent (with $+$ for east, and $-$ for west) is given, instead of actual geographical latitude, to save you trouble, in the lists of places on pp. 326–32. For places not named in these lists, look up latitude and longitude in the atlas or gazetteer, or inquire about nearest big cities, one of which is probably in the lists, and use latitude and longitude of that (if possible, with a correction according to miles east or west, south or north, from it, the amount of longitude or latitude for miles being tabulated for different parts of the world in a little table on p. 333).

107. Precision and Correctness are two different things. Whole degrees in a horoscope are more correct than degrees and minutes *if* the whole degrees are reliable and the minutes are not. Roughly, a difference of four minutes of time in a moment of birth makes a difference of about 1° on house cusps (it may be double this in some cases, or even more). So, Ascendant worked out in fractions of a degree, or in degrees and minutes, is absolutely *incorrect* because it is so precise, if birth time is uncertain to within about five minutes either way. Similarly, a degree error in the geographical longitude or latitude of birthplace may in some cases make up to 3° (most often about 1°) of difference to the Ascendant and other house cusps. And in places like London every mile from the official centre of the town, whose latitude and longitude are given in gazetteers, etc., may make about 1′ of difference to the latitude and longitude of the actual birthplace; it is a number of miles from Hampstead to Kennington if the birthplace is given merely as London! Slovenly lack of precision is bad in what professes to be exact and careful work, but really worse is a misleading amount of precision that ignores probable margins of error unavoidable from incomplete information. Never try to be more precise than justified by reliable, accurate, precise information available, or you will be *less* correct than you would be with less precision.

108. The Two Birth Times. These, of course, are really two methods of stating one birth-moment. Out of the many different ways that might be used for stating the moment of birth, two different ones must be used in casting the horoscope, and have to be arrived at from the reported time of birth, which may be given in some third way. The two ways in which birth-moment must be expressed for casting a horoscope are:

1. Greenwich Mean Time (GMT) of birth, for finding the planet's places from an ephemeris;

2. Local Sidereal Time of birth for finding the house cusps from the tables of houses.

Of these, GMT is found from reported time of birth by Steps I and II (below) in most cases (*special* cases will be easy for anyone with common sense to handle *if* he can get hold of the information needed for each case, often difficult in those special ones).

Local Sidereal Time is found from GMT, after that has been found, by Steps II, III and IV.

STEP I: TURNING SUMMER TIME INTO STANDARD OR ZONE TIME (never needed for births in a year before 1916). Make sure whether the reported time is the standard or zone time of the land of birth, or whether it is the legal 'summer time', 'daylight-saving time', etc., which is the standard or zone time with one hour (occasionally, as in British Double Summer Time, two hours) added. Details of this kind of 'summer time' are given on p. 340, but are in some cases incomplete due to lack of records. Details of *British* summer time are at the top of each page of ephemeris, 1916–1990 (see p. 340 for details of Double Summer Time (DST) and Central European Time (CET)). From the reported time of birth in such cases subtract the extra hour(s) of summer time. The result is standard or zone time.

STEP II: TURNING STANDARD OR ZONE TIME INTO GMT. Details of Standard and Zone Times for different countries, as far as ascertainable, are given on p. 341. They are given in the form plus (+) or minus (−) so many hours and minutes, and occasionally seconds, as for Paris in certain years. This means how fast (+) or slow (−) the Standard or Zone Time is compared with Greenwich. If the amount is '+' (more than Greenwich), it must be subtracted, making it less, to turn it into Greenwich time; if it is less than Greenwich, marked '−', it must be added, to increase it and make it into Greenwich time. This step is never needed in Great Britain, nor in Eire or Northern Ireland after October 1916.

Steps I and II, or whichever, if either, is needed, give you the GMT of birth. Use this for finding the planets' places. And use it as starting point for the following additional steps, which find the local

Sidereal Time of birth, but note (see Step III) the possibility of the
Greenwich-time *date* being the *day* before or after the reported day of
birth.

STEP III: FINDING THE GREENWICH SIDEREAL TIME AT MID-
NIGHT (ooh oom) FOR THE REPORTED DATE OF BIRTH. The sidereal
time for any date is found by adding:

A. Sidereal time for the year (1 January at midnight given at the
top of each yearly page of the planetary ephemeris).
B. Sidereal time for the month (given on p. 166). It is important
to select the leap or common year figure appropriate to the
year in question.
C. Sidereal time for the day of the month (given on p. 166).

As the figure we are interested in is less than 24h, if the number is at
any stage in excess of that, subtract 24 to keep the number small and
reduce the chance of error. With births in Britain in summer time,
during the first hour of the morning (see Step I), the GMT birth
date will be the day *before* the reported birth date. Similarly with
births in other countries, where the zone time is, for instance, + 5h,
any birth before 05h will give a GMT birth date *before* the reported
one (see Step II). Conversely, with late p.m. births and large
Western zone times the addition to find GMT may well give the
GMT birth date as the day *after* the reported birth date. Fortunately
this does not occur frequently, but it is essential to know the rules in
order to produce good results. In these rather rare cases it is crucial
to find the sidereal time for the GMT date of birth and *not* for the
reported date (even though failure to do so will make the calculation
only about 3m 56s out, assuming the rest of the figures and their
addition are correct).

STEP IV: TURNING GREENWICH SIDEREAL TIME AT MIDNIGHT
INTO GREENWICH SIDEREAL TIME AT MOMENT OF BIRTH. Add to
the Greenwich sidereal time found in Step III the hours and
minutes of GMT of birth a.m. or p.m. (as found by Steps I and II)
plus the acceleration. This 'acceleration' is the difference between a
certain amount of time expressed in figures as *mean time* and the

same actual length of time expressed as hours and minutes and seconds of *sidereal time*. It is: ten seconds for every hour or one minute for every six hours, less one second for anything from 3½ to 10½ hours, and less another second for anything over 10½ hours. But it may be found at sight from the table on the same page as the additions for month and day (p. 166).

STEP V: TURNING GREENWICH SIDEREAL TIME INTO LOCAL SIDEREAL TIME. To or from the Greenwich sidereal time found by Step IV, add or subtract the longitude equivalent of the birthplace. Add if the place is east of Greenwich (longitude equivalent marked ' + ' in this book's list of places, or longitude marked E in an atlas or gazetteer) and subtract if west (marked ' − ' or W). The result of this addition or subtraction is the local sidereal time of birth.

109. Examples of Finding the Two Birth Times

EXAMPLE A: Born in Cardiff, Wales (Britain), longitude (from gazetteer) 3°10′ W; longitude equivalent (calculated from this) 12m 40s (given in List of Places in Britain as − 12m 40s), 2 July 1910, at 7.30 p.m.

Step I. Not needed.

Step II. Not needed.

GMT for planets therefore is 7.30 p.m., or 19h 30m.*

	h	m	s
Step III. From ephemeris for 1910, sidereal time			
midnight 1 Jan.	6	39	3
From p. 166 add for July (common year)	11	53	36
Add for 2nd of the month	0	3	57
	18	36	36

* Because we use midnight in the ephemeris it is important to state times on the 24-hour clock in order not to accidentally drop half a day's travel.

	h	m	s
Step IV. Add GMT of birth	19	30	0
Add acceleration for 19h 30m (12h)	0	1	58
(7h 30m)	0	1	14
	38	9	48
Step V. Longitude equivalent (subtract because W) .	0	12	40
	37	57	8
Subtract 24 to give less than 24	24	0	0
Local Sidereal Time of birth	13	57	8

The seconds may not be correct, because they were not given in the reported birth time, but we used seconds in adding the different items because omitting 20s, for example, every time *might possibly* have added up to an error of 2m. Now, however, we round off by calling more than 30s a minute, or less than 30s 'no minutes', and say:

Local sidereal time of birth (used for houses) is 13h 57m.

EXAMPLE B: Born in Yarmouth, Norfolk, England, longitude 1°43′ E, longitude equivalent +6m 52s, 2 July 1951, at 10.24 a.m.

	h	m	s
Step I. Reported time	10	24	0
British Summer Time	1	0	0
Standard Time	9	24	0

Step II. Not needed, so time just found is GMT.
Step III. From ephemeris for 1951, sidereal time

	h	m	s
MIDNIGHT	6	39	20
Addition for July (as in Example A)	11	53	56
2nd day	0	3	57
Step IV. GMT a.m.	9	24	0
Acceleration for 9h 24m	0	1	33

Step V. Longitude equivalent (add for E or +)	o	6	52
	28	9	38
Deduct 24h and round off to whole minutes ...	24	o	o
Local Sidereal Time of birth	4	10	

EXAMPLE C: Born in Albany, New York, USA, Eastern Standard Time (− 5h), longitude 74° W, longitude equivalent − 4h 56m, 31 July 1951 at 10.24 p.m.

	h	m	s
Step I. From reported time, Summer Time	22	24	o
Subtract Summer Time	1	o	o
Zone time (Eastern Standard Time, USA)	21	24	o
Step II. Add the zone time difference	5	o	o
GMT of birth is therefore p.m. 31 July	26	24	o
Which is a.m. of the Greenwich-time date,			
1 Aug. 1951	2	24	o
Step III. (Remember Greenwich-time date, 1 Aug., so there is no need to add for the day of the month.) Sidereal Time ephemeris, 1951,			
1 Jan...............................	6	39	20
Add for August (common year)	13	55	50
Step IV. GMT of birth	2	24	o
Acceleration for 2h 24m	o	o	24
Greenwich Sidereal Time of birth	22	59	34

Step V. Subtract for west longitude (− longitude
    equivalent) 4 56 0
                                          ———————

Local Sidereal Time of birth (rounded off to
    whole minutes) 18   4

EXAMPLE D: Born in Peking (longitude 116°30′ E; longitude
equivalent 7h 46m 0s; but zone time is + 8h), on 1 Jan. 1952 at 7
a.m.

	h	m	s
Step I. Not needed.			
Step II. Reported time ....a.m.	7	0	0
Subtract zone time (because east)	8	0	0
Eight hours before 7 a.m is previous day ...p.m.	11	0	0
Which gives GMT on Greenwich-time date			
31 Dec. 1951.			
Step III. 1 Jan. 1951	6	39	20
Add for Dec. (common year)	21	56	49
And for 31st	1	58	17
Giving midnight 31 Dec. 1951	30	34	26
Subtract 24h	24	0	0
	6	34	26
Step IV. Add GMT of birth, 23h	23	0	0
Add acceleration for 23h (12h)	0	1	58
(11h)	0	1	48
	29	38	12
Step V. Add for east longitude equivalent	7	46	0
	37	24	12

	h	m	s
Too big again: subtract 24 and round off to whole minutes	24	0	0
Local Sidereal Time of birth	13	24	0

NB: In the interest of newcomers to astrology midnight tables were chosen for their simplicity. Providing one has the sidereal time for the right day, the additions are always positive (no subtractions). It is possible, and in some cases preferable, to subtract the time difference between the GMT of birth and the midnight immediately following it. This could be done with the last example quite simply:

	h	m	s
Step III. Find sidereal time for 1 Jan. 1952	6	38	23
Subtract difference of GMT from midnight . . .	1	0	0
Step IV. GMT of birth	5	38	23
Subtract acceleration for 1h	0	0	10
	5	38	13
Step V. Add (in this case) longitude equivalent	7	46	0
Local Sidereal Time of birth	13	24	13

The second of difference between this result and the above result makes no difference, as the seconds should be dropped anyway. The main thing to grasp here is that if one subtracts the interval between GMT of birth and the following midnight, the acceleration on that interval must also be subtracted.

VIII
Casting the Horoscope: the House Cusps

---

*110. **Finding the Cusps** of the houses depends on the system of house division chosen. Whichever system this is, the Ascendant will be cusp I. And, except in the Equal House system, the MC will be cusp X. Even in the Equal House system it is necessary to find the MC, though it is not a cusp of any house, because it should be marked inside a house, or against the outside of the 'wheel', to show where it comes. It is customary in careful work to aim at a standard of precision giving the nearest 1′ (one-sixtieth of a degree) on the Ascendant and MC, and for all planets, etc., but only the nearest degree on the cusps of the intermediate houses. For them, that is all that is permitted by the most-used tables of houses (Placidus) published in Britain. In quick or short work it is usually sufficient to give whole degrees only for everything, including Ascendant, MC and planets. In many cases, in fact, greater precision would be definitely wrong, as not being justified by precision of available data. Naturally, Evans is referring to books such as this. Using computers, much greater precision is possible and indeed desirable for some branches of astrology.*

*111. **The Condensed Tables of Houses** in this book give MC and Ascendant in degrees and minutes, and the intermediate cusps (XI, XII, II, III) in whole degrees (to the nearest degree), for every twelve minutes of sidereal time, with a separate table for each latitude. The intermediate-house cusps are given five times over, according to five different systems of house division: Regio-montanus, Campanus, Placidus, Natural Graduation, Koch (in what is believed to be their order of age). It is usually easy to see at a glance whether the differences between cusps at two consecutive* latitudes for which tables are provided are sufficient to make it advisable to correct those for the nearest latitude given by a proportionate part of the difference between the cusps given for that latitude and the cusps given for the next following or preceding latitude, or whether cusps given for the nearest latitude are good enough without correction. If birth time is known to within only about ten minutes either way, the nearest time given in the tables is good enough; if it is known more accurately, take cusps at two consecutive times between which the birth time lies, and use a proportion of the difference to get them correct for the actual birth time. The working out of Ascendant and MC and all cusps by each system in the Example Horoscope below will show what is meant, and will illustrate a way of arranging the work. In working these out the standard of precision used will be closer than usually worth while. In presenting final results, however, minutes, even when found, will not be given for the intermediate cusps; these will be rounded off to the nearest degree.

112. The Example Horoscope: Ascendant and MC (wanted whatever system of house division be used):

Man born at Cardiff, Wales; lat. 51°28′ N; long. 3°10′ W; 7.30 p.m., GMT, 2 July 1910. This is not, by the way, the horoscope of any real person but an imaginary case.

Local sidereal time (found as shown in the preceding chapter): 13h 57m. As this is between 13h 48m and 14h 0m, and the latitude is between 51° and 52°, we extract from the tables of houses the MC at both sidereal times given there, and the Ascendant at both times and both latitudes, to see how much difference 12m of time makes (and thence estimate how much difference 9m makes, to be added to 13h 48m in order to make the required 13h 57m), and how much difference 1° of latitude makes (to adjust the Ascendant given in tables for lat. 51° and make it correct for lat. 51°28′, by allowing for a proportionate part of the difference for 1° lat.). We find:

REMARKS. Note whether Ascendant moves forwards or backwards in the zodiac when the geographical latitude increases: backwards always if sidereal time is between 6h and 18h; otherwise forwards; in the present example backwards, so the difference for 28′

	Ascendants		Diff. for		Asc. for	MC
Sidereal time	lat. 51°	lat. 52°	1°	28′	51°28′	long.
13h 48m	25 ♐ 12	24 ♐ 3	− 1°9′	32.2′	24 ♐ 40	29 ♎ 3
14h 0m	27 ♐ 51	26 ♐ 40	− 1°11′	33.1′	27 ♐ 18	2 ♏ 11
Diff. for 12m					2° 38′	3° 8′
Difference for 9m (9/12 or ¾ of 12m)					1° 58′	2° 21′
Add differences to Asc. and MC at 13h 48m					24 ♐ 40	29 ♎ 3
Result: 13h 57m, lat. 51°28′ N					26 ♐ 38	1 ♏ 24
					Asc.	MC

has to be taken away from Ascendant at lat. 51°, not added. In the five systems of house division for which cusps XI, XII, II, III are given in the condensed tables of houses, those cusps sometimes move forward and sometimes backwards, sometimes some cusps one way and some the other at the same sidereal time, when the latitude of a place increases. A glance at tables for two consecutive latitudes shows which. Differences that are to be subtracted are marked ' − ', as done above. Difference for difference of time is always to be added, for changing any cusp at an earlier time to what is wanted for a later time.*

113. Opposite Cusps. In the following sections, where we find the other cusps (XI, XII, II, III) by various systems of house division, we do not bother to calculate cusps from IV to IX

* As an example in interpolation (finding intermediate amounts between amounts given in a table) we have dealt with 51°28′ as if the tables of houses gave nothing between 51° and 52°. As a matter of fact, because of the great number of London births, a table has been given for lat. 51°30′ (for London), which is close enough to 51°28′ to have rendered this work unnecessary.

inclusive, for the simple reason that once cusps X, XI, XII, I, II, III have been found, all that has to be done is to put the same degrees (and minutes if any) of the opposite signs on the opposite cusps. Opposite cusps are those that differ by 6 – the first and seventh, the third and ninth, the fourth and tenth, for example. Opposite signs, if not already known, can be learned from Section 34.

114. Southern Latitudes. The condensed tables of houses are calculated for northern latitudes. When a horoscope has to be erected for a southern latitude, proceed thus: pretend the sidereal time is twelve hours earlier or later, and pretend that the latitude is the equal northern latitude. Calculate the cusps accordingly, but change every sign to the opposite sign. This gives correct cusps for the real latitude (south) and time. For example, if a horoscope is needed for 51°28′ S, at sidereal time 1h 57m, we pretend it is for 51°28′ N at 13h 57m, and find Ascendant and MC as above to be 26 ♐ 38 and 1 ♏ 24, but changing these to the opposite sign we give the real Ascendant and MC as 26 ♊ 38 and 1 ♉ 24. If we found cusp XI was, let us suppose, 18 ♏ 39 by a certain system of house division, we should take this to mean that cusp XI is really 18 ♉ 39 by that system.

115. Intercepted Signs. These cannot occur in the Equal House system; in other systems it may happen that the same sign is on more than one cusp, and some other sign (perhaps more than one in the same half of the horoscope) seems to be omitted altogether. For example, there may be ♒ on one cusp and ♈ on the next, with ♓ omitted. In this case the 'omitted' sign is said to be intercepted – it begins after one cusp and ends before the next cusp. It is usual to mark it between the cusps, roughly nearer to whatever cusp it is really near (for example, if the cusp in ♒ was near the end of ♒ and the cusp in ♈ was near the beginning of ♈, obviously ♓ begins nearer the preceding cusp than the following one). If a sign is intercepted, the opposite sign must also be intercepted between the opposite cusps. Thus in the case just mentioned, ♍ is intercepted as well as ♓.

116. For Latitude 0° (which is omitted in the tables of houses here) the following rule will prove very simple. MC is the same as at any other latitude, so take it from a table of houses for some other latitude. Ascendant is the same as MC at sidereal time six hours later. The methods that will be taught for the Equal House and Porphyry systems will then apply. For the Natural Graduation system, the difference from Porphyry houses is so slight at latitude 0° as not to matter greatly, but a condensed table of Natural Graduation cusps for houses XI, XII, II, III is given on p. 282. For all other systems: XI is MC two hours later; XII is MC four hours later; II, eight hours later; and III is the MC ten hours later.

Special example for latitude 0°: sidereal time 3h 48m; Placidus system:

X (MC) is the MC at 3h 48m	29 ♉ 13
XI is the MC at 5h 48m	27 ♓ 15
XII is the MC at 7h 49m	25 ♋ 3
I (Asc.) is the MC at 9h 48m	24 ♌ 42
II is the MC at 11h 48m	26 ♍ 44
III is the MC at 13h 48m	29 ♈ 3

All these MCs used as different cusps are found in the MC column of the table of houses for any latitude.

117. Example Horoscope: Equal House System. The Ascendant is cusp I. The signs of the zodiac are put in their proper order on all the other cusps, starting at the sign on the Ascendant, and continuing all round. For the sake of giving, for every system, the houses X, XI, XII, I, II, III here, we have worked backwards from Ascendant to cusp X (which in this system is not the MC) and forwards from Ascendant to cusp III. But in practice you can simply go forward from I to XII in consecutive order right round the 'wheel'. The same degree is put on every cusp, and the same minutes if minutes are used. Here, for the sake of giving results in a similar form (for comparison) by all systems, we are keeping degrees and minutes on houses X and I but rounding off '26°38''' on the other cusps to the nearest degree, 27°. Thus we get:

House:	X	XI	XII	I	II	III
Cusp:	26 ♍ 38	27 ♏	27	26 ♐ 38	27 ♑	27 ♒
MC	1 ♏ 24 (between cusps XI and XII in this case)					

118. Example Horoscope: Porphyry System. For this system the distance in the zodiac from the MC to the Ascendant must be found and divided by three, and the result added to the MC to give the cusp of house XI, and added again to XI to give XII. Two whole signs forward from XII is II. Four whole signs forward from XI is III. Of course, X is the MC and I is the Ascendant.

From MC (1 ♏ 24) to end of sign (♏)	28°	36′
From beginning of Ascendant sign (♐) to Ascendant	26°	38′
Add 30° for each whole sign in between (none in this case)		
	3) 55°	14′
Divide by 3 and round up 24.6 to 25′ = ...	18°	24.6′
Add this to MC	1 ♏ 24	
Result for Cusp XI	19 ♏ 49	
Again add 18°25′ (change sign each 30°)	18°	25′
Result for Cusp XII	8 ♐ 14′	
The Ascendant is	26 ♐ 38	
Cusp XII (8 ♐ 14) plus two signs = Cusp II	8 ♒ 14	
Cusp XI (19 ♏ 49) plus four signs = Cusp III	19 ♓ 49	

Notice that as cusp X is in ♏, cusp IV will be the opposite sign, ♉, and therefore between cusps III (in ♓) and IV (♉) there is ♈ intercepted − which you might have overlooked, though seeing at once that ♒ is intercepted between ♑ and ♓. So we have:

House:	X	XI	XII	I	II	III
Cusp:	1 ♏ 24	20♏	8 ♐	26 ♐ 38	8♒	20 ♓
Intercepted	....				♑	.... ♈ .

Strictly speaking, one should not round fractions up or down until the calculations are finished. In this case we have used 18°24.6′, which was rounded up to 18°25′ and added twice; two 0.6′ = 1.2′ so the result for cusp XII should be less by 1′. This is not so important, as we shall be looking at only whole degrees.

119. Example Horoscope: Regiomontanus System. Use Ascendant and MC as cusps I and X as in the Porphyry system, but simply copy cusps XI, XII, II, III, as given under those house numbers* and under the name Regiomontanus in the tables of houses. A glance will usually be enough to show whether any correction is needed for a sidereal time or a geographical latitude in between the nearest ones given in the tables, when using the nearest time and latitude in the tables; and, if it is, a mental estimate of how much the correction should be is usually quite easy, as we are working only in whole degrees. But we will, for form's sake, do the work more elaborately, with an arrangement of the work that can be used in all cases:

We found cusps for 51°28′ by comparing those for 51 and 52° N latitude at each time in turn, noting that in this example greater

time	lat. 51° (in tables)				lat. 52° (in tables)				lat. 51°28′ (estimated)			
	XI	XII	II	III	XI	XII	II	III	XI	XII	II	III
13h 48m	18♏	5♐	2♒	26♓	1♏	4♐	1♒	25♓	1·♏ 4♐ 32	1♒ 32		25 ♓ 32
14h 0m	21♏	7♐	6♒	0♈	2♏	6♐	5♒	0♈	2♏ 6♐ 32	5♒ 32		0♈
12m time makes difference of									3° 2°	4°		4° 28′
So 9m time (¾ of 12m) makes a difference of									2°15′1° 30′3°	3°		21′
Add to 13h 48m									18'♏ 4♐ 32	1♒ 32		25 ♓ 32
Gives us cusps									20♏ 6♐	5♒		29 ♓ †

* Arabic numerals (11, 12, 2, 3) in the tables of houses.

† We can take the trouble to work in minutes of arc in interpolation of tables as long as we round up or down to the nearest whole degree. Obviously, as the house cusps are already rounded off in degrees, extra minutes calculated will not be that accurate.

latitude moves cusps *backwards* in the zodiac (it may move them either backwards or forwards, or some cusps one way and the others the other), and so subtracting from cusps at 51° latitude 28/60ths of the difference made by 1° latitude (slightly less than half the difference). In this particular example, as the difference made by 1° latitude is 1° or 0°, less than half that difference is always 0° in whole degrees, we need not have bothered with the table for latitude 52° but simply used cusps for latitude 51° for these houses, though not for the Ascendant (but see footnote to Section 112).

Thus we get, for the Regiomontanus system:

House:	X	XI	XII	I	II	III
Cusp:	1 ♏ 24	20♏	6 ♐	26 ♐ 38	5 ♒	29 ♓
Intercepted				♑		♈

120. Example Horoscope: Campanus System.* Method is exactly the same as that explained and shown above for the Regiomontanus system (section 119), only copying cusps from columns under Campanus in the tables of houses. For the Example Horoscope this gives:

House:	X	XI	XII	I	II	III
Cusp:	1 ♏ 24	14♏	29♏	26 ♐ 38	29♒	13♈
Intercepted				♑	♓	

121. Example Horoscope: Placidus System. Exactly the same method of work as for the Regiomontanus and Campanus systems, sections 119 and 120, only copying the cusps from columns under the name Placidus in the tables of houses.

For the Example Horoscope this gives:

House:	X	XI	XII	I	II	III
Cusp:	1 ♏ 24	23♏	10 ♐	26 ♐ 38	11♒	29♓
Intercepted				♑	♈	

* The table of houses for 51°30′ N is used for examples section 120 onwards.

In this case we round 10 ♐ 30 down to 10 ♐ , as 30′ is not over half a degree.

122. Example Horoscope: Natural Graduation System.
Exactly the same method as for Regiomontanus, Campanus or Placidus. This gives:

House:	X	XI	XII	I	II	III
Cusp:	1 ♏ 24	22 ♏	6 ♐	26 ♐ 38	2 ♒	25 ♓
Intercepted					♑	♈

122a. Example Horoscope: Koch System. Exactly the same method is used as for previous examples. This gives:

House:	X	XI	XII	I	II	III
Cusp:	1 ♏ 24	18 ♏	6 ♐	26 ♐ 38	22 ♑	5 ♓
Intercepted					♒	♈

IX
Casting the Horoscope: Planets

---

123. Finding the Planets' Places. In the new condensed ephemeris the Moon and Mercury longitudes (zodiacal positions) are given, as in previous editions, for every two and six days respectively. The other planets, Chiron and the mean North Node are given for every ten days from 1 January each year. This allows the same fractions to be used for each body, simplifying the process of calculating positions and reducing the chances of making mistakes. All positions are for midnight GMT (ooh oom) of the date given.

To calculate planetary positions, one must find the average daily travel of each body. This is multiplied by the number of days elapsed to midnight of the date of birth and added to the earlier position in the tables (subtracted if the planetary motion is retrograde). This gives the planetary position for ooh oom on the date of birth.

To find the position at the time of birth, the proportion of daily travel from ooh oom to the time of birth (i.e., hours elapsed divided by 24, multiplied by average daily motion) is added (subtracted if retrograde) to the ooh oom position found earlier.

This process is far from difficult, but there are several points to remember.

1. Always work in the same units; i.e., degrees and minutes, or hours and minutes.
2. There are 60′ to each degree of arc; therefore 1.5° is not 1°50′, but 1°30′.
3. There are 30° to each sign from the beginning of the zodiac (0° ♈). To add or subtract different signs, you must first convert them to degrees and minutes. For example, 22 ♋ 16 really

means 3 signs (90°) and 22° + 16′ from the beginning of the zodiac, or 112° 16′. See also Section 129.

Various examples of this process follow.

124. Example E: Moon's place wanted for 7.20 p.m. GMT (19h 20m) on 3 January 1950.

From ephemeris: 5 January 1950 . . . . 22 ♋ 16
       3 January 1950 . . . . 26 ♊ 19

Subtract to find 2 days' motion . . . . 25° 57′
Divide by 2 to find average daily motion . . . . 12° 58′

We know the 00h 00m position on the date of birth and the average motion for that date. By dividing 19h 20m by 24 to get the proportion of daily motion and multiplying this fraction by the average daily motion, we will find the motion travelled between 00h 00m and GMT of birth.

There are two ways to do this calculation. We can express 19h 20m in the decimal system as 19.3333 (20m is one-third — 0.3333 — of an hour). Then, perhaps using a calculator:

$$19.3333 \div 24 = 0.8055.$$

We can also convert 19h 20m to units of 20m:

$$(19 \times 3) + 1 = 58.$$

To keep the units the same, we must convert 24h to units of 20m:

$$24 \times 3 = 72. \quad \text{Then } 58 \div 72 = 0.8055.$$

In order to multiply the daily motion by this decimal fraction, we must reduce the 12° to minutes and add them to the 58′, or multiply the degrees and minutes separately and add them together later. Using the first method:

$$12 \times 60 = 720 + 58 = 778 \times 0.8055 = 626.7'.$$

We can round up the 0.7, making the result 627′. We divide 627′ by 60 to get whole degrees and minutes again: 10°27′. Then we add this to 00h 00m GMT on 3 January:

Midnight position 3 January . . . .   26 Ⅱ 19
Travel from 00h 00m to 19h 20m . . . .   10° 27

Result: Moon position 19h 20m on 3 January   . . . .   6 ♋ 46

Calculating the average motion of the planets is not an absolutely accurate method of calculating their position, but it is close enough for natal charts. We shall look at a more accurate method for the Moon later in this chapter (see Section 134).

125. *Example F:* Find Mercury's place at 7.00 a.m. GMT on 16 November 1950.

From ephemeris: 19 November 1950 . . . .   5 ♐ 59
            13 November 1950 . . . .   26 ♏ 42

Subtract to find 6 days' motion . . . .   9° 7′
Divide by 6 to find average daily motion . . . .   1° 31.2′
Multiply by 3 to find travel in 3 days . . . .   4° 33.6′
Find proportion of daily travel (GMT ÷ 24) and
   multiply by average daily motion (1°31.2′) to find
   travel from 00h 00m to 7.00 a.m. . . . .   0° 26.6′

Add: 00h 00m position 13 November . . . .   26° 42′
   Travel in 3 days (for 00h 00m 16 November) . .   4° 33.6′
   Travel from 00h 00m to 7.00 a.m. . . . .   0° 26.6′

Result: Mercury at 7.00 a.m. on 16 November 1950 .   1 ♐ 42.2
Round down to . . . .   1 ♐ 42

126. *Example G:* Find the position for Mars at 8.30 p.m. GMT (20h 30m) on 15 March 1982. In this case Mars is retrograde, so it is important to *subtract* movements instead of adding them.

From ephemeris: 12 March 1982	16 ♎ 49℞	
22 March 1982	13 ♎ 51℞	

Subtract to find 10 days' travel	− 2°	58′
Divide by 10 to find average daily motion	− 0°	17.8′
Multiply by 3 to find travel in 3 days (from 12 to 15 March)	− 0°	53.4′
Find proportion of daily motion (20.5 ÷ 24 = 0.854) and multiply by average daily motion (17.8) to find travel from 00h 00m to 20h 30m	− 0°	15.2′

Subtract from 00h 00m position 12 March the last two figures. To do this, first add them together:	16 ♎ 49℞	
− 53.4′ + − 15.2′ = − 68.6′ = − 69′ = ..	− 1°	9′

Result: Mars at 8.30 p.m. 15 March 1982	15 ♎ 40℞	

127. Example H: Find the position for Venus at 1 p.m. GMT (13h 00m) on 6 August 1983. In this case the ephemeris gives a direct position for 30 July and retrograde position for 9 August. This means the planet must have been in station during this period, and we should look to see when this station occurred. It is given as 4 August, with a position of 9 ♍ 30. Had we not checked this, we could have believed that the ten-day period encompassed a motion of only 6′ of arc. We can now use the midnight position for 4 August instead of 30 July.

From ephemeris: 4 August 1983	9 ♍ 30	
9 August 1983.	8 ♍ 59	

Subtract to find 5 days' travel (remember, the minus figure indicates retrograde motion)	− 0°	31′
Divide by 5 to find average daily motion	− 0°	6.2′
Multiply by 2 to find travel in 2 days	− 0°	12.4′

Find proportion of daily travel ($13 \div 24 = 0.541$),
  multiply by daily motion (-6.2) and round up to
  find travel from ooh oom to 13h oom . . . . $-0°$ $3.3'$

Subtract the last two figures ($-12.4 + -3.3 =$
  $-15.7 = -16$) from ooh oom position 4 August   9 ♍ 30
                                                  $-0°$ $16'$

Result: Venus at 1 p.m. 6 August 1983 . . . .   9 ♍ 14

Although often good enough, this is still not quite right, for a planet near its station goes much more slowly the day or two before and after station than a few days earlier or later still. A method for getting greater accuracy in such cases, with the faster planets, is given later in this chapter.

128. Example I: Find the position of Pluto on 24 September 1989 at 1 a.m. GMT.

From ephemeris: 28 September 1989 . . . .   13 ♏ 35
                  18 September 1989 . . . .   13 ♏ 16

10 days' travel . . . . $0°$ $19'$

Daily motion . . . . $0°$ $1.9'$

With the outer planets it is not worth finding the hourly proportion of a day's motion: they move so slowly that getting to the nearest midnight or noon will suffice. Rounding 1.9 up to 2, we can add six days' travel to the position on 18 September or subtract four days' travel from the position on 28 September.

Result: Pluto at 1 a.m. GMT 24 September 1989 13 ♏ 28, 13 ♏ 27 respectively.

129. Finding the Part of Fortune. Add the Moon's zodiacal longitude to the Ascendant and subtract the Sun's longitude or place in the zodiac. But how can you add (say) 13 ♉ to 29 ♒ and subtract 14 ♍? Remember that 13 ♉ really means 'one sign and 13° from the beginning of the zodiac', and 29 ♒ means '9 signs and 29°', and 14 ♍ means '5 signs and 14°'. Of course, ♍ is the sixth sign, but we say '5ˢ14°' because there are only five whole signs before Virgo, and then the 14° of Virgo are added. Make sure you can say offhand how many signs from the beginning of the zodiac any sign is:

>   ♈ is 1st sign, so before it there are   0 signs;
>   ♉ is 2nd sign, so before it there is   1 sign;
>   ♊ is 3rd sign, so before it there are   2 signs;
>   and so on.

Another way is to memorize how many degrees from the beginning of the zodiac 0° of each sign is, thus:

0 ♈ = 0°	0 ♋ = 90°	0 ♎ = 180°	0 ♑ = 270°
0 ♉ = 30°	0 ♌ = 120°	0 ♏ = 210°	0 ♒ = 300°
0 ♊ = 60°	0 ♍ = 150°	0 ♐ = 240°	0 ♓ = 330°

then add the degrees and minutes in the sign to the degrees equivalent to 0° of that sign. For example, 17 ♐ 23 is 240° (for 0 ♐) + 17°23′, making 257°23′.

130. Example J. Find Part of Fortune when Ascendant is 17 ♎ 43, ☽ is in 11 ♌ 46, and ☉ is in 14 ♑ 34:

Either this way		*Or this way*	
17 ♎ 43 is	6ˢ17°43′ Ascendant	17 ♎ 43 is	197°43′ Ascendant
11 ♌ 46 is	4ˢ11°46′ ☽	11 ♌ 46 is	131°46′ ☽
Add:	10ˢ29°29′		329°29′
14 ♑ 34 is	9ˢ14°34′ ☉	14 ♑ 34 is	284°34′ ☉
Subtract:	1ˢ14°55′		44°55′

Result: ⊕   14 ♉ 55

131. Example K. Find the Part of Fortune when the Sun is
9 ♐ 44, Moon is 20 ♉ 41 and Ascendant is 21 ♈ 30.

	Either this way	*Or this way*
Ascendant	0ˢ21°30′ (21 ♈ 30)	21°30′
☽ add	1ˢ20°41′ (20 ♉ 41)	50°41′
	2ˢ12°11′	72°11′
☉ subtract	9ˢ 9°44′ (9 ♐ 44)	279°44′

We cannot subtract the Sun's longitude from a *lesser* longitude, so
we add 12ˢ or 360° (the whole zodiac) to make a subtraction possible:

Ascendant + ☽	2ˢ42°11′	or	72°11′
add	12ˢ 0° 0′	or	360° 0′
	14ˢ12°11′		432°11′
☉	9ˢ 9°44′		279°44′
	4ˢ32°27′		152°27′
which is	5ˢ 2°27′		

Making the result 2 ♍ 27

(If Ascendant and ☽ add up to more than twelve signs or more
than 360°, we subtract twelve signs or 360° before proceeding, unless
we shall need them because the Sun is more than the remaining
signs and degrees would be.)

132. Completing the Example Horoscope. When finding
the places of all the planets for one nativity it is convenient to work
out together planets for which the same dates are given in the ephemeris.

By now you should realize the usefulness of a calculator, especially
if it has a memory facility, and particularly if you are given a birth
time to the nearest minute. For example, if the birth time is
5.17 p.m., or 17h 17m, you can convert 17 hours to minutes (× 60)

and add the 17 minutes to the result, making sure that when you divide by 24 (hours), you divide again by 60 so that the units (minutes) are the same. As the resulting fraction (the proportion of daily motion) is common to each calculation, it can sit in the memory until required.

Planetary positions required for 7.30 p.m. GMT (19h 30m) 2 July 1910.

☽ *Moon*

3 July (midnight)	17 ♉ 31
1 July (midnight)	18 ♈ 51
in 2 days	28° 40′
in 1 day	14° 20′
in 19½h (14°20′ × 0.812)	11° 39′
in 1 day 19½h	25° 59′
Add result to 1 July	18 ♈ 51
Result 7.30 p.m., 2 July 1910 . . .	14 ♉ 50

☿ *Mercury*

7 July (midnight)	29 ♊ 44
1 July (midnight)	19 ♊ 13
in 6 days	10° 31′
in 1 day	1° 45.1′
in 19½h (× 0.812)	1° 25.4′
in 1 day 19½h	3° 10.5′ (round down)
Add result to 1 July	19 ♊ 13
Result 7.30 p.m. 2 July 1910	22 ♊ 23

	⊙ *Sun*	♀ *Venus*	♂ *Mars*	♃ *Jupiter*
10 July	16 ♋ 52	11 ♊ 56	13 ♌ 1	6 ♎ 42
30 June	7 ♋ 19	0 ♊ 14	6 ♌ 47	5 ♎ 46
in 10 days	9° 33′	11° 42′	6° 14′	0° 56′
in 1 day	0° 57.3′	1° 10.2′	0° 37.4′	0° 5.6′
in 19½h (× 0.812)...	0 46.5	0 57	0 30.4	0 4.5
in 2 days	1 54.6	2 20.4	1 14.8	0 11.2
in 2 days 19½h	2° 41.1′	3° 17.4′	1° 45.2′	0° 16′
Add result to 30 June	7 ♋ 19	0 ♊ 14	6 ♌ 47	5 ♎ 46
Result	10 ♋ 0	3 ♊ 31	8 ♌ 32	6 ♎ 2

	♄ *Saturn*	♆ *Neptune*	♇ *Pluto*
10 July	5 ♉ 12	18 ♋ 59	26 ♊ 54
30 June	4 ♉ 28	18 ♋ 37	26 ♊ 40
in 10 days	0° 44′	0° 22′	0° 14′
in 1 day	0° 4.4′	0° 2.2′	0° 1.4′
in 19½h	0 3.5	0 1.7	0 1.1
in 2 days	0 8.8	0 4.4	0 2.8
in 2 days 19½h	0° 12′	0° 6′	0° 4′
Add result to 30 June	4 ♉ 28	18 ♋ 37	26 ♊ 40
Result	4 ♉ 40	18 ♋ 43	26 ♊ 44

When the numbers involved are relatively small, it is easier to add separate lines together without rewriting them. With practice, you can get quite used to this as well as to converting degrees to minutes, etc.

Chiron, Uranus and the North Node will be worked together as they are all retrograde; remember this requires subtraction.

	♄ Chiron	♅ Uranus	☊ North Node
30 June	2 ♓ 27℞	23 ♑ 54℞	26 ♉ 14℞
10 July	2 ♓ 11	23 ♑ 31	25 ♉ 42
in 10 days	−0 16	−0 23	−0 32
in 1 day	−0° 1.6′	−0° 2.3′	−0° 3.2′
in 19½h	−0 1.3	−0 1.8	−0 2.6
in 2 days	−0 3.2	−0 4.6	−0 6.4
in 2 days 19½h	−0° 4′	−0° 6′	−0° 9′
Subtract result from 30 June	2 ♓ 27℞	23 ♑ 54℞	26 ♉ 14℞
Result	2 ♓ 23℞	23 ♑ 48℞	26 ♉ 5℞

With the slower moving planets it may be easier to 'guesstimate'.

For the Part of Fortune

Add:

Ascendant	26 ♐ 38	=266°	38′
☽	14 ♉ 50	= 44	50
		311°	28′

Subtract:

Sun .... $10 \odot 0 = 100 \quad 00$

Part of Fortune .... $211° \quad 28'$

which is .... $\oplus \quad 1 \, ♏ \, 28$

133. Faster Planets Near Stations. The table below shows what fraction of X days' movement is made in Y days, reckoned backwards or forwards from the day of station. Look in the column headed with the number of days from the ephemeris date before the station to the day of the station, or from the day of the station to the ephemeris date after that; and look in the line for the number of days from the day of birth to the day of the station, or from the day of the station to the day of birth. The fraction found is what proportion of the movement that is made in the number of days named at the head of the column occurs in the number of days shown at the beginning of the line.

For days	of 12 days	of 11 days	of 10 days	of 9 days	of 8 days	of 7 days	of 6 days	of 5 days	of 4 days	of 3 days	of 2 days
1	$\frac{1}{64}$	$\frac{1}{50}$	$\frac{1}{45}$	$\frac{1}{32}$	$\frac{1}{30}$	$\frac{1}{22}$	$\frac{1}{16}$	$\frac{1}{12}$	$\frac{1}{8}$	$\frac{1}{5}$	$\frac{2}{5}$
2	$\frac{1}{25}$	$\frac{1}{20}$	$\frac{1}{16}$	$\frac{1}{12}$	$\frac{1}{11}$	$\frac{1}{8}$	$\frac{1}{6}$	$\frac{1}{5}$	$\frac{1}{3}$	$\frac{1}{2}$	...
3	$\frac{1}{12}$	$\frac{1}{10}$	$\frac{1}{8}$	$\frac{1}{7}$	$\frac{1}{6}$	$\frac{1}{5}$	$\frac{1}{3}$	$\frac{2}{5}$	$\frac{3}{5}$	...	...
4	$\frac{1}{8}$	$\frac{1}{7}$	$\frac{1}{6}$	$\frac{1}{6}$	$\frac{1}{3}$	$\frac{1}{4}$	$\frac{1}{2}$	$\frac{2}{3}$	...	...	...
5	$\frac{1}{6}$	$\frac{1}{5}$	$\frac{1}{5}$	$\frac{1}{3}$	$\frac{2}{5}$	$\frac{1}{2}$	$\frac{3}{4}$	...	...	...	...
6	$\frac{1}{4}$	$\frac{1}{3}$	$\frac{1}{3}$	$\frac{1}{2}$	$\frac{1}{2}$	$\frac{2}{3}$	...	...	...	...	...
7	$\frac{1}{3}$	$\frac{2}{5}$	$\frac{1}{2}$	$\frac{3}{5}$	$\frac{3}{4}$	...	...	...	...	...	...
8	$\frac{1}{2}$	$\frac{3}{5}$	$\frac{2}{3}$	$\frac{4}{5}$	...	...	...	...	...	...	...
9	$\frac{3}{5}$	$\frac{2}{3}$	$\frac{4}{5}$	...	...	...	...	...	...	...	...
10	$\frac{3}{4}$	$\frac{4}{5}$	...	...	...	...	...	...	...	...	...
11	$\frac{4}{5}$	...	...	...	...	...	...	...	...	...	...

EXAMPLE: Wanted, Mercury's place at 00h 00m on 3 October 1989.

The ephemeris gives station on 4 October as 25 ♍ 44 and on ephemeris date 1 October as 26 ♍ 31℞. This suggests a total movement of − 47′ over three days. From the station date to the birth date is one day, so we align the 1 in the 'for days' column with the 'of 3 days' column and find ⅓. We apply this figure to the total movement to find the distance travelled over a period of days (in this case one day) to or from the station: ⅓ of − 47′ = − 9′. The result is added (because motion was retrograde prior to station) to 25 ♍ 44, which gives 25 ♍ 53. This figure is accurate to within 4′ of arc, which is far closer than if we had simply added ⅓ of the total motion to the station, resulting in 26♍ , over 10′ of arc out. Obviously this method gives an improvement on accuracy, yet is insufficient for advanced precision work, to which a daily ephemeris is more suited. Note whether the birthday is before or after the station date, we always *subtract* the fractional part of total movement if station is where planet changes from direct to retrograde, but *add* if planet is changing from retrograde to direct.

(Apology to mathematicians and astronomers: this table professes to be nothing better than *roughly* approximate, *convenient* fractions, based empirically on a few typical cases. It is a development of the method given by Waite in his original work, though much extended and rearranged. *Evans.*)

134. Correction of Moon's Position for Varying Speed. If this optional method of obtaining a little closer accuracy for the Moon's place is adopted, it is necessary to copy from the ephemeris in this book *four* days' midnight positions of the Moon: the two between which the time and date of the horoscope fall, and the one before those and one after those. We thus have (usually) three intervals of two days each. Near the end or the beginning of a month it may be one interval of one day and two intervals of two days each; cases that are to be dealt with in a special way; see below.

Using first the ordinary method of finding the position as if speed were uniform, taught above, we get an *uncorrected position*, based solely on the Moon's movements during the middle interval (the interval inside which is our required birth date or birth time). For the correction: find the difference between the distance moved in the preceding and in the following period (ignoring that middle period). Take a fraction of this difference (as shown in the brief table on p. 123) and add it to or subtract it from the uncorrected position: *add* if the Moon is moving more *slowly* after the birth date; *subtract* if the Moon is moving more *quickly* after the birth date (that is, *add* if the movement is less in the third period; *subtract* if the movement is more in the third period than in the first period).

EXAMPLE: Required Moon's place at 00h 00m on 24 September 1989. The ephemeris gives:

21 September	14 ♊ 2	
		first period 27°11′
23 September	11 ♋ 13	
		second period 25°47′
25 September	7 ♌ 0	
		third period 24°45′
27 September	1 ♍ 45	

We find the uncorrected position by taking half of the second period and adding it to 23 September:

$$25°47′ \div 2 + 7 ♌ 0 = 24 ♌ 7.$$

For the correction, we compare the movement in the first period (27°11′) with that in the third period (24°45′), and find a difference between them of 2°26′. The part of a period wanted to reach 00h 00m on 24 September from 00h 00m on 23 September is 24 hours. The fraction given in the table opposite for 24 hours is $\frac{1}{16}$. So we take $\frac{1}{16}$ of the difference between movements in the first and third periods, or $\frac{1}{16}$ of 2°26′. This is $-0°9′$.

As the movement is slowing (it's less in the third period than the first), we add it to the uncorrected position (24 ♋ 7), which gives us the corrected position of 24 ♋ 16. This is exactly correct by an ephemeris giving positions every day at 00 h 00 m, and thus remedies the slight inaccuracy caused by using an ephemeris that gives the Moon only every two days.

If the first or third period in the condensed ephemeris is one day (31st of one month to 1st of next month, for example), double the

Table of Correction Fractions for Moon*

For or	3h 45h	6h 42h	9h 39h	12h 36h	15h 33h	18h 30h	21h 27h	24h 24h
FRACTION	0	$\frac{1}{36}$	$\frac{1}{25}$	$\frac{1}{21}$	$\frac{1}{18}$	$\frac{1}{16}$	$\frac{1}{16}$	$\frac{1}{16}$

movement in that period before finding the difference of movements in the first and third periods.

If the time of birth is in a day that happens to be a one-day period in the condensed ephemeris, the correction is not needed.

135. Day of Week. Most astrologers (and the present writer thinks wisely) ignore the day of the week in horoscope work, except when it helps to determine an uncertainly remembered date of birth ('I *think* it was 3 January 1942, but I *know* it was a Wednesday'). Some, however, attach importance to the 'ruling planet' of each day of the week: ☉ SUNDAY, ☽ MONDAY, ♂ TUESDAY, ☿ WEDNESDAY, ♃ THURSDAY, ♀ FRIDAY, ♄ SATURDAY.

136. The Chart in modern practice is almost always circular: a 'wheel' with the twelve spokes representing the cusps, usually a small circle in the middle, and the outer rim consisting of two circles between which are written the longitudes on the cusps of the houses. Inside the wheel, against the spokes, are written the planets, etc., with their degrees in their signs – the sign itself seldom needs writing, being indicated by that on the cusp. Planets in intercepted signs are written parallel to the rim of the wheel, against the intercepted sign; others, parallel to the nearest cusp-line, or 'spoke', on the correct side of it (before or after the cusp). The charts for the Example Horoscope according to the seven different systems of house division catered for in this book are on pp. 132–8. For the sake of legibility in charts reproduced on the small scale needed here, only whole degrees have been given, even for Ascendant, MC and planets.

* The fractions are convenient ones approximating the Besselian interpolation-coefficients for second differences, adapted for use with parts of two-day intervals.

137. The Aspects in the Example Horoscope. These should be tabulated after filling in the chart, and before trying to 'judge' the horoscope:

Sun is in 10 ♋ (to nearest whole degree). Allowing fairly wide orbs for major aspects (conjunction, sextile, square, trine, opposition), we look for bodies in from 2° to 18° of any sign except those adjacent to the one the Sun is in, and those adjacent to the Sun's opposite sign. This allows an orb of 8° either way (8° more or less than Sun's 10°). In the same sign (conjunction) is Neptune. For sextile aspects, we look in the next-but-one sign on either side of Cancer (in Taurus and Virgo), and we find Moon and Saturn (15 ♉ and 5 ♉). Look next for squares in signs of the same 'qualities' (cardinal, fixed or mutable; in this case, cardinal) as the Sun's sign (Cancer), other than the opposite sign. We find Jupiter in Libra. For trines, we look in signs of the same element (in this case Water), or four signs away in either direction, namely in Scorpio and Pisces, but find nothing; Sun has no trine aspects. We write Sun's aspects thus:

$$☉: ☌ \, ♆; ⚹ \, ☽ \, ♄; □ \, ♃.$$

A similar search for aspects to the other bodies gives us:

☽: ⚹ ☉ ♆; □ ♂.

☿: ☌ ♆.

♀: (as this is *very* near the beginning of a sign, in addition to looking in the proper signs for aspects, we must also make sure whether anything is very near the end of a sign preceding the sign that would make an aspect): ⚹ ♂; △ ♃; □ ⚷.

♂: ⚹ ♀ ♃; □ ☽ ♄.

♃: ⚹ ♂; □ ☉; △ ♀.

♄: ⚹ ☉; □ ♂.

⚷: △ MC; △ ⊕.

♅: ☍ ♆.

♆: ☍ ♅.

♇: ☌ ☿.

(Students sufficiently advanced or experienced to make proper use of the minor aspects need no instruction in finding them.)

To obviate oversights, a table in this form is useful:

	☉	☽	☿	♀	♂	♃	♄	⚷	♅	♆	♇	☊
☉		✶				□	✶			☌		
☽	✶				□					✶		
☿											☌	
♀					✶	△		□				
♂		□		✶		✶	□					
♃	□			△	✶							
♄	✶				□							
⚷				□								
♅												
♆	☌	✶										
♇			☌									
☊												
⊕							△					
Asc.											☍	
MC							△					

NB: In the above table, each aspect has been inserted twice: once under each of the two bodies concerned. This is not usual and not necessary; it has been done here so that the beginner may not overlook any major aspect, whether looking down a column or along a row to find aspects to a single planet. The normal and, for more experienced students, the better way is to enter each aspect only in the row belonging to the planet first in order, in the column under the other planet.

138. Summary: Example Horoscope by Seven Systems.

House System	X	XI	XII	I	II	III	Notes
Equal	26 ♍ 38	27 ♎	27 ♏	26 ♐ 38	27 ♑	27 ♒	MC 1♏ 24
Porphyry	1 ♏ 24	20 ♏	8 ♐	26 ♐ 38	8 ♒	20 ♓	intercepted ♑ ♈
Regiomontanus	1 ♏ 24	20 ♏	6 ♐	26 ♐ 38	5 ♒	29 ♓	intercepted ♑ ♈
Campanus	1 ♏ 24	14 ♏	29 ♏	26 ♐ 38	29 ♒	13 ♈	intercepted ♑ ♓
Placidus	1 ♏ 24	23 ♏	10 ♐	26 ♐ 38	11 ♒	29 ♓	intercepted ♑ ♈
Natural Graduation	1 ♏ 24	22 ♏	6 ♐	26 ♐ 38	2 ♒	25 ♓	intercepted ♑ ♈
Koch	1 ♏ 24	18 ♏	6 ♐	26 ♐ 38	22 ♑	5 ♓	intercepted ♒ ♈

PLANETARY POSITIONS

☉ 10♋; ☽ 14♉50; ☿ 22♊23; ♀ 3♊31; ♂ 8♌30; ♃ 6♎2; ♄ 4♉40; ⚷ 2♓24R; ♅ 23♑48R; ♆ 18♋43; ♇ 26♊44; Ω 26♉5R; ⊕ 1♏28.

(The North Node is always retrograde so there is no real need to note this.)

ASPECTS

Harmonious Aspects	Doubtful Aspects	Discordant Aspects
☉, ✶☽; ✶♄;	☉ ☌♆;	☉□♃
☽✶♆;		☽□♂
	☿☌♅;	
♀, ✶♂; Δ♃		♀□⚷
♂✶♃		♂□♄
⚷, ΔMC; Δ⊕;		
		♆☍Asc

(Each aspect is entered only once.)

X

The Judgement of the Horoscope

139. Scheme. With experience, it will be found best not to follow any cut-and-dried scheme in writing out a judgement of a chart. The having of such a scheme, however, from which to depart as and when it seems desirable, is useful. For the beginner and for short, 'summary' readings, the following may be suggested:

I. YOU AS PORTRAYED IN THE SKIES AT BIRTH:

Character: the Sun sign; aspects to the Sun.

Disposition: the Moon sign; aspects to the Moon.

Personality: the Ascendant sign; sign position of the ruling planet of the Ascendant; aspects to that planet; planet(s) in the Ascendant sign or rising; aspects to it or them.

Mentality: Mercury's sign and house position and aspects.

Affections: Venus in sign position and with aspects.

II. YOUR LIFE-PATTERN POTENTIALITIES:

Money: sign on cusp of second house; planet(s) in that house, and aspects; ruling planet of that sign, its sign position and aspects.

People: parents (tenth and fourth houses), relatives (third house), friends (eleventh house), lovers and children (fifth house), husband or wife (seventh house; also, Moon in man's horoscope, Sun in woman's).

Career: business, fame, success (tenth house); any indications in second house of kind of activity associated with income; in sixth house, of work as employee; in seventh house, of partnership business.

Health: sixth house mostly; any physical inferences from Ascendant and aspects to Sun.

Religio-philosophical and spiritual developments: ninth house; Neptune and Jupiter.

Travel: third and ninth houses.

140. The Specimen Reading that follows does not keep to the foregoing scheme, or any other fixed scheme. It simply illustrates the way one student might read the chart at first sight. Another might, quite as legitimately, pick out as most outstanding quite other factors, and in some details differently interpret the same factors. As this is not the horoscope of a real person, about whom it would be important to arrive at as true a conclusion as possible, but merely an imaginary horoscope dealt with for illustrative purposes, it does not matter what system of house division is used to obtain a chart on which to practise. The Natural Graduation has been used, as it happens. It would, however, be instructive, and useful practice for the student, to see what differences, in his opinion, would be made in the reading if the chart according to one of the other systems had been used instead.

141. A Short Judgement of the Example Horoscope (according to the Natural Graduation system). For the chart see Appendix I, Fig. 6.

1. Ascendant in Sagittarius suggests a vigorous, energetic, rather many-sided personality, and possibly a fairly tall man, though height may be reduced by Sun's square aspect to the Ascendant-sign ruler, Jupiter. His air and manner are likely as a rule to be 'jovial', optimistic, cheery and sociable; he is likely to be of a hospitable type, and possibly fond of horses and outdoor sport. But the planet Uranus rising is apt to suggest that a certain brusquerie or an occasionally offensive abruptness may come as a nasty change to his normally genial manner, and he can prove extremely independent and individualistic, not always co-operative.

2. Sun in Cancer makes his real fundamental character, even though not always shown as near the surface as the Ascendant personality, one marked by great sensitivity, with feelings more easily hurt than the Sagittarian exterior would lead casual acquaintances to suspect, and with much capacity for sympathy and perhaps

intuition, and a feminine streak of sentiment in his make-up. This may include a strong sentiment for things of historical and anti-quarian interest or associations. The conjunction of Neptune with the Sun adds to his intuitive gifts and, possibly, psychic faculties, especially being in Cancer (a sign congenial to mediums, for example).

3. Moon in Taurus gives an instinctive resistance against any change in his set ways or opposition to his purposes, a certain obstinacy, a taste and need for the material pleasures of the senses, including good food (and drink, probably, with Neptune conjunct Sun), and the company of the opposite sex (especially as the Moon is in his fifth house). Moon's square aspect to Mars can make the love instinct, in its more physical manifestations, a very strong one, and a source of much temptation at times. A gift of artistic imagination, besides a further indication of possible psychic powers, is indicated by Moon's sextile aspect to Neptune.

4. The financial fortunes may be marked by considerable difficulties during his life, with Uranus in the second house, and Saturn, traditional ruler of Aquarius (sign on cusp II) square to Mars, making for losses. On the other hand, Uranus being well-placed by sign in its own joint-rulership, Aquarius, and Saturn being in good aspect (sextile) to the Sun, makes for an influence of prosperity, if real wisdom is used to cope with the Saturn–Mars risks and tribulations in money matters.

5. With Taurus on the fifth house cusp, and Moon and Ascending Node there, and with Venus, ruler of Taurus, in good aspect to the passionate and virile Mars and to the expansive and prospering Jupiter, creative art, the professions or businesses dealing with pleasure and amusement, and the bringing up of his children if he has any (probably daughters) and the emotional life can be sources of rich benefit and enjoyment, provided that too much self-indulgent misuse of the capacity for a very full love life is not allowed to bring penalties too easily risked; for he is probably very 'successful' and popular with women. And some fickleness and changeability in matters of the affections may be likely with 'inconstant Moon' in the fifth house, and that house's accidental ruler (Venus), which is also the love planet, in the dualistic and changeful sign of Gemini.

6. Marriage, or the opportunity for it, may be something that will be

more than once a factor in this man's life, with the dualistic signs of Sagittarius and Gemini on the horizon, especially with Gemini on the seventh house, and its ruler Mercury almost on the cusp itself. Pluto conjunct Gemini on this cusp may possibly point (but our knowledge is too incomplete to speak with any positiveness) to bereavement and remarriage and a very great change in general outlook and life following this.

7. Venus in the sixth house in good aspect to Jupiter, ruler of the Ascendant, makes for the utmost beneficial influences for the best possible treatment and recuperation if illness is experienced at any time, but there is no real indication in this particular map of more illness than is perhaps common to all mankind. Much caution, however, with Uranus rising, Gemini on the sixth cusp, and Jupiter (the expansive and exaggerating) square to the Sun, is called for, to guard against excesses, rash risks and especially nerve-strain and nervous tension. Too foolhardy a disregard of any such caution *could* even give the Mars-in-eighth-house influence an opportunity to work out in terms of death by violence, though there could be no justification at all for predicting that such an end is more than a possibility. This position of Mars, in strong good aspects to the two most fortunate planets, Venus and Jupiter, but discordant (square) aspect to Moon and Saturn, may very probably point to much benefit from inheritance or legacies or the handling of wife's or partner's business or finances, but much grief from bereavements.

8. Pisces on the third house, with its ruler Jupiter on the overlap of the ninth and tenth houses, and its co-ruler Neptune conjunct with the Sun, and with Virgo on the ninth house, its ruler Mercury strongly placed on an angular cusp and dignified in its other rulership sign of Gemini, a sign favourable to movement and travel and to intellectual activities, all point to the likelihood of much travel, with beneficial effects both on career (tenth house) and on intellectual, and philosophic-religious, developments (ninth house).

9. In spite of the mixed influences affecting the house of money, referred to above, the potentialities for a successful career in the eyes of the world seem very good with Jupiter elevated, not far from the Midheaven, and the Part of Fortune situated there.

APPENDIX I
Charts of Example Horoscope According to Seven Systems

The following seven illustrations give the chart, or figure of the heavens, or map, of the Example Horoscope, according to the seven different systems of house division in current use for general astrological purposes in Europe and America.

Simply because a diagram overcrowded with numerals is not very easy for the unaccustomed person to follow at a glance when reduced to very small size to fit these pages, all longitudes have been rounded off to the nearest whole-degree value – even the Ascendant and MC (and cusp X of the Equal House chart), and the planets, although in Chapters VIII and IX these were found in degrees and minutes. Printed blank charts are available from various sources, including some bookshops that specialize in astrological or occult works.

To draw one's own wheel with a pair of compasses and a ruler is not difficult, and it is not very expensive to get a rubber stamp made of the horoscope wheel to one's own design or requirements and of the size one prefers (limited by size of inking-pads obtainable). The wheel is usually drawn with an extreme diameter of from 3 inches/ 7.5 cm (or a little less) to 5 inches/12.5 cm (or a little more).

'Zenith', often printed against the tenth cusp is wrong; 'East Point', sometimes put as an alternative to 'Ascendant' against cusp I, is equally wrong. So are 'North Point', and 'South Point', printed sometimes against cusps X and IV. If you get horoscope blanks so printed, do not let these wordings mislead you.

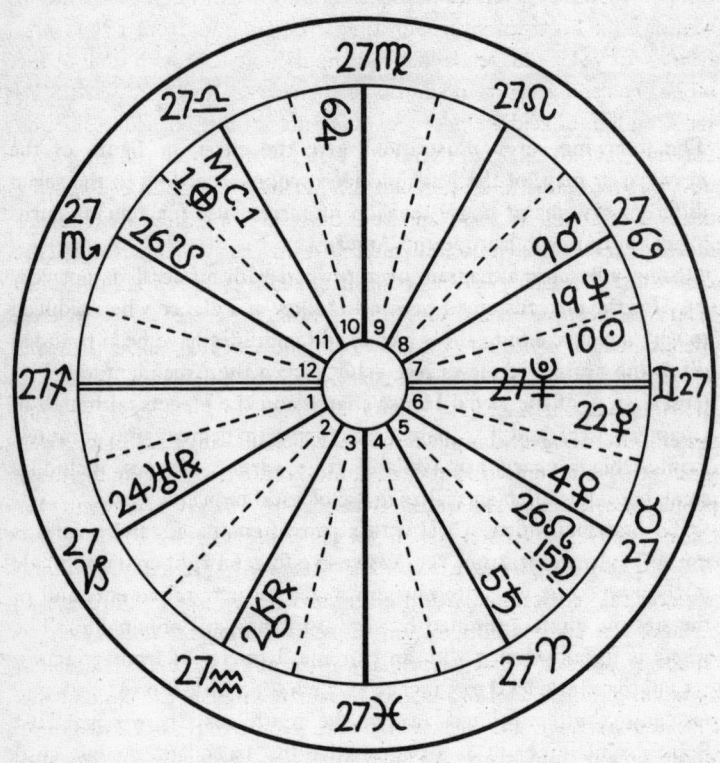

Figure 1. The Example Horoscope by the Equal
House system. Ignore dotted lines (not usually
printed on horoscope-chart blanks) if cusps considered beginnings of houses.

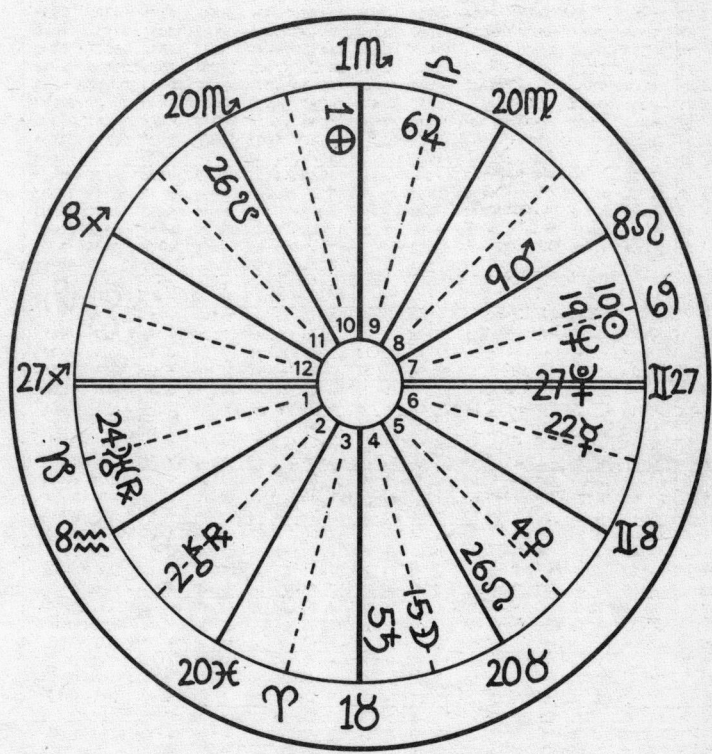

Figure 2. The Example Horoscope by the Porphyry system. Dotted lines are boundaries between houses when cusps considered centres of houses.

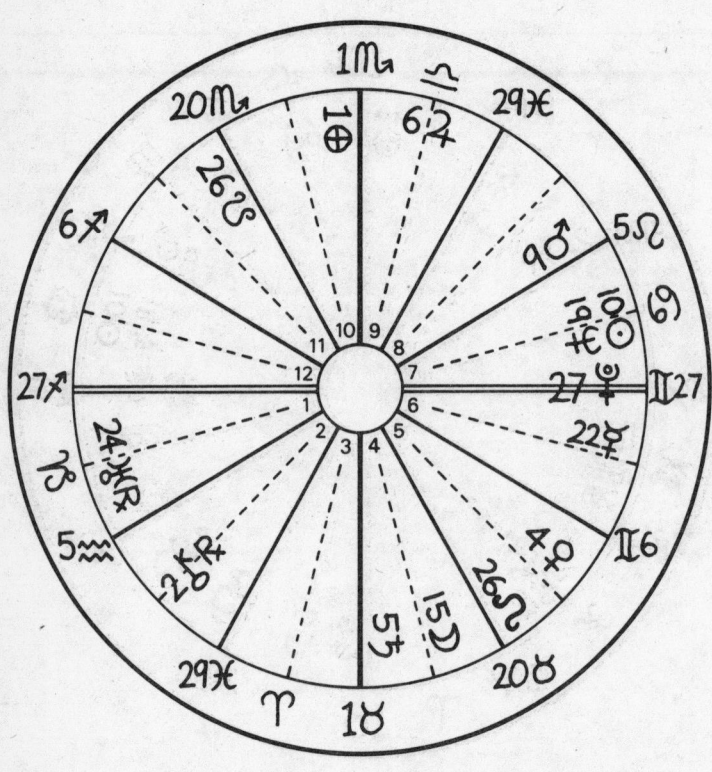

Figure 3. The Example Horoscope by the Regiomontanus system. Ignore dotted lines, as cusps
are (usually) considered beginnings of houses.

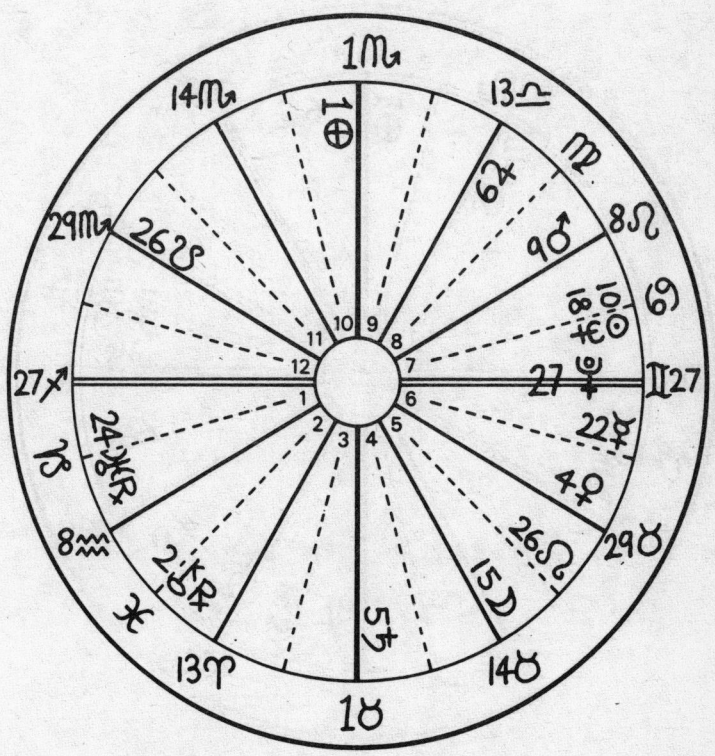

Figure 4. The Example Horoscope by the Campanus system. Cusps usually considered centres of houses, so dotted lines represent house boundaries.

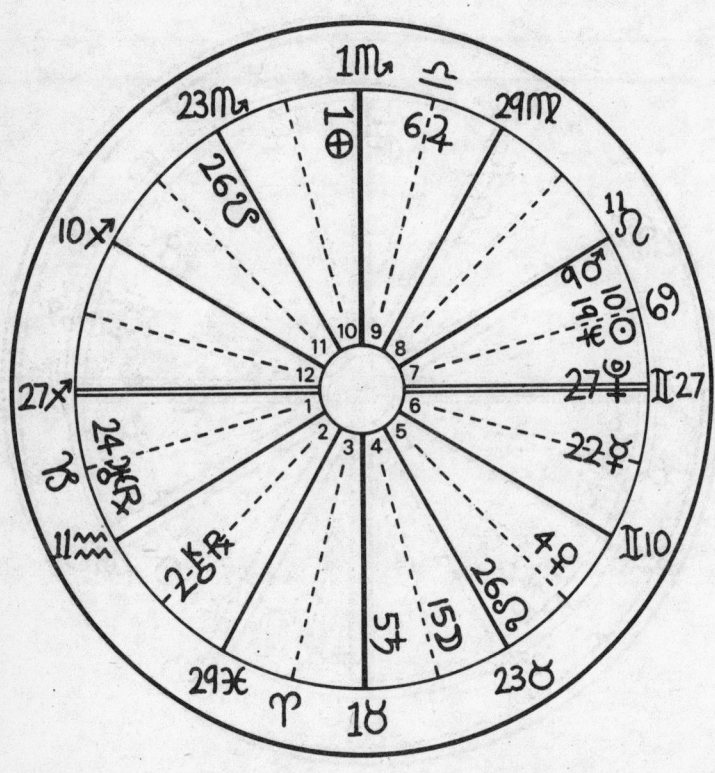

Figure 5. The Example Horoscope by the Placidus system. Cusps usually considered beginning of houses; dotted lines ignored.

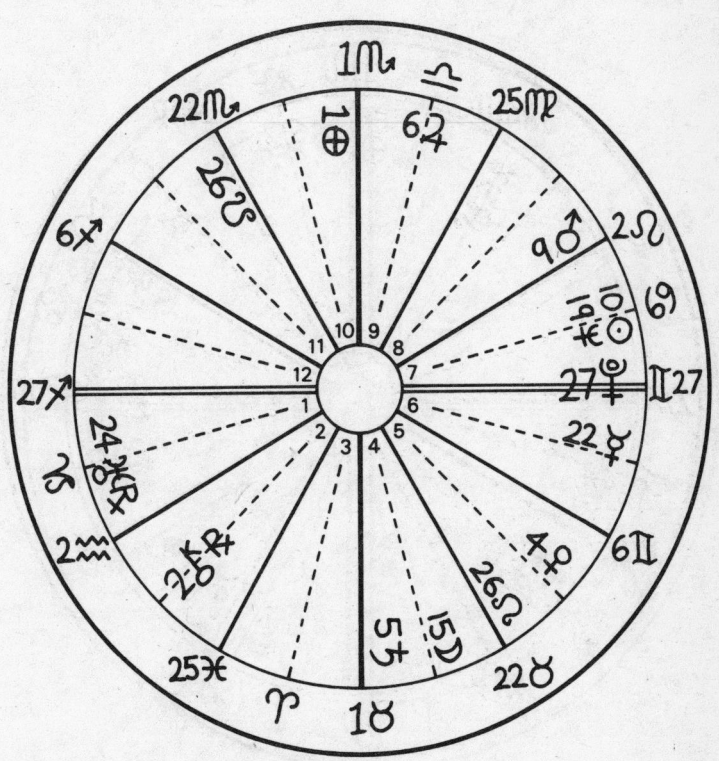

Figure 6. The Example Horoscope by the Natural Graduation system. Cusps sometimes considered centres of houses, then dotted lines are where houses begin.

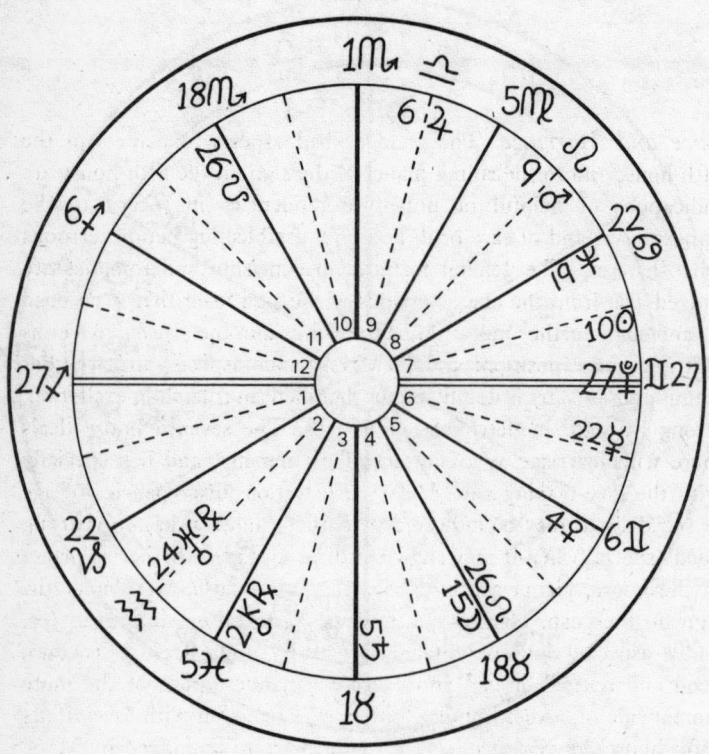

Figure 7. The Example Horoscope by the Koch
system. Ignore dotted lines as cusps are usually
considered beginning of houses.

APPENDIX II
Love, Money and Health

Love and Marriage. The good or bad aspects to planets in the fifth house and to the ruling planet of the sign on the fifth house are indications of helpful or unhelpful tendencies in regard to the opposite sex, and of ease or difficulty in establishing happy relations with that sex. The general fortunes in courtship and romance are judged also from the characteristics of the sign itself that is on cusp V; and some further indication is to be found in the aspects to Venus and her house position, and in Mars–Venus aspects, and whether Venus and/or Mars is debilitated or dignified (in rulership, exaltation, strong by sign, in detriment or in fall). The seventh house deals more with marriage as a contract of partnership, and less specially with the love-making side. Delays, frustration, discrepancies of age or social status may be indicated by Saturn, unless it has only strong good aspects (when it may show steadfast loyalty), whether as planet in the house, planet aspecting planet in the house, or ruler of the sign on the cusp. Harmony, affection, co-operation, by Venus (or, badly aspected and debilitated, sensuality and pleasure-seeking); good and normal or bad and excessive manifestations of the more animal side of sexual impulse, either in connection with love affairs (fifth house) or marriage (seventh house) are to be judged by Mars, its sign position, house position, and aspects; especially significant if either in or ruling the seventh or fifth house. If the interpretation is corroborated by other indications, Mars or Uranus not very harmoniously aspected in either house may show either quarrels or bereavement.

The Moon is said to symbolize the female marriage partner in a male chart, and the Sun the male spouse in a woman's horoscope.

The first planet making aspect to either, after birth, and the kind of aspect, denote the type of partner, and the success or otherwise of the match. In comparing two people's horoscopes of birth, Mars in one chart with Venus in the other, making strong aspect (good or bad) to one another, is significant of likelihood of amorous attraction, desirably or the reverse; aspect between Sun in one chart and Moon in the other is very significant for marriage. Ascendant signs and/or Sun signs in good or bad aspect are significant for general compatibility or incompatibility. But no one factor alone is at all conclusive.

Money in general is denoted in the second house; Taurus is a specially favourable sign here; Libra, Leo and Sagittarius are rather fortunate. Any planets in the second house are important as indicating a tendency to be subject to good or bad fortunes in financial matters (Mars bad through losses, extravagance, rashness; Saturn, through restriction of means, losses, frustration, meanness; Uranus, through the unforeseen and sudden, unless very well-aspected – then equally unforeseen strokes of luck; Neptune, more luck than judgement, some muddle; Jupiter, extremely fortunate unless ill-aspected – then extravagance or great expenditure; Moon, changeable fortunes; Venus very fortunate unless very badly aspected, then loss through self-indulgence or females; Mercury, gain through brainwork if well aspected, or through commerce, and some fluctuations of fortune). The planet ruling the sign on cusp II is equally important – and is *most* important if no planets are in the second house. Financial speculation or gambles are influenced by the same factors that affected love affairs in the fifth house. The tenth house, especially when it is related in any way to the second (by a planet in, or ruling, one of them and aspecting a planet in, or ruling, the other, for example) shows the factors primarily connected with career or public position or profession as affecting financial fortunes. Eighth house shows legacies, inheritance and other people's money you handle or are affected by, especially husband's or wife's.

Health. It is wrong and dangerous for any but the most experienced and expert student to be at all detailed or definite on matters of health and longevity. Only very tentative suggestions of possibilities should be made by any student who still needs such instruction as this book can give. Good planets and aspects affecting sixth house point to favourable protecting and helping influences to secure good recovery and recuperation in cases of illness. Saturn's influence makes rather for chronic (that is more or less permanent – not *necessarily* very bad) illnesses, and Mars more for acute (short and sharp) ones; Saturn, for chills and effects of cold, weakness; Mars for feverish conditions, cuts, burns; Uranus for shock, physical or mental, neuroses (bad aspects to Mercury here are an indication also), and hurts from electricity or explosions, and sudden unlooked-for accidents; Neptune, to toxins, drugs, drink, delusions; Jupiter, to protection, immunity, or, badly aspected, ill effects of excess or overdoing things. Below is a table of parts of the body ruled by each sign. The sign on the Ascendant or containing the Sun, or containing the ruler of the Ascendant, or on the sixth house, or containing its ruler, are all to be looked at in judging parts of the body most liable to be affected by illness or injury:

- ♈ Aries: head and face.
- ♉ Taurus: throat and neck.
- ♊ Gemini: lungs, nervous system, hands, arms, shoulders.
- ♋ Cancer: breast and stomach.
- ♌ Leo: heart, sides, upper back.
- ♍ Virgo: bowels, solar plexus.
- ♎ Libra: loins, kidneys, ovaries.
- ♏ Scorpio: bladder, anus, genitals.
- ♐ Sagittarius: liver, hips, thighs.
- ♑ Capricorn: knees, spleen.
- ♒ Aquarius: calves, ankles.
- ♓ Pisces: feet, reaction of body to fluids, medicine, drugs, alcohol, tobacco.

APPENDIX III
The Planets in the Zodiac Signs

Interpretation: The descriptions given in Chapter V, under the heading 'Planets in Houses', should be interpreted only in general terms, as experience will justify. Only by co-ordinating the influences of the aspects with the relationships of the signs and the signs in which the planets appear can a detailed analysis be made. This will be fully appreciated from experience, but initially is is necessary to master the fundamental influences of the planets in the houses of the chart.

A good astrologer will consider all influences before attempting to make an interpretation. He will consider a planet in a sign to have a comparatively weak influence in the horoscope if it is not supported by an aspect or an appropriate sign.

EXAMPLE: Mars is aggressive, combative, ardent and bold. Detriment in Libra is both pleasure- and beauty-loving. The discord between the planet and the sign of its detriment emphasizes the less desirable aspect of both – the violent, pleasure-seeking 'lover' and the sensual artist or the work-shy gangster, in the extreme case, but the sign of Mars, which is virile, heroic, courageous and adventuresome in the Fire sign of Sagittarius, which is cheerful, enterprising and energetic, produces a person who is very active, a traveller and one who is prepared to fight doggedly for his opinion in matters of religious or philosophical belief. In contrast to Mars in the sign of Sagittarius, Venus in the sign of Sagittarius (in which this planet is 'strong') will produce a gentler, idealistic and more artistic type of person with the ability to appreciate beauty, metaphysical ideas and capable of achieving success abroad.

The following information may help to clarify the associations between planets and signs.

The Sun in (denotes the fundamental ego of an individual):

Sign	General	Good Aspects	Bad Aspects
ARIES	Originality	Leadership	Egotism
	Independence		Selfishness
TAURUS	Creative	Enterprising	Possessiveness
	Practical		Laziness
	Constructive		Complacency
GEMINI	Awareness	Inventiveness	Lack of
	Intellectual	Adaptability	concentration
	Duality		Impatience
CANCER	Emotional	Protective	Possessiveness
	Imaginative	Shrewd	Anxiety
LEO	Creative	Inspiring	Egotism
	Self-expressive	Organizing	Vanity
VIRGO	Dutiful	Analytical	Intolerant
	Dedicated	Discriminating	Fussy
			Vague
LIBRA	Harmonious	Helpful	Suspicious
	Just	Diplomatic	Disbelieving
SCORPIO	Energetic	Self-control	Jealousy
	Determined		Ruthlessness
SAGITTARIUS	Joviality	Wisdom	Superficial
	Purposeful	Understanding	Careless
CAPRICORN	Dutiful	Cautious	Suspicious
	Integrity	Dependable	Snobbish
		Practical	Bone idle
AQUARIUS	Knowledge seeking	Humanitarian	Remote
	Intellectual	Co-ordinating	Vacant
PISCES	Sympathetic	Placid	Lazy
	Understanding	Adaptable	Unstable
		Imaginative	

The Moon in (controls instincts and desires):

Sign	General	Good Aspects	Bad Aspects
ARIES	Hasty	Independence	Restless
	Enthusiastic		Militant
	Impetuous		
TAURUS	Endurance	Resourceful	Over-sensuous
	Determined	Intuitive	Reminiscing
GEMINI	Poetic	Alert	Crafty
	Self-expressive	Conversationalist	Scheming
	Unusual pursuits	Controlling influence	Moody
CANCER	Imaginative	Sympathetic	Idealistic
	Romantic		
	Sociable		
LEO	Generous	Optimism in	Fame-seeking
	Loyal	leadership	Conceited
			Outspoken
VIRGO	Industrious	Reassuring	Over-critical
	Fastidious	Comforting	Nagging
LIBRA	Pacifist	Hospitable	Evasive
	Tolerant	Friendly	Sulky
	Accommodating	Self-reliant	
SCORPIO	Sexually attractive	Capable	Tormenting
	Seductive	Enthusiastic	
SAGITTARIUS	Forthright	Independent	Superficial
	Enthusiastic	Jovial	Unstable ideas
	Impulsive		Easily led
CAPRICORN	Prudent	Austere	Habit-forming
	Reliable	Diligent	Slow to rouse
	Ambitious		Jealous
			Pessimistic
			Self-centred
AQUARIUS	Humanitarian	Progressive	Obstinate
	Unconventional	Ingenious	Erratic
	Unpredictable	Friendly	
PISCES	Passive	Intense	Lazy
	Sentimental	Kind	Indecisive
	Gentle	Cheerful	Restless

Mercury in (mental activity):

Sign	General	Good Aspects	Bad Aspects
ARIES	Alert Forceful	Good concentration Decisive Conclusive	Argumentative
TAURUS	Practical Diplomatic	Organized Inspired Fluent	Inflexible Dogmatic
GEMINI	Active Lively	Inventive Versatile Witty	Easily misled Superficial
CANCER	Receptive Imaginative	Expressive Dedicated	Uninspired
LEO	Authoritative Comprehensive	Creative Self-sufficient	Diversified
VIRGO	Logical Observant Scientific	Accurate Attentive Decisive	Hesitating Dithering Hypercritical
LIBRA	Surmising Judicial Rational	Good concentration Suave	Easily dis- tracted Perfectionist
SCORPIO	Thorough Shrewd Secretive	Resourceful Astute Searching	Intolerant Bitter Critical
SAGITTARIUS	Inspiring Independent	Impulsive Enthralling Encouraging Good teacher	Argumentative Reactionary Sarcastic
CAPRICORN	Cautious Profound Painstaking Careful	Methodical Precise	Suspicious Dogmatic
AQUARIUS	Warm Poetic Clever	Original Tolerant	Uncertain Vague Detached
PISCES	Humorous Illogical Prejudiced	Subtle Diplomatic	Confused Wandering

Venus in (affections and artistic taste):

Sign	General	Good Aspects	Bad Aspects
ARIES	Impetuous Impulsive	Devoted	Fickle (changes of heart)
TAURUS	Steadfast Obedient	Generous Sociable Charming	Slow Slothful
GEMINI	Spontaneous	Humorous Sympathetic	Flirtatious
CANCER	Devoted Materialist	Romantic Gentle Warm-hearted	Possessive
LEO	Inspiring Reliable Sincere Noble	Generous	Indecisive Self-satisfying
VIRGO	Moral Pure	Dutiful	Fear of self-indulgence
LIBRA	Refined Idealistic	Sense of proportion Charming	Inflexible
SCORPIO	Passionate Direct	Loyal Expressive	Jealous Self-indulgent Desirous Secret
SAGITTARIUS	Adventurous High-spirited Impulsive	Freedom-loving Sincere	Evasive
CAPRICORN	Consistent Protective	Sincere	Stubborn
AQUARIUS	Impersonal Artistic	Altruistic	Insecure Unenterprising
PISCES	Devoted Changeable	Self-sacrificial	Lack of will-power

Mars in (dynamic activity, impulses):

Sign	General	Good Aspects	Bad Aspects
ARIES	Forceful	Independent	Impatient
	Positive	Spontaneous	Aggressive
	Direct		Quick-tempered
TAURUS	Persistent	Determined	Inflexible
		Enterprising	Single-minded
GEMINI	Spontaneous	Observant	Vulnerable
	Excitable	Quick-witted	Fearful of criticism
CANCER	Emotional	Conservative	Resentful
	Imaginative	Sympathetic	Spiteful
LEO	Dominating	Respected	Rebellious
	Dramatic		Self-indulgent
VIRGO	Calculating	Diplomatic	Hypercritical
	Self-disciplined	Consulting	Scheming
	Scientific		
LIBRA	Co-ordinated	Compromising	Easily influenced
		Courteous	Intolerant
SCORPIO	Persevering	Regimented	Callous
	Energetic	Perceptive	Insidious
	Probing	Authoritarian	
SAGITTARIUS	Frank	Courteous	Insatiable
	Spontaneous	Dedicated	Unscrupulous
	Optimistic	Just	
CAPRICORN	Orthodox	Efficient	Slow-witted
	Persistent	Suave	Humourless
	Organizing	Conscientious	Unimaginative
AQUARIUS	Original	Understanding	Disturbing
	Dynamic	Humane	Susceptible to changes of heart
	Theoretical		
PISCES	Receptive	Intuitive	Shy
	Unassuming	Humorous	Devious
	Co-operative		Scheming

Jupiter in (energy in expansion):

Sign	General
ARIES	Active desire for freedom, adventurous
TAURUS	Constructive, acquiring, self-helping
GEMINI	Creative, witty, scientific
CANCER	Domestic abilities, power of expression, good actor, diplomatic, fanciful
LEO	Assertion through example, vital, generous, vain, autocratic
VIRGO	Probing, researching, expansion through discovery
LIBRA	Harmonious, artistic expression, philosophical, humanitarian approach
SCORPIO	Attractive, inspiring devotion
SAGITTARIUS	Physically active, socially accepted, sporting interests
CAPRICORN	Devoted to duty, organizing, responsible, orthodox
AQUARIUS	Philosophical, original, reformer
PISCES	Receptive, sympathetic care of others

Saturn in (limitation, restrictions, discipline, caution):

Sign	General
ARIES	Overwrought, difficult in reconciliation, frustration, self-reliant
TAURUS	Determined, insecure, fear of dependence, prudent
GEMINI	Seeks unification, fear of being stereotyped, happy in situations requiring versatility and quick thought
CANCER	Emotional, opinionated, intolerant, fear of suppression
LEO	Sense of honour, jealous, hypocritical, dread of being ignored or overlooked
VIRGO	Cautious, discriminating, lack of confidence, seeking security, fear of unknown
LIBRA	Judgement, honourable, dislike of sentimentality, impartial
SCORPIO	Egotistical, exacting, self-disciplined, with bad aspects, callous, intolerant, afraid of becoming emotionally dependent
SAGITTARIUS	Issues of control and limitation may require attention. Freedom of thought and action will allow dignity in old age. Lack of freedom could lead to resentment
CAPRICORN	Well-controlled, organizing ability, seeks recognition, lacks originality
AQUARIUS	Detached, reserved, treasures independence, dread of over-involvement
PISCES	Intuitive, passive, pessimistic, dislikes own company, fear of being isolated

Uranus in any sign adds a touch of inspiration, expressiveness, will-power and inventiveness. It is the spark from which the fire is kindled. As joint ruler of Aquarius, it encourages originality, progressive thinking and analysis, while in the sign of Leo, Uranus produces over-confidence, pride and a quest for power.

Neptune in a sign produces intuitiveness, imagination, mysticism and the ability to overcome obstacles associated with the sign and the house in which it appears. This planet causes self-sacrifice, renunciation, expansion and achievement beyond normal boundaries, the breaking down of conventions, spiritualism and vagueness.

Pluto in a sign represents the potential for transformation, rejuvenation or rebirth within the sign or house in which it appears. It enables one to start afresh to find new beginnings. Pluto works well in Scorpio where the regenerative process is in harmony, but in Taurus it finds conflict with the steadfast, unchanging attitudes of Taurus.

APPENDIX IV
An Introduction to Chiron

———

Chiron was discovered in October 1977 by Charles T. Kowal. He named the planet, which is highly unusual for an astronomer. Also unusual is the fact that a planetary ephemeris* was available for Chiron within six months of its discovery, bearing in mind that it took nearer a decade to produce an ephemeris for Pluto.

In Astronomy. Not a vast amount is known about Chiron,† which was designated Minor Planet 2060 in August 1978. It has a possibly unstable orbit around the Sun, varying between 2,850 and 1,275 million km from it over a period of 50.7 years. Its highly eccentric orbit crosses the orbit of Saturn, approaches that of Jupiter and extends outwards almost to the orbit of Uranus. The gravitational pull of Saturn and Uranus may diminish Chiron's orbit, taking it closer to the Sun.

Chiron has been growing brighter since November 1987, as its orbit takes it nearer the Sun. The *New Scientist* reported: 'A rather faint fuzzy patch of light to the south-east of Chiron was discerned at Kitt Peak National Observatory in Arizona during April 1989.'‡ This patch resembles the coma of a comet, indicating the possibility that Chiron is a giant comet rather than a minor planet. This is an interesting development, as it is unlikely that any astrologers would have researched Chiron if it had been identified as a comet at the

———

* Eve S. Gregory, *The Chiron Ephemeris*, New York, CAO Times, 1985.

† A concise history of our knowledge of Chiron may be found in Erminie Lanterno, *A Continuing Discovery of Chiron*, York Beach, Maine, Samuel Weiser, 1983.

‡ 'Planet is a comet', *New Scientist*, vol. 122, no. 1664, May 1989, p. 35.

time of its discovery. Thus its inaccurate identification led to research that yielded valuable information – a typically Chironic situation.

In Mythology. The following is a brief account of the mythological figure Chiron; a more detailed account of which can be found in Erminie Lanterno's book* and other sources. Naturally, there are some variations in the story according to source.

Prometheus tricked the gods out of good meat by offering them one of two sacks. Both sacks contained the parts of a sacrificed bull: the first sack was filled with the good meat covered with a layer of bones, while the second sack held bones and fat, with the meatiest fat on top.

Zeus chose the second sack and, being displeased with the result, withdrew fire from humanity, to whom Prometheus had given the sack of good meat. Prometheus then took fire from the gods and gave it back to humanity. This so enraged Zeus that he sentenced Prometheus to be chained to a rock and have his liver eaten by a bird every day and grow back overnight to be eaten again.

Zeus had overreacted and wanted to release Prometheus, but as a god he could not be seen to lose face, especially as through Prometheus's intervention humanity was becoming almost like the gods themselves. However, Zeus promised to release Prometheus if an immortal would enter Hades on his behalf.

Chiron, the centaur, was an immortal, the son of Chronos (Saturn). Abandoned at birth by his mother, Philra, he was fostered by Apollo and was taught warrior skills as well as the arts of healing and music. Chiron, in turn, taught these disciplines to others.

One of Chiron's students was Hercules, who had known Prometheus prior to his punishment. While carrying out one of his twelve labours, Hercules accidentally wounded Chiron with an arrow dipped in the Hydra's blood. This blood was fatal to mortals, but its effect on the immortal Chiron was to leave him in perpetual pain. He became known as the Wounded Healer because he did not – perhaps

* Lanterno, op. cit.

could not – heal himself. However, it was Chiron who entered Hades and brought about the release of Prometheus.

Analysing this story, we see that Chiron was born half beast and half man (opposing natures), and he taught warrior skills and healing arts (opposing disciplines – warriors kill people, healers mend people). He taught his students one of the skills totally, with just enough of the other skill to enable them to survive; thus he produced for example, Asclepius the healer, and Jason the warrior. Chiron not only mastered his animal nature, but must also have resolved the conflict between killing and healing within himself in order to teach the subjects so well.

In Astrology. I have found that the main principle of Chiron revolves around the resolution of suffering, and that there are three distinct, vertical levels of Chironic experience. They are not the only faces of Chiron, but are perhaps the most consistent in daily life.

1. Suffering: something that we are all familiar with, though, naturally, some more than others.
2. Non-suffering: coming to terms with our suffering, at least in part, and being able to help and/or heal others and ourselves in the process.
3. Unsuffering: having given up suffering (and thus ego/personality), surrendering ourselves entirely to creation (God).

Suffering is the pain we experience as a result of own guilt, fear or ignorance. It can be so powerful that it drives some people to suicide. Used positively, however, suffering helps to strengthen and purify the individual. This brings one to non-suffering, even if only in a small way, for now one is in a position to offer a helping hand to others who may be suffering in a way with which one is familiar. This allows for growth and development for both parties.

Unsuffering is the final step of surrendering to creation (although in the first instance this is rarely a permanent transition), attuning to our higher nature and becoming that which we truly are, acknowledging and utilizing the gifts that are our own and bringing the healing light of love into the world.

THE LIFE OF CHIRON RELATED TO CHIRON EXPERIENCE

1. Suffering: Chiron grew up without a real mother or father, and was taught several disciplines. Growing up is a painful experience even with real parents, and the first steps of any valid discipline are rarely easy.

2. Non-suffering: having mastered the teachings he received, Chiron taught and practised them – that is, he shared them with others and occasionally healed them. However, during this phase he was seriously wounded: he had not mastered non-suffering to the point of unsuffering. This suggests that within non-suffering there is still some suffering.

3. Unsuffering: Chiron entered Hades to release Prometheus from his suffering. Chiron made this last redemptive step, but this does not mean that we have to die in order to overcome suffering.

In this case sacrifice is associated not only with Chiron's redemption, but also with Prometheus's release from suffering, Zeus saving face and achieving a clear conscience, and the reunion of Prometheus and Hercules.* Thus redemption is not a selfish act.

IN NATAL CHARTS. Chiron is often prominent by transit (an aspect made by a moving planet to a natal planet, cusp or other part of the birth chart) when a dramatic change in a native's life is under way. It seems to embody some of the qualities of Saturn and Uranus as well as qualities of its own, and has attracted many keywords, including the wounded healer, eccentric, key, maverick, door, bridge, guide, ironic and chronic.†

In the natal chart Chiron suggests a wound within the native and,

---

* In some accounts it is Hercules who mediates with Zeus for Prometheus's release. In another version Hercules shoots the bird with an arrow. In either case he is actively involved in the Chiron–Prometheus exchange, probably easing his conscience over wounding Chiron.

† See Melanie Reinhart, *Chiron and the Healing Journey*, London, Arkana, 1989; and Zane B. Stein, *Essence and Application*, New York, CAO Times, 1986.

paradoxically, an area where one can do much good if only the wound is acknowledged and treated to some extent.

The seven naked-eye planets represent or radiate energies that human beings are able to transcend and control. The outer planets, being so remote, receive more energy from outside our solar system than from within it. Thus they act as transformers or transducers of other-world energies, which humans are subject to and, in some circumstances, are able to channel, yet not consciously control. Chiron appears to act as a bridge for contacting the higher inter-planetary energies and may well help us to become aware of con-sciously channelling them.

Saturn is traditionally associated with time, and it is possible that Chiron is too, but in a different manner. Recently I observed two friends meeting each other, partly by design, mainly by chance. They had arranged a place to meet but not the time, yet they actually arrived simultaneously, approaching from opposite direc-tions. The combination of surprise and delight on their faces was very 'Chironic'.

Examples 1. Barney Camfield, a well-known healer in England, has 27° of Pisces on the sixth house cusp (a physical weak spot in the native generally). He has Chiron (17°) conjunct with the Sun (18.5°) and Mercury (22°) all in Aries and the sixth house. In the introduc-tion to his first book he mentions seventeen complaints he has suffered from 'apart from the usual plethora of childhood ailments'.*
He has been hospitalized in twenty-four hospitals and treated by eight specialists, including healers (sixth house – health/service, Chiron = suffering). He is now a devoted healer (Sun conjunct Chiron). He has innovated (Aries) a therapy (Chiron) using words and phrases (Mercury) that people use. He is also a lay priest (sixth house = service), not belonging to an orthodox Church with apostolic succession. He suffers from gout (Jupiter) affecting his feet (sixth house cusp = Pisces, rules feet). His natal Jupiter (associated with

* Barney Camfield, *Healing, Harmony and Health*, Bodmin, Cornwall, Bossiney Books, 1985.

gout) is quincunx his natal Chiron within 6′ of orb and is also retrograde.

2. Mr X has Chiron in the first house 15° past the ascendant. In his book, A. T. Mann gives a logarithmic time scale relating to planetary positions and their distance from the Ascendant.* In the case of 15° this is three months after birth. When asked about this period in his life, Mr X had this to say:

> About this time I had my first near-death experience. I had choked and was apparently black and blue, with no heartbeat and had stopped breathing. Meanwhile, somewhere else, I was aware of a seemingly endless dark tunnel. The end was very close and so very far away at the same time, with the light of impersonal love beckoning to me. I moved on towards it. However, the personal love generated by my father, who was holding me upside down and slapping my back at the time, was enough for me to return to my body. Reluctantly, I might add. Not that I had to; there was a choice involved; I could have left my body and joined the light. I *know that*.

Mr X had forgotten this early experience until a much later and far more unpleasant occurrence jolted the memory free. Remembering it was a key to getting his life into perspective. Chiron was also involved in this later experience.

SUMMARY. The three levels of Chiron experience are not linear consecutive phases of being we find ourselves in. Rather, they can, and do, change from moment to moment, suggesting a vertical axis of changing awareness growing towards the light, or not growing. If we begin to feel sorry for ourselves, it is easy to sink into despair, yet by hauling ourselves up 'by the boot-straps' we can learn to accept life's lessons and make the best of them.

The warrior/healer paradox of Chiron signifies different faces of the same being (like Janus). They are horizontal and deal with

---

* A. T. Mann, *Life Time Astrology*, London, Unwin, 1985.

application, that is, doing things. They may seem to contradict each other, yet they are different modes of expression of essentially the same energy (that is, at a higher level the energy is the same). Another way of seeing this is to accept that paradox is something that *is*, and minds cannot always accept the apparent contradictions involved. Clearly then, paradox and the inner truths of Chiron are beyond intellect.

The wound/healing paradox manifests itself in different ways too. One can 'project' one's requirement to learn on to others, thereby accentuating one's own wound because it remains unhealed in oneself, and one can find friends who are like bandages that compensate for one's wound, enabling one to pass over it as healed. Neither of these is actually coming to terms with the real issues. Conversely, acknowledging and coming to terms with one's wound helps to heal oneself and enables one to help others.

The themes mentioned in the following three sections are likely to be involved in transits, where appropriate, especially with outer planetary transits and, of course, with Chiron transits to natal Chiron and planets in aspect with Chiron natally. The healing aspects of Chiron relate not only to the potential of the native to heal others, but also to the therapies to which they are likely to respond.

In transits, often a part of the natal chart is brought to life in a new or different way. Sometimes pain is involved, but invariably there is much to gain, as if there is now a door where there was not one before.

Chiron by House Position. The following observations have been made using the Natural Graduation house system, yet also seem to apply to other house systems.

HOUSE I	Eccentric, inquisitive, original and scarred (physically or otherwise). Catalyst. Self-healing. Sense of separation. Potential natural healer.
HOUSE II	Materially/financially insecure. Earth and/or body rejection. Massage and/or touch therapy potential.

HOUSE III   Intelligent, quick. Intellectual/educational, time-wasting. Need to truly communicate (i.e., in depth). Important issues with siblings/neighbours.

HOUSE IV   Parental difficulties, home or base problems. Inner need to discover/uncover one's roots. Intuitional healing.

HOUSE V   Creative dilemmas/frustrations. Important lessons gained through one's own, or others', children.

HOUSE VI   Health and/or work difficulties. Creative dissatisfaction with systems or routine. Service, gifted healers potentially. Body healers.

HOUSE VII   Friendship, marital relationship dilemmas; worthwhile, sometimes painful lessons through these. Counsellors.

HOUSE VIII   Early exposure to death. Difficulties with one's sexuality, own resources, inner nature and other people's energy. Intuitional healing.

HOUSE IX   Religio–philosophical dilemmas (possibly from childhood). Travel issues, physical or other. Potential teachers.

HOUSE X   Career frustrations (though successful). Hollow ambitions. Difficulty in finding one's place in society. Vocational healing, possibly priesthood.

HOUSE XI   Need/fear of groups. Extensive social requirements. Difficulties fitting in. Group catalyst.

HOUSE XII   Compassionate/naïve. Victim. Isolated, exiled. Requirement to separate inner from outer, intuitional healing.

Chiron by Sign. Melanie Reinhart suggests that Chiron rules Sagittarius, is in exaltation in Virgo, falls in Pisces and is in detriment in Gemini. This information may be of benefit to those interested and I extend my thanks to her for her assistance with Chiron, especially by signs.

ARIES

Eccentric, innovative, courageous/foolhardy. Pioneering, wilful. New therapies.

TAURUS

Charismatic, sensual/mystical, natural. Creative with substance (possibly including money). Lack of imagination. Physical healing, using hands.

GEMINI

Gift/block for accessing non-physical dimensions. Problems with logical thinking. Gifted communicators. Translators, able to bridge different faiths, religions or cultural forms. Healing with words.

CANCER

Centred/wounded emotional nature. Clinging/nurturing. Possessive, fear of loneliness. Telepathic with loved ones.

LEO

Compulsion to express self regardless of others. Fear of/inability in self-expression. Blocked/dramatic spontaneity. Sense of drama. Inner nobility.

VIRGO

Feeling for natural timing and organic growth cycles. Devoted, desire to contribute. Potential linking of mind and body. Kind disposition. Homeopathy.

LIBRA

Need for harmony, beauty. Oversensitive to discord. Unconscious competitiveness and exploitation of others. Uses other people as mirror. Healing/wounding through relationships.

SCORPIO

Intense, searching, obsessive. Fearless (even ruthless) honesty with self and others. Futile struggles with negative emotions. Depth of being, instinctive knowing/healing.

SAGITTARIUS

Crusading/fanatical. Inspired. Over-extension of self. Wise. Crisis of meaning with regard to religion/faith. Indiscriminate deification. Wisdom teacher.

CAPRICORN

Patronizing/dignified. Burdened, resentful/dutiful. Tendency to be scapegoat. Willing to shoulder responsibility. Capacity to support others' individuality. Contact healing.

AQUARIUS   Rebellious eccentricity. Aloof, disdainful.
                  Idealistic/iconoclastic. Paradoxical issues regarding
                  strong super-ego. Utopian. Distant/crystal heal-
                  ing.

PISCES   Mystical/confused. Addictive, imaginative. Soul-
                  ful, unable to accept limits or boundaries.
                  Pantheism. Fascination with/fear of the occult.
                  Highly sensitive/healers, aromatherapy.

Chiron in Aspect. The following are issues that will be
raised. They will modify the picture drawn by Chiron by house and
by sign. Stronger aspects will be more observable. Discordant aspects
may well indicate amplification of the issues involved with the natal
chart. I initially used a 1° orb for Chiron with aspects, and extended
this to 4° or 5° where appropriate. Exact aspects will naturally be
more noticeable.

SUN/CHIRON   Issues around individuality. Probably projecting
                  self on to others, feeling insignificant as a result.
                  Catalyst and potential healer.

MOON   Emotional insecurity/wounds, possibly mother-
                  based. Leading to emotional understanding.

MERCURY   Quick/original mind. Intuitively logical. Teaching
                  ability.

VENUS   Highly sensitive and intuitive. Potential abuse of
                  partners/friends or vice versa. Intuitive healing.

MARS   Dangerously impulsive/repressed dynamism.
                  Perhaps subject to anger in childhood. Un-
                  directed compulsive activities. Distortions of
                  will-power/potential to energize others.

JUPITER   Insecurity in belief system(s) and direction.
                  Excesses. Ironic joviality. Zeal, capacity to in-
                  spire.

SATURN   Fear, isolation. Requirement to 'break the
                  mould'. Resolution of ancestral patterns on the
                  father's side.

URANUS	Unique sense of individuality. Eccentric, magical. Leading to wisdom.
NEPTUNE	Highly sensitive. Compassionate, self-sacrificing. Understanding/prophecy.
PLUTO	Originality with transformative energies. Dicing with death. Resolution of ancestral patterns on the mother's side.

APPENDIX V
Avenues for Further Study

By now, one hopes, any newcomer to astrology will have noticed the breadth of the subject. There is also a depth to it. At this stage there are only two books that one can seriously recommend to the beginner. They are:

1. Alan Oken, *Complete Astrology*, London, Bantam, 1980. Oken covers much of the subject matter in considerable detail.
2. Gregory Szanto, *The Marriage of Heaven and Earth*, London, Arkana, 1985. This book looks at some of the deeper issues in astrology without requiring the reader to have a thorough understanding of the astrological language.

Astrology does involve another language and beginners can be swamped by it. Once one is reasonably familiar with the language, it can be of great value to join a group, society or 'gathering of like minds' to further understanding and familiarity with the subject.

Here is a brief, by no means exhaustive, list of special interest subjects and authors.

Composite charts: This is an increasingly popular method used in synastry. By finding, literally, the mid-points of the planets and MC respectively, one can generate one chart from two. The Ascendant is found from the table of houses at the latitude of 'the relationship' according to the new MC. (The mid-point ascendant is also marked on the composite chart.) However, these charts have no 'reality' physically and must be interpreted as such (i.e., they will show potentials and issues relating to the friendship of those involved).

Esoteric astrology: deals with deeper issues and significances of the subject and normally requires a spiritual maturity in order to comprehend it.

Harmonics in astrology: another method for acquiring more detail by multiplying the whole natal chart by a given number to highlight particular aspects of the native. It requires some understanding of numerology.

Hereditary genetic astrology: looks at ancestral or hierarchic patterns through generations as an aid to counselling and understanding.

Karmic astrology: seeks to involve past life experiences as an aid to counselling.

Medical astrology: involved with the diagnosis or prevention of illness using the natal chart and transits, etc.

Psychological astrology: seeks to approach astrology from a psychological angle, often Jungian, in order to aid in-depth counselling.

Qabalistic astrology: approaching astrology with an understanding of Qabalah, it can lead to a greater comprehension of the process of creation than is perhaps possible using only 'pure astrology'. Invariably, however, one needs some form of teacher for this.

Synastry: the term used to denote that one is comparing or investigating two people's charts.

Books

ESOTERIC ASTROLOGY

Alice Bailey, *Esoteric Astrology*, Vol. III of *A Treatise on the Seven Rays*, London, Luscis Publishing Co., 1951.

GENETIC ASTROLOGY

See relevant sections of Liz Greene, *The Astrology of Fate*, London, Unwin Hyman, 1985.

HARMONIC ASTROLOGY

Books by John Addey.

KARMIC ASTROLOGY

Martin Schullman, *Karmic Astrology*, Vols. I–IV, York Beach, Maine, Samuel Weiser, 1975–1979.

Judy Hall, *The Karmic Journey*, London, Arkana, 1990.

PSYCHOLOGICAL ASTROLOGY

Liz Greene and Howard Sasportas, *Dynamics of the Unconscious*, London, Arkana, 1989; also other books by Liz Greene and books by S. Arroyo.

Should one decide to take up astrology seriously, it is almost essential to acquire a daily ephemeris or suitable computer. A worthwhile addition to your library would be definitive works on world time zones and changes. The following give this information as well as longitudes and latitudes.

The American Atlas, San Diego, ACS Publications, 1978.

The International Atlas, San Diego, ACS Publications, 1985.

XI
Condensed Ephemeris

———————

(a) Calculated for midnight (00 h 00 m) GMT, 19.00 to 20.10 inclusive, with rapid tables for finding Sidereal Time and a table for converting moving equinox zodiac to the stellar zodiac.

Accuracy of the planetary longitudes is plus or minus $\frac{1}{2}'$ of arc. (Seconds of arc have been rounded up or down to the nearest whole minute.)

(b) Longitudes are given in ° ′ of zodiacal longitude, at intervals of: ☽ every two days from the 1st of each month; ☿ every six days from the first of each month; ☉♀♂♃♄♅♆♇☊ every ten days from the 1 January each year. They are shown thus 12 ♈ 02 means 12° 02′ of ♈ (Aries).

(c) Retrograde, is shown only once in each column instead of the zodiac sign. However the zodiac sign takes precedence over ℞ and Direct symbols, so care must be taken not to overlook retrograde motion when taking figures from the top of any column. (Planetary longitude decreases when the planet is retrograde.)

(d) Stations, of all planets, are given in the lower right-hand block. They are given to make it possible to get more accurate results from the tables when planets are close to their stations. (See section 133.) As the time of the station is not given the dates given are to the nearest midnight and are not precise. Occasionally this results in the station appearing in the wrong year (1 January or 31 December rounded back or forwards). See the ephemeris for 1931, ☿ stations: 1/1 obviously applies to 1/1 1932. Check positions in year before or after if in doubt.

Tables for Sidereal Time

(e) Sidereal Time for midnight GMT 1 January is given on the left of the top line for each year. To calculate the Sidereal Time at Greenwich for any given day a simple addition of:

Sid. Time 1 January (year)
Sid. Time for month (note if leap or common)
Sid. Time for day

is necessary. The last two figures are selected from the tables below.

ADDITION FOR MONTH

Kind of year: (see Ephemeris)			FEB h m s	MAR h m s	APR h m s	MAY h m s	JUN h m s
Common year			2 2 13	3 51 37	5 54 50	7 53 7	9 55 20
Leap year			2 2 13	3 56 33	5 58 46	7 57 3	9 59 16

Kind of year:	JUL h m s	AUG h m s	SEP h m s	OCT h m s	NOV h m s	DEC h m s
Common	11 53 36	13 55 50	15 58 3	17 56 19	19 58 33	21 56 49
Leap	11 57 33	13 59 46	16 1 59	18 0 16	20 4 29	22 0 46

ADDITION FOR DAY

day	m	s	day	m	s	day	h	m	s	day	h	m	s	day	h	m	s
2nd	3	57	8th	27	36	14th	0	51	15	20th	1	14	56	26th	1	38	34
3rd	7	53	9th	31	32	15th	0	55	12	21st	1	18	51	27th	1	42	30
4th	11	50	10th	35	29	16th	0	59	8	22nd	1	22	48	28th	1	46	27
5th	15	46	11th	39	26	17th	1	3	5	23rd	1	26	44	29th	1	50	24
6th	19	43	12th	43	22	18th	1	7	1	24th	1	30	41	30th	1	54	20
7th	23	39	13th	47	19	19th	1	10	58	25th	1	34	37	31st	1	58	17

ACCELERATION

Mean Time min.	Whole Hours of Mean Time											
	0 h m s	1 h m s	2 h m s	3 h m s	4 h m s	5 h m s	6 h m s	7 h m s	8 h m s	9 h m s	10 h m s	11 h m s
0	0 0	0 10	0 20	0 30	0 39	0 49	0 59	1 9	1 19	1 29	1 39	1 48
6	0 1	0 11	0 21	0 31	0 40	0 50	1 0	1 10	1 20	1 30	1 40	1 49
12	0 2	0 12	0 22	0 32	0 41	0 51	1 1	1 11	1 21	1 31	1 41	1 50
18	0 3	0 13	0 23	0 33	0 42	0 52	1 2	1 12	1 22	1 32	1 42	1 51
24	0 4	0 14	0 24	0 34	0 43	0 53	1 3	1 13	1 23	1 33	1 43	1 52
30	0 5	0 15	0 25	0 34	0 44	0 54	1 4	1 14	1 24	1 34	1 43	1 53
36	0 6	0 16	0 26	0 35	0 45	0 55	1 5	1 15	1 25	1 35	1 44	1 54
42	0 7	0 17	0 27	0 36	0 46	0 56	1 6	1 16	1 26	1 36	1 45	1 55
48	0 8	0 18	0 28	0 37	0 47	0 57	1 7	1 17	1 27	1 37	1 46	1 56
54	0 9	0 19	0 29	0 38	0 48	0 58	1 8	1 18	1 28	1 38	1 47	1 57
60	0 10	0 20	0 30	0 39	0 49	0 59	1 9	1 19	1 29	1 39	1 48	1 58

SID M/N 1st JAN 6 h 40 m 43 s 1900 LEAP BST NONE

DAY	JAN	FEB	MAR	APR	MAY	JUN	JUL	AUG	SEP	OCT	NOV	DEC
1	2♑25	25♒04	3♓09	26♈54	3♊48	21♋43	24♌35	8♎38	22♏58	26♐50	16♒28	25♓00
☽ 3	1♒35	25♓16	3♈46	25♉48	0♋53	16♌37	18♍37	2♏25	17♐51	23♑07	14♓58	23♈54
5	1♓08	24♈20	3♉21	22♊50	26♋23	10♍41	12♎23	26♏52	14♑19	21♒14	14♈41	23♉05
7	0♈08	21♉42	1♊04	18♋11	20♌45	4♎28	6♏30	22♐36	12♒45	21♓02	14♉43	21♊47
9	28♈03	17♊34	26♊59	12♌27	14♍33	28♎35	1♐34	20♑07	12♓48	21♈36	13♊56	19♋20
11	24♉46	12♋23	21♋38	6♍13	8♎24	23♏33	28♐02	19♒18	13♈19	21♉32	11♋34	15♌24
13	20♊30	6♌36	15♌36	29♍59	2♏44	19♐37	26♑00	19♓19	12♉56	19♊51	7♌30	10♍09
15	15♋28	0♍30	9♍21	24♎05	27♏48	16♑50	25♒00	18♈56	10♊53	16♋21	2♍07	4♎03
17	9♌49	24♍15	3♎09	18♏42	23♐45	14♒55	24♓11	17♉20	7♋10	11♌24	25♍59	27♎44
19	3♍44	18♎05	27♎11	13♐58	20♑34	13♓24	22♈49	14♊19	2♌14	5♍33	19♎40	21♏51
21	27♍28	12♏20	21♏39	10♑09	18♒14	11♈51	20♉32	10♋08	26♌33	29♍18	13♏38	16♐49
23	21♎24	7♐32	16♐56	7♒28	16♓37	9♉58	17♊18	5♌08	20♍27	23♎01	8♐11	12♑52
25	16♏09	4♑16	13♑29	6♓03	15♈24	7♊27	13♋14	29♌31	14♎09	16♏57	3♑31	9♒56
27	12♐17	2♒55	11♒43	5♈34	14♉05	4♋07	8♌24	23♍28	7♏53	11♐20	29♑43	7♓42
29	10♑15		11♓29	5♉09	12♊03	29♋50	2♍52	17♎09	1♐57	6♑29	26♒53	5♈52
31	9♒53		11♈54		8♋49		26♍47	10♏54		2♒47		4♉10
1	19♐00	5♒25	25♓30	28♓37	14♈45	12♊10	4♌24	8♌51	26♌11	20♎12	1♐38	20♏13
☿ 7	27 03	15 39	4♈04	26R33	23 29	25 06	10 16	4R57	7♍40	29 29	5 41	23 48
13	5♑40	26 21	8 42	27D41	3♉27	7♋03	14 02	3D55	19 07	8♏17	5R34	0♐28
19	14 40	7♓26	8R22	1♈30	14 36	17 39	15R15	7 03	0♎04	16 35	29♏49	8 31
25	24 02	18 32	4 09	7 20	26 54	26 47	13 34	14 14	10 25	24 11	22 22	17 11
31	3♒46		29♓15		9♊58		9 37	24 20		0♐43		26 10

DATE	☉	♀	♂	♃	♄	⚷	♅	♆	♇	☊	STATIONS
1 1	10♑09	6♒23	13♑52	1♐08	27♐43	18♐54	10♐09	25♊13	15♊15	19♐09	
11	20 21	18 48	21 36	3 02	28 52	20 00	10 40	24R57	15R05	18 38	☿ 16/3 9♈10
21	0♒32	1♓09	29 24	4 47	29 58	21 01	11 09	24 43	14 56	18 06	☿ 8/4 26♓31
31	10 42	13 27	7♒13	6 22	1♑00	21 58	11 34	24 31	14 50	17 34	☿ 19/7 15♌15
10 2	20 50	25 39	15 05	7 46	1 57	22 48	11 55	24 22	14 45	17 02	☿ 12/8 3♌48
20	0♓55	7♈44	22 58	8 55	2 48	23 31	12 11	24 15	14 42	16 31	☿ 10/11 6♐17
1 3	10 59	19 41	0♓51	9 50	3 32	24 07	12 22	24 12	14D41	15 59	☿ 30/11 20♏07
11	20 59	1♉27	8 44	10 28	4 08	24 33	12 28	24D13	14 43	15 27	♀ 17/6 23♋59
21	0♈55	13 00	16 36	10 48	4 36	24 51	12R28	24 17	14 47	14 55	♀ 30/7 7♋29
31	10 49	24 17	24 26	10R50	4 53	24 59	12 23	24 24	14 53	14 23	♃ 28/3 10♐52
10 4	20 39	5♊14	2♈13	10 33	5 02	24R58	12 14	24 35	15 01	13 52	♃ 29/7 1♐01
20	0♉26	15 43	9 57	9 58	5R00	24 47	11 59	24 48	15 11	13 20	♄ 14/4 5♑02
30	10 09	25 38	17 37	9 07	4 49	24 28	11 41	25 04	15 22	12 48	♄ 3/9 28♐26
10 5	19 50	4♋45	25 13	8 04	4 28	24 01	11 20	25 22	15 34	12 16	♅ 18/3 12♐29
20	29 28	12 44	2♉43	6 51	4 00	23 28	10 57	25 41	15 47	11 45	♅ 18/8 8♐27
30	9♊04	19 06	10 09	5 35	3 24	22 50	10 32	26 02	16 01	11 13	♆ 6/3 24♊12
9 6	18 38	23 06	17 29	4 21	2 44	22 10	10 08	26 24	16 14	10 41	♆ 3/10 29♊16
19	28 11	23R49	24 44	3 13	2 01	21 29	9 44	26 47	16 28	10 09	♇ 27/2 14♊41
29	7♋43	20 40	1♊52	2 16	1 17	20 50	9 22	27 09	16 42	9 38	⚷ 4/4 25♐00
9 7	17 15	14 49	8 54	1 34	0 34	20 14	9 03	27 31	16 54	9 06	⚷ 23/8 18♐55
19	26 48	9 30	15 49	1 08	29♐55	19 43	8 47	27 51	17 06	8 34	
29	6♌21	7 29	22 37	1D01	29 21	19 19	8 36	28 11	17 16	8 02	
8 8	15 56	9D15	29 19	1 12	28 54	19 03	8 29	28 28	17 25	7 30	
18	25 32	14 01	5♋53	1 40	28 36	18 55	8D27	28 43	17 32	6 59	
28	5♍11	20 53	12 19	2 26	28 27	18D57	8 30	28 56	17 38	6 27	
7 9	14 52	29 13	18 37	3 27	28D27	19 07	8 39	29 05	17 41	5 55	
17	24 37	8♌35	24 45	4 43	28 37	19 26	8 52	29 12	17R42	5 23	
27	4♎24	18 43	0♌44	6 11	28 57	19 54	9 10	29 15	17 41	4 52	
7 10	14 15	29 23	6 32	7 50	29 26	20 29	9 33	29R15	17 37	4 20	
17	24 10	10♍30	12 07	9 39	0♑03	21 12	9 59	29 12	17 32	3 48	
27	4♏07	21 57	17 27	11 36	0 48	22 01	10 29	29 05	17 25	3 16	
6 11	14 08	3♎40	22 30	13 40	1 40	22 55	11 02	28 55	17 16	2 44	
16	24 12	15 36	27 13	15 49	2 38	23 54	11 36	28 43	17 06	2 13	
26	4♐19	27 41	1♍30	18 02	3 41	24 56	12 12	28 29	16 55	1 41	
6 12	14 27	9♏53	5 17	20 17	4 47	26 00	12 49	28 13	16 43	1 09	
16	24 37	22 11	8 26	22 34	5 56	27 06	13 26	27 56	16 32	0 37	
26	4♑49	4♐33	10 48	24 50	7 07	28 11	14 01	27 39	16 21	0 06	

SID M/N 1st JAN 6 h 39 m 46 s 1901 COMMON BST NONE

	DAY	JAN	FEB	MAR	APR	MAY	JUN	JUL	AUG	SEP	OCT	NOV	DEC
	1	18♉19	9♋34	19♋31	6♍53	9♎57	24♏09	27♐07	15♒05	6♈49	15♉38	8♋32	15♌04
☽	3	16♊23	5♌50	15♌05	1♎01	3♏35	18♐19	22♑37	12♓49	5♉51	14♊46	6♌05	11♍12
	5	13♋52	1♍17	9♍58	24♎46	27♏18	13♑12	19♒05	11♈03	4♊23	12♋42	2♍03	5♎52
	7	10♌22	25♍50	4♎12	18♏23	21♐23	8♒58	16♓21	9♉22	2♋11	9♌23	26♍50	29♎41
	9	5♍40	19♎42	27♎56	12♐13	16♑10	5♓43	14♈15	7♊32	29♋12	5♍01	20♎52	23♏14
	11	29♍56	13♏20	21♏33	6♑44	12♒02	3♈31	12♉37	5♋25	25♌25	29♍47	14♏31	16♐57
	13	23♎39	7♐24	15♐34	2♒31	9♓19	2♉20	11♊15	2♌47	20♍47	23♎54	8♐06	11♑07
	15	17♏28	2♑37	10♑40	0♓02	8♈06	1♊44	9♋44	29♌18	15♎17	17♏34	1♑56	5♒54
	17	12♐05	29♑31	7♒29	29♓19	7♉59	0♋59	7♌27	24♍43	9♏07	11♐07	26♑20	1♓31
	19	7♑59	28♒07	6♓13	29♈39	8♊01	29♋12	3♍56	19♎06	2♐41	5♑01	21♒45	28♓12
	21	5♒21	27♓41	6♈15	29♉49	7♋06	25♌53	29♍02	12♏49	26♐35	29♑51	18♓36	26♈11
	23	3♓47	27♈10	6♉26	28♊43	4♌35	21♍02	23♎05	6♐31	21♑30	26♒09	17♈07	25♉26
	25	2♈33	25♉44	5♊35	25♋55	0♍22	15♎06	16♏44	0♑53	18♒00	24♓16	17♉03	25♊24
	27	1♉01	23♊08	3♋14	21♌33	24♍51	8♏44	10♐40	26♑33	16♓16	23♈58	17♊28	25♋00
	29	28♉54		29♋28	16♍05	18♎38	2♐35	5♑30	23♒48	15♈48	24♉19	17♋06	23♌12
	31	26♊10		24♌37		12♏15		1♒35	22♓19		24♊08		19♍33
	1	27♐41	18♒34	21♓36	13♓04	25♈06	28♊20	25♋58	18♋54	11♍45	29♎45	16♏16	21♏09
☿	7	6♑56	29 14	17R09	18 55	6♉49	7♋51	24R16	25 18	22 41	7♏20	8R46	0♐02
	13	16 26	9♓26	11 27	26 16	19 27	15 36	20 41	4♌45	2♎54	13 51	4 30	9 11
	19	26 13	17 43	8 20	4♈49	2♊32	21 25	17 12	16 09	12 28	18 39	6D38	18 26
	25	6♒20	21 54	8D49	14 26	15 11	25 00	15D58	28 09	21 26	20R23	12 58	27 49
	31	16 48		12 16		26 35		18 10	9♍52		17 18		7♑19

DATE	☉	♀	♂	♃	♄	⚷	♅	♆	♇	☊	STATIONS
1 1	9♑54	10♐45	11♍38	25♐58	7♑42	28♐44	14♐19	27♊31	16♊15	29♏50	
11	20 06	23 11	12 30	28 11	8 53	29 48	14 52	27R15	16R05	29 18	☿ 27/2 22♓05
21	0♒17	5♑38	12R09	0♑21	10 02	0♑49	15 22	27 00	15 57	28 46	☿ 21/3 8♓07
31	10 27	18 06	10 28	2 26	11 08	1 46	15 49	26 48	15 50	28 14	☿ 30/6 26♋00
10 2	20 35	0♒34	7 35	4 24	12 11	2 39	16 11	26 38	15 45	27 43	☿ 24/7 15♋57
20	0♓41	13 02	3 50	6 14	13 09	3 26	16 30	26 31	15 42	27 11	☿ 25/10 20♏24
2 3	10 44	25 30	29♌55	7 55	14 01	4 06	16 43	26 27	15D41	26 39	☿ 14/11 4♏26
12	20 44	7♓57	26 31	9 24	14 46	4 39	16 51	26D27	15 42	26 07	♂ 13/1 12♍32
22	0♈41	20 23	24 11	10 40	15 24	5 04	16 54	26 30	15 46	25 36	♂ 4/4 23♌03
1 4	10 35	2♈48	23 07	11 41	15 53	5 20	16R52	26 36	15 52	25 04	♃ 1/5 13♑03
11	20 25	15 11	23D19	12 26	16 12	5 27	16 44	26 46	15 59	24 32	♃ 31/8 3♑13
21	0♉12	27 34	24 38	12 54	16 22	5R26	16 32	26 58	16 09	24 00	♄ 26/4 16♑23
1 5	9 55	9♉55	26 53	13R03	16R22	5 15	16 16	27 13	16 20	23 28	♄ 15/9 9♑47
11	19 36	22 14	29 54	12 53	16 13	4 57	15 56	27 31	16 32	22 57	♅ 22/3 16♐54
21	29 14	4♊33	3♍33	12 25	15 54	4 32	15 34	27 50	16 45	22 25	♅ 23/8 12♐53
31	8♊50	16 50	7 42	11 40	15 27	4 00	15 10	28 11	16 58	21 53	♆ 8/3 26♊26
10 6	18 24	29 07	12 15	10 41	14 53	3 25	14 45	28 33	17 12	21 21	♆ 5/10 1♋29
20	27 57	11♋22	17 10	9 31	14 14	2 46	14 21	28 55	17 26	20 50	♇ 1/3 15♊41
30	7♋30	23 37	22 23	8 15	13 31	2 07	13 58	29 17	17 40	20 18	⚷ 14/4 5♑28
10 7	17 02	5♌51	27 51	6 59	12 47	1 29	13 37	29 39	17 53	19 46	⚷ 4/9 29♐31
20	26 34	18 04	3♎32	5 47	12 04	0 54	13 20	0♋00	18 04	19 14	
30	6♌07	0♍15	9 26	4 46	11 24	0 24	13 06	0 20	18 15	18 42	
9 8	15 42	12 25	15 31	3 58	10 48	29♐59	12 57	0 38	18 24	18 11	
19	25 18	24 32	21 47	3 26	10 20	29 42	12 53	0 54	18 31	17 39	
29	4♍57	6♎37	28 12	3 13	10 00	29 33	12D54	1 07	18 37	17 07	
8 9	14 38	18 39	4♏47	3D19	9 49	29D32	13 00	1 17	18 40	16 35	
18	24 23	0♏38	11 30	3 44	9D47	29 40	13 11	1 25	18 42	16 04	
28	4♎10	12 32	18 22	4 27	9 56	29 56	13 26	1 29	18R41	15 32	
8 10	14 01	24 22	25 22	5 26	10 14	0♑20	13 47	1R29	18 38	15 00	
18	23 55	6♐05	2♐29	6 41	10 41	0 52	14 11	1 27	18 33	14 28	
28	3♏53	17 41	9 44	8 09	11 17	1 31	14 40	1 21	18 26	13 57	
7 11	13 54	29 06	17 06	9 49	12 01	2 16	15 11	1 12	18 17	13 25	
17	23 58	10♑16	24 34	11 40	12 53	3 06	15 45	1 00	18 07	12 53	
27	4♐04	21 06	2♑08	13 39	13 50	4 00	16 20	0 46	17 56	12 21	
7 12	14 12	1♒27	9 47	15 46	14 52	4 58	16 57	0 31	17 45	11 49	
17	24 23	11 07	17 31	17 58	15 58	5 58	17 33	0 14	17 33	11 18	
27	4♑34	19 45	25 18	20 14	17 07	6 59	18 09	29♊57	17 22	10 46	

SID M/N 1st JAN 6 h 38 m 48 s 1902 COMMON BST NONE

DAY	JAN	FEB	MAR	APR	MAY	JUN	JUL	AUG	SEP	OCT	NOV	DEC
1	2♎06	16♏06	23♏52	7♑23	10♒11	27♓58	5♉02	28♊25	21♌38	28♍10	15♏05	17♐51
☽ 3	26♎17	9♐43	17♐31	1♒55	5♓53	25♈55	4♊11	28♋05	19♍30	24♎09	9♐18	11♑35
5	19♏53	3♑45	11♑37	27♒45	3♈14	25♉29	4♋21	27♌12	16♎01	19♏03	3♑06	5♒20
7	13♐33	28♑42	6♒45	25♓10	2♉14	25♊55	4♌23	24♍53	11♏08	13♐08	26♑50	29♒29
9	7♑45	24♒44	3♓14	23♈59	2♊18	25♋56	3♍04	20♎49	5♐16	6♑52	21♒03	24♓34
11	2♒45	21♓43	0♈58	23♉29	2♋19	24♌27	29♍51	15♏21	29♐00	0♒51	16♓22	21♈11
13	28♒33	19♈18	29♈27	22♊46	1♌14	21♍06	24♎58	9♐10	23♑00	25♒41	13♈15	19♉42
15	25♓06	17♉16	28♉05	21♋10	28♌34	16♎10	19♏00	2♑54	17♒48	21♓49	11♉52	19♊50
17	22♈24	15♊28	26♊27	18♌27	24♍24	10♏16	12♐39	27♑07	13♓42	19♈23	11♊41	20♋26
19	20♉33	13♋47	24♋19	14♍37	19♎08	3♐57	6♑27	22♒06	10♈40	18♉04	11♋39	20♌06
21	19♊27	11♌51	21♌33	9♎51	13♏12	27♐38	0♒42	17♓56	8♉27	17♊12	10♌40	17♍59
23	18♋37	9♍07	17♍57	4♏18	6♐55	21♑36	25♒35	14♈32	6♊42	16♋03	8♍13	14♎04
25	17♌11	5♎10	13♎23	28♏14	0♑36	16♒03	21♓09	11♉51	5♋06	14♌07	4♎23	8♏51
27	14♍23	29♎57	7♏55	21♐53	24♑32	11♓12	17♈35	9♊52	3♌21	11♍15	29♎29	2♐55
29	9♎58		1♐46	15♑42	19♒04	7♈25	15♉04	8♋30	1♍10	7♎25	23♏53	26♐41
31	4♏15		25♐26		14♓38		13♊43	7♌21		2♏43		20♑25
1	8♑55	29♒11	20♒55	16♓33	12♉02	2♋14	27♊53	26♋14	25♍08	1♏59	19♎40	1♐29
☿ 7	18 40	4♓43	21D01	25 51	24 52	5 28	27D18	8♌28	4♎22	4 20	25 13	10 55
13	28 38	4℞38	24 20	6♈04	6♊48	6℞01	29 44	20 47	12 51	2℞38	3♏26	20 20
19	8♒47	29♒13	29 52	17 12	17 04	4 03	5♋13	2♍30	20 29	26♎28	12 36	29 49
25	18 49	23 08	6♓54	29 16	25 21	0 42	13 34	13 25	27 02	20 03	22 02	9♑24
31	27 53		15 05		1♋27		24 16	23 32		19D11		19 04

DATE	☉	♀	♂	♃	♄	⚷	♅	♆	♇	☊	STATIONS
1 1	9♑40	23♒32	29♑13	21♑24	17♑42	7♑29	18♐27	29♊49	17♊16	10♏30	
11	19 51	29 38	7♒05	23 44	18 53	8 30	19 01	29℞32	17℞06	9 58	☿ 10/2 5♓28
21	0♒02	3♓00	14 59	26 05	20 04	9 29	19 32	29 17	16 57	9 26	☿ 4/3 20♒29
31	10 12	2℞38	22 53	28 25	21 14	10 26	20 00	29 04	16 50	8 55	☿ 11/6 6♋08
10 2	20 20	28♒21	0♓48	0♒44	22 21	11 19	20 25	28 54	16 45	8 23	☿ 5/7 27♊11
20	0♓26	22 17	8 42	2 59	23 24	12 08	20 45	28 46	16 42	7 51	☿ 8/10 4♏22
2 3	10 29	18 09	16 34	5 10	24 23	12 51	21 01	28 41	16D40	7 19	☿ 29/10 18♎43
12	20 30	17D54	24 24	7 15	25 16	13 28	21 11	28D40	16 42	6 48	♀ 25/1 3♓21
22	0♈27	21 15	2♈11	9 12	26 03	13 58	21 16	28 42	16 45	6 16	♀ 8/3 17♒31
1 4	10 20	27 13	9 55	11 00	26 42	14 20	21℞16	28 48	16 50	5 44	♃ 6/6 17♒15
11	20 11	4♓57	17 34	12 38	27 12	14 34	21 11	28 57	16 58	5 12	♃ 4/10 7♒25
21	29 57	13 52	25 09	14 03	27 34	14 40	21 01	29 09	17 07	4 41	♄ 8/5 27♑48
1 5	9♉41	23 35	2♉40	15 15	27 46	14℞37	20 47	29 23	17 18	4 09	♄ 26/9 21♑11
11	19 22	3♈52	10 05	16 11	27℞48	14 26	20 29	29 40	17 30	3 37	♅ 27/3 21♐17
21	29 00	14 33	17 25	16 50	27 40	14 08	20 08	29 59	17 43	3 05	♅ 27/8 17♐16
31	8♊36	25 33	24 39	17 11	27 23	13 43	19 44	0♋20	17 57	2 33	♆ 11/3 28♊40
10 6	18 11	6♉46	1♊48	17℞14	26 58	13 13	19 20	0 41	18 10	2 02	♆ 8/10 3♋43
20	27 44	18 09	8 52	16 57	26 25	12 39	18 56	1 03	18 24	1 30	♇ 2/3 16♊40
30	7♋16	29 42	15 50	16 22	25 47	12 02	18 32	1 26	18 38	0 58	⚷ 23/ 4 14♑40
10 7	16 48	11♊22	22 43	15 30	25 05	11 24	18 10	1 48	18 51	0 26	⚷ 15/ 9 8♑52
20	26 20	23 08	29 31	14 25	24 20	10 48	17 51	2 09	19 03	29♎55	
30	5♌53	5♋01	6♋13	13 11	23 37	10 14	17 36	2 29	19 14	29 23	
9 8	15 28	17 00	12 50	11 53	22 56	9 44	17 25	2 47	19 23	28 51	
19	25 04	29 05	19 21	10 37	22 19	9 21	17 18	3 04	19 31	28 19	
29	4♍43	11♌14	25 48	9 28	21 49	9 04	17D16	3 18	19 37	27 47	
8 9	14 24	23 29	2♌09	8 32	21 27	8 54	17 20	3 29	19 40	27 16	
18	24 08	5♍48	8 24	7 51	21 14	8D53	17 28	3 37	19 42	26 44	
28	3♎56	18 11	14 33	7 29	21D11	8 59	17 42	3 42	19℞41	26 12	
8 10	13 47	0♎38	20 36	7D26	21 18	9 14	18 00	3℞43	19 38	25 40	
18	23 41	13 07	26 32	7 43	21 34	9 36	18 23	3 42	19 33	25 09	
28	3♏38	25 38	2♍20	8 19	22 00	10 06	18 49	3 36	19 27	24 37	
7 11	13 39	8♏11	7 59	9 13	22 35	10 42	19 19	3 28	19 18	24 05	
17	23 43	20 44	13 28	10 24	23 18	11 24	19 52	3 17	19 08	23 33	
27	3♐49	3♐19	18 45	11 49	24 08	12 11	20 26	3 04	18 58	23 02	
7 12	13 58	15 53	23 48	13 28	25 05	13 02	21 02	2 49	18 46	22 30	
17	24 08	28 28	28 34	15 18	26 07	13 56	21 39	2 32	18 35	21 58	
27	4♑19	11♑03	2♎59	17 18	27 13	14 52	22 15	2 15	18 23	21 26	

SID M/N 1st JAN 6 h 37 m 51 s 1903 COMMON BST NONE

	DAY	JAN	FEB	MAR	APR	MAY	JUN	JUL	AUG	SEP	OCT	NOV	DEC
	1	2♒19	18♓03	27♓28	16♉48	25♊09	18♌55	26♍59	15♏47	1♑23	3♒28	17♓20	20♈06
☽	3	26♒21	13♈21	23♈23	14♊42	24♋01	16♍53	23♎35	10♐31	25♑11	27♒18	12♈19	16♉42
	5	20♓57	9♉41	20♉09	13♋01	22♌22	13♎36	18♏55	4♑34	18♒57	21♓37	8♉33	14♊54
	7	16♈33	7♊23	17♊51	11♌28	19♍57	9♏17	13♐27	28♑20	13♓02	16♈46	6♊00	14♋07
	9	13♉43	6♋32	16♋27	9♍41	16♎42	4♐14	7♑31	22♒07	7♈40	12♉51	4♋15	13♌22
	11	12♊43	6♌34	15♌35	7♎18	12♏38	28♐36	1♒19	16♓07	3♉01	9♊50	2♌44	11♍54
	13	13♋06	6♍19	14♍31	3♏58	7♐45	22♑32	25♒03	10♈36	29♉20	7♋35	1♍01	9♎26
	15	13♌37	4♎41	12♎29	29♏31	2♑08	16♒15	19♓01	5♉59	26♊48	5♌55	28♍54	6♏04
	17	12♍51	1♏13	8♏59	24♐04	26♑00	10♓10	13♈42	2♊43	25♋27	4♍32	26♎14	1♐57
	19	10♎07	26♏12	4♐06	17♑59	19♒48	4♈52	9♉41	1♋06	24♌52	3♎03	22♏53	27♐08
	21	5♏35	20♐14	28♐14	11♒49	14♓05	0♉58	7♊28	0♌52	24♍17	0♏56	18♐37	21♑36
	23	29♏53	13♑56	22♑00	6♓10	9♈31	28♉56	7♋03	1♍07	22♎47	27♏41	13♑23	15♒27
	25	23♐38	7♒51	16♒00	1♈34	6♉32	28♊37	7♌35	0♎36	19♏48	23♐11	7♒22	9♓03
	27	17♑20	2♓19	10♓43	28♈20	5♊12	29♋00	7♍42	28♎27	15♐18	17♑35	1♓02	2♈58
	29	11♒18		6♈24	26♉22	4♋52	28♌45	6♎16	24♏34	9♑40	11♒23	25♓03	27♈53
	31	5♓40		3♉07		4♌27		3♏00	19♐20		5♓13		24♉28
	1	20♑41	14♒22	12♒17	28♓08	27♉31	13♊18	16♊20	13♌27	3♎28	12♎12	24♎46	12♐52
☿	7	0♒18	7R22	19 14	9♈34	6♊09	10R02	24 16	25 01	10 05	5R38	4♏36	22 13
	13	9 20	3 41	27 16	21 47	12 13	7 49	4♋24	5♍41	15 09	2D55	14 22	1♑33
	19	16 27	4D28	6♓09	4♉26	15 31	7D57	16 15	15 26	17 52	6 18	23 59	10 49
	25	19R09	8 27	15 50	16 42	15R55	10 50	28 56	24 18	17R06	13 50	3♐28	19 43
	31	15 29		26 18		13 49		11♌26	2♎14		23 09		27 32

DATE	☉	♀	♂	♃	♄	⚷	♅	♆	♇	☊	STATIONS
1 1	9♑25	17♑20	5♎02	18♒20	27♑47	15♑21	22♐33	2♋07	18♊18	21♎10	
11	19 36	29 54	8 46	20 31	28 57	16 18	23 07	1R50	18R07	20 39	☿ 25/1 19♒10
21	29 47	12♒27	11 55	22 47	0♒08	17 15	23 40	1 35	17 58	20 07	☿ 15/2 3♒30
31	9♒57	24 58	14 19	25 08	1 19	18 10	24 09	1 21	17 51	19 35	☿ 23/5 16♊05
10 2	20 05	7♓28	15 50	27 31	2 29	19 03	24 35	1 10	17 45	19 03	☿ 16/6 7♊32
20	0♓11	19 56	16R15	29 55	3 37	19 52	24 58	1 02	17 42	18 31	☿ 21/9 18♎04
2 3	10 15	2♈20	15 27	2♓19	4 42	20 36	25 15	0 56	17 40	18 00	☿ 13/10 2♎54
12	20 15	14 41	13 21	4 42	5 42	21 16	25 28	0 54	17D41	17 28	♀ 28/8 1♎43
22	0♈12	26 58	10 10	7 03	6 36	21 49	25 36	0D56	17 44	16 56	♀ 9/10 15♍39
1 4	10 06	9♉10	6 23	9 19	7 24	22 15	25R38	1 00	17 50	16 24	♂ 19/2 16♎16
11	19 56	21 16	2 40	11 30	8 05	22 34	25 35	1 08	17 57	15 53	♂ 10/5 27♍25
21	29 43	3♊16	29♍42	13 35	8 38	22 46	25 28	1 19	18 06	15 21	♃ 14/7 23♓18
1 5	9♉27	15 09	27 54	15 32	9 01	22R49	25 15	1 33	18 17	14 49	♃ 10/11 13♓25
11	19 08	26 53	27D26	17 19	9 15	22 45	24 59	1 50	18 29	14 17	♄ 20/5 9♒19
21	28 46	8♋27	28 12	18 56	9R19	22 33	24 39	2 08	18 41	13 46	♄ 8/10 2♒41
31	8♊22	19 50	0♎03	20 19	9 14	22 15	24 17	2 28	18 55	13 14	♅ 1/4 25♐38
10 6	17 57	0♌58	2 49	21 29	8 59	21 50	23 53	2 49	19 09	12 42	♅ 1/9 21♐38
20	27 30	11 46	6 20	22 23	8 36	21 20	23 29	3 12	19 23	12 10	♆ 13/3 0♋54
30	7♋02	22 11	10 27	22 59	8 04	20 46	23 04	3 34	19 37	11 38	♆ 10/10 5♋57
10 7	16 34	2♍03	15 06	23 17	7 27	20 11	22 42	3 56	19 50	11 07	♇ 3/3 17♊40
20	26 06	11 12	20 10	23R15	6 45	19 35	22 21	4 18	20 02	10 35	♇ 21/9 20♊42
30	5♌39	19 18	25 36	22 54	6 01	19 00	22 04	4 38	20 13	10 03	⚷ 30/4 22♑49
9 8	15 14	25 55	1♏21	22 14	5 17	18 27	21 51	4 57	20 23	9 31	⚷ 25/9 17♑11
19	24 50	0♎21	7 23	21 18	4 35	18 00	21 42	5 14	20 30	9 00	
29	4♍29	1R41	13 40	20 09	3 57	17 37	21 38	5 28	20 36	8 28	
8 9	14 10	29♍13	20 10	18 52	3 25	17 21	21D39	5 40	20 40	7 56	
18	23 54	23 42	26 52	17 33	3 01	17 12	21 45	5 49	20 42	7 24	
28	3♎42	18 09	3♐46	16 17	2 46	17D11	21 56	5 55	20R42	6 52	
8 10	13 32	15 41	10 49	15 10	2 41	17 17	22 12	5 57	20 39	6 21	
18	23 26	17D07	18 01	14 17	2D46	17 32	22 33	5R56	20 35	5 49	
28	3♏24	21 47	25 22	13 41	3 01	17 53	22 58	5 52	20 28	5 17	
7 11	13 25	28 43	2♑50	13 26	3 25	18 21	23 26	5 44	20 20	4 45	
17	23 28	7♎14	10 24	13D30	3 59	18 56	23 57	5 34	20 10	4 14	
27	3♐34	16 50	18 04	13 55	4 41	19 36	24 31	5 21	20 00	3 42	
7 12	13 43	27 12	25 48	14 40	5 31	20 21	25 06	5 06	19 48	3 10	
17	23 53	8♏07	3♒35	15 42	6 27	21 09	25 42	4 50	19 36	2 38	
27	4♑04	19 25	11 25	17 01	7 28	22 01	26 18	4 33	19 25	2 07	

SID M/N 1st JAN 6 h 36 m 54 s 1904 LEAP BST NONE

	DAY	JAN	FEB	MAR	APR	MAY	JUN	JUL	AUG	SEP	OCT	NOV	DEC
	1	8♊30	0♌53	24♌08	17♎17	23♏56	11♑46	14♒37	28♓32	13♉20	18♊05	8♌33	17♍17
☽	3	7♋49	1♍25	24♍28	15♏54	20♐51	6♒29	8♓24	22♈19	8♊33	14♋39	6♍45	15♎41
	5	7♌59	1♎12	23♎51	12♐55	16♑19	0♓22	2♈01	16♉55	5♋16	12♌39	5♎51	14♏16
	7	7♍43	29♎21	21♏33	8♑21	10♒36	24♓01	26♈09	12♊58	3♌43	12♍00	5♏18	12♐27
	9	6♎09	25♏50	17♐31	2♒35	4♓18	18♈10	21♉28	10♋49	3♍36	12♎05	4♐12	9♑35
	11	3♏07	20♐59	12♑10	26♒15	28♓05	13♉25	18♊27	10♌16	3♎57	11♏50	1♑42	5♒18
	13	28♏55	15♑16	6♒02	19♓57	22♈34	10♊09	17♋03	10♍26	3♏35	10♐11	27♑31	29♒45
	15	23♐53	9♒05	29♒39	14♈11	18♉09	8♋12	16♌34	10♎10	1♐40	6♑44	21♒56	23♓28
	17	18♑14	2♓44	23♓24	9♉14	14♊54	6♌57	16♍01	8♏37	28♐00	1♒42	15♓38	17♈09
	19	12♒08	26♓26	17♈35	5♊12	12♋33	5♍42	14♎38	5♐35	22♑57	25♒39	9♈18	11♉31
	21	5♓45	20♈31	12♉27	2♋04	10♌40	3♎58	12♏09	1♑15	17♒00	19♓14	3♉32	7♊04
	23	29♓25	15♉25	8♊15	29♋44	8♍56	1♏37	8♐38	25♑56	10♓39	13♈00	28♉42	3♋54
	25	23♈41	11♊36	5♋12	28♌06	7♎10	28♏36	4♑12	19♒58	4♈17	7♉17	24♊51	1♌43
	27	19♉11	9♋29	3♌26	26♍56	5♏08	24♐50	28♑58	13♓39	28♈13	2♊19	21♋47	29♌59
	29	16♊30	8♌59	2♍46	25♎46	2♐33	20♑10	23♒05	7♈15	22♉43	28♊09	19♌18	28♍17
	31	15♋44		2♎32		28♐59		16♓45	1♉09		24♋51		26♎23
	1	28♑38	17♑34	20♒00	16♈16	26♉19	18♉36	28♊06	29♌08	1♎12	19♍33	8♏31	24♐50
☿	7	2♒52	21 15	29 28	28 27	25R32	22 24	10♋50	8♍10	0R25	26 51	18 09	3♑22
	13	1R06	27 10	9♓36	9♉28	22 32	28 28	23 44	16 09	25♍59	6♎27	27 34	10 56
	19	24♑00	4♒26	20 27	18 11	19 11	6♊32	6♌00	22 53	19 56	16 42	6♐49	16 09
	25	18 07	12 37	2♈02	23 54	17 25	16 29	17 17	28 02	16 54	26 56	15 55	16R30
	31	17D16		14 12		18D13		27 31	0♎59		6♏53		10 28

DATE	☉	♀	♂	♃	♄	⚷	♅	♆	♇	☊	STATIONS
1 1	9♑10	25♏11	15♒21	17♓46	8♒01	22♑27	26♐36	4♋25	19♊19	1♎51	
11	19 21	6♐52	23 12	19 25	9 08	23 20	27 11	4R08	19R09	1 19	☿ 8/1 3♒05
21	29 32	18 45	1♓04	21 16	10 18	24 14	27 45	3 53	19 00	0 47	☿ 29/1 17♑00
31	9♒42	0♑44	8 54	23 16	11 30	25 07	28 16	3 38	18 52	0 15	☿ 2/5 26♉24
10 2	19 51	12 50	16 43	25 25	12 41	25 59	28 43	3 27	18 46	29♍44	☿ 26/5 17♉22
20	29 57	24 59	24 30	27 39	13 52	26 48	29 07	3 17	18 42	29 12	☿ 3/9 1♎21
1 3	10♓00	7♒10	2♈13	29 59	15 01	27 33	29 27	3 11	18 41	28 40	☿ 25/9 16♍53
11	20 01	19 24	9 52	2♈21	16 07	28 13	29 42	3 08	18D42	28 08	☿ 22/12 17♑08
21	29 58	1♓39	17 28	4 46	17 08	28 49	29 52	3D09	18 44	27 36	♃ 20/8 0♉13
31	9♈52	13 54	24 59	7 11	18 04	29 18	29 57	3 13	18 49	27 05	♃ 16/12 20♈15
10 4	19 42	26 09	2♉25	9 36	18 54	29 41	29R56	3 20	18 56	26 33	♄ 1/6 21♒00
20	29 29	8♈25	9 46	11 59	19 37	29 57	29 51	3 30	19 05	26 01	♄ 19/10 14♒21
30	9♉13	20 40	17 02	14 19	20 11	0♒06	29 41	3 44	19 16	25 29	♅ 4/4 29♐57
10 5	18 54	2♉56	24 13	16 35	20 37	0R07	29 26	3 59	19 27	24 58	♅ 5/9 25♐57
20	28 32	15 11	1♊19	18 45	20 53	0 01	29 08	4 17	19 40	24 26	♆ 15/3 3♋08
30	8♊09	27 26	8 20	20 49	21 00	29♑47	28 47	4 37	19 54	23 54	♆ 12/10 8♋11
9 6	17 43	9♊42	15 16	22 44	20R57	29 28	28 24	4 58	20 08	23 22	♇ 3/3 18♊41
19	27 16	21 58	22 08	24 30	20 45	29 02	27 59	5 20	20 22	22 51	♇ 22/9 21♊43
29	6♋48	4♋14	28 55	26 05	20 23	28 32	27 35	5 42	20 36	22 19	⚷ 6/5 0♒07
9 7	16 20	16 32	5♋38	27 27	19 53	28 00	27 12	6 04	20 49	21 47	⚷ 2/10 24♑37
19	25 52	28 50	12 17	28 34	19 17	27 25	26 50	6 26	21 01	21 15	
29	5♌26	11♌09	18 52	29 25	18 36	26 50	26 31	6 47	21 13	20 43	
8 8	15 00	23 29	25 23	29 58	17 52	26 17	26 16	7 06	21 22	20 12	
18	24 36	5♍50	1♌51	0♉13	17 07	25 47	26 05	7 24	21 31	19 40	
28	4♍15	18 11	8 16	0R07	16 24	25 20	25 59	7 39	21 37	19 08	
7 9	13 56	0♎32	14 37	29♈42	15 44	25 00	25D57	7 51	21 41	18 36	
17	23 40	12 53	20 55	28 58	15 11	24 45	26 01	8 01	21 43	18 05	
27	3♎27	25 14	27 10	27 58	14 45	24 38	26 10	8 08	21R43	17 33	
7 10	13 18	7♏34	3♍22	26 45	14 28	24D38	26 24	8 11	21 41	17 01	
17	23 12	19 53	9 30	25 25	14 21	24 45	26 42	8R11	21 36	16 29	
27	3♏09	2♐11	15 34	24 05	14D24	24 59	27 05	8 07	21 30	15 57	
6 11	13 10	14 28	21 35	22 49	14 37	25 21	27 31	8 01	21 22	15 26	
16	23 14	26 43	27 30	21 44	15 00	25 49	28 01	7 51	21 13	14 54	
26	3♐20	8♑56	3♎21	20 55	15 32	26 22	28 34	7 39	21 02	14 22	
6 12	13 28	21 05	9 05	20 25	16 13	27 01	29 08	7 24	20 51	13 50	
16	23 38	3♒10	14 42	20D15	17 02	27 44	29 44	7 08	20 39	13 19	
26	3♑49	15 08	20 11	20 25	17 57	28 31	0♑20	6 52	20 27	12 47	

SID M/N 1st JAN 6 h 39 m 53 s 1905 COMMON BST NONE

	DAY	JAN	FEB	MAR	APR	MAY	JUN	JUL	AUG	SEP	OCT	NOV	DEC
	1	10♏20	1♑10	11♑06	27♒29	29♓59	14♉12	17♊30	5♌53	27♍49	6♏42	29♐38	5♒31
☽	3	7♐54	26♑47	6♒08	21♓13	23♈37	8♊52	13♋32	4♍04	27♎26	6♐19	27♑05	1♓20
	5	4♑47	21♒35	0♓24	14♈49	17♉37	4♋19	10♌31	2♎48	26♏25	4♑22	22♒44	25♓49
	7	0♒41	15♓39	24♓12	8♉35	12♊11	0♌33	8♍11	1♏30	24♐14	0♒45	17♓10	19♈36
	9	25♒29	9♈18	17♈49	2♊46	7♋26	27♌33	6♎19	29♏46	20♑50	25♒50	10♈59	13♉19
	11	19♓26	2♉59	11♉34	27♊38	3♌33	25♍21	4♏42	27♐19	16♒21	20♓07	4♉41	7♊22
	13	13♈02	27♉16	5♊51	23♋35	0♍46	23♎57	3♐05	24♑01	11♓04	13♈59	28♉33	1♋57
	15	6♉58	22♊46	1♋12	20♌58	29♍16	23♏02	1♑02	19♒46	5♈12	7♉42	22♊45	27♋10
	17	1♊54	19♋57	28♋05	19♍59	28♎52	21♐53	28♑05	14♓37	28♈59	1♊30	17♋27	23♌06
	19	28♊20	18♌48	26♌44	20♎10	28♏43	19♑40	23♒56	8♈43	22♉42	25♊40	12♌59	19♍58
	21	26♋17	18♍42	26♍48	20♏27	27♐42	15♒55	18♓38	2♉27	16♊48	20♋36	9♍47	17♎59
	23	25♌16	18♎35	27♎13	19♐32	24♑59	10♓45	12♈35	26♉19	11♋49	16♌49	8♎10	17♏04
	25	24♍28	17♏30	26♏45	16♑44	20♒30	4♈40	6♉19	20♊54	8♌18	14♍46	7♏59	16♐38
	27	23♎11	14♐59	24♐37	12♒09	14♓45	28♈23	0♊30	16♋46	6♍34	14♎28	8♐19	15♑40
	29	21♏04		20♑42	6♓21	8♈25	22♉30	25♊41	14♌11	6♎21	15♏04	7♑48	13♒19
	31	18♐01		15♒27		2♉09		22♋10	13♍03		15♐10		9♓17
	1	9♑06	18♑34	1♓55	29♈02	28♈42	17♉22	16♋20	5♍18	4♍20	28♍16	20♏00	29♐13
☿	7	2℞25	26 47	12 53	5♉10	27℞13	26 56	28 17	10 31	0℞46	9♎01	29 00	1℞14
	13	1D03	5♒38	24 27	7 26	28D30	8♊01	9♌05	13 34	2D01	19 28	7♐43	27♐10
	19	4 14	15 01	6♈21	6℞01	2♉18	20 25	18 42	13℞44	8 14	29 29	16 00	19 16
	25	10 02	24 58	17 52	2 17	8 14	3♋30	27 08	10 35	17 37	9♏08	23 29	15 04
	31	17 16		27 40		15 56		4♍15	5 13		18 28		16D40

DATE	☉	♀	♂	♃	♄	⚷	♅	♆	♇	☊	STATIONS
1 1	9♑56	22♒15	23♎23	20♈42	18♒33	29♑00	0♑42	6♋41	20♊21	12♍28	
11	20 08	3♓57	28 35	21 24	19 37	29 50	1 17	6℞25	20℞10	11 56	☿ 11/1 0♑52
21	0♒19	15 25	3♏32	22 25	20 45	0♒41	1 51	6 09	20 01	11 24	☿ 13/4 7♉27
31	10 29	26 32	8 13	23 42	21 56	1 31	2 23	5 54	19 53	10 52	☿ 7/5 27♈13
10 2	20 37	7♈13	12 32	25 13	23 08	2 21	2 51	5 42	19 47	10 21	☿ 16/8 14♍04
20	0♓43	17 16	16 26	26 57	24 20	3 09	3 17	5 33	19 43	9 49	☿ 9/9 0♍35
2 3	10 46	26 28	19 47	28 51	25 32	3 54	3 38	5 26	19 42	9 17	☿ 6/12 1♑17
12	20 46	4♉26	22 27	0♉53	26 41	4 35	3 54	5 23	19D42	8 45	☿ 26/12 14♐59
22	0♈43	10 37	24 16	3 03	27 48	5 11	4 06	5D23	19 45	8 14	♀ 6/4 14♉43
1 4	10 36	14 12	25 03	5 18	28 50	5 42	4 13	5 26	19 50	7 42	♀ 19/5 28♈17
11	20 27	14℞14	24℞40	7 36	29 48	6 07	4℞14	5 33	19 57	7 10	♂ 3/4 25♏05
21	0♉14	10 20	23 00	9 58	0♓39	6 26	4 11	5 43	20 06	6 38	♂ 17/6 8♏17
1 5	9 57	4 14	20 12	12 21	1 23	6 38	4 02	5 56	20 16	6 07	♃ 26/9 6♊31
11	19 38	29♈28	16 42	14 43	1 59	6 43	3 49	6 11	20 28	5 35	♄ 14/6 2♓54
21	29 16	28D23	13 11	17 05	2 27	6℞40	3 32	6 29	20 41	5 03	♄ 31/10 26♒12
31	8♊52	0♉58	10 20	19 25	2 45	6 31	3 12	6 48	20 54	4 31	♅ 9/4 4♑14
10 6	18 26	6 18	8 39	21 42	2 53	6 15	2 50	7 09	21 08	3 59	♅ 10/9 0♑15
20	27 59	13 32	8D20	23 54	2℞52	5 54	2 26	7 31	21 23	3 28	♆ 17/3 5♋22
30	7♋32	22 03	9 20	26 00	2 41	5 28	2 01	7 53	21 36	2 56	♆ 14/10 10♋25
10 7	17 04	1♊28	11 30	27 59	2 20	4 58	1 38	8 15	21 50	2 24	♇ 5/3 19♊42
20	26 36	11 31	14 39	29 50	1 52	4 25	1 15	8 37	22 02	1 52	♇ 23/9 22♊45
30	6♌09	22 02	18 37	1♊31	1 16	3 51	0 55	8 58	22 14	1 21	⚷ 13/5 6♒43
9 8	15 44	2♋56	23 15	3 00	0 35	3 18	0 39	9 17	22 23	0 49	⚷ 10/10 1♒20
19	25 20	14 07	28 26	4 16	29♒51	2 47	0 26	9 35	22 32	0 17	
29	4♍59	25 33	4♐05	5 16	29 06	2 19	0 18	9 51	22 38	29♌45	
8 9	14 40	7♌12	10 07	6 00	28 22	1 55	0 15	10 04	22 42	29 13	
18	24 24	19 02	16 29	6 25	27 41	1 37	0D17	10 14	22 45	28 42	
28	4♎12	1♍01	23 07	6℞30	27 07	1 25	0 23	10 21	22℞45	28 10	
8 10	14 03	13 08	29 59	6 16	26 40	1 20	0 35	10 25	22 42	27 38	
18	23 57	25 22	7♑03	5 42	26 21	1D22	0 52	10℞25	22 38	27 06	
28	3♏55	7♎42	14 17	4 50	26 13	1 31	1 13	10 22	22 32	26 35	
7 11	13 56	20 07	21 39	3 43	26D15	1 47	1 39	10 16	22 24	26 03	
17	23 59	2♏35	29 07	2 26	26 27	2 10	2 07	10 07	22 14	25 31	
27	4♐06	15 06	6♒40	1 04	26 49	2 39	2 39	9 55	22 04	24 59	
7 12	14 14	27 38	14 16	29♉44	27 21	3 13	3 13	9 41	21 52	24 28	
17	24 24	10♐12	21 54	28 33	28 01	3 51	3 48	9 25	21 40	23 56	
27	4♑36	22 46	29 34	27 34	28 50	4 34	4 24	9 08	21 29	23 24	

SID M/N 1st JAN 6 h 38 m 56 s 1906 COMMON BST NONE

DAY	JAN	FEB	MAR	APR	MAY	JUN	JUL	AUG	SEP	OCT	NOV	DEC
1	21♓43	5♉35	13♉25	27♊19	0♌27	18♍44	26♎36	20♐20	12♒43	18♓47	5♉27	8♊18
☽ 3	15♈53	29♉22	7♊11	21♋50	26♌05	16♎48	25♏45	19♑18	9♓47	14♈17	29♉33	1♋58
5	9♉37	23♊37	1♋23	17♌39	23♍30	16♏31	25♐35	17♒37	5♈51	9♉01	23♊15	25♋42
7	3♊32	18♋50	26♋36	15♍15	22♎49	16♐59	25♑05	14♓45	0♉51	3♊02	16♋55	19♌55
9	28♊06	15♌17	23♌19	14♎36	23♏21	16♑52	23♒17	10♈30	25♉00	26♊43	11♌04	15♍08
11	23♋32	12♍52	21♍35	14♏51	23♐42	15♒07	19♓49	5♉05	18♊45	20♋37	6♍23	11♎57
13	19♌50	11♎12	20♎54	14♐43	22♑38	11♓31	14♈54	28♉59	12♋43	15♌24	3♎30	10♏40
15	16♍54	9♏47	20♏19	13♑13	19♒42	6♈28	9♉01	22♊47	7♌34	11♍42	2♏33	10♐51
17	14♎39	8♐09	19♐00	10♒06	15♓11	0♉33	2♊46	17♋05	3♍45	9♎49	2♐52	11♑21
19	12♏57	6♑01	16♑35	5♓41	9♈39	24♉16	26♊40	12♌18	1♎23	9♏18	3♑07	10♒51
21	11♐34	3♒12	13♒03	0♈23	3♉34	18♊04	21♋06	8♍37	0♏04	9♐08	2♒08	8♓35
23	10♑02	29♒32	8♓38	24♈33	27♉18	12♋11	16♌17	5♎57	29♏03	8♑13	29♒28	4♈37
25	7♒43	24♓57	3♈30	18♉24	21♊05	6♌50	12♍19	4♏01	27♐38	6♒02	25♓20	29♈22
27	4♓13	19♈30	27♈46	12♊07	15♋07	2♍14	9♎18	2♐25	25♑27	2♓37	20♈12	23♉23
29	29♓26		21♉37	5♋59	9♌43	28♍45	7♏11	0♑48	22♒30	28♓16	14♉26	17♊05
31	23♈40		15♊21		5♍21		5♐51	28♑53		23♈12		10♋48
1	17♐20	27♑39	16♓39	17♈30	13♈12	0♊07	0♌11	25♌49	19♌41	12♎05	28♏58	6♐05
☿ 7	22 56	7♒16	28 01	13℞03	19 17	12 59	8 54	23℞06	28 28	22 04	6♐20	29℞58
13	0♑11	17 21	8♈19	9 01	26 57	26 09	16 10	18 26	9♍15	1♏36	12 17	0D01
19	8 18	27 56	15 52	7D34	6♉01	8♋42	21 44	14 33	20 32	10 43	15 23	4 43
25	16 58	9♓02	19 13	9 07	16 24	20 06	25 11	14D14	1♎34	19 25	13℞24	11 44
31	26 05		18℞03		28 04		25℞59	18 33		27 39		19 50

DATE	☉	♀	♂	♃	♄	⚷	♅	♆	♇	☊	STATIONS
1 1	9♑41	29♐03	3♓23	27♉11	29♒17	4♒56	4♑42	9♋00	21♊23	23♌08	
11	19 53	11♑37	11 02	26℞39	0♓15	5 42	5 17	8℞43	21℞13	22 36	☿ 26/3 19♈20
21	0♒04	24 12	18 39	26 28	1 19	6 30	5 52	8 27	21 03	22 05	☿ 19/4 7♈34
31	10 14	6♒45	26 15	26D37	2 27	7 18	6 24	8 12	20 55	21 33	☿ 30/7 26♌04
10 2	20 22	19 18	3♈47	27 06	3 38	8 06	6 54	7 59	20 49	21 01	☿ 22/8 13♌49
20	0♓28	1♓50	11 15	27 54	4 50	8 53	7 21	7 49	20 45	20 29	☿ 20/11 15♐28
2 3	10 31	14 20	18 40	28 59	6 03	9 37	7 44	7 42	20 43	19 57	☿ 10/12 29♏14
12	20 31	26 49	26 01	0♊18	7 16	10 19	8 03	7 37	20D43	19 26	♀ 10/11 14♐45
22	0♈28	9♈16	3♉17	1 51	8 27	10 56	8 17	7D37	20 46	18 54	♀ 21/12 29♏26
1 4	10 22	21 40	10 28	3 35	9 35	11 29	8 26	7 39	20 50	18 22	♃ 22/1 26♉28
11	20 12	4♉02	17 36	5 29	10 39	11 56	8 29	7 45	20 57	17 50	♃ 30/10 11♋05
21	29 59	16 21	24 38	7 30	11 38	12 18	8℞28	7 54	21 06	17 19	♄ 27/6 15♓02
1 5	9♉43	28 38	1♊36	9 37	12 32	12 33	8 22	8 06	21 16	16 47	♄ 13/11 8♓18
11	19 24	10♊51	8 30	11 49	13 18	12 41	8 11	8 21	21 28	16 15	♅ 13/4 8♑30
21	29 02	23 02	15 20	14 04	13 57	12℞43	7 56	8 38	21 41	15 43	♅ 14/9 4♑30
31	8♊38	5♋09	22 06	16 22	14 27	12 38	7 37	8 57	21 54	15 12	♆ 20/3 7♋36
10 6	18 13	17 12	28 48	18 41	14 49	12 27	7 16	9 18	22 08	14 40	♆ 17/10 12♋39
20	27 45	29 11	5♋27	20 59	15 00	12 09	6 52	9 39	22 22	14 08	♇ 6/3 20♊43
30	7♋18	11♌06	12 03	23 16	15℞02	11 46	6 28	10 01	22 36	13 36	♇ 24/9 23♊47
10 7	16 50	22 55	18 36	25 31	14 53	11 19	6 04	10 24	22 50	13 04	⚷ 19/5 12♒43
20	26 22	4♍37	25 06	27 42	14 36	10 49	5 41	10 46	23 02	12 33	⚷ 17/10 7♒28
30	5♌55	16 11	1♌34	29 49	14 09	10 17	5 20	11 07	23 14	12 01	
9 8	15 30	27 36	8 00	1♋49	13 35	9 45	5 02	11 27	23 24	11 29	
19	25 06	8♎48	14 24	3 42	12 55	9 13	4 47	11 45	23 32	10 57	
29	4♍45	19 45	20 47	5 26	12 11	8 43	4 37	12 01	23 39	10 26	
8 9	14 26	0♏23	27 08	6 59	11 25	8 17	4 31	12 15	23 44	9 54	
18	24 10	10 33	3♍29	8 20	10 40	7 56	4D31	12 26	23 46	9 22	
28	3♎58	20 08	9 48	9 27	9 58	7 40	4 35	12 34	23℞46	8 50	
8 10	13 48	28 51	16 06	10 17	9 21	7 31	4 45	12 38	23 45	8 18	
18	23 43	6♐17	22 23	10 50	8 52	7D28	4 59	12℞39	23 40	7 47	
28	3♏40	11 50	28 39	11 04	8 31	7 32	5 18	12 37	23 34	7 15	
7 11	13 41	14 36	4♎54	10℞58	8 20	7 43	5 42	12 32	23 27	6 43	
17	23 45	13℞39	11 08	10 32	8D19	8 00	6 09	12 23	23 17	6 11	
27	3♐51	9 02	17 21	9 47	8 29	8 23	6 39	12 12	23 07	5 40	
7 12	13 59	3 11	23 33	8 47	8 50	8 52	7 12	11 58	22 55	5 08	
17	24 10	29♏43	29 42	7 34	9 20	9 27	7 46	11 43	22 44	4 36	
27	4♑21	0D13	5♏50	6 14	9 59	10 05	8 22	11 27	22 32	4 04	

SID M/N 1st JAN 6 h 37 m 59 s 1907 COMMON BST NONE

DAY	JAN	FEB	MAR	APR	MAY	JUN	JUL	AUG	SEP	OCT	NOV	DEC
1	22♋45	8♍53	18♍06	8♏33	17♐11	10♒34	18♓01	6♉25	21♊26	23♋04	6♍55	10♎08
☽ 3	16♌58	4♎51	14♎54	7♐10	16♑17	8♓28	14♈39	1♊03	15♋03	16♌53	2♎19	7♏09
5	11♍53	1♏46	12♏28	5♑40	14♒29	5♈00	9♉53	24♊52	8♌47	11♍30	29♎12	5♐47
7	7♎53	29♏40	10♐31	3♒44	11♓40	0♉25	4♊09	18♋26	3♍07	7♎17	27♏22	5♑23
9	5♏18	28♐26	8♑49	1♓15	7♈57	25♉00	27♊54	12♌13	28♍20	4♏11	26♐09	4♒57
11	4♐14	27♑40	7♒11	28♓11	3♉25	19♊00	21♋29	6♍30	24♎26	1♐52	24♑53	3♓41
13	4♑10	26♒38	5♓16	24♈21	28♉08	12♋39	15♌13	1♎31	21♏22	29♐56	23♒07	1♈14
15	4♒07	24♓34	2♈37	19♉34	22♊11	6♌14	9♍25	27♎28	19♐00	28♑07	20♓43	27♈37
17	2♓59	21♈01	28♈51	13♊53	15♋48	0♍13	4♎29	24♏30	17♑19	26♒17	17♈38	23♉03
19	0♈10	16♉02	23♉50	7♋35	9♌28	25♍08	0♏48	22♐43	16♒07	24♓16	13♉45	17♊40
21	25♈42	10♊03	17♊52	1♌17	3♍49	21♎32	28♏41	21♑58	14♓58	21♈38	8♊58	11♋41
23	20♉02	3♋42	11♋32	25♌40	29♍30	19♏46	28♐04	21♒40	13♈06	18♉00	3♋18	5♌19
25	13♊46	27♋38	5♌30	21♍24	27♎00	19♐34	28♑15	20♓51	9♉56	13♊08	27♋01	28♌57
27	7♋28	22♌21	0♍26	18♎50	26♏13	19♑57	28♒10	18♈41	5♊16	7♋15	20♌38	23♍04
29	1♌31		26♍45	17♏43	26♐18	19♒43	26♓46	14♉48	29♊26	0♌52	14♍47	18♎16
31	26♌14		24♎23		26♑05		23♈37	9♊28		24♌42		15♏03
1	21♐15	9♒47	27♓19	18♓41	17♈06	18♊36	3♌09	27♋05	1♍25	23♎50	29♏10	17♏29
☿ 7	29 58	20 19	1♈39	20 18	27 05	0♋36	6 28	26D43	13 04	2♏36	28℞49	24 23
13	9♑00	1♓11	0℞45	24 31	8♉13	11 11	7℞10	0♌18	24 12	10 48	23 01	2♐38
19	18 21	12 05	25♓58	0♈39	20 26	20 13	5 05	7 40	4♎40	18 15	15 41	11 27
25	28 02	22 03	20 58	8 15	3♊26	27 37	1 07	17 53	14 32	24 32	13D41	20 31
31	8♒04		18 44		16 29		27♋28	29 27		28 46		29 46

DATE	☉	♀	♂	♃	♄	⚷	♅	♆	♇	☊	STATIONS
1 1	9♑26	1♐51	8♏53	5♋33	10♓22	10♒25	8♑40	11♋18	22♊26	3♌48	
11	19 38	7 15	14 56	4℞14	11 13	11 08	9 16	11℞01	22℞15	3 17	☿ 9/3 1♈56
21	29 49	14 43	20 56	3 04	12 11	11 53	9 51	10 45	22 06	2 45	☿ 1/4 18♓41
31	9♒59	23 33	26 51	2 06	13 14	12 39	10 24	10 30	21 58	2 13	☿ 11/7 7♌15
10 2	20 07	3♑20	2♐42	1 25	14 22	13 25	10 55	10 16	21 51	1 41	☿ 5/8 26♋24
20	0♓13	13 45	8 25	1 04	15 33	14 10	11 23	10 05	21 47	1 10	☿ 4/11 29♏38
2 3	10 17	24 37	14 01	1D02	16 46	14 54	11 48	9 57	21 45	0 38	☿ 24/11 13♏33
12	20 17	5♒47	19 27	1 20	18 00	15 35	12 09	9 52	21D45	0 06	♂ 5/6 18♑53
22	0♈14	17 12	24 40	1 56	19 14	16 13	12 25	9 51	21 47	29♋34	♂ 9/8 6♑58
1 4	10 08	28 47	29 38	2 50	20 26	16 47	12 36	9D52	21 51	29 02	♃ 26/2 1♋00
11	19 58	10♓29	4♑17	3 59	21 35	17 16	12 42	9 57	21 58	28 31	♃ 1/12 13♌37
21	29 45	22 17	8 31	5 21	22 41	17 40	12℞43	10 06	22 06	27 59	♄ 10/7 27♓28
1 5	9♉29	4♈09	12 14	6 56	23 43	17 58	12 39	10 17	22 16	27 27	♄ 25/11 20♓41
11	19 10	16 05	15 17	8 40	24 39	18 09	12 30	10 31	22 28	26 55	♅ 18/4 12♑43
21	28 48	28 03	17 31	10 33	25 28	18 15	12 16	10 48	22 41	26 24	♅ 19/9 8♑44
31	8♊24	10♉04	18 43	12 32	26 10	18℞13	11 59	11 06	22 54	25 52	♆ 22/3 9♋51
10 6	17 59	22 06	18℞45	14 37	26 43	18 06	11 39	11 26	23 08	25 20	♆ 19/10 14♋54
20	27 32	4♊11	17 32	16 46	27 08	17 52	11 17	11 48	23 22	24 48	♇ 7/3 21♊44
30	7♋04	16 18	15 15	18 58	27 23	17 33	10 53	12 10	23 36	24 16	♇ 26/9 24♊49
10 7	16 36	28 27	12 23	21 12	27℞28	17 09	10 29	12 32	23 50	23 45	⚷ 24/5 18♒15
20	26 08	10♋39	9 37	23 26	27 23	16 41	10 05	12 54	24 03	23 13	⚷ 24 10 13♒06
30	5♌41	22 54	7 40	25 40	27 08	16 11	9 43	13 16	24 14	22 41	
9 8	15 16	5♌11	6 58	27 52	26 43	15 39	9 23	13 36	24 25	22 09	
19	24 52	17 31	7D39	0♌01	26 11	15 08	9 07	13 55	24 34	21 38	
29	4♍31	29 53	9 37	2 06	25 32	14 38	8 55	14 11	24 40	21 06	
8 9	14 12	12♍18	12 43	4 06	24 49	14 10	8 47	14 26	24 45	20 34	
18	23 56	24 44	16 43	5 58	24 03	13 46	8 44	14 37	24 48	20 02	
28	3♎43	7♎12	21 28	7 43	23 17	13 28	8D46	14 46	24℞49	19 31	
8 10	13 34	19 40	26 48	9 17	22 33	13 14	8 54	14 51	24 47	18 59	
18	23 28	2♏10	2♒35	10 39	21 54	13 07	9 06	14 53	24 43	18 27	
28	3♏26	14 39	8 43	11 48	21 22	13D07	9 23	14℞52	24 37	17 55	
7 11	13 26	27 09	15 07	12 41	20 59	13 13	9 44	14 48	24 30	17 23	
17	23 30	9♐39	21 44	13 18	20 45	13 26	10 10	14 40	24 21	16 52	
27	3♐36	22 09	28 29	13 35	20D42	13 45	10 39	14 29	24 10	16 20	
7 12	13 45	4♑38	5♓22	13℞33	20 49	14 09	11 10	14 16	23 59	15 48	
17	23 55	17 06	12 19	13 12	21 07	14 39	11 44	14 01	23 47	15 16	
27	4♑06	29 34	19 19	12 31	21 35	15 13	12 19	13 45	23 35	14 45	

SID M/N 1st JAN 6 h 37 m 1 s 1908 LEAP BST NONE

DAY	JAN	FEB	MAR	APR	MAY	JUN	JUL	AUG	SEP	OCT	NOV	DEC
1	29♏07	21♑27	14♒53	8♈03	14♉38	1♋44	4♌21	18♍35	4♏10	9♐27	0♒27	9♓39
☽ 3	28♐29	21♒53	14♓58	6♉19	10♊57	26♋02	28♌03	12♎37	29♏32	6♑05	28♒42	7♈59
5	28♑45	21♓49	14♈18	3♊00	5♋57	19♌47	21♍49	7♏24	26♐10	4♒00	27♓36	6♉01
7	28♒44	20♈11	11♉58	28♊07	0♌00	13♍33	16♎10	3♐28	24♑27	3♓12	26♈35	3♊22
9	27♓27	16♉40	7♊46	22♋08	23♌41	7♎57	11♏40	1♑14	24♒16	3♈06	24♉50	29♊42
11	24♈31	11♊35	2♋10	15♌46	17♍41	3♏33	8♐46	0♒42	24♓44	2♉35	21♊45	24♋56
13	20♉06	5♋32	25♋51	9♍42	12♎36	0♐39	7♑32	1♓10	24♈29	0♊37	17♋10	19♌14
15	14♊38	29♋08	19♌28	4♎25	8♏45	29♐08	7♒27	1♈20	22♉30	26♊50	11♌29	13♍02
17	8♋33	22♌48	13♍32	0♏09	6♐07	28♑25	7♓28	0♉03	18♊36	21♋34	5♍15	6♎54
19	2♌11	16♍51	8♎18	26♏47	4♑18	27♒40	6♈31	26♉53	13♋13	15♌26	29♍08	1♏28
21	25♌51	11♎28	3♏51	24♐08	2♒50	26♓14	4♉03	22♊07	7♌03	9♍08	23♎41	27♏13
23	19♍49	6♏50	0♐08	22♑00	1♓17	23♈46	0♊07	16♋21	0♍42	3♎11	19♏14	24♐23
25	14♎27	3♐13	27♐14	20♒16	29♓23	20♉12	25♊02	10♌06	24♍35	27♎55	15♐50	22♑46
27	10♏12	0♑54	25♑16	18♓46	26♈54	15♊40	19♋14	3♍46	18♎55	23♏24	13♑18	21♒46
29	7♐28	29♑57	24♒10	17♈05	23♉35	10♋19	13♌03	27♍36	13♏49	19♐38	11♒20	20♓38
31	6♑26		23♓30		19♊16		6♍43	21♎50		16♑39		18♈50
1	1♑19	22♒57	8♓21	13♓34	2♉28	2♋34	14♋50	20♋04	18♍34	2♏33	0♏54	25♏47
☿ 7	10 47	2♓55	2R49	21 17	15 08	9 44	11R13	0♌02	28 46	8 37	27D52	5♐04
13	20 30	11 02	0 38	0♈05	28 09	14 47	8 34	11 44	8♎17	12 43	1♏06	14 24
19	0♒29	14 58	2D06	9 54	10♊38	17 24	8D35	23 55	17 07	13R29	8 05	23 48
25	10 46	13R08	6 18	20 41	21 47	17R20	11 58	5♍43	25 16	9 22	16 39	3♑18
31	21 13		12 25		1♋11		18 39	16 48		2 00		12 56

DATE	☉	♀	♂	♃	♄	⚷	♅	♆	♇	☊	STATIONS
1 1	9♑12	5♒47	22♓50	12♌05	21♓53	15♒32	12♑37	13♋36	23♊30	14♋29	
11	19 23	18 11	29 51	11R01	22 35	16 12	13 13	13R19	23R19	13 57	☿ 20/2 15♓04
21	29 34	0♓32	6♈53	9 47	23 25	16 54	13 48	13 03	23 09	13 25	☿ 13/3 0♓37
31	9♒44	12 50	13 53	8 27	24 22	17 37	14 22	12 47	23 00	12 53	☿ 22/6 17♋42
10 2	19 52	25 01	20 52	7 08	25 25	18 21	14 54	12 33	22 54	12 22	☿ 16/7 8♋11
20	29 59	7♈06	27 49	5 56	26 32	19 06	15 23	12 22	22 49	11 50	☿ 17/10 13♏42
1 3	10♓02	19 02	4♉44	4 55	27 44	19 48	15 49	12 13	22 47	11 18	☿ 7/11 27♎52
11	20 02	0♉47	11 36	4 10	28 57	20 29	16 12	12 07	22D46	10 46	♀ 15/6 21♋51
21	0♈00	12 19	18 25	3 42	0♈11	21 08	16 30	12 05	22 48	10 15	♀ 28/7 5♋21
31	9 53	23 34	25 11	3D34	1 26	21 42	16 43	12D06	22 53	9 43	♃ 30/3 3♌34
10 4	19 44	4♊27	1♊54	3 44	2 39	22 13	16 51	12 10	22 59	9 11	♃ 31/12 14♍31
20	29 31	14 54	8 34	4 13	3 51	22 38	16 55	12 17	23 07	8 39	♄ 22/7 10♈11
30	9♉15	24 43	15 12	4 59	4 59	22 58	16R53	12 28	23 17	8 07	♄ 7/12 3♈23
10 5	18 56	3♋43	21 47	6 00	6 03	23 13	16 46	12 41	23 28	7 36	♅ 21/4 16♑55
20	28 34	11 32	28 19	7 15	7 01	23 21	16 35	12 57	23 41	7 04	♅ 22/9 12♑56
30	8♊10	17 38	4♋50	8 42	7 53	23R23	16 19	13 15	23 54	6 32	♆ 24/3 12♋05
9 6	17 45	21 15	11 18	10 19	8 38	23 18	16 01	13 35	24 08	6 00	♆ 20/10 17♋07
19	27 18	21R28	17 44	12 05	9 15	23 08	15 39	13 56	24 23	5 29	♇ 7/3 22♊46
29	6♋50	17 51	24 09	13 59	9 44	22 52	15 16	14 18	24 37	4 57	♇ 26/9 25♊51
9 7	16 22	11 51	0♌33	15 58	10 02	22 31	14 52	14 40	24 50	4 25	⚷ 28/5 23♒23
19	25 54	6 52	6 56	18 02	10 11	22 06	14 28	15 03	25 03	3 53	⚷ 29 10 18♒20
29	5♌28	5D22	13 18	20 10	10R09	21 38	14 05	15 24	25 15	3 21	
8 8	15 02	7 35	19 40	22 20	9 58	21 08	13 44	15 45	25 26	2 50	
18	24 38	12 40	26 01	24 31	9 36	20 37	13 26	16 04	25 35	2 18	
28	4♍17	19 46	2♍23	26 42	9 06	20 07	13 12	16 21	25 42	1 46	
7 9	13 58	28 15	8 45	28 51	8 29	19 38	13 02	16 36	25 47	1 14	
17	23 42	7♌43	15 08	0♍58	7 46	19 13	12 57	16 49	25 50	0 43	
27	3♎29	17 54	21 31	3 02	7 00	18 51	12D57	16 58	25R51	0 11	
7 10	13 20	28 38	27 56	5 00	6 13	18 35	13 02	17 04	25 50	29♊39	
17	23 14	9♍47	4♎21	6 52	5 28	18 25	13 12	17 07	25 46	29 07	
27	3♏11	21 15	10 48	8 36	4 47	18 20	13 27	17R07	25 41	28 36	
6 11	13 12	3♎00	17 16	10 10	4 12	18D23	13 46	17 03	25 33	28 04	
16	23 15	14 56	23 46	11 32	3 46	18 31	14 10	16 56	25 24	27 32	
26	3♐21	27 02	0♏17	12 41	3 29	18 46	14 37	16 46	25 14	27 00	
6 12	13 30	9♏15	6 50	13 34	3 23	19 07	15 07	16 33	25 03	26 28	
16	23 40	21 34	13 24	14 11	3D27	19 32	15 40	16 19	24 51	25 57	
26	3♑51	3♐56	19 59	14 29	3 43	20 03	16 15	16 03	24 39	25 25	

SID M/N 1st JAN 6 h 40 m 1 s 1909 COMMON BST NONE

	DAY	JAN	FEB	MAR	APR	MAY	JUN	JUL	AUG	SEP	OCT	NOV	DEC
	1	2♉37	22♊22	2♋01	17♌41	20♍00	4♏16	7♐26	26♑13	19♓03	27♈57	20♊09	25♋26
☽	3	29♉30	17♋19	26♋38	11♍26	13♎51	29♏12	3♑54	25♒16	19♈15	27♉34	17♋27	21♌16
	5	25♊32	11♌42	20♌40	5♎12	8♏07	25♐05	1♒38	24♓52	18♉23	25♊27	13♌04	15♍49
	7	20♋44	5♍40	14♍28	29♎13	3♐01	21♑58	0♓11	24♈00	15♊56	21♋36	7♍30	9♎38
	9	15♌13	29♍25	8♎14	23♏39	28♐40	19♒39	28♓57	22♉05	12♋03	16♌30	1♎20	3♏20
	11	9♍09	23♎14	2♏10	18♐45	25♑14	17♓55	27♈22	19♊00	7♌08	10♍39	25♎01	27♏27
	13	2♎53	17♏34	26♏35	14♑52	22♒48	16♈26	25♉10	14♋58	1♍34	4♎26	18♏55	22♐18
	15	26♎55	13♐00	21♐55	12♒22	21♓23	14♉52	22♊12	10♌10	25♍32	28♎08	13♐18	18♑04
	17	21♏54	10♑08	18♑46	11♓23	20♈36	12♊45	18♋25	4♍42	19♎15	21♏58	8♑22	14♒45
	19	18♐22	9♒11	17♒28	11♈24	19♉44	9♋43	13♌48	28♍43	12♏56	16♐13	4♒22	12♓14
	21	16♑34	9♓34	17♓41	11♉17	17♊57	5♌32	8♍20	22♎24	7♐00	11♑19	1♓32	10♈23
	23	16♒09	9♈57	18♈14	9♊55	14♋44	0♍16	2♎16	16♏12	2♑01	7♒46	29♓59	9♉00
	25	16♓06	9♉04	17♉43	6♋47	10♌05	24♍15	26♎00	10♐43	28♑38	5♓56	29♈25	7♊43
	27	15♈18	6♊21	15♊20	2♌02	4♍23	18♎03	20♏10	6♑38	27♒12	5♈39	29♉04	5♋58
	29	13♉08		11♋08	26♌15	28♍12	12♏16	15♐24	4♒24	27♓22	6♉02	27♊59	3♌10
	31	9♊34		5♌41		22♎06		12♑12	3♓55		5♊49		29♌03
	1	14♑34	28♒21	14♒28	21♓22	20♉21	27♊36	19♊46	4♌09	0♎01	27♎33	20♎10	6♐55
☿	7	24 25	26R53	18 33	1♈41	2♊02	27R01	23 19	16 35	8 18	24R49	28 51	16 20
	13	4♒22	20 35	24 36	12 53	11 53	24 20	29 41	28 20	15 39	18 15	8♏18	25 46
	19	14 05	14 54	2♓00	24 57	19 33	21 03	8♋38	9♍15	21 47	12 44	17 54	5♑15
	25	22 38	13D19	10 25	7♉40	24 48	19 08	19 43	19 18	26 06	13D08	27 27	14 47
	31	27 58		19 44		27 26		2♌04	28 33		18 53		24 11

DATE	☉	♀	♂	♃	♄	⚷	♅	♆	♇	☊	STATIONS
1 1	9♑58	11♐23	23♏57	14♍31	3♈57	20♒24	16♑36	15♋53	24♊32	25♊06	
11	20 09	23 49	0♐35	14R19	4 29	21 00	17 11	15R36	24R21	24 34	☿ 3/2 28♒36
21	0♒20	6♑17	7 14	13 48	5 10	21 40	17 47	15 19	24 11	24 02	☿ 24/2 13♒17
31	10 30	18 45	13 54	12 59	5 59	22 21	18 21	15 03	24 03	23 31	☿ 3/6 27♊42
10 2	20 38	1♒14	20 35	11 56	6 56	23 04	18 54	14 49	23 56	22 59	☿ 27/6 19♊01
20	0♓44	13 42	27 17	10 43	7 58	23 46	19 24	14 37	23 51	22 27	☿ 30/9 27♎34
2 3	10 48	26 10	3♑59	9 25	9 06	24 28	19 51	14 28	23 49	21 55	☿ 22/10 12♎06
12	20 48	8♓37	10 42	8 08	10 17	25 09	20 15	14 22	23D49	21 23	♂ 23/8 6♈50
22	0♈45	21 03	17 25	6 57	11 31	25 47	20 34	14 19	23 50	20 52	♂ 24/10 25♓28
1 4	10 38	3♈28	24 07	5 56	12 46	26 22	20 49	14D19	23 55	20 20	♃ 2/5 4♍32
11	20 29	15 52	0♒48	5 11	14 01	26 53	20 59	14 23	24 01	19 48	♄ 5/8 23♈14
21	0♉15	28 14	7 26	4 42	15 16	27 19	21 04	14 30	24 09	19 16	♄ 20/12 16♈23
1 5	9 59	10♉35	14 01	4 32	16 29	27 41	21R04	14 40	24 19	18 45	♅ 26/4 21♑05
11	19 40	22 55	20 32	4D40	17 38	27 57	20 59	14 53	24 30	18 13	♅ 27/9 17♑07
21	29 18	5♊13	26 55	5 06	18 44	28 07	20 49	15 09	24 43	17 41	♆ 26/3 14♋19
31	8♊54	17 31	3♓09	5 48	19 45	28 11	20 35	15 26	24 56	17 09	♆ 23/10 19♋21
10 6	18 28	29 47	9 11	6 46	20 40	28R09	20 18	15 46	25 10	16 37	♇ 9/3 23♊48
20	28 01	12♋03	14 56	7 58	21 28	28 01	19 57	16 07	25 25	16 06	♇ 27/9 26♊54
30	7♋33	24 17	20 19	9 21	22 07	27 48	19 35	16 29	25 39	15 34	⚷ 2/6 28♒11
10 7	17 05	6♌31	25 14	10 55	22 39	27 29	19 11	16 51	25 53	15 02	⚷ 3 11 23♒14
20	26 38	18 43	29 30	12 38	23 00	27 07	18 47	17 13	26 06	14 30	
30	6♌11	0♍54	2♈59	14 29	23 12	26 40	18 23	17 35	26 18	13 59	
9 8	15 46	13 03	5 27	16 26	23R13	26 11	18 02	17 56	26 28	13 27	
19	25 22	25 09	6 43	18 28	23 05	25 41	17 43	18 15	26 37	12 55	
29	5♍01	7♎13	6R35	20 34	22 46	25 11	17 27	18 33	26 45	12 23	
8 9	14 42	19 14	5 07	22 42	22 18	24 42	17 16	18 48	26 50	11 52	
18	24 26	1♏11	2 37	24 52	21 42	24 16	17 09	19 01	26 53	11 20	
28	4♎14	13 04	29♓43	27 01	20 59	23 54	17D07	19 11	26R54	10 48	
8 10	14 05	24 52	27 14	29 10	20 13	23 35	17 10	19 17	26 53	10 16	
18	23 59	6♐33	25 45	1♎16	19 26	23 23	17 18	19 21	26 49	9 44	
28	3♏57	18 05	25D34	3 19	18 39	23 16	17 31	19R21	26 44	9 13	
7 11	13 57	29 26	26 40	5 16	17 57	23D15	17 49	19 18	26 36	8 41	
17	24 01	10♑32	28 54	7 07	17 20	23 20	18 12	19 11	26 27	8 09	
27	4♐08	21 15	2♈03	8 49	16 51	23 32	18 38	19 01	26 17	7 37	
7 12	14 16	1♒27	5 56	10 21	16 32	23 49	19 07	18 49	26 06	7 06	
17	24 26	10 54	10 24	11 42	16 23	24 12	19 39	18 35	25 54	6 34	
27	4♑37	19 13	15 17	12 49	16D26	24 40	20 13	18 19	25 42	6 02	

SID M/N 1st JAN 6 h 39 m 3 s 1910 COMMON BST NONE

	DAY	JAN	FEB	MAR	APR	MAY	JUN	JUL	AUG	SEP	OCT	NOV	DEC
	1	11♍30	25♎18	3♏19	17♐21	21♑05	10♓28	18♈51	12♊12	4♌03	9♍55	25♎56	28♏24
☽	3	5♎40	18♏58	26♏56	11♑58	17♒04	8♈33	17♉31	10♋27	0♍34	4♎54	19♏38	22♐04
	5	29♎21	13♐11	21♐05	8♒02	14♓41	7♉49	16♊36	8♌12	26♍10	29♎08	13♐12	16♑05
	7	23♏15	8♑37	16♑27	5♓58	13♈57	7♊40	15♋28	4♍56	20♎45	22♏50	6♑58	10♒44
	9	17♐56	5♒38	13♒35	5♈36	14♉12	7♋06	13♌21	0♎24	14♏36	16♐24	1♒24	6♓20
	11	13♑49	4♓05	12♓30	5♉59	14♊17	5♌14	9♍47	24♎45	8♐11	10♑22	27♒00	3♈14
	13	10♒55	3♈14	12♈24	5♊51	13♋07	1♍40	4♎45	18♏27	2♑13	5♒25	24♓16	1♉41
	15	8♓54	2♉12	12♉08	4♋18	10♌14	26♍37	28♎43	12♐12	27♑21	2♓05	23♈17	1♊29
	17	7♈14	0♊24	10♊48	1♌07	5♍45	20♎35	22♏22	6♑42	24♒06	0♈33	23♉31	1♋46
	19	5♉30	27♊44	8♋07	26♌36	0♎07	14♏12	16♐20	2♒28	22♓25	0♉20	23♊51	1♌19
	21	3♊30	24♋18	4♌15	21♍06	23♎52	8♐01	11♑09	29♒37	21♈43	0♊26	23♋06	29♌12
	23	1♋07	20♌08	29♌30	15♎02	17♏29	2♑28	7♒04	27♓48	21♉04	29♊45	20♌37	25♍13
	25	28♋07	15♍14	24♍04	8♏42	11♐20	27♑43	4♓01	26♈24	19♊43	27♋40	16♍26	19♎45
	27	24♌14	9♎33	18♎05	2♐22	5♑40	23♒53	1♈40	24♉52	17♋24	24♌09	10♎59	13♏29
	29	19♍18		11♏45	26♐21	0♒46	20♓56	29♈44	22♊56	14♌06	19♍28	4♏50	7♐02
	31	13♎26		5♐23		26♒55		28♉02	20♋29		13♎56		0♑53
	1	25♑43	29♑11	14♒26	5♈17	0♊23	0♊22	19♊13	20♌47	4♎47	27♍52	0♏25	18♐07
☿	7	4♒18	26℞32	22 41	17 27	5 33	29℞06	29 44	1♍23	9 14	26D27	10 19	27 20
	13	10 40	28D18	1♓44	29 59	7 41	0D24	11♋51	11 02	11 06	0♎53	19 59	6♑22
	19	12℞10	2♒59	11 30	12♉00	6℞53	4 21	24 40	19 43	9℞20	9 03	29 29	14 56
	25	7 16	9 27	22 02	22 24	4 00	10 41	7♌12	27 24	3 50	18 44	8♐51	22 11
	31	0 07		3♈20		0 48		18 56	3♎51		28 45		26 13

DATE		☉	♀	♂	♃	♄	⚷	♅	♆	♇	☊	STATIONS
1	1	9♑43	22♒48	17♈52	13♎17	16♈31	24♒56	20♑30	18♋11	25♊36	5♊46	
11		19 55	28 19	23 14	14 00	16 50	25 30	21 05	17℞54	25℞25	5 14	☿ 17/1 12♒24
21		0♒06	0♓52	28 49	14 26	17 19	26 07	21 41	17 37	25 15	4 43	7/2 26♑32
31		10 16	29℞30	4♉35	14℞33	17 58	26 46	22 16	17 21	25 06	4 11	14/5 7♊44
10	2	20 24	24 29	10 28	14 21	18 45	27 26	22 49	17 06	24 59	3 39	7/6 29♉06
20		0♓30	18 35	16 26	13 50	19 40	28 08	23 20	16 54	24 54	3 07	13/9 11♎07
2	3	10 33	15 19	22 29	13 03	20 42	28 49	23 49	16 44	24 52	2 36	5/10 26♍13
12		20 33	16D03	28 36	12 01	21 48	29 28	24 14	16 37	24D51	2 04	♀ 23/1 0♓56
22		0♈30	20 08	4♊44	10 50	22 59	0♓06	24 35	16 33	24 53	1 32	5/3 15♒08
1	4	10 24	26 37	10 54	9 33	24 13	0 42	24 52	16D33	24 56	1 00	♃ 30/1 14♎33
11		20 14	4♓41	17 05	8 17	25 29	1 14	25 04	16 36	25 02	0 28	2/6 4♎37
21		0♉01	13 50	23 16	7 06	26 45	1 41	25 12	16 42	25 10	29♉57	♄ 19/8 6♉35
1	5	9 45	23 43	29 28	6 06	28 01	2 05	25℞14	16 51	25 20	29 25	♅ 30/4 25♑14
11		19 26	4♈07	5♋40	5 20	29 15	2 23	25 11	17 03	25 31	28 53	2/10 21♑16
21		29 04	14 54	11 53	4 50	0♉27	2 35	25 03	17 18	25 44	28 21	♆ 29/3 16♋32
31		8♊40	25 57	18 06	4 37	1 35	2 42	24 51	17 36	25 57	27 50	25/10 21♋35
10	6	18 14	7♉13	24 19	4D43	2 39	2℞43	24 35	17 55	26 11	27 18	♇ 10/3 24♊51
20		27 47	18 39	0♌32	5 06	3 37	2 38	24 16	18 15	26 26	26 46	28/9 27♊57
30		7♋20	0♊14	6 47	5 46	4 28	2 27	23 54	18 37	26 40	26 14	⚷ 7/6 2♓43
10	7	16 52	11 56	13 01	6 42	5 12	2 11	23 31	18 59	26 54	25 42	9/11 27♒51
20		26 24	23 44	19 17	7 51	5 47	1 51	23 07	19 21	27 07	25 11	
30		5♌57	5♋38	25 34	9 13	6 13	1 27	22 43	19 43	27 19	24 39	
9	8	15 32	17 38	1♍53	10 45	6 30	0 59	22 20	20 04	27 30	24 07	
19		25 08	29 43	8 13	12 27	6 35	0 31	22 00	20 24	27 39	23 35	
29		4♍47	11♌53	14 35	14 17	6℞31	0 01	21 43	20 42	27 47	23 04	
8	9	14 28	24 08	20 59	16 14	6 16	29♒32	21 30	20 58	27 53	22 32	
18		24 12	6♍28	27 25	18 15	5 51	29 05	21 21	21 12	27 56	22 00	
28		4♎00	18 51	3♎54	20 21	5 17	28 41	21 17	21 22	27 57	21 28	
8	10	13 50	1♎18	10 26	22 30	4 37	28 21	21D17	21 30	27℞56	20 57	
18		23 44	13 47	17 00	24 40	3 51	28 05	21 23	21 34	27 53	20 25	
28		3♏42	26 19	23 37	26 51	3 03	27 55	21 34	21℞35	27 48	19 53	
7	11	13 43	8♏51	0♏18	29 00	2 16	27 51	21 50	21 32	27 41	19 21	
17		23 46	21 25	7 02	1♏07	1 31	27D54	22 10	21 26	27 32	18 49	
27		3♐53	3♐59	13 49	3 11	0 51	28 02	22 35	21 18	27 21	18 18	
7	12	14 01	16 34	20 40	5 09	0 19	28 16	23 02	21 06	27 10	17 46	
17		24 11	29 09	27 35	7 01	29♈56	28 36	23 33	20 52	26 58	17 14	
27		4♑22	11♑43	4♐32	8 44	29 44	29 00	24 06	20 37	26 47	16 42	

SID M/N 1st JAN 6 h 38 m 6 s — 1911 COMMON — BST NONE

DAY	JAN	FEB	MAR	APR	MAY	JUN	JUL	AUG	SEP	OCT	NOV	DEC
1	13♑01	0♓03	9♓01	29♈51	8♊19	1♌47	8♍55	26♎31	10♐56	12♑32	26♒47	0♈13
☽ 3	7♒48	26♓39	6♈27	28♉54	7♋51	29♌52	5♎22	20♏53	4♑39	6♒37	22♓21	27♈14
5	3♓19	23♈54	4♉29	27♊42	6♌19	26♍13	0♏17	14♐38	28♑41	1♓36	19♈28	26♉05
7	29♓41	21♉44	2♊43	25♋50	3♍25	21♎12	24♏15	8♑21	23♒30	27♓48	18♉05	26♊14
9	27♈04	20♊09	0♋56	23♌06	29♍15	15♏20	17♐53	2♒32	19♓16	25♈12	17♊34	26♋29
11	25♉35	18♋54	28♋59	19♍29	24♎06	9♐04	11♑39	27♒22	15♈55	23♉29	16♋59	25♌38
13	25♊01	17♌25	26♌34	14♎58	18♏18	2♑44	5♒48	22♓56	13♉18	22♊08	15♌32	23♍04
15	24♋37	14♍57	23♍19	9♏36	12♐05	26♑37	0♓29	19♈14	11♊15	20♋38	12♍54	18♎58
17	23♌21	11♎02	18♎57	3♐35	5♑45	20♒58	25♓54	16♉25	9♋37	18♌41	9♎08	13♏46
19	20♍25	5♏44	13♏31	27♐15	29♑40	16♓08	22♈19	14♊33	8♌08	16♍02	4♏27	7♐56
21	15♎46	29♏34	7♐22	21♑07	24♒16	12♈33	20♉01	13♋33	6♍21	12♎32	29♏02	1♑47
23	9♏53	23♐13	1♑03	15♒45	20♓05	10♉34	19♊07	12♌52	3♎43	8♏05	23♐06	25♑30
25	3♐29	17♑23	25♑15	11♓44	17♈33	10♊09	19♋06	11♍34	29♎51	2♐45	16♑50	19♒19
27	27♐14	12♒36	20♒34	9♈22	16♉43	10♋35	18♌53	8♎52	24♏45	26♐44	10♒35	13♓34
29	21♑40		17♓20	8♉29	16♊57	10♌32	17♍18	4♏34	18♐48	20♑27	4♓51	8♈44
31	17♒02		15♈27		17♋07		13♎52	29♏00		14♒28		5♉25
1	26♑22	15♑49	23♒34	21♈52	16♉48	15♉10	4♋21	2♍04	22♍58	20♍27	12♏35	27♐19
☿ 7	23R18	22 13	3♓38	2♉47	13R19	21 37	17 21	9 57	18R25	0♎15	22 01	4♑38
13	15 44	29 47	14 22	11 18	10 04	29 55	29 44	16 31	12 42	10 43	1♐13	9 37
19	10 42	8♒10	25 47	16 36	8D51	9♊58	11♌08	21 24	10D06	21 08	10 14	9R47
25	10D56	17 12	7♈47	18R20	10 19	21 35	21 25	23 58	12 59	1♏13	19 00	3 38
31	14 55		19 54		14 17		0♍38	23R25		10 59		26♐21

DATE	☉	♀	♂	♃	♄	⚷	♅	♆	♇	☊	STATIONS
1 1	9♑28	18♑00	8♐03	9♏32	29♈42	29♒14	24♑23	20♋28	26♊41	16♉26	
11	19 40	0♒34	15 06	10 59	29D46	29 46	24 58	20R12	26R29	15 55	☿ 1/1 26♑23
21	29 51	13 07	22 12	12 14	0♉02	0♓20	25 34	19 55	26 19	15 23	22/1 10♑12
31	10♒01	25 38	29 22	13 14	0 28	0 57	26 09	19 38	26 10	14 51	25/4 18♉20
10 2	20 09	8♓08	6♑35	13 58	1 04	1 36	26 43	19 23	26 03	14 19	19/5 8♉51
20	0♓15	20 35	13 52	14 25	1 49	2 16	27 15	19 10	25 58	13 48	27/8 24♍10
2 3	10 18	2♈59	21 11	14R33	2 42	2 56	27 45	19 00	25 55	13 16	19/9 10♍06
12	20 19	15 20	28 32	14 23	3 42	3 35	28 11	18 52	25D54	12 44	16/12 10♑29
22	0♈16	27 36	5♒56	13 54	4 47	4 13	28 34	18 47	25 55	12 12	♀ 25/8 29♍28
1 4	10 10	9♉47	13 22	13 08	5 58	4 49	28 53	18D46	25 59	11 41	7/10 13♍22
11	20 00	21 52	20 49	12 08	7 11	5 21	29 07	18 48	26 04	11 09	♂ 18/10 11♊00
21	29 47	3♊51	28 16	10 58	8 27	5 50	29 17	18 53	26 12	10 37	30/12 24♉20
1 5	9♉31	15 42	5♓44	9 42	9 44	6 15	29 21	19 02	26 22	10 05	♃ 1/3 14♏33
11	19 12	27 25	13 10	8 27	11 00	6 34	29R20	19 14	26 33	9 33	3/7 4♏40
21	28 50	8♋57	20 34	7 16	12 16	6 49	29 15	19 28	26 45	9 02	♄ 2/1 29♈42
31	8♊26	20 16	27 54	6 15	13 30	6 58	29 05	19 45	26 59	8 30	3/9 20♉14
10 6	18 01	1♌20	5♈10	5 27	14 40	7 02	28 50	20 03	27 13	7 58	♅ 5/5 29♑21
20	27 34	12 04	12 20	4 55	15 47	6R59	28 33	20 23	27 27	7 26	6/10 25♑24
30	7♋06	22 22	19 22	4 41	16 48	6 51	28 12	20 45	27 41	6 55	♆ 31/3 18♋46
10 7	16 38	2♍05	26 14	4D45	17 43	6 38	27 49	21 07	27 55	6 23	28/10 23♋48
20	26 10	11 00	2♉53	5 06	18 31	6 20	27 25	21 29	28 09	5 51	♇ 11/3 25♊54
30	5♌43	18 48	9 18	5 45	19 11	5 58	27 01	21 51	28 21	5 19	30/9 29♊01
9 8	15 18	24 58	15 24	6 39	19 41	5 32	26 38	22 12	28 32	4 47	⚷ 11/6 7♓02
19	24 54	28 44	21 07	7 48	20 02	5 05	26 17	22 33	28 42	4 16	14/11 2♓14
29	4♍33	29R12	26 23	9 09	20 13	4 36	25 58	22 51	28 49	3 44	
8 9	14 14	25 50	1♊05	10 42	20R12	4 07	25 43	23 08	28 55	3 12	
18	23 58	19 58	5 04	12 25	20 02	3 39	25 32	23 22	28 59	2 40	
28	3♎45	14 56	8 12	14 16	19 40	3 14	25 26	23 33	29 01	2 09	
8 10	13 36	13D24	10 14	16 14	19 10	2 52	25D24	23 42	29R00	1 37	
18	23 30	15 41	11 00	18 18	18 32	2 35	25 28	23 47	28 57	1 05	
28	3♏27	20 57	10R19	20 26	17 48	2 22	25 37	23R48	28 52	0 33	
7 11	13 28	28 19	8 11	22 37	17 00	2 16	25 50	23 47	28 45	0 02	
17	23 32	7♎07	4 56	24 50	16 11	2D15	26 09	23 42	28 36	29♈30	
27	3♐38	16 55	1 12	27 03	15 24	2 20	26 31	23 33	28 26	28 58	
7 12	13 46	27 25	27♉49	29 15	14 42	2 31	26 57	23 22	28 15	28 26	
17	23 56	8♏26	25 26	1♐25	14 07	2 47	27 27	23 09	28 03	27 54	
27	4♑08	19 48	24 23	3 31	13 40	3 09	27 59	22 54	27 51	27 23	

SID M/N 1st JAN 6 h 37 m 9 s 1912 LEAP BST NONE

DAY	JAN	FEB	MAR	APR	MAY	JUN	JUL	AUG	SEP	OCT	NOV	DEC
1	19♉28	12♋23	6♌22	29♍02	5♏03	21♐44	24♑34	9♓06	25♈05	1♊00	23♋04	2♍24
☽ 3	18♊57	12♌50	6♍00	26♎31	0♐47	15♑56	18♒18	3♈13	20♉45	28♊11	21♌23	0♎19
5	19♋35	12♍39	4♎46	22♏43	25♐36	9♒44	12♓06	28♈05	17♊42	26♋19	19♍42	27♎33
7	19♌57	10♎47	1♏58	17♐41	19♑40	3♓32	6♈25	24♉15	16♋06	25♌12	17♎45	24♏07
9	18♍45	6♏59	27♏33	11♑46	13♒27	27♓54	1♉53	22♊10	15♌43	24♍19	15♏09	19♐56
11	15♎36	1♐43	21♐56	5♒34	7♓31	23♈28	29♉05	21♋47	15♍40	22♎57	11♐34	14♑54
13	10♏48	25♐38	15♑44	29♒39	2♈29	20♉46	28♊11	22♌15	14♎52	20♏26	6♑50	9♒03
15	5♐01	19♑19	9♒33	24♓33	28♈50	19♊48	28♋34	22♍15	12♏31	16♐29	1♒07	2♓44
17	28♐47	13♒12	3♓52	20♈35	26♉42	19♋49	28♌52	20♎41	8♐30	11♑15	24♒52	26♓30
19	22♑30	7♓33	28♓57	17♉46	25♊41	19♌37	27♍53	17♏17	3♑11	5♒12	18♓43	21♈01
21	16♒23	2♈29	24♈53	15♊51	24♋58	18♍13	25♎09	12♐26	27♑06	28♒56	13♈19	17♉00
23	10♓36	28♈08	21♉41	14♋20	23♌44	15♎20	20♏52	6♑38	20♒50	23♓05	9♉13	14♊47
25	5♈24	24♉44	19♊16	12♌48	21♍32	11♏13	15♐33	0♒26	14♓51	18♈04	6♊34	14♋02
27	1♉10	22♊33	17♋32	10♍53	18♎19	6♐12	9♑38	24♒12	9♈26	14♉07	5♋01	13♌48
29	28♉25	21♋33	16♌14	8♎22	14♏14	0♑35	3♒27	18♓11	4♉46	11♊10	3♌52	12♍58
31	27♊22		14♍54		9♐24		27♒12	12♈37		8♋59		10♎59
1	25♐35	20♑59	8♓40	28♈38	19♈02	22♉12	23♋52	4♍17	23♌37	4♎53	24♏49	24♐21
☿ 7	24D26	29 52	20 07	29R36	21 20	3♊31	4♌31	6 30	26D06	15 24	3♐21	19R10
13	27 54	9♒14	1♈51	26 55	26 00	16 04	13 56	5R42	3♍08	25 29	11 22	11 24
19	3♑57	19 06	13 02	22 40	2♉35	29 12	22 03	1 51	13 02	5♏08	18 24	8D22
25	11 21	29 32	22 15	19 32	10 47	12♋01	28 44	26♌42	23 57	14 25	23 25	10 58
31	19 33		28 04		20 27		3♍40	23 41		23 22		16 49

DATE	☉	♀	♂	♃	♄	⚷	♅	♆	♇	☊	STATIONS
1 1	9♑13	25♏36	24♉22	4♐32	13♉31	3♓22	28♑16	22♋46	27♊45	27♈07	
11	19 25	7♐21	25 16	6 30	13R20	3 50	28 50	22R29	27R34	26 35	☿ 5/1 24♐11
21	29 36	19 15	27 14	8 21	13D20	4 23	29 25	22 12	27 24	26 03	5/4 29♈45
31	9♒46	1♑17	0♊03	10 02	13 32	4 58	0♒01	21 56	27 15	25 31	29/4 18♈52
10 2	19 54	13 23	3 34	11 32	13 54	5 35	0 35	21 40	27 07	25 00	9/8 6♍36
20	0♓00	25 34	7 36	12 50	14 27	6 14	1 08	21 27	27 01	24 28	1/9 23♌37
1 3	10 04	7♒46	12 03	13 53	15 09	6 53	1 39	21 16	26 58	23 56	29/11 24♐39
11	20 04	20 01	16 49	14 41	15 59	7 31	2 07	21 07	26 57	23 24	19/12 8♐22
21	0♈01	2♓16	21 51	15 12	16 57	8 09	2 31	21 02	26D58	22 53	♃ 1/4 15♐24
31	9 55	14 32	27 04	15 24	18 01	8 45	2 52	20 59	27 01	22 21	3/8 5♐33
10 4	19 46	26 48	2♋28	15R17	19 10	9 18	3 08	21D01	27 07	21 49	♄ 16/1 13♉18
20	29 33	9♈04	7 59	14 52	20 23	9 47	3 19	21 05	27 14	21 17	16/9 4♊07
30	9♉17	21 20	13 36	14 10	21 38	10 13	3 26	21 13	27 24	20 45	♅ 8/5 3♒28
10 5	18 58	3♉36	19 19	13 13	22 55	10 35	3R28	21 24	27 35	20 14	9/10 29♑31
20	28 36	15 51	25 07	12 05	24 13	10 51	3 24	21 37	27 47	19 42	♆ 2/4 20♋59
30	8♊12	28 06	0♌59	10 50	25 30	11 02	3 16	21 53	28 00	19 10	29/10 26♋01
9 6	17 47	10♊22	6 54	9 34	26 45	11 08	3 04	22 12	28 14	18 38	♇ 11/3 26♊57
19	27 20	22 38	12 54	8 22	27 58	11R08	2 47	22 31	28 28	18 07	30/9 0♋05
29	6♋52	4♋55	18 56	7 18	29 07	11 03	2 28	22 53	28 43	17 35	⚷ 14/6 11♓09
9 7	16 24	17 12	25 01	6 28	0♊11	10 52	2 06	23 14	28 57	17 03	17/11 6♓26
19	25 56	29 31	1♍10	5 53	1 10	10 36	1 43	23 37	29 10	16 31	
29	5♌29	11♌50	7 23	5 35	2 02	10 16	1 19	23 59	29 23	16 00	
8 8	15 04	24 10	13 38	5D36	2 46	9 52	0 55	24 20	29 34	15 28	
18	24 40	6♍31	19 57	5 55	3 21	9 26	0 33	24 41	29 44	14 56	
28	4♍19	18 52	26 20	6 32	3 47	8 58	0 13	25 00	29 52	14 24	
7 9	14 00	1♎12	2♎47	7 25	4 02	8 29	29♑56	25 17	29 59	13 52	
17	23 44	13 33	9 18	8 33	4R07	8 02	29 43	25 32	0♋03	13 21	
27	3♎31	25 53	15 53	9 55	4 01	7 35	29 35	25 44	0 04	12 49	
7 10	13 22	8♏13	22 32	11 29	3 44	7 12	29 31	25 53	0R04	12 17	
17	23 16	20 31	29 16	13 13	3 17	6 53	29D33	25 59	0 01	11 45	
27	3♏13	2♐48	6♏04	15 06	2 42	6 39	29 39	26 01	29♊57	11 14	
6 11	13 14	15 04	12 57	17 07	1 59	6 29	29 50	26R01	29 50	10 42	
16	23 17	27 19	19 54	19 14	1 12	6 26	0♒07	25 56	29 41	10 10	
26	3♐23	9♑30	26 57	21 25	0 23	6D28	0 27	25 49	29 31	9 38	
6 12	13 32	21 38	4♐04	23 40	29♉35	6 36	0 52	25 39	29 20	9 07	
16	23 42	3♒42	11 16	25 57	28 50	6 50	1 20	25 26	29 09	8 35	
26	3♑53	15 38	18 32	28 14	28 12	7 09	1 51	25 11	28 57	8 03	

SID M/N 1st JAN 6 h 40 m 8 s   1913 COMMON   BST   NONE

	DAY	JAN	FEB	MAR	APR	MAY	JUN	JUL	AUG	SEP	OCT	NOV	DEC
	1	24♎32	13♐28	22♐49	8♒00	9♓53	23♈55	27♉22	16♋58	9♍56	18♎26	10♐24	15♑34
☽	3	20♏52	8♑10	17♑20	1♓39	3♈41	19♉14	24♊28	16♌27	10♎09	18♏02	7♑42	11♒10
	5	16♐23	2♒17	11♒12	25♓20	28♈08	15♊51	22♋57	16♍20	9♏23	16♐03	3♒15	5♓29
	7	11♑13	26♒02	4♓50	19♈28	23♉34	13♋35	22♌06	15♎36	7♐02	12♑15	27♒31	29♓08
	9	5♒27	19♓39	28♓32	14♉18	20♊01	11♌55	21♍05	13♏39	3♑07	7♒02	21♓09	22♈52
	11	29♒11	13♈25	22♈35	10♊00	17♋18	10♍19	19♎22	10♐25	28♑00	0♓56	14♈49	17♉18
	13	22♓47	7♉51	17♉17	6♋41	15♌12	8♎30	16♏48	6♑07	22♒06	24♓31	9♉01	12♊49
	15	16♈45	3♊29	13♊01	4♌24	13♍31	6♏20	13♐25	0♒56	15♓47	18♈14	4♊01	9♋25
	17	11♉46	0♋54	10♋10	3♍06	12♎03	3♐39	9♑14	25♒06	9♈23	12♉24	29♊51	6♌49
	19	8♊30	0♌09	8♌50	2♎26	10♏28	0♑10	4♒12	18♓49	3♉13	7♊12	26♋27	4♍40
	21	7♋12	0♍33	8♍42	1♏40	8♐12	25♑40	28♒24	12♈24	27♉38	2♋51	23♌49	2♎45
	23	7♌20	0♎52	8♎48	29♏59	4♑46	20♒09	22♓05	6♉17	23♊02	29♋34	21♍57	0♏58
	25	7♍38	29♎53	8♏01	26♐48	0♒00	13♓56	15♈44	1♊02	19♋51	27♌33	20♎47	29♏08
	27	6♎55	27♏09	5♐36	22♑05	24♒10	7♈36	9♉58	27♊14	18♌18	26♍44	19♏51	26♐50
	29	4♏36		1♑30	16♒14	17♓50	1♉52	5♊28	25♋13	18♍08	26♎35	18♐22	23♑31
	31	0♐48		26♑03		11♈42		2♋42	24♌48		26♏05		18♒56
	1	17♐59	3♒09	23♓19	3♈43	13♈45	8♊40	3♌41	14♌05	23♌43	18♎02	1♐21	22♏55
☿	7	25 36	13 13	3♈07	0R12	21 51	21 48	10 28	9R36	4♍50	27 32	6 41	24D07
	13	3♑56	23 45	9 50	29D44	1♉14	4♋15	15 22	6 46	16 19	6♏33	8R51	29 35
	19	12 45	4♓44	11R56	2♈15	11 51	15 29	17 59	7D45	27 28	15 07	5 41	7♐04
	25	21 57	15 59	9 25	7 06	23 40	25 19	17R47	13 05	8♎02	23 07	28♏01	15 27
	31	1♒31		4 31		6♊29		14 48	21 59		0♐17		24 16

DATE	☉	♀	♂	♃	♄	⚷	♅	♆	♇	☊	STATIONS
1 1	10♑00	22♒43	22♐56	29♐36	27♉52	7♓23	2♒11	25♋01	28♊49	7♈44	
11	20 11	4♓23	0♑20	1♑51	27R28	7 49	2 45	24R45	28R38	7 12	☿ 19/3 11♈57
21	0♒22	15 46	7 47	4 03	27 13	8 19	3 20	24 28	28 28	6 40	11/4 29♓32
31	10 32	26 48	15 18	6 11	27D10	8 53	3 55	24 11	28 18	6 09	22/7 18♌15
10 2	20 40	7♈22	22 53	8 13	27 19	9 29	4 29	23 56	28 11	5 37	15/8 6♌36
20	0♓46	17 15	0♒31	10 08	27 38	10 06	5 03	23 42	28 05	5 05	13/11 8♐51
2 3	10 49	26 13	8 11	11 53	28 08	10 44	5 34	23 30	28 02	4 33	3/12 22♏39
12	20 50	3♉50	15 54	13 28	28 48	11 22	6 03	23 21	28 00	4 01	♀ 4/4 12♉30
22	0♈47	9 30	23 37	14 51	29 36	11 59	6 29	23 15	28D01	3 30	16/5 26♈04
1 4	10 40	12 20	1♓22	16 00	0♊32	12 35	6 51	23 13	28 05	2 58	♂ 27/11 24♋35
11	20 30	11R26	9 06	16 53	1 34	13 08	7 08	23D14	28 10	2 26	♃ 6/5 17♑50
21	0♉17	6 46	16 50	17 30	2 42	13 38	7 21	23 18	28 18	1 54	5/9 8♑01
1 5	10 01	0 39	24 33	17 48	3 54	14 05	7 30	23 25	28 27	1 23	♄ 29/1 27♉10
11	19 42	26♈39	2♈12	17R48	5 09	14 27	7 33	23 35	28 38	0 51	1/10 18♊10
21	29 20	26D29	9 49	17 29	6 26	14 45	7R31	23 48	28 50	0 19	♅ 13/5 7♒33
31	8♊56	29 48	17 22	16 52	7 44	14 58	7 25	24 04	29 03	29♓47	14/10 3♒37
10 6	18 30	5♉40	24 50	15 59	9 01	15 05	7 14	24 22	29 17	29 16	♆ 4/4 23♋13
20	28 03	13 15	2♉12	14 53	10 18	15R07	6 59	24 41	29 32	28 44	1/11 28♋15
30	7♋35	22 01	9 27	13 40	11 32	15 03	6 40	25 02	29 46	28 12	♇ 13/3 28♊00
10 7	17 07	1♊36	16 35	12 23	12 43	14 54	6 19	25 24	0♋00	27 40	2/10 1♋09
20	26 40	11 46	23 34	11 08	13 50	14 40	5 56	25 46	0 14	27 08	⚷ 18/6 15♓07
30	6♌13	22 23	0♊24	10 01	14 51	14 22	5 32	26 09	0 27	26 37	22/11 10♓27
9 8	15 47	3♋21	7 02	9 06	15 46	13 59	5 09	26 30	0 38	26 05	
19	25 24	14 36	13 29	8 27	16 33	13 34	4 46	26 51	0 48	25 33	
29	5♍03	26 04	19 42	8 05	17 12	13 07	4 25	27 10	0 56	25 01	
8 9	14 44	7♌45	25 38	8D02	17 42	12 39	4 07	27 28	1 03	24 30	
18	24 28	19 36	1♋16	8 18	18 01	12 11	3 53	27 43	1 07	23 58	
28	4♎16	1♍37	6 32	8 52	18 10	11 45	3 43	27 55	1 09	23 26	
8 10	14 07	13 45	11 21	9 44	18R08	11 21	3 38	28 05	1R08	22 54	
18	24 01	26 00	15 39	10 52	17 54	11 00	3D37	28 11	1 06	22 22	
28	3♏58	8♎21	19 17	12 15	17 31	10 44	3 42	28 14	1 01	21 51	
7 11	13 59	20 46	22 06	13 50	16 58	10 33	3 52	28R14	0 54	21 19	
17	24 03	3♏15	23 56	15 36	16 17	10 28	4 06	28 10	0 46	20 47	
27	4♐09	15 45	24R35	17 32	15 31	10D28	4 25	28 03	0 36	20 15	
7 12	14 18	28 18	23 52	19 36	14 42	10 34	4 49	27 53	0 25	19 44	
17	24 28	10♐52	21 46	21 46	13 53	10 45	5 16	27 41	0 13	19 12	
27	4♑39	23 26	18 28	24 01	13 07	11 02	5 46	27 26	0 01	18 40	

SID M/N 1st JAN 6 h 39 m 11 s 1914 COMMON BST NONE

DAY	JAN	FEB	MAR	APR	MAY	JUN	JUL	AUG	SEP	OCT	NOV	DEC
1	1♓12	14♈46	23♈03	7♊45	12♋14	2♍09	10♎50	4♐20	25♑36	0♓45	16♈06	18♉36
☽ 3	25♓06	8♉30	16♉47	2♋39	8♌21	0♎05	9♏22	2♑09	21♒23	25♓10	9♉49	12♊36
5	18♈43	2♊57	11♊10	28♋49	5♍49	29♎05	8♐07	29♑12	16♓18	19♈08	3♊37	7♋01
7	12♉46	28♊44	6♋47	26♌38	4♎47	28♏38	6♑29	25♒13	10♈32	12♉51	27♊42	2♌00
9	7♊53	26♋12	4♌04	26♍06	4♏50	27♐49	3♒48	20♓10	4♉19	6♊37	22♋20	27♌46
11	4♋24	25♌05	3♍04	26♎32	4♐55	25♑39	29♒43	14♈17	28♉03	0♋48	17♌57	24♍42
13	2♌13	24♍41	3♎11	26♏41	3♑48	21♒46	24♓22	8♉01	22♊16	25♋54	15♍04	23♎04
15	0♍48	24♎02	3♏19	25♐24	0♒49	16♓27	18♈14	1♊58	17♋33	22♌28	13♎58	22♏42
17	29♍29	22♏28	2♐21	22♑14	26♒05	10♈16	11♉59	26♊43	14♌21	20♍52	14♏14	22♐43
19	27♎49	19♐44	29♐47	17♒25	20♓11	3♉57	6♊15	22♋46	12♍50	20♎52	14♐43	21♑54
21	25♏37	15♑53	25♑41	11♓31	13♈48	28♉05	1♋30	20♌15	12♎34	21♏24	13♑59	19♒24
23	22♐47	11♒05	20♒25	5♈09	7♉31	23♊02	27♋55	18♍54	12♏30	21♐06	11♒19	15♓07
25	19♑10	5♓32	14♓26	28♈47	1♊43	18♋52	25♌21	18♎03	11♐37	19♑05	6♓49	9♈32
27	14♒37	29♓26	8♈07	22♉42	26♊35	15♌30	23♍27	16♏58	9♑18	15♒16	1♈08	3♉18
29	9♓09		1♉45	17♊06	22♋11	12♍51	21♎51	15♐09	5♒35	10♓07	24♈53	27♉04
31	2♈59		25♉37		18♌36		20♏14	12♑22		4♈12		21♊16
1	25♐46	16♒05	24♓47	13♓43	22♈33	25♊58	28♋55	19♋54	8♍55	28♎17	21♏24	19♏39
☿ 7	4♑54	26 47	22℞30	18 38	3♉48	6♋16	28℞35	24 33	20 06	6♏16	14℞53	28 14
13	14 17	7♓24	16 57	25 16	16 06	14 53	25 47	2♌39	0♎36	13 24	8 13	7♐14
19	23 57	16 52	12 19	3♈15	29 06	21 43	21 52	13 18	10 26	19 11	7D29	16 25
25	3♒57	23 16	11D03	12 22	12♊04	26 31	19 10	25 08	19 39	22 37	12 11	25 43
31	14 19		13 06		24 06		19D29	6♍59		22℞01		5♑10

DATE	☉	♀	♂	♃	♄	⚷	♅	♆	♇	☊	STATIONS
1 1	9♑45	29♐44	16♋33	25♑10	12♊46	11♓13	6♒02	27♋18	29♊55	18♓24	
11	19 56	12♑18	12℞35	27 30	12℞08	11 37	6 35	27℞02	29℞44	17 52	☿ 1/3 24♓48
21	0♒07	24 52	9 09	29 52	11 40	12 05	7 09	26 45	29 33	17 21	☿ 24/3 11♓00
31	10 17	7♒26	6 47	2♒13	11 21	12 37	7 44	26 28	29 23	16 49	☿ 3/7 29♋07
10 2	20 25	19 59	5 45	4 33	11 13	13 11	8 19	26 12	29 16	16 17	☿ 28/7 18♋52
20	0♓31	2♓31	5D59	6 51	11D17	13 47	8 53	25 58	29 10	15 45	☿ 27/10 22♏59
2 3	10 35	15 01	7 21	9 04	11 32	14 24	9 25	25 46	29 06	15 14	☿ 17/11 6♏58
12	20 35	27 30	9 38	11 12	11 57	15 01	9 55	25 36	29 04	14 42	♀ 7/11 12♐17
22	0♈32	9♈56	12 40	13 14	12 33	15 38	10 22	25 30	29D05	14 10	♀ 18/12 26♏58
1 4	10 26	22 21	16 17	15 07	13 18	16 14	10 46	25 26	29 08	13 38	♂ 13/2 5♋41
11	20 16	4♉42	20 22	16 50	14 11	16 48	11 05	25D26	29 13	13 06	♃ 11/6 22♒17
21	0♉03	17 01	24 50	18 23	15 10	17 19	11 20	25 29	29 21	12 35	♃ 9/10 12♒27
1 5	9 47	29 17	29 35	19 42	16 16	17 46	11 31	25 36	29 30	12 03	♄ 12/2 11♊13
11	19 28	11♊30	4♌36	20 46	17 26	18 10	11 36	25 45	29 40	11 31	♄ 15/10 2♋20
21	29 06	23 40	9 49	21 34	18 40	18 29	11℞37	25 58	29 53	10 59	♅ 17/5 11♒37
31	8♊42	5♋47	15 12	22 05	19 56	18 44	11 32	26 13	0♋06	10 28	♅ 18/10 7♒41
10 6	18 16	17 49	20 45	22 17	21 14	18 53	11 23	26 30	0 20	9 56	♆ 7/4 25♋26
20	27 49	29 47	26 25	22℞10	22 32	18 57	11 10	26 49	0 34	9 24	♆ 3/11 0♌28
30	7♋22	11♌41	2♍13	21 44	23 49	18℞56	10 53	27 10	0 49	8 52	♇ 14/3 29♊04
10 7	16 54	23 28	8 08	21 01	25 05	18 49	10 33	27 32	1 03	8 21	♇ 3/10 2♋14
20	26 26	5♍08	14 09	20 02	26 18	18 37	10 11	27 54	1 17	7 49	⚷ 22/6 18♓57
30	5♌59	16 40	20 16	18 52	27 27	18 21	9 47	28 16	1 30	7 17	⚷ 26/11 14♓20
9 8	15 34	28 02	26 29	17 36	28 32	18 00	9 23	28 38	1 41	6 45	
19	25 10	9♎10	2♎48	16 18	29 30	17 36	9 00	28 59	1 52	6 13	
29	4♍49	20 03	9 13	15 04	0♋21	17 10	8 38	29 19	2 00	5 42	
8 9	14 30	0♏34	15 43	14 01	1 05	16 43	8 19	29 37	2 07	5 10	
18	24 14	10 36	22 20	13 12	1 39	16 15	8 03	29 52	2 11	4 38	
28	4♎01	19 59	29 02	12 40	2 03	15 48	7 51	0♌05	2 13	4 06	
8 10	13 52	28 24	5♏50	12 27	2 17	15 23	7 44	0 16	2℞13	3 35	
18	23 46	5♐26	12 44	12D34	2℞20	15 01	7 41	0 23	2 11	3 03	
28	3♏44	10 22	19 44	13 01	2 11	14 44	7D43	0 27	2 07	2 31	
7 11	13 45	12 17	26 49	13 47	1 52	14 30	7 51	0℞27	2 00	1 59	
17	23 48	10℞20	4♐01	14 50	1 23	14 23	8 04	0 24	1 52	1 27	
27	3♐55	5 04	11 18	16 09	0 45	14D20	8 21	0 18	1 42	0 56	
7 12	14 03	29♏31	18 40	17 41	0 01	14 24	8 42	0 09	1 31	0 24	
17	24 13	27 00	26 08	19 26	29♊13	14 33	9 08	29♋57	1 19	29♒52	
27	4♑24	28D27	3♑40	21 22	28 24	14 47	9 36	29 43	1 07	29 20	

SID M/N 1st JAN 6 h 38 m 13 s 1915 COMMON BST NONE

DAY	JAN	FEB	MAR	APR	MAY	JUN	JUL	AUG	SEP	OCT	NOV	DEC
1	3♋36	20♌56	29♌23	20♎47	29♏36	22♑57	29♒18	16♈19	0♊40	2♋18	16♌35	20♍30
☽ 3	28♋50	18♍08	27♍28	20♏40	29♐35	20♒50	25♓34	10♉45	24♊26	26♋19	12♍13	17♎44
5	24♌47	16♎01	26♎19	20♐01	28♑03	16♓55	20♈25	4♊35	18♋30	21♌19	9♎40	16♏54
7	21♍32	14♏17	25♏14	18♑07	24♒47	11♈41	14♉26	28♊24	13♌25	17♍48	8♏54	17♐20
9	19♎09	12♐41	23♐37	14♒52	20♓09	5♉43	8♊09	22♋42	9♍34	15♎54	9♐04	17♑41
11	17♏40	10♑51	21♑11	10♓30	14♈38	29♉27	2♋02	17♌48	6♎57	15♏05	8♑51	16♒44
13	16♐45	8♒27	17♒54	5♈22	8♉38	23♊13	26♋21	13♍51	5♏12	14♐24	7♒21	14♓01
15	15♑41	5♓06	13♓46	29♈41	2♊24	17♋13	21♌18	10♎49	3♐45	13♑03	4♓22	9♈46
17	13♒40	0♈38	8♈50	23♉36	26♊08	11♌42	17♍05	8♏35	2♑09	10♒40	0♈10	4♉27
19	10♓11	25♈11	3♉12	17♊18	20♋06	7♍01	13♎54	6♐57	0♒06	7♓20	25♈08	28♉29
21	5♈17	19♉04	27♉03	11♋12	14♌42	3♎36	11♏54	5♑36	27♒27	3♈13	19♉31	22♊14
23	29♈24	12♊53	20♊49	5♌47	10♍31	1♏47	10♐55	4♒06	24♓04	28♈23	13♊27	15♋55
25	23♉09	7♋13	15♋04	1♍44	8♎04	1♐25	10♑25	1♓57	19♈47	22♉51	7♋06	9♌48
27	17♊09	2♌37	10♌24	29♍32	7♏29	1♑39	9♒29	28♓43	14♉34	16♊45	0♌48	4♍12
29	11♋54		7♍21	29♎08	8♐01	1♒16	7♓22	24♈15	8♊35	10♋24	25♌03	29♍37
31	7♌40		5♎59		8♑19		3♈41	18♉42		4♌19		26♎33
1	6♑46	27♒57	25♒07	15♓02	8♉39	2♋40	2♋20	23♋31	22♍58	2♏24	21♎17	29♏24
☿ 7	16 26	5♓20	23D16	23 54	21 36	7 14	0R20	5♌19	2♎31	6 12	24 41	8♐49
13	26 20	8R07	25 08	3♈42	4♊04	9 15	1D06	17 39	11 21	6R39	1♏54	18 13
19	6♒29	4 55	29 40	14 26	15 11	8R34	5 01	29 38	19 25	2 23	10 42	27 41
25	16 42	28♒32	6♓00	26 07	24 27	5 45	12 00	10♍52	26 33	25♎11	20 00	7♑15
31	26 27		13 39		1♋40		21 41	21 18		21 18		16 56

DATE	☉	♀	♂	♃	♄	⚷	♅	♆	♇	☊	STATIONS
1 1	9♑30	0♐29	7♑28	22♒23	27♊59	14♓57	9♒52	29♋35	1♋01	29♒05	
11	19 42	6 28	15 07	24 31	27R13	15 18	10 24	29R19	0R50	28 33	☿ 13/2 8♓07
21	29 53	14 20	22 50	26 45	26 33	15 45	10 58	29 02	0 39	28 01	☿ 7/3 23♒16
31	10♒03	23 26	0♒35	29 03	26 00	16 14	11 33	28 45	0 29	27 29	☿ 14/6 9♋19
10 2	20 11	3♑24	8 23	1♓26	25 37	16 47	12 08	28 29	0 21	26 57	☿ 9/7 0♋14
20	0♓17	13 57	16 14	3 50	25 25	17 22	12 42	28 15	0 15	26 26	☿ 11/10 6♏58
2 3	10 20	24 55	24 05	6 14	25D23	17 58	13 15	28 02	0 11	25 54	☿ 1/11 21♎16
12	20 21	6♒10	1♓57	8 38	25 33	18 35	13 46	27 52	0 09	25 22	♂ 1/1 29♌49
22	0♈18	17 38	9 48	11 00	25 54	19 11	14 14	27 44	0D09	24 50	♃ 19/7 28♓30
1 4	10 11	29 16	17 38	13 19	26 25	19 47	14 39	27 40	0 12	24 19	♃ 15/11 18♓37
11	20 02	11♓00	25 27	15 33	27 06	20 21	15 00	27D39	0 17	23 47	♄ 26/2 25♊22
21	29 49	22 50	3♈13	17 42	27 55	20 53	15 17	27 41	0 24	23 15	♄ 30/10 16♋30
1 5	9♉33	4♈43	10 55	19 43	28 52	21 21	15 30	27 47	0 33	22 43	♅ 21/5 15♒40
11	19 14	16 40	18 34	21 35	29 55	21 46	15 37	27 56	0 44	22 11	♅ 23/10 11♒44
21	28 52	28 39	26 09	23 18	1♋03	22 07	15 40	28 08	0 56	21 40	♆ 9/4 27♋39
31	8♊28	10♉41	3♉38	24 49	2 15	22 23	15R38	28 22	1 09	21 08	♆ 6/11 2♌40
10 6	18 02	22 44	11 03	26 06	3 30	22 34	15 31	28 39	1 23	20 36	♇ 15/3 0♋09
20	27 35	4♊50	18 21	27 08	4 47	22 41	15 19	28 58	1 37	20 04	♇ 4/10 3♋19
30	7♋08	16 57	25 33	27 54	6 05	22R41	15 04	29 18	1 52	19 33	⚷ 26/6 22♓42
10 7	16 40	29 07	2♊38	28 22	7 23	22 37	14 45	29 39	2 06	19 01	⚷ 30/11 18♓07
20	26 12	11♋19	9 37	28R30	8 40	22 27	14 24	0♌01	2 20	18 29	
30	5♌45	23 34	16 27	28 19	9 54	22 12	14 01	0 24	2 33	17 57	
9 8	15 20	5♌52	23 11	27 49	11 06	21 54	13 37	0 46	2 45	17 26	
19	24 56	18 12	29 45	27 01	12 12	21 31	13 13	1 07	2 56	16 54	
29	4♍34	0♍34	6♋11	25 59	13 14	21 06	12 51	1 27	3 04	16 22	
8 9	14 16	12 59	12 27	24 45	14 09	20 39	12 30	1 45	3 11	15 50	
18	24 00	25 25	18 32	23 26	14 56	20 12	12 13	2 02	3 16	15 18	
28	3♎47	7♎53	24 25	22 07	15 35	19 45	11 59	2 15	3 19	14 47	
8 10	13 38	20 21	0♌05	20 55	16 04	19 19	11 50	2 26	3R19	14 15	
18	23 32	2♏50	5 28	19 54	16 22	18 56	11 45	2 34	3 17	13 43	
28	3♏29	15 20	10 33	19 09	16 30	18 37	11D45	2 39	3 13	13 11	
7 11	13 30	27 49	15 16	18 43	16R27	18 22	11 50	2R40	3 06	12 40	
17	23 34	10♐19	19 32	18D37	16 12	18 12	12 01	2 38	2 58	12 08	
27	3♐40	22 48	23 15	18 52	15 47	18 07	12 16	2 33	2 49	11 36	
7 12	13 48	5♑17	26 17	19 27	15 13	18D08	12 36	2 24	2 38	11 04	
17	23 58	17 45	28 29	20 20	14 31	18 15	12 59	2 13	2 26	10 32	
27	4♑09	0♒12	29 40	21 31	13 45	18 27	13 27	2 00	2 14	10 01	

SID M/N 1st JAN 6 h 37 m 16 s   1916 LEAP   BST 21/5 to 1/10

DAY	JAN	FEB	MAR	APR	MAY	JUN	JUL	AUG	SEP	OCT	NOV	DEC
1	10♏41	3♑53	28♑01	19♓55	25♈49	12♊11	14♋48	29♌21	16♎12	22♏53	15♑22	24♒25
☽ 3	10♐09	3♒37	26♒46	16♈49	21♉08	6♋03	8♌23	23♍48	12♏29	20♐28	13♒36	22♓17
5	10♑31	2♓50	24♓53	12♉42	15♊37	29♋37	2♍14	19♎09	9♐42	18♑31	11♓34	19♈14
7	10♒32	0♈42	21♈49	7♊28	9♋26	23♌21	26♍48	15♏40	7♑53	16♒55	9♈08	15♉20
9	9♓07	26♈55	17♉20	1♋23	3♌02	17♍49	22♎35	13♐36	6♒55	15♓27	6♉01	10♊35
11	5♈55	21♉43	11♊40	25♋02	27♌04	13♎41	20♏02	12♑52	6♓18	13♈35	1♊57	5♋02
13	1♉10	15♊37	5♋23	19♌06	22♍13	11♏23	19♐09	12♒52	5♈09	10♉44	26♊48	28♋52
15	25♉23	9♋16	29♋09	14♍15	19♎03	10♐46	19♑23	12♓36	2♉43	6♊31	20♋46	22♌27
17	19♊06	3♌12	23♌37	10♎55	17♏37	11♑01	19♒35	11♈03	28♉37	1♋01	14♌22	16♍18
19	12♋47	27♌50	19♍11	9♏01	17♐16	10♒56	18♓39	7♉44	23♊09	24♋46	8♍16	11♎05
21	6♌46	23♍21	15♎58	7♐56	16♑55	9♓35	16♈01	2♊50	16♋53	18♌26	3♎09	7♏21
23	1♍16	19♎47	13♏42	6♑51	15♒43	6♈40	11♉44	26♊52	10♌32	12♍45	29♎33	5♐25
25	26♍33	17♏03	11♐54	5♒11	13♓19	2♉24	6♊15	20♋27	4♍42	8♎14	27♏29	4♑55
27	22♎50	15♐03	10♑10	2♓48	9♈47	27♉06	0♋03	14♌10	29♍48	5♏02	26♐30	4♒56
29	20♏21	13♑37	8♒19	29♓41	5♉18	21♊08	23♋38	8♍24	25♎55	2♐52	25♑43	4♓25
31	19♐08		6♓10		0♊03		17♌21	3♎23		1♑11		2♈38
1	18♑33	19♒50	13♒00	27♓21	27♉10	17♊37	17♊11	12♌22	3♎39	16♎45	24♎20	12♐20
☿ 7	28 18	13R12	19 31	8♈35	6♊32	14R27	24 19	24 09	10 42	10R05	4♏03	21 43
13	7♒47	7 33	27 13	20 39	13 29	11 37	3♋48	5♍02	16 21	5 39	13 48	1♑06
19	16 06	6D18	5♓51	3♉17	17 48	10D45	15 13	15 01	19 58	7D17	23 25	10 27
25	21 14	8 53	15 18	15 48	19 16	12 36	27 45	24 08	20R27	13 51	2♐55	19 35
31	20R35		25 34		18R02		10♌19	2♎23		22 45		27 56

DATE	☉	♀	♂	♃	♄	⚷	♅	♆	♇	☊	STATIONS
1 1	9♑15	6♒25	29♌49	22♓12	13♋20	18♓35	13♒41	1♌52	2♋08	9♒45	
11	19 27	18 49	29R09	23 45	12R31	18 55	14 13	1R36	1R56	9 13	☿ 27/1 21♒47
21	29 38	1♓09	27 09	25 30	11 43	19 19	14 46	1 19	1 45	8 41	☿ 18/2 6♒12
31	9♒48	13 25	23 58	27 26	11 00	19 47	15 21	1 02	1 35	8 10	☿ 25/5 19♊16
10 2	19 56	25 36	20 05	29 31	10 24	20 18	15 55	0 46	1 27	7 38	☿ 18/6 10♊43
20	0♓02	7♈39	16 13	1♈42	9 56	20 51	16 30	0 31	1 21	7 06	☿ 23/9 20♎43
1 3	10 06	19 33	13 03	3 59	9 39	21 27	17 03	0 18	1 16	6 34	☿ 14/10 5♎28
11	20 06	1♉16	11 02	6 20	9 33	22 03	17 35	0 07	1 14	6 02	♀ 12/6 19♋43
21	0♈03	12 45	10 20	8 44	9D38	22 39	18 05	29♋59	1D14	5 31	♀ 25/7 3♋12
31	9 57	23 56	10D51	11 08	9 54	23 15	18 31	29 54	1 17	4 59	♂ 22/3 10♌19
10 4	19 48	4♊45	12 25	13 33	10 21	23 49	18 54	29 52	1 21	4 27	♃ 25/8 5♉24
20	29 35	15 04	14 53	15 57	10 57	24 21	19 13	29D53	1 28	3 55	♃ 21/12 25♈25
30	9♉19	24 44	18 03	18 19	11 42	24 51	19 27	29 58	1 37	3 24	♄ 12/3 9♋33
10 5	19 00	3♋30	21 47	20 37	12 35	25 17	19 37	0♌06	1 47	2 52	♄ 12/11 0♌36
20	28 38	10 58	25 59	22 50	13 35	25 39	19 41	0 17	1 59	2 20	♅ 25/5 19♒42
30	8♊14	16 35	0♍35	24 57	14 40	25 57	19R41	0 31	2 12	1 48	♅ 26/10 15♒46
9 6	17 49	19 30	5 29	26 57	15 50	26 10	19 36	0 47	2 26	1 16	♆ 10/4 29♋52
19	27 22	18R50	10 40	28 48	17 04	26 18	19 27	1 06	2 41	0 45	♆ 7/11 4♌53
29	6♋54	14 26	16 05	0♉28	18 20	26 21	19 13	1 26	2 55	0 13	♇ 16/3 1♋14
9 7	16 26	8 20	21 42	1 57	19 37	26R18	18 56	1 47	3 10	29♑41	♇ 5/10 4♋25
19	25 58	4 01	27 30	3 12	20 55	26 11	18 35	2 09	3 24	29 09	⚷ 29/ 6 26♓21
29	5♌31	3D26	3♎28	4 12	22 12	25 58	18 13	2 31	3 37	28 38	⚷ 3/12 21♓48
8 8	15 06	6 24	9 36	4 54	23 28	25 41	17 50	2 53	3 49	28 06	
18	24 42	12 01	15 52	5 19	24 40	25 20	17 26	3 15	4 00	27 34	
28	4♍20	19 28	22 17	5R23	25 49	24 56	17 03	3 35	4 09	27 02	
7 9	14 02	28 12	28 51	5 08	26 53	24 30	16 41	3 54	4 16	26 31	
17	23 46	7♌51	5♏32	4 34	27 51	24 03	16 22	4 11	4 21	25 59	
27	3♎33	18 09	12 21	3 41	28 42	23 36	16 07	4 25	4 24	25 27	
7 10	13 23	28 59	19 17	2 34	29 25	23 09	15 55	4 37	4R25	24 55	
17	23 17	10♍12	26 20	1 17	29 58	22 46	15 48	4 46	4 23	24 23	
27	3♏15	21 44	3♐31	29♈56	0♌21	22 25	15D46	4 51	4 19	23 52	
6 11	13 15	3♎31	10 48	28 37	0 34	22 08	15 49	4 53	4 13	23 20	
16	23 19	15 29	18 11	27 26	0R35	21 56	15 58	4R52	4 06	22 48	
26	3♐25	27 37	25 41	26 29	0 25	21 49	16 11	4 48	3 56	22 16	
6 12	13 33	9♏51	3♑15	25 48	0 05	21D48	16 28	4 40	3 45	21 45	
16	23 43	22 11	10 55	25 28	29♋34	21 52	16 51	4 29	3 34	21 13	
26	3♑55	4♐34	18 39	25D28	28 55	22 02	17 16	4 16	3 21	20 41	

SID M/N 1st JAN 6 h 40 m 15 s — 1917 COMMON — BST 8/4 to 17/9

DAY		JAN	FEB	MAR	APR	MAY	JUN	JUL	AUG	SEP	OCT	NOV	DEC
	1	16♈11	4♊26	13♊18	27♋43	29♌21	13♎45	17♏32	7♑19	0♓31	9♈17	0♊54	5♋31
☽	3	12♉20	28♊45	7♋32	21♌19	23♍24	9♏31	14♐53	7♒01	1♈02	8♉49	27♊45	0♌45
	5	7♊24	22♋29	1♌11	15♍15	18♎22	6♐39	13♑43	7♓22	0♉32	6♊38	23♋01	24♌58
	7	1♋43	16♌06	24♌48	9♎55	14♏27	4♑55	13♒23	7♈08	28♉10	2♋34	17♌10	18♍44
	9	25♋32	9♍51	18♍48	5♏26	11♐32	3♒45	12♓55	5♉23	23♊57	27♋05	10♍53	12♎41
	11	19♌09	4♎02	13♎23	1♐45	9♑19	2♓33	11♈31	1♊56	18♋26	20♌52	4♎48	7♏22
	13	12♍52	28♎53	8♏41	28♐47	7♒28	0♈52	8♉50	27♊06	12♌15	14♍33	29♎22	3♐12
	15	7♎07	24♏47	4♐48	26♑31	5♓48	28♈25	4♊55	21♋22	5♍54	8♎34	24♏48	0♑14
	17	2♏25	22♐05	1♑56	24♒57	4♈04	25♉05	0♋00	15♌11	29♍43	3♏10	21♐06	28♑14
	19	29♏15	20♑59	0♒16	23♓51	1♉56	20♊49	24♋21	8♍52	23♎55	28♏24	18♑10	26♒43
	21	27♐52	21♒05	29♒41	22♈37	28♉58	15♋39	18♌14	2♎38	18♏39	24♐21	15♒53	25♓12
	23	27♑54	21♓20	29♓27	20♉27	24♊51	9♌45	11♍54	26♎48	14♐13	21♑13	14♓09	23♈22
	25	28♒19	20♈29	28♈28	16♊48	19♋36	3♍27	5♎43	21♏44	10♑59	19♒11	12♈46	20♉56
	27	27♓52	17♉48	25♉54	11♋43	13♌33	27♍16	0♏10	17♐54	9♒17	18♓14	11♉16	17♊45
	29	25♈46		21♊32	5♌41	7♍15	21♎47	25♏47	15♑45	9♓00	17♈47	9♊00	13♋39
	31	21♉54		15♋51		1♎21		23♐02	15♒18		16♉51		8♌37
	1	29♑10	19♑43	18♒12	13♈07	28♉32	20♉49	25♊09	27♌02	3♎02	20♍12	6♏16	23♐04
☿	7	4♒42	22 24	27 22	25 30	29R25	23 15	7♋28	6♍32	4R00	25 36	16 00	1♑52
	13	4R57	27 42	7♓13	7♉14	27 29	28 09	20 23	15 02	1 16	4♎21	25 29	10 04
	19	28♑57	4♒34	17 46	17 10	24 06	5♊13	2♌58	22 24	25♍26	14 22	4♐49	16 42
	25	22 03	12 29	29 04	24 24	21 19	14 16	14 40	28 25	20 18	24 35	14 01	19 42
	31	19D38		11♈04		20D40		25 21	2♎34		4♏37		16R28

DATE	☉	♀	♂	♃	♄	⚷	♅	♆	♇	☊	STATIONS
1 1	10♑01	12♐01	23♑19	25♈38	28♋29	22♓11	17♒33	4♌07	3♋14	20♑22	
11	20 13	24 28	1♒09	26 11	27R42	22 29	18 04	3R52	3R02	19 50	☿ 10/1 5♒40
21	0♒24	6♑56	9 01	27 02	26 53	22 51	18 37	3 35	2 51	19 18	☿ 31/1 19♑38
31	10 34	19 24	16 54	28 11	26 04	23 18	19 11	3 18	2 41	18 47	☿ 6/5 29♉30
10 2	20 42	1♒53	24 49	29 35	25 20	23 48	19 45	3 02	2 33	18 15	☿ 30/5 20♉35
20	0♓48	14 22	2♓43	1♉12	24 41	24 21	20 20	2 46	2 26	17 43	☿ 6/9 4♎04
2 3	10 51	26 50	10 37	3 01	24 11	24 55	20 54	2 33	2 22	17 11	☿ 28/9 19♍30
12	20 51	9♓17	18 29	4 59	23 50	25 30	21 26	2 21	2 20	16 40	☿ 25/12 19♑42
22	0♈48	21 44	26 19	7 05	23 41	26 06	21 56	2 13	2D20	16 08	♃ 1/10 11♊31
1 4	10 42	4♈09	4♈06	9 16	23D42	26 42	22 24	2 07	2 22	15 36	♄ 26/3 23♋40
11	20 32	16 32	11 49	11 33	23 54	27 16	22 48	2 05	2 27	15 04	♄ 26/11 14♌32
21	0♉19	28 55	19 29	13 53	24 16	27 49	23 08	2D06	2 34	14 32	♅ 29/5 23♒43
1 5	10 03	11♉16	27 03	16 14	24 49	28 19	23 23	2 10	2 42	14 01	♅ 30/10 19♒47
11	19 44	23 36	4♉33	18 37	25 31	28 46	23 35	2 18	2 53	13 29	♆ 13/4 2♌05
21	29 22	5♊54	11 58	20 59	26 20	29 09	23 41	2 29	3 05	12 57	♆ 10/11 7♌07
31	8♊58	18 11	19 17	23 19	27 17	29 28	23R43	2 42	3 18	12 25	♇ 17/3 2♋19
10 6	18 32	0♋28	26 31	25 37	28 20	29 42	23 39	2 58	3 32	11 54	♇ 6/10 5♋32
20	28 05	12 43	3♊39	27 51	29 28	29 52	23 31	3 16	3 46	11 22	⚷ 3/7 29♓56
30	7♋37	24 57	10 42	0♊00	0♌40	29 56	23 19	3 36	4 01	10 50	⚷ 7/12 25♓24
10 7	17 09	7♌10	17 39	2 03	1 55	29R55	23 03	3 57	4 16	10 18	
20	26 42	19 22	24 29	3 58	3 11	29 49	22 43	4 18	4 30	9 47	
30	6♌15	1♍32	1♋14	5 43	4 28	29 38	22 22	4 41	4 43	9 15	
9 8	15 49	13 40	7 53	7 18	5 46	29 22	21 58	5 03	4 55	8 43	
19	25 26	25 46	14 26	8 41	7 01	29 02	21 35	5 24	5 06	8 11	
29	5♍04	7♎49	20 53	9 49	8 15	28 39	21 11	5 45	5 15	7 39	
8 9	14 46	19 49	27 13	10 41	9 25	28 14	20 49	6 04	5 23	7 08	
18	24 30	1♏45	3♌27	11 15	10 31	27 47	20 29	6 21	5 28	6 36	
28	4♎18	13 36	9 33	11 30	11 30	27 20	20 12	6 36	5 31	6 04	
8 10	14 08	25 21	15 31	11R26	12 24	26 53	20 00	6 48	5R32	5 32	
18	24 03	7♐00	21 20	11 01	13 09	26 29	19 51	6 58	5 30	5 01	
28	4♏00	18 29	27 00	10 17	13 45	26 07	19 47	7 04	5 26	4 29	
7 11	14 01	29 46	2♍28	9 17	14 11	25 49	19D49	7 06	5 20	3 57	
17	24 05	10♑46	7 42	8 04	14 27	25 36	19 55	7R06	5 12	3 25	
27	4♐11	21 23	12 41	6 44	14R32	25 27	20 07	7 02	5 03	2 53	
7 12	14 20	1♒25	17 20	5 23	14 25	25 24	20 23	6 54	4 52	2 22	
17	24 30	10 37	21 36	4 06	14 08	25D27	20 44	6 44	4 40	1 50	
27	4♑41	18 35	25 23	3 01	13 40	25 35	21 08	6 31	4 28	1 18	

SID M/N 1st JAN 6 h 39 m 18 s   **1918 COMMON**   BST 24/3 to 30/9

DAY		JAN	FEB	MAR	APR	MAY	JUN	JUL	AUG	SEP	OCT	NOV	DEC
	1	20♌47	4♎43	13♎20	28♏34	3♑28	24♒15	3♈31	26♉41	16♋50	21♌29	6♎33	8♏48
☽	3	14♍42	28♎34	7♏14	23♐35	29♑53	22♓28	1♉55	23♊44	12♌03	15♍42	0♏14	2♐52
	5	8♎27	23♏03	1♐40	19♑48	27♒33	21♈15	29♉58	19♋56	6♍38	9♎33	24♏04	27♐33
	7	2♏38	18♐47	27♐12	17♒39	26♓30	20♉07	27♊21	15♌22	0♎42	3♏13	18♐16	23♑01
	9	27♏51	16♑18	24♑26	17♓10	26♈13	18♊24	23♋53	10♍03	24♎26	26♏58	13♑09	19♒24
	11	24♐33	15♒35	23♒36	17♈35	25♉43	15♋32	19♌23	4♎06	18♏06	21♐10	9♒06	16♓47
	13	22♑47	15♓50	24♓05	17♉34	24♊01	11♌21	13♍56	27♎48	12♐15	16♑21	6♓29	15♈09
	15	22♒04	15♈47	24♈32	15♊59	20♋40	5♍59	7♎51	21♏42	7♑30	13♒06	5♈25	14♉15
	17	21♓29	14♉22	23♉37	12♋31	15♌49	29♍55	1♏39	16♐25	4♒30	11♓45	5♉23	13♊28
	19	20♈12	11♊19	20♊49	7♌31	9♍59	23♎44	25♏57	12♑36	3♓26	11♈55	5♊22	12♋01
	21	17♉48	6♋54	16♋21	1♍36	3♎45	18♏01	21♐21	10♒36	3♈44	12♉27	4♋15	9♌14
	23	14♊18	1♌35	10♌48	25♍20	27♎40	13♐13	18♑12	10♓03	4♉06	12♊01	1♌26	4♍57
	25	9♋53	25♌44	4♍42	19♎10	22♏08	9♑32	16♒25	10♈00	3♊15	9♋50	26♌59	29♍25
	27	4♌44	19♍36	28♍27	13♏20	17♐22	6♒55	15♓27	9♉17	0♋42	5♌53	21♍20	23♎12
	29	29♌00		22♎16	8♐02	13♑27	5♓03	14♈28	7♊15	26♋37	0♍39	15♎06	16♏56
	31	22♍52		16♏21		10♒26		12♉50	3♋54		24♍41		11♐11
	1	15♑20	17♑24	29♒27	27♈41	3♉34	16♉07	13♋04	4♍49	9♍46	25♍46	18♏00	29♐22
☿	7	7℞36	25 15	10♓10	5♉30	0℞51	24 55	25 26	10 55	4℞42	6♎29	27 08	3♑29
	13	3 35	3♒48	21 31	9 44	0D39	5♊18	6♌44	15 10	3D24	17 02	6♐01	2℞26
	19	4D52	12 57	3♈24	10℞09	3 10	17 09	16 53	16 53	7 25	27 12	14 35	25♐27
	25	9 34	22 39	15 17	7 27	8 01	0♋02	25 52	15℞21	15 34	6♏59	22 34	18 48
	31	16 10		26 05		14 49		3♍39	10 43		16 27		17D52

DATE		☉	♀	♂	♃	♄	⚷	♅	♆	♇	☊	STATIONS	
1	1	9♑47	21♒56	27♍04	2♊34	13♌23	25♓41	21♒22	6♌24	4♋22	1♑02		
11		19 58	26 50	29 55	1℞52	12℞43	25 57	21 51	6℞09	4℞10	0 30	☿ 14/1	3♑28
21		0♒09	28℞30	1♎56	1 31	11 58	26 18	22 23	5 52	3 59	29♐59	☿ 17/4	10♉25
31		10 19	26 08	2 58	1D30	11 09	26 43	22 57	5 35	3 49	29 27	☿ 10/5	0♉24
10	2	20 27	20 34	2℞50	1 49	10 21	27 12	23 31	5 19	3 40	28 55	☿ 19/8	16♍53
20		0♓33	15 02	1 25	2 28	9 35	27 43	24 06	5 03	3 33	28 23	☿ 12/9	3♍14
2	3	10 37	12 45	28♍45	3 24	8 54	28 16	24 40	4 49	3 29	27 52	☿ 9/12	3♑51
12		20 37	14D23	25 10	4 36	8 20	28 51	25 13	4 37	3 26	27 20	☿ 29/12	17♐32
22		0♈34	19 09	21 16	6 02	7 55	29 27	25 44	4 28	3D26	26 48	♀ 20/1	28♒30
1	4	10 28	26 06	17 46	7 40	7 41	0℞02	26 12	4 22	3 28	26 16	♀ 3/3	12♒44
11		20 18	4♓29	15 15	9 29	7D37	0D37	26 38	4 18	3 32	25 45	♂ 4/2	3♎04
21		0♉05	13 50	14 00	11 26	7 44	1♈10	27 00	4D19	3 39	25 13	♂ 26/4	13♍51
1	5	9 49	23 53	14D01	13 29	8 02	1 41	27 17	4 22	3 47	24 41	♃ 27/1	1♊28
11		19 30	4♈24	15 13	15 39	8 30	2 09	27 30	4 29	3 58	24 09	♃ 4/11	15♋50
21		29 08	15 15	17 24	17 52	9 07	2 33	27 39	4 39	4 09	23 37	♄ 10/4	7♌37
31		8♊44	26 23	20 24	20 08	9 53	2 54	27 42	4 52	4 22	23 06	♄ 10/12	28♌14
10	6	18 18	7♉42	24 04	22 26	10 46	3 10	27℞41	5 07	4 36	22 34	♅ 2/6	27♒43
20		27 51	19 10	28 17	24 44	11 45	3 21	27 35	5 24	4 51	22 02	♅ 4/11	23♒47
30		7♋23	0♊46	2♎57	27 01	12 51	3 27	27 25	5 44	5 06	21 30	♆ 15/4	4♌18
10	7	16 56	12 30	8 00	29 17	14 00	3℞28	27 10	6 04	5 20	20 59	♆ 12/11	9♌20
20		26 28	24 19	13 23	1♋29	15 13	3 24	26 52	6 26	5 35	20 27	♇ 18/3	3♋26
30		6♌01	6♋14	19 04	3 38	16 28	3 15	26 31	6 48	5 48	19 55	♇ 7/10	6♋39
9	8	15 35	18 15	24 59	5 41	17 45	3 01	26 09	7 10	6 01	19 23	⚷ 31/3	29♓59
19		25 12	0♌21	1♏08	7 37	19 01	2 43	25 45	7 32	6 12	18 52	⚷ 1/4	0♈02
29		4♍50	12 32	7 30	9 25	20 17	2 21	25 21	7 53	6 21	18 20	⚷ 7/7	3♈29
8	9	14 32	24 48	14 03	11 04	21 32	1 56	24 58	8 13	6 29	17 48	⚷ 11 12	28♓58
18		24 16	7♍08	20 47	12 30	22 43	1 30	24 37	8 30	6 34	17 16		
28		4♎03	19 32	27 41	13 43	23 50	1 03	24 19	8 46	6 38	16 44		
8	10	13 54	1♎59	4♐43	14 42	24 52	0 36	24 05	8 59	6℞39	16 13		
18		23 48	14 28	11 55	15 23	25 47	0 11	23 54	9 09	6 38	15 41		
28		3♏46	27 00	19 14	15 45	26 36	29♓48	23 48	9 16	6 34	15 09		
7	11	13 46	9♏32	26 40	15℞49	27 15	29 29	23D48	9 19	6 28	14 37		
17		23 50	22 06	4♑13	15 32	27 45	29 13	23 52	9℞19	6 21	14 06		
27		3♐56	4♐40	11 51	14 55	28 05	29 03	24 01	9 16	6 11	13 34		
7	12	14 05	17 15	19 34	14 02	28 14	28 58	24 15	9 09	6 01	13 02		
17		24 15	29 50	27 21	12 54	28℞11	28D59	24 34	9 00	5 49	12 30		
27		4♑26	12♑24	5♒11	11 36	27 58	29 05	24 57	8 48	5 37	11 58		

SID M/N 1st JAN 6 h 38 m 21 s — 1919 COMMON — BST 30/3 to 29/9

DAY	JAN	FEB	MAR	APR	MAY	JUN	JUL	AUG	SEP	OCT	NOV	DEC
1	23♐39	11♒33	19♒46	11♈56	20♉33	13♋16	19♌21	6♎10	20♏11	21♐49	6♒41	11♓24
☽ 3	19♑23	9♓41	18♓39	12♉07	20♊25	11♌09	15♍36	0♏26	13♐49	15♑56	2♓36	8♈41
5	16♒08	8♈21	18♈12	11♊32	18♋52	7♍18	10♎24	24♏06	7♑59	11♒14	0♈17	7♉39
7	13♓41	6♉52	17♉25	9♋31	15♌36	2♎02	4♏17	17♐55	3♒18	8♓12	29♈40	7♊52
9	11♈43	4♊55	15♊39	6♌05	10♍55	25♎56	27♏55	12♑28	0♓08	6♈50	29♉57	8♋13
11	10♉01	2♋24	12♋48	1♍30	5♎15	19♏32	21♐53	8♒12	28♓20	6♉29	29♊58	7♌29
13	8♊21	29♋17	9♌02	26♍06	29♎02	13♐20	16♑37	5♓08	27♈14	6♊08	28♋42	4♍57
15	6♋25	25♌26	4♍29	20♎09	22♏39	7♑38	12♒18	2♈56	26♉05	4♋55	25♌48	0♎38
17	3♌46	20♍42	29♍15	13♏50	16♐25	2♒40	8♓54	1♉07	24♊23	2♌31	21♍26	25♎01
19	0♍02	15♎05	23♎21	7♐28	10♑37	28♒36	6♈16	29♉23	22♋00	28♌56	16♎00	18♏44
21	25♍04	8♏50	17♏01	1♑24	5♒37	25♓36	4♉17	27♊32	18♌54	24♍22	9♏55	12♐17
23	19♎08	2♐30	10♐41	26♑12	1♓49	23♈43	2♊48	25♋24	14♍59	19♎00	3♐32	6♑04
25	12♏49	26♐49	4♑55	22♒25	29♓32	22♉48	1♋32	22♌41	10♎10	13♏00	27♐09	0♒20
27	6♐46	22♑26	0♒26	20♓28	28♈44	22♊21	0♌00	19♍01	4♏31	6♐37	21♑04	25♒16
29	1♑39		27♒46	20♈08	28♉49	21♋28	27♌30	14♎11	28♏14	0♑12	15♒40	21♓06
31	27♑54		26♓55		28♊43		23♍38	8♏20		24♑17		18♈04
1	18♐14	25♑39	13♓51	21♈47	13♈52	27♉04	28♋13	28♌59	19♌25	9♎38	27♏35	12♐24
☿ 7	22 32	5♒04	25 23	18℞24	18 58	9♊33	7♌35	27℞45	26 38	19 49	5♐25	4℞41
13	29 05	14 58	6♈25	13 53	25 51	22 42	15 35	23 46	6♍40	29 31	12 13	1D47
19	6♑48	25 21	15 29	11 00	4♉14	5♋36	22 03	18 59	17 48	8♏49	16 57	4 38
25	15 13	6♓18	20 59	11D02	14 00	17 32	26 39	16 34	28 56	17 43	17℞39	10 43
31	24 07		22℞01		25 05		28 53	18D37		26 13		18 22

DATE	☉	♀	♂	♃	♄	⚷	♅	♆	♇	☊	STATIONS
1 1	9♑32	18♑41	9♒07	10♋56	27♌47	29♓10	25♒10	8♌41	5♋31	11♐43	
11	19 43	1♒15	17 00	9℞35	27℞19	29 24	25 38	8℞26	5℞19	11 11	☿ 29/3 22♈11
21	29 54	13 47	24 53	8 20	26 42	29 43	26 09	8 09	5 07	10 39	☿ 22/4 10♈39
31	10♒04	26 18	2♓47	7 16	25 59	0♈06	26 42	7 52	4 57	10 07	☿ 2/8 29♌00
10 2	20 13	8♓48	10 39	6 27	25 11	0 33	27 16	7 36	4 48	9 35	☿ 25/8 16♌33
20	0♓19	21 14	18 29	5 56	24 23	1 03	27 50	7 20	4 41	9 04	☿ 23/11 18♐02
2 3	10 22	3♈38	26 17	5 45	23 36	1 36	28 25	7 05	4 36	8 32	☿ 13/12 1♐46
12	20 22	15 58	4♈02	5D54	22 53	2 10	28 58	6 53	4 33	8 00	♀ 23/8 27♍14
22	0♈19	28 13	11 43	6 21	22 17	2 45	29 30	6 43	4D33	7 28	♀ 4/10 11♍06
1 4	10 13	10♉24	19 19	7 07	21 48	3 20	0♓00	6 36	4 34	6 57	♃ 3/3 5♋45
11	20 04	22 28	26 51	8 09	21 30	3 55	0 27	6 32	4 38	6 25	♃ 5/12 18♌09
21	29 51	4♊26	4♉18	9 25	21 21	4 29	0 50	6D31	4 45	5 53	♄ 24/4 21♌21
1 5	9♉35	16 15	11 41	10 53	21D24	5 00	1 09	6 34	4 53	5 21	♄ 23/12 11♍40
11	19 16	27 56	18 57	12 33	21 37	5 29	1 24	6 40	5 03	4 50	♅ 7/6 1♓42
21	28 54	9♋26	26 09	14 21	22 00	5 55	1 35	6 49	5 15	4 18	♅ 8/11 27♒46
31	8♊30	20 42	3♊16	16 17	22 33	6 17	1 41	7 01	5 28	3 46	♆ 18/4 6♌31
10 6	18 04	1♌42	10 17	18 19	23 14	6 35	1℞41	7 16	5 42	3 14	♆ 15/11 11♌33
20	27 37	12 20	17 14	20 26	24 03	6 48	1 37	7 33	5 56	2 42	♇ 20/3 4♋32
30	7♋10	22 31	24 05	22 36	25 00	6 56	1 29	7 52	6 11	2 11	♇ 9/10 7♋47
10 7	16 42	2♍04	0♋52	24 48	26 02	6 59	1 16	8 12	6 26	1 39	⚷ 11/7 6♈59
20	26 14	10 45	7 35	27 02	27 09	6℞57	1 00	8 34	6 40	1 07	⚷ 15/12 2♈29
30	5♌47	18 13	14 12	29 16	28 20	6 50	0 40	8 56	6 54	0 35	
9 8	15 22	23 53	20 46	1♌28	29 33	6 37	0 18	9 18	7 07	0 04	
19	24 58	26 57	27 16	3 38	0♍49	6 21	29♒54	9 40	7 18	29♏32	
29	4♍36	26℞29	3♌41	5 45	2 05	6 00	29 31	10 01	7 28	29 00	
8 9	14 18	22 19	10 02	7 47	3 20	5 37	29 07	10 21	7 36	28 28	
18	24 02	16 18	16 20	9 43	4 35	5 11	28 45	10 39	7 42	27 56	
28	3♎49	11 57	22 33	11 31	5 47	4 44	28 26	10 55	7 45	27 25	
8 10	13 40	11D21	28 41	13 09	6 55	4 17	28 10	11 09	7 47	26 53	
18	23 34	14 25	4♍45	14 37	7 58	3 51	27 57	11 20	7℞46	26 21	
28	3♏31	20 15	10 44	15 52	8 56	3 27	27 49	11 27	7 43	25 49	
7 11	13 32	27 59	16 37	16 52	9 46	3 06	27 46	11 32	7 37	25 18	
17	23 35	7♎03	22 24	17 36	10 29	2 50	27D49	11℞33	7 30	24 46	
27	3♐42	17 01	28 03	18 02	11 02	2 37	27 56	11 30	7 21	24 14	
7 12	13 50	27 39	3♎34	18℞08	11 25	2 30	28 08	11 24	7 10	23 42	
17	24 00	8♏46	8 54	17 55	11 38	2D29	28 25	11 16	6 58	23 11	
27	4♑11	20 13	14 02	17 23	11℞39	2 33	28 46	11 04	6 46	22 39	

SID M/N 1st JAN 6 h 37 m 23 s   1920 LEAP   BST 28/3 to 25/10

DAY	JAN	FEB	MAR	APR	MAY	JUN	JUL	AUG	SEP	OCT	NOV	DEC
1	2♉04	25♊12	19♋43	11♍19	16♎44	2♐19	4♑53	20♒02	7♈37	14♉31	7♋30	16♌36
☽ 3	1♊06	24♋28	18♌00	7♎34	11♏25	26♐01	28♑45	15♓01	4♉19	12♊36	6♌08	14♍29
5	1♋03	23♌21	15♍35	2♏49	5♐29	19♑44	23♒01	10♈43	1♊45	10♋57	3♍58	10♎58
7	0♌55	20♍59	12♎00	27♏10	29♐11	13♒46	17♓56	7♉21	29♊58	9♌17	0♎53	6♏20
9	29♌33	16♎57	7♏06	20♐56	22♑55	8♓30	13♈50	5♊10	28♋46	7♍19	26♎54	0♐56
11	26♍21	11♏30	1♐12	14♑39	17♒12	4♈27	11♉07	4♋11	27♌40	4♎38	22♏04	25♐02
13	21♎26	5♐14	24♐51	8♒57	12♓34	2♉01	9♊59	3♌55	25♍53	0♏57	16♐30	18♑49
15	15♏24	28♐53	18♑47	4♓26	9♈31	1♊16	10♋04	3♍20	22♎48	26♏09	10♑23	12♒32
17	8♐58	23♑06	13♒37	1♈27	8♉09	1♋37	10♌18	1♎26	18♏15	20♐25	4♒05	6♓31
19	2♑43	18♒18	9♓44	29♈55	8♊01	1♌50	9♍23	27♎46	12♐34	14♑12	28♒08	1♈19
21	27♑04	14♓31	7♈06	29♉14	8♋05	0♍44	6♎36	22♏35	6♑21	8♒04	23♓08	27♈32
23	22♒13	11♈35	5♉21	28♊34	7♌16	27♍46	2♏02	16♐30	0♒13	2♓38	19♈36	25♉35
25	18♓08	9♉12	3♊55	27♋11	4♍58	23♎10	26♏16	10♑12	24♒47	28♓24	17♉48	25♊25
27	14♈48	7♊12	2♋20	24♌45	1♎09	17♏28	19♐58	4♒15	20♓21	25♈35	17♊22	26♋01
29	12♉18	5♋31	0♌23	21♍14	26♎09	11♐13	13♑41	29♒00	17♈00	23♉59	17♋20	25♌59
31	10♊42		27♌51		20♏22		7♒47	24♓33		22♊59		24♍17

DAY	JAN	FEB	MAR	APR	MAY	JUN	JUL	AUG	SEP	OCT	NOV	DEC
1	19♐43	7♒24	27♓48	21♓49	16♈54	17♊26	4♌28	0♌53	0♍28	23♎25	0♐54	18♏25
☿ 7	28 11	17 47	3♈35	22D23	26 33	29 46	8 38	29D15	12 08	2♏21	2℞03	24 35
13	7♑04	28 35	4℞22	25 46	7♉21	10♋47	10 18	1♌29	23 22	10 45	27♏47	2♐30
19	16 17	9♓37	0 36	1♈18	19 17	20 18	9℞09	7 45	3♎58	18 29	20 04	11 08
25	25 48	20 15	25♓20	8 26	2♊09	28 15	5 36	17 14	13 59	25 15	16 06	20 06
31	5♒42		22 03		15 17		1 27	28 31		0♐19		29 17

DATE	☉	♀	♂	♃	♄	⚷	♅	♆	♇	☊	STATIONS
1 1	9♑17	26♏02	16♎31	17♌00	11♍36	2♈37	28♒58	10♌57	6♋40	22♏23	
11	19 28	7♐49	21 15	16℞03	11℞21	2 49	29 25	10℞43	6℞28	21 51	☿ 11/3 4♈41
21	29 40	19 46	25 39	14 52	10 56	3 06	29 55	10 27	6 16	21 19	☿ 3/4 21♓39
31	9♒49	1♑49	29 39	13 35	10 22	3 27	0♓27	10 10	6 06	20 48	☿ 14/7 10♌18
10 2	19 58	13 58	3♏07	12 15	9 41	3 53	1 00	9 53	5 57	20 16	☿ 7/8 29♋15
20	0♓04	26 09	5 56	10 59	8 55	4 22	1 35	9 37	5 49	19 44	☿ 6/11 2♐12
1 3	10 07	8♒23	7 58	9 53	8 08	4 54	2 09	9 22	5 44	19 12	☿ 26/11 16♏05
11	20 08	20 38	9 00	9 01	7 20	5 27	2 43	9 09	5 41	18 40	♂ 15/3 9♏06
21	0♈05	2♓54	8℞54	8 25	6 36	6 02	3 15	8 58	5D40	18 09	♂ 1/6 21♎15
31	9 59	15 10	7 31	8 08	5 57	6 37	3 46	8 51	5 41	17 37	♃ 4/4 8♌06
10 4	19 49	27 27	4 56	8D09	5 26	7 12	4 14	8 46	5 45	17 05	♄ 7/5 4♍49
20	29 37	9♈43	1 28	8 30	5 04	7 46	4 39	8D44	5 51	16 33	♅ 10/6 5♓40
30	9♉21	21 59	27♎44	9 08	4 51	8 18	5 00	8 46	5 59	16 02	♅ 11/11 1♓45
10 5	19 02	4♉15	24 28	10 02	4D49	8 48	5 17	8 52	6 09	15 30	♆ 19/4 8♌44
20	28 40	16 31	22 13	11 10	4 58	9 15	5 29	9 00	6 21	14 58	♆ 16/11 13♌46
30	8♊16	28 47	21 17	12 32	5 16	9 39	5 37	9 11	6 33	14 26	♇ 20/3 5♋40
9 6	17 51	11♊03	21D40	14 04	5 45	9 58	5 40	9 25	6 47	13 55	♇ 9/10 8♋55
19	27 24	23 19	23 15	15 46	6 22	10 13	5℞38	9 42	7 02	13 23	⚷ 14/7 10♈29
29	6♋56	5♋36	25 52	17 36	7 08	10 23	5 32	10 00	7 17	12 51	⚷ 18/12 5♈58
9 7	16 28	17 53	29 20	19 33	8 00	10 28	5 21	10 20	7 32	12 19	
19	26 00	0♌12	3♏29	21 35	8 59	10℞28	5 06	10 41	7 46	11 47	
29	5♌33	12 31	8 14	23 41	10 04	10 23	4 47	11 03	8 00	11 16	
8 8	15 08	24 51	13 28	25 49	11 12	10 12	4 26	11 25	8 13	10 44	
18	24 44	7♍11	19 06	28 00	12 24	9 57	4 03	11 47	8 25	10 12	
28	4♍22	19 32	25 06	0♍11	13 38	9 38	3 39	12 09	8 35	9 40	
7 9	14 03	1♎52	1♐23	2 21	14 53	9 16	3 16	12 29	8 43	9 09	
17	23 48	14 12	7 57	4 29	16 09	8 51	2 53	12 48	8 49	8 37	
27	3♎35	26 32	14 44	6 34	17 23	8 24	2 32	13 05	8 53	8 05	
7 10	13 25	8♏51	21 43	8 35	18 35	7 57	2 15	13 19	8 55	7 33	
17	23 19	21 09	28 53	10 29	19 44	7 30	2 01	13 30	8℞54	7 01	
27	3♏17	3♐26	6♑12	12 17	20 49	7 06	1 51	13 39	8 51	6 30	
6 11	13 17	15 41	13 38	13 55	21 48	6 44	1 46	13 44	8 46	5 58	
16	23 21	27 54	21 11	15 22	22 40	6 25	1D45	13 46	8 39	5 26	
26	3♐27	10♑05	28 48	16 37	23 25	6 11	1 51	13℞44	8 30	4 54	
6 12	13 35	22 11	6♒30	17 37	24 01	6 02	2 01	13 39	8 20	4 23	
16	23 45	4♒13	14 14	18 21	24 27	5 58	2 16	13 31	8 08	3 51	
26	3♑56	16 07	21 59	18 47	24 43	6D00	2 35	13 20	7 56	3 19	

	DAY	JAN	FEB	MAR	APR	MAY	JUN	JUL	AUG	SEP	OCT	NOV	DEC
	1	7♎44	24♏53	3♐17	17♑27	19♒07	3♈36	7♉33	27♊59	21♌42	0♎12	20♏57	25♐28
☽	3	3♏25	19♐00	27♐29	11♒13	13♓17	29♈25	5♊05	27♋58	21♍55	29♎03	17♐26	20♑31
	5	28♏00	12♑43	21♑13	5♓21	8♈23	26♉52	4♋25	28♌32	21♎01	26♏29	12♑39	14♒39
	7	21♐59	6♒27	15♒02	0♈15	4♉45	25♊50	4♌42	28♍17	18♏23	22♐20	6♒50	8♓21
	9	15♑45	0♓28	9♓18	26♈08	2♊26	25♋29	4♍39	26♎19	14♐05	16♑55	0♓34	2♈13
	11	9♒29	24♓55	4♈13	23♉00	1♋00	24♌48	3♎13	22♏36	8♑35	10♒47	24♓30	26♈57
	13	3♓25	19♈58	29♈52	20♊39	29♋50	23♍02	0♏09	17♐35	2♒28	4♓33	19♈12	23♉07
	15	27♓48	15♉59	26♉21	18♋52	28♌19	20♎03	25♏47	11♑46	26♒12	28♓41	15♉04	20♊55
	17	23♈06	13♊21	23♊48	17♌20	26♍08	16♏02	20♐31	5♒35	20♓09	23♈34	12♊10	19♋53
	19	19♉51	12♋14	22♋14	15♍44	23♎10	11♐12	14♑42	29♒20	14♈34	19♉21	10♋11	19♌07
	21	18♊27	12♌13	21♌23	13♎37	19♏23	5♑45	8♒34	23♓13	9♉40	16♊02	8♌34	17♍49
	23	18♋39	12♍12	20♍32	10♏37	14♐46	29♑48	2♓17	17♈31	5♊40	13♋33	6♍53	15♎35
	25	19♌17	10♎59	18♎51	6♐30	9♑21	23♒33	26♓08	12♉37	2♋50	11♌44	4♎55	12♏29
	27	18♍54	7♏58	15♏45	1♑18	3♒20	17♓22	20♈35	8♊59	1♌14	10♍22	2♏29	8♐37
	29	16♎38		11♐11	25♑20	27♒06	11♈49	16♉12	7♋00	0♍36	9♎03	29♏25	4♑02
	31	12♏30		5♑31		21♓13		13♊34	6♌34		7♏13		28♑43
	1	0♑50	22♒21	14♓03	13♓01	29♈26	1♋13	19♋33	18♋59	15♍59	1♏39	6♏44	23♏52
☿	7	10 14	2♓38	8R02	20 05	11♉46	9 21	16R15	27 44	26 29	8 25	0R59	3♐03
	13	19 54	11 34	4 03	28 23	24 45	15 32	12 45	8♌47	6♎17	13 38	1D29	12 21
	19	29 50	17 01	3D48	7♈43	7♊37	19 29	11 09	20 50	15 25	16 14	7 02	21 42
	25	10♒06	17R00	6 45	18 04	19 26	20 51	12D45	2♍48	23 55	14R32	15 00	1♑09
	31	20 36		11 58		29 41		17 49	14 10		8 02		10 45

DATE	☉	♀	♂	♃	♄	⚷	♅	♆	♇	☊	STATIONS
1 1	10♑03	23♒11	26♒39	18♍54	24♍47	6♈04	2♓49	13♌12	7♋49	3♏00	
11	20 15	4♓47	4♓25	18R50	24R45	6 14	3 14	12R58	7R37	2 28	☿ 22/2 17♓45
21	0♒26	16 06	12 09	18 27	24 33	6 30	3 43	12 42	7 25	1 56	☿ 16/3 3♓28
31	10 36	27 03	19 52	17 45	24 10	6 51	4 14	12 25	7 14	1 25	☿ 25/6 20♋51
10 2	20 44	7♈29	27 32	16 48	23 38	7 15	4 47	12 08	7 05	0 53	☿ 19/7 11♋09
20	0♓50	17 11	5♈09	15 39	22 59	7 43	5 22	11 52	6 58	0 21	☿ 20/10 16♏18
2 3	10 53	25 53	12 42	14 23	22 15	8 14	5 56	11 37	6 52	29♎49	☿ 9/11 0♏24
12	20 53	3♉07	20 11	13 04	21 28	8 47	6 30	11 24	6 49	29 18	♀ 1/4 10♉17
22	0♈50	8 13	27 36	11 50	20 41	9 22	7 03	11 13	6D48	28 46	♀ 14/5 23♈52
1 4	10 44	10 16	4♉55	10 45	19 56	9 57	7 34	11 05	6 49	28 14	♃ 4/1 18♍55
11	20 34	8R25	12 10	9 53	19 16	10 32	8 03	10 59	6 53	27 42	♃ 6/5 8♍56
21	0♉21	3 07	19 21	9 16	18 43	11 06	8 29	10 58	6 59	27 11	♄ 4/1 24♍47
1 5	10 05	27♈12	26 26	8 58	18 18	11 39	8 51	10D59	7 07	26 39	♄ 21/5 17♍58
11	19 45	24 02	3♊27	8D58	18 03	12 10	9 10	11 04	7 17	26 07	♅ 14/6 9♓38
21	29 24	24D47	10 23	9 16	17D58	12 38	9 24	11 11	7 28	25 35	♅ 15/11 5♓43
31	9♊00	28 47	17 15	9 51	18 04	13 02	9 33	11 22	7 41	25 03	♆ 22/4 10♌58
10 6	18 34	5♉07	24 02	10 42	18 19	13 23	9 38	11 36	7 55	24 32	♆ 19/11 15♌59
20	28 07	13 02	0♋46	11 48	18 44	13 39	9R37	11 52	8 10	24 00	♇ 21/3 6♋48
30	7♋39	22 01	7 26	13 06	19 19	13 51	9 32	12 10	8 24	23 28	♇ 11/10 10♋04
10 7	17 11	1♊45	14 03	14 35	20 01	13 57	9 23	12 30	8 39	22 56	⚷ 18/7 13♈59
20	26 44	12 03	20 36	16 15	20 51	13R59	9 09	12 51	8 54	22 25	⚷ 21/12 9♈28
30	6♌17	22 45	27 07	18 02	21 48	13 55	8 52	13 13	9 08	21 53	
9 8	15 51	3♋47	3♌35	19 57	22 50	13 46	8 31	13 35	9 21	21 21	
19	25 28	15 04	10 00	21 56	23 57	13 32	8 09	13 57	9 33	20 49	
29	5♍06	26 36	16 24	24 01	25 07	13 14	7 45	14 19	9 43	20 17	
8 9	14 48	8♌18	22 45	26 08	26 20	12 52	7 21	14 39	9 52	19 46	
18	24 32	20 11	29 04	28 17	27 34	12 28	6 58	14 58	9 58	19 14	
28	4♎19	2♍13	5♍21	0♎27	28 49	12 01	6 37	15 15	10 02	18 42	
8 10	14 10	14 23	11 37	2 36	0♎02	11 34	6 18	15 30	10 04	18 10	
18	24 04	26 39	17 51	4 43	1 14	11 07	6 03	15 42	10R03	17 39	
28	4♏02	9♎00	24 02	6 48	2 23	10 42	5 51	15 51	10 01	17 07	
7 11	14 03	21 25	0♎12	8 48	3 28	10 19	5 45	15 56	9 55	16 35	
17	24 07	3♏54	6 19	10 41	4 28	9 59	5D43	15 59	9 48	16 03	
27	4♐13	16 25	12 24	12 27	5 21	9 44	5 46	15R57	9 39	15 32	
7 12	14 21	28 58	18 26	14 04	6 07	9 33	5 55	15 53	9 29	15 00	
17	24 31	11♐32	24 24	15 30	6 44	9 28	6 08	15 45	9 18	14 28	
27	4♑43	24 07	0♏18	16 43	7 12	9D29	6 26	15 35	9 05	13 56	

SID M/N 1st JAN 6 h 39 m 25 s — 1922 COMMON — BST 26/3 to 8/10

DAY	JAN	FEB	MAR	APR	MAY	JUN	JUL	AUG	SEP	OCT	NOV	DEC
1	10♒48	24♓47	3♈37	19♉14	24♊53	16♌36	25♍49	18♏24	8♑02	12♒11	26♓32	28♈30
☽ 3	4♓33	18♈33	27♈33	14♊44	21♋54	14♍50	23♎56	15♐09	2♒58	6♓05	20♈12	22♉56
5	28♓10	13♉04	22♉11	11♋23	19♌46	13♎07	21♏28	11♑00	27♒10	29♓42	14♉18	18♊18
7	22♈16	9♊00	18♊01	9♌20	18♍20	11♏17	18♐22	6♒01	20♓55	23♈23	9♊05	14♋35
9	17♉34	6♋51	15♋30	8♍31	17♎19	8♐58	14♑27	0♓18	14♈30	17♉24	4♋39	11♌35
11	14♊40	6♌30	14♌41	8♎20	16♏09	5♑45	9♒36	24♓04	8♉16	12♊03	1♌04	9♍10
13	13♋35	7♍01	14♍59	7♏50	14♐06	1♒21	3♓51	17♈38	2♊40	7♋39	28♌29	7♎16
15	13♌35	7♎02	15♎11	6♐05	10♑39	25♒48	27♓33	11♉35	28♊14	4♌34	26♍58	5♏50
17	13♍27	5♏35	14♏09	2♑41	5♒46	19♓33	21♈14	6♊31	25♋25	2♍59	26♎19	4♐28
19	12♎11	2♐26	11♐22	27♑44	29♒50	13♈16	15♉38	3♋02	24♌20	2♎41	25♏49	2♑32
21	9♏30	27♐53	6♑57	21♒45	23♓28	7♉39	11♊22	1♌22	24♍28	2♏51	24♐29	29♑23
23	5♐35	22♑22	1♒21	15♓22	17♈23	3♊16	8♋47	1♍05	24♎45	2♐21	21♑34	24♒46
25	0♑47	16♒18	25♒07	9♈09	12♉06	0♋19	7♌39	1♎12	24♏00	0♑15	16♒58	18♓57
27	25♑19	9♓58	18♓43	3♉32	7♊56	28♋32	7♍10	0♏35	21♐35	26♑20	11♓08	12♈36
29	19♒20		12♈32	28♉45	4♋52	27♌14	6♎21	28♏37	17♑31	20♒57	4♈45	6♉24
31	13♓00		6♉50		2♌35		4♏39	25♐12		14♓45		1♊01
1	12♑22	29♒29	16♒13	19♓20	17♉10	29♊57	22♊10	0♌56	28♍14	29♎55	19♎19	4♐48
☿ 7	22 11	1℞01	18 58	29 16	29 27	0℞51	24 09	13 25	6♎55	29℞20	27 08	14 14
13	2♒10	26♒33	24 08	10♈05	10♊13	29♊11	29 06	25 28	14 45	24 14	6♏17	23 40
19	12 09	19 57	0♓54	21 48	18 59	25 58	6♋49	6♍43	21 33	17 20	15 48	3♑09
25	21 29	16 17	8 51	4♉19	25 29	23 03	16 59	17 07	26 53	14D42	25 20	12 43
31	28 40		17 46		29 32		28 52	26 43		18 16		22 16

DATE	☉	♀	♂	♃	♄	⚷	♅	♆	♇	☊	STATIONS
1 1	9♑48	0♑24	3♏13	17♎14	7♎22	9♈31	6♓37	15♌28	8♋59	13♎40	
11	20 00	12 59	8 59	18 04	7 34	9 39	7 01	15℞14	8℞47	13 09	☿ 5/2 1♓14
21	0♒11	25 33	14 38	18 38	7℞35	9 53	7 29	14 59	8 35	12 37	☿ 27/2 16♒02
31	10 21	8♒07	20 09	18 53	7 26	10 12	7 59	14 42	8 24	12 05	☿ 6/6 0♋54
10 2	20 29	20 40	25 31	18℞49	7 06	10 35	8 31	14 25	8 15	11 33	☿ 30/6 22♊08
20	0♓35	3♓12	0♐40	18 26	6 37	11 02	9 05	14 09	8 07	11 01	☿ 3/10 0♏12
2 3	10 38	15 42	5 34	17 46	6 01	11 32	9 39	13 54	8 01	10 30	☿ 24/10 14♎40
12	20 39	28 10	10 10	16 50	5 18	12 04	10 14	13 40	7 58	9 58	♀ 5/11 9♐49
22	0♈36	10♈37	14 23	15 42	4 33	12 39	10 47	13 28	7 56	9 26	♀ 16/12 24♏30
1 4	10 29	23 01	18 06	14 28	3 46	13 14	11 19	13 19	7D57	8 54	♂ 8/5 25♐16
11	20 20	5♉22	21 13	13 11	3 00	13 49	11 49	13 13	8 01	8 23	♂ 17/7 11♐06
21	0♉07	17 41	23 34	11 57	2 19	14 24	12 16	13 11	8 06	7 51	♃ 3/2 18♎54
1 5	9 51	29 57	24 57	10 52	1 44	14 57	12 40	13D11	8 14	7 19	♃ 6/6 8♎58
11	19 31	12♊09	25℞13	9 59	1 17	15 29	13 00	13 15	8 24	6 47	♄ 17/1 7♎36
21	29 10	24 19	24 15	9 21	0 58	15 58	13 16	13 22	8 35	6 16	♄ 4/6 0♎49
31	8♊46	6♋24	22 05	9 01	0 50	16 24	13 27	13 32	8 48	5 44	♅ 19/6 13♓36
10 6	18 20	18 26	19 04	8D59	0D51	16 46	13 34	13 45	9 02	5 12	♅ 20/11 9♓41
20	27 53	0♌23	15 50	9 15	1 03	17 04	13℞36	14 01	9 16	4 40	♆ 24/4 13♌10
30	7♋25	12 15	13 06	9 48	1 24	17 18	13 33	14 18	9 31	4 08	♆ 21/11 18♌11
10 7	16 57	24 01	11 27	10 36	1 55	17 26	13 25	14 38	9 46	3 37	♇ 23/3 7♋56
20	26 30	5♍39	11D10	11 40	2 34	17 30	13 13	14 58	10 01	3 05	♇ 12/10 11♋13
30	6♌03	17 08	12 15	12 56	3 21	17℞28	12 57	15 20	10 15	2 33	⚷ 21/7 17♈30
9 8	15 37	28 27	14 34	14 24	4 15	17 21	12 38	15 42	10 29	2 01	⚷ 25/12 12♈58
19	25 14	9♎31	17 55	16 03	5 15	17 09	12 16	16 04	10 41	1 30	
29	4♍52	20 19	22 08	17 49	6 19	16 53	11 53	16 26	10 51	0 58	
8 9	14 34	0♏43	27 02	19 43	7 28	16 32	11 29	16 47	11 00	0 26	
18	24 18	10 36	2♑30	21 43	8 39	16 09	11 06	17 06	11 07	29♍54	
28	4♎05	19 46	8 26	23 48	9 52	15 43	10 43	17 24	11 11	29 22	
8 10	13 56	27 53	14 42	25 55	11 06	15 16	10 23	17 39	11 13	28 51	
18	23 50	4♐27	21 17	28 05	12 19	14 48	10 06	17 52	11℞13	28 19	
28	3♏48	8 43	28 05	0♏16	13 31	14 22	9 53	18 01	11 11	27 47	
7 11	13 48	9℞43	5♒04	2 26	14 40	13 58	9 45	18 08	11 06	27 15	
17	23 52	6 48	12 11	4 35	15 46	13 37	9 41	18 11	10 59	26 44	
27	3♐58	1 06	19 24	6 40	16 46	13 20	9D42	18℞11	10 50	26 12	
7 12	14 07	26♏04	26 41	8 41	17 41	13 07	9 48	18 07	10 40	25 40	
17	24 17	24D32	4♓01	10 36	18 28	12 60	10 00	18 00	10 28	25 08	
27	4♑28	26 53	11 22	12 23	19 07	12D58	10 16	17 50	10 16	24 37	

SID M/N 1st JAN 6 h 38 m 28 s 1923 COMMON BST 22/4 to 16/9

DAY		JAN	FEB	MAR	APR	MAY	JUN	JUL	AUG	SEP	OCT	NOV	DEC
☽	1	13♊47	2♌22	10♌16	2♎27	11♏05	3♑55	9♒41	25♓50	9♉47	11♊52	27♋22	2♍34
	3	10♋15	1♍05	9♍26	2♏53	11♐10	1♒39	5♓33	19♈55	3♊34	6♋08	23♌13	29♍45
	5	7♌47	0♎13	9♎22	2♐42	9♑46	27♒32	0♈04	13♉39	27♊56	1♌30	20♍46	28♎37
	7	5♍53	29♎02	9♏00	0♑57	6♒27	22♓01	23♈53	7♊41	23♋27	28♌26	20♎08	28♏45
	9	4♎08	27♏08	7♐32	27♑26	1♓28	15♈45	17♉38	2♋35	20♌29	27♍10	20♏40	29♐03
	11	2♏18	24♐22	4♑40	22♒28	25♓28	9♉25	11♊56	28♋42	18♍59	27♎12	21♐00	28♑09
	13	0♐15	20♑43	0♒31	16♓35	19♈03	3♊32	7♋10	26♌05	18♎26	27♏25	19♑53	25♒20
	15	27♐46	16♒11	25♒22	10♈16	12♉45	28♊20	3♌23	24♍22	17♏52	26♐38	16♒48	20♓45
	17	24♑30	10♓49	19♓31	3♉53	6♊51	23♋55	0♍28	23♎03	16♐32	24♑12	12♓03	14♈59
	19	20♒10	4♈47	13♈17	27♉43	1♋32	20♌16	28♍11	21♏37	14♑01	20♒12	6♈17	8♉42
	21	14♓45	28♈24	6♉54	22♊01	26♋56	17♍25	26♎22	19♐44	10♒21	15♓03	0♉04	2♊28
	23	8♈34	22♉11	0♊44	17♋07	23♌17	15♎27	24♏49	17♑08	5♓42	9♈14	23♉47	26♊36
	25	2♉12	16♊44	25♊14	13♌24	20♍51	14♏18	23♐14	13♒40	0♈18	3♉04	17♊42	21♋17
	27	26♉20	12♋39	20♋57	11♍15	19♎45	13♐31	21♑05	9♓15	24♈21	26♉48	11♋57	16♌36
	29	21♊37		18♌18	10♎42	19♏36	12♑15	17♒55	3♈56	18♉06	20♊38	6♌47	12♍42
	31	18♋25		17♍24		19♐24		13♓29	27♈55		14♋55		9♎49
☿	1	23♑51	4♒45	13♒21	2♈23	29♉43	5♊08	17♊38	18♌02	4♎32	3♎01	28♎10	16♐06
	7	2♒59	29℞51	21 10	14 17	6♊19	2℞42	27 14	29 02	9 58	28℞56	8♏05	25 23
	13	10 42	29D39	29 51	26 47	10 03	2D33	8♋42	9♍05	13 15	0D46	17 49	4♑34
	19	14 51	3♒04	9♓18	9♉13	10℞48	5 05	21 18	18 12	13℞23	7 30	27 22	13 30
	25	12℞51	8 44	19 29	20 30	8 55	10 11	4♌01	26 23	9 30	16 38	6♐46	21 35
	31	5 56		0♈29		5 40		16 06	3♎29		26 30		27 29

DATE	☉	♀	♂	♃	♄	⚷	♅	♆	♇	☊	STATIONS
1 1	9♑34	29♏16	15♓02	13♏13	19♎23	12♈59	10♓26	17♌44	10♋10	24♍21	
11	19 45	5♐47	22 23	14 46	19 48	13 06	10 48	17℞31	9℞58	23 49	☿ 20/1 15♒00
21	29 56	14 01	29 42	16 06	20 03	13 18	11 14	17 15	9 46	23 17	☿ 10/2 29♑12
31	10♒06	23 23	6♈59	17 13	20℞07	13 35	11 43	16 59	9 35	22 45	☿ 18/5 10♊53
10 2	20 14	3♑31	14 14	18 04	20 00	13 57	12 15	16 42	9 25	22 14	☿ 10/6 2♊18
20	0♓20	14 11	21 26	18 39	19 43	14 22	12 48	16 26	9 17	21 42	☿ 16/9 13♎48
2 3	10 24	25 15	28 34	18 55	19 17	14 51	13 22	16 10	9 11	21 10	☿ 8/10 28♍48
12	20 24	6♒34	5♉39	18℞53	18 43	15 23	13 57	15 56	9 07	20 38	♃ 6/3 18♏56
22	0♈21	18 05	12 40	18 32	18 02	15 57	14 31	15 44	9 05	20 06	♃ 7/7 9♏04
1 4	10 15	29 45	19 37	17 53	17 17	16 32	15 03	15 34	9D06	19 35	♄ 30/1 20♎07
11	20 06	11♓32	26 30	16 59	16 31	17 07	15 34	15 27	9 09	19 03	♄ 17/6 13♎22
21	29 53	23 23	3♊20	15 53	15 46	17 43	16 02	15 24	9 14	18 31	♅ 23/6 17♓33
1 5	9♉36	5♈18	10 06	14 39	15 04	18 17	16 28	15D23	9 22	17 59	♅ 24/11 13♓38
11	19 17	17 16	16 49	13 23	14 27	18 50	16 49	15 26	9 31	17 28	♆ 27/4 15♌23
21	28 56	29 16	23 28	12 10	13 57	19 20	17 07	15 33	9 43	16 56	♆ 23/11 20♌24
31	8♊32	11♉18	0♋05	11 04	13 36	19 47	17 20	15 42	9 55	16 24	♇ 24/3 9♋05
10 6	18 06	23 22	6 39	10 09	13 24	20 11	17 29	15 54	10 09	15 52	♇ 14/10 12♋23
20	27 39	5♊28	13 10	9 30	13D22	20 31	17 33	16 09	10 23	15 21	⚷ 25/7 21♈03
30	7♋12	17 36	19 39	9 08	13 31	20 47	17℞32	16 26	10 39	14 49	
10 7	16 44	29 47	26 06	9D04	13 48	20 57	17 26	16 45	10 54	14 17	
20	26 16	11♋59	2♌32	9 18	14 16	21 03	17 16	17 06	11 09	13 45	
30	5♌49	24 15	8 57	9 49	14 52	21℞03	17 02	17 27	11 23	13 13	
9 8	15 24	6♌33	15 20	10 37	15 36	20 58	16 44	17 49	11 36	12 42	
19	25 00	18 53	21 42	11 39	16 27	20 48	16 24	18 11	11 49	12 10	
29	4♍38	1♍15	28 04	12 56	17 24	20 33	16 01	18 33	12 00	11 38	
8 9	14 19	13 40	4♍26	14 24	18 27	20 14	15 37	18 54	12 09	11 06	
18	24 04	26 06	10 48	16 03	19 33	19 51	15 13	19 14	12 16	10 35	
28	3♎51	8♎34	17 09	17 51	20 43	19 26	14 50	19 32	12 20	10 03	
8 10	13 42	21 02	23 31	19 46	21 55	18 59	14 29	19 48	12 23	9 31	
18	23 36	3♏31	29 54	21 48	23 08	18 32	14 11	20 01	12℞23	8 59	
28	3♏33	16 00	6♎16	23 55	24 21	18 05	13 56	20 12	12 21	8 27	
7 11	13 34	28 29	12 40	26 05	25 32	17 39	13 45	20 19	12 17	7 56	
17	23 37	10♐59	19 04	28 17	26 42	17 17	13 39	20 23	12 10	7 24	
27	3♐43	23 28	25 28	0♐31	27 48	16 58	13D38	20℞24	12 01	6 52	
7 12	13 52	5♑56	1♏53	2 44	28 49	16 44	13 43	20 21	11 51	6 20	
17	24 02	18 24	8 18	4 56	29 44	16 34	13 52	20 14	11 40	5 49	
27	4♑13	0♒50	14 43	7 04	0♏33	16 31	14 06	20 05	11 28	5 17	

SID M/N 1st JAN 6 h 37 m 31 s 1924 LEAP BST 13/4 to 21/9

	DAY	JAN	FEB	MAR	APR	MAY	JUN	JUL	AUG	SEP	OCT	NOV	DEC
	1	23♎50	17♐24	12♑05	2♓35	7♈23	22♉41	25♊18	10♌30	28♍31	5♏59	29♐36	8♒08
☽	3	22♏45	16♑02	9♒32	28♓02	1♉42	16♊25	19♋17	5♍49	25♎59	4♐52	28♑19	5♓50
	5	22♐22	14♒03	6♓10	22♈48	25♉38	10♋12	13♌43	2♎02	24♏05	3♑31	25♒46	2♈02
	7	21♑42	10♓55	1♈53	16♉59	19♊22	4♌19	8♍52	29♎11	22♐29	1♒32	22♓08	27♈09
	9	19♒47	6♈28	26♈40	10♊46	13♋09	29♌07	5♎03	27♏18	20♑52	28♒49	17♈38	21♉32
	11	16♓10	0♉56	20♉43	4♋32	7♌25	25♍07	2♏35	26♐09	18♒54	25♓22	12♉29	15♊30
	13	11♈04	24♉46	14♊29	28♋50	2♍44	22♎49	1♐31	25♑15	16♓17	21♈09	6♊44	9♋11
	15	5♉03	18♊37	8♋31	24♌18	29♍43	22♏15	1♑22	23♒53	12♈41	16♉07	0♋31	2♌52
	17	28♉47	13♋04	3♌26	21♍27	28♎39	22♐43	1♒06	21♓23	7♉58	10♊19	24♋08	26♌53
	19	22♊49	8♌33	29♌45	20♎25	29♏00	22♑51	29♒42	17♈30	2♊18	4♋02	18♌06	21♍48
	21	17♋33	5♍13	27♍37	20♏30	29♐29	21♒30	26♓38	12♉20	26♊05	27♋49	13♍05	18♎12
	23	13♌08	2♎57	26♎39	20♐30	28♑46	18♓18	22♈01	6♊20	19♋57	22♌19	9♎44	16♏29
	25	9♍33	1♏19	26♏03	19♑19	26♒14	13♈32	16♉18	0♋06	14♌31	18♍13	8♏22	16♐26
	27	6♎44	29♏50	24♐55	16♒34	22♓03	7♉46	10♊05	24♋12	10♍19	15♎53	8♐28	16♑59
	29	4♏36	28♐07	22♑46	12♓27	16♈44	1♊33	3♋53	19♌08	7♎34	15♏04	8♑49	16♒48
	31	3♐03		19♒33		10♉47		28♋08	15♍07		14♐51		14♓58
	1	28♑06	15♑57	23♒04	20♈58	20♉45	16♉29	3♋06	1♍57	26♍30	20♍27	12♏00	27♐19
☿	7	28℞09	21 30	2♓59	2♉23	17℞50	22 13	16 07	10 12	22℞55	29 43	21 30	5♑06
	13	21 58	28 33	13 33	11 46	14 18	29 54	28 42	17 14	17 03	10♎03	0♐46	11 03
	19	15 01	6♒34	24 49	18 10	12 13	9♊25	10♌21	22 44	12 59	20 26	9 52	12℞58
	25	12D50	15 18	6♈44	21 09	12D40	20 36	20 57	26 11	14D09	0♏35	18 46	8 31
	31	15 14		18 57		15 44		0♍28	26℞45		10 24		0 43

DATE	☉	♀	♂	♃	♄	⚷	♅	♆	♇	☊	STATIONS
1 1	9♑19	7♒03	17♏56	8♐07	0♏54	16D31	14♓15	20♌00	11♋22	5♍01	
11	19 30	19 26	24 22	10 08	1 30	16♈35	14 36	19℞47	11℞09	4 29	☿ 4/1 28♑57
21	29 41	1♓46	0♐47	12 02	1 57	16 45	15 00	19 32	10 57	3 57	☿ 24/1 12♑49
31	9♒51	14 01	7 12	13 47	2 14	17 01	15 28	19 16	10 46	3 26	☿ 27/4 21♉23
10 2	20 00	26 11	13 36	15 23	2 20	17 21	15 59	18 59	10 36	2 54	☿ 21/5 12♉04
20	0♓06	8♈12	19 59	16 47	2℞16	17 45	16 32	18 42	10 27	2 22	☿ 29/8 26♍56
1 3	10 09	20 04	26 20	17 57	2 02	18 13	17 05	18 26	10 21	1 50	☿ 21/9 12♍43
11	20 10	1♉45	2♑39	18 52	1 38	18 44	17 40	18 11	10 17	1 19	☿ 18/12 13♑03
21	0♈07	13 10	8 55	19 30	1 06	19 18	18 14	17 59	10 15	0 47	♀ 10/6 17♋34
31	10 01	24 17	15 08	19 51	0 27	19 52	18 47	17 49	10D15	0 15	♀ 23/7 1♋03
10 4	19 51	5♊00	21 15	19℞53	29♎44	20 28	19 19	17 41	10 18	29♌43	♂ 24/7 5♓18
20	29 38	15 12	27 15	19 36	28 59	21 04	19 48	17 37	10 23	29 11	♂ 22/9 25♒20
30	9♉22	24 41	3♒06	19 02	28 13	21 39	20 15	17D36	10 30	28 40	♃ 6/4 19♐55
10 5	19 03	3♋12	8 46	18 11	27 30	22 12	20 38	17 38	10 40	28 08	♃ 7/8 10♐03
20	28 42	10 19	14 11	17 08	26 52	22 44	20 58	17 43	10 51	27 36	♄ 11/2 2♏20
30	8♊18	15 23	19 15	15 56	26 21	23 13	21 13	17 52	11 03	27 04	♄ 29/6 25♎38
9 6	17 52	17 33	23 54	14 39	25 57	23 39	21 24	18 03	11 17	26 33	♅ 26/6 21♓31
19	27 25	15℞58	27 59	13 25	25 43	24 00	21 30	18 17	11 31	26 01	♅ 27/11 17♓36
29	6♋58	10 54	1♓21	12 16	25 38	24 18	21℞31	18 34	11 46	25 29	♆ 28/4 17♌36
9 7	16 30	4 55	3 47	11 19	25D43	24 30	21 27	18 53	12 02	24 57	♆ 25/11 22♌36
19	26 02	1 24	5 07	10 37	25 57	24 38	21 19	19 13	12 17	24 25	♇ 24/3 10♋15
29	5♌35	1D42	5℞10	10 11	26 22	24 40	21 06	19 34	12 31	23 54	♇ 14/10 13♋34
8 8	15 10	5 21	3 57	10D03	26 55	24℞38	20 50	19 56	12 45	23 22	⚷ 29/12 16♈30
18	24 46	11 27	1 44	10 14	27 36	24 29	20 30	20 18	12 57	22 50	⚷ 29/7 24♈40
28	4♍24	19 14	29♒07	10 43	28 25	24 16	20 09	20 40	13 09	22 18	
7 9	14 05	28 12	26 50	11 29	29 20	23 59	19 45	21 02	13 18	21 47	
17	23 49	8♌00	25 31	12 31	0♏20	23 37	19 21	21 22	13 25	21 15	
27	3♎37	18 26	25D28	13 47	1 25	23 13	18 58	21 40	13 30	20 43	
7 10	13 27	29 21	26 44	15 16	2 33	22 46	18 36	21 57	13 33	20 11	
17	23 21	10♍38	29 09	16 57	3 44	22 19	18 16	22 11	13℞34	19 40	
27	3♏18	22 13	2♓32	18 46	4 56	21 51	17 59	22 22	13 32	19 08	
6 11	13 19	4♎02	6 40	20 45	6 09	21 25	17 47	22 30	13 28	18 36	
16	23 23	16 03	11 25	22 49	7 20	21 01	17 39	22 35	13 21	18 04	
26	3♐29	28 12	16 36	24 59	8 30	20 40	17 36	22℞36	13 13	17 32	
6 12	13 37	10♏27	22 09	27 13	9 36	20 24	17D38	22 34	13 03	17 01	
16	23 47	22 48	27 57	29 30	10 37	20 13	17 45	22 28	12 52	16 29	
26	3♑58	5♐11	3♈57	1♑47	11 34	20 07	17 57	22 20	12 40	15 57	

SID M/N 1st JAN 6 h 40 m 30 s 1925 COMMON BST 19/4 to 4/10

DAY	JAN	FEB	MAR	APR	MAY	JUN	JUL	AUG	SEP	OCT	NOV	DEC
1	28♓23	15♉04	23♉08	7♋03	8♌35	23♍21	28♎00	19♐07	12♒35	20♓57	11♉31	15♊55
☽ 3	24♈02	9♊12	17♊20	0♌44	2♍45	19♎30	25♏50	18♑51	12♓20	19♈25	7♊38	10♋29
5	18♉33	2♋52	11♋01	24♌53	28♍07	17♏30	25♐21	19♒08	11♈17	16♉39	2♋29	4♌19
7	12♊28	26♋36	4♌49	20♍08	25♎07	17♐00	25♑41	18♓47	8♉41	12♊21	26♋25	27♌55
9	6♋08	20♌46	29♌16	16♎45	23♏39	17♑03	25♒40	16♈56	4♊21	6♋44	20♌02	21♍52
11	29♋53	15♍36	24♍43	14♏34	22♐57	16♒30	24♓18	13♉18	28♊43	0♌25	14♍02	16♎53
13	23♌57	11♎17	21♎11	13♐02	22♑08	14♓43	21♈18	8♊11	22♋23	24♌08	9♎06	13♏28
15	18♍37	7♏55	18♏31	11♑32	20♒31	11♈34	16♉50	2♋09	16♌02	18♍30	5♏35	11♐43
17	14♎18	5♐34	16♐25	9♒42	17♓58	7♉15	11♊18	25♋44	10♍10	13♎57	3♐24	11♑06
19	11♏21	4♑12	14♑41	7♓26	14♈31	2♊04	5♋09	19♌25	5♎06	10♏31	2♑01	10♒41
21	9♐58	3♒27	13♒07	4♈38	10♉16	26♊13	28♋45	13♍31	0♏55	7♐57	0♒43	9♓37
23	9♑48	2♓39	11♓25	1♉05	5♊13	19♋56	22♌24	8♎17	27♏34	5♑52	29♒03	7♈27
25	9♒54	0♈57	9♈05	26♉36	29♊26	13♌30	16♍26	3♏56	25♐00	3♒59	26♓50	4♉08
27	9♓08	27♈48	5♉40	21♊08	23♋08	7♍20	11♎13	0♐40	23♑09	2♓12	24♈00	29♉50
29	6♈44		0♊58	14♋57	16♌45	1♎58	7♏13	28♐37	21♒57	0♈21	20♉25	24♊41
31	2♉39		25♊11		10♍52		4♐45	27♑44		28♈01		18♋52
1	29♐39	20♑47	5♓58	29♈29	22♈04	20♉01	21♋04	5♍04	26♌56	2♎17	23♏01	27♐09
☿ 7	26D46	29 30	17 15	2♉33	22D56	0♊42	2♌15	8 35	26D57	12 57	1♐45	24R52
13	29 02	8♒44	28 59	1R37	26 25	12 44	12 14	9R22	2♍00	23 11	10 06	17 19
19	4♑24	18 28	10♈37	27♈57	2♉02	25 43	20 58	6 57	10 47	2♏59	17 44	11 31
25	11 26	28 46	20 59	24 01	9 25	8♋46	28 24	2 00	21 21	12 25	23 57	11D45
31	19 24		28 34		18 23		4♍16	27♌24		21 32		16 18

DATE	☉	♀	♂	♃	♄	⚷	♅	♆	♇	☊	STATIONS
1 1	10♑05	12♐39	7♈38	3♑10	12♏04	20♈06	18♓07	22♌14	12♋32	15♌38	
11	20 17	25 06	13 51	5 26	12 49	20D09	18 26	22R01	12R20	15 06	☿ 7/1 26♐46
21	0♒28	7♑35	20 10	7 41	13 26	20 18	18 50	21 46	12 08	14 35	☿ 8/4 2♉40
31	10 37	20 04	26 32	9 51	13 54	20 32	19 17	21 30	11 56	14 03	☿ 2/5 22♈01
10 2	20 46	2♒33	2♉57	11 56	14 11	20 51	19 47	21 13	11 46	13 31	☿ 12/8 9♍28
20	0♓51	15 02	9 23	13 55	14 19	21 14	20 19	20 57	11 38	12 59	☿ 4/9 26♌18
2 3	10 55	27 30	15 49	15 45	14R16	21 42	20 52	20 41	11 31	12 27	☿ 2/12 27♐13
12	20 55	9♓58	22 16	17 25	14 03	22 12	21 26	20 26	11 27	11 56	☿ 22/12 10♐55
22	0♈52	22 24	28 43	18 54	13 40	22 45	22 01	20 13	11 25	11 24	♃ 11/5 22♑32
1 4	10 46	4♈49	5♊08	20 10	13 10	23 20	22 34	20 02	11D25	10 52	♃ 9/9 12♑41
11	20 36	17 13	11 33	21 11	12 32	23 56	23 06	19 54	11 28	10 20	♄ 22/2 14♏19
21	0♉23	29 36	17 57	21 56	11 50	24 32	23 36	19 49	11 33	9 49	♄ 12/7 7♏38
1 5	10 07	11♉57	24 19	22 23	11 05	25 08	24 04	19D48	11 40	9 17	♅ 1/7 25♓29
11	19 47	24 16	0♋41	22R32	10 20	25 42	24 29	19 49	11 49	8 45	♅ 1/12 21♓34
21	29 26	6♊35	7 02	22 21	9 37	26 15	24 49	19 54	12 00	8 13	♆ 1/5 19♌48
31	9♊02	18 52	13 21	21 53	8 58	26 45	25 06	20 03	12 13	7 41	♆ 27/11 24♌48
10 6	18 36	1♋08	19 41	21 07	8 26	27 12	25 18	20 14	12 27	7 10	♇ 26/3 11♋25
20	28 09	13 23	25 59	20 07	8 01	27 35	25 26	20 27	12 41	6 38	♇ 16/10 14♋45
30	7♋41	25 37	2♌18	18 57	7 45	27 54	25 29	20 44	12 56	6 06	⚷ 1/1 20♈06
10 7	17 13	7♌50	8 36	17 41	7 38	28 09	25R27	21 02	13 12	5 34	⚷ 2/8 28♈22
20	26 46	20 01	14 54	16 24	7D41	28 18	25 20	21 22	13 27	5 03	
30	6♌19	2♍10	21 13	15 13	7 54	28 22	25 09	21 43	13 41	4 31	
9 8	15 53	14 18	27 33	14 11	8 17	28R21	24 54	22 05	13 55	3 59	
19	25 30	26 23	3♍54	13 24	8 48	28 14	24 35	22 27	14 08	3 27	
29	5♍08	8♎25	10 15	12 53	9 27	28 03	24 14	22 49	14 19	2 56	
8 9	14 50	20 23	16 39	12 41	10 15	27 46	23 51	23 11	14 29	2 24	
18	24 34	2♏17	23 03	12D48	11 08	27 26	23 27	23 31	14 36	1 52	
28	4♎21	14 07	29 30	13 15	12 07	27 02	23 03	23 50	14 41	1 20	
8 10	14 12	25 50	5♎59	13 59	13 11	26 36	22 40	24 06	14 45	0 48	
18	24 06	7♐26	12 30	15 00	14 19	26 08	22 20	24 21	14R45	0 17	
28	4♏04	18 52	19 03	16 16	15 29	25 40	22 02	24 32	14 43	29♋45	
7 11	14 05	0♑05	25 39	17 46	16 40	25 13	21 48	24 41	14 39	29 13	
17	24 08	10 59	2♏17	19 28	17 52	24 48	21 39	24 46	14 33	28 41	
27	4♐15	21 28	8 58	21 20	19 03	24 26	21 34	24 48	14 25	28 10	
7 12	14 23	1♒19	15 42	23 21	20 12	24 08	21D34	24R46	14 15	27 38	
17	24 33	10 15	22 29	25 29	21 18	23 56	21 40	24 41	14 04	27 06	
27	4♑44	17 51	29 19	27 42	22 20	23 48	21 51	24 33	13 51	26 34	

SID M/N 1st JAN 6 h 39 m 33 s — 1926 COMMON — BST 18/4 to 3/10

	DAY	JAN	FEB	MAR	APR	MAY	JUN	JUL	AUG	SEP	OCT	NOV	DEC
	1	0♌46	14♍55	23♍55	10♏28	16♐38	8♒42	17♓57	10♉24	29♊04	2♌25	16♍25	18♎26
☽	3	24♌23	9♎00	18♎20	6♐30	14♑02	7♓10	16♈14	6♊48	23♋30	26♌09	10♎20	13♏11
	5	18♍05	3♏52	13♏28	3♑22	11♒59	5♈24	13♉31	2♋00	17♌20	19♍50	4♏50	8♐57
	7	12♎25	29♏58	9♐33	1♒10	10♓23	3♉10	9♊45	26♋23	11♍00	13♎47	0♐05	5♑43
	9	7♏59	27♐43	6♑54	29♒57	8♈59	0♊10	5♋03	20♌17	4♎47	8♏12	26♐03	3♒16
	11	5♐14	27♑06	5♒42	29♓21	7♉16	26♊10	29♋34	13♍59	28♎51	3♐13	22♑47	1♓20
	13	4♑13	27♒30	5♓37	28♈30	4♊36	21♋08	23♌31	7♎43	23♏31	29♐01	20♒23	29♓40
	15	4♒21	27♓40	5♈40	26♉26	0♋35	15♌16	17♍12	1♏53	19♐08	25♑56	18♓51	28♈00
	17	4♓28	26♈27	4♉39	22♊41	25♋18	8♍58	11♎03	26♏58	16♑12	24♒14	17♈55	25♉59
	19	3♈31	23♉21	1♊48	17♋27	19♌12	2♎51	5♏40	23♐27	14♒58	23♓48	16♉54	23♊11
	21	0♉58	18♊36	27♊11	11♌18	12♍55	27♎32	1♐34	21♑43	15♓08	23♈47	14♊55	19♋18
	23	26♉53	12♋44	21♋19	4♍57	7♎06	23♏30	29♐08	21♒35	15♈35	23♉02	11♋29	14♌19
	25	21♊40	6♌23	14♌56	29♍03	2♏19	20♐58	28♑16	22♓07	14♉58	20♊36	6♌35	8♍27
	27	15♋43	0♍00	8♍37	23♎59	28♏44	19♑39	28♒16	21♈56	12♊26	16♋23	0♍42	2♎13
	29	9♌25		2♎50	19♏53	26♐16	18♒54	28♓02	20♉07	8♋04	10♌49	24♍26	26♎12
	31	3♍03		27♎44		24♑29		26♈39	16♊27		4♍35		21♏01
	1	17♐19	0♒57	20♓50	9♈09	13♈09	5♊13	2♌34	19♌04	21♌39	15♎47	0♐39	27♏03
☿	7	24 20	10 50	1♈29	4℞39	20 32	18 22	10 10	14℞45	2♍08	25 28	6 57	25D23
	13	2♑20	21 12	9 53	2 36	29 18	1♋13	16 05	10 37	13 31	4♏42	10 55	29 11
	19	10 56	2♓03	14 19	3D39	9♉20	13 01	19 56	9D29	24 47	13 30	10℞29	5♐52
	25	19 57	13 18	14℞00	7 22	20 37	23 30	21℞14	12 43	5♎34	21 49	4 19	13 51
	31	29 21		9 59		3♊03		19 36	20 06		29 28		22 27

DATE	☉	♀	♂	♃	♄	⚷	♅	♆	♇	☊	STATIONS
1 1	9♑50	20♒56	2♐45	28♑51	22♏49	23♈46	21♓58	24♌28	13♋45	26♋18	
11	20 02	25 08	9 39	1♒10	23 42	23D47	22 15	24℞16	13℞33	25 47	☿ 22/3 14♈45
21	0♒13	25℞52	16 35	3 31	24 28	23 54	22 37	24 02	13 20	25 15	☿ 14/4 2♈34
31	10 23	22 34	23 35	5 53	25 06	24 06	23 03	23 46	13 09	24 43	☿ 25/7 21♌15
10 2	20 31	16 39	0♑37	8 15	25 35	24 23	23 32	23 30	12 58	24 11	☿ 18/8 9♌22
20	0♓37	11 42	7 42	10 34	25 55	24 45	24 03	23 13	12 50	23 40	☿ 16/11 11♐24
2 3	10 40	10D24	14 49	12 50	26 04	25 12	24 36	22 56	12 43	23 08	☿ 5/12 25♏11
12	20 40	12 55	21 58	15 01	26℞03	25 41	25 10	22 41	12 38	22 36	♀ 18/1 26♒04
22	0♈38	18 18	29 09	17 06	25 52	26 14	25 44	22 28	12 36	22 04	♀ 28/2 10♒20
1 4	10 31	25 40	6♒22	19 04	25 32	26 49	26 18	22 17	12D36	21 32	♂ 29/9 19♉28
11	20 22	4♓20	13 36	20 53	25 03	27 25	26 51	22 08	12 38	21 01	♂ 7/12 4♉32
21	0♉09	13 54	20 50	22 31	24 27	28 01	27 22	22 02	12 43	20 29	♃ 16/6 27♒11
1 5	9 52	24 04	28 04	23 57	23 46	28 38	27 51	22 00	12 50	19 57	♃ 14/10 17♒19
11	19 33	4♈42	5♓16	25 09	23 02	29 13	28 16	22D01	12 59	19 25	♄ 6/3 26♏05
21	29 12	15 38	12 26	26 05	22 17	29 47	28 39	22 05	13 10	18 54	♄ 24/7 19♏25
31	8♊48	26 49	19 32	26 45	21 34	0♉19	28 57	22 12	13 22	18 22	♅ 5/7 29♓27
10 6	18 22	8♉10	26 32	27 07	20 54	0 48	29 12	22 23	13 36	17 50	♅ 6/12 25♓32
20	27 55	19 41	3♈24	27℞09	20 20	1 13	29 21	22 36	13 50	17 18	♆ 3/5 22♌00
30	7♋27	1♊19	10 07	26 53	19 54	1 34	29 26	22 51	14 05	16 46	♆ 30/11 27♌00
10 7	16 59	13 04	16 36	26 18	19 35	1 51	29℞26	23 09	14 21	16 15	♇ 27/3 12♋35
20	26 32	24 55	22 49	25 26	19 26	2 03	29 21	23 29	14 36	15 43	♇ 17/10 15♋57
30	6♌05	6♋51	28 40	24 21	19D27	2 09	29 12	23 49	14 51	15 11	⚷ 4/1 23♈46
9 8	15 39	18 53	4♉05	23 07	19 37	2℞10	28 59	24 11	15 05	14 39	⚷ 6/8 2♉10
19	25 16	1♌00	8 57	21 48	19 57	2 06	28 41	24 33	15 18	14 08	
29	4♍54	13 11	13 06	20 32	20 26	1 56	28 21	24 56	15 29	13 36	
8 9	14 35	25 28	16 22	19 23	21 03	1 42	27 59	25 17	15 39	13 04	
18	24 20	7♍48	18 34	18 26	21 48	1 23	27 35	25 38	15 47	12 32	
28	4♎07	20 12	19 27	17 45	22 40	0 60	27 11	25 57	15 53	12 01	
8 10	13 58	2♎40	18℞53	17 23	23 38	0 34	26 48	26 14	15 56	11 29	
18	23 52	15 09	16 53	17D20	24 41	0 06	26 26	26 29	15℞57	10 57	
28	3♏49	27 41	13 48	17 38	25 47	29♈38	26 07	26 42	15 56	10 25	
7 11	13 50	10♏13	10 19	18 15	26 56	29 10	25 52	26 51	15 52	9 53	
17	23 54	22 47	7 15	19 10	28 07	28 44	25 40	26 57	15 46	9 22	
27	4♐00	5♐21	5 13	20 22	29 19	28 20	25 33	27 00	15 38	8 50	
7 12	14 08	17 56	4 32	21 48	0♐29	28 01	25D32	26℞59	15 28	8 18	
17	24 18	0♑30	5D10	23 28	1 38	27 46	25 35	26 55	15 17	7 46	
27	4♑30	13 04	6 56	25 19	2 45	27 36	25 44	26 48	15 05	7 15	

SID M/N 1st JAN 6 h 38 m 35 s — 1927 COMMON — BST 10/4 to 2/10

	DAY	JAN	FEB	MAR	APR	MAY	JUN	JUL	AUG	SEP	OCT	NOV	DEC
	1	3♐53	22♑35	0♒27	23♓18	2♉13	24♊18	29♋33	15♍32	29♎42	2♐02	18♑00	24♒02
☽	3	0♑39	21♒51	29♒57	23♈55	1♊54	21♋29	25♌06	9♎35	23♏25	26♐17	14♒04	21♓32
	5	28♑42	21♓44	0♈26	23♉44	0♋05	17♌10	19♍37	3♏20	17♐43	21♑40	11♓50	20♈19
	7	27♒32	21♈08	0♉32	21♊47	26♋28	11♍40	13♎30	27♏20	13♑15	18♒48	11♈17	19♉58
	9	26♓25	19♉18	29♉08	17♋59	21♌24	5♎32	7♏20	22♐16	10♒34	17♓54	11♉40	19♊35
	11	24♈48	16♊04	25♊57	12♌47	15♍26	29♎22	1♐45	18♑39	9♓43	18♈19	11♊44	18♋13
	13	22♉23	11♋43	21♋19	6♍48	9♎10	23♏40	27♐13	16♒40	9♈54	18♉45	10♋23	15♌17
	15	19♊07	6♌34	15♌47	0♎33	3♏04	18♐47	23♑58	15♓52	9♉51	17♊54	7♌12	10♍44
	17	15♋00	0♍52	9♍46	24♎21	27♏27	14♑52	21♒52	15♈20	8♊31	15♋16	2♍27	5♎02
	19	10♌05	24♍47	3♎33	18♏25	22♐28	11♒53	20♓27	14♉10	5♋38	11♌03	26♍41	28♎45
	21	4♍26	18♎31	27♎20	12♐56	18♑16	9♓40	19♈06	11♊55	1♌28	5♍44	20♎25	22♏30
	23	28♍17	12♏25	21♏20	8♑13	15♒02	8♈01	17♉22	8♋37	26♌24	29♍46	14♏07	16♐45
	25	22♎03	6♐58	15♐55	4♒39	12♓53	6♉37	15♊02	4♌26	20♍44	23♎31	8♐05	11♑46
	27	16♏17	2♑48	11♑35	2♓36	11♈45	5♊02	11♋57	29♌31	14♎39	17♏13	2♑34	7♒42
	29	11♐35		8♒56	2♈02	11♉07	2♋49	8♌03	23♍58	8♏19	11♐05	27♑47	4♓31
	31	8♑29		8♓09		10♊10		3♍15	17♎52		5♑28		2♈09
	1	23♐56	13♒36	26♓40	14♓59	20♈13	23♊17	1♌05	21♋51	6♍00	26♎40	25♏19	18♏26
☿	7	2♑55	24 16	26R58	18 47	1♉00	4♋18	2R12	24 37	17 25	4♏59	20R58	26 33
	13	12 11	5♓05	22 37	24 37	12 52	13 44	0 36	1♌08	28 10	12 35	13 21	5♐21
	19	21 44	15 20	17 08	1♈57	25 38	21 29	26♋57	10 44	8♎16	19 08	9 32	14 26
	25	1♒36	23 28	14 08	10 32	8♊45	27 22	23 14	22 09	17 45	23 55	12D02	23 40
	31	11 51		14D36		21 18		21D46	4♍02		25R31		3♑03

DATE	☉	♀	♂	♃	♄	⚷	♅	♆	♇	☊	STATIONS
1 1	9♑35	19♑21	8♉12	26♒18	3♐16	27♈33	25♓50	26♌43	14♋59	6♋59	
11	19 47	1♒55	11 18	28 23	4 16	27D32	26 05	26R31	14R46	6 27	☿ 4/3 27♓31
21	29 58	14 27	15 04	0♓34	5 10	27 36	26 26	26 18	14 34	5 55	☿ 27/3 13♓55
31	10♒08	26 58	19 20	2 51	5 57	27 46	26 50	26 02	14 22	5 23	☿ 6/7 2♌13
10 2	20 16	9♓27	24 00	5 12	6 36	28 02	27 17	25 46	14 11	4 52	☿ 31/7 21♋46
20	0♓22	21 54	28 58	7 36	7 06	28 23	27 47	25 29	14 02	4 20	☿ 30/10 25♏33
2 3	10 26	4♈17	4♊11	10 01	7 27	28 48	28 20	25 12	13 55	3 48	☿ 19/11 9♏31
12	20 26	16 36	9 34	12 25	7 38	29 17	28 53	24 57	13 50	3 16	♀ 20/8 24♍59
22	0♈23	28 51	15 06	14 48	7R39	29 49	29 28	24 43	13 47	2 45	♀ 2/10 8♍51
1 4	10 17	11♉00	20 45	17 09	7 30	0♉23	0♈02	24 31	13D47	2 13	♃ 24/7 3♈32
11	20 07	23 04	26 30	19 26	7 12	0 59	0 35	24 22	13 49	1 41	♃ 20/11 23♓37
21	29 54	5♊00	2♋19	21 38	6 45	1 36	1 07	24 15	13 54	1 09	♄ 18/3 7♐40
1 5	9♉38	16 48	8 11	23 43	6 11	2 13	1 37	24 12	14 00	0 37	♄ 6/8 1♐02
11	19 19	28 27	14 07	25 40	5 31	2 50	2 04	24D12	14 09	0 06	♅ 9/7 3♈25
21	28 58	9♋54	20 05	27 28	4 48	3 25	2 28	24 16	14 20	29♊34	♅ 10/12 29♓30
31	8♊34	21 07	26 06	29 05	4 03	3 58	2 48	24 22	14 32	29 02	♆ 6/5 24♌12
10 6	18 08	2♌02	2♌09	0♈29	3 20	4 29	3 04	24 32	14 45	28 30	♆ 2/12 29♌12
20	27 41	12 35	8 14	1 40	2 39	4 56	3 16	24 44	15 00	27 59	♇ 29/3 13♋47
30	7♋14	22 38	14 21	2 34	2 04	5 20	3 23	24 59	15 15	27 27	♇ 19/10 17♋10
10 7	16 46	2♍00	20 30	3 11	1 36	5 39	3R25	25 16	15 31	26 55	⚷ 8/1 27♈31
20	26 18	10 26	26 42	3 30	1 15	5 53	3 22	25 36	15 46	26 23	⚷ 11/8 6♉06
30	5♌51	17 32	2♍56	3R29	1 04	6 02	3 15	25 56	16 01	25 51	
9 8	15 25	22 39	9 13	3 08	1D02	6 06	3 03	26 18	16 15	25 20	
19	25 02	24 57	15 32	2 29	1 10	6R04	2 48	26 40	16 28	24 48	
29	4♍40	23R34	21 54	1 33	1 28	5 57	2 29	27 02	16 40	24 16	
8 9	14 21	18 41	28 20	0 24	1 55	5 44	2 07	27 24	16 50	23 44	
18	24 05	12 44	4♎49	29♓07	2 30	5 27	1 44	27 45	16 59	23 13	
28	3♎53	9 11	11 21	27 47	3 13	5 05	1 20	28 04	17 05	22 41	
8 10	13 43	9D31	17 57	26 30	4 04	4 40	0 56	28 22	17 09	22 09	
18	23 37	13 19	24 37	25 23	5 00	4 13	0 33	28 38	17 10	21 37	
28	3♏35	19 39	1♏21	24 29	6 02	3 44	0 13	28 51	17R09	21 06	
7 11	13 35	27 44	8 09	23 54	7 07	3 15	29♓56	29 01	17 05	20 34	
17	23 39	7♎01	15 01	23 38	8 16	2 48	29 43	29 08	17 00	20 02	
27	3♐45	17 10	21 58	23D42	9 26	2 23	29 34	29 11	16 52	19 30	
7 12	13 54	27 55	28 59	24 08	10 37	2 01	29 30	29R11	16 42	18 58	
17	24 04	9♏07	6♐04	24 52	11 48	1 44	29D31	29 08	16 31	18 27	
27	4♑15	20 38	13 14	25 55	12 57	1 32	29 38	29 01	16 19	17 55	

SID M/N 1st JAN 6 h 37 m 38 s 1928 LEAP BST 22/4 to 7/10

	DAY	JAN	FEB	MAR	APR	MAY	JUN	JUL	AUG	SEP	OCT	NOV	DEC
	1	16♈13	9♊28	3♋56	23♌42	28♍10	12♏58	15♐14	0♒46	19♓48	27♈33	21♊01	29♋07
☽	3	14♉47	7♋17	0♌45	18♍50	22♎15	6♐36	9♑28	26♒54	18♈03	26♉52	19♋57	27♌02
	5	13♊36	4♌34	26♌52	13♎17	15♏58	0♑30	4♒28	23♓57	16♉33	25♊40	17♌28	23♍14
	7	12♋07	1♍00	22♍12	7♏12	9♐35	24♑58	0♓20	21♈39	14♊53	23♋34	13♍39	18♎03
	9	9♌42	26♍22	16♎45	0♐49	3♑26	20♒17	27♓07	19♉45	12♋51	20♌32	8♎45	12♏02
	11	5♍57	20♎43	10♏37	24♐32	27♑56	16♓44	24♈49	18♊07	10♌21	16♍37	3♏04	5♐39
	13	0♎52	14♏27	4♐14	18♑54	23♒35	14♈31	23♉22	16♋31	7♍10	11♎52	26♏53	29♐16
	15	24♎51	8♐11	28♐11	14♒35	20♓49	13♉36	22♊29	14♌32	3♎04	6♏18	20♐27	23♑09
	17	18♏31	2♑39	23♑13	12♓05	19♈46	13♊28	21♋34	11♍38	27♎56	0♐08	14♑07	17♒34
	19	12♐33	28♑27	19♒54	11♈22	19♉54	13♋09	19♌49	7♎27	21♏56	23♐41	8♒20	12♓52
	21	7♑29	25♒50	18♓24	11♉39	20♊08	11♌40	16♍38	2♏02	15♐32	17♑30	3♓36	9♈25
	23	3♒38	24♓28	18♈05	11♊41	19♋19	8♍30	11♎55	25♏50	9♑23	12♒14	0♈26	7♉31
	25	0♓55	23♈32	17♉52	10♋28	16♌49	3♎45	6♏04	19♐30	4♒13	8♓29	29♈04	7♊05
	27	28♓57	22♉16	16♊46	7♌39	12♍40	27♎53	29♏43	13♑46	0♓33	6♈32	29♉07	7♋25
	29	27♈13	20♊14	14♋24	3♍26	7♎17	21♏31	23♐33	9♒11	28♓29	6♉03	29♊32	7♌17
	31	25♉26		10♌51		1♏09		18♑06	5♓58		6♊08		5♍37
	1	4♑37	26♒13	29♒21	15♓05	7♉27	3♋35	6♋39	22♋54	22♍21	3♏16	23♎59	28♏55
☿	7	14 13	4♓56	26R13	23 38	20 23	9 01	3R52	4♌18	2♎06	7 52	25D41	8♐18
	13	24 03	10 12	26D58	3♈10	3♊07	12 00	3D29	16 33	11 08	9R34	2♏01	17 41
	19	4♒09	9R48	0♓43	13 39	14 41	12R18	6 16	28 38	19 27	6 47	10 25	27 08
	25	14 27	4 23	6 30	25 05	24 33	10 08	12 16	10♍02	26 55	29♎53	19 34	6♑41
	31	24 36		13 45		2♋28		21 11	20 40		24 20		16 23

DATE	☉	♀	♂	♃	♄	⚷	♅	♆	♇	☊	STATIONS
1 1	9♑20	26♏29	16♐50	26♓32	13♐31	1♉28	29♓43	28♌57	16♋13	17♊39	
11	19 32	8♐19	24 06	27 59	14 35	1 24	29 57	28R46	16R00	17 07	☿ 16/2 10♓47
21	29 43	20 18	1♑25	29 38	15 35	1D26	0♈15	28 33	15 48	16 35	☿ 9/3 26♒04
31	9♒53	2♑23	8 49	1♈29	16 30	1 34	0 37	28 18	15 36	16 04	☿ 17/6 12♋30
10 2	20 01	14 32	16 16	3 29	17 18	1 48	1 04	28 02	15 25	15 32	☿ 11/7 3♋16
20	0♓07	26 44	23 46	5 38	17 58	2 07	1 33	27 45	15 16	15 00	☿ 13/10 9♏34
1 3	10 11	8♒59	1♒19	7 52	18 30	2 31	2 04	27 28	15 08	14 28	☿ 2/11 23♎49
11	20 11	21 15	8 55	10 11	18 52	2 59	2 37	27 12	15 03	13 57	♂ 12/11 9♋18
21	0♈09	3♓32	16 33	12 34	19 05	3 30	3 11	26 58	15 00	13 25	♃ 30/8 10♉26
31	10 03	15 49	24 12	14 58	19R08	4 04	3 46	26 46	14D59	12 53	♃ 26/12 0♉26
10 4	19 53	28 06	1♓51	17 23	19 01	4 41	4 19	26 36	15 01	12 21	♄ 29/3 19♐08
20	29 40	10♈22	9 31	19 47	18 44	5 18	4 52	26 29	15 05	11 50	♄ 17/8 12♐30
30	9♉24	22 39	17 10	22 10	18 19	5 56	5 23	26 25	15 12	11 18	♅ 13/7 7♈24
10 5	19 05	4♉55	24 47	24 30	17 46	6 34	5 51	26D24	15 20	10 46	♅ 13/12 3♈28
20	28 44	17 11	2♈22	26 45	17 08	7 10	6 17	26 26	15 30	10 14	♆ 7/5 26♌24
30	8♊20	29 27	9 53	28 55	16 25	7 45	6 39	26 32	15 43	9 42	♆ 4/12 1♍24
9 6	17 54	11♊43	17 19	0♉59	15 41	8 18	6 57	26 41	15 56	9 11	♇ 29/3 14♋59
19	27 27	24 00	24 40	2 55	14 57	8 47	7 10	26 53	16 10	8 39	♇ 19/10 18♋24
29	7♋00	6♋17	1♉54	4 41	14 16	9 13	7 19	27 07	16 26	8 07	⚷ 12/1 1♉24
9 7	16 32	18 34	9 00	6 15	13 40	9 35	7 24	27 24	16 41	7 35	⚷ 14/8 10♉11
19	26 04	0♌53	15 57	7 38	13 10	9 52	7R23	27 42	16 57	7 04	
29	5♌37	13 12	22 43	8 45	12 48	10 03	7 18	28 03	17 12	6 32	
8 8	15 12	25 31	29 16	9 37	12 34	10 10	7 08	28 24	17 26	6 00	
18	24 48	7♍52	5♊34	10 10	12D31	10R10	6 54	28 46	17 40	5 28	
28	4♍26	20 12	11 36	10 25	12 36	10 05	6 36	29 08	17 52	4 56	
7 9	14 07	2♎32	17 17	10R20	12 52	9 55	6 15	29 30	18 03	4 25	
17	23 51	14 52	22 33	9 55	13 17	9 39	5 53	29 52	18 11	3 53	
27	3♎38	27 11	27 21	9 11	13 50	9 19	5 29	0♍12	18 18	3 21	
7 10	13 29	9♏29	1♋33	8 10	14 32	8 55	5 05	0 30	18 22	2 49	
17	23 23	21 46	5 01	6 58	15 21	8 28	4 42	0 46	18 24	2 18	
27	3♏20	4♐02	7 34	5 38	16 16	7 60	4 20	1 00	18R23	1 46	
6 11	13 21	16 17	9 02	4 17	17 17	7 30	4 02	1 11	18 20	1 14	
16	23 24	28 29	9R12	3 01	18 22	7 02	3 47	1 18	18 14	0 42	
26	3♐30	10♑39	7 56	1 56	19 30	6 35	3 36	1 23	18 07	0 11	
6 12	13 39	22 44	5 18	1 07	20 40	6 11	3 30	1R23	17 58	29♉39	
16	23 49	4♒44	1 41	0 36	21 50	5 52	3D29	1 21	17 47	29 07	
26	4♑00	16 36	27♊46	0D26	23 01	5 37	3 33	1 15	17 35	28 35	

SID M/N 1st JAN 6 h 40 m 37 s 1929 COMMON BST 21/4 to 6/10

	DAY	JAN	FEB	MAR	APR	MAY	JUN	JUL	AUG	SEP	OCT	NOV	DEC
	1	19♍04	5♏07	12♏55	26♐32	28♑20	13♓48	18♈57	10♊18	4♌01	12♍28	2♏09	6♐04
☽	3	14♎38	29♏01	6♐54	20♑17	22♒45	10♈02	16♉36	9♋48	3♍22	10♎11	27♏31	0♑17
	5	8♏54	22♐35	0♑32	14♒44	18♓23	7♉59	15♊55	9♌55	1♎49	6♏41	22♐01	24♑06
	7	2♐32	16♑28	24♑31	10♓24	15♈36	7♊32	16♋18	9♍28	28♎44	1♐54	15♑54	17♒48
	9	26♐07	11♒06	19♒25	7♈30	14♉22	7♋51	16♌29	7♎25	24♏03	26♐07	9♒38	11♓54
	11	20♑04	6♓37	15♓30	5♉48	14♊03	7♌43	15♍16	3♏30	18♐15	19♑52	3♓50	6♈56
	13	14♒38	2♈57	12♈37	4♊42	13♋40	6♍10	12♎08	28♏07	11♑59	13♒49	29♓04	3♉31
	15	9♓54	29♈59	10♉26	3♋32	12♌23	2♎54	7♏21	21♐57	5♒53	8♓31	25♈47	1♊56
	17	6♈00	27♉39	8♊35	1♌50	9♍48	28♎11	1♐29	15♑38	0♓27	4♈22	24♉01	1♋50
	19	3♉05	25♊58	6♋49	29♌23	5♎58	22♏29	25♐10	9♒39	25♓56	1♉26	23♊18	2♌08
	21	1♊21	24♋46	5♌00	26♍04	1♏05	16♐19	18♑53	4♓16	22♈18	29♉28	22♋44	1♍34
	23	0♋42	23♌31	2♍49	21♎50	25♏27	9♑59	12♒53	29♓35	19♉25	27♊58	21♌30	29♍25
	25	0♌27	21♍25	29♍53	16♏43	19♐21	3♒47	7♓23	25♈37	17♊10	26♋30	19♍09	25♎39
	27	29♌32	17♎54	25♎52	10♐51	13♑02	27♒58	2♈32	22♉31	15♋27	24♌41	15♎41	20♏43
	29	27♍04		20♏43	4♑34	6♒50	22♓53	28♈39	20♊26	14♌01	22♍17	11♏16	15♐02
	31	22♎48		14♐42		1♓14		26♉03	19♋20		19♎05		8♑58
	1	18♑00	23♒41	13♒05	24♓53	24♉45	21♊59	17♊32	9♌11	2♎24	21♎43	22♎27	10♐14
☿	7	27 50	18℞05	18 49	5♈46	5♊08	19℞28	23 23	21 17	9 59	15℞58	1♏55	19 38
	13	7♒32	11 36	25 58	17 30	13 18	16 12	1♋45	2♍32	16 23	9 39	11 37	29 03
	19	16 24	8 55	4♓10	29 59	19 00	14 05	12 20	12 53	21 08	8D20	21 16	8♑29
	25	22 48	10D25	13 15	12♉43	22 00	14D24	24 28	22 23	23 20	12 55	0♐48	17 49
	31	24℞06		23 09		22℞12		7♌06	1♎03		20 57		26 43

DATE	☉	♀	♂	♃	♄	⚷	♅	♆	♇	☊	STATIONS
1 1	10♑07	23♒38	25♊37	0♉30	23♐43	5♉31	3♈38	1♍10	17♋27	28♉16	
11	20 18	5♓11	22℞49	0 53	24 51	5 26	3 50	1℞00	17℞14	27 44	☿ 29/1 24♒24
21	0♒29	16 26	21 16	1 36	25 55	5D26	4 07	0 47	17 02	27 13	☿ 20/2 8♒54
31	10 39	27 16	21D04	2 36	26 55	5 33	4 28	0 32	16 50	26 41	☿ 28/5 22♊27
10 2	20 47	7♈33	22 05	3 53	27 50	5 45	4 54	0 16	16 39	26 09	☿ 21/6 13♊52
20	0♓53	17 04	24 06	5 24	28 38	6 03	5 22	29♌59	16 30	25 37	☿ 26/9 23♎22
2 3	10 57	25 29	26 56	7 06	29 19	6 26	5 53	29 42	16 22	25 06	☿ 17/10 8♎02
12	20 57	2♉18	0♋24	9 00	29 51	6 53	6 25	29 26	16 16	24 34	♀ 30/3 8♉03
22	0♈54	6 47	4 22	11 01	0♑14	7 24	6 59	29 12	16 13	24 02	♀ 12/5 21♈39
1 4	10 47	7℞59	8 45	13 10	0 28	7 58	7 33	28 59	16D12	23 30	♂ 28/1 21♊00
11	20 38	5 12	13 26	15 24	0℞31	8 34	8 07	28 49	16 14	22 58	♃ 5/10 16♊24
21	0♉25	29♈25	18 23	17 42	0 25	9 12	8 40	28 41	16 18	22 27	♄ 10/4 0♑31
1 5	10 08	23 54	23 33	20 02	0 09	9 51	9 12	28 37	16 24	21 55	♄ 29/8 23♐54
11	19 49	21 39	28 52	22 24	29♐45	10 29	9 41	28D36	16 33	21 23	♅ 17/7 11♈23
21	29 28	23D15	4♌21	24 46	29 13	11 07	10 08	28 38	16 43	20 51	♅ 17/12 7♈27
31	9♊04	27 54	9 57	27 07	28 35	11 44	10 31	28 43	16 55	20 20	♆ 10/5 28♌36
10 6	18 38	4♉40	15 40	29 26	27 53	12 18	10 50	28 51	17 09	19 48	♆ 6/12 3♍35
20	28 11	12 52	21 28	1♊42	27 09	12 50	11 05	29 03	17 23	19 16	♇ 30/3 16♋12
30	7♋43	22 04	27 23	3 53	26 25	13 17	11 16	29 17	17 39	18 44	♇ 21/10 19♋38
10 7	17 15	1♊57	3♍22	5 59	25 44	13 41	11 22	29 33	17 54	18 12	⚷ 15/1 5♉25
20	26 47	12 21	9 27	7 58	25 07	14 00	11℞23	29 51	18 10	17 41	⚷ 19/8 14♉26
30	6♌21	23 08	15 36	9 48	24 36	14 15	11 19	0♍11	18 25	17 09	
9 8	15 55	4♋13	21 50	11 28	24 13	14 23	11 11	0 33	18 40	16 37	
19	25 32	15 34	28 09	12 56	23 59	14 26	10 58	0 55	18 54	16 05	
29	5♍10	27 07	4♎34	14 12	23 54	14℞23	10 41	1 17	19 06	15 34	
8 9	14 51	8♌52	11 03	15 11	23D59	14 15	10 22	1 39	19 16	15 02	
18	24 36	20 47	17 37	15 54	24 14	14 01	9 59	2 00	19 25	14 30	
28	4♎23	2♍50	24 16	16 19	24 38	13 42	9 36	2 21	19 32	13 58	
8 10	14 14	15 00	1♏01	16℞24	25 10	13 19	9 12	2 39	19 36	13 27	
18	24 08	27 17	7 51	16 08	25 51	12 52	8 48	2 56	19 38	12 55	
28	4♏06	9♎39	14 46	15 34	26 40	12 24	8 26	3 10	19℞38	12 23	
7 11	14 06	22 05	21 47	14 41	27 35	11 54	8 06	3 21	19 35	11 51	
17	24 10	4♏34	28 53	13 33	28 35	11 24	7 50	3 29	19 29	11 19	
27	4♐16	17 06	6♐05	12 16	29 40	10 56	7 38	3 34	19 22	10 48	
7 12	14 25	29 39	13 22	10 55	0♑47	10 31	7 30	3℞35	19 13	10 16	
17	24 35	12♐13	20 44	9 35	1 57	10 10	7 27	3 33	19 02	9 44	
27	4♑46	24 47	28 10	8 24	3 08	9 53	7D30	3 28	18 50	9 12	

SID M/N 1st JAN 6 h 39 m 40 s — 1930 COMMON — BST 13/4 to 5/10

	DAY	JAN	FEB	MAR	APR	MAY	JUN	JUL	AUG	SEP	OCT	NOV	DEC
☽	1	20♑52	5♓31	14♓33	1♉25	7♊49	0♌45	10♍01	1♏38	19♐26	22♑27	6♓14	8♈01
	3	14♒35	29♓48	9♈16	27♉55	5♋58	29♌38	8♎11	27♏40	13♑50	16♒16	0♈13	2♉54
	5	8♓27	24♈46	4♉39	25♊15	4♌26	27♍40	4♏57	22♐35	7♒42	10♓01	24♈55	29♉08
	7	2♈52	20♉52	0♊58	23♋22	2♍50	24♎45	0♐37	16♑49	1♓26	4♈07	20♉39	26♊45
	9	28♈22	18♊35	28♊29	22♌04	0♎52	20♏57	25♐29	10♒41	25♓19	28♈50	17♊24	25♋17
	11	25♉32	18♋00	27♋17	20♍54	28♎15	16♐22	19♑48	4♓25	19♈34	24♉19	14♋58	24♌00
	13	24♊37	18♌27	26♌57	19♎13	24♏47	11♑04	13♒43	28♓14	14♉28	20♊42	13♌04	22♍22
	15	25♋07	18♍33	26♍32	16♏27	20♐20	5♒09	7♓26	22♈28	10♊24	18♋06	11♍24	20♎08
	17	25♌39	17♎08	24♎59	12♐20	14♑57	28♒55	1♈17	17♉36	7♋43	16♌28	9♎45	17♏16
	19	24♍53	13♏47	21♏45	7♑03	8♒54	22♓48	25♈51	14♊12	6♌32	15♍33	7♏45	13♐45
	21	22♎10	8♐49	16♐59	1♒00	2♓42	17♈25	21♉44	12♋39	6♍25	14♎43	5♐02	9♑25
	23	17♏43	2♑52	11♑09	24♒48	26♓57	13♉26	19♊29	12♌40	6♎21	13♏11	1♑14	4♒13
	25	12♐08	26♑34	4♒54	19♓03	22♈13	11♊12	19♋03	13♍10	5♏13	10♐21	26♑15	28♒13
	27	6♑00	20♒22	28♒48	14♈11	18♉56	10♋33	19♌31	12♎48	2♐26	6♑03	20♒20	21♓51
	29	29♑42		23♓15	10♉28	17♊05	10♌33	19♍32	10♏44	28♐01	0♒33	14♓02	15♈45
	31	23♒31		18♈29		16♋09		18♎02	6♐53		24♒23		10♉35
☿	1	28♑06	22♑28	16♒35	9♈59	29♉51	23♉50	22♊30	24♌44	4♎09	22♍05	4♏00	21♐12
	7	5♒11	23D19	25 25	22 23	2♊27	24D49	4♋14	4♍41	6 39	25 06	13 48	0♑12
	13	8 15	27 30	4♓58	4♉36	1R57	28 26	17 00	13 39	5R48	2♎34	23 23	8 49
	19	4R55	3♒40	15 13	15 31	29♉10	4♊23	29 47	21 35	1 09	12 08	2♐46	16 25
	25	27♑34	11 06	26 13	24 07	25 51	12 27	11♌52	28 19	24♍57	22 15	12 02	21 30
	31	22 47		7♈58		23 55		22 59	3♎29		2♏20		21R24

DATE	☉	♀	♂	♃	♄	⚷	♅	♆	♇	☊	STATIONS
1 1	9♑52	1♑05	1♑55	7♊53	3♑43	9♉47	7♈33	3♍24	18♋43	8♉56	
11	20 03	13 39	9 29	7R03	4 54	9 39	7 43	3R14	18R31	8 25	☿ 13/1 8♒15
21	0♒14	26 14	17 06	6 32	6 02	9D37	7 58	3 02	18 18	7 53	☿ 3/2 22♑17
31	10 24	8♒47	24 47	6 21	7 07	9 41	8 18	2 48	18 06	7 21	☿ 9/5 2♊36
10 2	20 33	21 20	2♒30	6D31	8 08	9 51	8 41	2 32	17 55	6 49	☿ 2/6 23♉48
20	0♓39	3♓52	10 17	7 00	9 03	10 07	9 08	2 15	17 45	6 18	☿ 9/9 6♎47
2 3	10 42	16 22	18 05	7 48	9 52	10 28	9 38	1 58	17 37	5 46	☿ 1/10 22♍05
12	20 42	28 51	25 54	8 52	10 34	10 54	10 10	1 42	17 31	5 14	☿ 28/12 22♑17
22	0♈39	11♈17	3♓43	10 11	11 08	11 24	10 44	1 27	17 28	4 42	♀ 2/11 7♐22
1 4	10 33	23 41	11 33	11 44	11 33	11 58	11 18	1 14	17D26	4 10	♀ 13/12 22♏02
11	20 23	6♉02	19 21	13 27	11 48	12 34	11 52	1 03	17 28	3 39	♂ 19/12 16♌49
21	0♉10	18 21	27 07	15 19	11 53	13 12	12 26	0 55	17 31	3 07	♃ 31/1 6♊21
1 5	9 54	0♊36	4♈51	17 20	11R49	13 52	12 58	0 50	17 38	2 35	♃ 8/11 20♋31
11	19 35	12 48	12 31	19 26	11 35	14 31	13 28	0 48	17 46	2 03	♄ 21/4 11♑53
21	29 14	24 57	20 08	21 37	11 12	15 11	13 56	0D49	17 56	1 32	♄ 10/9 5♑16
31	8♊50	7♋02	27 40	23 51	10 42	15 49	14 21	0 53	18 08	1 00	♅ 21/7 15♈23
10 6	18 24	19 02	5♉06	26 08	10 05	16 25	14 42	1 01	18 21	0 28	♅ 21/12 11♈27
20	27 57	0♌58	12 27	28 25	9 24	16 59	14 59	1 12	18 36	29♈56	♆ 12/5 0♍48
30	7♋29	12 49	19 42	0♋42	8 40	17 30	15 11	1 25	18 51	29 25	♆ 8/12 5♍47
10 7	17 01	24 33	26 49	2 59	7 56	17 57	15 19	1 41	19 07	28 53	♇ 1/4 17♋26
20	26 34	6♍09	3♊49	5 12	7 14	18 19	15 23	1 59	19 22	28 21	♇ 22/10 20♋54
30	6♌07	17 36	10 41	7 23	6 36	18 36	15R21	2 18	19 38	27 49	⚷ 19/1 9♉36
9 8	15 41	28 51	17 24	9 28	6 03	18 48	15 14	2 39	19 53	27 17	⚷ 24/8 18♉55
19	25 18	9♎52	23 57	11 27	5 39	18 54	15 04	3 01	20 07	26 46	
29	4♍56	20 33	0♋20	13 19	5 23	18R54	14 49	3 23	20 19	26 14	
8 9	14 37	0♏50	6 32	15 02	5 16	18 48	14 30	3 45	20 30	25 42	
18	24 21	10 33	12 30	16 34	5D19	18 37	14 09	4 07	20 39	25 10	
28	4♎09	19 29	18 13	17 53	5 32	18 20	13 46	4 28	20 46	24 39	
8 10	14 00	27 15	23 39	18 59	5 54	17 58	13 21	4 47	20 51	24 07	
18	23 54	3♐19	28 45	19 48	6 26	17 33	12 57	5 04	20 54	23 35	
28	3♏51	6 52	3♌26	20 19	7 05	17 04	12 34	5 18	20R53	23 03	
7 11	13 52	6R54	7 37	20 31	7 53	16 34	12 13	5 30	20 51	22 32	
17	23 55	3 05	11 13	20R23	8 47	16 04	11 56	5 39	20 46	22 00	
27	4♐02	27♏11	14 03	19 55	9 46	15 34	11 42	5 45	20 39	21 28	
7 12	14 10	22 50	15 59	19 09	10 50	15 07	11 32	5 47	20 29	20 56	
17	24 20	22D18	16 48	18 07	11 58	14 43	11 27	5R46	20 19	20 24	
27	4♑31	25 30	16R21	16 54	13 08	14 24	11D27	5 42	20 07	19 53	

SID M/N 1st JAN 6 h 38 m 43 s 1931 COMMON BST 19/4 to 4/10

DAY	JAN	FEB	MAR	APR	MAY	JUN	JUL	AUG	SEP	OCT	NOV	DEC
1	23♉35	13♋06	21♋15	14♍23	22♎59	14♐37	19♑54	5♓39	19♈40	22♉23	9♋23	16♌11
☽ 3	20♊54	12♌56	20♌55	14♎34	22♏08	11♑33	15♒10	29♓25	13♉25	16♊58	5♌47	13♍42
5	19♋48	13♍16	21♍25	14♏06	20♐08	7♒07	9♓25	23♈01	7♊55	12♋42	3♍27	12♎04
7	19♌28	12♎49	21♎28	12♐07	16♑32	1♓29	3♈07	17♉04	3♋44	9♌57	2♎26	11♏06
9	18♍47	10♏52	20♏01	8♑23	11♒28	25♓12	26♈52	12♊13	1♌18	8♍51	2♏17	10♐13
11	17♎03	7♐24	16♐50	3♒13	5♓25	18♈58	21♉25	9♋02	0♍35	8♎57	2♐03	8♑32
13	14♏10	2♑47	12♑10	27♒08	29♓02	13♉25	17♊19	7♌34	0♎48	9♏13	0♑39	5♒22
15	10♐20	27♑21	6♒29	20♓44	22♈57	9♊02	14♋46	7♍12	0♏49	8♐27	27♑29	0♓35
17	5♑45	21♒23	0♓16	14♈29	17♉36	5♋54	13♌26	6♎55	29♏37	5♑58	22♒38	24♓40
19	0♒28	15♓05	23♓53	8♉45	13♊14	3♌45	12♍30	5♏49	26♐49	1♒45	16♓39	18♈16
21	24♒35	8♈41	17♈37	3♊44	9♋50	2♍02	11♎15	3♐31	22♑33	26♒14	10♈14	12♉07
23	18♓15	2♉34	11♉46	29♊37	7♌13	0♎22	9♏18	0♑01	17♒13	20♓00	4♉00	6♊47
25	11♈53	27♉14	6♊40	26♋31	5♍13	28♎30	6♐34	25♑30	11♓11	13♈35	28♉21	2♋32
27	6♉03	23♊19	2♋44	24♌32	3♎40	26♏18	3♑04	20♒11	4♈50	7♉23	23♊30	29♋17
29	1♊28		0♌18	23♍31	2♏18	23♐32	28♑44	14♓14	28♈28	1♊38	19♋28	26♌43
31	28♊44		29♌24		0♐42		23♒32	7♈53		26♊35		24♍34
1	20♑42	16♑30	27♒04	25♈44	8♉44	15♉18	9♋40	3♍59	15♍15	23♍26	15♏56	28♐54
☿ 7	13℞41	23 53	7♓32	4♉58	5℞12	23 16	22 23	10 51	9℞37	3♎58	25 12	4♑35
13	7 20	2♒06	18 39	11 01	3 36	2♊53	4♌09	16 06	6 02	14 34	4♐13	6℞17
19	6D17	10 59	0♈23	13 23	4D41	14 06	14 48	19 11	7D31	24 52	12 59	1 44
25	9 35	20 26	12 26	12℞12	8 20	26 36	24 19	19℞21	13 59	4♏47	21 21	23♐53
31	15 22		23 57		14 09		2♍42	16 05		14 22		20 08

DATE	☉	♀	♂	♃	♄	⚷	♅	♆	♇	☊	STATIONS
1 1	9♑37	28♏13	15♌36	16♋14	13♑43	14♉16	11♈30	5♍38	20♋01	19♈37	
11	19 49	5♐13	13℞08	14℞53	14 54	14 05	11 38	5℞29	19℞48	19 05	☿ 17/1 6♑03
21	0♒00	13 46	9 36	13 35	16 04	14 00	11 51	5 17	19 35	18 33	☿ 20/4 13♉25
31	10 10	23 22	5 38	12 26	17 13	14D02	12 08	5 03	19 23	18 01	☿ 14/5 3♉35
10 2	20 18	3♑40	1 57	11 29	18 19	14 09	12 30	4 48	19 11	17 30	☿ 22/8 19♍41
20	0♓24	14 27	29♋12	10 50	19 20	14 23	12 56	4 31	19 01	16 58	☿ 14/9 5♍53
2 3	10 27	25 35	27 42	10 30	20 17	14 43	13 25	4 14	18 53	16 26	☿ 12/12 6♑24
12	20 28	6♒59	27D30	10D29	21 07	15 07	13 56	3 58	18 47	15 54	☿ 1/1 20♐06
22	0♈25	18 33	28 29	10 48	21 50	15 36	14 29	3 43	18 43	15 23	♂ 9/3 27♋26
1 4	10 19	0♓15	0♌26	11 25	22 26	16 10	15 03	3 29	18 41	14 51	♃ 7/3 10♋27
11	20 09	12 04	3 11	12 19	22 52	16 46	15 37	3 18	18D42	14 19	♃ 10/12 22♌38
21	29 56	23 56	6 35	13 28	23 09	17 24	16 11	3 09	18 46	13 47	♄ 3/5 23♑17
1 5	9♉40	5♈53	10 31	14 51	23 16	18 04	16 44	3 03	18 52	13 15	♄ 22/9 16♑39
11	19 21	17 52	14 51	16 25	23℞14	18 45	17 15	3 00	19 00	12 44	♅ 26/7 19♈23
21	29 00	29 53	19 31	18 09	23 02	19 26	17 44	3D00	19 10	12 12	♅ 26/12 15♈26
31	8♊36	11♉56	24 29	20 01	22 41	20 06	18 10	3 04	19 21	11 40	♆ 15/5 3♍00
10 6	18 10	24 00	29 41	22 00	22 12	20 45	18 33	3 11	19 34	11 08	♆ 11/12 7♍59
20	27 43	6♊07	5♍05	24 04	21 36	21 21	18 52	3 21	19 49	10 37	♇ 2/4 18♋41
30	7♋15	18 16	10 40	26 12	20 56	21 54	19 06	3 33	20 04	10 05	♇ 24/10 22♋10
10 7	16 47	0♋26	16 26	28 23	20 12	22 24	19 17	3 49	20 20	9 33	⚷ 24/1 13♉60
20	26 20	12 40	22 20	0♌36	19 28	22 50	19 22	4 06	20 36	9 01	⚷ 30/8 23♉39
30	5♌53	24 55	28 22	2 49	18 45	23 10	19℞22	4 25	20 51	8 30	
9 8	15 27	7♌13	4♎32	5 02	18 06	23 25	19 18	4 46	21 07	7 58	
19	25 04	19 34	10 50	7 13	17 32	23 35	19 09	5 08	21 21	7 26	
29	4♍42	1♍56	17 15	9 21	17 06	23 38	18 56	5 30	21 34	6 54	
8 9	14 23	14 21	23 47	11 25	16 48	23℞36	18 38	5 52	21 45	6 22	
18	24 07	26 47	0♏27	13 24	16 40	23 27	18 18	6 14	21 54	5 51	
28	3♎55	9♎14	7 13	15 15	16D41	23 13	17 56	6 35	22 02	5 19	
8 10	13 45	21 43	14 06	16 58	16 52	22 53	17 32	6 54	22 07	4 47	
18	23 39	4♏11	21 06	18 30	17 13	22 29	17 07	7 12	22 10	4 15	
28	3♏37	16 40	28 12	19 51	17 43	22 01	16 44	7 27	22℞10	3 44	
7 11	13 37	29 09	5♐25	20 58	18 21	21 31	16 22	7 40	22 08	3 12	
17	23 41	11♐38	12 44	21 49	19 08	20 60	16 03	7 49	22 03	2 40	
27	3♐47	24 07	20 08	22 22	20 01	20 29	15 47	7 56	21 56	2 08	
7 12	13 55	6♑35	27 39	22 37	21 00	19 59	15 35	7 59	21 47	1 36	
17	24 05	19 03	5♑14	22℞33	22 04	19 33	15 28	7℞59	21 37	1 05	
27	4♑16	1♒29	12 54	22 09	23 11	19 11	15D26	7 55	21 25	0 33	

SID M/N 1st JAN 6 h 37 m 46 s 1932 LEAP BST 17/4 to 2/10

	DAY	JAN	FEB	MAR	APR	MAY	JUN	JUL	AUG	SEP	OCT	NOV	DEC
	1	8♎36	1♐40	26♐01	15♒02	18♓42	2♉55	5♊15	21♋16	10♍35	18♎19	12♐10	20♑03
☽	3	6♏50	29♐04	22♑28	9♓35	12♈25	26♉43	29♊56	17♌54	9♎20	18♏15	11♑26	17♒51
	5	5♐08	25♑44	17♒57	3♈31	6♉01	21♊03	25♋29	15♍26	8♏24	17♐34	8♒54	13♓44
	7	3♑06	21♒30	12♓37	27♈11	29♉50	16♋02	21♌51	13♎34	7♐07	15♑34	4♓40	8♈17
	9	0♒09	16♓17	6♈40	20♉50	24♊04	11♌45	18♍57	11♏56	5♑03	12♒10	29♓17	2♉08
	11	25♒55	10♈16	0♉20	14♊48	18♋57	8♍21	16♎45	10♐18	2♒04	7♓37	23♈17	25♉49
	13	20♓28	3♉53	24♉00	9♋28	14♌47	6♎02	15♏13	8♑20	28♒08	2♈14	17♉02	19♊43
	15	14♈14	27♉45	18♊11	5♌18	11♍55	4♏53	14♐04	5♒41	23♓18	26♈19	10♊48	13♋58
	17	7♉54	22♊30	13♋27	2♍43	10♎36	4♐29	12♑41	2♓02	17♈44	20♉06	4♋45	8♌44
	19	2♊10	18♋42	10♌19	1♎52	10♏33	3♑55	10♒23	27♓16	11♉37	13♊50	29♋11	4♍14
	21	27♊36	16♌32	8♍56	2♏11	10♐47	2♒10	6♓40	21♈35	5♊20	7♋51	24♌29	0♎50
	23	24♋26	15♍37	8♎50	2♐31	10♑03	28♒42	1♈35	15♉22	29♊22	2♌40	21♍12	28♎52
	25	22♌25	15♎09	9♏01	1♑37	7♒31	23♓39	25♈36	9♊12	24♋21	28♌51	19♎43	28♏19
	27	20♍59	14♏15	8♐20	28♑52	3♓08	17♈37	19♉19	3♋43	20♌45	26♍49	19♏48	28♐25
	29	19♎32	12♐22	6♑09	24♒23	27♓26	11♉17	13♊24	29♋25	18♍51	26♎31	20♐24	27♑58
	31	17♏44		2♒24		21♈07		8♋22	26♌32		27♏02		25♒56
	1	20♐06	23♑45	12♓58	25♈02	15♈40	26♉09	27♋43	1♍36	20♌43	8♎52	27♏27	17♐06
☿	7	22 39	2♒58	24 32	22℞47	20 01	8♊21	7♌28	1℞26	26 42	19 09	5♐32	9℞15
	13	28 17	12 40	5♈53	18 25	26 19	21 24	15 55	28♌13	6♍04	28 58	12 47	4 30
	19	5♑29	22 51	15 45	14 48	4♉12	4♋27	22 55	23 16	16 58	8♏22	18 22	5D51
	25	13 35	3♓36	22 30	13D47	13 32	16 40	28 13	19 39	28 06	17 23	20℞35	11 09
	31	22 15		25 02		24 14		1♍20	20D09		26 03		18 22

DATE	☉	♀	♂	♃	♄	⚷	♅	♆	♇	☊	STATIONS
1 1	9♑22	7♒41	16♑46	21♌50	23♑46	19♉02	15♈27	7♍52	21♋19	0♈17	
11	19 34	20 03	24 32	20℞59	24 56	18 48	15 33	7℞43	21℞06	29♓45	☿ 31/3 25♈03
21	29 45	2♓22	2♒20	19 54	26 08	18 40	15 44	7 32	20 53	29 14	☿ 24/4 13♈45
31	9♒55	14 37	10 12	18 39	27 18	18D38	16 00	7 19	20 41	28 42	☿ 4/8 1♍55
10 2	20 03	26 45	18 05	17 19	28 28	18 43	16 20	7 04	20 29	28 10	☿ 27/8 19♌16
20	0♓09	8♈45	25 58	16 02	29 34	18 55	16 45	6 47	20 19	27 38	☿ 25/11 20♐35
1 3	10 13	20 35	3♓52	14 51	0♒37	19 12	17 12	6 31	20 10	27 06	☿ 14/12 4♐19
11	20 13	2♉13	11 45	13 52	1 34	19 35	17 42	6 14	20 04	26 35	♀ 8/6 15♋26
21	0♈11	13 35	19 37	13 09	2 26	20 03	18 15	5 58	19 59	26 03	♀ 21/7 28♊55
31	10 04	24 37	27 26	12 43	3 11	20 36	18 48	5 44	19 57	25 31	♃ 9/4 12♌36
10 4	19 55	5♊15	5♈13	12D36	3 48	21 12	19 22	5 32	19D58	24 59	♄ 15/5 4♒45
20	29 42	15 18	12 56	12 48	4 16	21 50	19 57	5 23	20 01	24 28	♄ 3/10 28♑07
30	9♉26	24 36	20 35	13 18	4 35	22 31	20 30	5 16	20 06	23 56	♅ 29/7 23♈23
10 5	19 07	2♋50	28 09	14 05	4 44	23 13	21 02	5 12	20 14	23 24	♅ 29/12 19♈27
20	28 46	9 33	5♉39	15 07	4℞44	23 55	21 32	5D12	20 24	22 52	♆ 16/5 5♍12
30	8♊22	14 03	13 03	16 23	4 34	24 37	22 00	5 15	20 35	22 20	♆ 12/12 10♍11
9 6	17 56	15℞24	20 22	17 50	4 15	25 18	22 24	5 21	20 49	21 49	♇ 3/4 19♋57
19	27 29	12 55	27 35	19 28	3 48	25 57	22 45	5 30	21 03	21 17	♇ 24/10 23♋28
29	7♋02	7 19	4♊42	21 14	3 13	26 34	23 01	5 42	21 18	20 45	⚷ 28/1 18♉38
9 7	16 34	1 39	11 42	23 07	2 33	27 06	23 13	5 57	21 34	20 13	⚷ 4/9 28♉41
19	26 06	28♊59	18 37	25 07	1 50	27 35	23 21	6 13	21 50	19 42	
29	5♌39	0D08	25 25	27 10	1 06	27 60	23 23	6 32	22 06	19 10	
8 8	15 13	4 26	2♋06	29 18	0 22	28 19	23℞21	6 53	22 21	18 38	
18	24 50	10 59	8 41	1♍27	29♑42	28 32	23 14	7 14	22 36	18 06	
28	4♍28	19 04	15 09	3 38	29 07	28 39	23 02	7 36	22 49	17 35	
7 9	14 09	28 15	21 28	5 48	28 39	28℞40	22 47	7 58	23 00	17 03	
17	23 53	8♌12	27 40	7 57	28 19	28 35	22 28	8 20	23 10	16 31	
27	3♎40	18 45	3♌43	10 03	28 08	28 24	22 06	8 42	23 18	15 59	
7 10	13 31	29 44	9 36	12 06	28D08	28 06	21 43	9 01	23 24	15 27	
17	23 25	11♍05	15 19	14 03	28 17	27 44	21 18	9 19	23 27	14 56	
27	3♏22	22 43	20 48	15 54	28 36	27 17	20 54	9 35	23℞27	14 24	
6 11	13 23	4♎34	26 03	17 36	29 05	26 47	20 31	9 49	23 26	13 52	
16	23 26	16 36	1♍01	19 08	29 42	26 15	20 11	9 59	23 21	13 20	
26	3♐32	28 47	5 38	20 28	0♒28	25 43	19 53	10 07	23 15	12 49	
6 12	13 41	11♏03	9 50	21 34	1 20	25 12	19 40	10 11	23 06	12 17	
16	23 51	23 25	13 30	22 25	2 19	24 43	19 31	10℞11	22 56	11 45	
26	4♑02	5♐49	16 32	22 59	3 22	24 18	19 27	10 08	22 44	11 13	

SID M/N 1st JAN 6 h 40 m 45 s   1933 COMMON   BST 9/4 to 8/10

DAY	JAN	FEB	MAR	APR	MAY	JUN	JUL	AUG	SEP	OCT	NOV	DEC
1	9♓12	24♈37	2♉22	16♊13	18♋23	4♍10	9♎54	2♐08	25♑49	3♓44	22♈41	26♉36
☽ 3	4♈31	18♉35	26♉23	10♋03	12♌45	0♎25	7♏44	1♑26	24♒18	0♈38	17♉44	20♊39
5	28♈42	12♊21	20♊10	4♌32	8♍20	28♎32	7♐09	1♒00	22♓00	26♈39	12♊05	14♋21
7	22♉26	6♋29	14♋18	0♍15	5♎41	28♏23	7♑25	29♒54	18♈30	21♉42	5♋52	7♌59
9	16♊15	1♌27	9♌23	27♍38	4♏54	29♐01	7♒19	27♓24	13♉45	15♊54	29♋31	2♍02
11	10♋34	27♌23	5♍47	26♎35	5♐16	28♑58	5♓46	23♈21	8♊00	9♋37	23♌37	27♍08
13	5♌33	24♍18	3♎29	26♏21	5♑25	27♒15	2♈25	18♉00	1♋46	3♌30	18♍52	23♎54
15	1♍15	21♎58	2♏08	25♐50	4♒14	23♓42	27♈32	11♊55	25♋42	28♌12	15♎52	22♏39
17	27♍44	20♏07	1♐01	24♑14	1♓20	18♈45	21♉42	5♋41	20♌21	24♍17	14♏42	22♐53
19	25♎06	18♐32	29♐32	21♒18	27♓00	12♉55	15♊27	29♋48	16♍09	21♎59	14♐42	23♑22
21	23♏26	16♑52	27♑21	17♓14	21♈41	6♊42	9♋14	24♌39	13♎10	20♏54	14♑37	22♒46
23	22♐30	14♒44	24♒20	12♈20	15♉49	0♋26	3♌24	20♍23	11♏10	20♐11	13♒25	20♓27
25	21♑39	11♓43	20♓30	6♉49	9♊39	24♋20	28♌07	17♎03	9♐36	18♑58	10♓45	16♈32
27	19♒59	7♈35	15♈50	0♊51	3♋22	18♌38	23♍37	14♏34	8♑02	16♒49	6♈51	11♉27
29	16♓55		10♉23	24♊35	27♋13	13♍40	20♎07	12♐48	6♒08	13♓45	2♉03	5♊38
31	12♈21		4♊21		21♌36		17♏50	11♑27		9♈53		29♊27
1	19♐41	6♒44	26♓27	25♓46	15♈23	14♊02	4♌30	5♌42	27♌38	21♎24	1♐32	19♏13
☿ 7	27 57	17 02	4♈07	24D40	24 28	26 48	9 47	2R30	9♍15	0♏34	4 38	23 54
13	6♑42	27 47	7 24	26 42	4♉45	8♋26	12 48	2D40	20 39	9 14	3R03	1♐07
19	15 48	8♓52	5R41	1♈12	16 12	18 40	13R08	7 01	1♎30	17 20	26♏11	9 25
25	25 15	19 48	0 47	7 34	28 43	27 23	10 39	15 07	11 44	24 40	19 39	18 13
31	5♒03		26♓17		11♊51		6 26	25 44		0♐43		27 17

DATE	☉	♀	♂	♃	♄	⚷	♅	♆	♇	☊	STATIONS
1 1	10♑09	13♐17	17♍59	23♍11	4♒02	24♉06	19♈27	10♍05	22♋37	10♓54	
11	20 20	25 45	19 40	23R15	5 11	23 49	19 31	9R57	22R24	10 22	☿ 14/3 7♈27
21	0♒31	8♑14	20 16	23 00	6 22	23 38	19 41	9 46	22 11	9 51	☿ 6/4 24♓38
31	10 41	20 43	19R38	22 26	7 34	23 34	19 55	9 33	21 58	9 19	☿ 17/7 13♌21
10 2	20 49	3♒13	17 41	21 35	8 45	23D37	20 14	9 18	21 46	8 47	☿ 10/8 2♌05
20	0♓55	15 42	14 35	20 31	9 55	23 46	20 37	9 02	21 36	8 15	☿ 8/11 4♐46
2 3	10 58	28 10	10 45	19 17	11 02	24 02	21 03	8 45	21 27	7 44	☿ 28/11 18♏37
12	20 59	10♓38	6 54	17 59	12 05	24 23	21 33	8 28	21 21	7 12	♂ 21/1 20♍16
22	0♈56	23 04	3 42	16 43	13 04	24 50	22 04	8 13	21 16	6 40	♂ 12/4 0♍51
1 4	10 49	5♈30	1 38	15 33	13 56	25 22	22 38	7 58	21 14	6 08	♃ 8/1 23♍16
11	20 40	17 54	0 51	14 35	14 42	25 58	23 12	7 46	21D15	5 36	♃ 10/5 13♍17
21	0♉27	0♉16	1D19	13 52	15 20	26 37	23 46	7 36	21 18	5 05	♄ 27/5 16♒22
1 5	10 10	12 37	2 52	13 25	15 49	27 19	24 20	7 29	21 23	4 33	♄ 15/10 9♒43
11	19 51	24 57	5 19	13D17	16 10	28 02	24 53	7 25	21 31	4 01	♅ 3/8 27♈25
21	29 29	7♊15	8 31	13 27	16 21	28 46	25 23	7D24	21 40	3 29	♆ 19/5 7♍24
31	9♊05	19 32	12 18	13 55	16R22	29 30	25 52	7 26	21 52	2 58	♆ 15/12 12♍23
10 6	18 40	1♋48	16 36	14 39	16 13	0♊13	26 17	7 32	22 05	2 26	♇ 4/4 21♋14
20	28 13	14 03	21 17	15 38	15 55	0 54	26 39	7 40	22 19	1 54	♇ 26/10 24♋46
30	7♋45	26 16	26 20	16 51	15 29	1 34	26 57	7 52	22 35	1 22	⚷ 1/2 23♉34
10 7	17 17	8♌29	1♎40	18 16	14 55	2 10	27 11	8 06	22 50	0 51	⚷ 10/9 4♊05
20	26 49	20 40	7 16	19 51	14 15	2 42	27 20	8 23	23 07	0 19	
30	6♌23	2♍48	13 06	21 35	13 32	3 10	27 24	8 41	23 23	29♒47	
9 8	15 57	14 55	19 08	23 26	12 48	3 33	27R24	9 01	23 38	29 15	
19	25 33	26 59	25 22	25 24	12 04	3 50	27 18	9 23	23 53	28 43	
29	5♍12	9♎00	1♏46	27 26	11 22	4 01	27 08	9 45	24 06	28 12	
8 9	14 53	20 57	8 20	29 32	10 46	4 05	26 54	10 07	24 18	27 40	
18	24 38	2♏50	15 04	1♎40	10 17	4R03	26 36	10 29	24 28	27 08	
28	4♎25	14 37	21 57	3 50	9 56	3 54	26 15	10 50	24 36	26 36	
8 10	14 16	26 18	28 58	6 00	9 45	3 39	25 52	11 10	24 42	26 05	
18	24 10	7♐51	6♐06	8 08	9D43	3 19	25 28	11 29	24 45	25 33	
28	4♏08	19 14	13 23	10 14	9 52	2 53	25 03	11 45	24R46	25 01	
7 11	14 08	0♑22	20 46	12 16	10 10	2 24	24 40	11 59	24 44	24 29	
17	24 12	11 10	28 16	14 12	10 38	1 52	24 18	12 10	24 40	23 57	
27	4♐18	21 30	5♑52	16 02	11 16	1 19	24 00	12 18	24 33	23 26	
7 12	14 27	1♒09	13 33	17 42	12 01	0 46	23 45	12 22	24 25	22 54	
17	24 37	9 49	21 18	19 13	12 53	0 15	23 34	12R23	24 14	22 22	
27	4♑48	16 59	29 07	20 32	13 52	29♉47	23 29	12 21	24 03	21 50	

SID M/N 1st JAN 6 h 39 m 48 s — 1934 COMMON — BST 22/4 to 7/10

DAY	JAN	FEB	MAR	APR	MAY	JUN	JUL	AUG	SEP	OCT	NOV	DEC
1	11♋17	25♌56	4♍45	22♎19	29♏23	22♑42	1♓26	22♈33	9♊55	12♋23	25♌44	27♍37
☽ 3	4♌58	20♍34	29♍59	19♏45	28♐15	21♒41	29♓38	18♉37	4♋08	6♌01	19♍50	22♎51
5	28♌55	16♎02	26♎07	17♐48	26♑58	19♓33	26♈20	13♊22	27♋46	29♌45	14♎59	19♏38
7	23♍30	12♏36	23♏08	16♑02	25♒07	16♈18	21♉47	7♋19	21♌24	24♍06	11♏25	17♐51
9	19♎16	10♐28	20♐57	14♒16	22♓36	12♉06	16♊19	0♌55	15♍28	19♎25	8♐57	16♑54
11	16♏40	9♑34	19♑26	12♓18	19♈23	7♊06	10♋15	24♌33	10♎12	15♏41	7♑06	15♒58
13	15♐48	9♒21	18♒19	9♈53	15♉24	1♋23	3♌52	18♍32	5♏45	12♐44	5♒23	14♓25
15	16♑06	8♓51	17♓03	6♉38	10♊34	25♋09	27♌28	13♎09	2♐12	10♑23	3♓32	12♈04
17	16♒20	7♈07	14♈59	2♊15	4♋51	18♌43	21♍26	8♏44	29♐39	8♒31	1♈28	8♉52
19	15♓20	3♉45	11♉35	26♊47	28♋34	12♍35	16♎16	5♐36	28♑07	7♓03	28♈59	4♊49
21	12♈33	28♉51	6♊46	20♋34	22♌13	7♎22	12♏28	3♑57	27♒24	5♈39	25♉45	29♊54
23	8♉08	22♊54	0♋53	14♌15	16♍30	3♏43	10♐25	3♒33	26♓50	3♉42	21♊28	24♋13
25	2♊33	16♋33	24♋33	8♍33	12♎04	1♐55	9♑57	3♓40	25♈29	0♊34	16♋05	17♌57
27	26♊21	10♌21	18♌26	4♎04	9♏23	1♑38	10♒19	3♈10	22♉38	26♊00	9♌55	11♍33
29	20♋00		13♍07	1♏05	8♐16	1♒51	10♓17	1♉11	18♊09	20♋15	3♍31	5♎35
31	13♌51		8♎57		7♑55		8♈54	27♉24		13♌54		0♏42
1	28♐49	19♒56	19♓05	12♓51	26♈34	29♊26	23♋42	18♋38	13♍18	0♏30	12♏53	22♏05
☿ 7	8♑08	0♓29	13℞44	19 12	8♉31	8♋28	21℞17	25 57	24 05	7 49	5℞34	1♐06
13	17 41	10 19	8 25	26 55	21 19	15 40	17 33	6♌03	4♎10	13 54	3D00	10 19
19	27 31	17 43	6 20	5♈46	4♊22	20 49	14 38	17 46	13 35	17 59	6 32	19 37
25	7♒41	20℞27	7D47	15 39	16 45	23 36	14D26	29 49	22 23	18℞34	13 35	29 01
31	18 10		11 57		27 46		17 44	11♍26		14 05		8♑34

DATE	☉	♀	♂	♃	♄	⚷	♅	♆	♇	☊	STATIONS
1 1	9♑54	19♒47	3♒02	21♎06	14♒23	29♉35	23♈28	12♍18	23♋56	21♒35	
11	20 05	23 14	10 54	22 03	15 29	29 15	23D30	12℞11	23℞44	21 03	☿ 25/2 20♓27
21	0♒16	23℞00	18 48	22 43	16 38	29 01	23 37	12 01	23 31	20 31	☿ 19/3 6♓20
31	10 26	18 49	26 43	23 06	17 49	28 53	23 49	11 48	23 18	19 59	☿ 28/6 24♋00
10 2	20 34	12 47	4♓37	23℞11	19 01	28D52	24 06	11 33	23 06	19 27	☿ 22/7 14♋07
20	0♓40	8 36	12 30	22 56	20 13	28 58	24 28	11 18	22 55	18 56	☿ 23/10 18♏53
2 3	10 44	8D18	20 21	22 23	21 24	29 11	24 53	11 01	22 46	18 24	☿ 12/11 2♏56
12	20 44	11 37	28 10	21 33	22 32	29 30	25 21	10 44	22 39	17 52	♀ 15/1 23♒38
22	0♈41	17 34	5♈55	20 30	23 37	29 56	25 52	10 28	22 34	17 20	♀ 26/2 7♒56
1 4	10 35	25 19	13 36	19 18	24 37	0♊26	26 25	10 14	22 32	16 49	♃ 7/2 23♎11
11	20 25	4♓15	21 14	18 02	25 31	1 01	26 59	10 01	22D32	16 17	♃ 11/6 13♎16
21	0♉12	13 59	28 46	16 46	26 19	1 40	27 33	9 50	22 35	15 45	♄ 9/6 28♒11
1 5	9 56	24 18	6♉14	15 37	26 59	2 22	28 07	9 42	22 40	15 13	♄ 27/10 21♒30
11	19 37	5♈01	13 36	14 38	27 31	3 06	28 40	9 37	22 47	14 41	♅ 2/1 23♈28
21	29 15	16 01	20 54	13 54	27 54	3 52	29 12	9 36	22 56	14 10	♅ 7/8 1♉27
31	8♊52	27 15	28 05	13 26	28 07	4 38	29 42	9D37	23 08	13 38	♆ 21/5 9♍36
10 6	18 26	8♉40	5♊12	13 16	28℞11	5 24	0♉09	9 42	23 21	13 06	♆ 17/12 14♍35
20	27 59	20 13	12 13	13D24	28 04	6 08	0 32	9 50	23 35	12 34	♇ 6/4 22♋32
30	7♋31	1♊53	19 09	13 50	27 49	6 51	0 52	10 01	23 50	12 03	♇ 28/10 26♋05
10 7	17 03	13 39	26 00	14 32	27 24	7 31	1 08	10 14	24 06	11 31	⚷ 6/2 28♉51
20	26 36	25 31	2♋46	15 29	26 52	8 07	1 19	10 30	24 22	10 59	⚷ 17/9 9♊56
30	6♌09	7♋28	9 27	16 40	26 14	8 39	1 25	10 48	24 38	10 27	
9 8	15 43	19 31	16 02	18 03	25 31	9 07	1℞27	11 08	24 54	9 56	
19	25 19	1♌38	22 33	19 37	24 46	9 29	1 24	11 29	25 09	9 24	
29	4♍58	13 51	29 00	21 21	24 01	9 44	1 15	11 51	25 23	8 52	
8 9	14 39	26 08	5♌21	23 12	23 19	9 54	1 03	12 13	25 35	8 20	
18	24 23	8♍29	11 37	25 09	22 41	9℞56	0 46	12 35	25 45	7 48	
28	4♎11	20 53	17 48	27 12	22 10	9 52	0 27	12 57	25 54	7 17	
8 10	14 01	3♎20	23 53	29 19	21 47	9 40	0 04	13 17	26 00	6 45	
18	23 56	15 50	29 52	1♏28	21 33	9 23	29♈40	13 36	26 04	6 13	
28	3♏53	28 21	5♍45	3 39	21D30	8 60	29 16	13 53	26℞05	5 41	
7 11	13 54	10♏54	11 30	5 50	21 36	8 32	28 52	14 08	26 04	5 10	
17	23 57	23 28	17 06	8 00	21 53	8 00	28 29	14 19	26 00	4 38	
27	4♐04	6♐02	22 32	10 07	22 20	7 26	28 09	14 28	25 54	4 06	
7 12	14 12	18 36	27 46	12 10	22 55	6 52	27 53	14 33	25 45	3 34	
17	24 22	1♑11	2♎45	14 08	23 40	6 19	27 40	14 35	25 35	3 02	
27	4♑33	13 45	7 28	15 59	24 31	5 48	27 32	14℞33	25 23	2 31	

SID M/N 1st JAN 6 h 38 m 50 s — 1935 COMMON — BST 14/4 to 6/10

	DAY	JAN	FEB	MAR	APR	MAY	JUN	JUL	AUG	SEP	OCT	NOV	DEC
	1	13♏51	3♑45	12♑17	5♓24	14♈15	5♊31	10♋18	25♌29	9♎50	13♏09	0♑48	7♒59
☽	3	11♐27	3♒31	11♒36	5♈16	12♉57	1♋45	4♌58	19♍11	3♏51	8♐01	27♑22	5♓49
	5	10♑38	3♓56	11♓54	4♉37	10♊28	26♋47	28♌56	12♎56	28♏32	3♑49	25♒04	4♈14
	7	10♒35	3♈46	12♈00	2♊29	6♋26	20♌53	22♍38	7♏11	24♐21	0♒58	23♓56	2♉57
	9	10♓13	2♉04	10♉43	28♊31	1♌03	14♍36	16♎35	2♐29	21♑48	29♒44	23♈32	1♊24
	11	8♈44	28♉37	7♊31	23♋05	24♌52	8♎33	11♏23	29♐19	21♒02	29♓47	22♉54	28♊56
	13	5♉52	23♊41	2♋37	16♌50	18♍35	3♏23	7♐32	27♑56	21♓29	0♉04	21♊02	25♋10
	15	1♊44	17♋50	26♋39	10♍28	12♎50	29♏28	5♑17	27♒54	21♈51	29♉14	17♋28	20♌07
	17	26♊37	11♌31	20♌14	4♎33	8♏03	26♐52	4♒22	28♓10	20♉52	26♊32	12♌22	14♍11
	19	20♋49	5♍09	13♍55	29♎23	4♐20	25♑15	4♓00	27♈33	17♊57	22♋01	6♍21	7♎56
	21	14♌35	28♍58	8♎02	25♏03	1♑31	24♒02	3♈17	25♉18	13♋19	16♌16	0♎04	2♏00
	23	8♍12	23♎16	2♏44	21♐28	29♑20	22♓42	1♉31	21♊26	7♌35	9♍59	24♎06	26♏56
	25	2♎00	18♏20	28♏10	18♑37	27♒30	20♈50	28♉31	16♋21	1♍19	3♎43	18♏50	23♐02
	27	26♎28	14♐33	24♐29	16♒32	25♓52	18♉14	24♊22	10♌30	25♍00	27♎50	14♐25	20♑16
	29	22♏07		21♑56	15♓12	24♈10	14♊44	19♋17	4♍16	18♎53	22♏32	10♑50	18♒20
	31	19♐25		20♒38		21♉57		13♌32	27♍57		17♐51		16♓48
	1	10♑10	29♒30	18♒51	17♓28	13♉51	1♋32	25♊26	27♋49	26♍18	1♏24	19♎13	2♐42
☿	7	19 56	3♓43	20D00	27 01	26 32	3 54	25D48	10♌13	5♎21	2℞46	25 45	12 07
	13	29 55	1℞56	24 04	7♈26	8♊06	3℞34	29 12	22 28	13 36	29♎47	4♏23	21 33
	19	10♒01	25♒42	0♓06	18 47	17 51	0 59	5♋34	4♍03	20 57	22 58	13 44	1♑02
	25	19 50	20 16	7 30	1♉01	25 30	27♊37	14 37	14 47	27 06	17 40	23 13	10 36
	31	28 21		15 58		0♋52		25 49	24 43		18D30		20 15

DATE	☉	♀	♂	♃	♄	⚷	♅	♆	♇	☊	STATIONS
1 1	9♑39	20♑02	9♎41	16♏51	25♒00	5♊34	27♈30	14♍31	25♋17	2♒15	
11	19 50	2♒35	13 50	18 28	26 01	5 10	27D30	14℞25	25℞04	1 43	☿ 8/2 3♓52
21	0♒01	15 07	17 30	19 54	27 06	4 51	27 35	14 15	24 51	1 11	☿ 2/3 18♒47
31	10 11	27 38	20 34	21 07	28 15	4 40	27 45	14 03	24 38	0 40	☿ 9/6 4♋05
10 2	20 20	10♓07	22 52	22 05	29 27	4 35	28 01	13 49	24 26	0 08	☿ 3/7 25♊13
20	0♓26	22 33	24 16	22 47	0♓39	4D37	28 20	13 33	24 15	29♑36	☿ 6/10 2♏49
2 3	10 29	4♈56	24℞33	23 11	1 52	4 47	28 44	13 17	24 06	29 04	☿ 27/10 17♎13
12	20 30	17 15	23 36	23℞17	3 04	5 04	29 11	13 00	23 58	28 32	♀ 18/8 22♍46
22	0♈27	29 29	21 23	23 04	4 13	5 27	29 41	12 44	23 53	28 01	♀ 30/9 6♍35
1 4	10 21	11♉37	18 07	22 33	5 19	5 56	0♉13	12 29	23 51	27 29	♂ 27/2 24♎36
11	20 11	23 39	14 19	21 46	6 21	6 30	0 46	12 15	23D50	26 57	♂ 18/5 6♎02
21	29 58	5♊34	10 42	20 44	7 17	7 08	1 21	12 04	23 52	26 25	♃ 10/3 23♏17
1 5	9♉42	17 20	7 55	19 34	8 07	7 50	1 55	11 56	23 57	25 54	♃ 12/7 13♏25
11	19 23	28 57	6 20	18 18	8 50	8 35	2 29	11 50	24 04	25 22	♄ 21/6 10♓13
21	29 01	10♋21	6D05	17 03	9 24	9 22	3 01	11 47	24 13	24 50	♄ 8/11 3♓30
31	8♊38	21 31	7 04	15 53	9 50	10 10	3 32	11D48	24 25	24 18	♅ 6/1 27♈30
10 6	18 12	2♌21	9 08	14 53	10 06	10 58	4 00	11 52	24 37	23 46	♅ 11/8 5♉30
20	27 45	12 48	12 05	14 07	10 13	11 46	4 25	11 59	24 52	23 15	♆ 24/5 11♍47
30	7♋17	22 43	15 47	13 37	10℞09	12 32	4 47	12 09	25 07	22 43	♆ 20/12 16♍46
10 7	16 49	1♍53	20 05	13 25	9 56	13 16	5 05	12 22	25 23	22 11	♇ 7/4 23♋50
20	26 22	10 03	24 54	13D31	9 34	13 57	5 18	12 38	25 39	21 39	♇ 29/10 27♋25
30	5♌55	16 44	0♏08	13 55	9 04	14 34	5 27	12 55	25 55	21 08	⚷ 12/2 4♊35
9 8	15 29	21 16	5 44	14 36	8 26	15 07	5 30	13 15	26 11	20 36	⚷ 24/9 16♊20
19	25 05	22℞45	11 40	15 32	7 44	15 34	5℞29	13 36	26 26	20 04	
29	4♍44	20 26	17 52	16 43	6 59	15 56	5 23	13 57	26 40	19 32	
8 9	14 25	14 59	24 19	18 06	6 14	16 10	5 12	14 19	26 53	19 01	
18	24 09	9 20	0♐59	19 41	5 30	16 18	4 57	14 42	27 04	18 29	
28	3♎56	6 39	7 51	21 25	4 51	16℞19	4 39	15 03	27 12	17 57	
8 10	13 47	7D52	14 53	23 18	4 18	16 12	4 17	15 24	27 19	17 25	
18	23 41	12 20	22 05	25 18	3 52	15 59	3 54	15 43	27 23	16 53	
28	3♏38	19 08	29 26	27 23	3 36	15 39	3 30	16 01	27 25	16 22	
7 11	13 39	27 32	6♑54	29 32	3 30	15 13	3 05	16 16	27℞24	15 50	
17	23 43	7♎03	14 28	1♐45	3D34	14 43	2 42	16 28	27 20	15 18	
27	3♐49	17 21	22 07	3 58	3 49	14 09	2 20	16 38	27 15	14 46	
7 12	13 57	28 13	29 51	6 12	4 14	13 34	2 02	16 44	27 07	14 15	
17	24 07	9♏29	7♒38	8 25	4 49	12 58	1 48	16 46	26 57	13 43	
27	4♑18	21 04	15 27	10 35	5 32	12 25	1 38	16℞45	26 45	13 11	

SID M/N 1st JAN 6 h 37 m 53 s 1936 LEAP BST 19/4 to 4/10

DAY	JAN	FEB	MAR	APR	MAY	JUN	JUL	AUG	SEP	OCT	NOV	DEC
1	1♈02	23♉58	17♊45	5♌38	8♍50	22♎57	25♏10	11♑13	1♓09	9♈24	3♊14	10♋24
☽ 3	29♈18	20♊46	13♋39	29♌56	2♎37	16♏57	20♐05	8♒24	0♈48	9♉49	2♋21	8♌02
5	27♉06	16♋37	8♌33	23♍48	26♎22	11♐34	16♑04	6♓50	0♉34	9♊17	29♋40	3♍56
7	24♊12	11♌42	2♍52	17♎33	20♏25	6♑56	13♒07	5♈50	29♉28	7♋06	25♌20	28♍32
9	20♋24	6♍09	26♍48	11♏24	14♐55	3♒10	11♓01	4♉38	27♊03	3♌20	19♍52	22♎23
11	15♌39	0♎07	20♎34	5♐33	10♑05	0♓19	9♈23	2♊46	23♋26	28♌27	13♎47	16♏02
13	10♍02	23♎51	14♏22	0♑19	6♒12	28♓21	7♉50	0♋04	18♌55	22♍49	7♏28	9♐57
15	3♎52	17♏48	8♐37	26♑12	3♓34	27♈06	6♊03	26♋34	13♍42	16♎46	1♐13	4♑25
17	27♎40	12♐33	3♑50	23♒40	2♈18	26♉05	3♋43	22♌16	7♎55	10♏28	25♐16	29♑37
19	22♏04	8♑43	0♒39	22♓53	1♉59	24♊39	0♌34	17♍10	1♏42	4♐08	19♑54	25♒42
21	17♐37	6♒42	29♒23	23♈15	1♊42	22♋10	26♌22	11♎23	25♏21	28♐09	15♒31	22♓48
23	14♑41	6♓19	29♓40	23♉28	0♋24	18♌19	21♍10	5♏08	19♐19	23♑02	12♓32	20♈57
25	13♒11	6♈33	0♉14	22♊18	27♋27	13♍13	15♎12	28♏55	14♑15	19♒22	11♈08	19♉58
27	12♓31	6♉09	29♉41	19♋15	22♌55	7♎16	8♏58	23♐23	10♒48	17♓36	10♉59	19♊19
29	11♈45	4♊17	27♊18	14♌34	17♍15	1♏03	3♐05	19♑11	9♓19	17♈31	11♊08	18♋10
31	10♉10		23♋11		11♎04		28♐10	16♒45		18♉07		15♌48
1	21♑51	10♒50	13♒41	1♈29	29♉55	9♊35	17♊51	17♌05	5♎04	7♎39	27♎36	15♐37
☿ 7	1♒19	4R17	21 10	13 13	7♊24	6R37	26 48	28 18	11 02	2R11	7♏29	24 56
13	9 57	1 52	29 36	25 38	12 11	5D30	7♋45	8♍36	15 08	2D10	17 14	4♑12
19	16 09	3D43	8♓49	8♉13	14 02	7 00	20 07	17 59	16R26	7 41	26 48	13 19
25	17R14	8 24	18 49	19 59	13R04	11 11	2♌51	26 28	13 49	16 16	6♐15	21 49
31	12 04		29 36		10 09		15 07	3♎56		25 58		28 39

DATE	☉	♀	♂	♃	♄	⚷	♅	♆	♇	☊	STATIONS
1 1	9♑24	26♏56	19♒22	11♐39	5♓56	12♊09	1♉35	16♍44	26♋39	12♑55	
11	19 36	8♐49	27 12	13 43	6 50	11 41	1D33	16R38	26R26	12 23	☿ 23/1 17♒36
21	29 47	20 50	5♓02	15 41	7 51	11 18	1 35	16 29	26 13	11 52	☿ 13/2 1♒52
31	9♒57	2♑56	12 50	17 31	8 56	11 01	1 44	16 18	26 00	11 20	☿ 20/5 14♊03
10 2	20 05	15 07	20 36	19 11	10 05	10 52	1 57	16 04	25 48	10 48	☿ 13/6 5♊29
20	0♓11	27 20	28 20	20 41	11 17	10D50	2 14	15 49	25 36	10 16	☿ 18/9 16♎28
1 3	10 15	9♒36	6♈00	21 57	12 30	10 56	2 36	15 32	25 27	9 44	☿ 10/10 1♎23
11	20 15	21 52	13 37	23 00	13 44	11 09	3 02	15 16	25 19	9 13	♃ 11/4 24♐26
21	0♈12	4♓09	21 09	23 46	14 56	11 29	3 31	14 59	25 13	8 41	♃ 12/8 14♐35
31	10 06	16 27	28 36	24 15	16 07	11 56	4 02	14 44	25 10	8 09	♄ 4/7 22♓31
10 4	19 57	28 45	5♉59	24 26	17 15	12 28	4 35	14 30	25D09	7 37	♄ 19/11 15♓47
20	29 44	11♈02	13 16	24R17	18 18	13 06	5 09	14 18	25 11	7 06	♅ 11/1 1♉33
30	9♉28	23 19	20 29	23 51	19 17	13 48	5 44	14 09	25 16	6 34	♅ 15/8 9♉35
10 5	19 09	5♉35	27 37	23 08	20 09	14 34	6 18	14 03	25 22	6 02	♆ 25/5 13♍59
20	28 48	17 51	4♊40	22 10	20 55	15 22	6 51	13 59	25 31	5 30	♆ 21/12 18♍58
30	8♊24	0♊08	11 38	21 01	21 32	16 12	7 23	13D59	25 42	4 59	♇ 8/4 25♋09
9 6	17 58	12 24	18 31	19 46	22 01	17 03	7 52	14 02	25 55	4 27	♇ 30/10 28♋46
19	27 31	24 40	25 20	18 30	22 21	17 53	8 19	14 09	26 09	3 55	⚷ 18/2 10♊50
29	7♋04	6♋57	2♋05	17 18	22 30	18 43	8 42	14 18	26 24	3 23	⚷ 1/10 23♊22
9 7	16 36	19 15	8 46	16 15	22R30	19 32	9 02	14 30	26 40	2 51	
19	26 08	1♌33	15 23	15 25	22 20	20 18	9 17	14 45	26 56	2 20	
29	5♌41	13 52	21 57	14 52	22 00	20 60	9 28	15 02	27 13	1 48	
8 8	15 15	26 12	28 27	14 36	21 32	21 38	9 34	15 21	27 29	1 16	
18	24 52	8♍32	4♌54	14D39	20 56	22 12	9R35	15 42	27 44	0 44	
28	4♍30	20 52	11 18	15 00	20 15	22 39	9 31	16 03	27 59	0 13	
7 9	14 11	3♎12	17 40	15 38	19 30	23 00	9 22	16 25	28 12	29♐41	
17	23 55	15 31	23 58	16 33	18 44	23 15	9 09	16 48	28 23	29 09	
27	3♎42	27 50	0♍14	17 44	17 59	23 22	8 52	17 10	28 32	28 37	
7 10	13 33	10♏07	6 28	19 08	17 18	23R21	8 32	17 31	28 39	28 06	
17	23 27	22 24	12 38	20 43	16 42	23 13	8 09	17 50	28 44	27 34	
27	3♏24	4♐39	18 45	22 30	16 15	22 57	7 45	18 08	28 46	27 02	
6 11	13 24	16 53	24 49	24 25	15 56	22 35	7 20	18 24	28R45	26 30	
16	23 28	29 04	0♎49	26 27	15 47	22 07	6 56	18 37	28 42	25 58	
26	3♐34	11♑12	6 45	28 36	15D49	21 34	6 34	18 47	28 37	25 27	
6 12	13 42	23 16	12 37	0♑49	16 02	20 59	6 14	18 54	28 29	24 55	
16	23 52	5♒14	18 22	3 05	16 24	20 22	5 58	18 57	28 19	24 23	
26	4♑03	17 04	24 01	5 23	16 57	19 45	5 46	18R57	28 08	23 51	

SID M/N 1st JAN 6 h 40 m 52 s — 1937 COMMON — BST 18/4 to 3/10

DAY	JAN	FEB	MAR	APR	MAY	JUN	JUL	AUG	SEP	OCT	NOV	DEC
1	29♌03	14♎24	22♎17	6♐07	8♑31	25♒09	1♈47	24♉22	17♋33	25♌17	13♎42	17♏06
☽ 3	24♍24	8♏19	16♏09	29♐52	3♒03	21♓44	29♈39	23♊03	15♌24	21♍39	8♏11	10♐47
5	18♎38	1♐59	9♐48	24♑23	28♒54	19♈54	28♉37	21♋53	12♍34	17♎08	2♐05	4♑22
7	12♏20	26♐07	3♑53	20♒21	26♓32	19♉28	28♊12	20♌15	8♎40	11♏42	25♐40	28♑10
9	6♐08	21♑18	29♑08	18♓12	25♈54	19♊40	27♋36	17♍29	3♏34	5♐33	19♑19	22♒32
11	0♑34	17♒52	26♒02	17♈40	26♉14	19♋21	25♌52	13♎15	27♏32	29♐07	13♒37	17♓56
13	25♑59	15♓40	24♓32	17♉48	26♊19	17♌37	22♍30	7♏44	21♐10	23♑03	9♓09	14♈49
15	22♒25	14♈10	23♈55	17♊24	25♋06	14♍09	17♎35	1♐29	15♑08	18♒01	6♈25	13♉25
17	19♓42	12♉42	23♉12	15♋43	22♌13	9♎10	11♏37	25♐11	10♒08	14♓34	5♉26	13♊26
19	17♈36	10♊52	21♊39	12♌36	17♍50	3♏13	5♐15	19♑31	6♓34	12♈49	5♊35	13♋54
21	15♉51	8♋33	19♋05	8♍19	12♎23	26♏50	29♐04	14♒55	4♈25	12♉15	5♋43	13♌31
23	14♊16	5♌41	15♌35	3♎08	6♏17	20♐32	23♑34	11♓30	3♉07	11♊54	4♌47	11♍25
25	12♋32	2♍08	11♍18	27♎20	29♏55	14♑39	18♒57	9♈02	1♊56	10♋53	2♍16	7♎29
27	10♌12	27♍41	6♎17	21♏06	23♐36	9♒26	15♓15	7♉04	0♋21	8♌45	28♍14	2♏08
29	6♍48		0♏34	14♐42	17♑38	5♓05	12♈22	5♊16	28♋09	5♍27	23♎02	25♏58
31	2♎10		24♏20		12♒23		10♉12	3♋29		1♎10		19♐32
1	29♑29	17♑17	21♒04	17♈57	24♉26	17♉31	29♊48	0♍12	29♍41	19♍36	9♏48	25♐47
☿ 7	1℞25	22 08	0♓41	29 55	22℞43	22 05	12♋42	8 58	27℞51	27 44	19 23	4♑04
13	26♑51	28 45	10 59	10♉25	19 19	28 47	25 32	16 37	22 39	7♎41	28 45	11 08
19	19 21	6♒29	21 59	18 20	16 17	7♊24	7♌36	22 56	17 03	18 02	7♐57	15 19
25	15 33	15 00	3♈41	23 05	15D18	17 50	18 38	27 30	15D29	28 15	16 59	13℞57
31	16D43		15 54		16 59		28 38	29 38		8♏10		6 48

DATE	☉	♀	♂	♃	♄	⚷	♅	♆	♇	☊	STATIONS
1 1	10♑10	24♒04	27♎20	6♑46	17♓21	19♊24	5♉41	18♍56	28♋00	23♐32	
11	20 22	5♓33	2♏46	9 03	18 08	18 52	5℞37	18℞50	27℞48	23 00	☿ 6/1 1♒32
21	0♒33	16 43	8 00	11 19	19 02	18 25	5D38	18 42	27 34	22 29	☿ 26/1 15♑26
31	10 43	27 27	13 01	13 32	20 02	18 04	5 45	18 31	27 21	21 57	☿ 30/4 24♉26
10 2	20 51	7♈36	17 46	15 41	21 07	17 50	5 56	18 17	27 09	21 25	☿ 24/5 15♉17
20	0♓57	16 53	22 10	17 43	22 17	17 44	6 12	18 02	26 57	20 53	☿ 1/9 29♍41
2 3	11 00	25 00	26 10	19 38	23 29	17D45	6 33	17 46	26 47	20 22	☿ 24/9 15♍20
12	21 00	1♉21	29 38	21 23	24 43	17 55	6 58	17 29	26 39	19 50	☿ 21/12 15♑37
22	0♈57	5 10	2♐26	22 58	25 57	18 12	7 26	17 13	26 34	19 18	♀ 28/3 5♉49
1 4	10 51	5℞28	4 26	24 21	27 11	18 37	7 56	16 57	26 30	18 46	♀ 9/5 19♈26
11	20 41	1 48	5 26	25 30	28 23	19 08	8 29	16 43	26D30	18 15	♂ 15/4 5♐31
21	0♉28	25♈44	5℞16	26 23	29 32	19 45	9 03	16 31	26 31	17 43	♂ 27/6 19♏30
1 5	10 12	20 48	3 50	26 59	0♈37	20 26	9 37	16 22	26 36	17 11	♃ 16/5 27♑19
11	19 53	19D29	1 14	27 17	1 37	21 13	10 11	16 15	26 42	16 39	♃ 14/9 17♑28
21	29 31	21 54	27♏53	27℞16	2 32	22 02	10 45	16 11	26 51	16 07	♄ 17/7 5♈08
31	9♊07	27 08	24 25	26 56	3 19	22 54	11 18	16D10	27 02	15 36	♄ 2/12 28♓21
10 6	18 42	4♉18	21 35	26 18	3 59	23 47	11 48	16 13	27 15	15 04	♅ 14/1 5♉37
20	28 15	12 46	19 53	25 25	4 31	24 41	12 16	16 19	27 29	14 32	♅ 19/8 13♉41
30	7♋47	22 09	19D33	24 19	4 53	25 35	12 40	16 28	27 44	14 00	♆ 28/5 16♍10
10 7	17 19	2♊10	20 33	23 05	5 05	26 28	13 01	16 40	28 00	13 29	♆ 23/12 21♍09
20	26 51	12 40	22 46	21 48	5℞07	27 19	13 18	16 54	28 16	12 57	♇ 9/4 26♋30
30	6♌24	23 31	25 58	20 33	4 59	28 06	13 31	17 11	28 33	12 25	♇ 1/11 0♌08
9 8	15 59	4♋40	0♐01	19 26	4 42	28 51	13 38	17 30	28 49	11 53	⚷ 23/2 17♊43
19	25 35	16 04	4 45	18 31	4 15	29 30	13 41	17 50	29 05	11 21	⚷ 10/10 1♋13
29	5♍14	27 40	10 03	17 52	3 41	0♋04	13℞39	18 11	29 19	10 50	
8 9	14 55	9♌26	15 48	17 31	3 00	0 32	13 32	18 33	29 32	10 18	
18	24 39	21 22	21 57	17D30	2 15	0 53	13 20	18 56	29 44	9 46	
28	4♎27	3♍26	28 24	17 47	1 29	1 07	13 04	19 18	29 53	9 14	
8 10	14 18	15 38	5♑08	18 23	0 43	1 13	12 45	19 39	0♌00	8 43	
18	24 12	27 55	12 05	19 17	0 00	1℞11	12 23	19 59	0 05	8 11	
28	4♏09	10♎18	19 13	20 26	29♓23	1 00	11 59	20 17	0 08	7 39	
7 11	14 10	22 44	26 29	21 50	28 53	0 43	11 34	20 33	0℞07	7 07	
17	24 14	5♏14	3♒52	23 27	28 33	0 18	11 10	20 46	0 04	6 36	
27	4♐20	17 46	11 19	25 16	28 22	29♊47	10 47	20 57	29♋59	6 04	
7 12	14 28	0♐19	18 51	27 13	28D22	29 12	10 26	21 04	29 51	5 32	
17	24 39	12 53	26 24	29 19	28 33	28 34	10 08	21 08	29 42	5 00	
27	4♑50	25 28	3♓58	1♒30	28 55	27 56	9 55	21℞09	29 30	4 28	

SID M/N 1st JAN 6 h 39 m 55 s — 1938 COMMON — BST 10/4 to 2/10

DAY	JAN	FEB	MAR	APR	MAY	JUN	JUL	AUG	SEP	OCT	NOV	DEC
1	1♑20	16♒25	25♒06	13♈21	20♉25	13♋50	22♌30	13♎15	29♏45	1♑49	15♒19	17♓29
☽ 3	25♑12	11♓41	21♓00	11♉19	19♊43	13♌15	20♍52	9♏02	23♐49	25♑33	9♓40	12♈49
5	19♒35	7♈43	17♈47	9♊45	18♋50	11♍17	17♎25	3♐29	17♑31	19♒33	5♈05	9♉43
7	14♓40	4♉32	15♉12	8♋12	17♌11	7♎49	12♏28	27♐16	11♒26	14♓20	1♉53	8♊18
9	10♈44	2♊16	13♊05	6♌23	14♍30	3♏06	6♐35	20♑56	5♓57	10♈08	29♉57	8♋01
11	8♉03	0♋57	11♋22	4♍05	10♎47	27♏31	0♑18	14♒54	1♈15	6♉57	28♊48	7♌50
13	6♊48	0♌16	9♌52	1♎05	6♏07	21♐25	24♑00	9♓22	27♈18	4♊32	27♋42	6♍44
15	6♋41	29♌26	8♍07	27♎09	0♐40	15♑07	17♒55	4♈27	24♉06	2♋38	26♌07	4♎14
17	6♌45	27♍28	5♎32	22♏12	24♐38	8♒52	12♓17	0♉19	21♊42	0♌59	23♍45	0♏25
19	5♍47	23♎52	1♏39	16♐23	18♑19	3♓02	7♈24	27♉13	20♋07	29♌19	20♎30	25♏36
21	3♎03	18♏42	26♏27	10♑06	12♒09	28♓03	3♉37	25♊23	19♌06	27♍17	16♏22	20♐07
23	28♎30	12♐34	20♐23	3♒55	6♓40	24♈24	1♊21	24♋45	18♍00	24♎28	11♐24	14♑09
25	22♏40	6♑11	14♑03	28♒29	2♈26	22♉27	0♋41	24♌37	16♎00	20♏34	5♑42	7♒54
27	16♐16	0♒12	8♒09	24♓20	29♈50	22♊07	0♌59	23♍50	12♏34	15♐32	29♑31	1♓39
29	9♑55		3♓17	21♈44	28♉51	22♋34	1♍03	21♎30	7♐42	9♑39	23♒16	25♓47
31	4♒04		29♓41		28♊49		29♍40	17♏22		3♒23		20♈53
1	5♑28	19♑19	3♓20	29♈22	25♈54	18♉10	18♋04	5♍18	1♍19	29♍41	21♏07	28♐43
☿ 7	29℞57	27 44	14 25	4♉26	25D17	28 09	29 45	9 57	28D58	10♎26	0♐02	29℞18
13	0D01	6♒43	26 03	5℞30	27 25	9♊37	10♌16	12 12	1♍41	20 49	8 37	23 40
19	4 07	16 14	7♈54	3 04	1♉58	22 15	19 35	11℞24	8 57	0♏47	16 42	16 04
25	10 26	26 18	19 05	29♈02	8 28	5♋22	27 40	7 26	18 52	10 21	23 47	13D29
31	17 58		28 09		16 39		4♍21	2 06		19 36		16 18

DATE	☉	♀	♂	♃	♄	⚷	♅	♆	♇	☊	STATIONS
1 1	9♑55	1♑45	7♓45	2♒38	29♓09	27♊37	9♉50	21♍08	29♋24	4♐13	
11	20 07	14 20	15 19	4 56	29 45	27 01	9℞44	21℞03	29℞11	3 41	☿ 10/1 29♐20
21	0♒18	26 54	22 51	7 17	0♈30	26 28	9D43	20 55	28 58	3 09	☿ 12/4 5♉36
31	10 28	9♒28	0♈21	9 40	1 23	26 02	9 47	20 45	28 45	2 37	☿ 5/5 25♈10
10 2	20 36	22 01	7 47	12 02	2 23	25 42	9 56	20 32	28 32	2 05	☿ 15/8 12♍19
20	0♓42	4♓33	15 11	14 23	3 27	25 29	10 11	20 17	28 20	1 34	☿ 7/9 28♌58
2 3	10 45	17 03	22 30	16 41	4 37	25 25	10 29	20 01	28 10	1 02	☿ 5/12 29♐46
12	20 46	29 31	29 46	18 56	5 49	25D29	10 52	19 45	28 02	0 30	☿ 24/12 13♐28
22	0♈43	11♈58	6♉57	21 04	7 03	25 42	11 19	19 28	27 56	29♏58	♀ 31/10 4♐56
1 4	10 37	24 21	14 04	23 06	8 18	26 02	11 49	19 12	27 52	29 27	♀ 11/12 19♏34
11	20 27	6♉42	21 07	25 00	9 33	26 30	12 20	18 58	27D51	28 55	♃ 22/6 2♓15
21	0♉14	19 00	28 05	26 44	10 46	27 05	12 54	18 45	27 52	28 23	♃ 19/10 22♒23
1 5	9 58	1♊15	4♊59	28 17	11 57	27 45	13 28	18 35	27 56	27 51	♄ 31/7 18♈03
11	19 39	13 27	11 49	29 37	13 05	28 31	14 03	18 27	28 02	27 20	♄ 15/12 11♈13
21	29 17	25 35	18 35	0♓42	14 07	29 21	14 37	18 23	28 11	26 48	♅ 18/1 9♉42
31	8♊53	7♋39	25 18	1 31	15 05	0♋14	15 10	18D21	28 22	26 16	♅ 24/8 17♉49
10 6	18 28	19 39	1♋57	2 02	15 56	1 09	15 42	18 23	28 34	25 44	♆ 30/5 18♍21
20	28 01	1♌34	8 34	2 14	16 39	2 07	16 11	18 28	28 48	25 12	♆ 26/12 23♍20
30	7♋33	13 23	15 07	2℞08	17 14	3 04	16 37	18 36	29 03	24 41	♇ 11/4 27♋51
10 7	17 05	25 05	21 38	1 42	17 40	4 02	17 00	18 48	29 19	24 09	♇ 2/11 1♌31
20	26 37	6♍39	28 07	0 59	17 56	4 58	17 19	19 01	29 36	23 37	⚷ 2/3 25♊25
30	6♌11	18 03	4♌34	0 00	18 02	5 52	17 33	19 18	29 52	23 05	⚷ 20/10 10♋03
9 8	15 45	29 14	10 59	28♒50	17℞58	6 43	17 43	19 36	0♌09	22 34	
19	25 21	10♎10	17 22	27 33	17 44	7 30	17 48	19 56	0 25	22 02	
29	5♍00	20 46	23 45	26 14	17 20	8 12	17℞48	20 17	0 40	21 30	
8 9	14 41	0♏55	0♍06	25 00	16 48	8 49	17 43	20 39	0 53	20 58	
18	24 25	10 27	6 27	23 57	16 09	9 19	17 33	21 01	1 05	20 26	
28	4♎13	19 07	12 47	23 07	15 25	9 41	17 19	21 23	1 15	19 55	
8 10	14 03	26 31	19 06	22 35	14 38	9 56	17 01	21 45	1 22	19 23	
18	23 57	2♐02	25 25	22 23	13 51	10 03	16 40	22 05	1 28	18 51	
28	3♏55	4 47	1♎44	22D31	13 06	10℞00	16 17	22 24	1 30	18 19	
7 11	13 55	3℞50	8 02	22 58	12 27	9 50	15 52	22 40	1℞30	17 48	
17	23 59	29♏14	14 20	23 45	11 54	9 31	15 28	22 54	1 28	17 16	
27	4♐05	23 23	20 37	24 49	11 30	9 04	15 04	23 06	1 23	16 44	
7 12	14 14	19 52	26 53	26 09	11 17	8 32	14 42	23 14	1 16	16 12	
17	24 24	20D19	3♏09	27 42	11D14	7 55	14 23	23 19	1 06	15 41	
27	4♑35	24 18	9 23	29 28	11 21	7 16	14 07	23℞20	0 55	15 09	

SID M/N 1st JAN 6 h 38 m 58 s — **1939 COMMON** — BST 16/4 to 19/11

	DAY	JAN	FEB	MAR	APR	MAY	JUN	JUL	AUG	SEP	OCT	NOV	DEC
☽	1	3♉59	24♊17	3♋29	27♌09	5♎52	26♏04	0♑34	15♒48	0♈22	3♉53	22♊19	0♌15
	3	1♊35	24♋12	2♌48	26♍29	3♏39	21♐43	25♑01	9♓32	24♈30	29♉07	19♋34	28♌35
	5	1♋03	24♌53	2♍59	25♎08	0♐27	16♑32	18♒59	3♈18	19♉19	25♊21	17♌34	26♍51
	7	1♌34	24♍52	2♎48	22♏27	26♐04	10♒39	12♓42	27♈32	15♊20	22♋50	16♍10	24♎49
	9	1♍46	23♎04	1♏09	18♐13	20♑39	4♓25	6♈37	22♉50	12♋58	21♌34	14♎58	22♏21
	11	0♎28	19♏19	27♏39	12♑47	14♒34	28♓24	1♉21	19♊47	12♌16	21♍10	13♏25	19♐10
	13	27♎21	14♐07	22♐37	6♒39	8♓23	23♈13	27♉32	18♋39	12♍34	20♎44	10♐55	15♑02
	15	22♏43	8♑05	16♑39	0♓28	2♈45	19♉26	25♊36	18♌57	12♎38	19♏19	7♑07	9♒51
	17	17♐08	1♒47	10♒21	24♓44	28♈07	17♊18	25♋16	19♍24	11♏19	16♐21	2♒02	3♓50
	19	11♑04	25♒34	4♓15	19♈50	24♉47	16♋27	25♌32	18♎42	8♐12	11♑50	26♒03	27♓30
	21	4♒49	19♓39	28♓37	15♉53	22♊40	16♌01	25♍06	16♏13	3♑31	6♒11	19♓45	21♈31
	23	28♒35	14♈10	23♈38	12♊53	21♋16	15♍01	23♎11	12♐06	27♑48	29♒57	13♈49	16♉34
	25	22♓34	9♉24	19♉25	10♋39	19♌59	12♎55	19♏45	6♑50	21♒36	23♓45	8♉46	13♊09
	27	17♈06	5♊42	16♊05	8♌56	18♍19	9♏41	15♐08	0♒55	15♓21	18♈02	4♊54	11♋15
	29	12♉43		13♋48	7♍28	16♎00	5♐30	9♑45	24♒42	9♈22	13♉04	2♋12	10♌17
	31	9♊57		12♌31		12♏55		3♒52	18♓27		9♊00		9♍21
☿	1	17♐08	28♑49	18♓09	14♈29	12♈58	1♊52	1♌06	23♌28	20♌09	13♎26	29♏38	2♐32
	7	23 20	8♒32	29 19	9R45	19 34	14 53	9 26	20R01	29 39	23 20	6♐40	27R52
	13	0♑54	18 43	9♈02	6 18	27 39	27 58	16 13	15 19	10♍44	2♏46	11 59	29D26
	19	9 13	29 23	15 33	5D47	7♉05	10♋17	21 12	12 19	22 04	11 46	13R56	4♐59
	25	18 01	10♓33	17R34	8 12	17 48	21 22	23 53	13D19	3♎01	20 20	10 20	12 26
	31	27 15		15 11		29 46		23R46	18 50		28 22		20 45

DATE	☉	♀	♂	♃	♄	⚷	♅	♆	♇	☊	STATIONS
1 1	9♑41	27♏18	12♏30	0♓25	11♈29	6♋56	14♉01	23♍19	0♌49	14♏53	
11	19 52	4♐45	18 41	2 26	11 53	6 16	13R53	23R16	0R36	14 21	☿ 25/3 17♈35
21	0♒03	13 36	24 51	4 35	12 27	5 39	13 50	23 09	0 23	13 49	☿ 17/4 5♈37
31	10 13	23 24	0♐58	6 50	13 10	5 06	13D52	22 59	0 09	13 18	☿ 28/7 24♌13
10 2	20 21	3♑50	7 02	9 09	14 02	4 39	13 59	22 46	29♋57	12 46	☿ 21/8 12♌08
20	0♓27	14 44	13 01	11 32	15 00	4 19	14 11	22 32	29 45	12 14	☿ 18/11 13♐58
2 3	10 31	25 57	18 55	13 57	16 04	4 08	14 28	22 16	29 34	11 42	☿ 8/12 27♏44
12	20 31	7♒24	24 43	16 22	17 12	4D05	14 49	22 00	29 25	11 10	♂ 23/6 4♒43
22	0♈29	19 01	0♑23	18 46	18 25	4 12	15 15	21 43	29 19	10 39	♂ 24/8 23♑56
1 4	10 22	0♓46	5 53	21 09	19 39	4 27	15 43	21 27	29 15	10 07	♃ 30/7 8♈47
11	20 13	12 36	11 09	23 28	20 55	4 50	16 14	21 12	29 13	9 35	♃ 25/11 28♓52
21	0♉00	24 30	16 10	25 43	22 11	5 21	16 47	20 59	29D14	9 03	♄ 14/8 1♉16
1 5	9 44	6♈28	20 50	27 51	23 25	5 59	17 21	20 48	29 18	8 32	♄ 28/12 24♈25
11	19 25	18 28	25 04	29 53	24 38	6 43	17 56	20 40	29 24	8 00	♅ 22/1 13♉50
21	29 03	0♉30	28 44	1♈46	25 48	7 33	18 30	20 35	29 32	7 28	♅ 28/8 21♉58
31	8♊40	12 33	1♒40	3 30	26 53	8 26	19 04	20 33	29 42	6 56	♆ 2/6 20♍32
10 6	18 14	24 39	3 43	5 01	27 53	9 24	19 36	20D34	29 55	6 25	♆ 28/12 25♍31
20	27 47	6♊46	4 40	6 19	28 48	10 23	20 07	20 38	0♌08	5 53	♇ 12/4 29♋13
30	7♋19	18 55	4R23	7 23	29 35	11 25	20 34	20 45	0 24	5 21	♇ 4/11 2♌55
10 7	16 51	1♋06	2 55	8 09	0♉14	12 27	20 59	20 56	0 40	4 49	⚷ 10/3 4♋05
20	26 24	13 20	0 30	8 38	0 44	13 29	21 20	21 09	0 56	4 17	⚷ 1 11 20♋04
30	5♌57	25 36	27♑46	8R47	1 04	14 29	21 36	21 24	1 13	3 46	
9 8	15 31	7♌54	25 26	8 37	1 15	15 27	21 48	21 42	1 30	3 14	
19	25 07	20 15	24 06	8 08	1R15	16 22	21 56	22 02	1 46	2 42	
29	4♍46	2♍37	24D06	7 20	1 04	17 13	21R58	22 23	2 01	2 10	
8 9	14 27	15 02	25 26	6 17	0 44	17 59	21 55	22 45	2 15	1 39	
18	24 11	27 28	27 58	5 03	0 14	18 39	21 47	23 07	2 27	1 07	
28	3♎58	9♎55	1♒31	3 44	29♈37	19 13	21 35	23 29	2 37	0 35	
8 10	13 49	22 23	5 52	2 25	28 54	19 38	21 19	23 51	2 45	0 03	
18	23 43	4♏52	10 51	1 11	28 07	19 55	20 59	24 11	2 51	29♎31	
28	3♏40	17 21	16 19	0 10	27 20	20 03	20 36	24 30	2 54	29 00	
7 11	13 41	29 49	22 11	29♓25	26 33	20R02	20 12	24 47	2R55	28 28	
17	23 44	12♐18	28 20	28 58	25 51	19 52	19 47	25 02	2 53	27 56	
27	3♐51	24 47	4♓41	28D52	25 16	19 33	19 23	25 14	2 48	27 24	
7 12	13 59	7♑14	11 13	29 07	24 49	19 06	19 00	25 23	2 41	26 53	
17	24 09	19 41	17 51	29 42	24 31	18 33	18 39	25 29	2 32	26 21	
27	4♑20	2♒07	24 35	0♈36	24 25	17 55	18 22	25 31	2 21	25 49	

SID M/N 1st JAN 6 h 38 m 0 s 1940 LEAP BST 25/2 to 31/12

	DAY	JAN	FEB	MAR	APR	MAY	JUN	JUL	AUG	SEP	OCT	NOV	DEC
	1	23♍40	15♏47	8♐57	26♑18	29♒02	12♈40	14♉45	1♋23	22♌00	0♎08	23♏35	0♑41
☽	3	21♎39	12♐11	4♑43	20♒30	22♓42	6♉44	10♊02	29♋12	21♍54	0♏30	22♐45	28♑13
	5	18♏48	7♑38	29♑26	14♓11	16♈23	1♊41	6♋42	28♌16	21♎51	0♐04	20♑10	24♒00
	7	15♐12	2♒22	23♒29	7♈48	10♉33	27♊45	4♌36	27♍40	20♏52	28♐03	15♒48	18♓24
	9	10♑53	26♒32	17♓12	1♉41	5♊30	24♋50	3♍08	26♎35	18♐29	24♑19	10♓09	12♈04
	11	5♒48	20♓16	10♈49	26♉06	1♋20	22♌35	1♎42	24♏35	14♑45	19♒15	3♈49	5♉44
	13	29♒58	13♈50	4♉37	21♊19	28♋05	20♍44	29♎56	21♐36	9♒55	13♓18	27♈25	29♉56
	15	23♓39	7♉44	29♉01	17♋39	25♌43	19♎03	27♏40	17♑43	4♓18	6♈58	21♉23	25♊01
	17	17♈19	2♊34	24♊31	15♌18	24♍11	17♏22	24♐49	13♒00	28♓10	0♉35	15♊56	21♋00
	19	11♉40	28♊59	21♋36	14♍17	23♎12	15♐19	21♑13	7♓29	21♈46	24♉28	11♋14	17♌46
	21	7♊23	27♋21	20♌28	14♎06	22♏14	12♑26	16♒39	1♈22	15♉26	18♊54	7♌22	15♍08
	23	4♋58	27♌20	20♍37	13♏49	20♐31	8♒22	11♓07	24♈56	9♊37	14♋12	4♍29	13♎07
	25	4♌14	27♍48	20♎57	12♐28	17♑28	3♓04	4♈54	18♉44	4♋51	10♌46	2♎45	11♏38
	27	4♍15	27♎27	20♏17	9♑27	12♒54	26♓56	28♈33	13♊23	1♌38	8♍51	2♏00	10♐25
	29	3♎48	25♏32	17♐55	4♒50	7♓09	20♈36	22♉43	9♋30	0♍11	8♎20	1♐39	8♑47
	31	2♏08		13♑51		0♈50		18♊05	7♌26		8♏34		6♒02
	1	22♐11	11♒09	28♓10	17♓13	19♈45	22♊20	3♌06	24♋40	5♍00	26♎23	28♏07	18♏45
☿	7	1♑01	21 43	0℞12	20 09	0♉13	3♋47	5 12	26D07	16 31	4♏54	25℞24	26 27
	13	10 09	2♓35	27♓09	25 21	11 48	13 42	4℞33	1♌28	27 25	12 46	18 05	5♐03
	19	19 34	13 18	21 40	2♈12	24 23	22 01	1 24	10 14	7♎40	19 45	12 30	14 01
	25	29 19	22 43	17 40	10 24	7♊30	28 35	27♋21	21 14	17 18	25 14	13D17	23 11
	31	9♒25		17D00		20 18		24 48	3♍02		28 03		2♑31

DATE	☉	♀	♂	♃	♄	⚷	♅	♆	♇	☊	STATIONS
1 1	9♑26	8♒19	27♓58	1♈09	24♈25	17♋34	18♉15	25♍31	2♌15	25♎33	
11	19 37	20 40	4♈45	2 28	24 35	16 52	18℞05	25℞28	2℞02	25 01	☿ 6/3 0♈15
21	29 48	2♓59	11 34	4 01	24 56	16 11	17 59	25 22	1 49	24 30	☿ 29/3 16♓50
31	9♒58	15 12	18 23	5 46	25 27	15 32	17D59	25 12	1 35	23 58	☿ 9/7 5♌18
10 2	20 07	27 19	25 11	7 42	26 08	14 58	18 04	25 01	1 22	23 26	☿ 2/8 24♋38
20	0♓13	9♈17	1♉59	9 46	26 57	14 30	18 14	24 47	1 10	22 54	☿ 1/11 28♏07
1 3	10 16	21 05	8 44	11 58	27 54	14 10	18 29	24 31	0 59	22 23	☿ 21/11 12♏03
11	20 17	2♉40	15 28	14 14	28 56	13 59	18 48	24 15	0 50	21 51	♀ 5/6 13♋18
21	0♈14	13 59	22 10	16 35	0♉04	13D57	19 12	23 58	0 43	21 19	♀ 19/7 26♊47
31	10 08	24 56	28 49	18 58	1 16	14 05	19 39	23 42	0 39	20 47	♃ 4/9 15♉41
10 4	19 59	5♊27	5♊26	21 23	2 30	14 22	20 09	23 27	0 37	20 15	♃ 31/12 5♉40
20	29 46	15 22	12 01	23 48	3 47	14 47	20 41	23 13	0D37	19 44	♄ 27/8 14♉47
30	9♉30	24 28	18 34	26 11	5 03	15 21	21 15	23 02	0 40	19 12	♅ 27/1 17♉58
10 5	19 11	2♋24	25 04	28 33	6 19	16 02	21 50	22 53	0 46	18 40	♅ 1/9 26♉09
20	28 49	8 40	1♋33	0♉50	7 33	16 50	22 25	22 47	0 54	18 08	♆ 3/6 22♍43
30	8♊26	12 32	7 59	3 03	8 45	17 43	22 59	22 44	1 04	17 37	♆ 30/12 27♍42
9 6	18 00	13℞02	14 25	5 11	9 53	18 41	23 32	22D44	1 16	17 05	♇ 13/4 0♌37
19	27 33	9 41	20 48	7 10	10 56	19 42	24 04	22 47	1 30	16 33	♇ 5/11 4♌20
29	7♋05	3 44	27 11	9 02	11 54	20 46	24 33	22 54	1 45	16 01	⚷ 18/3 13♋57
9 7	16 37	28♊33	3♌33	10 43	12 45	21 52	24 59	23 04	2 01	15 30	⚷ 13/11 1♌30
19	26 10	26D47	9 54	12 12	13 28	22 59	25 21	23 16	2 18	14 58	
29	5♌43	28 45	16 15	13 27	14 02	24 06	25 40	23 31	2 35	14 26	
8 8	15 17	3♋38	22 36	14 27	14 27	25 11	25 54	23 49	2 52	13 54	
18	24 53	10 35	28 57	15 10	14 42	26 15	26 04	24 08	3 08	13 22	
28	4♍32	18 57	5♍19	15 35	14℞47	27 15	26 08	24 28	3 23	12 51	
7 9	14 13	28 19	11 41	15℞40	14 41	28 11	26℞08	24 50	3 38	12 19	
17	23 57	8♌25	18 05	15 25	14 24	29 03	26 02	25 12	3 50	11 47	
27	3♎44	19 04	24 29	14 51	13 58	29 47	25 52	25 34	4 01	11 15	
7 10	13 35	0♍08	0♎55	13 58	13 23	0♌25	25 37	25 56	4 10	10 44	
17	23 28	11 33	7 22	12 51	12 42	0 55	25 19	26 17	4 16	10 12	
27	3♏26	23 13	13 51	11 34	11 56	1 16	24 58	26 37	4 19	9 40	
6 11	13 26	5♎07	20 22	10 13	11 08	1 28	24 34	26 54	4℞20	9 08	
16	23 30	17 11	26 55	8 54	10 20	1℞29	24 09	27 10	4 19	8 36	
26	3♐36	29 22	3♏29	7 42	9 36	1 21	23 44	27 22	4 15	8 05	
6 12	13 44	11♏40	10 06	6 44	8 57	1 04	23 20	27 32	4 08	7 33	
16	23 54	24 02	16 44	6 04	8 26	0 38	22 59	27 39	3 59	7 01	
26	4♑05	6♐27	23 25	5 43	8 05	0 04	22 40	27 42	3 48	6 29	

SID M/N 1st JAN 6 h 41 m 0 s — 1941 COMMON — DST 4/5 to 10/8

	DAY	JAN	FEB	MAR	APR	MAY	JUN	JUL	AUG	SEP	OCT	NOV	DEC
	1	19♒06	3♈59	12♈02	25♉59	29♊01	16♌29	23♍32	16♏26	9♑40	16♒55	4♈15	7♉16
☽	3	14♓08	27♈42	5♉42	19♊57	23♋52	13♍06	21♎22	14♐59	6♒56	12♓32	28♈21	0♊59
	5	8♈08	21♉24	29♉24	14♋43	19♌50	11♎04	20♏07	13♑24	3♓19	7♈22	22♉10	24♊49
	7	1♉44	15♊47	23♊43	10♌50	17♍19	10♏22	19♐25	11♒07	28♓43	1♉34	15♊53	18♋57
	9	25♉42	11♋25	19♋16	8♍41	16♎28	10♐24	18♑27	7♓42	23♈13	25♉22	9♋47	13♌34
	11	20♊35	8♌34	16♌27	8♎10	16♏46	10♑02	16♒18	2♈59	17♉06	19♊05	4♌14	9♍02
	13	16♋42	6♍58	15♍16	8♏33	17♐03	8♒12	12♓32	27♈15	10♊51	13♋11	29♌44	5♎51
	15	13♌55	5♎58	15♎02	8♐34	16♑04	4♓30	7♈19	21♉00	5♋01	8♌14	26♍51	4♏21
	17	11♍49	4♏51	14♏46	7♑12	13♒10	29♓14	1♉14	14♊54	0♌13	4♍46	25♎50	4♐19
	19	9♎59	3♐08	13♐34	4♒04	8♓31	23♈05	24♉57	9♋33	26♌51	3♎05	26♏13	4♑46
	21	8♏10	0♑37	11♑02	29♒25	2♈42	16♉43	19♊04	5♌20	25♍00	2♏52	26♐45	4♒16
	23	6♐15	27♑16	7♒12	23♓44	26♈21	10♊40	14♋01	2♍22	24♎13	3♐08	26♑01	1♓55
	25	4♑00	23♒01	2♓19	17♈31	19♉59	5♋15	9♌56	0♎23	23♏40	2♑36	23♒23	27♓43
	27	1♒03	17♓54	26♓40	11♉08	13♊57	0♌35	6♍44	28♎55	22♐31	0♒32	18♓59	22♈10
	29	27♒03		20♈31	4♊53	8♋25	26♌39	4♎13	27♏30	20♑17	26♒53	13♈25	15♉58
	31	21♓55		14♉09		3♌35		2♏16	25♐45		22♓00		9♊40
	1	4♑05	25♒51	4♓53	14♓00	4♉11	3♋01	11♋42	20♋53	19♍58	2♏54	27♎59	26♏54
☿	7	13 38	5♓12	0R03	22 02	16 59	9 34	8R13	1♌26	0♎01	8 30	26D41	6♐14
	13	23 26	11 47	28D58	1♈07	29 57	13 53	6 20	13 25	9 22	11 48	1♏12	15 36
	19	3♒30	13R15	1♓21	11 10	12♊09	15 39	7D24	25 37	18 01	11R20	8 50	25 01
	25	13 49	9 06	6 12	22 11	22 51	14R43	11 47	7♍17	25 56	5 59	17 40	4♑32
	31	24 10		12 46		1♋44		19 21	18 13		28♎50		14 11

DATE	☉	♀	♂	♃	♄	⚷	♅	♆	♇	☊	STATIONS
1 1	10♑12	13♐56	27♏26	5♉40	7♉58	29♋41	22♉30	27♍42	3♌41	6♎10	
11	20 24	26 24	4♐10	5 53	7D54	28 60	22R18	27R39	3R28	5 39	☿ 17/2 13♓27
21	0♒35	8♑53	10 56	6 25	8 01	28 16	22 11	27 34	3 15	5 07	☿ 12/3 28♒53
31	10 44	21 23	17 43	7 17	8 19	27 33	22D09	27 25	3 01	4 35	☿ 20/6 15♋40
10 2	20 53	3♒52	24 32	8 25	8 48	26 53	22 12	27 13	2 48	4 03	☿ 14/7 6♋17
20	0♓59	16 22	1♑23	9 49	9 27	26 17	22 20	27 00	2 36	3 31	☿ 15/10 12♏10
2 3	11 02	28 50	8 16	11 25	10 14	25 48	22 34	26 44	2 25	3 00	☿ 5/11 26♎22
12	21 02	11♓18	15 09	13 13	11 09	25 28	22 52	26 28	2 16	2 28	♂ 7/9 23♈44
22	0♈59	23 45	22 03	15 10	12 11	25 17	23 14	26 12	2 09	1 56	♂ 10/11 11♈06
1 4	10 53	6♈10	28 58	17 15	13 18	25D16	23 40	25 55	2 04	1 24	♃ 10/10 21♊27
11	20 43	18 34	5♒53	19 26	14 29	25 24	24 09	25 40	2 02	0 53	♄ 10/1 7♉53
21	0♉30	0♉57	12 47	21 41	15 44	25 43	24 41	25 26	2D02	0 21	♄ 11/9 28♉33
1 5	10 14	13 18	19 39	24 00	17 00	26 11	25 14	25 14	2 05	29♍49	♅ 30/1 22♉09
11	19 55	25 38	26 28	26 21	18 17	26 47	25 49	25 05	2 11	29 17	♅ 6/9 0♊21
21	29 33	7♊56	3♓13	28 42	19 34	27 31	26 24	24 58	2 18	28 46	♆ 6/6 24♍54
31	9♊09	20 13	9 52	1♊03	20 50	28 22	26 58	24 55	2 29	28 14	♇ 15/4 2♌02
10 6	18 44	2♋28	16 22	3 23	22 03	29 19	27 32	24D55	2 41	27 42	♇ 7/11 5♌47
20	28 17	14 43	22 40	5 40	23 13	0♌21	28 04	24 58	2 54	27 10	⚷ 28/3 25♋15
30	7♋49	26 56	28 42	7 53	24 19	1 27	28 35	25 04	3 10	26 38	⚷ 27/11 14♌34
10 7	17 21	9♌08	4♈24	10 02	25 19	2 36	29 02	25 13	3 26	26 07	
20	26 53	21 18	9 40	12 04	26 13	3 47	29 26	25 25	3 42	25 35	
30	6♌26	3♍26	14 21	13 58	26 59	4 59	29 46	25 40	3 59	25 03	
9 8	16 01	15 32	18 18	15 43	27 37	6 11	0♊02	25 57	4 16	24 31	
19	25 37	27 35	21 19	17 17	28 06	7 22	0 13	26 16	4 33	24 00	
29	5♍16	9♎35	23 11	18 39	28 25	8 32	0 20	26 36	4 49	23 28	
8 9	14 57	21 30	23R44	19 47	28 33	9 38	0R21	26 58	5 03	22 56	
18	24 41	3♏22	22 49	20 38	28R30	10 40	0 17	27 20	5 16	22 24	
28	4♎29	15 07	20 38	21 12	28 17	11 37	0 09	27 42	5 27	21 52	
8 10	14 19	26 46	17 38	21 26	27 54	12 28	29♉56	28 04	5 36	21 21	
18	24 14	8♐16	14 36	21R21	27 21	13 11	29 38	28 25	5 42	20 49	
28	4♏11	19 35	12 17	20 55	26 41	13 46	29 18	28 45	5 46	20 17	
7 11	14 12	0♑38	11 10	20 11	25 56	14 12	28 55	29 03	5R47	19 45	
17	24 16	11 19	11D23	19 10	25 08	14 28	28 30	29 19	5 46	19 14	
27	4♐22	21 30	12 50	17 57	24 19	14 34	28 05	29 32	5 42	18 42	
7 12	14 30	0♒56	15 20	16 37	23 33	14R29	27 40	29 42	5 35	18 10	
17	24 40	9 17	18 40	15 15	22 52	14 14	27 18	29 49	5 27	17 38	
27	4♑51	15 59	22 40	14 00	22 19	13 49	26 58	29 52	5 16	17 07	

SID M/N 1st JAN 6 h 40 m 2 s   **1942 COMMON**   DST 5/4 to 9/8

	DAY	JAN	FEB	MAR	APR	MAY	JUN	JUL	AUG	SEP	OCT	NOV	DEC
	1	21♊37	7♌01	15♌17	3♎44	11♏09	5♑13	13♒29	3♈22	19♉31	21♊33	5♌03	7♍24
☽	3	15♋51	2♍44	11♍36	2♏29	11♐16	4♒49	11♓38	29♈04	13♊39	15♋17	29♌19	2♎45
	5	10♌38	29♍16	9♎01	1♐47	10♑57	2♓41	7♈57	23♉33	7♋25	9♌16	24♍50	29♎56
	7	6♍03	26♎34	7♏11	0♑46	9♒19	28♓51	2♉52	17♊24	1♌23	4♍06	22♎03	29♏01
	9	2♎20	24♏36	5♐39	28♑53	6♓11	23♈46	26♉56	11♋09	26♌03	0♎15	20♏54	29♐17
	11	29♎45	23♐12	4♑02	25♒58	1♈50	17♉58	20♊41	5♌14	21♍43	27♎47	20♐33	29♑25
	13	28♏27	21♑59	2♒01	22♓06	26♈38	11♊48	14♋27	29♌55	18♎25	26♏18	19♑56	28♒17
	15	28♐04	20♒18	29♒21	17♈26	20♉53	5♋31	8♌29	25♍23	15♏59	25♐05	18♒17	25♓34
	17	27♑39	17♓32	25♓51	12♉06	14♊46	29♋20	3♍02	21♎45	14♐08	23♑33	15♓26	21♈27
	19	26♒08	13♈27	21♈22	6♊10	8♋29	23♌33	28♍21	19♏08	12♑33	21♒23	11♈36	16♉23
	21	22♓57	8♉09	15♉59	29♊55	2♌19	18♍36	24♎51	17♐29	10♒56	18♓33	7♉00	10♊41
	23	18♈11	2♊05	9♊56	23♋46	26♌48	15♎02	22♏48	16♑32	8♓56	15♈00	1♊45	4♋34
	25	12♉20	25♊53	3♋42	18♌19	22♍31	13♏16	22♐07	15♒41	6♈11	10♉39	25♊53	28♋14
	27	6♊04	20♋07	27♋55	14♍11	20♎03	13♐08	22♑08	14♓09	2♉22	5♊27	19♋36	21♌56
	29	29♊58		23♌08	11♎50	19♏28	13♑40	21♒43	11♈21	27♉24	29♊30	13♌15	16♍07
	31	24♋28		19♍49		19♐59		19♓55	7♉07		23♋11		11♎20
	1	15♑49	27♒01	13♒43	22♓35	21♉58	25♊38	18♊37	5♌56	0♎56	25♎41	20♎51	8♐08
☿	7	25 39	23R53	18 29	3♈06	3♊13	24R15	23 04	18 17	8 59	21R44	29 54	17 33
	13	5♒32	17 05	24 58	14 29	12 30	21 09	0♋13	29 52	16 01	14 52	9♏29	26 58
	19	15 00	12 21	2♓41	26 42	19 28	18 10	9 48	10♍36	21 41	10 41	19 07	6♑26
	25	22 54	11D57	11 22	9♉28	23 55	17D01	21 20	20 28	25 17	12D44	28 40	15 54
	31	26 55		20 54		25 38		3♌50	29 30		19 28		25 09

DATE	☉	♀	♂	♃	♄	⚷	♅	♆	♇	☊	STATIONS
1 1	9♑57	18♒28	24♈51	13♊25	22♉06	13♌34	26♉49	29♍53	5♌10	16♍51	
11	20 09	21 07	29 34	12R28	21R47	12 58	26R35	29R51	4R57	16 19	☿ 1/2 27♒01
21	0♒20	19R52	4♉37	11 47	21 39	12 16	26 26	29 46	4 44	15 47	☿ 23/2 11♒37
31	10 30	14 56	9 55	11 26	21D42	11 31	26 21	29 38	4 30	15 15	☿ 1/6 25♊39
10 2	20 38	9 02	15 26	11D25	21 56	10 46	26D22	29 27	4 17	14 44	☿ 25/6 17♊01
20	0♓44	5 44	21 06	11 45	22 21	10 03	26 28	29 14	4 04	14 12	☿ 29/9 26♎00
2 3	10 47	6D24	26 53	12 23	22 56	9 24	26 39	28 59	3 53	13 40	☿ 20/10 10♎36
12	20 48	10 28	2♊46	13 19	23 41	8 53	26 55	28 43	3 43	13 08	♀ 13/1 21♒12
22	0♈45	16 57	8 43	14 31	24 33	8 30	27 16	28 27	3 36	12 36	♀ 23/2 5♒31
1 4	10 39	25 02	14 42	15 56	25 33	8 16	27 41	28 10	3 31	12 05	♃ 5/2 11♊23
11	20 29	4♓12	20 45	17 34	26 38	8D13	28 08	27 55	3 28	11 33	♃ 13/11 25♋15
21	0♉16	14 07	26 49	19 21	27 48	8 20	28 39	27 40	3D28	11 01	♄ 23/1 21♉38
1 5	10 00	24 33	2♋54	21 17	29 02	8 37	29 12	27 28	3 31	10 29	♄ 25/9 12♊32
11	19 41	5♈21	9 01	23 20	0♊18	9 05	29 46	27 18	3 36	9 58	♅ 4/2 26♉21
21	29 19	16 26	15 08	25 28	1 35	9 42	0♊21	27 11	3 43	9 26	♅ 10/9 4♊35
31	8♊55	27 43	21 17	27 40	2 52	10 27	0 56	27 07	3 53	8 54	♆ 1/1 29♍53
10 6	18 30	9♉10	27 27	29 55	4 09	11 19	1 30	27D06	4 05	8 22	♆ 8/6 27♍06
20	28 03	20 45	3♌37	2♋11	5 24	12 19	2 03	27 08	4 19	7 51	♇ 16/4 3♌28
30	7♋35	2♊27	9 49	4 28	6 37	13 24	2 35	27 13	4 34	7 19	♇ 8/11 7♌16
10 7	17 07	14 14	16 02	6 44	7 45	14 33	3 03	27 22	4 50	6 47	⚷ 9/4 8♌13
20	26 39	26 07	22 16	8 59	8 48	15 46	3 29	27 33	5 07	6 15	⚷ 14/12 29♌23
30	6♌13	8♋06	28 32	11 10	9 46	17 02	3 51	27 47	5 24	5 43	
9 8	15 47	20 09	4♍50	13 18	10 36	18 19	4 09	28 04	5 41	5 12	
19	25 23	2♌17	11 10	15 20	11 19	19 37	4 23	28 22	5 58	4 40	
29	5♍02	14 30	17 32	17 15	11 52	20 54	4 31	28 42	6 14	4 08	
8 9	14 43	26 48	23 56	19 01	12 16	22 10	4 35	29 04	6 28	3 36	
18	24 27	9♍09	0♎23	20 38	12 29	23 23	4R34	29 26	6 42	3 05	
28	4♎14	21 34	6 53	22 03	12R31	24 32	4 27	29 48	6 53	2 33	
8 10	14 05	4♎01	13 26	23 15	12 23	25 37	4 16	0♎10	7 02	2 01	
18	23 59	16 31	20 03	24 11	12 04	26 35	4 01	0 31	7 09	1 29	
28	3♏57	29 02	26 42	24 51	11 35	27 27	3 41	0 51	7 14	0 57	
7 11	13 57	11♏35	3♏26	25 11	10 58	28 10	3 19	1 10	7 16	0 26	
17	24 01	24 09	10 13	25R13	10 14	28 43	2 55	1 26	7R15	29♌54	
27	4♐07	6♐43	17 03	24 54	9 26	29 07	2 30	1 40	7 11	29 22	
7 12	14 15	19 17	23 58	24 16	8 37	29 20	2 05	1 51	7 05	28 50	
17	24 25	1♑51	0♐56	23 21	7 49	29R22	1 41	1 58	6 56	28 19	
27	4♑37	14 26	7 58	22 12	7 06	29 13	1 20	2 03	6 46	27 47	

SID M/N 1st JAN 6 h 39 m 5 s — 1943 COMMON — DST 4/4 to 15/8

DAY	JAN	FEB	MAR	APR	MAY	JUN	JUL	AUG	SEP	OCT	NOV	DEC
1	24♎33	15♐46	25♐39	19♒02	27♓20	17♉02	21♊19	6♌02	20♍35	24♎37	14♐06	22♑14
☽ 3	22♏24	15♑25	24♑32	17♓30	24♈28	12♊15	15♋21	29♌38	15♎08	20♏35	11♑49	20♒47
5	22♐02	15♒37	23♒56	15♈28	20♉47	6♋40	9♌01	23♍30	10♏30	17♐21	9♒51	18♓58
7	22♑34	15♓10	23♓03	12♉24	16♊05	0♌28	2♍35	18♎03	6♐54	14♑55	8♓05	16♈39
9	22♒39	13♈13	21♈04	8♊02	10♋24	24♌03	26♍34	13♏42	4♑34	13♒18	6♈21	13♉43
11	21♓15	9♉31	17♉31	2♋29	4♌06	18♍00	21♎32	10♐52	3♒29	12♓17	4♉18	10♊00
13	18♈03	4♊22	12♊31	26♋14	27♌49	13♎00	18♏03	9♑41	3♓15	11♈20	1♊22	5♋19
15	13♉22	28♊19	6♋31	19♌58	22♍15	9♏39	16♐23	9♒42	2♈58	9♉38	27♊11	29♋41
17	7♊42	21♋57	0♌09	14♍21	18♎01	8♐06	16♑14	9♓58	1♉36	6♊30	21♋47	23♌26
19	1♋32	15♌44	24♌04	9♎54	15♏26	7♑48	16♒34	9♈17	28♉32	1♋49	15♌34	17♍03
21	25♋12	10♍01	18♍43	6♏48	14♐09	7♒42	16♓13	6♉56	23♊48	25♋57	9♍13	11♎14
23	18♌58	5♎01	14♎22	4♐44	13♑24	6♓48	14♈23	2♊51	17♋54	19♌34	3♎26	6♏37
25	13♍07	0♏52	10♏59	3♑10	12♒20	4♈37	10♉57	27♊26	11♌30	13♍23	28♎49	3♐37
27	7♎59	27♏43	8♐25	1♒33	10♓28	1♉09	6♊10	21♋15	5♍13	7♎59	25♏38	2♑11
29	3♏57		6♑24	29♒39	7♈42	26♉39	0♋28	14♌49	29♍31	3♏41	23♐39	1♒38
31	1♐25		4♒46		4♉07		24♋14	8♍33		0♐26		1♓02
1	26♑38	26♑22	15♒08	6♈56	0♊20	27♉37	20♊14	22♌15	4♎40	25♍21	1♏43	19♐16
☿ 7	4♒46	25D02	23 37	19 11	4 35	27D10	1♋14	2♍37	8 28	25D35	11 35	28 24
13	10 06	27 47	2♓51	1♉39	5R42	29 22	13 38	12 01	9R23	1♎16	21 14	7♑18
19	9R53	3♒05	12 48	13 20	4 02	4♊06	26 29	20 27	6 30	10 03	0♐42	15 34
25	3 41	9 57	23 29	23 09	0 48	11 07	8♌54	27 49	0 27	19 58	10 01	22 09
31	27♑04		4♈57		27♉55		20 25	3♎50		0♏03		24R51

DATE	☉	♀	♂	♃	♄	⚷	♅	♆	♇	☊	STATIONS
1 1	9♑42	20♑42	11♐30	21♋34	6♊46	29♌04	1♊11	2♎04	6♌40	27♌31	
11	19 54	3♒15	18 38	20R14	6R14	28 39	0R55	2R03	6R28	26 59	☿ 16/1 10♒51
21	0♒05	15 48	25 49	18 54	5 50	28 06	0 43	1 59	6 14	26 27	☿ 6/2 24♑56
31	10 15	28 18	3♑04	17 40	5 38	27 25	0 36	1 51	6 00	25 56	☿ 12/5 5♊44
10 2	20 23	10♓47	10 23	16 37	5D36	26 40	0D35	1 41	5 47	25 24	☿ 5/6 27♉01
20	0♓29	23 12	17 45	15 50	5 46	25 54	0 38	1 29	5 34	24 52	☿ 12/9 9♎29
2 3	10 33	5♈34	25 09	15 21	6 07	25 08	0 47	1 14	5 22	24 20	☿ 4/10 24♍41
12	20 33	17 53	2♒36	15 11	6 38	24 26	1 01	0 58	5 13	23 49	☿ 31/12 24♑51
22	0♈30	0♉06	10 06	15D20	7 19	23 51	1 20	0 42	5 05	23 17	♀ 16/8 20♍32
1 4	10 24	12 13	17 37	15 48	8 08	23 23	1 43	0 25	4 59	22 45	♀ 27/9 4♍20
11	20 15	24 14	25 09	16 34	9 05	23 05	2 09	0 10	4 56	22 13	♂ 28/10 22♊14
21	0♉02	6♊08	2♓42	17 36	10 08	22 57	2 39	29♍55	4D55	21 41	♃ 12/3 15♋11
1 5	9 46	17 52	10 15	18 52	11 17	23D01	3 11	29 42	4 58	21 10	♃ 14/12 27♌04
11	19 27	29 26	17 46	20 20	12 29	23 15	3 45	29 31	5 02	20 38	♄ 6/2 5♊35
21	29 05	10♋48	25 15	21 59	13 44	23 40	4 19	29 24	5 10	20 06	♄ 10/10 26♊38
31	8♊41	21 53	2♈41	23 47	15 01	24 14	4 55	29 19	5 19	19 34	♅ 8/2 0♊34
10 6	18 16	2♌39	10 02	25 42	16 19	24 59	5 29	29 17	5 31	19 03	♅ 15/9 8♊51
20	27 49	12 59	17 17	27 43	17 37	25 51	6 03	29D18	5 44	18 31	♆ 4/1 2♎04
30	7♋21	22 45	24 25	29 49	18 53	26 51	6 36	29 23	5 59	17 59	♆ 11/6 29♍17
10 7	16 53	1♍43	1♉25	1♌58	20 07	27 57	7 06	29 30	6 15	17 27	♇ 18/4 4♌55
20	26 26	9 35	8 13	4 10	21 18	29 08	7 33	29 41	6 32	16 55	♇ 10/11 8♌45
30	5♌59	15 49	14 48	6 23	22 24	0♍24	7 57	29 55	6 49	16 24	⚷ 23/4 22♌57
9 8	15 33	19 42	21 07	8 35	23 25	1 43	8 17	0♎11	7 07	15 52	
19	25 09	20R19	27 08	10 47	24 19	3 04	8 33	0 29	7 24	15 20	
29	4♍48	17 07	2♊46	12 56	25 06	4 27	8 44	0 48	7 40	14 48	
8 9	14 29	11 17	7 56	15 01	25 44	5 50	8 50	1 09	7 55	14 17	
18	24 13	6 07	12 32	17 02	26 12	7 11	8R51	1 31	8 09	13 45	
28	4♎00	4D21	16 27	18 56	26 31	8 31	8 47	1 54	8 21	13 13	
8 10	13 51	6 25	19 30	20 43	26 38	9 48	8 38	2 16	8 31	12 41	
18	23 45	11 30	21 30	22 19	26R35	10 60	8 24	2 37	8 38	12 10	
28	3♏42	18 43	22 14	23 45	26 20	12 07	8 06	2 58	8 43	11 38	
7 11	13 43	27 24	21R32	24 58	25 55	13 07	7 45	3 17	8 45	11 06	
17	23 46	7♎07	19 24	25 55	25 21	13 59	7 22	3 34	8R45	10 34	
27	3♐52	17 34	16 06	26 36	24 40	14 42	6 57	3 48	8 41	10 02	
7 12	14 01	28 32	12 17	26 59	23 53	15 15	6 32	4 00	8 36	9 31	
17	24 11	9♏53	8 46	27R03	23 04	15 37	6 07	4 08	8 28	8 59	
27	4♑22	21 31	6 13	26 47	22 15	15 48	5 45	4 13	8 17	8 27	

SID M/N 1st JAN 6 h 38 m 8 s **1944 LEAP** DST 2/4 to 15/7

DAY	JAN	FEB	MAR	APR	MAY	JUN	JUL	AUG	SEP	OCT	NOV	DEC
1	15♓29	7♉19	29♉57	16♋30	18♌38	2♎11	4♏34	21♐36	12♒21	20♓46	14♉27	21♊15
☽ 3	13♈34	3♊35	25♊32	10♌26	12♍17	26♎36	0♐12	19♑36	12♓31	21♈19	13♊22	18♋13
5	10♉34	28♊38	19♋54	4♍01	6♎12	22♏05	27♐16	19♒01	12♈58	21♉04	10♋27	13♌40
7	6♊33	22♋52	13♌38	27♍48	0♏53	18♐45	25♑38	19♓00	12♉23	18♊59	5♌49	7♍58
9	1♋39	16♌38	7♍14	22♎09	26♏29	16♑24	24♒44	18♈28	10♊01	14♋59	0♍00	1♎44
11	26♋01	10♍16	1♎02	17♏11	22♐57	14♒37	23♓49	16♉39	5♋55	9♌35	23♍43	25♎37
13	19♌51	4♎01	25♎17	12♐58	20♑07	13♓03	22♈17	13♊23	0♌35	3♍25	17♎31	20♏08
15	13♍26	28♎15	20♏10	9♑33	17♒54	11♈22	19♉49	8♋52	24♌33	27♍04	11♏50	15♐35
17	7♎15	23♏23	15♐58	7♒07	16♓14	9♉20	16♊22	3♌28	18♍15	20♎56	6♐49	12♑02
19	1♏51	19♐53	13♑00	5♓45	14♈55	6♊38	11♋57	27♌31	11♎58	15♏11	2♑32	9♒19
21	27♏49	18♑05	11♒30	5♈10	13♉27	2♋59	6♌42	21♍15	5♏56	9♐58	29♑00	7♓13
23	25♐32	17♒52	11♓17	4♉33	11♊08	28♋14	0♍47	14♎57	0♐22	5♑29	26♒20	5♈29
25	24♑54	18♓20	11♈29	2♊53	7♋30	22♌33	24♍30	8♏57	25♐42	2♒05	24♓37	3♉53
27	25♒05	18♈13	10♉49	29♊34	2♌31	16♍20	18♎17	3♐46	22♑23	0♓04	23♈40	2♊04
29	24♓58	16♉31	8♊26	24♋38	26♌33	10♎07	12♏40	29♐53	20♒48	29♓26	22♉50	29♊35
31	23♈36		4♋11		20♍15		8♐14	27♑45		29♈31		26♋04
1	24♑42	15♑55	26♒27	25♈10	13♉13	16♉01	8♋24	4♍09	19♍35	22♍59	15♏24	29♐13
☿ 7	19R57	22 44	6♓46	5♉11	9R31	23 22	21 15	11 28	14R07	3♎17	24 44	5♑42
13	12 21	0♒34	17 45	12 20	7 05	2♊28	3♌17	17 19	9 21	13 51	3♐51	8 56
19	8 43	9 09	29 23	15 58	7D10	13 13	14 14	21 13	9D07	24 11	12 44	6R17
25	10D11	18 20	11♈28	16R01	9 55	25 24	24 05	22R27	14 14	4♏10	21 18	28♐37
31	14 55		23 18		14 58		2♍49	20 17		13 49		23 11

DATE	☉	♀	♂	♃	♄	⚷	♅	♆	♇	☊	STATIONS
1 1	9♑28	27♏24	5♊25	26♌32	21♊52	15R49	5♊34	4♎15	8♌12	8♌11	
11	19 39	9♐19	4D52	25R49	21R08	15♍42	5R16	4R15	7R59	7 39	☿ 20/1 8♑39
21	29 50	21 22	5 34	24 49	20 32	15 24	5 03	4 11	7 46	7 08	☿ 22/4 16♉25
31	10♒00	3♑30	7 22	23 38	20 05	14 56	4 54	4 05	7 32	6 36	☿ 16/5 6♉47
10 2	20 08	15 42	10 03	22 20	19 47	14 19	4 50	3 55	7 18	6 04	☿ 24/8 22♍29
20	0♓15	27 56	13 26	21 01	19 41	13 36	4D51	3 43	7 05	5 32	☿ 16/9 8♍31
1 3	10 18	10♒12	17 21	19 47	19D46	12 50	4 58	3 29	6 53	5 01	☿ 14/12 8♑58
11	20 19	22 30	21 42	18 43	20 02	12 03	5 10	3 14	6 43	4 29	♂ 10/1 4♊51
21	0♈16	4♓48	26 22	17 52	20 29	11 17	5 27	2 57	6 35	3 57	♃ 13/4 17♌02
31	10 10	17 06	1♋19	17 19	21 06	10 37	5 48	2 41	6 29	3 25	♄ 21/2 19♊41
10 4	20 00	29 24	6 28	17 03	21 52	10 04	6 13	2 25	6 25	2 54	♄ 23/10 10♋48
20	29 48	11♈41	11 48	17D07	22 45	9 39	6 41	2 10	6D24	2 22	♅ 12/2 4♊50
30	9♉32	23 58	17 15	17 29	23 46	9 25	7 12	1 56	6 26	1 50	♅ 18/9 13♊09
10 5	19 13	6♉15	22 51	18 08	24 52	9D22	7 45	1 45	6 30	1 18	♆ 6/1 4♎15
20	28 51	18 32	28 32	19 03	26 02	9 30	8 19	1 37	6 37	0 46	♆ 12/6 1♎28
30	8♊28	0♊48	4♌18	20 12	27 16	9 49	8 55	1 31	6 46	0 15	♇ 19/4 6♌24
9 6	18 02	13 04	10 09	21 34	28 33	10 19	9 30	1 28	6 58	29♋43	♇ 11/11 10♌16
19	27 35	25 21	16 04	23 07	29 50	10 59	10 04	1D29	7 11	29 11	⚷ 31/12 15♍49
29	7♋07	7♋38	22 03	24 49	1♋08	11 49	10 38	1 33	7 26	28 39	⚷ 8/5 9♍22
9 7	16 39	19 56	28 07	26 39	2 26	12 46	11 09	1 40	7 42	28 08	
19	26 12	2♌14	4♍14	28 36	3 41	13 51	11 38	1 49	7 59	27 36	
29	5♌45	14 33	10 25	0♍37	4 54	15 01	12 03	2 02	8 16	27 04	
8 8	15 19	26 53	16 40	2 43	6 02	16 18	12 25	2 18	8 34	26 32	
18	24 55	9♍12	22 59	4 51	7 06	17 38	12 43	2 35	8 51	26 00	
28	4♍34	21 32	29 22	7 01	8 04	19 01	12 57	2 55	9 07	25 29	
7 9	14 15	3♎51	5♎49	9 11	8 54	20 26	13 05	3 15	9 23	24 57	
17	23 59	16 10	12 21	11 21	9 37	21 52	13 08	3 37	9 37	24 25	
27	3♎46	28 28	18 57	13 28	10 10	23 19	13R07	3 59	9 49	23 53	
7 10	13 36	10♏45	25 38	15 32	10 33	24 43	13 00	4 22	10 00	23 22	
17	23 30	23 01	2♏24	17 31	10 45	26 06	12 48	4 43	10 08	22 50	
27	3♏28	5♐16	9 14	19 25	10R47	27 25	12 32	5 04	10 13	22 18	
6 11	13 28	17 28	16 09	21 10	10 37	28 39	12 12	5 23	10 16	21 46	
16	23 32	29 38	23 10	22 47	10 16	29 47	11 50	5 41	10R16	21 15	
26	3♐38	11♑45	0♐15	24 12	9 46	0♎47	11 25	5 56	10 13	20 43	
6 12	13 46	23 48	7 26	25 24	9 07	1 40	11 00	6 08	10 08	20 11	
16	23 56	5♒44	14 41	26 21	8 23	2 22	10 35	6 18	10 00	19 39	
26	4♑07	17 31	22 01	27 02	7 34	2 54	10 11	6 24	9 50	19 07	

SID M/N 1st JAN 6 h 41 m 7 s 1945 COMMON DST 2/4 to 15/7 END BST 7/10

DAY	JAN	FEB	MAR	APR	MAY	JUN	JUL	AUG	SEP	OCT	NOV	DEC
1	8♌52	23♍39	2♎01	16♏27	19♐51	7♒54	15♓40	9♉11	1♋41	8♌10	24♍55	27♎40
☽ 3	3♍39	17♎26	25♎46	10♐32	14♑52	4♓55	13♈53	7♊21	28♋12	3♍20	18♎52	21♏20
5	27♍39	11♏16	19♏35	5♑19	10♒59	3♈04	12♉29	4♋54	23♌54	27♍51	12♏35	15♐12
7	21♎25	5♐43	13♐55	1♒24	8♓35	2♉12	11♊05	1♌43	18♍52	21♎53	6♐17	9♑29
9	15♏33	1♑23	9♑23	29♒17	7♈47	1♊41	9♋10	27♌40	13♎12	15♏35	0♑12	4♒26
11	10♐38	28♑42	6♒35	28♓58	7♉56	0♋34	6♌15	22♍41	7♏01	9♐14	24♑46	0♓22
13	7♑01	27♒37	5♓41	29♈34	7♊53	28♋08	2♍07	16♎54	0♐41	3♑17	20♒28	27♓31
15	4♒43	27♓23	6♈01	29♉40	6♋29	24♌10	26♍52	10♏40	24♐46	28♑20	17♓49	26♈02
17	3♓20	26♈55	6♉17	28♊09	3♌17	18♍54	20♎51	4♐33	19♑57	25♒02	16♈57	25♉37
19	2♈11	25♉22	5♊15	24♋44	28♌30	12♎52	14♏39	29♐12	16♒51	23♓42	17♉16	25♊25
21	0♉42	22♊29	2♋28	19♌49	22♍42	6♏39	8♐52	25♑12	15♓36	23♈55	17♊33	24♋25
23	28♉31	18♋25	28♋09	14♍00	16♎27	0♐47	4♑01	22♒49	15♈36	24♉27	16♋36	21♌54
25	25♊32	13♌30	22♌50	7♎47	10♏17	25♐39	0♒24	21♓44	15♉38	23♊58	13♌51	17♍44
27	21♋42	7♍59	16♍56	1♏33	4♐29	21♑25	27♒59	21♈08	14♊35	21♋44	9♍26	12♎15
29	17♌02		10♎47	25♏30	29♐16	18♒07	26♓21	20♉05	12♋02	17♌50	3♎52	6♏03
31	11♍36		4♏32		24♑47		24♈57	18♊05		12♍45		29♏44
1	22♐51	23♑25	10♓11	27♈34	17♈28	23♉30	25♋18	3♍27	22♌10	6♎19	25♏49	22♐04
☿ 7	24D01	2♒30	21 41	27℞16	20 35	5♊10	5♌38	4℞48	26 00	16 47	4♐12	15℞33
13	28 51	12 04	3♈19	23 44	25 54	17 55	14 42	3 04	4♍01	26 46	11 57	8 28
19	5♑37	22 09	14 07	19 30	3♉00	1♋04	22 26	28♌37	14 22	6♏20	18 32	7D06
25	13 27	2♓46	22 32	17 03	11 38	13 43	28 39	23 48	25 25	15 31	22 40	10 50
31	21 57		27 12		21 41		2♍57	22D00		24 22		17 17

DATE	☉	♀	♂	♃	♄	⚷	♅	♆	♇	☊	STATIONS
1 1	10♑14	24♒29	26♐27	27♍18	7♋04	3♎08	9♊58	6♎26	9♌43	18♋48	
11	20 25	5♓55	3♑54	27 30	6℞16	3 22	9℞39	6℞26	9℞31	18 17	☿ 3/1 22♐40
21	0♒36	17 00	11 25	27℞22	5 31	3℞23	9 24	6 23	9 18	17 45	☿ 4/4 27♈56
31	10 46	27 37	19 00	26 56	4 52	3 13	9 13	6 17	9 04	17 13	☿ 27/4 16♈52
10 2	20 54	7♈35	26 38	26 12	4 22	2 52	9 07	6 08	8 50	16 41	☿ 7/8 4♍49
20	1♓00	16 39	4♒19	25 13	4 01	2 21	9D07	5 56	8 37	16 10	☿ 30/8 21♌59
2 3	11 04	24 24	12 03	24 03	3 51	1 42	9 12	5 42	8 25	15 38	☿ 27/11 23♐09
12	21 04	0♉16	19 48	22 46	3D52	0 57	9 22	5 27	8 14	15 06	☿ 17/12 6♐52
22	1♈01	3 20	27 34	21 29	4 05	0 10	9 37	5 11	8 06	14 34	♀ 25/3 3♉35
1 4	10 55	2℞42	5♓21	20 16	4 28	29♍23	9 57	4 54	7 59	14 02	♀ 7/5 17♈12
11	20 45	28♈14	13 07	19 13	5 01	28 39	10 20	4 38	7 56	13 31	♂ 5/12 3♌13
21	0♉32	22 06	20 52	18 23	5 44	28 00	10 48	4 23	7D55	12 59	♃ 12/1 27♍30
1 5	10 16	17 54	28 36	17 49	6 34	27 30	11 18	4 09	7 56	12 27	♃ 15/5 17♍32
11	19 57	17D32	6♈16	17 33	7 32	27 09	11 50	3 58	8 00	11 55	♄ 6/3 3♋50
21	29 35	20 42	13 54	17D36	8 36	26 58	12 24	3 49	8 07	11 24	♄ 6/11 24♋54
31	9♊11	26 28	21 27	17 56	9 45	26D59	13 00	3 43	8 16	10 52	♅ 16/2 9♊06
10 6	18 45	3♉59	28 55	18 33	10 57	27 11	13 35	3 40	8 27	10 20	♅ 23/9 17♊28
20	28 18	12 43	6♉17	19 26	12 13	27 34	14 10	3D40	8 41	9 48	♆ 7/1 6♎26
30	7♋51	22 16	13 32	20 33	13 30	28 08	14 44	3 43	8 55	9 16	♆ 15/6 3♎39
10 7	17 23	2♊25	20 41	21 52	14 48	28 52	15 16	3 50	9 12	8 45	♇ 20/4 7♌54
20	26 55	13 00	27 41	23 23	16 05	29 45	15 46	3 59	9 29	8 13	♇ 13/11 11♌49
30	6♌28	23 56	4♊32	25 03	17 22	0♎45	16 13	4 12	9 46	7 41	⚷ 17/1 3♎24
9 8	16 03	5♋08	11 13	26 51	18 35	1 53	16 37	4 26	10 04	7 09	⚷ 25/5 26♍57
19	25 39	16 34	17 44	28 46	19 46	3 07	16 56	4 44	10 21	6 38	
29	5♍18	28 12	24 01	0♎46	20 51	4 25	17 11	5 03	10 38	6 06	
8 9	14 59	10♌00	0♋05	2 51	21 51	5 48	17 22	5 23	10 54	5 34	
18	24 43	21 58	5 52	4 58	22 45	7 13	17 27	5 45	11 08	5 02	
28	4♎31	4♍03	11 20	7 08	23 30	8 40	17℞27	6 07	11 21	4 31	
8 10	14 21	16 16	16 26	9 17	24 06	10 08	17 22	6 30	11 31	3 59	
18	24 15	28 34	21 05	11 26	24 33	11 35	17 12	6 51	11 40	3 27	
28	4♏13	10♎57	25 11	13 33	24 49	13 00	16 57	7 12	11 45	2 55	
7 11	14 14	23 24	28 37	15 37	24℞54	14 23	16 39	7 32	11 48	2 23	
17	24 17	5♏54	1♌13	17 36	24 48	15 41	16 17	7 50	11℞48	1 52	
27	4♐24	18 26	2 49	19 28	24 31	16 54	15 53	8 05	11 46	1 20	
7 12	14 32	0♐59	3℞12	21 13	24 04	18 01	15 28	8 18	11 41	0 48	
17	24 42	13 34	2 13	22 48	23 28	18 59	15 02	8 28	11 33	0 16	
27	4♑53	26 08	29♋53	24 12	22 45	19 49	14 38	8 34	11 23	29♊45	

SID M/N 1st JAN 6 h 40 m 10 s — **1946 COMMON** — BST 14/4 to 6/10

	DAY	JAN	FEB	MAR	APR	MAY	JUN	JUL	AUG	SEP	OCT	NOV	DEC
	1	11♐41	27♑05	5♒06	24♓24	2♉11	25♊57	3♌45	23♍24	9♏16	11♐05	24♑41	27♒39
☽	3	6♑04	23♒29	2♓04	23♈49	2♊29	25♋26	1♍51	19♎02	3♐12	4♑41	19♒08	23♓17
	5	1♒16	20♓55	0♈22	23♉35	2♋12	23♌19	28♍13	13♏23	26♐50	28♑45	14♓59	20♈36
	7	27♒21	18♈57	29♈18	22♊41	0♌31	19♍32	23♎06	7♐05	20♑54	23♒56	12♈36	19♉41
	9	24♓19	17♉12	28♉06	20♋37	27♌19	14♎23	17♏02	0♑48	15♒59	20♓40	11♉49	19♊56
	11	22♈06	15♊23	26♊15	17♌21	22♍48	8♏24	10♐39	25♑08	12♓24	18♈55	11♊48	20♋14
	13	20♉34	13♋23	23♋40	13♍08	17♎23	2♐02	4♑27	20♒25	9♈59	18♉03	11♋29	19♌25
	15	19♊27	10♌55	20♌24	8♎08	11♏22	25♐42	28♑49	16♓44	8♉14	17♊11	10♌01	16♍51
	17	18♋11	7♍40	16♍25	2♏29	5♐02	19♑42	23♒58	13♈52	6♊38	15♋43	7♍10	12♎39
	19	16♌08	3♎21	11♎37	26♏18	28♐40	14♒19	20♓00	11♉37	4♋51	13♌23	3♎04	7♏13
	21	12♍46	27♎57	5♏59	19♐54	22♑37	9♓51	16♈58	9♊48	2♌46	10♍10	27♎59	1♐05
	23	8♎00	21♏47	29♏45	13♑43	17♒22	6♈38	14♉54	8♋15	0♍12	6♎06	22♏11	24♐40
	25	2♏09	15♐28	23♐23	8♒23	13♓24	4♉50	13♊42	6♌43	26♍54	1♏12	15♐56	18♑19
	27	25♏50	9♑41	17♑34	4♓32	11♈08	4♊16	13♋00	4♍39	22♎36	25♏29	9♑30	12♒17
	29	19♐42		12♒59	2♈33	10♉31	4♋15	12♌02	1♎30	17♏14	19♐13	3♒14	6♓53
	31	14♑21		10♓09		10♊49		10♍00	27♎00		12♑47		2♈26
	1	18♐30	4♒26	24♓31	0♈31	14♈12	10♊34	4♌03	10♌54	25♌00	19♎17	1♐33	21♏09
☿	7	26 24	14 34	3♈39	27R49	22 40	23 37	10 18	6R41	6♍23	28 40	6 10	23D47
	13	4♑55	25 11	9 13	28D18	2♉23	5♋48	14 34	4D53	17 53	7♏34	7R05	0♐01
	19	13 50	6♓13	9R54	1♈37	13 18	16 41	16 20	7 08	28 56	15 58	2 24	7 51
	25	23 08	17 23	6 17	7 05	25 24	26 07	15R16	13 34	9♎24	23 45	24♏38	16 25
	31	2♒47		1 15		8♊22		11 39	23 12		0♐33		25 21

DATE	☉	♀	♂	♃	♄	⚷	♅	♆	♇	☊	STATIONS
1 1	9♑59	2♑26	28♋16	24♎49	22♋21	20♎10	14♊27	8♎36	11♌18	29♊29	
11	20 11	15 01	24R28	25 52	21R32	20 45	14R06	8R37	11R06	28 57	☿ 17/3 10♈14
21	0♒22	27 35	20 32	26 40	20 43	21 08	13 49	8 35	10 52	28 25	☿ 9/4 27♓37
31	10 31	10♒09	17 13	27 10	19 56	21 19	13 36	8 30	10 38	27 53	☿ 20/7 16♌22
10 2	20 40	22 42	15 01	27 22	19 15	21R18	13 28	8 22	10 24	27 22	☿ 13/8 4♌53
20	0♓46	5♓14	14 07	27R15	18 41	21 05	13 25	8 11	10 11	26 50	☿ 11/11 7♐20
2 3	10 49	17 44	14D30	26 49	18 16	20 42	13D27	7 57	9 58	26 18	☿ 1/12 21♏09
12	20 49	0♈12	15 58	26 06	18 01	20 10	13 35	7 42	9 48	25 46	♀ 28/10 2♐29
22	0♈47	12 38	18 20	25 09	17D57	19 30	13 48	7 26	9 39	25 15	♀ 8/12 17♏07
1 4	10 40	25 02	21 26	24 00	18 05	18 45	14 06	7 10	9 32	24 43	♂ 22/2 14♋06
11	20 31	7♉22	25 06	22 45	18 23	17 58	14 28	6 53	9 28	24 11	♃ 11/2 27♎22
21	0♉18	19 40	29 13	21 28	18 52	17 12	14 54	6 38	9 26	23 39	♃ 15/6 17♎27
1 5	10 02	1♊54	3♌42	20 16	19 30	16 29	15 23	6 24	9D27	23 07	♄ 20/3 17♋57
11	19 43	14 05	8 30	19 12	20 16	15 52	15 54	6 12	9 31	22 36	♄ 21/11 8♌54
21	29 21	26 13	13 32	18 22	21 11	15 23	16 28	6 02	9 37	22 04	♅ 20/2 13♊25
31	8♊57	8♋16	18 47	17 47	22 11	15 04	17 03	5 55	9 46	21 32	♅ 28/9 21♊48
10 6	18 32	20 15	24 13	17 29	23 18	14 55	17 38	5 51	9 57	21 00	♆ 10/1 8♎37
20	28 05	2♌08	29 49	17D30	24 28	14D57	18 13	5D51	10 10	20 29	♆ 17/6 5♎51
30	7♋37	13 56	5♍32	17 48	25 42	15 11	18 48	5 53	10 25	19 57	♇ 22/4 9♌26
10 7	17 09	25 36	11 24	18 23	26 58	15 35	19 21	,5 59	10 41	19 25	♇ 15/11 13♌22
20	26 41	7♍08	17 22	19 14	28 15	16 10	19 52	6 08	10 58	18 53	⚷ 4/2 21♎20
30	6♌14	18 29	23 28	20 20	29 33	16 54	20 21	6 19	11 15	18 21	⚷ 13/6 14♎55
9 8	15 49	29 37	29 40	21 38	0♌50	17 48	20 46	6 34	11 33	17 50	
19	25 25	10♎28	5♎58	23 08	2 04	18 49	21 08	6 51	11 51	17 18	
29	5♍04	20 58	12 23	24 48	3 16	19 57	21 25	7 09	12 08	16 46	
8 9	14 45	0♏58	18 54	26 36	4 24	21 10	21 38	7 29	12 24	16 14	
18	24 29	10 18	25 31	28 31	5 26	22 28	21 46	7 51	12 39	15 43	
28	4♎16	18 42	2♏15	0♏32	6 23	23 50	21R48	8 13	12 52	15 11	
8 10	14 07	25 41	9 05	2 38	7 11	25 15	21 46	8 35	13 03	14 39	
18	24 01	0♐35	16 01	4 47	7 52	26 41	21 38	8 57	13 12	14 07	
28	3♏58	2 29	23 03	6 57	8 23	28 07	21 25	9 19	13 18	13 36	
7 11	13 59	0R33	0♐11	9 09	8 43	29 33	21 08	9 39	13 22	13 04	
17	24 03	25♏18	7 25	11 19	8 53	0♏56	20 48	9 57	13R22	12 32	
27	4♐09	19 44	14 45	13 28	8R51	2 16	20 25	10 13	13 20	12 00	
7 12	14 17	17 09	22 10	15 33	8 39	3 32	20 00	10 26	13 16	11 28	
17	24 27	18D33	29 40	17 34	8 15	4 42	19 34	10 37	13 08	10 57	
27	4♑38	23 14	7♑16	19 28	7 43	5 45	19 09	10 44	12 59	10 25	

SID M/N 1st JAN 6 h 39 m 12 s | 1947 COMMON | DST 13/4 to 10/8

DAY	JAN	FEB	MAR	APR	MAY	JUN	JUL	AUG	SEP	OCT	NOV	DEC
1	15♈42	7♊11	17♊36	10♌57	19♍10	8♏00	11♐37	26♑07	11♓14	15♈37	5♊29	13♋47
☽ 3	13♉25	6♋23	16♋08	9♍00	15♎42	2♐35	5♑24	20♒01	6♈18	12♉05	3♋50	13♌02
5	12♊43	6♌12	15♌06	6♎23	11♏18	26♐36	29♑06	14♓20	2♉05	9♊17	2♌20	11♍30
7	13♋01	5♍37	13♍48	2♏43	6♐01	20♑19	22♒57	9♈16	28♉41	7♋08	0♍38	8♎52
9	13♌09	3♎36	11♎26	27♏51	0♑03	14♒03	17♓15	5♉04	26♊21	5♌32	28♍27	5♏11
11	11♍55	29♎45	7♏32	22♐01	23♑44	8♓15	12♈25	2♊08	25♋05	4♍12	25♎33	0♐37
13	8♎48	24♏22	2♐14	15♑42	17♒37	3♈27	8♉53	0♋43	24♌33	2♎37	21♏43	25♐19
15	3♏58	18♐07	26♐04	9♒35	12♓18	0♉08	7♊02	0♌34	23♍51	0♏08	16♐55	19♑27
17	28♏00	11♑43	19♑43	4♓19	8♈20	28♉33	6♋46	0♍44	22♎00	26♏21	11♑15	13♒12
19	21♐34	5♒44	13♒54	0♈19	5♉58	28♊24	7♌15	29♍57	18♏29	21♐17	5♒04	6♓58
21	15♑13	0♓33	9♓03	27♈42	5♊00	28♋41	7♍09	27♎24	13♐27	15♑20	28♒52	1♈14
23	9♒17	26♓12	5♈21	26♉07	4♋40	28♌11	5♎24	23♏01	7♑27	9♒05	23♓16	26♈37
25	3♓57	22♈39	2♉35	24♊58	4♌03	26♍09	1♏46	17♐21	1♒10	3♓10	18♈51	23♉39
27	29♓22	19♉46	0♊25	23♋39	2♍24	22♎27	26♏37	11♑05	25♒12	28♓07	15♉56	22♊31
29	25♈39		28♊34	21♌47	29♍30	17♏27	20♐36	4♒49	19♓58	24♈15	14♊27	22♋36
31	23♉02		26♋50		25♎25		14♑16	28♒57		21♉31		22♌44
1	26♐51	17♒27	23♓01	13♓10	23♈55	27♊16	27♋07	19♋06	10♍30	29♎09	18♏33	20♏27
☿ 7	6♑04	28 08	19℞23	18 40	5♉25	7♋08	25℞57	24 48	21 34	6♏54	11℞18	29 14
13	15 31	8♓31	13 35	25 44	17 54	15 15	22 38	3♌42	1♎55	13 41	5 52	8♐20
19	25 14	17 21	9 46	4♈03	0♊58	21 30	18 55	14 49	11 36	18 55	6D49	17 34
25	5♒17	22 33	9D32	13 27	13 46	25 34	17 04	26 47	20 41	21 25	12 32	26 55
31	15 42		12 26		25 28		18D30	8♍35		19℞25		6♑24

DATE	☉	♀	♂	♃	♄	⚷	♅	♆	♇	☊	STATIONS
1 1	9♑44	26♏30	11♑05	20♏22	7♌23	6♏13	18♊57	10♎46	12♌53	10♊09	
11	19 56	4♐22	18 46	22 03	6℞40	7 04	18℞35	10 49	12℞41	9 37	☿ 28/2 23♓09
21	0♒07	13 29	26 31	23 34	5 52	7 44	18 16	10℞47	12 28	9 05	☿ 22/3 9♓12
31	10 17	23 28	4♒19	24 53	5 03	8 15	18 01	10 43	12 14	8 34	☿ 1/7 27♋08
10 2	20 25	4♑03	12 09	25 58	4 15	8 33	17 51	10 35	12 00	8 02	☿ 26/7 17♋03
20	0♓31	15 02	20 01	26 47	3 31	8 41	17 46	10 25	11 46	7 30	☿ 26/10 21♏27
2 3	10 34	26 20	27 54	27 19	2 54	8℞36	17D46	10 12	11 34	6 58	☿ 15/11 5♏29
12	20 35	7♒50	5♓46	27 33	2 25	8 21	17 51	9 57	11 22	6 27	♃ 14/3 27♏34
22	0♈32	19 30	13 38	27℞28	2 06	7 56	18 02	9 41	11 13	5 55	♃ 16/7 17♏42
1 4	10 26	1♓17	21 28	27 05	1 58	7 22	18 17	9 25	11 06	5 23	♄ 4/4 1♌57
11	20 17	13 09	29 17	26 24	2D00	6 41	18 37	9 08	11 01	4 51	♄ 4/12 22♌41
21	0♉04	25 04	7♈02	25 29	2 13	5 56	19 02	8 53	10 59	4 20	♅ 25/2 17♊45
1 5	9 48	7♈03	14 44	24 22	2 37	5 10	19 29	8 38	11D00	3 48	♅ 3/10 26♊11
11	19 29	19 04	22 21	23 07	3 11	4 25	20 00	8 26	11 03	3 16	♆ 12/1 10♎49
21	29 07	1♉07	29 54	21 51	3 53	3 44	20 33	8 16	11 09	2 44	♆ 20/6 8♎02
31	8♊43	13 11	7♉22	20 38	4 43	3 10	21 07	8 08	11 17	2 12	♇ 24/4 10♌59
10 6	18 18	25 17	14 45	19 34	5 41	2 43	21 42	8 03	11 28	1 41	♇ 17/11 14♌58
20	27 51	7♊25	22 02	18 42	6 44	2 25	22 18	8D02	11 41	1 09	⚷ 21/2 8♏41
30	7♋23	19 35	29 12	18 05	7 52	2 18	22 53	8 04	11 55	0 37	⚷ 2/7 2♏18
10 7	16 55	1♋46	6♊16	17 45	9 04	2D22	23 27	8 08	12 11	0 05	
20	26 27	14 00	13 13	17D43	10 19	2 36	24 00	8 16	12 28	29♉34	
30	6♌01	26 16	20 04	18 00	11 35	3 01	24 30	8 27	12 46	29 02	
9 8	15 35	8♌35	26 47	18 34	12 52	3 36	24 57	8 41	13 04	28 30	
19	25 11	20 56	3♋22	19 24	14 09	4 20	25 21	8 57	13 22	27 58	
29	4♍50	3♍18	9 48	20 29	15 24	5 13	25 40	9 16	13 39	27 26	
8 9	14 31	15 43	16 06	21 47	16 37	6 13	25 55	9 35	13 56	26 55	
18	24 15	28 09	22 15	23 18	17 46	7 19	26 05	9 57	14 11	26 23	
28	4♎02	10♎36	28 12	24 58	18 51	8 31	26 10	10 19	14 24	25 51	
8 10	13 53	23 04	3♌57	26 48	19 49	9 48	26℞10	10 41	14 36	25 19	
18	23 47	5♏32	9 29	28 46	20 41	11 07	26 05	11 03	14 45	24 48	
28	3♏44	18 01	14 45	0♐49	21 25	12 29	25 54	11 25	14 52	24 16	
7 11	13 44	0♐29	19 41	2 58	21 59	13 52	25 39	11 45	14 56	23 44	
17	23 48	12 58	24 15	5 09	22 24	15 14	25 20	12 04	14℞58	23 12	
27	3♐54	25 26	28 21	7 23	22 38	16 36	24 58	12 20	14 56	22 41	
7 12	14 02	7♑53	1♍52	9 38	22℞41	17 54	24 34	12 34	14 52	22 09	
17	24 12	20 20	4 42	11 52	22 32	19 10	24 08	12 46	14 45	21 37	
27	4♑24	2♒45	6 39	14 04	22 13	20 20	23 43	12 54	14 36	21 05	

SID M/N 1st JAN 6 h 38 m 15 s 1948 LEAP BST 14/3 to 30/10

	DAY	JAN	FEB	MAR	APR	MAY	JUN	JUL	AUG	SEP	OCT	NOV	DEC
	1	7♍26	28♎38	20♏28	6♑20	8♒20	21♓59	24♈26	11♊45	3♌17	12♍05	5♏06	11♐28
☽	3	5♎38	24♏33	15♐50	0♒21	2♓07	16♈27	20♉04	10♋02	3♍36	12♎11	3♐21	8♑01
	5	2♏14	19♐12	10♑05	24♒04	26♓12	12♉03	17♊25	9♌58	4♎01	11♏25	0♑11	3♒21
	7	27♏35	13♑11	3♒50	18♓04	21♈03	9♊07	16♋25	10♍24	3♏13	9♐04	25♑32	27♒38
	9	22♐06	6♒55	27♒34	12♈39	16♉59	7♋30	16♌18	10♎01	0♐38	5♑00	19♒48	21♓22
	11	16♑09	0♓41	21♓36	8♉01	14♊01	6♌33	15♍53	8♏01	26♐23	29♑39	13♓33	15♈12
	13	9♒56	24♓39	16♈07	4♊14	11♋54	5♍29	14♎20	4♐23	20♑58	23♒33	7♈24	9♉47
	15	3♓40	19♈02	11♉16	1♋19	10♌17	3♎44	11♏25	29♐33	14♒56	17♓16	1♉52	5♊39
	17	27♓37	14♉13	7♊17	29♋15	8♍44	1♏05	7♐22	23♑57	8♓40	11♈14	27♉16	2♋53
	19	22♈14	10♊42	4♋29	27♌53	6♎56	27♏34	2♑28	17♒55	2♈28	5♉43	23♊42	1♌10
	21	18♉07	8♋55	3♌03	26♍50	4♏36	23♐15	26♑57	11♓40	26♈34	0♊56	21♋01	29♌49
	23	15♊48	8♌46	2♍40	25♎25	1♐27	18♑11	20♒58	5♈25	21♉14	27♊01	18♌56	28♍15
	25	15♋22	9♍18	2♎27	23♏01	27♐18	12♒26	14♓42	29♈28	16♊50	24♋07	17♍14	26♎10
	27	16♌01	9♎06	1♏16	19♐16	22♑09	6♓14	8♈28	24♉19	13♋48	22♌16	15♎39	23♏32
	29	16♍18	7♏10	28♏29	14♑14	16♒14	0♈02	2♉48	20♊32	12♌19	21♍17	13♏52	20♐17
	31	15♎01		24♐02		10♓01		28♉20	18♋35		20♎35		16♑15
	1	8♑00	28♒39	22♒04	17♓17	12♉38	3♋10	29♊06	26♋53	25♍50	2♏53	20♎36	2♐10
☿	7	17 42	5♓03	22D01	26 33	25 29	6 31	28D23	9♌05	5♎05	5 22	26 01	11 35
	13	27 38	6R13	25 14	6♈44	7♊28	7R11	0♋40	21 24	13 35	3R50	4♏09	21 01
	19	7♒46	1 37	0♓41	17 51	17 49	5 19	6 03	3♍09	21 15	27♎47	13 18	0♑30
	25	17 52	25♒14	7 41	29 53	26 10	2 00	14 18	14 05	27 51	21 15	22 43	10 04
	31	27 15		15 49		2♋22		24 56	24 13		20D09		19 45

DATE	☉	♀	♂	♃	♄	⚷	♅	♆	♇	☊	STATIONS
1 1	9♑29	8♒56	7♍15	15♐09	21♌59	20♏53	23♊30	12♎56	14♌31	20♉49	
11	19 41	21 17	7R34	17 15	21R26	21 53	23R07	13 00	14R19	20 18	☿ 11/2 6♓31
21	29 52	3♓35	6 36	19 16	20 45	22 46	22 46	12R59	14 05	19 46	☿ 4/3 21♒33
31	10♒02	15 47	4 18	21 11	19 59	23 30	22 30	12 55	13 51	19 14	☿ 11/6 7♋16
10 2	20 10	27 52	0 56	22 56	19 10	24 05	22 17	12 48	13 37	18 42	☿ 6/7 28♊18
20	0♓16	9♈49	27♌00	24 31	18 22	24 28	22 09	12 39	13 23	18 10	☿ 8/10 5♏25
1 3	10 20	21 34	23 14	25 54	17 37	24 41	22D07	12 26	13 10	17 39	☿ 29/10 19♎46
11	20 20	3♉06	20 18	27 03	16 57	24R43	22 10	12 12	12 59	17 07	♀ 3/6 11♋09
21	0♈18	14 21	18 34	27 57	16 25	24 34	22 18	11 56	12 49	16 35	♀ 16/7 24♊38
31	10 12	25 14	18D07	28 34	16 01	24 15	22 32	11 40	12 41	16 03	♂ 9/1 7♍36
10 4	20 02	5♊38	18 52	28 54	15 48	23 46	22 50	11 24	12 36	15 32	♂ 30/3 18♌06
20	29 50	15 23	20 39	28R54	15D46	23 10	23 12	11 08	12 34	15 00	♃ 15/4 28♐56
30	9♉34	24 15	23 17	28 36	15 55	22 29	23 38	10 53	12D34	14 28	♃ 16/8 19♐06
10 5	19 15	1♋52	26 36	28 01	16 14	21 45	24 08	10 40	12 37	13 56	♄ 17/4 15♌46
20	28 53	7 40	0♍28	27 09	16 42	21 00	24 40	10 29	12 42	13 25	♄ 17/12 6♍13
30	8♊29	10 50	4 47	26 05	17 21	20 18	25 13	10 21	12 50	12 53	♅ 1/3 22♊07
9 6	18 04	10R27	9 29	24 52	18 07	19 39	25 49	10 15	13 01	12 21	♅ 6/10 0♋35
19	27 37	6 17	14 30	23 36	19 01	19 08	26 24	10 13	13 13	11 49	♆ 15/1 13♎00
29	7♋09	0 12	19 47	22 21	20 01	18 44	27 00	10D14	13 27	11 17	♆ 21/6 10♎13
9 7	16 41	25♊39	25 19	21 14	21 06	18 29	27 35	10 18	13 43	10 46	♇ 25/4 12♌33
19	26 14	24D47	1♎02	20 17	22 16	18 24	28 08	10 25	14 00	10 14	♇ 17/11 16♌34
29	5♌47	27 31	6 57	19 36	23 29	18D30	28 40	10 36	14 18	9 42	⚷ 8/3 24♏44
8 8	15 21	2♋57	13 03	19 12	24 44	18 46	29 08	10 49	14 36	9 10	⚷ 19/7 18♏24
18	24 57	10 16	19 18	19D07	26 00	19 12	29 34	11 04	14 54	8 39	
28	4♍36	18 54	25 43	19 20	27 16	19 47	29 55	11 22	15 12	8 07	
7 9	14 17	28 27	2♏16	19 51	28 32	20 31	0♋13	11 41	15 29	7 35	
17	24 01	8♌40	8 58	20 39	29 45	21 23	0 25	12 02	15 44	7 03	
27	3♎48	19 25	15 48	21 43	0♍55	22 21	0 33	12 24	15 58	6 31	
7 10	13 38	0♍33	22 45	23 02	2 01	23 26	0R35	12 47	16 10	6 00	
17	23 32	12 01	29 50	24 33	3 02	24 36	0 32	13 09	16 20	5 28	
27	3♏29	23 44	7♐03	26 15	3 56	25 49	0 24	13 30	16 28	4 56	
6 11	13 30	5♎40	14 22	28 07	4 43	27 05	0 11	13 51	16 32	4 24	
16	23 33	17 45	21 47	0♑07	5 20	28 23	29♊54	14 10	16 34	3 53	
26	3♐39	29 58	29 19	2 14	5 49	29 41	29 33	14 27	16R33	3 21	
6 12	13 48	12♏17	6♑56	4 26	6 06	0♐58	29 09	14 42	16 29	2 49	
16	23 58	24 40	14 37	6 42	6 13	2 14	28 44	14 54	16 23	2 17	
26	4♑09	7♐05	22 23	9 00	6R08	3 26	28 18	15 03	16 14	1 46	

SID M/N 1st JAN 6 h 41 m 14 s — 1949 COMMON — BST 3/4 to 30/10

DAY	JAN	FEB	MAR	APR	MAY	JUN	JUL	AUG	SEP	OCT	NOV	DEC
1	28♑53	13♓42	22♓19	6♉44	10♊30	29♋39	7♍58	1♏20	23♐17	29♑21	15♓22	17♈32
☽ 3	23♒29	7♈19	15♈55	1♊00	6♋06	27♌09	6♎15	29♏11	19♑32	24♒15	9♈03	11♉12
5	17♓22	1♉01	9♉40	26♊08	2♌43	25♍17	4♏28	26♐19	14♒52	18♓23	2♉39	5♊21
7	11♈00	25♉27	4♊06	22♋34	0♍28	23♎52	2♐28	22♑42	9♓24	12♈05	26♉31	0♋15
9	5♉04	21♊19	29♊48	20♌36	29♍19	22♏37	29♐58	18♒13	3♈21	5♉41	20♊54	25♋56
11	0♊16	19♋05	27♋17	20♍05	28♎50	20♐57	26♑39	12♓51	26♈57	29♉29	16♋00	22♌24
13	27♊08	18♌36	26♌37	20♎18	28♏13	18♑15	22♒14	6♈45	20♉37	23♊51	12♌05	19♍41
15	25♋39	18♍53	27♍02	20♏06	26♐35	14♒10	16♓43	0♉21	14♊52	19♋14	9♍26	17♎51
17	25♌08	18♎38	27♎16	18♐32	23♑23	8♓47	10♈29	24♉13	10♋20	16♌06	8♎09	16♏51
19	24♍32	17♏02	26♏12	15♑11	18♒37	2♈35	4♉10	19♊04	7♌29	14♍39	7♏56	16♐07
21	23♎03	13♐55	23♐25	10♒19	12♓44	26♈16	28♉28	15♋28	6♍25	14♎35	7♐54	14♑48
23	20♏27	9♑35	19♑04	4♓24	6♈22	20♉29	24♊00	13♌36	6♎30	14♏57	6♑54	12♒03
25	16♐53	4♒22	13♒37	28♓02	0♉09	15♊46	21♋04	13♍00	6♏38	14♐32	4♒11	7♓39
27	12♑32	28♒33	7♓30	21♈42	24♉34	12♋17	19♌25	12♎43	5♐44	12♑28	29♒42	1♈57
29	7♒29		1♈08	15♉46	19♊54	9♌50	18♍21	11♏48	3♑17	8♒37	23♓55	25♈36
31	1♓47		24♈48		16♋11		17♎08	9♐45		3♓21		19♉19
1	21♑22	15♒40	13♒06	28♓47	28♉14	14♊35	17♊11	14♌04	4♎14	13♎30	25♎28	13♐32
☿ 7	1♒01	8℞39	20 01	10♈12	6♊58	11℞19	25 01	25 40	10 55	6℞53	5♏16	22 54
13	10 05	4 48	28 00	22 24	13 09	9 00	5♋04	6♍21	16 03	3D57	15 03	2♑15
19	17 18	5D26	6♓52	5♉03	16 34	9D01	16 53	16 08	18 53	7 08	24 40	11 31
25	20℞13	9 19	16 31	17 21	17℞05	11 47	29 33	25 02	18℞16	14 34	4♐09	20 27
31	16 45		26 58		15 05		12♌03	3♎00		23 51		28 21

DATE	☉	♀	♂	♃	♄	⚷	♅	♆	♇	☊	STATIONS
1 1	10♑16	14♐34	27♑04	10♑23	6♍00	4♐07	28♊03	15♎07	16♌08	1♉26	
11	20 27	27 03	4♒55	12 42	5℞39	5 13	27℞39	15 10	15℞56	0 55	☿ 25/1 20♒13
21	0♒38	9♑32	12 48	15 00	5 07	6 12	27 17	15℞10	15 43	0 23	☿ 15/2 4♒33
31	10 48	22 02	20 42	17 15	4 29	7 03	26 59	15 07	15 29	29♈51	☿ 23/5 17♊13
10 2	20 56	4♒32	28 37	19 26	3 44	7 47	26 45	15 00	15 14	29 19	☿ 16/6 8♊40
20	1♓02	17 02	6♓31	21 32	2 56	8 22	26 35	14 51	15 00	28 48	☿ 21/9 19♎08
2 3	11 05	29 31	14 25	23 31	2 08	8 47	26 31	14 39	14 47	28 16	☿ 13/10 3♎57
12	21 06	11♓59	22 16	25 22	1 22	9 02	26D32	14 25	14 35	27 44	♃ 21/5 2♒10
22	1♈03	24 25	0♈04	27 03	0 41	9℞06	26 38	14 10	14 25	27 12	♃ 19/9 22♑20
1 4	10 57	6♈51	7 50	28 32	0 06	8 60	26 50	13 53	14 18	26 41	♄ 1/5 29♌19
11	20 47	19 15	15 31	29 48	29♌41	8 44	27 06	13 37	14 12	26 09	♄ 30/12 19♍27
21	0♉34	1♉38	23 09	0♒49	29 25	8 19	27 27	13 21	14 09	25 37	♅ 5/3 26♊31
1 5	10 18	13 59	0♉41	1 34	29 19	7 47	27 52	13 06	14D09	25 05	♅ 11/10 5♋01
11	19 59	26 18	8 09	2 02	29D24	7 08	28 21	12 53	14 12	24 33	♆ 16/1 15♎11
21	29 37	8♊36	15 31	2℞10	29 39	6 27	28 52	12 41	14 17	24 02	♆ 24/6 12♎24
31	9♊13	20 53	22 48	2 00	0♍05	5 43	29 25	12 33	14 25	23 30	♇ 26/4 14♌09
10 6	18 47	3♋08	29 59	1 31	0 39	5 01	0♋00	12 27	14 36	22 58	♇ 19/11 18♌12
20	28 20	15 23	7♊05	0 46	1 23	4 22	0 36	12 24	14 48	22 26	⚷ 21/3 9♐06
30	7♋53	27 36	14 05	29♑45	2 13	3 48	1 12	12D24	15 02	21 55	⚷ 4/8 2♐52
10 7	17 25	9♌47	21 00	28 35	3 11	3 21	1 47	12 28	15 18	21 23	
20	26 57	21 57	27 49	27 18	4 14	3 02	2 21	12 35	15 35	20 51	
30	6♌30	4♍04	4♋33	26 01	5 21	2 53	2 54	12 45	15 53	20 19	
9 8	16 05	16 09	11 11	24 50	6 33	2D53	3 24	12 57	16 11	19 47	
19	25 41	28 11	17 43	23 48	7 46	3 03	3 50	13 13	16 30	19 16	
29	5♍20	10♎09	24 10	23 01	9 02	3 22	4 14	13 30	16 47	18 44	
8 9	15 01	22 04	0♌31	22 31	10 17	3 51	4 33	13 49	17 04	18 12	
18	24 45	3♏53	6 46	22 20	11 32	4 28	4 47	14 10	17 20	17 40	
28	4♎32	15 37	12 54	22D29	12 46	5 13	4 57	14 32	17 35	17 09	
8 10	14 23	27 13	18 55	22 56	13 56	6 05	5 01	14 54	17 47	16 37	
18	24 17	8♐40	24 48	23 42	15 03	7 03	5℞00	15 16	17 57	16 05	
28	4♏15	19 54	0♍33	24 44	16 05	8 07	4 54	15 38	18 05	15 33	
7 11	14 16	0♑52	6 08	26 02	17 00	9 14	4 43	15 59	18 10	15 02	
17	24 19	11 26	11 31	27 34	17 48	10 24	4 27	16 18	18 12	14 30	
27	4♐25	21 27	16 41	29 18	18 27	11 36	4 07	16 36	18℞11	13 58	
7 12	14 34	0♒39	21 35	1♒12	18 58	12 49	3 44	16 51	18 08	13 26	
17	24 44	8 39	26 09	3 14	19 17	14 02	3 20	17 03	18 02	12 54	
27	4♑55	14 50	0♎18	5 24	19 26	15 13	2 54	17 13	17 53	12 23	

SID M/N 1st JAN 6 h 40 m 17 s — 1950 COMMON — BST 16/4 to 22/10

	DAY	JAN	FEB	MAR	APR	MAY	JUN	JUL	AUG	SEP	OCT	NOV	DEC
	1	1♊25	17♋25	25♋15	14♍53	22♎40	16♐36	24♑27	13♓32	28♈50	0♊46	14♋57	18♌29
☽	3	26♊19	14♌31	22♌40	14♎32	23♏07	16♑12	22♒18	8♈46	22♉42	24♊31	9♌31	14♍05
	5	22♋16	12♍36	21♍26	14♏42	23♐12	14♒06	18♓22	2♉56	16♊29	18♋45	5♍19	11♎16
	7	19♌07	11♎06	20♎51	14♐15	21♑48	10♓06	12♈59	26♉40	10♋47	14♌03	2♎51	10♏17
	9	16♍36	9♏33	20♏03	12♑25	18♒32	4♈39	6♉47	20♊37	6♌09	10♍53	2♏12	10♐40
	11	14♎29	7♐39	18♐25	9♒02	13♓41	28♈25	0♊29	15♋19	2♍54	9♎22	2♐38	11♑10
	13	12♏41	5♑16	15♑43	4♓20	7♈49	22♉02	24♊36	11♌05	0♎55	9♏00	2♑49	10♒24
	15	11♐04	2♒14	11♒59	28♓44	1♉29	15♊56	19♋28	7♍53	29♎44	8♐48	1♒36	7♓39
	17	9♑16	28♒18	7♓18	22♈36	25♉07	10♋23	15♌09	5♎30	28♏40	7♑46	28♒34	3♈07
	19	6♒41	23♓22	1♈50	16♉15	18♊59	5♌29	11♍37	3♏38	27♐10	5♒23	23♓59	27♈26
	21	2♓49	17♈33	25♈47	9♊57	13♋20	1♍21	8♎49	2♐00	24♑54	1♓40	18♈26	21♉12
	23	27♓40	11♉13	19♉25	4♋03	8♌24	28♍11	6♏48	0♑21	21♒43	26♓55	12♉22	14♊55
	25	21♈34	4♊58	13♊10	28♋58	4♍32	26♎13	5♐27	28♑20	17♓37	21♈25	6♊07	8♋52
	27	15♉12	29♊27	7♋36	25♌11	2♎06	25♏24	4♑25	25♒33	12♈39	15♉27	29♊53	3♌11
	29	9♊15		3♌15	23♍06	1♏14	25♐10	2♒58	21♓41	6♉57	9♊12	23♋54	28♌04
	31	4♋22		0♍34		1♐26		0♓23	16♈41		2♋57		23♍46
	1	29♑27	18♑32	19♒11	14♈49	27♉12	19♉16	26♊42	28♌13	1♎59	19♍37	7♏33	24♐05
☿	7	3♒51	22 07	28 31	27 06	27℞04	22 32	9♋17	7♍28	1℞58	26 10	17 15	2♑43
	13	2℞19	27 58	8♓32	8♉28	24 24	28 09	22 13	15 40	28♍12	5♎28	26 42	10 34
	19	25♑19	5♒11	19 14	17 43	20 57	5♊49	4♌39	22 41	22 08	15 40	5♐59	16 27
	25	19 18	13 20	0♈41	24 05	18 44	15 23	16 08	28 12	18 08	25 54	15 07	18℞00
	31	18D16		12 46		18D58		26 34	1♎40		5♏55		13 06

DATE	☉	♀	♂	♃	♄	⚷	♅	♆	♇	☊	STATIONS
1 1	10♑01	16♒59	2♎13	6♒31	19♍27	15♐47	2♋41	17♎16	17♌48	12♈07	
11	20 12	18℞45	5 36	8 48	19℞19	16 53	2℞16	17 20	17℞36	11 35	☿ 9/1 4♒07
21	0♒23	16 30	8 18	11 09	19 01	17 55	1 53	17℞21	17 23	11 03	☿ 29/1 18♑03
31	10 33	11 00	10 10	13 31	18 33	18 52	1 33	17 19	17 09	10 31	☿ 4/5 27♉31
10 2	20 41	5 27	11 00	15 54	17 57	19 42	1 17	17 13	16 55	10 00	☿ 28/5 18♉30
20	0♓47	3 07	10℞39	18 17	17 14	20 24	1 05	17 04	16 40	9 28	☿ 4/9 2♎25
2 3	10 51	4D43	9 01	20 37	16 28	20 58	0 58	16 53	16 27	8 56	☿ 26/9 17♍57
12	20 51	9 28	6 10	22 54	15 40	21 23	0D57	16 39	16 15	8 24	☿ 24/12 18♑11
22	0♈48	16 25	2 30	25 06	14 54	21 39	1 01	16 24	16 04	7 53	♀ 11/1 18♒45
1 4	10 42	24 49	28♍39	27 12	14 11	21 44	1 10	16 08	15 56	7 21	♀ 21/2 3♒06
11	20 33	4♓12	25 19	29 11	13 34	21℞40	1 24	15 52	15 50	6 49	♂ 12/2 11♎02
21	0♉20	14 16	23 02	1♓01	13 05	21 27	1 43	15 35	15 47	6 17	♂ 4/5 22♍00
1 5	10 04	24 49	22 03	2 40	12 46	21 05	2 06	15 20	15D46	5 45	♃ 27/6 7♓27
11	19 45	5♈42	22D20	4 07	12 36	20 35	2 33	15 06	15 48	5 14	♃ 24/10 27♒35
21	29 23	16 51	23 45	5 20	12D37	20 00	3 03	14 55	15 53	4 42	♄ 15/5 12♍35
31	8♊59	28 11	26 09	6 18	12 48	19 21	3 36	14 45	16 01	4 10	♅ 10/3 0♋56
10 6	18 34	9♉40	29 20	6 59	13 09	18 40	4 10	14 39	16 11	3 38	♅ 16/10 9♋29
20	28 07	21 17	3♎11	7 22	13 39	17 58	4 45	14 35	16 23	3 07	♆ 19/1 17♎21
30	7♋39	3♊01	7 34	7℞26	14 19	17 19	5 21	14D35	16 37	2 35	♆ 26/6 14♎35
10 7	17 11	14 49	12 24	7 11	15 06	16 45	5 57	14 38	16 53	2 03	♇ 28/4 15♌46
20	26 43	26 44	17 37	6 37	16 00	16 16	6 32	14 44	17 10	1 31	♇ 21/11 19♌52
30	6♌16	8♋43	23 09	5 45	17 00	15 54	7 06	14 53	17 28	1 00	⚷ 2/4 21♐44
9 8	15 51	20 47	28 59	4 41	18 05	15 41	7 37	15 05	17 46	0 28	⚷ 19/8 15♐37
19	25 27	2♌56	5♏04	3 26	19 15	15 37	8 06	15 19	18 04	29♓56	
29	5♍06	15 10	11 23	2 07	20 27	15D41	8 31	15 36	18 23	29 24	
8 9	14 47	27 28	17 55	0 50	21 41	15 55	8 52	15 55	18 40	28 52	
18	24 31	9♍49	24 38	29♒41	22 56	16 18	9 09	16 16	18 56	28 21	
28	4♎18	22 14	1♐31	28 43	24 10	16 50	9 21	16 37	19 11	27 49	
8 10	14 09	4♎42	8 34	28 02	25 24	17 29	9 28	16 59	19 24	27 17	
18	24 03	17 12	15 46	27 39	26 35	18 15	9℞29	17 22	19 35	26 45	
28	4♏00	29 43	23 06	27D37	27 42	19 08	9 26	17 44	19 43	26 14	
7 11	14 01	12♏16	0♑33	27 54	28 45	20 05	9 17	18 05	19 49	25 42	
17	24 04	24 50	8 07	28 32	29 41	21 07	9 03	18 25	19 51	25 10	
27	4♐11	7♐24	15 46	29 27	0♎31	22 12	8 45	18 43	19℞51	24 38	
7 12	14 19	19 58	23 30	0♓39	1 13	23 18	8 23	18 58	19 48	24 07	
17	24 29	2♑32	1♒17	2 07	1 46	24 26	7 59	19 11	19 42	23 35	
27	4♑40	15 06	9 07	3 47	2 08	25 34	7 34	19 21	19 34	23 03	

SID M/N 1st JAN 6 h 39 m 20 s — 1951 COMMON — BST 15/4 to 21/10

DAY	JAN	FEB	MAR	APR	MAY	JUN	JUL	AUG	SEP	OCT	NOV	DEC
1	7♎03	29♏14	10♐09	3♒26	10♓54	28♈42	2♊04	16♋28	1♍33	6♎00	26♏46	5♑24
☽ 3	4♏44	28♐14	8♑36	0♓42	6♈40	22♉58	25♊49	10♌29	27♍00	3♏14	25♐57	5♒01
5	3♐56	27♑32	6♒56	27♓09	1♉39	16♊53	19♋34	5♍00	23♎22	1♐17	24♑50	3♓23
7	4♑04	26♒13	4♓42	22♈45	26♉04	10♋36	13♌30	0♎13	20♏37	29♐42	22♒54	0♈23
9	3♒55	23♓34	1♈29	17♉32	20♊00	4♌23	7♍54	26♎25	18♐39	28♑02	20♓05	26♈15
11	2♓20	19♈22	27♈07	11♊39	13♋43	28♌34	3♎11	23♏49	17♑16	26♒05	16♈28	21♉19
13	28♓53	13♉55	21♉41	5♋24	7♌36	23♍45	29♎49	22♐29	16♒05	23♓36	12♉08	15♊47
15	23♈51	7♊46	15♊36	29♋21	2♍14	20♎29	28♏09	22♑01	14♓31	20♈24	7♊04	9♋45
17	17♉51	1♋34	9♋24	24♌05	28♍16	19♏09	27♐57	21♒35	12♈00	16♉14	1♋16	3♌24
19	11♊33	25♋52	3♌44	20♍13	26♎09	19♐22	28♑18	20♓13	8♉13	11♊04	24♋59	27♌05
21	5♋28	21♌01	29♌06	18♎01	25♏45	19♑56	27♒55	17♈20	3♊10	5♋06	18♌40	21♍19
23	29♋54	17♍08	25♍47	17♏12	26♐08	19♒29	25♓53	12♉54	27♊14	28♋48	13♍00	16♎48
25	24♌59	14♎10	23♎42	16♐54	25♑56	17♓13	22♈04	7♊18	20♋59	22♌49	8♎40	14♏06
27	20♍48	11♏55	22♏23	16♑05	24♒16	13♈14	16♉52	1♋07	15♌02	17♍50	6♏09	13♐20
29	17♎26		21♐10	14♒07	20♓56	8♉00	10♊52	24♋55	9♍56	14♎19	5♐22	13♑45
31	15♏03		19♑31		16♈20		4♋35	19♌10		12♏20		14♒00
1	11♑47	18♑01	0♓49	28♈26	0♉27	16♉41	14♋52	5♍05	6♍30	27♍08	19♏09	29♐19
☿ 7	4R26	26 06	11 39	5♉18	28R26	25 56	27 01	10 41	2R14	7♎54	28 13	2♑19
13	1D56	4♒49	23 07	8 24	29D08	6♊44	8♌03	14 14	2D24	18 25	7♐00	29R32
19	4 22	14 06	5♈00	7R40	2♉27	18 54	17 54	15R03	7 42	28 31	15 24	21 49
25	9 45	23 56	16 42	4 16	7 57	1♋55	26 35	12 34	16 38	8♏14	23 06	16 27
31	16 45		26 58		15 18		3♍59	7 26		17 37		17D01

DATE	☉	♀	♂	♃	♄	⚷	♅	♆	♇	☊	STATIONS
1 1	9♑46	21♑23	13♒03	4♓42	2♎16	26♐07	7♋21	19♎25	19♌29	22♓47	
11	19 57	3♒56	20 55	6 38	2 22	27 12	6R55	19 30	19R18	22 15	☿ 13/1 1♑55
21	0♒09	16 28	28 48	8 44	2R18	28 14	6 31	19R32	19 05	21 44	☿ 15/4 8♉33
31	10 18	28 58	6♓40	10 56	2 03	29 12	6 10	19 30	18 51	21 12	☿ 8/5 28♈21
10 2	20 27	11♓26	14 30	13 13	1 38	0♑05	5 51	19 25	18 36	20 40	☿ 18/8 15♍09
20	0♓33	23 51	22 19	15 35	1 05	0 52	5 37	19 17	18 22	20 08	☿ 10/9 1♍38
2 3	10 36	6♈13	0♈04	17 59	0 24	1 32	5 28	19 06	18 08	19 36	☿ 7/12 2♑20
12	20 37	18 30	7 46	20 24	29♍39	2 04	5 24	18 53	17 56	19 05	☿ 27/12 16♐01
22	0♈34	0♉43	15 24	22 49	28 52	2 27	5D26	18 39	17 45	18 33	♀ 13/8 18♍19
1 4	10 28	12 49	22 58	25 13	28 06	2 42	5 33	18 23	17 36	18 01	♀ 25/9 2♍06
11	20 18	24 49	0♉27	27 35	27 22	2 48	5 45	18 06	17 30	17 29	♃ 4/8 14♈11
21	0♉06	6♊41	7 51	29 52	26 43	2R44	6 01	17 50	17 26	16 58	♃ 30/11 4♈14
1 5	9 50	18 24	15 10	2♈04	26 12	2 32	6 23	17 34	17D25	16 26	♄ 12/1 2♎22
11	19 31	29 55	22 24	4 10	25 49	2 11	6 48	17 20	17 26	15 54	♄ 29/5 25♍32
21	29 09	11♋14	29 33	6 08	25 36	1 44	7 17	17 08	17 31	15 22	♅ 14/3 5♋24
31	8♊45	22 15	6♊37	7 57	25D33	1 11	7 48	16 58	17 38	14 50	♅ 21/10 14♋00
10 6	18 20	2♌56	13 35	9 35	25 40	0 33	8 22	16 51	17 48	14 19	♆ 21/1 19♎32
20	27 53	13 09	20 29	11 01	25 57	29♐54	8 57	16 46	18 00	13 47	♆ 29/6 16♎45
30	7♋25	22 45	27 18	12 13	26 23	29 14	9 33	16D45	18 13	13 15	♇ 30/4 17♌25
10 7	16 57	1♍29	4♋03	13 09	26 59	28 36	10 09	16 47	18 29	12 43	♇ 23/11 21♌33
20	26 29	9 01	10 44	13 48	27 43	28 02	10 45	16 52	18 46	12 12	⚷ 12/4 2♑48
30	6♌02	14 46	17 20	14 08	28 34	27 33	11 19	17 01	19 04	11 40	⚷ 1/9 26♐48
9 8	15 37	17 58	23 53	14R08	29 31	27 10	11 52	17 12	19 22	11 08	
19	25 13	17R41	0♌22	13 49	0♎34	26 55	12 22	17 26	19 41	10 36	
29	4♍52	13 39	6 47	13 11	1 41	26 48	12 49	17 42	19 59	10 05	
8 9	14 33	7 38	13 08	12 16	2 52	26D50	13 12	18 01	20 17	9 33	
18	24 17	3 06	19 26	11 07	4 04	27 01	13 31	18 21	20 34	9 01	
28	4♎04	2D16	25 40	9 50	5 18	27 20	13 46	18 42	20 49	8 29	
8 10	13 54	5 07	1♍51	8 29	6 32	27 47	13 55	19 04	21 03	7 57	
18	23 48	10 47	7 57	7 12	7 45	28 22	14 00	19 27	21 14	7 26	
28	3♏46	18 23	13 59	6 04	8 57	29 04	13R58	19 49	21 23	6 54	
7 11	13 46	27 20	19 57	5 09	10 04	29 52	13 52	20 10	21 29	6 22	
17	23 50	7♎14	25 49	4 32	11 08	0♑45	13 40	20 30	21 32	5 50	
27	3♐56	17 48	1♎34	4 16	12 06	1 42	13 24	20 49	21R33	5 19	
7 12	14 04	28 52	7 13	4D19	12 57	2 42	13 04	21 05	21 30	4 47	
17	24 14	10♏17	12 43	4 44	13 40	3 44	12 41	21 19	21 25	4 15	
27	4♑25	21 58	18 04	5 28	14 15	4 46	12 16	21 30	21 17	3 43	

SID M/N 1st JAN 6 h 38 m 23 s — 1952 LEAP — BST 20/4 to 26/10

	DAY	JAN	FEB	MAR	APR	MAY	JUN	JUL	AUG	SEP	OCT	NOV	DEC
	1	28♒41	19♈05	10♉29	26♊08	27♋56	11♍28	14♎17	2♐30	24♑26	3♓09	25♈53	2♊17
☽	3	26♓47	15♉01	5♊55	20♋04	21♌35	6♎02	10♏15	0♑56	24♒20	2♈43	23♉46	28♊20
	5	23♈13	9♊41	0♋10	13♌43	15♍40	2♏03	8♐02	0♒50	24♓27	1♉43	20♊19	23♋14
	7	18♉24	3♋35	23♋51	7♍45	10♎50	29♏48	7♑26	1♓12	23♈39	29♉18	15♋25	17♌13
	9	12♊45	27♋14	17♌33	2♎41	7♏27	28♐54	7♒36	0♈52	21♉10	25♊11	9♌27	10♍50
	11	6♋39	20♌59	11♍44	28♎46	5♐25	28♑29	7♓21	29♈00	16♊56	19♋39	3♍04	4♎45
	13	0♌20	15♍07	6♎42	25♏54	4♑06	27♒36	5♈51	25♉25	11♋22	13♌22	26♍59	29♎39
	15	24♌02	9♎54	2♏33	23♐44	2♒50	25♓43	2♉53	20♊26	5♌05	7♍00	21♎49	26♏01
	17	18♍04	5♏34	29♏17	21♑55	1♓06	22♈45	28♉37	14♋32	28♌40	1♎09	17♏54	23♐52
	19	12♎53	2♐27	26♐53	20♒11	28♓48	18♉50	23♊23	8♌12	22♍34	26♎11	15♐07	22♑42
	21	9♏02	0♑42	25♑15	18♓22	25♈50	14♊04	17♋28	1♍47	17♎05	22♏09	13♑03	21♒44
	23	6♐55	0♒07	24♒09	16♈12	22♉09	8♋34	11♌09	25♍38	12♏21	18♐56	11♒15	20♓20
	25	6♑29	29♒59	23♓06	13♉16	17♊35	2♌27	4♍43	20♎01	8♐31	16♑22	9♓26	18♈11
	27	6♒55	29♓17	21♈21	9♊14	12♋06	26♌01	28♍32	15♏18	5♑41	14♒23	7♈29	15♉15
	29	6♓55	27♈10	18♉21	4♋01	5♌55	19♍45	23♎06	11♐50	3♒57	12♓53	5♉12	11♊28
	31	5♈29		13♊52		29♌32		18♏57	9♑52		11♈37		6♋50
	1	17♐34	26♑46	17♓18	18♈44	14♈06	0♊45	0♌54	26♌58	20♌30	12♎44	29♏42	7♐25
☿	7	22 40	6♒18	28 41	14R20	20 06	13 36	9 41	24R22	29 10	22 45	7♐07	1R07
	13	29 39	16 17	9♈03	10 15	27 43	26 45	17 00	19 43	9♍54	2♏17	13 08	0D57
	19	7♑37	26 47	16 43	8 41	6♉44	9♋20	22 39	15 43	21 11	11 25	16 24	5 32
	25	16 12	7♓48	20 15	10D07	17 04	20 46	26 12	15D14	2♎13	20 08	14R37	12 30
	31	25 14		19R16		28 42		27R06	19 23		28 23		20 34

DATE		☉	♀	♂	♃	♄	⚷	♅	♆	♇	☊	STATIONS
1	1	9♑31	27♏53	20♎39	5♈57	14♎29	5♑18	12♋03	21♎34	21♌12	3♓27	
11		19 43	9♐50	25 41	7 07	14 49	6 20	11R37	21 40	21R01	2 56	☿ 27/3 20♈25
21		29 54	21 55	0♏26	8 33	14 58	7 21	11 12	21 42	20 48	2 24	☿ 19/4 8♈41
31		10♒04	4♑04	4 51	10 12	14R57	8 19	10 49	21R42	20 35	1 52	☿ 30/7 27♌10
10	2	20 12	16 17	8 51	12 02	14 45	9 12	10 29	21 37	20 20	1 20	☿ 23/8 14♌53
20		0♓18	28 32	12 21	14 02	14 23	10 01	10 13	21 30	20 06	0 49	☿ 20/11 16♐31
1	3	10 22	10♒49	15 12	16 10	13 52	10 45	10 02	21 20	19 52	0 17	☿ 10/12 0♐16
11		20 22	23 07	17 15	18 24	13 14	11 21	9 55	21 07	19 39	29♒45	♂ 25/3 18♏27
21		0♈20	5♓26	18 20	20 42	12 30	11 51	9D54	20 53	19 27	29 13	♂ 10/6 1♏08
31		10 14	17 44	18R15	23 04	11 44	12 12	9 59	20 37	19 18	28 41	♃ 10/9 20♉59
10	4	20 04	0♈03	16 55	25 28	10 58	12 25	10 08	20 21	19 11	28 10	♄ 25/1 14♎59
20		29 51	12 21	14 23	27 52	10 13	12 29	10 23	20 04	19 07	27 38	♄ 11/6 8♎11
30		9♉35	24 38	10 59	0♉16	9 33	12R25	10 42	19 49	19 05	27 06	♅ 18/3 9♋54
10	5	19 17	6♉55	7 19	2 39	9 00	12 13	11 06	19 34	19D06	26 34	♅ 24/10 18♋32
20		28 55	19 12	4 07	4 58	8 34	11 53	11 33	19 21	19 10	26 03	♆ 23/1 21♎43
30		8♊31	1♊29	1 58	7 14	8 18	11 26	12 03	19 11	19 17	25 31	♆ 30/6 18♎56
9	6	18 06	13 45	1 08	9 24	8 11	10 54	12 36	19 03	19 26	24 59	♇ 1/5 19♌05
19		27 39	26 02	1D39	11 28	8D15	10 19	13 10	18 58	19 38	24 27	♇ 24/11 23♌16
29		7♋11	8♋19	3 22	13 23	8 28	9 41	13 46	18 56	19 51	23 55	⚷ 20/4 12♑29
9	7	16 43	20 37	6 07	15 10	8 52	9 03	14 22	18D57	20 07	23 24	⚷ 11/9 6♑38
19		26 16	2♌55	9 43	16 45	9 24	8 26	14 59	19 01	20 24	22 52	
29		5♌49	15 14	14 02	18 08	10 04	7 53	15 34	19 09	20 42	22 20	
8	8	15 23	27 33	18 56	19 16	10 53	7 24	16 08	19 20	21 00	21 48	
18		24 59	9♍52	24 19	20 08	11 47	7 02	16 39	19 33	21 19	21 17	
28		4♍38	22 12	0♐07	20 43	12 48	6 46	17 08	19 49	21 38	20 45	
7	9	14 19	4♎31	6 15	20 58	13 53	6 38	17 33	20 07	21 56	20 13	
17		24 03	16 49	12 42	20R54	15 02	6D39	17 55	20 26	22 13	19 41	
27		3♎50	29 07	19 24	20 29	16 13	6 48	18 12	20 48	22 29	19 10	
7	10	13 40	11♏23	26 19	19 46	17 26	7 05	18 24	21 09	22 43	18 38	
17		23 34	23 38	3♑26	18 46	18 39	7 30	18 30	21 32	22 55	18 06	
27		3♏31	5♐52	10 41	17 33	19 52	8 02	18R32	21 54	23 04	17 34	
6	11	13 32	18 03	18 05	16 14	21 03	8 40	18 28	22 16	23 11	17 02	
16		23 35	0♑13	25 35	14 52	22 11	9 25	18 19	22 36	23 15	16 31	
26		3♐41	12 18	3♒11	13 36	23 15	10 14	18 05	22 55	23R16	15 59	
6	12	13 49	24 19	10 50	12 31	24 14	11 07	17 46	23 12	23 14	15 27	
16		23 59	6♒13	18 31	11 41	25 06	12 03	17 25	23 26	23 09	14 55	
26		4♑10	17 57	26 13	11 09	25 51	13 01	17 00	23 38	23 02	14 24	

SID M/N 1st JAN 6 h 41 m 22 s 1953 COMMON BST 19/4 to 4/10

	DAY	JAN	FEB	MAR	APR	MAY	JUN	JUL	AUG	SEP	OCT	NOV	DEC
	1	19♋12	3♍39	12♍22	27♎16	1♐40	21♑29	29♒54	23♈31	15♊04	20♋15	5♍25	7♎21
☽	3	13♌22	27♍16	6♎07	22♏06	27♐50	19♒20	28♓34	21♉26	10♋51	14♌44	29♍05	1♏15
	5	7♍02	21♎11	0♏15	17♐42	24♑44	17♓33	26♈51	18♊08	5♌33	8♍34	22♎53	25♏46
	7	0♎41	15♏54	25♏04	14♑15	22♒28	15♈59	24♉30	13♋46	29♌36	2♎14	17♏07	21♐05
	9	24♎57	11♐57	20♐57	12♒03	21♓02	14♉17	21♊19	8♌33	23♍22	26♎02	11♐53	17♑12
	11	20♏27	9♑44	18♑19	11♓09	20♈09	11♊58	17♋11	2♍43	17♎03	20♏09	7♑20	14♒06
	13	17♐37	9♒10	17♒20	11♈02	19♉06	8♋34	12♌06	26♍29	10♏57	14♐48	3♒36	11♓43
	15	16♑26	9♓32	17♓32	10♉41	17♊01	3♌54	6♍14	20♎11	5♐24	10♑18	1♓00	10♈01
	17	16♒13	9♈35	17♈49	8♊58	13♋23	28♌12	29♍58	14♏15	0♑54	7♒05	29♓38	8♉46
	19	15♓58	8♉17	16♉56	5♋25	8♌16	21♍57	23♎48	9♐15	27♑57	5♓30	29♈13	7♊26
	21	14♈45	5♊13	14♊10	0♌16	2♍13	15♎48	18♏21	5♑43	26♒50	5♈24	28♉50	5♋20
	23	12♉13	0♋37	9♋38	24♌09	25♍54	10♏23	14♐10	3♒56	27♓07	5♉49	27♊23	1♌57
	25	8♊24	24♋58	3♌51	17♍46	19♎58	6♐08	11♑31	3♓38	27♈38	5♊23	24♋15	27♌13
	27	3♋33	18♌45	27♌31	11♎41	14♏54	3♑10	10♒17	3♈55	27♉02	3♋08	19♌30	21♍28
	29	27♋56		21♍08	6♏17	10♐52	1♒16	9♓47	3♉31	24♊33	29♋00	13♍38	15♎14
	31	21♌49		15♎06		7♑46		9♈09	1♊38		23♌29		9♏10
	1	21♐58	10♒27	28♓08	19♓47	17♈49	19♊13	4♌05	28♋16	2♍03	24♎32	0♐08	18♏19
☿	7	0♑40	20 58	2♈39	21D17	27 46	1♋15	7 30	27D44	13 43	3♏19	29℞58	25 09
	13	9 42	1♓51	1℞57	25 24	8♉51	11 54	8℞18	1♌10	24 51	11 32	24 20	3♐22
	19	19 02	12 46	27♓16	1♈27	21 03	21 00	6 20	8 25	5♎20	19 01	16 55	12 09
	25	28 42	22 47	22 13	9 01	4♊02	28 27	2 24	18 33	15 13	25 23	14D41	21 12
	31	8♒44		19 51		17 06		28♋41	0♍06		29 43		0♑27

DATE	☉	♀	♂	♃	♄	⚷	♅	♆	♇	☊	STATIONS
1 1	10♑17	24♒54	0♓51	11♉00	26♎14	13♑37	16♋45	23♎43	22♌56	14♒05	
11	20 29	6♓15	8 33	11D02	26 45	14 35	16℞19	23 50	22℞45	13 33	☿ 9/3 3♈00
21	0♒40	17 14	16 14	11 24	27 06	15 33	15 53	23 53	22 32	13 01	☿ 1/4 19♓47
31	10 50	27 44	23 53	12 05	27 17	16 29	15 30	23℞52	22 19	12 29	☿ 12/7 8♌22
10 2	20 58	7♈32	1♈29	13 05	27℞17	17 23	15 08	23 49	22 04	11 57	☿ 5/8 27♋30
20	1♓04	16 20	9 02	14 20	27 06	18 12	14 51	23 42	21 49	11 26	☿ 4/11 0♐41
2 3	11 07	23 43	16 31	15 50	26 46	18 56	14 37	23 32	21 35	10 54	☿ 24/11 14♏35
12	21 08	29 01	23 55	17 31	26 17	19 35	14 29	23 20	21 22	10 22	♀ 23/3 1♉20
22	1♈05	1♉19	1♉16	19 23	25 40	20 08	14 26	23 06	21 11	9 50	♀ 5/5 14♈58
1 4	10 58	29℞44	8 31	21 24	24 58	20 33	14D28	22 50	21 01	9 19	♃ 5/1 10♉58
11	20 49	24 35	15 42	23 31	24 13	20 51	14 36	22 34	20 54	8 47	♃ 15/10 26♊28
21	0♉36	18 35	22 48	25 44	23 27	21 00	14 49	22 17	20 49	8 15	♄ 5/2 27♎18
1 5	10 20	15 13	29 50	28 00	22 42	21℞02	15 06	22 01	20 47	7 43	♄ 24/6 20♎33
11	20 01	15D46	6♊47	0♊19	22 02	20 56	15 28	21 47	20D48	7 11	♅ 23/3 14♋26
21	29 39	19 38	13 40	2 40	21 27	20 42	15 54	21 34	20 52	6 40	♅ 29/10 23♋06
31	9♊15	25 54	20 29	5 01	21 00	20 21	16 23	21 23	20 59	6 08	♆ 25/1 23♎53
10 6	18 49	3♉45	27 13	7 21	20 42	19 55	16 55	21 14	21 08	5 36	♆ 3/7 21♎06
20	28 22	12 42	3♋54	9 38	20 33	19 23	17 29	21 09	21 19	5 04	♇ 3/5 20♌47
30	7♋55	22 25	10 32	11 53	20D35	18 48	18 05	21 06	21 33	4 33	♇ 27/11 25♌01
10 7	17 27	2♊41	17 07	14 04	20 46	18 12	18 41	21D07	21 48	4 01	⚷ 28/4 21♑02
20	26 59	13 21	23 39	16 09	21 07	17 35	19 18	21 11	22 05	3 29	⚷ 21/9 15♑20
30	6♌32	24 21	0♌08	18 06	21 37	17 00	19 54	21 18	22 23	2 57	
9 8	16 07	5♋37	6 35	19 56	22 15	16 29	20 28	21 28	22 42	2 26	
19	25 43	17 05	13 00	21 35	23 01	16 02	21 01	21 41	23 01	1 54	
29	5♍22	28 45	19 23	23 03	23 54	15 41	21 31	21 57	23 20	1 22	
8 9	15 03	10♌35	25 44	24 18	24 53	15 27	21 58	22 14	23 38	0 50	
18	24 47	22 34	2♍04	25 17	25 57	15 20	22 21	22 34	23 55	0 18	
28	4♎34	4♍40	8 22	26 00	27 04	15D21	22 40	22 55	24 11	29♑47	
8 10	14 25	16 54	14 39	26 23	28 14	15 30	22 54	23 17	24 26	29 15	
18	24 19	29 13	20 55	26℞28	29 26	15 47	23 03	23 39	24 38	28 43	
28	4♏17	11♎36	27 09	26 12	0♏39	16 11	23 06	24 01	24 48	28 11	
7 11	14 17	24 04	3♎22	25 36	1 51	16 42	23℞04	24 23	24 55	27 40	
17	24 21	6♏34	9 33	24 43	3 02	17 20	22 57	24 44	24 59	27 08	
27	4♐27	19 06	15 42	23 35	4 10	18 02	22 45	25 03	25℞01	26 36	
7 12	14 36	1♐40	21 50	22 18	5 14	18 49	22 28	25 20	24 59	26 04	
17	24 46	14 14	27 54	20 57	6 13	19 40	22 07	25 35	24 55	25 32	
27	4♑57	26 49	3♏56	19 37	7 05	20 33	21 44	25 47	24 47	25 01	

DAY	JAN	FEB	MAR	APR	MAY	JUN	JUL	AUG	SEP	OCT	NOV	DEC
1	21♏23	7♑28	15♑15	5♓17	13♈41	7♊37	14♋55	3♍17	18♎38	20♏48	5♑13	9♒14
☽ 3	16♐34	4♒53	12♒47	5♈17	14♉10	6♋40	12♌08	28♍21	12♏27	14♐28	29♑48	5♓09
5	12♑53	3♓36	12♓01	5♉53	14♊07	4♌08	7♍57	22♎32	6♐11	8♑37	25♒45	2♈35
7	10♒17	2♈54	12♈10	5♊39	12♋27	29♌57	2♎35	16♏18	0♑26	3♒55	23♓32	1♉37
9	8♓25	1♉55	11♉57	3♋41	8♌54	24♍30	26♎30	10♐17	25♑52	1♓00	23♈09	1♊43
11	6♈51	0♊03	10♊26	29♋57	3♍53	18♎23	20♏19	5♑05	22♒59	0♈01	23♉43	1♋47
13	5♉11	27♊08	7♋21	24♌53	27♍59	12♏09	14♐35	1♒10	21♓46	0♉17	23♊53	0♌42
15	3♊11	23♋17	3♌00	19♍04	21♎44	6♐16	9♑43	28♒39	21♈29	0♊31	22♋32	27♌52
17	0♋33	18♌37	27♌47	12♎54	15♏32	1♑00	5♒55	27♓13	21♉00	29♊31	19♌21	23♍23
19	27♋04	13♍16	22♍01	6♏40	9♐39	26♑31	3♓08	26♈08	19♊31	26♋52	14♍41	17♎44
21	22♌37	7♎21	15♎55	0♐32	4♑14	22♒54	1♈06	24♉44	16♋46	22♌47	9♎02	11♏29
23	17♍13	1♏07	9♏40	24♐47	29♑34	20♓15	29♈28	22♊40	12♌56	17♍42	2♏51	5♐09
25	11♎10	24♏58	3♐32	19♑46	25♒57	18♈30	27♉55	19♋49	8♍16	11♎59	26♏32	29♐09
27	4♏56	19♐28	27♐58	16♒01	23♓43	17♉26	26♊07	16♌11	2♎58	5♏51	20♐18	23♑44
29	29♏07		23♑33	14♓00	22♈50	16♊29	23♋42	11♍46	27♎05	29♏31	14♑26	19♒05
31	24♐20		20♒53		22♉43		20♌22	6♎31		23♐13		15♓22
1	2♑00	23♒38	10♓43	13♓13	1♉04	1♋57	16♋39	19♋26	17♍27	2♏11	3♏17	24♏56
☿ 7	11 28	3♓39	4R49	20 41	13 35	9 32	13R06	28 54	27 48	8 33	28R59	4♐12
13	21 10	11 51	1 50	29 16	26 36	15 03	10 03	10♌22	7♎26	13 09	1D05	13 31
19	1♒09	15 59	2D37	8♈53	9♊16	18 12	9D25	22 32	16 25	14R44	7 32	22 54
25	11 26	14R21	6 20	19 28	20 43	18R42	12 05	4♍26	24 42	11 39	15 54	2♑23
31	21 53		12 06		0♋29		18 07	15 39		4 30		12 00

DATE	☉	♀	♂	♃	♄	⚷	♅	♆	♇	☊	STATIONS
1 1	10♑03	3♑06	6♏56	19♊01	7♏29	20♑60	21♋31	25♎52	24♌43	24♑45	
11	20 14	15 41	12 52	17R56	8 10	21 55	21R05	25 59	24R32	24 13	☿ 20/2 16♓08
21	0♒25	28 16	18 43	17 06	8 43	22 50	20 39	26 03	24 20	23 41	☿ 15/3 1♓42
31	10 35	10♒50	24 28	16 35	9 06	23 44	20 15	26R03	24 06	23 10	☿ 23/6 18♋50
10 2	20 43	23 23	0♐07	16 24	9 18	24 36	19 52	26 00	23 51	22 38	☿ 17/7 9♋17
20	0♓49	5♓54	5 36	16D34	9R21	25 25	19 32	25 54	23 37	22 06	☿ 18/10 14♏46
2 3	10 53	18 24	10 55	17 03	9 13	26 11	19 17	25 45	23 22	21 34	☿ 8/11 28♎54
12	20 53	0♈53	16 01	17 50	8 55	26 51	19 06	25 33	23 09	21 02	♀ 26/10 0♐03
22	0♈50	13 18	20 50	18 53	8 28	27 26	19 01	25 20	22 57	20 31	♀ 6/12 14♏39
1 4	10 44	25 42	25 19	20 12	7 53	27 55	19D00	25 04	22 47	19 59	♂ 23/5 8♑30
11	20 35	8♉02	29 21	21 43	7 13	28 17	19 05	24 48	22 39	19 27	♂ 30/7 25♐33
21	0♉22	20 19	2♑51	23 25	6 28	28 32	19 16	24 32	22 34	18 55	♃ 10/2 16♊24
1 5	10 06	2♊33	5 39	25 16	5 43	28 39	19 31	24 16	22 32	18 24	♃ 17/11 29♋56
11	19 47	14 44	7 35	27 15	4 58	28R38	19 51	24 01	22D32	17 52	♄ 17/2 9♏21
21	29 25	26 50	8 28	29 19	4 17	28 30	20 15	23 47	22 35	17 20	♄ 7/7 2♏38
31	9♊01	8♋53	8R08	1♋29	3 41	28 15	20 43	23 36	22 41	16 48	♅ 28/3 19♋00
10 6	18 35	20 51	6 35	3 42	3 12	27 54	21 14	23 27	22 50	16 16	♅ 3/11 27♋42
20	28 08	2♌43	4 01	5 57	2 52	27 27	21 47	23 21	23 01	15 45	♆ 27/1 26♎04
30	7♋41	14 29	0 57	8 13	2 40	26 56	22 22	23 17	23 14	15 13	♆ 5/7 23♎17
10 7	17 13	26 07	28♐07	10 29	2D39	26 22	22 58	23D17	23 30	14 41	♇ 5/5 22♌31
20	26 45	7♍36	26 11	12 44	2 47	25 47	23 35	23 20	23 46	14 09	♇ 29/11 26♌47
30	6♌18	18 54	25D33	14 56	3 05	25 12	24 11	23 27	24 04	13 38	⚷ 5/5 28♑40
9 8	15 53	29 58	26 18	17 05	3 32	24 38	24 47	23 36	24 23	13 06	⚷ 1/10 23♑05
19	25 29	10♎44	28 20	19 09	4 08	24 09	25 20	23 48	24 42	12 34	
29	5♍08	21 07	1♑29	21 07	4 51	23 43	25 52	24 03	25 01	12 02	
8 9	14 49	0♏58	5 32	22 57	5 42	23 24	26 21	24 21	25 20	11 31	
18	24 33	10 06	10 20	24 39	6 39	23 11	26 46	24 40	25 38	10 59	
28	4♎20	18 10	15 42	26 09	7 41	23 05	27 07	25 00	25 54	10 27	
8 10	14 11	24 42	21 32	27 27	8 47	23D07	27 23	25 22	26 09	9 55	
18	24 05	28 57	27 44	28 30	9 56	23 17	27 35	25 44	26 22	9 23	
28	4♏02	29R57	4♒13	29 17	11 07	23 33	27 41	26 07	26 33	8 52	
7 11	14 03	27 03	10 56	29 46	12 19	23 57	27R42	26 29	26 40	8 20	
17	24 06	21 22	17 48	29 56	13 31	24 27	27 37	26 50	26 45	7 48	
27	4♐12	16 17	24 48	29R47	14 41	25 03	27 27	27 09	26 47	7 16	
7 12	14 21	14D41	1♓53	29 17	15 49	25 44	27 13	27 27	26R46	6 45	
17	24 31	16 59	9 02	28 30	16 54	26 29	26 54	27 42	26 43	6 13	
27	4♑42	22 19	16 12	27 27	17 53	27 17	26 31	27 55	26 36	5 41	

SID M/N 1st JAN 6 h 39 m 27 s — 1955 COMMON — BST 17/4 to 2/10

	DAY	JAN	FEB	MAR	APR	MAY	JUN	JUL	AUG	SEP	OCT	NOV	DEC
	1	28♓53	21♉41	2♊42	25♋17	2♍11	19♎28	22♏20	6♑18	21♒43	26♓41	18♉02	26♊21
☽	3	26♈47	20♊08	0♋46	22♌03	27♍41	13♏30	15♐56	0♒35	17♓57	24♈43	17♊39	26♋15
	5	25♉41	18♋34	28♋23	18♍03	22♎23	7♐11	9♑42	25♒41	15♈11	23♉25	16♋47	24♌54
	7	25♊06	16♌31	25♌28	13♎16	16♏29	0♑49	3♒56	21♓42	13♉02	22♊04	14♌54	21♍57
	9	24♋14	13♍30	21♍47	7♏46	10♐11	24♑42	28♒52	18♈33	11♊10	20♋18	11♍54	17♎36
	11	22♌16	9♎11	17♎09	1♐38	3♑47	19♒13	24♓43	16♉10	9♋24	17♌59	7♎53	12♏12
	13	18♍45	3♏42	11♏33	25♐14	27♑44	14♓47	21♈42	14♊30	7♌36	15♍00	2♏59	6♐10
	15	13♎47	27♏29	5♐18	19♑07	22♒33	11♈47	19♉54	13♋22	5♍25	11♎15	27♏21	29♐48
	17	7♏49	21♐12	28♐59	13♒58	18♓52	10♉24	19♊10	12♌15	2♎26	6♏33	21♐10	23♑25
	19	1♐28	15♑32	23♑19	10♓25	17♈01	10♊17	18♋53	10♍28	28♎16	0♐56	14♑43	17♒18
	21	25♐22	11♒01	18♒58	8♈44	16♉45	10♋30	18♌07	7♎22	22♏54	24♐40	8♒29	11♓52
	23	20♑00	7♓52	16♓16	8♉27	17♊07	9♌53	16♍00	2♏47	16♐43	18♑16	3♓02	7♈36
	25	15♒36	5♈49	15♈01	8♊28	16♋53	7♍40	12♎12	27♏00	10♑22	12♒24	29♓00	4♉56
	27	12♓12	4♉17	14♉22	7♋42	15♌12	3♎45	6♏56	20♐39	4♒32	7♓45	26♈44	3♊59
	29	9♈35		13♊24	5♌37	11♍53	28♎27	0♐47	14♑28	29♒53	4♈45	26♉07	4♋16
	31	7♉33		11♋34		7♎12		24♐24	9♒01		3♉20		4♌37
	1	13♑37	28♒55	15♒01	20♓26	18♉55	28♊30	20♊31	2♌41	29♍16	28♎37	19♎40	6♐01
☿	7	23 26	28R45	18 35	0♈35	0♊52	28R30	23 27	15 10	7♎43	26R48	28 03	15 27
	13	3♒24	23 04	24 17	11 36	11 07	26 09	29 15	27 04	15 17	20 46	7♏24	24 53
	19	13 13	16 50	1♓27	23 30	19 16	22 50	7♋42	8♍09	21 42	14 30	16 59	4♑21
	25	22 08	14 22	9 41	6♉08	25 02	20 29	18 25	18 22	26 28	13D36	26 32	13 53
	31	28 20		18 49		28 14		0♌35	27 46		18 29		23 21

DATE	☉	♀	♂	♃	♄	⚷	♅	♆	♇	☊	STATIONS
1 1	9♑48	25♏50	19♓48	26♋51	18♏21	27♑42	26♋19	28♎00	26♌32	5♑25	
11	19 59	4♐03	26 59	25R33	19 11	28 34	25R54	28 08	26R21	4 53	☿ 4/2 29♒39
21	0♒10	13 25	4♈09	24 12	19 53	29 26	25 28	28 13	26 09	4 22	☿ 25/2 14♒21
31	10 20	23 35	11 18	22 55	20 27	0♒17	25 02	28R14	25 55	3 50	☿ 4/6 28♊50
10 2	20 29	4♑17	18 24	21 47	20 51	1 08	24 38	28 12	25 41	3 18	☿ 28/6 20♊09
20	0♓35	15 22	25 28	20 52	21 06	1 57	24 17	28 07	25 26	2 46	☿ 2/10 28♎38
2 3	10 38	26 44	2♉29	20 14	21R10	2 42	24 00	27 58	25 11	2 15	☿ 23/10 13♎09
12	20 39	8♒17	9 27	19 55	21 05	3 23	23 47	27 47	24 58	1 43	♃ 17/3 19♋53
22	0♈36	20 00	16 22	19D55	20 49	4 00	23 38	27 34	24 45	1 11	♃ 18/12 1♍30
1 4	10 30	1♓48	23 13	20 15	20 24	4 31	23 35	27 19	24 35	0 39	♄ 1/3 21♏10
11	20 20	13 42	0♊01	20 52	19 51	4 56	23D38	27 03	24 26	0 07	♄ 19/7 14♏30
21	0♉07	25 39	6 46	21 46	19 12	5 15	23 46	26 47	24 21	29♐36	♅ 2/4 23♋35
1 5	9 51	7♈39	13 28	22 55	18 29	5 26	23 59	26 30	24 18	29 04	♅ 8/11 2♌20
11	19 33	19 41	20 06	24 18	17 44	5 31	24 16	26 15	24D18	28 32	♆ 30/1 28♎14
21	29 11	1♉44	26 42	25 51	17 00	5R28	24 39	26 01	24 20	28 00	♆ 8/7 25♎28
31	8♊47	13 49	3♋15	27 34	16 18	5 18	25 05	25 49	24 26	27 29	♇ 7/5 24♌17
10 6	18 22	25 56	9 46	29 25	15 41	5 01	25 34	25 39	24 34	26 57	♇ 1/12 28♌36
20	27 55	8♊04	16 15	1♌23	15 10	4 39	26 06	25 32	24 45	26 25	⚷ 12/5 5♒31
30	7♋27	20 14	22 41	3 27	14 47	4 12	26 41	25 28	24 58	25 53	⚷ 9/10 0♒05
10 7	16 59	2♋26	29 07	5 34	14 34	3 41	27 17	25D28	25 13	25 21	
20	26 31	14 40	5♌31	7 44	14D30	3 07	27 53	25 30	25 30	24 50	
30	6♌04	26 57	11 54	9 56	14 35	2 33	28 30	25 36	25 47	24 18	
9 8	15 39	9♌16	18 17	12 08	14 50	1 60	29 06	25 44	26 06	23 46	
19	25 15	21 37	24 39	14 20	15 15	1 28	29 41	25 56	26 26	23 14	
29	4♍53	3♍59	1♍01	16 29	15 48	1 00	0♌14	26 10	26 45	22 43	
8 9	14 35	16 24	7 22	18 36	16 30	0 37	0 44	26 27	27 04	22 11	
18	24 19	28 50	13 45	20 39	17 19	0 20	1 11	26 45	27 22	21 39	
28	4♎06	11♎17	20 07	22 36	18 14	0 09	1 35	27 06	27 39	21 07	
8 10	13 56	23 45	26 31	24 25	19 14	0 05	1 54	27 27	27 55	20 36	
18	23 50	6♏13	2♎55	26 06	20 19	0D08	2 08	27 49	28 08	20 04	
28	3♏48	18 41	9 20	27 37	21 27	0 18	2 16	28 12	28 19	19 32	
7 11	13 48	1♐09	15 46	28 55	22 37	0 35	2 20	28 34	28 28	19 00	
17	23 52	13 37	22 13	29 59	23 49	0 59	2R18	28 55	28 33	18 28	
27	3♐58	26 05	28 41	0♍47	25 00	1 29	2 10	29 15	28 36	17 57	
7 12	14 06	8♑32	5♏10	1 18	26 10	2 04	1 58	29 33	28R36	17 25	
17	24 16	20 58	11 40	1 30	27 18	2 44	1 41	29 49	28 32	16 53	
27	4♑27	3♒22	18 11	1R23	28 23	3 28	1 20	0♏03	28 26	16 21	

SID M/N 1st JAN 6 h 38 m 30 s 1956 LEAP BST 22/4 to 7/10

	DAY	JAN	FEB	MAR	APR	MAY	JUN	JUL	AUG	SEP	OCT	NOV	DEC
	1	19♌26	9♎38	0♏40	15♐46	17♑26	1♓26	4♈52	23♉31	15♋44	24♌53	17♎15	23♏04
☽	3	17♍47	5♏29	25♏51	9♑33	11♒11	26♓14	0♉52	21♊44	15♌25	23♍59	14♏16	18♐22
	5	14♎16	29♏53	19♐53	3♒17	5♓32	22♈25	28♉32	21♋29	15♍18	22♎21	10♐07	12♑53
	7	9♏12	23♐33	13♑30	27♒36	1♈02	20♉16	27♊54	21♌55	14♎14	19♏20	4♑52	6♒48
	9	3♐11	17♑08	7♒21	23♓01	28♈02	19♊35	28♋17	21♍42	11♏25	14♐48	28♑51	0♓31
	11	26♐47	11♒08	1♓59	19♈41	26♉23	19♋35	28♌25	19♎47	6♐52	9♑07	22♒36	24♓34
	13	20♑24	5♓47	27♓35	17♉22	25♊31	19♌09	27♍10	15♏58	1♑07	2♒53	16♓45	19♈34
	15	14♒21	1♈10	24♈05	15♊38	24♋40	17♍31	24♎06	10♐40	24♑50	26♒46	11♈52	16♉03
	17	8♓51	27♈20	21♉16	14♋03	23♌12	14♎23	19♏27	4♑33	18♒39	21♓18	8♉17	14♊13
	19	4♈07	24♉20	19♊00	12♌20	20♍47	9♏58	13♐46	28♑12	12♓58	16♈48	6♊00	13♋42
	21	0♉27	22♊20	17♋13	10♍14	17♎22	4♐36	7♑34	22♒04	8♈01	13♉18	4♋37	13♌31
	23	28♉09	21♋18	15♌46	7♎32	13♏00	28♐39	1♒15	16♓21	3♉47	10♊37	3♌30	12♍38
	25	27♊18	20♌47	14♍15	3♏55	7♐47	22♑23	25♒05	11♈13	0♊19	8♋32	2♍02	10♎28
	27	27♋25	19♍49	12♎01	29♏16	1♑54	16♒06	19♓17	6♉48	27♊40	6♌49	29♍53	6♏59
	29	27♌22	17♎29	8♏30	23♐39	25♑38	10♓07	14♈08	3♊23	25♋55	5♍13	26♎55	2♐26
	31	26♍01		3♐37		19♒23		10♉02	1♋16		3♎24		27♐09
	1	24♑54	1♒23	15♒11	5♈55	1♊14	1♊37	19♊56	21♌27	5♎38	29♍05	1♏06	18♐49
☿	7	3♒44	27R44	23 25	18 04	6 31	0R14	0♋24	2♍04	10 10	27D27	10 59	28 01
	13	10 43	28D42	2♓26	0♉36	8 47	1D25	12 28	11 44	12 10	1♎42	20 40	7♑05
	19	13R26	2♒54	12 11	12 40	8R06	5 15	25 16	20 28	10R33	9 47	0♐09	15 41
	25	9 42	9 04	22 41	23 09	5 17	11 29	7♌50	28 11	5 08	19 25	9 32	23 01
	31	2 27		3♈58		2 04		19 35	4♎41		29 26		27 12

DATE		☉	♀	♂	♃	♄	⚷	♅	♆	♇	☊	STATIONS
1	1	9♑33	9♒34	21♏27	1♍12	28♏53	3♒51	1♌09	0♏08	28♌22	16♐05	
11		19 44	21 54	27 59	0R36	29 51	4 38	0R44	0 17	28R12	15 34	☿ 19/1 13♒27
21		29 55	4♓10	4♐32	29♌43	0♐41	5 27	0 18	0 23	28 00	15 02	☿ 9/2 27♑35
31		10♒05	16 21	11 06	28 36	1 25	6 17	29♋52	0 25	27 47	14 30	☿ 14/5 8♊52
10	2	20 14	28 25	17 39	27 21	2 00	7 05	29 27	0R23	27 32	13 58	☿ 7/6 0♊14
20		0♓20	10♈20	24 13	26 02	2 26	7 53	29 04	0 19	27 17	13 27	☿ 14/9 12♎11
1	3	10 23	22 03	0♑47	24 45	2 42	8 38	28 45	0 11	27 02	12 55	☿ 6/10 27♍16
11		20 24	3♉32	7 20	23 36	2 49	9 20	28 30	0 01	26 48	12 23	♀ 1/6 9♋01
21		0♈21	14 43	13 52	22 39	2R45	9 57	28 19	29♎48	26 36	11 51	♀ 14/7 22♊30
31		10 15	25 30	20 22	21 58	2 31	10 30	28 14	29 33	26 25	11 19	♂ 11/8 23♓40
10	4	20 06	5♊47	26 49	21 34	2 08	10 58	28D13	29 18	26 16	10 48	♂ 10/10 13♓10
20		29 53	15 22	3♒13	21D30	1 37	11 19	28 19	29 01	26 10	10 16	♃ 18/4 21♌29
30		9♉37	23 59	9 31	21 43	1 00	11 34	28 29	28 45	26 06	9 44	♄ 12/3 2♐49
10	5	19 18	1♋15	15 43	22 15	0 18	11 42	28 45	28 30	26D05	9 12	♄ 31/7 26♏09
20		28 57	6 32	21 45	23 03	29♏33	11R44	29 05	28 15	26 07	8 41	♅ 5/4 28♋13
30		8♊33	8 57	27 35	24 06	28 49	11 38	29 29	28 03	26 12	8 09	♅ 12/11 6♌59
9	6	18 08	7R40	3♓07	25 22	28 07	11 26	29 57	27 52	26 20	7 37	♆ 1/2 0♏25
19		27 41	2 47	8 18	26 49	27 28	11 08	0♌28	27 45	26 31	7 05	♆ 9/7 27♎38
29		7♋13	26♊45	13 00	28 27	26 56	10 45	1 01	27 40	26 43	6 34	♇ 8/5 26♌05
9	7	16 45	22 58	17 04	0♍14	26 32	10 17	1 37	27 38	26 58	6 02	♇ 2/12 0♍27
19		26 17	22D59	20 20	2 07	26 16	9 46	2 13	27D40	27 14	5 30	⚷ 17/5 11♒44
29		5♌51	26 26	22 35	4 06	26 10	9 13	2 50	27 45	27 32	4 58	⚷ 15/10 6♒26
8	8	15 25	2♋22	23 37	6 10	26D13	8 40	3 27	27 53	27 51	4 26	
18		25 01	10 01	23R19	8 17	26 26	8 08	4 02	28 03	28 11	3 55	
28		4♍39	18 53	21 44	10 26	26 48	7 39	4 36	28 17	28 30	3 23	
7	9	14 20	28 36	19 14	12 36	27 19	7 13	5 08	28 33	28 50	2 51	
17		24 04	8♌57	16 31	14 46	27 59	6 52	5 37	28 51	29 08	2 19	
27		3♎52	19 47	14 20	16 54	28 46	6 37	6 03	29 11	29 26	1 48	
7	10	13 42	0♍59	13 14	18 59	29 39	6 28	6 24	29 33	29 42	1 16	
17		23 36	12 30	13D26	21 01	0♐38	6D26	6 40	29 55	29 56	0 44	
27		3♏33	24 16	14 54	22 57	1 42	6 31	6 52	0♏17	0♍07	0 12	
6	11	13 34	6♎13	17 28	24 46	2 49	6 42	6 58	0 39	0 17	29♏41	
16		23 37	18 20	20 55	26 26	3 59	7 01	6R59	1 01	0 23	29 09	
26		3♐43	0♏34	25 04	27 56	5 10	7 25	6 54	1 21	0 26	28 37	
6	12	13 51	12 54	29 46	29 13	6 21	7 56	6 44	1 40	0R27	28 05	
16		24 01	25 17	4♈52	0♎17	7 31	8 31	6 29	1 57	0 24	27 33	
26		4♑12	7♐44	10 18	1 05	8 39	9 10	6 10	2 11	0 18	27 02	

SID M/N 1st JAN 6 h 41 m 29 s — 1957 COMMON — BST 14/4 to 6/10

DAY	JAN	FEB	MAR	APR	MAY	JUN	JUL	AUG	SEP	OCT	NOV	DEC
1	9♑17	23♒53	2♓46	17♈57	22♉26	12♋53	21♌48	15♎25	5♐59	10♑31	25♒23	27♓04
☽ 3	3♒16	17♓40	26♓43	13♉05	19♊07	11♌30	20♍55	13♏02	1♑30	5♒00	19♓06	20♈58
5	27♒00	11♈44	21♈04	9♊00	16♋38	10♍06	19♎04	9♐15	26♑03	28♒52	12♈58	15♉38
7	20♓47	6♉28	16♉02	5♋54	14♌48	8♎18	16♏07	4♑27	20♒03	22♓35	7♉23	11♊26
9	15♈06	2♊27	12♊02	3♌55	13♍20	5♏52	12♐13	28♑58	13♓49	16♈29	2♊35	8♋23
11	10♉33	0♋12	9♋27	2♍55	11♎53	2♐40	7♑31	23♒02	7♈33	10♉48	28♊40	6♌12
13	7♊42	29♋48	8♌30	2♎21	9♏58	28♐37	2♒10	16♓48	1♉32	5♊47	25♋39	4♍26
15	6♋45	0♍27	8♍38	1♏20	7♐07	23♑40	26♒15	10♈30	26♉06	1♋42	23♌27	2♎43
17	7♌06	0♎43	8♎42	29♏02	3♑03	17♒57	20♓00	4♉33	21♊46	28♋50	21♍56	0♏49
19	7♍28	29♎22	7♏29	25♐11	27♑52	11♓45	13♈49	29♉32	19♋01	27♌20	20♎48	28♏33
21	6♎33	26♏03	4♐25	20♑00	21♒54	5♈37	8♉18	26♊05	18♌00	26♍51	19♏30	25♐41
23	3♏51	21♐09	29♐42	13♒59	15♓42	0♉11	4♊06	24♋33	18♍14	26♎37	17♐22	21♑52
25	29♏33	15♑17	23♑54	7♓45	9♈52	26♉02	1♋44	24♌37	18♎30	25♏34	13♑57	16♒59
27	24♐11	9♒02	17♒38	1♈51	4♉56	23♊29	1♌05	25♍10	17♏34	23♐01	9♒10	11♓08
29	18♑14		11♓26	26♈41	1♊14	22♋20	1♍16	24♎47	14♐52	18♑51	3♓21	4♈49
31	12♒01		5♈38		28♊46		1♎01	22♏41		13♒25		28♈41
1	27♑24	16♑39	24♒15	22♈31	18♉02	16♉03	4♋57	2♍48	24♍10	21♍11	13♏15	28♐04
☿ 7	24R33	22 59	4♓18	3♉30	14R37	22 25	17 57	10 44	19R42	0♎56	22 42	5♑27
13	17 02	0♒32	15 01	12 08	11 19	0♊40	0♌22	17 21	13 56	11 23	1♐55	10 33
19	11 50	8 53	26 25	17 34	10 00	10 38	11 47	22 19	11 09	21 48	10 56	10R55
25	11D53	17 54	8♈24	19 27	11D20	22 13	22 07	25 00	13D51	1♏53	19 43	4 57
31	15 46		20 32		15 11		1♍22	24R35		11 39		27♐35

DATE	☉	♀	♂	♃	♄	⚷	♅	♆	♇	☊	STATIONS
1 1	10♑19	15♐13	13♈41	1♎25	9♐18	9♒35	5♌57	2♏18	0♍14	26♏43	
11	20 31	27 42	19 28	1 45	10 20	10 19	5R33	2 27	0R04	26 11	☿ 2/1 27♑25
21	0♒42	10♑12	25 24	1R46	11 18	11 05	5 07	2 33	29♌52	25 39	☿ 22/1 11♑15
31	10 52	22 42	1♉27	1 27	12 09	11 52	4 41	2 36	29 39	25 07	☿ 25/4 19♉27
10 2	21 00	5♒12	7 36	0 51	12 52	12 39	4 16	2R35	29 24	24 35	☿ 19/5 10♉00
20	1♓06	17 42	13 47	29♍58	13 28	13 25	3 52	2 31	29 09	24 04	☿ 27/8 25♍15
2 3	11 09	0♓11	20 02	28 52	13 54	14 09	3 31	2 23	28 54	23 32	☿ 19/9 11♍09
12	21 09	12 39	26 17	27 37	14 11	14 50	3 14	2 13	28 40	23 00	☿ 16/12 11♑32
22	1♈07	25 06	2♊34	26 20	14 18	15 28	3 02	2 01	28 27	22 28	♃ 16/1 1♎48
1 4	11 00	7♈32	8 51	25 04	14R15	16 02	2 54	1 46	28 16	21 57	♃ 19/5 21♍50
11	20 51	19 56	15 09	23 57	14 02	16 31	2D52	1 31	28 06	21 25	♄ 24/3 14♐18
21	0♉38	2♉18	21 26	23 01	13 40	16 54	2 55	1 15	28 00	20 53	♄ 12/8 7♐40
1 5	10 22	14 39	27 43	22 20	13 10	17 11	3 03	0 58	27 56	20 21	♅ 10/4 2♌52
11	20 02	26 59	3♋59	21 56	12 34	17 22	3 17	0 43	27D55	19 50	♅ 17/11 11♌40
21	29 41	9♊17	10 16	21D51	11 53	17 26	3 35	0 28	27 57	19 18	♆ 2/2 2♏36
31	9♊17	21 33	16 32	22 03	11 09	17R24	3 58	0 15	28 02	18 46	♆ 12/7 29♎49
10 6	18 51	3♋49	22 47	22 33	10 24	17 15	4 25	0 05	28 09	18 14	♇ 10/5 27♌55
20	28 24	16 02	29 03	23 19	9 42	17 01	4 54	29♎57	28 19	17 42	♇ 4/12 2♍19
30	7♋57	28 15	5♌19	24 20	9 03	16 40	5 27	29 51	28 32	17 11	⚷ 22/5 17♒26
10 7	17 29	10♌26	11 36	25 34	8 31	16 15	6 02	29 49	28 47	16 39	⚷ 22/10 12♒15
20	27 01	22 35	17 53	27 00	8 05	15 47	6 38	29D50	29 03	16 07	
30	6♌34	4♍42	24 11	28 36	7 48	15 16	7 15	29 55	29 21	15 35	
9 8	16 09	16 46	0♍30	0♎21	7 41	14 44	7 52	0♏02	29 40	15 04	
19	25 45	28 47	6 50	2 13	7D43	14 12	8 28	0 13	29 59	14 32	
29	5♍23	10♎44	13 12	4 11	7 55	13 42	9 03	0 26	0♍19	14 00	
8 9	15 05	22 37	19 35	6 14	8 16	13 15	9 36	0 42	0 39	13 28	
18	24 49	4♏24	26 01	8 21	8 46	12 52	10 06	1 00	0 58	12 56	
28	4♎36	16 05	2♎28	10 30	9 24	12 34	10 33	1 19	1 16	12 25	
8 10	14 27	27 39	8 59	12 39	10 10	12 22	10 56	1 40	1 32	11 53	
18	24 21	9♐02	15 31	14 49	11 03	12 16	11 15	2 02	1 46	11 21	
28	4♏18	20 13	22 07	16 57	12 02	12D17	11 29	2 25	1 58	10 49	
7 11	14 19	1♑05	28 45	19 02	13 05	12 24	11 37	2 47	2 08	10 18	
17	24 23	11 31	5♏27	21 04	14 11	12 38	11 40	3 09	2 15	9 46	
27	4♐29	21 21	12 11	22 59	15 21	12 59	11R37	3 29	2 19	9 14	
7 12	14 37	0♒18	18 59	24 47	16 31	13 25	11 29	3 48	2R19	8 42	
17	24 47	7 54	25 50	26 27	17 42	13 56	11 16	4 05	2 17	8 11	
27	4♑59	13 31	2♐44	27 55	18 52	14 32	10 58	4 20	2 11	7 39	

SID M/N 1st JAN 6 h 40 m 32 s 1958 COMMON BST 20/4 to 5/10

DAY	JAN	FEB	MAR	APR	MAY	JUN	JUL	AUG	SEP	OCT	NOV	DEC
1	10♉54	27♊21	5♋24	26♌18	4♎53	28♏15	5♑26	23♒37	8♈39	10♉49	25♊49	0♌43
☽ 3	6♊18	25♋23	3♌19	26♍16	4♏51	26♐52	2♒20	18♓21	2♉15	4♊34	20♋51	27♌02
5	3♋14	24♌53	2♍59	26♎41	4♐25	24♑12	27♒57	12♈16	25♉57	28♊57	17♌03	24♍25
7	1♌35	24♍49	3♎25	26♏19	2♑40	19♒59	22♓23	5♉52	20♊20	24♋33	14♍46	23♎00
9	0♍37	24♎02	3♏19	24♐22	29♑12	14♓27	16♈08	29♉52	16♋05	21♌49	14♎01	22♏32
11	29♍29	21♏59	1♐45	20♑41	24♒12	8♈12	9♉51	24♊54	13♌35	20♍49	14♏13	22♐13
13	27♎40	18♐41	28♐35	15♒35	18♓12	1♉53	4♊15	21♋30	12♍42	21♎00	14♐16	20♑58
15	25♏02	14♑24	24♑04	9♓37	11♈48	26♉07	29♊51	19♌40	12♎41	21♏15	13♑01	18♒04
17	21♐42	9♒21	18♒37	3♈15	5♉34	21♊19	26♋49	18♍49	12♏24	20♐25	9♒56	13♓26
19	17♑38	3♓41	12♓35	26♈53	29♉53	17♋36	24♌51	18♎04	11♐00	17♑55	5♓10	7♈34
21	12♒49	27♓31	6♈15	20♉51	24♊59	14♌47	23♍20	16♏42	8♑14	13♒48	29♓16	1♉10
23	7♓11	21♈06	29♈52	15♊24	20♋59	12♍35	21♎47	14♐26	4♒13	8♓27	22♈53	24♉54
25	0♈57	14♉51	23♉46	10♋51	17♌55	10♎46	19♏54	11♑16	29♒12	2♈23	16♉32	19♊18
27	24♈34	9♊24	18♊23	7♌30	15♍47	9♏10	17♐34	7♒14	23♓27	26♈00	10♊35	14♋33
29	18♉41		14♋16	5♍33	14♎29	7♐32	14♑38	2♓22	17♈14	19♉39	5♋17	10♌40
31	14♊02		11♌51		13♏40		10♒53	26♓43		13♊37		7♍31
1	26♐46	21♑42	7♓27	29♈00	20♈01	21♉08	22♋38	4♍36	24♌48	3♎44	24♏04	25♐40
☿ 7	25D26	0♒33	18 49	0R50	21 46	2♊11	3♌31	7 22	26D15	14 21	2♐41	21R42
13	28 46	9 54	0♈32	28♈48	25 58	14 31	13 11	7R13	2♍29	24 30	10 50	13 48
19	4♑44	19 46	11 56	24 40	2♉11	27 36	21 34	3 56	11 57	4♏13	18 08	9 30
25	12 05	0♓11	21 41	21 07	10 04	10♋33	28 34	28♌47	22 46	13 34	23 42	11D09
31	20 16		28 17		19 26		3♍54	25 03		22 36		16 31

DATE	☉	♀	♂	♃	♄	⚷	♅	♆	♇	☊	STATIONS
1 1	10♑04	15♒17	6♐12	28♎35	19♐27	14♒51	10♌48	4♏26	2♍08	7♏23	
11	20 16	16R07	13 11	29 45	20 33	15 32	10R25	4 36	1R58	6 51	☿ 5/1 25♐14
21	0♒27	12 55	20 13	0♏39	21 36	16 15	10 00	4 43	1 47	6 19	☿ 7/4 0♉50
31	10 37	7 03	27 19	1 17	22 33	16 59	9 34	4 46	1 34	5 48	☿ 30/4 20♈00
10 2	20 45	2 05	4♑27	1 37	23 25	17 44	9 08	4R46	1 19	5 16	☿ 10/8 7♍42
20	0♓51	0D44	11 38	1R38	24 10	18 29	8 44	4 43	1 04	4 44	☿ 2/9 24♌41
2 3	10 54	3 13	18 52	1 20	24 46	19 12	8 21	4 36	0 49	4 12	☿ 30/11 25♐42
12	20 55	8 36	26 09	0 44	25 14	19 53	8 02	4 27	0 35	3 40	☿ 20/12 9♐25
22	0♈52	15 58	3♒27	29♎53	25 33	20 31	7 47	4 15	0 21	3 09	♀ 8/1 16♒17
1 4	10 46	24 40	10 48	28 48	25 42	21 06	7 37	4 01	0 09	2 37	♀ 18/2 0♒41
11	20 36	4♓15	18 09	27 35	25R40	21 36	7 32	3 46	0 00	2 05	♂ 10/10 2♊34
21	0♉23	14 28	25 31	26 19	25 29	22 01	7D33	3 30	29♌53	1 33	♂ 20/12 16♉36
1 5	10 07	25 06	2♓53	25 04	25 09	22 21	7 39	3 13	29 48	1 02	♃ 16/2 1♏40
11	19 48	6♈04	10 14	23 56	24 41	22 35	7 50	2 57	29 46	0 30	♃ 19/6 21♎45
21	29 27	17 17	17 33	23 00	24 06	22 42	8 06	2 42	29D48	29♎58	♄ 5/4 25♐42
31	9♊03	28 40	24 48	22 18	23 26	22R43	8 26	2 29	29 52	29 26	♄ 24/8 19♐05
10 6	18 37	10♉11	1♈59	21 53	22 42	22 38	8 51	2 18	29 59	28 55	♅ 15/4 7♌32
20	28 10	21 50	9 02	21D45	21 58	22 27	9 20	2 09	0♍09	28 23	♅ 22/11 16♌22
30	7♋43	3♊35	15 58	21 56	21 15	22 10	9 51	2 03	0 21	27 51	♆ 5/2 4♏47
10 7	17 15	15 25	22 42	22 24	20 36	21 48	10 25	2 00	0 35	27 19	♆ 14/7 2♏00
20	26 47	27 20	29 12	23 08	20 02	21 22	11 00	2D01	0 52	26 47	♇ 12/5 29♌46
30	6♌20	9♋21	5♉25	24 08	19 35	20 53	11 37	2 04	1 09	26 16	♇ 6/12 4♍14
9 8	15 55	21 26	11 17	25 21	19 16	20 23	12 14	2 11	1 28	25 44	⚷ 28/5 22♒43
19	25 31	3♌35	16 43	26 46	19 06	19 51	12 51	2 21	1 48	25 12	⚷ 28/10 17♒39
29	5♍09	15 49	21 36	28 22	19D06	19 21	13 27	2 33	2 08	24 40	
8 9	14 51	28 08	25 48	0♏07	19 16	18 53	14 01	2 48	2 28	24 09	
18	24 35	10♍30	29 09	2 00	19 35	18 28	14 33	3 06	2 47	23 37	
28	4♎22	22 55	1♊28	3 59	20 04	18 07	15 02	3 25	3 05	23 05	
8 10	14 13	5♎23	2 31	6 03	20 41	17 52	15 27	3 46	3 22	22 33	
18	24 07	17 53	2R08	8 11	21 25	17 42	15 48	4 08	3 37	22 01	
28	4♏04	0♏24	0 18	10 21	22 17	17 39	16 04	4 30	3 50	21 30	
7 11	14 05	12 57	27♉15	12 33	23 14	17D42	16 15	4 53	4 00	20 58	
17	24 08	25 31	23 38	14 45	24 17	17 52	16 21	5 15	4 08	20 26	
27	4♐14	8♐05	20 15	16 55	25 23	18 08	16R21	5 35	4 12	19 54	
7 12	14 23	20 39	17 49	19 02	26 32	18 30	16 16	5 55	4R14	19 23	
17	24 33	3♑13	16 41	21 05	27 42	18 57	16 05	6 12	4 12	18 51	
27	4♑44	15 46	16D53	23 03	28 53	19 29	15 49	6 27	4 07	18 19	

SID M/N 1st JAN 6 h 39 m 35 s — 1959 COMMON — BST 19/4 to 4/10

	DAY	JAN	FEB	MAR	APR	MAY	JUN	JUL	AUG	SEP	OCT	NOV	DEC
	1	21♍10	14♏02	24♏56	17♑19	23♒38	9♈54	12♉13	26♊15	12♌03	17♍02	8♏34	17♐08
☽	3	18♎59	12♐12	23♐02	13♒49	18♓41	3♉38	5♊54	20♋57	8♍44	15♎28	8♐47	17♑26
	5	17♏26	10♑09	20♑22	9♓13	12♈51	27♉14	29♊58	16♌34	6♎27	14♏45	8♑29	16♒12
	7	16♐17	7♒30	16♒51	3♈46	6♉35	21♊05	24♋41	13♍05	4♏49	14♐02	6♒47	13♓02
	9	14♑56	3♓51	12♓27	27♈45	0♊13	15♋23	20♌07	10♎19	3♐21	12♑34	3♓28	8♈16
	11	12♒35	29♓01	7♈11	21♉26	24♊01	10♌18	16♍19	8♏11	1♑42	10♒03	28♓52	2♉32
	13	8♓43	23♈11	1♉11	15♊07	18♋17	6♍05	13♎24	6♐33	29♑35	6♓27	23♈25	26♉21
	15	3♈27	16♉50	24♉49	9♋14	13♌22	3♎02	11♏30	5♑11	26♒43	1♈55	17♉27	20♊04
	17	27♈16	10♊39	18♊38	4♌19	9♍42	1♏25	10♐33	3♒34	22♓56	26♈37	11♊15	13♋57
	19	20♉55	5♋19	13♋13	0♍52	7♎40	1♐06	9♑59	1♓08	18♈08	20♉44	4♋59	8♌07
	21	15♊03	1♌19	9♌10	29♍12	7♏16	1♑14	8♒51	27♓25	12♉29	14♊30	28♋57	2♍53
	23	10♋13	28♌46	6♍47	29♎01	7♐43	0♒35	6♓19	22♈25	6♊17	8♋15	23♌36	28♍38
	25	6♌34	27♍18	5♎52	29♏22	7♑46	28♒15	2♈09	16♉30	0♋05	2♌32	19♍28	25♎52
	27	3♍54	26♎14	5♏39	29♐03	6♒16	24♓04	26♈38	10♊14	24♋28	27♌55	17♎05	24♏51
	29	1♎48		5♐08	27♑12	2♓50	18♈29	20♉26	4♋16	20♌00	24♍55	16♏33	25♐08
	31	29♎57		3♑35		27♓49		14♊11	29♋10		23♎40		25♑30
	1	17♐37	2♒11	22♓12	5♈49	13♈21	7♊05	3♌10	16♌04	22♌41	17♎05	1♐04	24♏28
☿	7	25 00	12 10	2♈23	1R48	21 10	20 15	10 18	11R35	3♍35	26 40	6 50	24D29
	13	3♑14	22 37	9 52	0D41	0♉17	2♋54	15 38	8 10	15 04	5♏47	9 49	29 18
	19	11 57	3♓32	12 59	2 37	10 39	14 23	18 46	8D16	26 17	14 26	7R51	6♐30
	25	21 05	14 46	11R19	7 02	22 15	24 30	19R11	12 44	6♎58	22 34	0 40	14 44
	31	0♒34		6 39		4♊54		16 43	21 02		29 57		23 29

DATE		☉	♀	♂	♃	♄	⚷	♅	♆	♇	☊	STATIONS
1	1	9♑49	22♑03	17♉27	23♏59	29♐28	19♒46	15♌40	6♏34	4♍04	18♎03	
11		20 01	4♒36	19 23	25 44	0♑38	20 24	15R19	6 45	3R55	17 31	☿ 20/3 13♈02
21		0♒12	17 08	22 12	27 20	1 44	21 04	14 55	6 52	3 44	17 00	☿ 12/4 0♈38
31		10 22	29 38	25 42	28 45	2 48	21 46	14 29	6 56	3 31	16 28	☿ 23/7 19♌22
10	2	20 30	12♓05	29 46	29 56	3 46	22 29	14 03	6R57	3 16	15 56	☿ 16/8 7♌41
20		0♓36	24 30	4♊14	0♐53	4 39	23 13	13 37	6 55	3 01	15 24	☿ 14/11 9♐53
2	3	10 40	6♈51	9 02	1 33	5 24	23 55	13 13	6 49	2 46	14 53	☿ 4/12 23♏42
12		20 40	19 08	14 06	1 55	6 02	24 36	12 53	6 40	2 31	14 21	♀ 11/8 16♍06
22		0♈38	1♉20	19 22	1R58	6 32	25 14	12 36	6 29	2 18	13 49	♀ 23/9 29♌52
1	4	10 32	13 25	24 47	1 43	6 52	25 49	12 23	6 15	2 05	13 17	♃ 19/3 1♐59
11		20 22	25 24	0♋20	1 10	7 02	26 21	12 16	6 00	1 55	12 45	♃ 20/7 22♏07
21		0♉09	7♊14	5 59	0 21	7R03	26 47	12D13	5 45	1 47	12 14	♄ 17/4 7♑04
1	5	9 53	18 55	11 44	29♏18	6 54	27 09	12 17	5 28	1 42	11 42	♄ 5/9 0♑27
11		19 34	0♋24	17 33	28 07	6 35	27 25	12 25	5 12	1 40	11 10	♅ 20/4 12♌13
21		29 13	11 39	23 25	26 51	6 09	27 35	12 39	4 57	1D41	10 38	♅ 27/11 21♌05
31		8♊49	22 36	29 21	25 36	5 35	27 39	12 57	4 43	1 44	10 07	♆ 7/2 6♏57
10	6	18 23	3♌11	5♌20	24 27	4 55	27R37	13 20	4 31	1 51	9 35	♆ 17/7 4♏11
20		27 57	13 17	11 21	23 29	4 13	27 29	13 47	4 22	2 00	9 03	♇ 14/5 1♍40
30		7♋29	22 42	17 26	22 45	3 29	27 15	14 17	4 15	2 12	8 31	♇ 9/12 6♍10
10	7	17 01	1♍12	23 33	22 17	2 45	26 57	14 49	4 12	2 26	8 00	⚷ 2/6 27♒39
20		26 33	8 22	29 43	22 07	2 05	26 33	15 24	4D11	2 42	7 28	⚷ 3/11 22♒41
30		6♌06	13 35	5♍56	22D16	1 30	26 07	16 01	4 14	3 00	6 56	
9	8	15 41	16 02	12 12	22 42	1 01	25 37	16 38	4 20	3 19	6 24	
19		25 17	14R50	18 31	23 25	0 41	25 07	17 15	4 29	3 38	5 52	
29		4♍55	10 04	24 54	24 24	0 29	24 37	17 51	4 41	3 59	5 21	
8	9	14 36	4 04	1♎20	25 37	0D27	24 08	18 27	4 55	4 19	4 49	
18		24 20	0 18	7 50	27 03	0 35	23 42	19 00	5 12	4 38	4 17	
28		4♎08	0D24	14 23	28 40	0 53	23 19	19 30	5 31	4 57	3 45	
8	10	13 58	3 59	21 01	0♐27	1 20	23 01	19 58	5 52	5 14	3 14	
18		23 52	10 09	27 43	2 21	1 55	22 49	20 21	6 13	5 30	2 42	
28		3♏49	18 07	4♏29	4 23	2 39	22 42	20 40	6 36	5 43	2 10	
7	11	13 50	27 18	11 20	6 30	3 29	22D41	20 53	6 58	5 54	1 38	
17		23 53	7♎22	18 15	8 41	4 26	22 47	21 02	7 20	6 03	1 06	
27		4♐00	18 04	25 14	10 55	5 27	22 59	21 05	7 41	6 08	0 35	
7	12	14 08	29 13	2♐18	13 10	6 33	23 17	21R02	8 01	6 10	0 03	
17		24 18	10♏42	9 27	15 25	7 42	23 41	20 54	8 19	6R09	29♍31	
27		4♑29	22 26	16 40	17 39	8 52	24 09	20 40	8 35	6 05	28 59	

SID M/N 1st JAN 6 h 38 m 37 s 1960 LEAP BST 10/4 to 2/10

DAY	JAN	FEB	MAR	APR	MAY	JUN	JUL	AUG	SEP	OCT	NOV	DEC
1	10♒15	29♓38	20♈20	5♊16	7♋14	21♌33	25♍21	14♏46	7♑44	16♒52	8♈17	13♉48
☽ 3	8♓23	25♈13	15♉19	29♊08	1♌00	16♍17	21♎25	13♐09	6♒58	15♓05	4♉38	8♊45
5	4♈35	19♉35	9♊24	22♋57	25♌20	12♎28	19♏15	12♑50	6♓07	12♈39	0♊08	3♋04
7	29♈18	13♊21	3♋10	17♌22	20♍51	10♏34	18♐51	12♒55	4♈22	9♉11	24♊45	26♋52
9	23♉13	7♋10	27♋14	12♍56	18♎03	10♐23	19♑23	12♓14	1♉13	4♊31	18♋40	20♌29
11	16♊54	1♌28	22♌07	9♎59	17♏00	10♑56	19♒29	10♈00	26♉38	28♊51	12♌20	14♍27
13	10♋48	26♌30	18♍05	8♏23	16♐58	10♒48	18♓02	6♉03	20♊58	22♋37	6♍24	9♎27
15	5♌07	22♍21	15♎10	7♐32	16♑46	9♓02	14♈44	0♊46	14♋45	16♌28	1♎33	6♏10
17	29♌58	19♎00	13♏06	6♑36	15♒26	5♈33	9♉55	24♊42	8♌36	11♍02	28♎20	4♐49
19	25♍31	16♏27	11♐29	4♒55	12♓38	0♉45	4♊09	18♋25	3♍02	6♎49	26♏47	4♑53
21	22♎02	14♐40	9♑54	2♓17	8♈34	25♉06	27♊57	12♌22	28♍23	3♏59	26♐16	5♒06
23	19♏48	13♑25	8♒04	28♓43	3♉36	19♊02	21♋40	6♍51	24♎46	2♐13	25♑43	4♓17
25	18♐52	12♒14	5♓40	24♈19	28♉02	12♋46	15♌36	2♎02	22♏04	0♑55	24♒17	1♈55
27	18♑39	10♓24	2♈28	19♉11	22♊01	6♌31	9♍56	28♎06	20♐02	29♑26	21♓43	28♈07
29	18♒07	7♈22	28♈18	13♊25	15♋45	0♍34	5♎00	25♏11	18♑24	27♒26	18♈09	23♉18
31	16♓14		23♉09		9♌31		1♏09	23♐20		24♓50		17♊46
1	24♐58	14♒59	25♓50	14♓39	23♈13	26♊38	29♋59	20♋53	9♍33	29♎01	22♏35	20♏24
☿ 7	4♑03	25 39	23R44	19 29	4♉27	6♋59	29R47	25 24	20 45	7♏01	16R12	28 56
13	13 23	6♓21	18 15	26 04	16 42	15 41	27 03	3♌23	1♎16	14 11	9 25	7♐56
19	23 00	16 11	13 32	4♈00	29 42	22 36	23 09	13 58	11 07	20 02	8D27	17 06
25	2♒56	23 23	12D07	13 04	12♊41	27 29	20 20	25 46	20 21	23 36	13 00	26 24
31	13 14		14 03		24 46		20D30	7♍37		23R11		5♑51

DATE	☉	♀	♂	♃	♄	⚷	♅	♆	♇	☊	STATIONS
1 1	9♑35	28♏23	20♐19	18♐45	9♑28	24♒25	20♌32	8♏42	6♍02	28♍44	
11	19 46	10♐22	27 38	20 54	10 38	24 60	20R12	8 53	5R53	28 12	☿ 2/3 25♓52
21	29 57	22 28	5♑02	22 58	11 48	25 37	19 50	9 02	5 43	27 40	☿ 24/3 12♓06
31	10♒07	4♑39	12 30	24 56	12 55	26 17	19 24	9 07	5 30	27 08	☿ 4/7 0♌15
10 2	20 16	16 53	20 01	26 46	13 59	26 58	18 58	9R08	5 16	26 36	☿ 28/7 19♋58
20	0♓22	29 09	27 35	28 26	14 58	27 40	18 32	9 07	5 01	26 05	☿ 28/10 24♏02
1 3	10 25	11♒27	5♒13	29 55	15 52	28 22	18 07	9 01	4 45	25 33	☿ 17/11 8♏01
11	20 26	23 45	12 52	1♑12	16 39	29 02	17 45	8 53	4 30	25 01	♂ 21/11 18♋40
21	0♈23	6♓04	20 33	2 13	17 18	29 40	17 26	8 43	4 16	24 29	♃ 20/4 3♑37
31	10 17	18 23	28 15	2 59	17 49	0♓16	17 11	8 30	4 03	23 58	♃ 21/8 23♐46
10 4	20 08	0♈42	5♓58	3 27	18 11	0 48	17 01	8 15	3 53	23 26	♄ 27/4 18♑26
20	29 55	13 00	13 40	3 37	18 23	1 16	16 56	7 59	3 44	22 54	♄ 16/9 11♑49
30	9♉39	25 18	21 22	3R28	18R25	1 39	16D57	7 43	3 38	22 22	♅ 24/4 16♌56
10 5	19 20	7♉35	29 01	3 00	18 18	1 57	17 03	7 27	3 35	21 50	♅ 1/12 25♌48
20	28 59	19 52	6♈37	2 16	18 02	2 10	17 14	7 11	3D35	21 19	♆ 10/2 9♏08
30	8♊35	2♊09	14 10	1 17	17 36	2 17	17 30	6 57	3 39	20 47	♆ 18/7 6♏22
9 6	18 10	14 26	21 38	0 08	17 04	2R17	17 50	6 45	3 44	20 15	♇ 15/5 3♍35
19	27 43	26 43	29 00	28♐52	16 26	2 12	18 15	6 35	3 53	19 43	♇ 10/12 8♍08
29	7♋15	9♋00	6♉16	27 36	15 43	2 02	18 44	6 28	4 05	19 12	⚷ 5/6 2♓18
9 7	16 47	21 18	13 24	26 24	14 59	1 45	19 15	6 23	4 18	18 40	⚷ 7/11 27♒25
19	26 19	3♌36	20 23	25 22	14 16	1 25	19 49	6D22	4 34	18 08	
29	5♌52	15 54	27 13	24 34	13 35	1 00	20 25	6 24	4 52	17 36	
8 8	15 27	28 14	3♊51	24 01	12 58	0 33	21 02	6 29	5 11	17 05	
18	25 03	10♍33	10 16	23 47	12 28	0 03	21 39	6 37	5 30	16 33	
28	4♍41	22 52	16 25	23D51	12 06	29♒34	22 16	6 48	5 51	16 01	
7 9	14 22	5♎10	22 18	24 14	11 53	29 05	22 52	7 02	6 11	15 29	
17	24 06	17 28	27 49	24 55	11D49	28 37	23 27	7 19	6 31	14 57	
27	3♎53	29 45	2♋57	25 53	11 55	28 13	23 59	7 37	6 50	14 26	
7 10	13 44	12♏01	7 34	27 05	12 11	27 53	24 28	7 57	7 08	13 54	
17	23 38	24 15	11 36	28 31	12 36	27 38	24 53	8 19	7 24	13 22	
27	3♏35	6♐28	14 53	0♑09	13 10	27 28	25 15	8 41	7 38	12 50	
6 11	13 35	18 38	17 15	1 58	13 52	27 25	25 31	9 03	7 50	12 19	
16	23 39	0♑46	18 31	3 55	14 42	27D27	25 42	9 26	7 59	11 47	
26	3♐45	12 51	18R29	5 59	15 38	27 36	25 48	9 47	8 05	11 15	
6 12	13 53	24 49	17 01	8 10	16 39	27 50	25R48	10 07	8 08	10 43	
16	24 03	6♒41	14 14	10 25	17 45	28 10	25 42	10 26	8R07	10 11	
26	4♑14	18 23	10 32	12 42	18 53	28 35	25 31	10 42	8 04	9 40	

SID M/N 1st JAN 6 h 41 m 37 s — 1961 COMMON — BST 26/3 to 29/10

DAY		JAN	FEB	MAR	APR	MAY	JUN	JUL	AUG	SEP	OCT	NOV	DEC
☽	1	29♊49	14♌15	22♌55	8♎12	13♏10	4♑39	13♒29	6♈37	26♉48	0♋52	15♌07	16♍31
	3	23♋38	8♍04	17♍01	4♏02	10♐48	3♒46	12♓45	4♉19	22♊18	25♋10	8♍43	10♎32
	5	17♌16	2♎19	11♎46	0♐49	9♑03	2♓27	10♈51	0♊29	16♋37	18♌49	2♎41	5♏35
	7	11♍02	27♎24	7♏20	28♐20	7♒26	0♈21	7♉41	25♊27	10♌19	12♍27	27♎31	2♐01
	9	5♎24	23♏44	3♐54	26♑25	5♓37	27♈26	3♊27	19♋36	3♍53	6♎33	23♏27	29♐42
	11	1♏01	21♐39	1♑34	24♒55	3♈30	23♉43	28♊21	13♌18	27♍43	1♏24	20♐19	28♑06
	13	28♏25	21♑04	0♒18	23♓31	0♉53	19♊12	22♋34	6♍52	22♎03	27♏05	17♑50	26♒38
	15	27♐41	21♒17	29♒44	21♈45	27♉31	13♋51	16♌18	0♎38	17♏08	23♐35	15♒45	24♓53
	17	28♑08	21♓07	29♓04	19♉03	23♊07	7♌47	9♍52	24♎57	13♐14	20♑55	13♓56	22♈44
	19	28♒25	19♈35	27♈27	15♊02	17♋40	1♍22	3♎41	20♏17	10♑35	19♒07	12♈18	20♉03
	21	27♓24	16♉17	24♉19	9♋44	11♌28	25♍11	28♎22	17♐05	9♒16	18♓04	10♉28	16♊37
	23	24♈37	11♊26	19♊38	3♌35	5♍08	19♎54	24♏30	15♑33	8♓59	17♈16	7♊54	12♋14
	25	20♉16	5♋34	13♋49	27♌16	29♍20	16♏08	22♐27	15♒25	8♈53	15♉55	4♋05	6♌52
	27	14♊49	29♋13	7♌28	21♍26	24♎44	14♐11	22♑00	15♓45	7♉53	13♊13	28♋58	0♍44
	29	8♋44		1♍15	16♎39	21♏44	13♑37	22♒19	15♈23	5♊15	8♋53	22♌54	24♍20
	31	2♌25		25♍39		20♐08		22♓10	13♉27		3♌14		18♎19
☿	1	7♑26	28♒42	26♒20	15♓47	9♉16	3♋32	3♋36	24♋11	23♍39	3♏16	22♎19	0♐05
	7	17 06	6♓12	24D20	24 36	22 13	8 13	1R29	5♌57	3♎13	7 10	25 32	9 30
	13	27 01	9R11	26 05	4♈23	4♊43	10 21	2D07	18 17	12 04	7R45	2♏39	18 54
	19	7♒09	6 11	0♓31	15 05	15 53	9R47	5 54	0♍16	20 10	3 40	11 24	28 22
	25	17 23	29♒50	6 48	26 44	25 13	7 02	12 46	11 31	27 21	26♎28	20 41	7♑55
	31	27 11		14 24		2♋32		22 22	21 59		22 22		17 36

DATE	☉	♀	♂	♃	♄	⚷	♅	♆	♇	☊	STATIONS
1 1	10♑21	25♒17	8♋09	14♑06	19♑35	28♒53	25♌23	10♏51	8♍00	9♍21	
11	20 32	6♓34	4R28	16 25	20 46	29 25	25R04	11 02	7R52	8 49	☿ 13/2 9♓11
21	0♒43	17 28	1 43	18 44	21 57	0♓00	24 43	11 11	7 42	8 17	☿ 7/3 24♒20
31	10 53	27 49	0 15	21 02	23 07	0 38	24 18	11 17	7 29	7 45	☿ 15/6 10♋28
10 2	21 02	7♈25	0D06	23 16	24 14	1 17	23 52	11 19	7 15	7 14	☿ 9/7 1♋21
20	1♓08	15 57	1 08	25 25	25 19	1 58	23 26	11R18	7 00	6 42	☿ 11/10 8♏02
2 3	11 11	22 55	3 10	27 28	26 18	2 38	23 01	11 13	6 45	6 10	☿ 1/11 22♎19
12	21 11	27 36	6 00	29 23	27 12	3 18	22 37	11 06	6 29	5 38	♀ 21/3 29♈05
22	1♈08	29R03	9 28	1♒10	28 00	3 56	22 17	10 55	6 15	5 06	♀ 2/5 12♈44
1 4	11 02	26 32	13 26	2 45	28 40	4 31	22 00	10 43	6 02	4 35	♂ 6/2 0♋00
11	20 52	20 51	17 48	4 09	29 12	5 04	21 48	10 28	5 51	4 03	♃ 26/5 7♒09
21	0♉40	15 13	22 29	5 18	29 34	5 32	21 41	10 12	5 42	3 31	♃ 24/9 27♑19
1 5	10 23	12 46	27 26	6 12	29 48	5 57	21D40	9 56	5 36	2 59	♄ 10/5 29♑51
11	20 04	14D11	2♌35	6 48	29R51	6 16	21 43	9 40	5 33	2 28	♄ 28/9 23♑14
21	29 43	18 43	7 55	7 07	29 45	6 30	21 52	9 24	5D32	1 56	♅ 29/4 21♌39
31	9♊19	25 25	13 24	7R06	29 29	6 39	22 06	9 10	5 35	1 24	♅ 6/12 0♍33
10 6	18 53	3♉34	19 01	6 47	29 05	6 42	22 25	8 57	5 41	0 52	♆ 11/2 11♏19
20	28 26	12 44	24 45	6 10	28 34	6R39	22 48	8 47	5 49	0 21	♆ 21/7 8♏33
30	7♋58	22 36	0♍36	5 16	27 56	6 30	23 15	8 39	6 01	29♌49	♇ 17/5 5♍32
10 7	17 30	2♊58	6 33	4 10	27 14	6 16	23 46	8 34	6 14	29 17	♇ 12/12 10♍08
20	27 03	13 44	12 35	2 56	26 30	5 57	24 19	8 33	6 30	28 45	⚷ 10/6 6♓42
30	6♌36	24 47	18 43	1 38	25 46	5 35	24 54	8D34	6 47	28 13	⚷ 12/11 1♓53
9 8	16 10	6♋06	24 57	0 23	25 04	5 09	25 31	8 39	7 06	27 42	
19	25 47	17 37	1♎16	29♑16	24 27	4 41	26 08	8 46	7 26	27 10	
29	5♍25	29 19	7 40	28 21	23 56	4 11	26 45	8 57	7 47	26 38	
8 9	15 07	11♌10	14 09	27 42	23 33	3 42	27 22	9 11	8 07	26 06	
18	24 51	23 10	20 45	27 22	23 19	3 15	27 57	9 27	8 27	25 35	
28	4♎38	5♍18	27 25	27D21	23D14	2 50	28 31	9 45	8 47	25 03	
8 10	14 29	17 32	4♏12	27 39	23 19	2 29	29 01	10 05	9 05	24 31	
18	24 23	29 52	11 04	28 16	23 34	2 12	29 28	10 26	9 22	23 59	
28	4♏20	12♎16	18 02	29 11	23 59	1 60	29 51	10 48	9 36	23 27	
7 11	14 21	24 44	25 05	0♒22	24 33	1 54	0♍10	11 11	9 48	22 56	
17	24 25	7♏14	2♐14	1 48	25 15	1D54	0 23	11 33	9 58	22 24	
27	4♐31	19 46	9 28	3 26	26 04	1 60	0 31	11 55	10 04	21 52	
7 12	14 39	2♐20	16 48	5 16	27 00	2 12	0R33	12 15	10 07	21 20	
17	24 49	14 55	24 13	7 15	28 01	2 29	0 30	12 34	10R08	20 49	
27	5♑00	27 30	1♑43	9 22	29 07	2 52	0 21	12 50	10 05	20 17	

SID M/N 1st JAN 6 h 40 m 39 s — 1962 COMMON — BST 25/3 to 28/10

	DAY	JAN	FEB	MAR	APR	MAY	JUN	JUL	AUG	SEP	OCT	NOV	DEC
	1	0♏40	17♐47	26♐15	17♒22	26♓11	19♉33	26♊30	13♌46	28♍31	1♏05	16♐47	22♑05
☽	3	26♏27	15♑58	24♑03	16♓58	25♈47	17♊35	22♋37	8♍02	22♎11	25♏06	12♑03	18♒42
	5	23♐51	15♒36	23♒32	17♈14	25♉04	14♋20	17♌39	1♎50	16♏05	19♐42	8♒19	16♓15
	7	22♑39	15♓47	23♓57	16♉54	23♊01	9♌40	11♍48	25♎33	10♐38	15♑19	5♓57	14♈49
	9	22♒06	15♈21	24♈04	14♊57	19♋14	3♍53	5♎32	19♏44	6♑24	12♒27	5♈06	14♉03
	11	21♓17	13♉33	22♉47	11♋06	13♌58	27♍36	29♎27	14♐59	3♒51	11♓22	5♉11	13♊12
	13	19♈37	10♊12	19♊37	5♌45	7♍48	21♎30	24♏10	11♑45	3♓05	11♈40	5♊04	11♋21
	15	16♉54	5♋32	14♋51	29♌32	1♎28	16♏10	20♐09	10♒09	3♈28	12♉10	3♋34	7♌57
	17	13♊10	29♋58	9♌00	23♍08	25♎33	11♐55	17♑33	9♓47	3♉43	11♊29	0♌11	3♍04
	19	8♋32	23♌51	2♍40	17♎01	20♏25	8♑47	16♒05	9♈39	2♊39	8♋52	25♌10	27♍11
	21	3♌07	17♍30	26♍18	11♏29	16♐11	6♒30	15♓09	8♉46	29♊46	4♌25	19♍10	20♎55
	23	27♌05	11♎12	20♎11	6♐39	12♑44	4♓44	14♈02	6♊32	25♋17	28♌45	12♎50	14♏54
	25	20♍43	5♏16	14♏32	2♑33	10♒00	3♈07	12♉16	2♋55	19♌45	22♍30	6♏44	9♐36
	27	14♎26	0♐07	9♐36	29♑21	7♓55	1♉25	9♊36	28♋11	13♍38	16♎11	1♐10	5♑15
	29	8♏47		5♑39	27♒13	6♈25	29♉20	5♋57	22♌40	7♎20	10♏06	26♐16	1♒51
	31	4♐23		3♒05		5♉13		1♌23	16♍38		4♐26		29♒13
	1	19♑14	21♒03	12♒55	26♓14	26♉05	19♊17	17♊07	10♌56	3♎08	18♎55	23♎28	11♐27
☿	7	29 00	14℞31	19 07	7♈18	5♊53	16℞18	23 45	22 53	10 24	12℞31	3♏06	20 50
	13	8♒31	8 45	26 37	19 12	13 22	13 14	2♋46	3♍56	16 23	7 09	12 51	0♑13
	19	16 53	7D19	5♓04	1♉46	18 15	11 51	13 51	14 06	20 30	7D32	22 30	9 36
	25	22 11	9 47	14 22	14 24	20 20	13D06	26 15	23 24	21℞44	13 18	2♐01	18 49
	31	21℞46		24 28		19℞38		8♌53	1♎49		21 54		27 24

DATE	☉	♀	♂	♃	♄	⚷	♅	♆	♇	☊	STATIONS
1 1	10♑06	3♑47	5♑29	10♒28	29♑41	3♓05	0♍15	12♏58	10♍02	20♌01	
11	20 18	16 22	13 06	12 44	0♒51	3 34	29℞59	13 10	9℞54	19 29	☿ 28/1 22♒50
21	0♒29	28 57	20 46	15 03	2 02	4 07	29 38	13 20	9 44	18 57	☿ 18/2 7♒15
31	10 39	11♒30	28 29	17 25	3 13	4 43	29 15	13 26	9 32	18 26	☿ 26/5 20♊24
10 2	20 47	24 03	6♒16	19 49	4 24	5 21	28 50	13 29	9 18	17 54	☿ 19/6 11♊51
20	0♓53	6♓35	14 04	22 12	5 32	5 60	28 24	13℞29	9 03	17 22	☿ 24/9 21♎47
2 3	10 56	19 05	21 54	24 34	6 37	6 39	27 58	13 25	8 47	16 50	☿ 16/10 6♎31
12	20 57	1♈33	29 45	26 53	7 38	7 18	27 33	13 18	8 32	16 19	♀ 23/10 27♏38
22	0♈54	13 59	7♓36	29 09	8 33	7 56	27 11	13 09	8 17	15 47	♀ 3/12 12♏12
1 4	10 48	26 22	15 26	1♓18	9 22	8 31	26 53	12 56	8 04	15 15	♂ 26/12 24♌48
11	20 38	8♉42	23 14	3 22	10 04	9 04	26 38	12 42	7 52	14 43	♃ 2/7 12♓41
21	0♉25	20 59	1♈01	5 16	10 38	9 34	26 29	12 27	7 43	14 11	♃ 29/10 2♓49
1 5	10 09	3♊12	8 44	7 02	11 03	9 60	26 24	12 11	7 36	13 40	♄ 22/5 11♒24
11	19 50	15 22	16 24	8 36	11 18	10 21	26D25	11 55	7 32	13 08	♄ 10/10 4♒45
21	29 29	27 28	24 00	9 57	11 24	10 37	26 31	11 39	7D31	12 36	♅ 4/5 26♌24
31	9♊05	9♋30	1♉31	11 03	11℞20	10 48	26 43	11 24	7 33	12 04	♅ 11/12 5♍18
10 6	18 39	21 26	8 56	11 54	11 06	10 53	27 00	11 11	7 38	11 33	♆ 14/2 13♏30
20	28 12	3♌17	16 16	12 26	10 44	10℞52	27 21	11 00	7 46	11 01	♆ 23/7 10♏43
30	7♋45	15 01	23 29	12 41	10 14	10 46	27 46	10 52	7 57	10 29	♇ 19/5 7♍31
10 7	17 17	26 38	0♊36	12℞35	9 37	10 35	28 15	10 46	8 10	9 57	♇ 15/12 12♍10
20	26 49	8♍04	7 35	12 11	8 56	10 18	28 46	10 43	8 26	9 26	⚷ 14/6 10♓53
30	6♌22	19 19	14 27	11 29	8 12	9 58	29 21	10D44	8 43	8 54	⚷ 17/11 6♓09
9 8	15 57	0♎19	21 11	10 31	7 27	9 34	29 57	10 48	9 02	8 22	
19	25 33	10 59	27 45	9 20	6 45	9 07	0♍34	10 55	9 22	7 50	
29	5♍11	21 15	4♋10	8 03	6 06	8 38	1 11	11 05	9 42	7 18	
8 9	14 52	0♏56	10 25	6 44	5 33	8 10	1 49	11 18	10 03	6 47	
18	24 37	9 49	16 28	5 30	5 08	7 42	2 25	11 33	10 24	6 15	
28	4♎24	17 34	22 17	4 25	4 52	7 16	2 59	11 51	10 44	5 43	
8 10	14 14	23 36	27 52	3 35	4 46	6 53	3 31	12 10	11 02	5 11	
18	24 08	27 07	3♌09	3 02	4D49	6 34	4 00	12 31	11 19	4 40	
28	4♏06	27℞10	8 05	2 49	5 02	6 20	4 25	12 53	11 35	4 08	
7 11	14 06	23 22	12 36	2D57	5 26	6 12	4 46	13 16	11 47	3 36	
17	24 10	17 28	16 36	3 24	5 58	6 09	5 02	13 38	11 58	3 04	
27	4♐16	13 04	19 59	4 10	6 39	6D12	5 13	14 00	12 05	2 32	
7 12	14 24	12D27	22 36	5 15	7 28	6 21	5 18	14 21	12 09	2 01	
17	24 34	15 36	24 16	6 35	8 23	6 35	5℞17	14 40	12℞10	1 29	
27	4♑45	21 32	24℞48	8 09	9 24	6 55	5 11	14 57	12 07	0 57	

SID M/N 1st JAN 6 h 39 m 42 s | 1963 COMMON | BST 31/3 to 27/10

	DAY	JAN	FEB	MAR	APR	MAY	JUN	JUL	AUG	SEP	OCT	NOV	DEC
	1	13♓08	6♉34	17♉10	8♋52	14♌16	29♍55	2♏05	16♐02	1♒51	7♓09	29♈32	8♊06
☽	3	11♈19	4♊35	15♊15	4♌54	9♍04	23♎45	25♏54	10♑54	29♒03	6♈18	0♊07	8♋11
	5	9♉44	1♋51	12♋04	29♌49	3♎08	17♏31	20♐10	6♒56	27♓39	6♉23	29♊55	6♌47
	7	8♊05	28♋19	7♌49	24♍05	26♎54	11♐34	15♑12	4♓10	26♈55	6♊08	28♋04	3♍33
	9	5♋54	23♌56	2♍47	18♎00	20♏41	6♑09	11♒08	2♈18	25♉58	4♋38	24♌32	28♍47
	11	2♌44	18♍44	27♍11	11♏45	14♐41	1♒24	7♓59	0♉48	24♊10	1♌42	19♍43	23♎01
	13	28♌22	12♎50	21♎09	5♐34	9♑07	27♒34	5♈40	29♉15	21♋24	27♌35	14♎04	16♏45
	15	22♍56	6♏36	14♏54	29♐46	4♒21	24♓52	4♉01	27♊18	17♌45	22♍37	7♏57	10♐25
	17	16♎50	0♐32	8♐47	24♑50	0♓49	23♈22	2♊43	24♋46	13♍21	17♎02	1♐39	4♑20
	19	10♏38	25♐14	3♑21	21♒23	28♓54	22♉45	1♋20	21♌28	8♎13	11♏00	25♐21	28♑43
	21	4♐58	21♑17	29♑14	19♓48	28♈31	22♊15	29♋17	17♍15	2♏24	4♐39	19♑21	23♒50
	23	0♑20	19♒01	26♒57	19♈53	28♉48	20♋54	26♌07	12♎05	26♏08	28♐20	14♒08	20♓01
	25	27♑00	18♓11	26♓27	20♉29	28♊30	18♌06	21♍43	6♏08	19♐51	22♑34	10♓13	17♈32
	27	24♒54	17♈55	26♈52	20♊12	26♋37	13♍45	16♎13	29♏52	14♑10	17♒59	8♈04	16♉25
	29	23♓33		26♉49	18♋08	22♌57	8♎13	10♏05	23♐54	9♒45	15♓13	7♉38	16♊13
	31	22♈19		25♊17		17♍50		3♐56	18♑51		14♈24		15♋58
	1	28♑42	20♑41	17♒28	11♈41	29♉03	21♉47	23♊52	26♌02	3♎31	20♍47	5♏17	22♐16
☿	7	4♒58	22D39	26 29	24 04	0℞37	23 40	5♋58	5♍44	5℞09	25 13	15 04	1♑09
	13	6℞29	27 31	6♓12	6♉02	29♉12	28 04	18 51	14 26	3 12	3♎29	24 36	9 32
	19	1 32	4♒07	16 37	16 25	25 58	4♊41	1♌32	22 03	27♍47	13 21	3♐57	16 36
	25	24♑13	11 51	27 46	24 15	22 54	13 20	13 26	28 22	22 06	23 34	13 11	20 34
	31	20 46		9♈39		21D44		24 19	2♎58		3♏38		18℞42

DATE	☉	♀	♂	♃	♄	⚷	♅	♆	♇	☊	STATIONS
1 1	9♑51	25♏16	24♌35	9♓01	9♒56	7♓07	5♍06	15♏05	12♍05	0♌41	
11	20 03	3♐49	23℞08	10 52	11 04	7 34	4℞53	15 18	11℞58	0 09	☿ 11/1 6♒42
21	0♒14	13 25	20 25	12 54	12 13	8 04	4 34	15 28	11 49	29♋38	☿ 1/2 20♑41
31	10 24	23 44	16 45	15 03	13 25	8 38	4 13	15 36	11 37	29 06	☿ 7/5 0♊37
10 2	20 32	4♑33	12 47	17 18	14 37	9 14	3 48	15 39	11 23	28 34	☿ 31/5 21♉44
20	0♓38	15 43	9 15	19 38	15 48	9 52	3 22	15℞40	11 08	28 02	☿ 7/9 5♎09
2 3	10 42	27 08	6 43	22 01	16 57	10 30	2 56	15 37	10 53	27 31	☿ 29/9 20♍33
12	20 42	8♒45	5 28	24 25	18 03	11 08	2 31	15 31	10 37	26 59	☿ 26/12 20♑45
22	0♈39	20 30	5D30	26 51	19 05	11 46	2 07	15 22	10 22	26 27	♂ 17/3 5♌20
1 4	10 33	2♓20	6 40	29 15	20 02	12 22	1 47	15 10	10 08	25 55	♃ 10/8 19♈29
11	20 24	14 15	8 47	1♈38	20 53	12 55	1 30	14 56	9 56	25 24	♃ 5/12 9♈32
21	0♉11	26 14	11 41	3 58	21 37	13 26	1 18	14 41	9 46	24 52	♄ 3/6 23♒07
1 5	9 55	8♈15	15 12	6 13	22 13	13 52	1 11	14 25	9 39	24 20	♄ 22/10 16♒27
11	19 36	20 17	19 12	8 22	22 40	14 15	1D09	14 09	9 34	23 48	♅ 9/5 1♍09
21	29 15	2♉22	23 38	10 25	22 58	14 33	1 13	13 53	9 32	23 16	♅ 16/12 10♍05
31	8♊51	14 27	28 23	12 19	23 06	14 45	1 22	13 38	9D34	22 45	♆ 16/2 15♏40
10 6	18 25	26 35	3♍25	14 03	23℞05	14 53	1 36	13 24	9 38	22 13	♆ 26/7 12♏54
20	27 58	8♊43	8 42	15 36	22 53	14℞55	1 55	13 13	9 46	21 41	♇ 21/5 9♍32
30	7♋31	20 54	14 12	16 55	22 33	14 51	2 18	13 04	9 56	21 09	♇ 17/12 14♍14
10 7	17 03	3♋06	19 52	18 00	22 04	14 42	2 45	12 57	10 09	20 38	⚷ 18/6 14♓55
20	26 35	15 21	25 43	18 48	21 29	14 28	3 15	12 54	10 24	20 06	⚷ 22/11 10♓14
30	6♌08	27 38	1♎43	19 18	20 48	14 09	3 48	12D54	10 41	19 34	
9 8	15 43	9♌56	7 51	19 29	20 04	13 47	4 24	12 57	10 59	19 02	
19	25 19	22 17	14 08	19℞20	19 19	13 21	5 00	13 03	11 19	18 31	
29	4♍57	4♍40	20 33	18 52	18 36	12 54	5 38	13 12	11 40	17 59	
8 9	14 38	17 05	27 06	18 06	17 56	12 26	6 16	13 25	12 01	17 27	
18	24 22	29 31	3♏46	17 03	17 21	11 58	6 52	13 40	12 22	16 55	
28	4♎10	11♎58	10 34	15 50	16 54	11 31	7 28	13 57	12 42	16 23	
8 10	14 00	24 25	17 28	14 30	16 36	11 07	8 01	14 16	13 01	15 52	
18	23 54	6♏53	24 30	13 10	16 27	10 47	8 32	14 37	13 19	15 20	
28	3♏51	19 21	1♐38	11 56	16D29	10 31	8 59	14 58	13 35	14 48	
7 11	13 52	1♐49	8 53	10 54	16 40	10 20	9 22	15 21	13 48	14 16	
17	23 55	14 17	16 15	10 07	17 02	10 14	9 41	15 43	13 59	13 45	
27	4♐01	26 44	23 42	9 40	17 33	10D15	9 54	16 05	14 07	13 13	
7 12	14 10	9♑11	1♑15	9D33	18 13	10 21	10 02	16 26	14 12	12 41	
17	24 20	21 36	8 52	9 46	19 01	10 33	10℞05	16 46	14℞14	12 09	
27	4♑31	4♒00	16 35	10 20	19 56	10 50	10 01	17 04	14 12	11 37	

SID M/N 1st JAN 6 h 38 m 45 s — 1964 LEAP — BST 22/3 to 25/10

	DAY	JAN	FEB	MAR	APR	MAY	JUN	JUL	AUG	SEP	OCT	NOV	DEC
	1	0♌30	19♍29	10♎17	25♏12	27♐12	11♒52	16♓27	6♉53	29♊52	8♌48	29♍46	4♏54
☽	3	28♌25	15♎03	5♏08	18♐52	20♑54	6♓53	12♈55	5♊05	28♋26	6♍28	25♎34	29♏18
	5	24♍38	9♏26	29♏07	12♑35	15♒19	3♈22	10♉48	4♋08	26♌56	3♎28	20♏30	23♐09
	7	19♎26	3♐09	22♐46	7♒02	11♓05	1♉36	10♊02	3♌33	24♍44	29♎30	14♐39	16♑45
	9	13♏21	26♐54	16♑48	2♓53	8♈40	1♊21	10♋03	2♍27	21♎17	24♏25	8♑18	10♒24
	11	6♐59	21♑18	11♒52	0♈30	7♉58	1♋43	9♌48	0♎04	16♏27	18♐25	1♒55	4♓36
	13	0♑53	16♒45	8♓24	29♈37	8♊11	1♌28	8♍17	26♎04	10♐33	12♑01	26♒08	29♓53
	15	25♑25	13♓21	6♈21	29♉19	8♋03	29♌44	5♎03	20♏39	4♑11	5♒54	21♓36	26♈46
	17	20♒46	10♈53	5♉06	28♊33	6♌42	26♍18	0♏14	14♐26	28♑05	0♓46	18♈47	25♉27
	19	17♓01	8♉56	3♊55	26♋45	3♍50	21♎26	24♏20	8♑05	22♒52	27♓07	17♉38	25♊31
	21	14♈08	7♊10	2♋13	23♌47	29♍38	15♏37	17♐58	2♒13	18♓55	24♈59	17♊28	25♋55
	23	12♉06	5♋22	29♋51	19♍51	24♎26	9♐19	11♑40	27♒13	16♈10	23♉53	17♋15	25♌25
	25	10♊45	3♌22	26♌50	15♎05	18♏34	2♑57	5♒51	23♓13	14♉13	23♊00	16♌04	23♍16
	27	9♋45	0♍50	23♍07	9♏38	12♐18	26♑48	0♓44	20♈05	12♊31	21♋39	13♍32	19♎25
	29	8♌26	27♍25	18♎35	3♐35	5♑54	21♒12	26♓29	17♉37	10♋46	19♌31	9♎44	14♏15
	31	6♍09		13♏11		29♑44		23♈10	15♊40		16♍34		8♐16
	1	17♑44	16♑57	0♓06	28♈25	4♉51	16♉54	13♋40	5♍37	11♍04	26♍27	18♏41	0♑12
☿	7	10R05	24 37	10 48	6♉21	2R03	25 38	26 04	11 48	5R55	7♎09	27 50	4 28
	13	4 58	3♒03	22 09	10 44	1D44	5♊58	7♌24	16 07	4D25	17 42	6♐43	3R37
	19	5D18	12 04	4♈01	11R19	4 08	17 46	17 35	17 57	8 15	27 52	15 18	26♐47
	25	9 28	21 40	15 56	8 43	8 53	0♋38	26 37	16R34	16 18	7♏40	23 20	19 59
	31	15 46		26 48		15 37		4♍27	12 01		17 08		18D51

DATE	☉	♀	♂	♃	♄	⚷	♅	♆	♇	☊	STATIONS
1 1	9♑36	10♒11	20♑27	10♈45	20♒25	11♓00	9♍57	17♏11	14♍10	11♋22	
11	19 48	22 30	28 15	11 46	21 28	11 25	9R46	17 25	14R04	10 50	☿ 15/1 4♑30
21	29 59	4♓46	6♒05	13 04	22 35	11 53	9 30	17 37	13 55	10 18	☿ 17/4 11♉32
31	10♒09	16 55	13 58	14 36	23 46	12 25	9 10	17 45	13 43	9 46	☿ 11/5 1♉32
10 2	20 17	28 58	21 52	16 21	24 57	12 59	8 47	17 49	13 30	9 14	☿ 20/8 17♍58
20	0♓24	10♈51	29 46	18 16	26 10	13 35	8 21	17R50	13 15	8 43	☿ 12/9 4♍18
1 3	10 27	22 31	7♓40	20 19	27 22	14 13	7 55	17 48	13 00	8 11	☿ 9/12 4♑53
11	20 28	3♉57	15 33	22 30	28 32	14 50	7 29	17 43	12 44	7 39	☿ 29/12 18♐35
21	0♈25	15 03	23 24	24 46	29 40	15 28	7 05	17 34	12 29	7 07	♀ 29/5 6♋52
31	10 19	25 45	1♈12	27 06	0♓43	16 03	6 43	17 23	12 14	6 36	♀ 12/7 20♊21
10 4	20 10	5♊53	8 58	29 28	1 42	16 37	6 24	17 10	12 02	6 04	♃ 15/9 26♉08
20	29 57	15 17	16 39	1♉52	2 35	17 08	6 10	16 55	11 51	5 32	♄ 15/6 5♓02
30	9♉41	23 39	24 16	4 16	3 21	17 36	6 00	16 40	11 43	5 00	♄ 2/11 28♒20
10 5	19 22	0♋32	1♉49	6 39	3 59	18 00	5 56	16 23	11 38	4 29	♅ 13/5 5♍55
20	29 01	5 14	9 16	8 59	4 29	18 20	5D56	16 07	11 36	3 57	♅ 20/12 14♍51
30	8♊37	6R52	16 38	11 17	4 50	18 34	6 03	15 52	11D36	3 25	♆ 18/2 17♏50
9 6	18 12	4 40	23 55	13 29	5 00	18 44	6 14	15 38	11 40	2 53	♆ 27/7 15♏04
19	27 45	29♊13	1♊06	15 36	5R02	18 48	6 31	15 26	11 47	2 21	♇ 23/5 11♍35
29	7♋17	23 25	8 11	17 36	4 53	18R46	6 52	15 16	11 57	1 50	♇ 18/12 16♍20
9 7	16 49	20 29	15 10	19 27	4 35	18 39	7 17	15 09	12 09	1 18	⚷ 21/6 18♓48
19	26 21	21D22	22 03	21 08	4 08	18 27	7 46	15 05	12 24	0 46	⚷ 25/11 14♓10
29	5♌54	25 28	28 50	22 37	3 34	18 11	8 17	15D04	12 40	0 14	
8 8	15 29	1♋52	5♋30	23 53	2 54	17 50	8 52	15 06	12 59	29♊43	
18	25 05	9 50	12 05	24 53	2 10	17 26	9 28	15 12	13 19	29 11	
28	4♍43	18 55	18 32	25 37	1 25	16 60	10 05	15 20	13 39	28 39	
7 9	14 24	28 47	24 53	26 02	0 41	16 32	10 43	15 32	14 00	28 07	
17	24 08	9♌14	1♌06	26R08	29♒59	16 04	11 20	15 46	14 22	27 35	
27	3♎55	20 09	7 12	25 53	29 23	15 37	11 57	16 03	14 42	27 04	
7 10	13 46	1♍26	13 09	25 19	28 54	15 13	12 31	16 21	15 02	26 32	
17	23 40	13 00	18 56	24 27	28 33	14 51	13 03	16 42	15 20	26 00	
27	3♏37	24 48	24 33	23 20	28 22	14 33	13 33	17 03	15 37	25 28	
6 11	13 37	6♎47	29 56	22 03	28D21	14 20	13 58	17 26	15 51	24 57	
16	23 41	18 55	5♍05	20 42	28 31	14 12	14 19	17 48	16 03	24 25	
26	3♐47	1♏10	9 56	19 22	28 51	14D10	14 35	18 10	16 12	23 53	
6 12	13 55	13 31	14 26	18 11	29 20	14 13	14 46	18 32	16 17	23 21	
16	24 05	25 55	18 30	17 12	29 59	14 22	14 51	18 52	16 20	22 50	
26	4♑16	8♐22	22 01	16 31	0♓46	14 37	14R50	19 10	16R19	22 18	

SID M/N 1st JAN 6 h 41 m 44 s — 1965 COMMON — BST 21/3 to 24/10

DAY	JAN	FEB	MAR	APR	MAY	JUN	JUL	AUG	SEP	OCT	NOV	DEC
1	20♐07	4♒19	12♒52	28♓45	3♉59	25♊37	4♌25	27♍40	17♏13	20♐35	4♒32	6♓07
☽ 3	13♑42	28♒30	7♓25	25♈13	2♊06	25♋13	4♍08	25♎23	12♐25	14♑46	28♒19	0♈19
5	7♒24	23♓18	2♈49	22♉32	0♋48	24♌19	2♎27	21♏16	6♑32	8♒29	22♓34	25♈33
7	1♓28	18♈52	28♈59	20♊24	29♋30	22♍20	29♎07	15♐50	0♒13	2♓23	17♈47	22♉14
9	26♓14	15♉22	25♉53	18♋34	27♌47	19♎08	24♏24	9♑42	24♒01	26♓55	14♉09	20♊23
11	22♈05	13♊05	23♊31	16♌53	25♍26	14♏50	18♐46	3♒22	18♓16	22♈17	11♊35	19♋31
13	19♉26	12♋04	21♋56	15♍06	22♎15	9♐39	12♑39	27♒11	13♈06	18♉29	9♋44	18♌47
15	18♊24	11♌55	20♌57	12♎48	18♏10	3♑49	6♒21	21♓21	8♉37	15♊25	8♌10	17♍27
17	18♋36	11♍36	19♍53	9♏29	13♐08	27♑36	0♓07	16♈03	4♊57	13♋04	6♍31	15♎05
19	18♌55	10♎01	17♎54	4♐56	7♑20	21♒18	24♓16	11♉35	2♋19	11♌21	4♎31	11♏42
21	18♍06	6♏36	14♏25	29♐18	1♒04	15♓21	19♈10	8♊19	0♌51	10♍03	1♏54	7♐24
23	15♎26	1♐32	9♐25	23♑04	24♒51	10♈16	15♉17	6♋34	0♍18	8♎41	28♏24	2♑20
25	10♏57	25♐26	3♑24	16♒51	19♓19	6♉34	13♊03	6♌15	29♍50	6♏33	23♐54	26♑38
27	5♐12	19♑00	27♑02	11♓19	14♈59	4♊36	12♋31	6♍32	28♎23	3♐10	18♑27	20♒28
29	28♐51		21♒02	6♈58	12♉13	4♋10	12♌58	6♎07	25♏18	28♐25	12♒22	14♓11
31	22♑25		15♓54		10♊55		13♍07	4♏00		22♑38		8♈16
1	19♐11	26♑20	14♓30	22♈56	14♈49	27♉42	28♋55	0♍04	20♌18	10♎17	28♏19	13♐43
☿ 7	23 22	5♒45	26 02	19℞41	19 50	10♊10	8♌20	28℞58	27 22	20 29	6♐11	5℞56
13	29 51	15 38	7♈06	15 10	26 39	23 18	16 23	25 03	7♍21	0♏12	13 02	2D49
19	7♑32	26 01	16 16	12 11	4♉58	6♋13	22 55	20 13	18 27	9 30	17 53	5 30
25	15 55	6♓56	21 56	12D06	14 41	18 11	27 36	17 39	29 35	18 25	18℞46	11 30
31	24 49		23℞09		25 44		29 56	19D31		26 56		19 06

DATE	☉	♀	♂	♃	♄	⚷	♅	♆	♇	☊	STATIONS
1 1	10♑23	15♐51	23♍49	16♉16	1♓18	14♓48	14♍47	19♏20	16♍17	21♊59	
11	20 34	28 21	26 13	16D07	2 15	15 11	14℞38	19 34	16℞11	21 27	☿ 30/3 23♈16
21	0♒45	10♑51	27 40	16 18	3 19	15 37	14 24	19 45	16 02	20 55	☿ 22/4 11♈46
31	10 55	23 22	28℞01	16 50	4 26	16 08	14 05	19 54	15 51	20 23	☿ 2/8 0♍06
10 2	21 03	5♒52	27 07	17 40	5 37	16 41	13 43	19 59	15 38	19 52	☿ 26/8 17♌37
20	1♓09	18 22	24 55	18 47	6 49	17 16	13 18	20℞01	15 23	19 20	☿ 23/11 19♐05
2 3	11 13	0♓51	21 38	20 10	8 02	17 52	12 52	19 59	15 08	18 48	☿ 13/12 2♐49
12	21 13	13 19	17 46	21 45	9 15	18 29	12 26	19 54	14 52	18 16	♂ 29/1 28♍03
22	1♈10	25 47	14 00	23 31	10 26	19 06	12 01	19 46	14 36	17 45	♂ 20/4 8♍44
1 4	11 04	8♈12	11 02	25 27	11 35	19 42	11 38	19 35	14 22	17 13	♃ 10/1 16♉07
11	20 54	20 36	9 14	27 30	12 40	20 16	11 18	19 22	14 09	16 41	♃ 20/10 1♋19
21	0♉41	2♉59	8D44	29 40	13 40	20 47	11 02	19 08	13 58	16 09	♄ 28/6 17♓13
1 5	10 25	15 20	9 27	1♊54	14 35	21 15	10 50	18 52	13 49	15 37	♄ 14/11 10♓29
11	20 06	27 39	11 14	4 11	15 22	21 40	10 44	18 36	13 44	15 06	♅ 19/5 10♍42
21	29 45	9♊57	13 53	6 30	16 02	22 01	10D42	18 20	13 41	14 34	♅ 25/12 19♍38
31	9♊21	22 14	17 15	8 50	16 34	22 17	10 46	18 04	13D41	14 02	♆ 20/2 20♏01
10 6	18 55	4♋29	21 12	11 10	16 57	22 27	10 56	17 50	13 45	13 30	♆ 30/7 17♏14
20	28 28	16 42	25 39	13 29	17 10	22 33	11 10	17 38	13 51	12 59	♇ 25/5 13♍41
30	8♋00	28 54	0♎29	15 44	17℞13	22℞33	11 29	17 28	14 01	12 27	♇ 21/12 18♍28
10 7	17 32	11♌05	5 40	17 57	17 06	22 28	11 53	17 20	14 13	11 55	⚷ 25/6 22♓34
20	27 05	23 13	11 09	20 04	16 50	22 18	12 20	17 16	14 27	11 23	⚷ 29/11 17♓58
30	6♌38	5♍19	16 54	22 05	16 25	22 03	12 51	17D14	14 44	10 51	
9 8	16 12	17 22	22 52	23 58	15 51	21 43	13 24	17 16	15 02	10 20	
19	25 49	29 22	29 03	25 42	15 12	21 21	14 00	17 21	15 22	9 48	
29	5♍27	11♎18	5♏26	27 15	14 28	20 55	14 37	17 29	15 43	9 16	
8 9	15 08	23 09	12 00	28 36	13 43	20 28	15 14	17 40	16 04	8 44	
18	24 53	4♏55	18 43	29 43	12 57	20 00	15 52	17 54	16 26	8 13	
28	4♎40	16 34	25 36	0♋33	12 15	19 33	16 29	18 10	16 47	7 41	
8 10	14 31	28 04	2♐38	1 06	11 37	19 08	17 04	18 29	17 07	7 09	
18	24 25	9♐24	9 48	1 19	11 07	18 45	17 38	18 49	17 25	6 37	
28	4♏22	20 30	17 06	1℞13	10 44	18 26	18 08	19 10	17 42	6 06	
7 11	14 23	1♑16	24 31	0 46	10 32	18 12	18 35	19 33	17 57	5 34	
17	24 26	11 34	2♑02	0 01	10D30	18 02	18 58	19 55	18 09	5 02	
27	4♐33	21 12	9 39	29♊00	10 38	17 58	19 16	20 17	18 19	4 30	
7 12	14 41	29 51	17 22	27 46	10 57	17D60	19 29	20 39	18 25	3 58	
17	24 51	7♒02	25 08	26 26	11 26	18 07	19 36	20 59	18 28	3 27	
27	5♑02	12 02	2♒57	25 05	12 04	18 20	19℞38	21 18	18℞28	2 55	

SID M/N 1st JAN 6 h 40 m 47 s — 1966 COMMON — BST 20/3 to 23/10

DAY	JAN	FEB	MAR	APR	MAY	JUN	JUL	AUG	SEP	OCT	NOV	DEC
1	20♈38	8♊00	17♊00	8♌52	18♍11	10♏52	17♐11	4♒03	18♓55	21♈36	7♊38	13♋30
☽ 3	16♉25	6♋14	14♋49	8♍22	17♎12	8♐01	12♑45	28♒12	12♈37	15♉46	3♋26	10♌55
5	13♊55	6♌12	14♌23	8♎17	15♏40	4♑11	7♒32	21♓59	6♉32	10♊35	0♌13	8♍55
7	13♋10	6♍53	14♍55	7♏28	12♐59	29♑19	1♓40	15♈42	1♊07	6♋29	28♌07	7♎16
9	13♌20	6♎49	15♎02	5♐06	8♑55	23♒33	25♓25	9♉50	26♊58	3♌51	27♍00	5♏44
11	13♍12	4♏59	13♏33	1♑02	3♒37	17♓22	19♈18	5♊02	24♋36	2♍48	26♎24	3♐57
13	11♎46	1♐18	10♐08	25♑38	27♒34	11♈19	13♉59	1♋55	24♌03	2♎50	25♏28	1♑24
15	8♏44	26♐13	5♑09	19♒31	21♓22	6♉01	10♊03	0♌43	24♍33	2♏52	23♐27	27♑42
17	4♐22	20♑21	29♑13	13♓16	15♈35	1♊59	7♋51	0♍54	24♎45	1♐46	19♑54	22♒45
19	29♐06	14♒08	22♒56	7♈21	10♉40	29♊22	7♌08	1♎11	23♏29	28♐57	14♒57	16♓50
21	23♑18	7♓52	16♓42	2♉05	6♊49	27♋54	6♍57	0♏21	20♐23	24♑29	9♓00	10♈31
23	17♒09	1♈44	10♈49	27♉35	4♋01	26♌54	6♎13	27♏52	15♑47	18♒53	2♈42	4♉29
25	10♓52	25♈58	5♉25	23♊56	1♌59	25♍38	4♏16	23♐52	10♒10	12♓41	26♈39	29♉21
27	4♈43	20♉53	0♊42	21♋12	0♍22	23♎39	1♐03	18♑50	4♓03	6♈25	21♉18	25♊31
29	29♈07		26♊58	19♌21	28♍49	20♏50	26♐48	13♒08	27♓47	0♉27	16♊55	23♋00
31	24♉38		24♋33		26♎59		21♑47	7♓02		25♉04		21♌20
1	20♐27	8♒03	27♓12	23♓13	16♈09	15♊54	4♌26	2♌42	29♌10	22♎34	1♐13	18♏36
☿ 7	28 54	18 26	3♈51	23D06	25 33	28 26	9 04	0℞24	10♍50	1♏36	3℞15	24 12
13	7♑46	29 14	5℞42	25 58	6♉07	9♋44	11 18	1D46	22 11	10 07	0 09	1♐51
19	16 58	10♓17	2 42	1♈06	17 51	19 34	10℞44	7 15	2♎55	18 01	22♏36	10 22
25	26 29	20 57	27♓26	7 56	0♊34	27 51	7 35	16 11	13 01	25 01	17 24	19 17
31	6♒22		23 34		13 43		3 20	27 13		0♐31		28 25

DATE	☉	♀	♂	♃	♄	⚷	♅	♆	♇	☊	STATIONS
1 1	10♑08	13♒23	6♒53	24♊26	12♓26	18♓28	19♍37	21♏26	18♍26	2♊39	
11	20 19	13℞15	14 46	23℞16	13 16	18 48	19℞30	21 41	18℞21	2 07	☿ 12/3 5♈45
21	0♒30	9 10	22 40	22 19	14 13	19 13	19 19	21 53	18 13	1 35	☿ 4/4 22♓45
31	10 40	3 09	0♓34	21 39	15 16	19 41	19 02	22 02	18 02	1 04	☿ 15/7 11♌26
10 2	20 49	28♑56	8 27	21 18	16 24	20 13	18 42	22 08	17 49	0 32	☿ 8/8 0♌20
20	0♓55	28D36	16 19	21D18	17 34	20 47	18 18	22 11	17 35	0 00	☿ 7/11 3♐15
2 3	10 58	1♒54	24 08	21 37	18 47	21 22	17 53	22℞10	17 19	29♉28	☿ 27/11 17♏07
12	20 59	7 51	1♈55	22 15	20 01	21 59	17 27	22 06	17 03	28 57	♀ 6/1 13♒50
22	0♈56	15 37	9 38	23 11	21 15	22 35	17 01	21 58	16 48	28 25	♀ 16/2 28♑15
1 4	10 50	24 34	17 17	24 22	22 27	23 11	16 37	21 48	16 33	27 53	♃ 15/2 21♊15
11	20 40	4♓20	24 52	25 46	23 37	23 45	16 15	21 36	16 19	27 21	♃ 21/11 4♌29
21	0♉27	14 41	2♉22	27 22	24 44	24 17	15 57	21 22	16 08	26 50	♄ 11/7 29♓41
1 5	10 11	25 25	9 46	29 09	25 47	24 46	15 43	21 06	15 59	26 18	♄ 27/11 22♓55
11	19 52	6♈28	17 06	1♋03	26 44	25 12	15 34	20 50	15 52	25 46	♅ 24/5 15♍29
21	29 31	17 43	24 20	3 05	27 34	25 34	15 29	20 34	15 49	25 14	♅ 30/12 24♍26
31	9♊07	29 09	1♊30	5 11	28 17	25 51	15D31	20 18	15D48	24 42	♆ 22/2 22♏11
10 6	18 41	10♉43	8 33	7 22	28 52	26 04	15 37	20 04	15 51	24 11	♆ 1/8 19♏24
20	28 14	22 23	15 32	9 35	29 18	26 12	15 49	19 51	15 57	23 39	♇ 27/5 15♍48
30	7♋47	4♊10	22 26	11 51	29 35	26℞14	16 06	19 40	16 06	23 07	♇ 23/12 20♍39
10 7	17 19	16 01	29 15	14 06	29 41	26 11	16 27	19 32	16 17	22 35	⚷ 29/6 26♓14
20	26 51	27 57	5♋59	16 21	29℞38	26 03	16 53	19 27	16 31	22 04	⚷ 3/12 21♓40
30	6♌24	9♋58	12 38	18 34	29 24	25 50	17 22	19 25	16 48	21 32	
9 8	15 58	22 04	19 13	20 44	29 01	25 32	17 54	19D26	17 06	21 00	
19	25 35	4♌14	25 43	22 50	28 30	25 11	18 28	19 30	17 26	20 28	
29	5♍13	16 29	2♌09	24 51	27 52	24 46	19 05	19 37	17 47	19 56	
8 9	14 54	28 48	8 31	26 44	27 09	24 20	19 42	19 47	18 08	19 25	
18	24 38	11♍10	14 47	28 29	26 23	23 53	20 20	20 01	18 30	18 53	
28	4♎26	23 36	21 00	0♌05	25 37	23 25	20 57	20 16	18 51	18 21	
8 10	14 16	6♎04	27 07	1 28	24 53	22 59	21 34	20 34	19 11	17 49	
18	24 10	18 34	3♍09	2 38	24 13	22 36	22 08	20 54	19 31	17 18	
28	4♏08	1♏05	9 05	3 32	23 40	22 15	22 41	21 15	19 48	16 46	
7 11	14 08	13 38	14 55	4 09	23 15	21 59	23 09	21 38	20 04	16 14	
17	24 12	26 11	20 38	4 27	23 00	21 48	23 34	22 00	20 17	15 42	
27	4♐18	8♐45	26 12	4℞26	22D55	21 41	23 55	22 22	20 27	15 11	
7 12	14 26	21 19	1♎35	4 05	23 01	21D41	24 11	22 44	20 34	14 39	
17	24 36	3♑53	6 47	3 25	23 17	21 45	24 21	23 05	20 38	14 07	
27	4♑47	16 27	11 45	2 29	23 44	21 56	24 25	23 24	20℞38	13 35	

SID M/N 1st JAN 6 h 39 m 49 s 1967 COMMON BST 19/3 to 29/10

	DAY	JAN	FEB	MAR	APR	MAY	JUN	JUL	AUG	SEP	OCT	NOV	DEC
	1	5♍37	28♎59	8♏56	29♐53	4♒49	20♓02	21♈46	5♊35	22♋00	27♌49	20♎14	28♏38
☽	3	4♎05	26♏39	6♐55	25♑53	29♒36	13♈43	15♉31	0♋47	19♌44	27♍08	20♏38	28♐31
	5	2♏09	23♐21	3♑28	20♒41	23♓31	7♉24	9♊58	27♋28	18♍51	27♎20	20♐30	27♑09
	7	29♏44	19♑16	28♑55	14♓43	17♈07	1♊36	5♋32	25♌29	18♎30	27♏14	18♑52	23♒56
	9	26♐44	14♒27	23♒35	8♈23	10♉50	26♊38	2♌17	24♍14	17♏43	25♐55	15♒24	19♓03
	11	22♑59	8♓56	17♓40	2♉00	5♊01	22♋37	29♌55	23♎01	15♐55	23♑02	10♓25	13♈02
	13	18♒20	2♈49	11♈23	25♉51	29♊54	19♌29	28♍02	21♏20	12♑59	18♒46	4♈28	6♉37
	15	12♓44	26♈24	4♉58	20♊17	25♋42	17♍07	26♎17	19♐02	9♒02	13♓27	28♈06	0♊21
	17	6♈30	20♉13	28♉50	15♋42	22♌35	15♎24	24♏30	16♑04	4♓12	7♈28	21♉44	24♊39
	19	0♉10	14♊58	23♊32	12♌33	20♍40	14♏09	22♐30	12♒19	28♓36	1♉08	15♊41	19♋41
	21	24♉28	11♋19	19♋40	11♍02	19♎49	12♐58	19♑56	7♓40	22♈27	24♉45	10♋11	15♌30
	23	20♊03	9♌35	17♌42	10♎52	19♏28	11♑10	16♒25	2♈07	16♉02	18♊37	5♌27	12♍06
	25	17♋20	9♍22	17♍25	11♏07	18♐44	8♒11	11♓44	25♈54	9♊47	13♋11	1♍49	9♎35
	27	16♌08	9♎33	17♎54	10♐38	16♑45	3♓44	5♈59	19♉30	4♋17	8♌55	29♍31	8♏01
	29	15♍36		17♏50	8♑36	13♒07	28♓04	29♈40	13♊34	0♌10	6♍13	28♎37	7♐15
	31	14♎45		16♐18		8♓00		23♉26	8♋48		5♎14		6♑33
	1	29♐58	21♒16	16♓12	12♓48	28♈06	0♋25	21♋10	18♋38	14♍49	1♏11	9♏21	23♏04
☿	7	9♑20	1♓40	10R18	19 36	10♉16	8 56	18R10	26 49	25 27	8 10	2R44	2♐12
	13	18 56	11 01	5 40	27 40	23 10	15 32	14 31	7♌29	5♎23	13 47	1D56	11 29
	19	28 49	17 22	4D39	6♈48	6♊08	19 59	12 22	19 26	14 39	17 02	6 42	20 49
	25	9♒02	18R32	7 00	16 57	18 14	21 56	13D14	1♍29	23 16	16R21	14 19	0♑15
	31	19 30		11 49		28 49		17 35	12 58		10 38		9 49

DATE	☉	♀	♂	♃	♄	⚷	♅	♆	♇	☊	STATIONS
1 1	9♑53	22♑43	14♎08	1♌55	24♓01	22♓03	24♍26	23♏32	20♍37	13♉19	
11	20 05	5♒16	18 38	0R41	24 42	22 21	24R22	23 48	20R33	12 48	☿ 23/2 18♓49
21	0♒16	17 47	22 44	29♋21	25 31	22 44	24 13	24 01	20 26	12 16	☿ 18/3 4♓33
31	10 26	0♓17	26 21	28 02	26 27	23 11	23 58	24 11	20 15	11 44	☿ 26/6 21♋59
10 2	20 34	12 45	29 22	26 49	27 29	23 41	23 40	24 18	20 03	11 12	☿ 20/7 12♋16
20	0♓40	25 09	1♏37	25 48	28 36	24 13	23 18	24 21	19 49	10 40	☿ 21/10 17♏21
2 3	10 43	7♈30	2 56	25 02	29 47	24 48	22 53	24R21	19 33	10 09	☿ 11/11 1♏27
12	20 44	19 46	3R08	24 34	1♈00	25 23	22 27	24 17	19 17	9 37	♀ 9/8 13♍54
22	0♈41	1♉56	2 06	24D26	2 15	25 59	22 01	24 11	19 01	9 05	♀ 20/9 27♌38
1 4	10 35	14 01	29♎48	24 36	3 29	26 35	21 36	24 01	18 46	8 33	♂ 9/3 3♏12
11	20 26	25 58	26 30	25 06	4 43	27 09	21 13	23 50	18 32	8 02	♂ 26/5 15♎00
21	0♉13	7♊47	22 44	25 52	5 55	27 42	20 53	23 36	18 20	7 30	♃ 21/3 24♋26
1 5	9 57	19 25	19 13	26 54	7 04	28 12	20 37	23 21	18 10	6 58	♃ 22/12 5♍50
11	19 38	0♋52	16 35	28 10	8 08	28 39	20 25	23 05	18 03	6 26	♄ 25/7 12♈28
21	29 17	12 03	15 11	29 38	9 08	29 02	20 18	22 48	17 59	5 55	♄ 9/12 5♈39
31	8♊53	22 56	15D08	1♌17	10 01	29 21	20D17	22 33	17D58	5 23	♅ 29/5 20♍17
10 6	18 27	3♌25	16 19	3 04	10 48	29 36	20 21	22 18	18 00	4 51	♆ 25/2 24♏21
20	28 00	13 22	18 33	4 58	11 26	29 45	20 30	22 04	18 05	4 19	♆ 4/8 21♏35
30	7♋33	22 36	21 41	6 59	11 56	29 49	20 44	21 53	18 13	3 47	♇ 30/5 17♍58
10 7	17 05	0♍50	25 33	9 04	12 16	29R48	21 03	21 44	18 24	3 16	♇ 26/12 22♍51
20	26 37	7 36	0♏02	11 13	12 27	29 42	21 27	21 38	18 38	2 44	⚷ 3/7 29♓50
30	6♌10	12 15	5 01	13 23	12R27	29 31	21 54	21 35	18 54	2 12	⚷ 7/12 25♓17
9 8	15 45	13R54	10 26	15 35	12 17	29 15	22 24	21D35	19 12	1 40	
19	25 21	11 46	16 12	17 47	11 57	28 56	22 58	21 39	19 31	1 09	
29	4♍59	6 24	22 18	19 57	11 28	28 33	23 33	21 45	19 52	0 37	
8 9	14 40	0 39	28 40	22 05	10 52	28 07	24 10	21 55	20 14	0 05	
18	24 24	27♌45	5♐16	24 09	10 10	27 40	24 48	22 08	20 36	29♈33	
28	4♎11	28D44	12 06	26 09	9 24	27 13	25 26	22 23	20 57	29 01	
8 10	14 02	3♍00	19 07	28 01	8 37	26 46	26 03	22 40	21 18	28 30	
18	23 56	9 38	26 18	29 46	7 51	26 22	26 39	23 00	21 38	27 58	
28	3♏53	17 55	3♑37	1♍21	7 09	26 00	27 12	23 21	21 56	27 26	
7 11	13 54	27 20	11 05	2 44	6 33	25 42	27 43	23 43	22 13	26 54	
17	23 57	7♎33	18 38	3 55	6 06	25 29	28 10	24 05	22 26	26 23	
27	4♐03	18 21	26 17	4 50	5 47	25 20	28 33	24 27	22 37	25 51	
7 12	14 11	29 35	4♒00	5 28	5 39	25 17	28 51	24 49	22 45	25 19	
17	24 21	11♏08	11 45	5 48	5D42	25D20	29 04	25 10	22 50	24 47	
27	4♑32	22 55	19 32	5R48	5 56	25 28	29 11	25 30	22R51	24 16	

SID M/N 1st JAN 6 h 38 m 52 s | 1968 LEAP | CET from 13/2

DAY	JAN	FEB	MAR	APR	MAY	JUN	JUL	AUG	SEP	OCT	NOV	DEC
1	20♑56	9♓38	0♈23	14♉54	17♊10	2♌38	7♍51	28♎44	22♐05	1♒02	21♓06	25♈28
☽ 3	18♒38	4♈48	24♈47	8♊32	11♋07	27♌55	4♎24	26♏54	20♑26	28♒08	16♈11	19♉31
5	14♓38	28♈53	18♉33	2♋24	5♌48	24♍23	2♏09	25♐47	18♒21	24♓20	10♉36	13♊19
7	9♈12	22♉31	12♊13	27♋06	1♍40	22♎25	1♐11	24♑49	15♓23	19♈39	4♊34	7♋04
9	2♉56	16♊25	6♋29	23♌11	29♍12	21♏59	0♑59	23♒13	11♈16	14♉09	28♊18	0♌59
11	26♉34	11♋12	1♌56	20♍58	28♎26	22♐22	0♒34	20♓18	6♉03	8♊04	22♋06	25♌21
13	20♊45	7♌17	28♌55	20♎17	28♏47	22♑16	28♒50	15♈52	0♊03	1♋47	16♌26	20♍38
15	15♋52	4♍36	27♍21	20♏22	29♐03	20♒36	25♓18	10♉15	23♊47	25♋50	11♍53	17♎24
17	12♌00	2♎44	26♎35	20♐06	28♑01	17♓00	20♈11	4♊01	17♋54	20♌50	8♎59	16♏01
19	8♍57	1♏11	25♏50	18♑36	25♒10	11♈49	14♉08	27♊51	12♌59	17♍16	7♏56	16♐12
21	6♎28	29♏32	24♐24	15♒34	20♓39	5♉43	7♊47	22♋20	9♍21	15♎21	8♐13	16♑50
23	4♏24	27♐33	22♑00	11♓11	14♈59	29♉19	1♋45	17♌47	7♎01	14♏45	8♑33	16♒27
25	2♐43	25♑07	18♒33	5♈49	8♉44	23♊07	26♋23	14♍16	5♏37	14♐32	7♒42	14♓10
27	1♑12	21♒57	14♓09	29♈49	2♊22	17♋23	21♌48	11♎37	4♐30	13♑42	5♓04	10♈01
29	29♑21	17♓50	8♈55	23♉31	26♊09	12♌15	17♍59	9♏34	3♑06	11♒38	0♈49	4♉33
31	26♒33		3♉01		20♋19		14♎57	7♐52		8♓14		28♉26
1	11♑25	29♒32	17♒14	20♓02	17♉47	0♋59	23♊17	1♌33	28♍57	0♏55	20♎08	5♐29
☿ 7	21 12	2R17	19 53	29 56	0♊06	2R00	25 08	14 02	7♎39	0R29	27 52	14 54
13	1♒11	28♒52	24 57	10♈44	10 56	0 26	29 57	26 06	15 31	25♎32	6♏59	24 21
19	11 12	22 14	1♓41	22 26	19 47	27♊15	7♋34	7♍22	22 22	18 35	16 29	3♑50
25	20 45	17 45	9 35	4♉56	26 23	24 17	17 39	17 48	27 46	15D44	26 00	13 24
31	28 33		18 28		0♋33		29 29	27 25		19 07		22 58

DATE	☉	♀	♂	♃	♄	⚷	♅	♆	♇	☊	STATIONS
1 1	9♑38	28♏53	23♒26	5♍41	6♈07	25♓34	29♍13	25♏39	22♍51	24♈00	
11	19 50	10♐54	1♓15	5R13	6 36	25 51	29R12	25 55	22R47	23 28	☿ 7/2 2♓17
21	0♒01	23 02	9 02	4 27	7 15	26 11	29 05	26 08	22 40	22 56	☿ 28/2 17♒06
31	10 11	5♑14	16 48	3 26	8 02	26 36	28 54	26 19	22 31	22 24	☿ 6/6 2♋02
10 2	20 19	17 29	24 31	2 14	8 57	27 05	28 37	26 27	22 19	21 53	☿ 30/6 23♊15
20	0♓25	29 46	2♈11	0 56	9 58	27 36	28 17	26 31	22 05	21 21	☿ 3/10 1♏15
1 3	10 29	12♒04	9 48	29♌38	11 05	28 10	27 53	26R32	21 50	20 49	☿ 25/10 15♎43
11	20 29	24 23	17 21	28 25	12 15	28 45	27 28	26 29	21 34	20 17	♃ 22/4 25♌50
21	0♈27	6♓43	24 49	27 22	13 29	29 20	27 02	26 23	21 17	19 45	♄ 7/8 25♈33
31	10 21	19 02	2♉13	26 34	14 44	29 56	26 36	26 15	21 02	19 14	♄ 21/12 18♈42
10 4	20 12	1♈21	9 32	26 03	15 59	0♈30	26 12	26 03	20 48	18 42	♅ 4/1 29♍13
20	29 59	13 40	16 46	25 50	17 14	1 04	25 51	25 50	20 35	18 10	♅ 2/6 25♍05
30	9♉43	25 58	23 55	25D56	18 28	1 34	25 32	25 35	20 25	17 38	♆ 27/2 26♏32
10 5	19 24	8♉16	0♊59	26 19	19 39	2 02	25 18	25 19	20 17	17 07	♆ 5/8 23♏45
20	29 03	20 33	7 59	27 00	20 46	2 27	25 09	25 03	20 12	16 35	♇ 31/5 20♍10
30	8♊39	2♊50	14 54	27 57	21 48	2 47	25 05	24 47	20 10	16 03	♇ 27/12 25♍06
9 6	18 13	15 06	21 45	29 07	22 45	3 03	25D06	24 32	20D11	15 31	⚷ 6/7 3♈22
19	27 47	27 23	28 31	0♍29	23 34	3 15	25 12	24 18	20 16	15 00	⚷ 10/12 28♓51
29	7♋19	9♋41	5♋14	2 03	24 17	3 21	25 24	24 06	20 23	14 28	
9 7	16 51	21 58	11 52	3 45	24 50	3R22	25 40	23 57	20 33	13 56	
19	26 23	4♌17	18 28	5 36	25 15	3 18	26 02	23 50	20 47	13 24	
29	5♌56	16 35	25 00	7 32	25 29	3 09	26 27	23 46	21 02	12 52	
8 8	15 31	28 54	1♌29	9 34	25R33	2 55	26 56	23D46	21 20	12 21	
18	25 07	11♍13	7 56	11 40	25 27	2 36	27 28	23 48	21 39	11 49	
28	4♍45	23 31	14 20	13 48	25 11	2 15	28 02	23 54	22 00	11 17	
7 9	14 26	5♎49	20 41	15 57	24 45	1 50	28 39	24 03	22 22	10 45	
17	24 10	18 07	27 00	18 07	24 11	1 24	29 16	24 15	22 44	10 14	
27	3♎57	0♏23	3♍17	20 16	23 30	0 57	29 54	24 29	23 06	9 42	
7 10	13 48	12 38	9 32	22 23	22 45	0 30	0♎32	24 46	23 27	9 10	
17	23 41	24 52	15 44	24 26	21 57	0 04	1 08	25 05	23 47	8 38	
27	3♏39	7♐04	21 54	26 25	21 10	29♓42	1 43	25 26	24 06	8 06	
6 11	13 39	19 13	28 01	28 17	20 26	29 22	2 15	25 48	24 23	7 35	
16	23 42	1♑20	4♎06	0♎01	19 48	29 07	2 44	26 10	24 38	7 03	
26	3♐48	13 23	10 07	1 35	19 17	28 57	3 09	26 33	24 49	6 31	
6 12	13 57	25 20	16 05	2 58	18 55	28 52	3 30	26 55	24 58	5 59	
16	24 07	7♒09	21 58	4 08	18 43	28D52	3 45	27 16	25 04	5 28	
26	4♑18	18 47	27 45	5 02	18D43	28 58	3 56	27 36	25 06	4 56	

SID M/N 1st JAN 6 h 41 m 51 s — 1969 COMMON — CET

	DAY	JAN	FEB	MAR	APR	MAY	JUN	JUL	AUG	SEP	OCT	NOV	DEC
	1	10♊17	24♋41	2♌57	18♍53	24♎11	16♐38	25♑40	18♓23	7♉09	10♊19	24♋17	25♌55
☽	3	4♋02	19♌14	27♌49	15♎51	23♏03	16♑55	25♒31	15♈50	2♊22	4♋33	18♌00	20♍01
	5	28♋02	14♍25	23♍38	13♏55	22♐38	16♒19	23♓39	11♉36	26♊33	28♋18	12♍12	15♎18
	7	22♌25	10♎21	20♎22	12♐36	21♑56	14♓09	20♈01	6♊08	20♋17	22♌13	7♎33	12♏20
	9	17♍25	7♏11	17♏53	11♑15	20♒14	10♈28	15♉03	0♋01	14♌09	16♍51	4♏25	11♐09
	11	13♎22	5♐04	15♐59	9♒28	17♓19	5♉38	9♊15	23♋44	8♍32	12♎34	2♐42	11♑02
	13	10♏41	3♑58	14♑27	6♓59	13♈22	0♊06	3♋04	17♌38	3♎42	9♏28	1♑44	10♒47
	15	9♐36	3♒21	12♒56	3♈43	8♉36	24♊06	26♋47	11♍57	29♎45	7♐16	0♒40	9♓26
	17	9♑41	2♓21	10♓58	29♈37	3♊12	17♋52	20♌37	6♎55	26♏44	5♑33	28♒55	6♈44
	19	9♒46	0♈06	8♈06	24♉39	27♊16	11♌35	14♍51	2♏48	24♐33	3♒55	26♓19	2♉54
	21	8♓37	26♈17	4♉03	18♊55	21♋00	5♍37	9♎50	29♏53	23♑05	2♓04	22♈58	28♉12
	23	5♈37	21♉06	28♉53	12♋43	14♌48	0♎30	6♏07	28♐18	21♒57	29♓50	18♉54	22♊51
	25	0♉55	15♊04	22♊55	6♌34	9♍12	26♎51	4♐05	27♑46	20♓38	26♈55	14♊04	16♋57
	27	25♉06	8♋50	16♋42	1♍04	4♎52	25♏06	3♑40	27♒30	18♈29	23♉05	8♋28	10♌39
	29	18♊49		10♌50	26♍49	2♏18	25♐04	4♒03	26♓29	15♉04	18♊12	2♌17	4♍16
	31	12♋38		5♍54		1♐33		3♓58	24♈01		12♋24		28♍19
	1	24♑33	6♒03	14♒08	3♈01	0♊30	6♊25	18♊24	18♌40	5♎21	4♎18	28♎51	16♐47
☿	7	3♒43	1R00	21 54	14 55	7 13	3R55	27 56	29 42	10 51	0R02	8♏45	26 04
	13	11 32	0D38	0♓33	27 24	11 05	3D38	9♋20	9♍47	14 14	1D39	18 29	5♑17
	19	15 51	3 57	9 59	9♉51	11R58	6 03	21 55	18 56	14R31	8 15	28 02	14 13
	25	14R05	9 33	20 09	21 12	10 11	11 03	4♌38	27 09	10 46	17 20	7♐27	22 22
	31	7 15		1♈07		6 57		16 45	4♎17		27 11		28 24

DATE	☉	♀	♂	♃	♄	⚷	♅	♆	♇	☊	STATIONS
1 1	10♑24	25♒40	1♏11	5♎27	18♈48	29♓04	3♎59	27♏47	25♍06	4♈37	
11	20 36	6♓52	6 49	5 55	19 05	29 19	4R00	28 03	25R03	4 05	☿ 20/1 16♒03
21	0♒47	17 39	12 18	6R03	19 33	29 38	3 56	28 17	24 56	3 33	☿ 10/2 0♒15
31	10 57	27 51	17 36	5 53	20 10	0R02	3 46	28 28	24 47	3 01	☿ 18/5 12♊01
10 2	21 05	7♈15	22 43	5 23	20 56	0D29	3 32	28 36	24 35	2 30	☿ 11/6 3♊26
20	1♓11	15 28	27 34	4 37	21 50	0♈60	3 13	28 41	24 22	1 58	☿ 17/9 14♎52
2 3	11 14	22 00	2♐06	3 36	22 51	1 33	2 51	28R42	24 06	1 26	☿ 8/10 29♍51
12	21 15	26 01	6 15	2 25	23 57	2 07	2 26	28 40	23 50	0 54	♀ 18/3 26♈50
22	1♈12	26R34	9 54	1 08	25 07	2 42	2 00	28 35	23 34	0 23	♀ 30/4 10♈30
1 4	11 06	23 08	12 56	29♍51	26 21	3 18	1 34	28 27	23 19	29♓51	♂ 27/4 16♐46
11	20 56	17 07	15 12	28 40	27 36	3 52	1 09	28 16	23 04	29 19	♂ 8/7 1♐42
21	0♉43	12 03	16 30	27 38	28 52	4 26	0 47	28 03	22 51	28 47	♃ 20/1 6♎03
1 5	10 27	10D32	16R41	26 51	0♉09	4 57	0 27	27 48	22 40	28 16	♃ 23/5 26♍06
11	20 08	12 47	15 37	26 20	1 23	5 26	0 11	27 32	22 32	27 44	♄ 21/8 8♉57
21	29 46	17 54	13 21	26 06	2 36	5 51	0 00	27 16	22 26	27 12	♅ 8/1 4♎01
31	9♊23	25 01	10 13	26D11	3 45	6 13	29♍53	27 00	22 24	26 40	♅ 7/6 29♍52
10 6	18 57	3♉27	6 51	26 34	4 49	6 30	29D52	26 45	22D25	26 08	♆ 1/3 28♏42
20	28 30	12 48	3 58	27 13	5 48	6 43	29 56	26 31	22 29	25 37	♆ 8/8 25♏56
30	8♋02	22 48	2 10	28 08	6 41	6 50	0♎06	26 19	22 36	25 05	♇ 3/6 22♍24
10 7	17 34	3♊17	1D43	29 16	7 26	6 53	0 20	26 09	22 46	24 33	♇ 30/12 27♍23
20	27 07	14 07	2 38	0♎37	8 03	6R50	0 40	26 02	22 59	24 01	⚷ 30/1 29♓59
30	6♌40	25 14	4 48	2 09	8 31	6 42	1 03	25 57	23 14	23 30	⚷ 31/1 0♈02
9 8	16 14	6♋35	8 00	3 51	8 49	6 30	1 31	25D56	23 32	22 58	⚷ 10/7 6♈53
19	25 51	18 09	12 04	5 40	8 57	6 13	2 02	25 58	23 51	22 26	⚷ 14/12 2♈22
29	5♍29	29 52	16 51	7 36	8R54	5 52	2 35	26 04	24 12	21 54	
8 9	15 10	11♌45	22 12	9 37	8 40	5 28	3 11	26 12	24 34	21 22	
18	24 54	23 47	28 01	11 43	8 17	5 02	3 48	26 24	24 56	20 51	
28	4♎42	5♍55	4♑13	13 51	7 45	4 35	4 26	26 38	25 18	20 19	
8 10	14 32	18 10	10 44	16 00	7 05	4 08	5 04	26 55	25 40	19 47	
18	24 27	0♎31	17 30	18 10	6 20	3 42	5 41	27 13	26 00	19 15	
28	4♏24	12 55	24 28	20 20	5 33	3 19	6 16	27 34	26 20	18 44	
7 11	14 25	25 23	1♒36	22 27	4 45	2 58	6 50	27 55	26 37	18 12	
17	24 28	7♏54	8 51	24 30	3 59	2 42	7 20	28 18	26 52	17 40	
27	4♐34	20 27	16 12	26 28	3 19	2 30	7 47	28 40	27 05	17 08	
7 12	14 43	3♐01	23 37	28 20	2 45	2 24	8 09	29 02	27 14	16 37	
17	24 53	15 35	1♓03	0♏03	2 21	2D23	8 27	29 24	27 20	16 05	
27	5♑04	28 10	8 31	1 37	2 07	2 27	8 39	29 44	27 23	15 33	

SID M/N 1st JAN 6 h 40 m 54 s — 1970 COMMON — CET

	DAY	JAN	FEB	MAR	APR	MAY	JUN	JUL	AUG	SEP	OCT	NOV	DEC
	1	10♎42	28♏57	8♐38	1♒06	10♓15	2♉13	8♊20	24♋39	9♍02	11♎47	28♏41	5♑08
☽	3	6♏36	27♐20	6♑35	29♒59	8♈28	28♉49	3♋26	18♌25	2♎46	6♏26	25♐12	3♒04
	5	4♐27	27♑15	5♒49	29♓04	6♉15	24♊32	27♋47	11♍59	26♎58	1♐52	22♑24	1♓13
	7	4♑05	27♒43	5♓44	27♈38	3♊08	19♋18	21♌34	5♎42	21♏58	28♐13	20♒15	29♓22
	9	4♒34	27♓25	5♈18	25♉01	28♊49	13♌15	15♍08	0♏01	18♐10	25♑39	18♓41	27♈25
	11	4♓31	25♈30	3♉36	20♊53	23♋20	6♍52	9♎01	25♏32	15♑51	24♒13	17♈30	25♉07
	13	3♈00	21♉49	0♊12	15♋27	17♌07	0♎47	3♏53	22♐41	15♒01	23♓41	16♉07	22♊03
	15	29♈48	16♊45	25♊16	9♌14	10♍48	25♎41	0♐19	21♑35	15♓09	23♈18	13♊46	17♋52
	17	25♉16	10♋48	19♋19	2♍55	5♎07	22♏09	28♐35	21♒44	15♈10	22♉03	9♋59	12♌31
	19	19♊50	4♌29	12♌57	27♍07	0♏38	20♐17	28♑16	22♓02	13♉59	19♊13	4♌45	6♍22
	21	13♋50	28♌10	6♍44	22♎18	27♏35	19♑32	28♒22	21♈18	11♊01	14♋40	28♌36	29♍59
	23	7♌33	22♍09	1♎03	18♏36	25♐42	18♒58	27♓46	18♉57	6♋22	8♌52	22♍13	24♎06
	25	1♍12	16♎41	26♎10	15♐51	24♑21	17♓46	25♈51	14♊57	0♌32	2♍29	16♎19	19♏20
	27	25♍06	12♏05	22♏11	13♑44	22♒55	15♈35	22♉31	9♋41	24♌10	26♍11	11♏26	16♐05
	29	19♎40		19♐06	11♒56	21♓03	12♉24	18♊00	3♌38	17♍47	20♎31	7♐47	14♑10
	31	15♏26		16♑54		18♈39		12♋36	27♌15		15♏44		13♒02
	1	29♑01	16♑50	22♒10	19♈35	22♉13	16♉41	1♋35	1♍11	27♍52	19♍55	11♏04	26♐39
☿	7	29R19	22 19	1♓57	1♉16	19R42	21 58	14 33	9 40	25R00	28 46	20 37	4♑40
	13	23 17	29 19	12 23	11 09	16 07	29 16	27 17	16 58	19 19	8♎58	29 56	11 07
	19	16 14	7♒17	23 32	18 13	13 36	8♊25	9♌08	22 49	14 30	19 23	9♐04	14 05
	25	13D52	16 00	5♈20	21 56	13D29	19 17	19 56	26 45	14D30	29 35	18 00	10R57
	31	16 08		17 33		16 01		29 40	27R59		9♏27		3 12

DATE		☉	♀	♂	♃	♄	⚷	♅	♆	♇	☊	STATIONS		
1	1	10♑10	4♑28	12♓15	2♏20	2♉04	2♈31	8♎43	29♏53	27♍23	15♓17			
11		20 21	17 03	19 42	3 35	2D06	2 44	8 47	0♐10	27R21	14 45	☿	4/1	0♒00
21		0♒32	29 37	27 07	4 36	2 20	3 01	8R46	0 25	27 15	14 14	☿	25/1	13♑52
31		10 42	12♒11	4♈31	5 21	2 44	3 23	8 39	0 37	27 07	13 42	☿	28/4	22♉30
10	2	20 50	24 44	11 51	5 49	3 19	3 49	8 26	0 46	26 55	13 10	☿	22/5	13♉12
20		0♓56	7♓16	19 09	5R58	4 02	4 19	8 10	0 51	26 42	12 38	☿	30/8	28♍01
2	3	11 00	19 46	26 22	5 48	4 54	4 50	7 49	0 53	26 27	12 06	☿	22/9	13♍47
12		21 00	2♈13	3♉32	5 20	5 53	5 24	7 26	0R52	26 11	11 35	☿	19/12	14♑05
22		0♈58	14 39	10 38	4 35	6 58	5 59	7 00	0 47	25 55	11 03	♀	21/10	25♏12
1	4	10 51	27 02	17 40	3 36	8 07	6 34	6 34	0 40	25 39	10 31	♀	1/12	9♏46
11		20 42	9♉21	24 37	2 26	9 20	7 09	6 09	0 29	25 24	9 59	♃	20/2	5♏58
21		0♉29	21 38	1♊31	1 10	10 36	7 43	5 45	0 17	25 10	9 28	♃	23/6	26♎04
1	5	10 13	3♊51	8 21	29♎54	11 53	8 15	5 24	0 03	24 59	8 56	♄	4/1	2♉03
11		19 54	16 00	15 07	28 43	13 10	8 45	5 06	29♏47	24 50	8 24	♄	5/9	22♉37
21		29 32	28 05	21 50	27 41	14 26	9 11	4 52	29 31	24 44	7 52	♅	13/1	8♎48
31		9♊09	10♋06	28 29	26 52	15 40	9 34	4 43	29 15	24 40	7 20	♅	12/6	4♎39
10	6	18 43	22 01	5♋06	26 20	16 51	9 53	4 39	28 59	24D40	6 49	♆	3/3	0♐53
20		28 16	3♌51	11 39	26 05	17 59	10 08	4D41	28 45	24 44	6 17	♆	10/8	28♏07
30		7♋48	15 33	18 11	26D08	19 01	10 17	4 47	28 32	24 50	5 45	♇	5/6	24♍40
10	7	17 20	27 08	24 40	26 29	19 57	10 22	4 59	28 22	25 00	5 13	⚷	14/7	10♈22
20		26 53	8♍31	1♌07	27 06	20 46	10R21	5 16	28 14	25 12	4 42	⚷	18/12	5♈52
30		6♌26	19 43	7 32	27 59	21 27	10 15	5 38	28 09	25 27	4 10			
9	8	16 00	0♎38	13 56	29 07	22 00	10 04	6 03	28 07	25 44	3 38			
19		25 37	11 13	20 19	0♏27	22 22	9 49	6 32	28D08	26 03	3 06			
29		5♍15	21 20	26 41	1 59	22 35	9 30	7 05	28 13	26 24	2 35			
8	9	14 56	0♏51	3♍03	3 41	22R36	9 07	7 39	28 21	26 45	2 03			
18		24 40	9 29	9 24	5 31	22 27	8 42	8 16	28 31	27 07	1 31			
28		4♎28	16 51	15 45	7 27	22 08	8 15	8 53	28 45	27 30	0 59			
8	10	14 18	22 20	22 06	9 30	21 39	7 48	9 31	29 01	27 52	0 27			
18		24 12	25 04	28 27	11 37	21 02	7 21	10 09	29 19	28 13	29♒56			
28		4♏09	24R08	4♎48	13 47	20 19	6 57	10 45	29 39	28 33	29 24			
7	11	14 10	19 33	11 09	15 59	19 31	6 35	11 20	0♐01	28 51	28 52			
17		24 14	13 41	17 30	18 11	18 42	6 17	11 51	0 23	29 07	28 20			
27		4♐20	10 06	23 51	20 22	17 55	6 04	12 20	0 46	29 20	27 49			
7	12	14 28	10D28	0♏12	22 31	17 12	5 55	12 45	1 08	29 31	27 17			
17		24 38	14 23	6 33	24 37	16 35	5 52	13 05	1 30	29 38	26 45			
27		4♑49	20 52	12 54	26 37	16 07	5D54	13 20	1 50	29 41	26 13			

SID M/N 1st JAN 6 h 39 m 57 s 1971 COMMON CET to 31/10

DAY	JAN	FEB	MAR	APR	MAY	JUN	JUL	AUG	SEP	OCT	NOV	DEC
1	27♒31	20♈41	0♉03	20♊44	25♋00	9♍33	11♎11	25♏25	12♑12	18♒12	11♈00	19♉48
☽ 3	26♓11	18♉29	28♉16	16♋34	19♌32	3♎14	5♏10	20♐53	10♒00	17♓34	11♉29	19♊19
5	24♈14	14♊59	24♊47	11♌02	13♍17	27♎10	0♐00	17♑51	9♓25	18♈04	11♊23	17♋31
7	21♉32	10♋25	19♋52	4♍47	6♎55	21♏50	26♐04	16♒16	9♈37	18♉24	9♋37	13♌56
9	18♊03	5♌00	14♌04	28♍23	0♏59	17♐30	23♑20	15♓36	9♉25	17♊18	5♌53	8♍50
11	13♋42	29♌01	7♍48	22♎13	25♏44	14♑06	21♒32	14♈59	7♊53	14♋16	0♍38	2♎49
13	8♌28	22♍42	1♎26	16♏33	21♐14	11♒26	20♓08	13♉39	4♋43	9♌35	24♍32	26♎31
15	2♍29	16♎21	25♎14	11♐30	17♑31	9♓20	18♈41	11♊14	0♌11	3♍51	18♎12	20♏31
17	26♍07	10♏26	19♏29	7♑16	14♒35	7♈38	16♉50	7♋42	24♌43	27♍38	12♏04	15♐11
19	19♎52	5♐26	14♐31	4♒07	12♓33	6♉08	14♊22	3♌09	18♍43	21♎20	6♐23	10♑38
21	14♏24	1♑55	10♑46	2♓19	11♈23	4♊26	11♋01	27♌49	12♎27	15♏10	1♑15	6♒53
23	10♐18	0♒10	8♒35	1♈46	10♉39	1♋58	6♌42	21♍53	6♏10	9♐21	26♑48	3♓53
25	7♑54	29♒56	8♓01	1♉48	9♊29	28♋17	1♍26	15♎36	0♐08	4♑08	23♒18	1♈40
27	7♒00	0♈19	8♈24	1♊12	7♋04	23♌21	25♍27	9♏21	24♐48	29♑54	21♓01	0♉08
29	6♓49		8♉30	29♊02	3♌01	17♍27	19♎10	3♐37	20♑39	27♒06	20♈01	29♉00
31	6♈19		7♊08		27♌36		13♏08	28♐58		26♓00		27♊38
1	1♑59	20♑07	4♓47	29♈26	23♈23	19♉06	19♋44	5♍09	28♌35	1♎07	22♏13	27♐54
☿ 7	27R55	28 43	15 58	3♉21	23D39	29 29	1♌09	9 08	27D35	11 51	1♐02	26R54
13	29D19	7♒50	27 39	3R12	26 37	11♊17	11 22	10R33	1♍40	22 10	9 28	20 01
19	4♑11	17 29	9♈23	29♈56	1♉49	24 07	20 22	8 48	9 52	2♏03	17 18	13 15
25	10 57	27 40	20 08	25 51	8 52	7♋14	28 04	4 11	20 12	11 33	23 54	12D18
31	18 45		28 23		17 31		4♍17	29♌12		20 43		16 11

DATE	☉	♀	♂	♃	♄	⚷	♅	♆	♇	☊	STATIONS
1 1	9♑55	24♏47	16♏04	27♏35	15♉57	5♈58	13♎25	2♐00	29♍42	25♒57	
11	20 06	3♐38	22 23	29 25	15R44	6 08	13 32	2 17	29R40	25 26	☿ 8/1 27♐48
21	0♒17	13 26	28 42	1♐06	15D42	6 24	13R34	2 33	29 36	24 54	☿ 10/4 3♉45
31	10 27	23 54	4♐59	2 36	15 52	6 44	13 29	2 45	29 28	24 22	☿ 3/5 23♈08
10 2	20 36	4♑50	11 15	3 53	16 13	7 09	13 19	2 55	29 17	23 50	☿ 13/8 10♍33
20	0♓42	16 05	17 28	4 57	16 44	7 37	13 05	3 01	29 04	23 19	☿ 5/9 27♌22
2 3	10 45	27 34	23 38	5 44	17 24	8 08	12 46	3 04	28 50	22 47	☿ 3/12 28♐16
12	20 46	9♒13	29 44	6 15	18 14	8 41	12 24	3R03	28 34	22 15	☿ 23/12 11♐57
22	0♈43	21 00	5♑46	6 27	19 10	9 15	12 00	3 00	28 17	21 43	♂ 11/7 21♒57
1 4	10 37	2♓53	11 41	6R20	20 13	9 50	11 34	2 53	28 01	21 11	♂ 10/9 11♒53
11	20 28	14 49	17 28	5 55	21 22	10 25	11 08	2 43	27 46	20 40	♃ 23/3 6♐27
21	0♉15	26 49	23 05	5 13	22 34	10 60	10 43	2 31	27 32	20 08	♃ 25/7 26♏36
1 5	9 59	8♈51	28 30	4 16	23 49	11 32	10 21	2 17	27 20	19 36	♄ 17/1 15♉42
11	19 40	20 54	3♒37	3 08	25 06	12 03	10 01	2 02	27 10	19 04	♄ 19/9 6♊31
21	29 19	2♉59	8 22	1 53	26 23	12 31	9 45	1 46	27 03	18 33	♅ 18/1 13♎34
31	8♊55	15 06	12 39	0 37	27 40	12 55	9 34	1 30	26 59	18 01	♅ 18/6 9♎26
10 6	18 29	27 14	16 20	29♏25	28 56	13 16	9 27	1 14	26D58	17 29	♆ 5/3 3♐04
20	28 02	9♊23	19 14	28 21	0♊10	13 32	9D26	0 59	27 01	16 57	♆ 13/8 0♐18
30	7♋35	21 34	21 10	27 31	1 19	13 44	9 30	0 46	27 06	16 25	♇ 2/1 29♍42
10 7	17 07	3♋46	21 56	26 55	2 25	13 50	9 39	0 35	27 15	15 54	♇ 8/6 26♍58
20	26 39	16 01	21R27	26 38	3 24	13R51	9 53	0 26	27 27	15 22	⚷ 18/7 13♈51
30	6♌12	28 18	19 48	26D38	4 17	13 47	10 12	0 21	27 41	14 50	⚷ 21/12 9♈21
9 8	15 46	10♌37	17 20	26 57	5 03	13 39	10 36	0 18	27 58	14 18	
19	25 23	22 58	14 45	27 33	5 40	13 25	11 03	0D19	28 17	13 47	
29	5♍01	5♍21	12 46	28 25	6 07	13 07	11 34	0 22	28 37	13 15	
8 9	14 42	17 46	11 54	29 32	6 24	12 45	12 07	0 29	28 59	12 43	
18	24 26	0♎12	12D22	0♐53	6 31	12 21	12 43	0 39	29 21	12 11	
28	4♎13	12 39	14 06	2 25	6R27	11 55	13 20	0 52	29 44	11 40	
8 10	14 04	25 06	16 58	4 08	6 12	11 27	13 58	1 08	0♎06	11 08	
18	23 58	7♏33	20 44	6 00	5 47	11 01	14 36	1 26	0 28	10 36	
28	3♏55	20 01	25 13	8 00	5 13	10 35	15 13	1 45	0 48	10 04	
7 11	13 55	2♐29	0♓15	10 05	4 31	10 12	15 48	2 06	1 07	9 32	
17	23 59	14 56	5 44	12 15	3 45	9 53	16 21	2 28	1 23	9 01	
27	4♐05	27 23	11 31	14 28	2 56	9 38	16 52	2 51	1 38	8 29	
7 12	14 13	9♑49	17 34	16 43	2 07	9 27	17 18	3 13	1 49	7 57	
17	24 23	22 14	23 48	18 59	1 22	9 22	17 41	3 35	1 57	7 25	
27	4♑34	4♒37	0♈10	21 14	0 42	9D22	17 58	3 56	2 01	6 54	

SID M/N 1st JAN 6 h 38 m 59 s — 1972 LEAP — BST 19/3 to 29/10

	DAY	JAN	FEB	MAR	APR	MAY	JUN	JUL	AUG	SEP	OCT	NOV	DEC
	1	11♋37	29♌30	20♍20	5♏03	7♐42	23♑34	29♒16	21♈10	14♊45	23♋03	12♍09	16♎08
☽	3	8♌38	24♍22	14♎35	28♏47	1♑47	19♒06	26♓20	19♉34	12♋31	19♌30	6♎55	10♏04
	5	4♍15	18♎27	8♏24	22♐44	26♑31	15♓49	24♈23	18♊02	9♌33	15♍06	1♏07	3♐45
	7	28♍43	12♏13	2♐11	17♑24	22♒26	14♈00	23♉15	16♋11	5♍48	10♎00	24♏56	27♐28
	9	22♎33	6♐15	26♐28	13♒24	20♓01	13♉29	22♊26	13♌39	1♎14	4♏17	18♐34	21♑26
	11	16♏23	1♑09	21♑53	11♓17	19♈24	13♊29	21♋10	10♍08	25♎51	28♏05	12♑19	16♒00
	13	10♐48	27♑24	18♒58	10♈58	19♉51	12♋51	18♌46	5♎28	19♏47	21♐43	6♒40	11♓35
	15	6♑14	25♒08	17♓49	11♉32	20♊03	10♌44	14♍56	29♎50	13♐28	15♑41	2♓13	8♈38
	17	2♒46	24♓00	17♈47	11♊33	18♋47	6♍54	9♎49	23♏39	7♑32	10♒39	29♓34	7♉20
	19	0♓18	23♈13	17♉41	9♋59	15♌39	1♎42	3♏51	17♐31	2♒38	7♓17	28♈49	7♊18
	21	28♓28	22♉00	16♊29	6♌37	10♍56	25♎41	27♏37	12♑04	29♒20	5♈52	29♉18	7♋32
	23	26♈52	19♊52	13♋46	1♍51	5♎12	19♏26	21♐43	7♒48	27♓43	5♉55	29♊40	6♌50
	25	25♉10	16♋45	9♌43	26♍12	29♎00	13♐25	16♑35	4♓54	27♈14	6♊14	28♋43	4♍27
	27	23♊05	12♌45	4♍44	20♎07	22♏45	7♑56	12♒28	3♈10	26♉48	5♋32	25♌57	0♎20
	29	20♋21	7♍59	29♍08	13♏53	16♐44	3♒10	9♓21	1♉58	25♊32	3♌14	21♍35	24♎54
	31	16♌42		23♎09		11♑08		7♈05	0♊37		29♌28		18♏45
	1	17♐08	0♒01	21♓30	10♈27	13♈58	5♊49	3♌20	20♌18	22♌22	16♎27	1♐26	28♏16
☿	7	23 50	9 50	2♈11	5℞54	21 18	18 59	10 59	16℞02	2♍47	26 09	7 48	26D23
	13	1♑41	20 06	10 42	3 44	0♉01	1♋50	16 58	11 50	14 09	5♏24	11 52	0♐01
	19	10 10	0♓51	15 19	4D40	10 01	13 41	20 56	10D31	25 26	14 13	11℞38	6 38
	25	19 06	12 03	15℞11	8 17	21 16	24 12	22℞21	13 36	6♎13	22 33	5 38	14 35
	31	28 26		11 16		3♊40		20 50	20 51		0♐14		23 10

DATE		☉	♀	♂	♃	♄	⚷	♅	♆	♇	☊	STATIONS		
1	1	9♑40	10♒48	3♈23	22♐21	0♊25	9♈24	18♎05	4♐06	2♎02	6♒38			
11		19 51	23 07	9 53	24 33	29℞57	9 33	18 15	4 24	2℞02	6 06	☿	22/3	15♈50
21		0♒03	5♓21	16 26	26 40	29 40	9 47	18 19	4 40	1 58	5 34	☿	14/4	3♈40
31		10 13	17 29	23 01	28 41	29 34	10 05	18℞17	4 53	1 51	5 02	☿	25/7	22♌21
10	2	20 21	29 30	29 37	0♑35	29D40	10 29	18 10	5 03	1 41	4 31	☿	18/8	10♌27
20		0♓27	11♈21	6♉13	2 21	29 56	10 55	17 58	5 11	1 28	3 59	☿	16/11	12♐27
1	3	10 31	22 59	12 49	3 56	0♊23	11 25	17 41	5 14	1 14	3 27	☿	6/12	26♏14
11		20 31	4♉21	19 24	5 19	1 00	11 58	17 21	5℞15	0 58	2 55	♀	27/5	4♋44
21		0♈29	15 23	25 57	6 28	1 46	12 32	16 58	5 12	0 42	2 24	♀	9/7	18♊13
31		10 23	25 58	2♊30	7 21	2 40	13 07	16 32	5 06	0 26	1 52	♃	25/4	8♑19
10	4	20 13	5♊58	9 00	7 58	3 41	13 42	16 07	4 57	0 10	1 20	♃	25/8	28♐29
20		0♉01	15 10	15 29	8 17	4 47	14 17	15 41	4 45	29♍55	0 48	♄	31/1	29♉34
30		9 45	23 14	21 56	8℞17	5 58	14 50	15 17	4 32	29 43	0 16	♄	3/10	20♊35
10	5	19 26	29 41	28 22	7 58	7 13	15 22	14 56	4 17	29 32	29♑45	♅	23/1	18♎19
20		29 05	3♋46	4♋46	7 22	8 29	15 51	14 38	4 01	29 25	29 13	♅	22/6	14♎11
30		8♊41	4℞34	11 09	6 29	9 47	16 17	14 24	3 45	29 20	28 41	♆	7/3	5♐15
9	6	18 15	1 29	17 31	5 24	11 05	16 39	14 15	3 29	29 18	28 09	♆	14/8	2♐29
19		27 48	25♊37	23 52	4 11	12 22	16 57	14 11	3 14	29D20	27 38	♇	4/1	2♎03
29		7♋21	20 16	0♌13	2 55	13 37	17 10	14D13	3 00	29 25	27 06	♇	9/6	29♍18
9	7	16 53	18 13	6 33	1 40	14 49	17 19	14 19	2 48	29 33	26 34	⚷	20/7	17♈22
19		26 25	19D56	12 52	0 33	15 57	17 22	14 31	2 39	29 44	26 02	⚷	24/12	12♈51
29		5♌58	24 38	19 12	29♐37	17 00	17℞20	14 47	2 33	29 57	25 30			
8	8	15 33	1♋27	25 32	28 57	17 56	17 13	15 09	2 29	0♎14	24 59			
18		25 09	9 42	1♍53	28 34	18 46	17 01	15 34	2D29	0 32	24 27			
28		4♍47	18 59	8 15	28D30	19 27	16 45	16 03	2 32	0 52	23 55			
7	9	14 28	28 59	14 37	28 44	20 00	16 24	16 35	2 38	1 14	23 23			
17		24 12	9♌33	21 01	29 17	20 22	16 01	17 10	2 47	1 36	22 52			
27		3♎59	20 33	27 27	0♑07	20 33	15 35	17 46	3 00	1 59	22 20			
7	10	13 49	1♍53	3♎54	1 13	20℞34	15 08	18 24	3 15	2 22	21 48			
17		23 43	13 30	10 23	2 34	20 24	14 41	19 01	3 32	2 44	21 16			
27		3♏40	25 20	16 54	4 07	20 03	14 15	19 39	3 51	3 05	20 45			
6	11	13 41	7♎21	23 28	5 51	19 32	13 51	20 15	4 12	3 24	20 13			
16		23 44	19 31	0♏03	7 45	18 54	13 30	20 50	4 34	3 41	19 41			
26		3♐50	1♏47	6 41	9 47	18 09	13 13	21 22	4 56	3 56	19 09			
6	12	13 58	14 08	13 22	11 55	17 20	13 00	21 50	5 19	4 08	18 37			
16		24 08	26 33	20 05	14 09	16 31	12 53	22 15	5 41	4 17	18 06			
26		4♑19	9♐01	26 50	16 26	15 44	12D51	22 35	6 02	4 23	17 34			

SID M/N 1st JAN 6 h 41 m 53 s   1973 COMMON   BST 18/3 to 28/10

DAY	JAN	FEB	MAR	APR	MAY	JUN	JUL	AUG	SEP	OCT	NOV	DEC
1	0♐34	14♑38	22♑36	8♓54	14♈48	7♊39	16♋18	8♍34	27♎10	0♐06	13♑47	15♒40
☽ 3	24♐16	9♒27	17♒45	6♈35	14♉13	7♋56	15♌58	6♎01	22♏13	24♐04	7♒27	9♓58
5	18♑21	5♓15	14♓13	5♉29	14♊11	7♌19	14♍09	1♏46	16♐13	17♑41	1♓51	5♈33
7	13♒04	1♈59	11♈51	4♊44	13♋36	5♍10	10♎36	26♏12	9♑50	11♒41	27♓36	2♉50
9	8♓34	29♈29	10♉09	3♋30	11♌49	1♎27	5♏34	19♐55	3♒47	6♓42	25♈01	1♊52
11	5♈04	27♉32	8♊33	1♌25	8♍42	26♎30	29♏36	13♑34	28♒35	3♈06	23♉52	1♋58
13	2♉41	25♊59	6♋43	28♌27	4♎29	20♏42	23♐14	7♒39	24♓30	0♉49	23♊22	2♌00
15	1♊24	24♋32	4♌31	24♍43	29♎24	14♐27	16♑54	2♓30	21♈26	29♉18	22♋37	0♍58
17	0♋50	22♌46	1♍51	20♎12	23♏40	8♑04	10♒58	28♓13	19♉03	27♊56	20♌58	28♍23
19	0♌12	20♍05	28♍28	14♏54	17♐28	1♒50	5♓40	24♈47	17♊04	26♋14	18♍14	24♎21
21	28♌37	16♎08	24♎08	8♐55	11♑03	26♒08	1♈14	22♉11	15♋17	24♌05	14♎31	19♏13
23	25♍31	10♏55	18♏46	2♑33	4♒51	21♓23	27♈54	20♊22	13♌35	21♍21	9♏53	13♐20
25	20♎53	4♐49	12♐38	26♑18	29♒25	18♈02	25♉50	19♋12	11♍39	17♎53	4♐28	7♑02
27	15♏06	28♐29	6♑17	20♒53	25♓22	16♉20	24♊57	18♌15	9♎00	13♏30	28♐25	0♒38
29	8♐46		0♒24	16♓56	23♈06	16♊02	24♋43	16♍48	5♏11	8♐08	22♑00	24♒24
31	2♑33		25♒41		22♉32		24♌14	14♎06		1♑59		18♓45
1	24♐38	14♒15	27♓37	15♓59	20♈54	23♊55	2♌05	22♋55	6♍38	27♎23	26♏25	19♏13
☿ 7	3♑37	24 56	28R07	19 41	1♉39	5♋00	3R20	25 32	18 04	5♏43	22R15	27 17
13	12 52	5♓45	23 54	25 26	13 29	14 29	1 50	1♌55	28 50	13 21	14 38	6♐04
19	22 25	16 03	18 25	2♈43	26 14	22 18	28♋14	11 25	8♎57	19 58	10 35	15 08
25	2♒16	24 18	15 16	11 15	9♊22	28 17	24 28	22 48	18 27	24 50	12D54	24 21
31	12 31		15D37		21 56		22D51	4♍40		26R35		3♑43

DATE	☉	♀	♂	♃	♄	⚷	♅	♆	♇	☊	STATIONS
1 1	10♑26	16♐30	0♐54	17♑49	15♊17	12♈53	22♎44	6♐14	4♎25	17♑15	
11	20 38	29 00	7 44	20 09	14R39	13 00	22 56	6 32	4R25	16 43	☿ 5/3 28♓35
21	0♒49	11♑31	14 36	22 29	14 08	13 13	23 02	6 49	4 21	16 11	☿ 27/3 15♓00
31	10 59	24 01	21 30	24 48	13 48	13 30	23R03	7 02	4 15	15 40	☿ 7/7 3♌21
10 2	21 07	6♒32	28 27	27 04	13 38	13 52	22 58	7 13	4 05	15 08	☿ 31/7 22♋51
20	1♓13	19 02	5♑25	29 16	13D40	14 18	22 48	7 21	3 53	14 36	☿ 30/10 26♏36
2 3	11 16	1♓32	12 26	1♒23	13 53	14 47	22 33	7 25	3 39	14 04	☿ 20/11 10♏33
12	21 17	14 00	19 29	3 23	14 17	15 19	22 14	7R26	3 23	13 32	♂ 20/9 9♉16
22	1♈14	26 27	26 33	5 14	14 51	15 53	21 52	7 23	3 07	13 01	♂ 26/11 25♈19
1 4	11 08	8♈53	3♒38	6 56	15 34	16 28	21 27	7 17	2 50	12 29	♃ 31/5 12♒07
11	20 58	21 17	10 45	8 26	16 25	17 03	21 01	7 09	2 34	11 57	♃ 29/9 2♒17
21	0♉45	3♉40	17 51	9 42	17 24	17 38	20 36	6 58	2 20	11 25	♄ 14/2 13♊38
1 5	10 29	16 01	24 56	10 44	18 29	18 12	20 11	6 45	2 06	10 54	♄ 17/10 4♋45
11	20 10	28 20	2♓00	11 30	19 38	18 45	19 49	6 30	1 56	10 22	♅ 27/1 23♎03
21	29 48	10♊38	9 00	11 58	20 51	19 14	19 30	6 14	1 47	9 50	♅ 27/6 18♎56
31	9♊24	22 54	15 56	12R07	22 07	19 41	19 14	5 58	1 42	9 18	♆ 9/3 7♐26
10 6	18 59	5♋09	22 45	11 58	23 25	20 05	19 03	5 42	1 40	8 46	♆ 17/8 4♐40
20	28 32	17 22	29 26	11 29	24 43	20 24	18 57	5 27	1D41	8 15	♇ 6/1 4♎25
30	8♋04	29 33	5♈54	10 44	26 01	20 39	18D56	5 13	1 45	7 43	♇ 12/6 1♎40
10 7	17 36	11♌43	12 07	9 44	27 17	20 49	19 00	5 01	1 53	7 11	⚷ 24/7 20♈54
20	27 09	23 51	18 00	8 33	28 30	20 54	19 10	4 51	2 04	6 39	
30	6♌42	5♍56	23 28	7 16	29 40	20R54	19 24	4 44	2 17	6 08	
9 8	16 16	17 58	28 23	5 59	0♋45	20 48	19 44	4 41	2 33	5 36	
19	25 52	29 57	2♉36	4 47	1 45	20 37	20 07	4D40	2 51	5 04	
29	5♍31	11♎51	5 58	3 45	2 37	20 22	20 35	4 42	3 11	4 32	
8 9	15 12	23 41	8 15	2 58	3 22	20 03	21 06	4 48	3 33	4 01	
18	24 56	5♏25	9 14	2 28	3 58	19 40	21 39	4 57	3 55	3 29	
28	4♎44	17 01	8R47	2 17	4 24	19 15	22 15	5 09	4 18	2 57	
8 10	14 34	28 29	6 55	2D26	4 40	18 48	22 52	5 23	4 41	2 25	
18	24 28	9♐45	3 58	2 54	4R44	18 21	23 30	5 40	5 03	1 53	
28	4♏26	20 45	0 38	3 41	4 38	17 54	24 08	5 59	5 25	1 22	
7 11	14 26	1♑25	27♈43	4 45	4 21	17 29	24 44	6 20	5 45	0 50	
17	24 30	11 33	25 51	6 04	3 53	17 07	25 20	6 42	6 02	0 18	
27	4♐36	20 59	25D19	7 37	3 17	16 49	25 53	7 04	6 18	29♐46	
7 12	14 45	29 19	26 05	9 22	2 34	16 35	26 23	7 27	6 30	29 15	
17	24 55	6♒02	28 00	11 17	1 46	16 26	26 49	7 49	6 40	28 43	
27	5♑06	10 20	0♉50	13 20	0 56	16 23	27 10	8 10	6 46	28 11	

SID M/N 1st JAN 6 h 41 m 1 s 1974 COMMON BST 17/3 to 27/10

DAY	JAN	FEB	MAR	APR	MAY	JUN	JUL	AUG	SEP	OCT	NOV	DEC
1	1♈17	20♉16	0♊28	23♋04	2♍20	23♎53	29♏18	14♑48	29♒15	2♈21	19♉43	26♊13
☽ 3	27♈23	18♊23	28♊13	21♌39	0♎12	19♏48	23♐48	8♒30	23♓24	27♈31	16♊46	24♋53
5	25♉11	17♋56	27♋03	20♍19	27♎22	14♐50	17♑47	2♓16	18♈03	23♉24	14♋29	23♌38
7	24♊40	18♌11	26♌34	18♎24	23♏34	9♑08	11♒30	26♓19	13♉22	20♊03	12♌39	22♍00
9	25♋06	17♍55	25♍53	15♏16	18♐41	2♒57	5♓15	20♈57	9♊39	17♋36	11♍04	19♎41
11	25♌16	16♎06	23♎59	10♐43	12♑54	26♒39	29♓24	16♉33	7♋13	16♌06	9♎25	16♏34
13	24♍02	12♏22	20♏22	5♑01	6♒37	20♓47	24♈26	13♊34	6♌12	15♍16	7♏13	12♐35
15	20♎56	7♐04	15♐10	28♑44	0♓28	15♈55	20♉52	12♋16	6♍08	14♎22	4♐01	7♑44
17	16♏12	0♑51	9♑02	22♒33	25♓05	12♉31	19♊02	12♌23	5♎57	12♏30	29♐38	2♒06
19	10♐22	24♑24	2♒39	17♓07	20♈57	10♊47	18♋47	12♍48	4♏30	9♐06	24♑10	25♒57
21	4♑02	18♒14	26♒39	12♈49	18♉17	10♋20	19♌12	12♎12	1♐12	4♑14	18♒02	19♓42
23	27♑37	12♓40	21♓29	9♉42	16♊49	10♌15	19♍01	9♏45	26♐16	28♑21	11♓50	13♈56
25	21♒27	7♈49	17♈15	7♊28	15♋56	9♍30	17♎15	5♐27	20♑18	22♒05	6♈10	9♉16
27	15♓45	3♉43	13♉51	5♋43	14♌54	7♎26	13♏42	29♐52	13♒59	16♓05	1♉35	6♊09
29	10♈46		11♊07	4♌06	13♍11	3♏58	8♐44	23♑39	7♓53	10♈49	28♉18	4♋41
31	6♉47		8♋57		10♎34		2♑54	17♒20		6♉31		4♌17
1	5♑18	26♒56	1♓31	14♓31	5♉57	3♋18	8♋32	21♋53	21♍20	3♏08	25♎29	28♏02
☿ 7	14 53	5♓44	27R36	22 52	18 50	9 11	5R25	2♌57	1♎13	8 10	25D55	7♐25
13	24 43	11 09	27D37	2♈13	1♊41	12 43	4D25	15 08	10 23	10 35	1♏33	16 48
19	4♒49	10R58	0♓49	12 30	13 33	13R36	6 32	27 17	18 51	8R49	9 40	26 14
25	15 07	5 41	6 15	23 45	23 47	11 53	11 53	8♍50	26 31	2 27	18 43	5♑46
31	25 18		13 14		2♋06		20 14	19 37		26♎03		15 26

DATE	☉	♀	♂	♃	♄	⚷	♅	♆	♇	☊	STATIONS
1 1	10♑11	11♒16	2♉33	14♒25	0♋32	16D23	27♎20	8♐20	6♎48	27♐55	
11	20 23	10R07	6 26	16 39	29R45	16♈28	27 34	8 39	6R49	27 23	☿ 16/2 11♓50
21	0♒34	5 16	10 49	18 57	29 03	16 39	27 43	8 56	6 47	26 52	☿ 10/3 27♒08
31	10 44	29♑23	15 35	21 18	28 29	16 55	27 46	9 10	6 41	26 20	☿ 18/6 13♋38
10 2	20 52	26 02	20 39	23 42	28 05	17 15	27R44	9 22	6 32	25 48	☿ 12/7 4♋23
20	0♓58	26D40	25 57	26 06	27 50	17 40	27 37	9 30	6 20	25 16	☿ 14/10 10♏38
2 3	11 02	0♒44	1♊26	28 29	27D47	18 08	27 24	9 35	6 07	24 45	☿ 4/11 24♎52
12	21 02	7 13	7 03	0♓50	27 55	18 39	27 07	9R37	5 51	24 13	♀ 3/1 11♒22
22	0♈59	15 19	12 47	3 07	28 14	19 13	26 46	9 35	5 35	23 41	♀ 13/2 25♑49
1 4	10 53	24 31	18 35	5 20	28 44	19 47	26 23	9 30	5 18	23 09	♃ 8/7 17♓52
11	20 44	4♓27	24 28	7 27	29 23	20 23	25 58	9 22	5 02	22 37	♃ 3/11 7♓59
21	0♉31	14 55	0♋24	9 27	0♋11	20 58	25 32	9 12	4 47	22 06	♄ 28/2 27♊47
1 5	10 15	25 45	6 22	11 17	1 06	21 33	25 07	8 59	4 33	21 34	♄ 1/11 18♋54
11	19 56	6♈52	12 23	12 57	2 08	22 06	24 43	8 44	4 22	21 02	♅ 1/2 27♎46
21	29 34	18 11	18 25	14 26	3 15	22 38	24 22	8 29	4 13	20 30	♅ 2/7 23♎39
31	9♊11	29 39	24 30	15 40	4 26	23 06	24 05	8 13	4 07	19 59	♆ 12/3 9♐37
10 6	18 45	11♉15	0♌36	16 39	5 41	23 31	23 51	7 57	4 04	19 27	♆ 19/8 6♐50
20	28 18	22 57	6 43	17 22	6 58	23 52	23 43	7 41	4D04	18 55	♇ 9/1 6♎49
30	7♋50	4♊45	12 52	17 46	8 16	24 09	23 39	7 27	4 07	18 23	♇ 14/6 4♎03
10 7	17 22	16 37	19 03	17R51	9 34	24 21	23D41	7 14	4 14	17 51	⚷ 28/12 16♈23
20	26 55	28 34	25 16	17 37	10 51	24 28	23 48	7 04	4 24	17 20	⚷ 28/7 24♈30
30	6♌28	10♋36	1♍31	17 04	12 06	24R30	24 00	6 57	4 37	16 48	
9 8	16 02	22 43	7 48	16 13	13 17	24 26	24 16	6 52	4 52	16 16	
19	25 39	4♌54	14 07	15 09	14 25	24 18	24 38	6 50	5 10	15 44	
29	5♍17	17 09	20 30	13 54	15 27	24 04	25 04	6D52	5 30	15 13	
8 9	14 58	29 28	26 54	12 35	16 23	23 46	25 33	6 57	5 51	14 41	
18	24 42	11♍51	3♎22	11 18	17 12	23 25	26 05	7 05	6 13	14 09	
28	4♎29	24 16	9 54	10 07	17 52	23 00	26 40	7 16	6 36	13 37	
8 10	14 20	6♎45	16 28	9 09	18 23	22 34	27 16	7 30	7 00	13 06	
18	24 14	19 15	23 06	8 27	18 44	22 06	27 54	7 46	7 22	12 34	
28	4♏11	1♏46	29 48	8 04	18 53	21 39	28 31	8 05	7 44	12 02	
7 11	14 12	14 19	6♏34	8D00	18R52	21 13	29 09	8 25	8 05	11 30	
17	24 15	26 52	13 24	8 18	18 39	20 49	29 45	8 47	8 23	10 58	
27	4♐21	9♐26	20 18	8 55	18 16	20 29	0♏19	9 09	8 39	10 27	
7 12	14 30	22 00	27 15	9 51	17 43	20 14	0 50	9 32	8 53	9 55	
17	24 40	4♑34	4♐17	11 03	17 02	20 03	1 18	9 54	9 03	9 23	
27	4♑51	17 07	11 23	12 30	16 16	19 58	1 42	10 16	9 11	8 51	

SID M/N 1st JAN 6 h 44 m 4 s 1975 COMMON BST 16/3 to 26/10

DAY	JAN	FEB	MAR	APR	MAY	JUN	JUL	AUG	SEP	OCT	NOV	DEC
1	19♌11	12♎32	21♎15	11♐05	14♑46	29♒14	0♈58	15♉19	2♋29	9♌15	2♎31	11♏05
☽ 3	18♍29	10♏14	19♏22	6♑43	9♒19	23♓02	24♈58	10♊46	0♌31	8♍42	2♏24	9♐43
5	16♎37	6♐17	15♐34	1♒07	3♓11	17♈03	19♉49	7♋57	0♍19	9♎07	1♐41	7♑22
7	13♏27	1♑10	10♑22	24♒55	26♓59	11♉51	16♊03	6♌56	0♎52	9♏11	29♐34	3♒38
9	9♐11	25♑22	4♒23	18♓39	21♈13	7♊48	13♋52	6♍59	0♏45	7♐49	25♑47	28♒33
11	4♑07	19♒14	28♒06	12♈42	16♉13	4♋58	12♌54	6♎52	29♏03	4♑38	20♒36	22♓33
13	28♑28	12♓58	21♓52	7♉17	12♊08	3♌06	12♍15	5♏34	25♐37	29♑55	14♓33	16♈14
15	22♒23	6♈46	15♈52	2♊32	8♋57	1♍40	11♎05	2♐46	20♑51	24♒11	8♈15	10♉16
17	16♓06	0♉56	10♉18	28♊38	6♌36	0♎11	8♏56	28♐43	15♒14	17♓59	2♉12	5♊10
19	9♈57	25♉56	5♊28	25♋48	4♍53	28♎16	5♐46	23♑46	9♓10	11♈42	26♉45	1♋12
21	4♉30	22♊20	1♋47	24♌08	3♎32	25♏44	1♑43	18♒11	2♈54	5♉40	22♊06	28♋20
23	0♊20	20♋38	29♋41	23♍24	2♏06	22♐25	26♑56	12♓11	26♈39	0♊04	18♋21	26♌13
25	28♊00	20♌39	29♌09	22♎54	0♐05	18♑12	21♒28	5♈54	20♉42	25♊12	15♌29	24♍25
27	27♋28	21♍21	29♍27	21♏40	26♐59	13♒05	15♓27	29♈38	15♊29	21♋22	13♍27	22♎40
29	27♌56		29♎18	19♐00	22♑39	7♓12	9♈09	23♉51	11♋31	18♌51	12♎07	20♏46
31	28♍01		27♏38		17♒14		3♉04	19♊11		17♍42		18♐29
1	17♑03	25♒13	13♒13	23♓50	23♉30	23♊23	17♊46	7♌43	1♎47	23♎28	21♎40	9♐21
☿ 7	26 52	20℞33	18 34	4♈33	4♊16	21℞16	23 04	19 57	9 34	18℞25	1♏00	18 45
13	6♒38	13 45	25 28	16 07	12 55	18 00	0♋56	1♍22	16 15	11 43	10 41	28 10
19	15 47	10 09	3♓28	28 29	19 09	15 29	11 07	11 54	21 24	9D07	20 21	7♑36
25	22 53	10D53	12 23	11♉14	22 44	15D13	23 01	21 34	24 13	12 40	29 54	16 59
31	25℞25		22 08		23℞31		5♌37	0♎24		20 13		26 02

DATE	☉	♀	♂	♃	♄	⚷	♅	♆	♇	☊	STATIONS
1 1	9♑57	23♑24	14♐58	13♓19	15♋52	19♈57	1♏52	10♐26	9♎13	8♐35	
11	20 08	5♒56	22 10	15 06	15℞02	20D00	2 09	10 45	9 15	8 04	☿ 30/1 25♒27
21	0♒19	18 27	[illegible] 26	17 02	14 14	20 09	2 21	11 03	9℞13	7 32	☿ 21/2 9♒58
31	10 29	0♓57	6♑46	19 08	13 30	20 23	2 27	11 18	9 08	7 00	☿ 30/5 23♊35
10 2	20 37	13 24	14 09	21 20	12 53	20 42	2℞28	11 30	9 00	6 28	☿ 23/6 15♊00
20	0♓44	25 48	21 36	23 38	12 24	21 05	2 23	11 39	8 49	5 57	☿ 27/9 24♎25
2 3	10 47	8♈08	29 05	25 59	12 05	21 32	2 12	11 45	8 36	5 25	☿ 18/10 9♎05
12	20 48	20 23	6♒37	28 23	11 57	22 03	1 57	11 47	8 21	4 53	♀ 6/8 11♍42
22	0♈45	2♉33	14 12	0♈48	12D00	22 35	1 39	11℞46	8 05	4 21	♀ 18/9 25♌25
1 4	10 39	14 36	21 47	3 13	12 14	23 10	1 16	11 42	7 48	3 50	♂ 7/11 2♋40
11	20 30	26 32	29 24	5 37	12 39	23 46	0 52	11 35	7 32	3 18	♃ 15/8 24♈42
21	0♉17	8♊19	7♓01	7 58	13 13	24 22	0 27	11 25	7 16	2 46	♃ 11/12 14♈45
1 5	10 01	19 55	14 38	10 16	13 57	24 57	0 01	11 13	7 02	2 14	♄ 14/3 11♋57
11	19 42	1♋19	22 13	12 28	14 49	25 31	29♎37	10 59	6 50	1 42	♄ 15/11 2♌58
21	29 20	12 26	29 45	14 35	15 47	26 04	29 14	10 43	6 40	1 11	♅ 6/2 2♏28
31	8♊57	23 15	7♈15	16 33	16 52	26 33	28 55	10 27	6 33	0 39	♅ 7/7 28♎21
10 6	18 31	3♌37	14 39	18 23	18 01	27 00	28 40	10 11	6 29	0 07	♆ 14/3 11♐47
20	28 04	13 26	21 59	20 01	19 14	27 23	28 29	9 56	6D29	29♏35	♆ 21/8 9♐01
30	7♋37	22 27	29 11	21 28	20 29	27 42	28 22	9 41	6 31	29 04	♇ 11/1 9♎15
10 7	17 09	0♍23	6♉15	22 41	21 47	27 56	28D21	9 28	6 37	28 32	♇ 17/6 6♎28
20	26 41	6 43	13 09	23 38	23 04	28 06	28 25	9 17	6 46	28 00	⚷ 1/1 19♈57
30	6♌14	10 45	19 51	24 17	24 22	28 10	28 35	9 09	6 58	27 28	⚷ 2/8 28♈10
9 8	15 48	11℞33	26 20	24 39	25 38	28℞08	28 49	9 04	7 13	26 56	
19	25 25	8 31	2♊32	24℞40	26 51	28 02	29 08	9 01	7 31	26 25	
29	5♍03	2 44	8 25	24 22	28 00	27 50	29 32	9D02	7 50	25 53	
8 9	14 44	27♌25	13 56	23 45	29 05	27 34	29 59	9 06	8 11	25 21	
18	24 28	25 25	18 58	22 50	0♌04	27 13	0♏30	9 13	8 33	24 49	
28	4♎15	27D15	23 27	21 42	0 56	26 50	1 03	9 24	8 56	24 18	
8 10	14 06	2♍08	27 14	20 24	1 40	26 23	1 39	9 37	9 20	23 46	
18	23 59	9 12	0♋10	19 04	2 15	25 56	2 16	9 53	9 43	23 14	
28	3♏57	17 46	2 03	17 46	2 40	25 28	2 54	10 11	10 05	22 42	
7 11	13 57	27 23	2℞40	16 37	2 55	25 01	3 31	10 31	10 26	22 11	
17	24 01	7♎45	1 53	15 41	2℞58	24 37	4 08	10 52	10 45	21 39	
27	4♐07	18 40	29♊40	15 04	2 50	24 15	4 43	11 14	11 02	21 07	
7 12	14 15	29 59	26 18	14 46	2 31	23 57	5 16	11 37	11 17	20 35	
17	24 25	11♏35	22 26	14D49	2 02	23 45	5 45	11 59	11 28	20 03	
27	4♑36	23 25	18 51	15 13	1 24	23 37	6 11	12 21	11 36	19 32	

SID M/N 1st JAN 6 h 39 m 7 s — 1976 LEAP — BST 21/3 to 24/10

DAY	JAN	FEB	MAR	APR	MAY	JUN	JUL	AUG	SEP	OCT	NOV	DEC
1	2♑06	19♒46	10♓48	25♈18	27♉57	14♋30	20♌59	13♎29	6♐44	14♑37	3♓10	6♈29
☽ 3	28♑37	14♓22	4♈46	18♉56	22♊17	10♌40	18♍35	11♏49	4♑14	10♒54	27♓37	0♉09
5	24♒02	8♈15	28♈22	12♊57	17♋27	7♍49	16♎40	9♐51	0♒54	6♓08	21♈26	23♉45
7	18♓24	1♉51	22♉02	7♋51	13♌47	5♎56	15♏05	7♑29	26♒44	0♈35	15♉03	17♊40
9	12♈09	25♉47	16♊20	4♌09	11♍32	4♏53	13♐35	4♒28	21♓42	24♈29	8♊44	12♋08
11	5♉54	20♊47	11♋57	2♍14	10♎39	4♐12	11♑45	0♓31	15♈54	18♉05	2♋48	7♌19
13	0♊21	17♋26	9♌25	1♎57	10♏37	3♑06	9♒01	25♓31	9♉35	11♊44	27♋34	3♍21
15	26♊06	15♌53	8♍43	2♏23	10♐25	0♒50	4♓58	19♈36	3♊12	5♋55	23♌26	0♎26
17	23♋24	15♍32	9♎02	2♐17	9♑03	26♒59	29♓40	13♉13	27♊22	1♌10	20♍46	28♎46
19	21♌54	15♎16	9♏06	0♑43	5♒59	21♓43	23♈30	7♊04	22♋44	28♌01	19♎43	28♏11
21	20♍52	14♏08	7♐53	27♑25	1♓19	15♈34	17♉10	1♋49	19♌49	26♍39	19♏49	28♐01
23	19♎32	11♐45	5♑05	22♒37	25♓29	9♉11	11♊21	28♋01	18♍35	26♎39	20♐04	27♑09
25	17♏30	8♑12	0♒53	16♓50	19♈07	3♊14	6♋37	25♌48	18♎25	26♏59	19♑13	24♒42
27	14♐45	3♒46	25♒39	10♈31	12♉47	28♊09	3♌13	24♍42	18♏12	26♐28	16♒35	20♓28
29	11♑18	28♒37	19♓46	4♉07	6♊55	24♋06	0♍56	23♎54	17♐05	24♑21	12♓10	14♈49
31	7♒09		13♈30		1♋45		29♍16	22♏39		20♒35		8♉29
1	27♑28	23♑55	17♒18	10♈37	0♊48	24♉59	23♊11	25♌24	5♎04	23♍09	4♏40	21♐54
☿ 7	5♒01	23D53	26 07	23 00	3 31	25D51	4♋52	5♍23	7 40	25D57	14 28	0♑55
13	9 09	27 30	5♓39	5♉14	3R10	29 21	17 36	14 23	6R58	3♎19	24 03	9 34
19	7R09	3♒20	15 53	16 14	0 27	5♊12	0♌24	22 21	2 26	12 49	3♐27	17 14
25	0 05	10 33	26 51	24 56	27♉07	13 12	12 30	29 08	26♍12	22 56	12 44	22 26
31	24♑24		8♈35		25 06		23 39	4♎23		3♏00		22R33

DATE	☉	♀	♂	♃	♄	⚷	♅	♆	♇	☊	STATIONS
1 1	9♑42	29♏24	17♊23	15♈32	1♌03	23♈35	6♏23	12♐32	11♎39	19♏16	
11	19 53	11♐27	15R23	16 25	0R17	23D36	6 42	12 51	11 42	18 44	☿ 14/1 9♒18
21	0♒04	23 36	14D44	17 34	29♋28	23 43	6 56	13 09	11R41	18 12	☿ 4/2 23♑20
31	10 14	5♑49	15 22	18 59	28 39	23 55	7 05	13 25	11 37	17 40	☿ 9/5 3♊44
10 2	20 23	18 05	17 04	20 38	27 53	24 12	7 08	13 38	11 30	17 09	☿ 2/6 24♉57
20	0♓29	0♒23	19 40	22 27	27 13	24 34	7R06	13 48	11 20	16 37	☿ 9/9 7♎51
1 3	10 32	12 42	22 58	24 26	26 40	25 00	6 58	13 54	11 07	16 05	☿ 1/10 23♍09
11	20 33	25 01	26 49	26 33	26 17	25 30	6 46	13 58	10 53	15 33	☿ 28/12 23♑19
21	0♈31	7♓21	1♋05	28 46	26 04	26 02	6 29	13R57	10 37	15 02	♂ 21/1 14♊44
31	10 25	19 41	5 42	1♉04	26D02	26 37	6 08	13 54	10 20	14 30	♃ 20/9 1♊12
10 4	20 15	2♈01	10 36	3 25	26 11	27 12	5 45	13 48	10 03	13 58	♄ 28/3 26♋02
20	0♉03	14 20	15 42	5 47	26 31	27 49	5 20	13 38	9 47	13 26	♄ 28/11 16♌52
30	9 47	26 38	20 59	8 11	27 01	28 25	4 54	13 27	9 33	12 55	♅ 11/2 7♏08
10 5	19 28	8♉56	26 26	10 34	27 40	28 60	4 29	13 13	9 20	12 23	♅ 11/7 3♏02
20	29 06	21 13	1♌59	12 56	28 28	29 34	4 06	12 58	9 09	11 51	♆ 16/3 13♐58
30	8♊43	3♊30	7 39	15 14	29 23	0♉05	3 45	12 42	9 02	11 19	♆ 23/8 11♐12
9 6	18 17	15 47	13 26	17 29	0♌24	0 33	3 28	12 26	8 57	10 47	♇ 14/1 11♎42
19	27 50	28 04	19 17	19 39	1 31	0 58	3 14	12 10	8D55	10 16	♇ 19/6 8♎55
29	7♋23	10♋21	25 13	21 42	2 42	1 19	3 05	11 55	8 57	9 44	⚷ 4/ 1 23♈35
9 7	16 55	22 39	1♍14	23 37	3 56	1 36	3 02	11 42	9 02	9 12	⚷ 5/ 8 1♉55
19	26 27	4♌57	7 19	25 24	5 12	1 47	3D03	11 30	9 10	8 40	
29	6♌00	17 16	13 29	26 59	6 29	1 54	3 10	11 21	9 22	8 09	
8 8	15 34	29 34	19 43	28 21	7 46	1R55	3 22	11 15	9 36	7 37	
18	25 11	11♍53	26 02	29 30	9 02	1 50	3 39	11 12	9 53	7 05	
28	4♍49	24 11	2♎25	0♊22	10 16	1 41	4 00	11D12	10 12	6 33	
7 9	14 30	6♎29	8 53	0 56	11 27	1 26	4 25	11 15	10 33	6 01	
17	24 14	18 45	15 25	1 12	12 34	1 07	4 54	11 22	10 55	5 30	
27	4♎01	1♏01	22 03	1R07	13 36	0 44	5 27	11 32	11 18	4 58	
7 10	13 51	13 15	28 45	0 43	14 31	0 19	6 01	11 44	11 41	4 26	
17	23 45	25 28	5♏33	29♉59	15 18	29♈51	6 37	11 59	12 04	3 54	
27	3♏42	7♐39	12 26	28 59	15 57	29 23	7 15	12 17	12 27	3 23	
6 11	13 43	19 48	19 24	27 46	16 26	28 55	7 52	12 36	12 49	2 51	
16	23 46	1♑53	26 27	26 26	16 44	28 29	8 29	12 57	13 09	2 19	
26	3♐52	13 54	3♐35	25 05	16 52	28 06	9 05	13 20	13 26	1 47	
6 12	14 00	25 49	10 49	23 49	16R48	27 47	9 39	13 42	13 42	1 16	
16	24 10	7♒36	18 07	22 43	16 34	27 32	10 10	14 05	13 54	0 44	
26	4♑21	19 11	25 31	21 53	16 09	27 22	10 38	14 27	14 03	0 12	

SID M/N 1st JAN 6 h 42 m 6 s — 1977 COMMON — BST 20/3 to 23/10

DAY	JAN	FEB	MAR	APR	MAY	JUN	JUL	AUG	SEP	OCT	NOV	DEC
1	20♉16	4♋28	12♋18	29♌11	5♎14	28♏09	7♑02	29♒11	17♈03	19♉42	3♋37	6♌03
☽ 3	14♊07	29♋53	7♌56	27♍12	4♏45	28♐39	6♒43	26♓15	11♉47	13♊37	27♋27	0♍28
5	8♋41	26♌27	4♍59	26♎29	5♐03	28♑21	4♓49	21♈40	5♊43	7♋22	21♌58	25♍59
7	4♌06	23♍52	3♎13	26♏12	4♑57	26♒18	1♈01	15♉54	29♊28	1♌33	17♍43	23♎10
9	0♍20	21♎46	2♏01	25♐25	3♒28	22♓23	25♈42	9♊37	23♋41	26♌46	15♎10	22♏14
11	27♍16	19♏54	0♐46	23♑31	0♓16	17♈02	19♉33	3♋28	18♌51	23♍23	14♏19	22♐40
13	24♎53	18♐06	29♐01	20♒20	25♓38	10♉54	13♊11	27♋57	15♍11	21♎28	14♐26	23♑09
15	23♏13	16♑13	26♑36	16♓02	19♈59	4♊30	7♋07	23♌17	12♎36	20♏33	14♑18	22♒20
17	22♐07	13♒52	23♒23	10♈49	13♉49	28♊16	1♌37	19♍30	10♏45	19♐49	12♒55	19♓36
19	20♑59	10♓34	19♓17	4♉58	7♊28	22♋24	26♌48	16♎29	9♐13	18♑32	9♓58	15♈10
21	19♒01	6♈03	14♈15	28♉42	1♋12	17♌06	22♍44	14♏08	7♑37	16♒16	5♈40	9♉38
23	15♓34	0♉27	8♉26	22♊21	25♋18	12♍36	19♎33	12♐24	5♒40	12♓58	0♉25	3♊32
25	10♈37	24♉11	2♊08	16♋19	20♌08	9♎15	17♏25	11♑04	3♓06	8♈43	24♉36	27♊17
27	4♉36	17♊54	25♊52	11♌08	16♍08	7♏20	16♐20	9♒40	29♓38	3♉39	18♊28	21♋05
29	28♉13		20♋13	7♍19	13♎44	6♐50	15♑51	7♓34	25♈08	27♉56	12♋11	15♌08
31	22♊10		15♌48		13♏02		15♒02	4♈14		21♊46		9♍41

DAY	JAN	FEB	MAR	APR	MAY	JUN	JUL	AUG	SEP	OCT	NOV	DEC
1	21♑55	17♑17	27♒44	26♈25	10♉01	16♉08	10♋16	4♍45	16♍32	24♍08	16♏37	29♐41
☿ 7	15R01	24 38	8♓11	5♉45	6R27	24 01	23 00	11 41	10R53	4♎38	25 53	5♑28
13	8 31	2♒50	19 17	11 57	4 45	3♊35	4♌48	17 00	7 09	15 14	4♐55	7R22
19	7D17	11 41	1♈01	14 28	5D43	14 44	15 29	20 12	8D26	25 32	13 42	3 02
25	10 27	21 07	13 04	13R26	9 16	27 13	25 03	20R29	14 45	5♏27	22 06	25♐09
31	16 10		24 38		14 59		3♍28	17 21		15 02		21 12

DATE	☉	♀	♂	♃	♄	⚷	♅	♆	♇	☊	STATIONS
1 1	10♑28	26♒01	29♐59	21♉32	15♌49	27♈19	10♏53	14♐39	14♎07	29♎53	
11	20 40	7♓08	7♑29	21R12	15R10	27D18	11 14	14 59	14 11	29 21	☿ 17/1 7♑06
21	0♒51	17 48	15 04	21D14	14 26	27 23	11 30	15 18	14R11	28 49	☿ 20/4 14♉31
31	11 00	27 51	22 42	21 35	13 38	27 34	11 41	15 33	14 07	28 18	☿ 14/5 4♉43
10 2	21 09	7♈01	0♒23	22 16	12 49	27 50	11 46	15 47	14 00	27 46	☿ 23/8 20♍46
20	1♓15	14 54	8 07	23 15	12 02	28 11	11R46	15 57	13 51	27 14	☿ 15/9 6♍57
2 3	11 18	20 56	15 53	24 30	11 20	28 36	11 41	16 04	13 38	26 42	☿ 12/12 7♑27
12	21 18	24 14	23 41	25 58	10 45	29 05	11 30	16 08	13 24	26 10	☿ 1/1 21♐09
22	1♈16	23R51	1♓29	27 39	10 19	29 37	11 15	16R08	13 08	25 39	♀ 16/3 24♈34
1 4	11 09	19 35	9 18	29 30	10 03	0♉12	10 55	16 05	12 52	25 07	♀ 27/4 8♈15
11	21 00	13 27	17 05	1♊29	9 57	0 47	10 33	15 59	12 35	24 35	♂ 13/12 11♌34
21	0♉47	9 04	24 51	3 35	10D02	1 24	10 09	15 50	12 19	24 03	♃ 15/1 21♉10
1 5	10 31	8D30	2♈35	5 46	10 18	2 01	9 44	15 39	12 04	23 32	♃ 24/10 6♋09
11	20 12	11 32	10 16	8 01	10 45	2 37	9 18	15 26	11 50	23 00	♄ 11/4 9♌57
21	29 50	17 13	17 53	10 19	11 20	3 12	8 54	15 11	11 39	22 28	♄ 11/12 0♍32
31	9♊26	24 41	25 26	12 38	12 04	3 44	8 32	14 55	11 31	21 56	♅ 15/2 11♏47
10 6	19 01	3♉23	2♉53	14 58	12 56	4 14	8 13	14 39	11 26	21 25	♅ 16/7 7♏41
20	28 34	12 55	10 15	17 16	13 55	4 41	7 58	14 23	11 24	20 53	♆ 18/3 16♐09
30	8♋06	23 03	17 31	19 33	14 59	5 04	7 48	14 08	11D25	20 21	♆ 25/8 13♐22
10 7	17 38	3♊37	24 39	21 47	16 08	5 22	7 42	13 54	11 29	19 49	♇ 16/1 14♎11
20	27 10	14 31	1♊39	23 56	17 20	5 36	7D41	13 42	11 37	19 17	♇ 21/6 11♎24
30	6♌44	25 42	8 31	26 00	18 35	5 44	7 46	13 33	11 48	18 46	⚷ 7/1 27♈18
9 8	16 18	7♋06	15 14	27 56	19 51	5 47	7 56	13 26	12 02	18 14	⚷ 9/8 5♉47
19	25 54	18 41	21 47	29 45	21 08	5R44	8 10	13 23	12 18	17 42	
29	5♍33	0♌27	28 08	1♋23	22 24	5 36	8 30	13D22	12 37	17 10	
8 9	15 14	12 21	4♋17	2 50	23 38	5 23	8 54	13 25	12 58	16 39	
18	24 58	24 24	10 11	4 03	24 50	5 05	9 21	13 31	13 20	16 07	
28	4♎46	6♍33	15 49	5 01	25 58	4 43	9 52	13 41	13 43	15 35	
8 10	14 36	18 49	21 08	5 42	27 01	4 18	10 26	13 53	14 06	15 03	
18	24 30	1♎10	26 03	6 05	27 57	3 50	11 01	14 08	14 30	14 32	
28	4♏28	13 35	0♌32	6R08	28 47	3 22	11 38	14 25	14 53	14 00	
7 11	14 28	26 03	4 26	5 50	29 28	2 54	12 16	14 44	15 15	13 28	
17	24 32	8♏34	7 39	5 14	29 59	2 27	12 53	15 05	15 35	12 56	
27	4♐38	21 07	10 01	4 20	0♍21	2 02	13 30	15 27	15 54	12 24	
7 12	14 46	3♐41	11 21	3 11	0 31	1 41	14 04	15 49	16 09	11 53	
17	24 56	16 16	11R27	1 53	0R31	1 25	14 36	16 12	16 22	11 21	
27	5♑07	28 51	10 12	0 32	0 19	1 13	15 06	16 34	16 32	10 49	

SID M/N 1st JAN 6 h 41 m 9 s 1978 COMMON BST 19/3 to 29/10

DAY	JAN	FEB	MAR	APR	MAY	JUN	JUL	AUG	SEP	OCT	NOV	DEC
1	22♍15	11♏50	22♏28	15♑45	24♒50	15♈14	20♉01	5♋12	19♌33	22♍30	10♏16	17♐17
☽ 3	18♎19	9♐59	20♐30	14♒03	22♓00	10♉31	14♊16	28♋55	13♍50	18♎03	8♐12	16♑46
5	16♏02	9♑23	19♑13	11♓54	18♈17	5♊08	8♋09	22♌45	8♎46	14♏36	6♑45	15♒58
7	15♐29	9♒16	18♒10	9♈01	13♉46	29♊15	1♌52	16♍55	4♏33	12♐01	5♒17	14♓13
9	15♑59	8♓31	16♓39	5♉10	8♊31	23♋02	25♌38	11♎43	1♐19	10♑03	3♓25	11♈23
11	16♒08	6♈13	14♈00	0♊17	2♋38	16♌44	19♍48	7♏33	29♐12	8♒28	1♈01	7♉39
13	14♓44	2♉11	9♉56	24♊32	26♋24	10♍50	14♎51	4♐49	28♑05	6♓59	28♈00	3♊12
15	11♈22	26♉47	4♊39	18♋20	20♌16	5♎54	11♏23	3♑39	27♒27	5♈11	24♉15	28♊03
17	6♉23	20♊39	28♊36	12♌16	14♍51	2♏35	9♐46	3♒37	26♓31	2♉36	19♊35	22♋14
19	0♊26	14♋24	22♋24	6♍55	10♎46	1♐13	9♑47	3♓40	24♈30	28♉53	14♋01	15♌57
21	24♊09	8♌31	16♌37	2♎49	8♏27	1♑21	10♒21	2♈39	21♉00	23♊57	7♌49	9♍35
23	17♋57	3♍19	11♍43	0♏12	7♐43	1♒48	10♓05	29♈57	16♊05	18♋05	1♍31	3♎45
25	12♌07	28♍53	7♎55	28♏47	7♑40	1♓13	8♈07	25♉35	10♋12	11♌49	25♍47	29♎09
27	6♍46	25♎15	5♏09	27♐53	7♒09	28♓56	4♉20	20♊02	3♌56	5♍47	21♎19	26♏23
29	2♎04		3♐09	26♑45	5♓24	25♈03	29♉14	13♋52	27♌53	0♎36	18♏32	25♐28
31	28♎17		1♑32		2♈15		23♊19	7♌36		26♎42		25♑39
1	21♐09	24♑27	11♓42	26♈07	16♈11	24♉54	26♋38	2♍21	21♌07	7♎46	26♏46	19♐21
☿ 7	23 33	3♒39	23 14	24℞36	20 03	6♊52	6♌40	2℞50	26 14	18 08	4♐58	11℞53
13	29 05	13 20	4♈44	20 28	25 58	19 48	15 22	0 12	5♍04	28 02	12 27	5 59
19	6♑14	23 31	15 01	16 29	3♉33	2♋55	22 41	25♌23	15 46	7♏31	18 29	6D13
25	14 18	4♓15	22 31	14 52	12 36	15 21	28 22	21 12	26 54	16 37	21 34	10 55
31	22 57		25 58		23 02		1♍59	20D43		25 21		17 51

DATE	☉	♀	♂	♃	♄	⚷	♅	♆	♇	☊	STATIONS
1 1	10♑13	5♑09	9♌04	29♊52	0♍09	1♉09	15♏19	16♐45	16♎36	10♎33	
11	20 25	17 44	5℞55	28℞37	29℞42	1 06	15 42	17 05	16 40	10 01	☿ 2/4 26♈08
21	0♒36	0♒18	2 02	27 33	29 06	1D09	16 00	17 24	16℞41	9 30	☿ 25/4 14♈52
31	10 46	12 52	28♋09	26 45	28 24	1 18	16 14	17 40	16 39	8 58	☿ 5/8 3♍01
10 2	20 54	25 25	24 59	26 15	27 37	1 32	16 22	17 54	16 33	8 26	☿ 29/8 20♌20
20	1♓00	7♓56	22 59	26 05	26 49	1 52	16℞24	18 05	16 24	7 54	☿ 26/11 21♐38
2 3	11 03	20 26	22 17	26D14	26 01	2 16	16 21	18 13	16 12	7 23	☿ 16/12 5♐21
12	21 04	2♈54	22D50	26 44	25 18	2 44	16 13	18 18	15 58	6 51	♀ 18/10 22♏48
22	1♈01	15 19	24 26	27 31	24 40	3 15	16 00	18℞19	15 43	6 19	♀ 29/11 7♏20
1 4	10 55	27 42	26 55	28 34	24 10	3 49	15 43	18 17	15 26	5 47	♂ 2/3 22♋17
11	20 46	10♉01	0♌05	29 52	23 50	4 25	15 22	18 12	15 10	5 15	♃ 20/2 26♊05
21	0♉33	22 17	3 49	1♋22	23 40	5 02	14 59	18 04	14 53	4 44	♃ 26/11 9♌04
1 5	10 17	4♊30	8 00	3 04	23D41	5 40	14 34	17 53	14 38	4 12	♄ 26/4 23♌39
11	19 58	16 38	12 33	4 54	23 52	6 17	14 08	17 40	14 24	3 40	♄ 25/12 13♍56
21	29 36	28 42	17 23	6 51	24 13	6 53	13 44	17 25	14 12	3 08	♅ 20/2 16♏24
31	9♊12	10♋42	22 29	8 55	24 44	7 27	13 21	17 10	14 03	2 37	♅ 21/7 12♏19
10 6	18 47	22 36	27 47	11 04	25 25	7 59	13 00	16 53	13 57	2 05	♆ 21/3 18♐19
20	28 20	4♌24	3♍16	13 15	26 13	8 28	12 43	16 37	13 54	1 33	♆ 28/8 15♐33
30	7♋52	16 05	8 55	15 29	27 08	8 53	12 30	16 22	13D54	1 01	♇ 19/1 16♎41
10 7	17 24	27 37	14 43	17 44	28 09	9 13	12 22	16 08	13 58	0 30	♇ 24/6 13♎54
20	26 57	8♍58	20 39	19 59	29 15	9 29	12 19	15 56	14 05	29♍58	⚷ 11/1 1♉06
30	6♌30	20 05	26 42	22 13	0♍25	9 40	12D21	15 46	14 15	29 26	⚷ 14/8 9♉46
9 8	16 04	0♎56	2♎53	24 24	1 38	9 46	12 28	15 38	14 28	28 54	
19	25 40	11 24	9 11	26 32	2 53	9℞46	12 40	15 34	14 44	28 22	
29	5♍19	21 23	15 36	28 34	4 09	9 40	12 57	15D33	15 02	27 51	
8 9	15 00	0♏42	22 07	0♌31	5 25	9 29	13 19	15 35	15 22	27 19	
18	24 44	9 03	28 46	2 20	6 40	9 13	13 44	15 40	15 44	26 47	
28	4♎31	16 01	5♏31	3 59	7 52	8 52	14 14	15 49	16 07	26 15	
8 10	14 22	20 54	12 22	5 28	9 01	8 28	14 46	16 00	16 31	25 44	
18	24 16	22 48	19 20	6 44	10 05	8 01	15 21	16 14	16 55	25 12	
28	4♏13	20℞53	26 24	7 45	11 03	7 32	15 57	16 31	17 18	24 40	
7 11	14 14	15 39	3♐35	8 30	11 55	7 03	16 34	16 50	17 40	24 08	
17	24 17	10 03	10 51	8 57	12 39	6 35	17 12	17 10	18 01	23 37	
27	4♐23	7 23	18 14	9℞04	13 13	6 09	17 49	17 32	18 20	23 05	
7 12	14 32	8D42	25 42	8 52	13 38	5 46	18 24	17 55	18 37	22 33	
17	24 41	13 20	3♑15	8 20	13 52	5 27	18 57	18 17	18 51	22 01	
27	4♑53	20 18	10 53	7 31	13℞55	5 13	19 28	18 39	19 02	21 29	

SID M/N 1st JAN 6 h 40 m 11 s — 1979 COMMON — BST 18/3 to 28/10

DAY		JAN	FEB	MAR	APR	MAY	JUN	JUL	AUG	SEP	OCT	NOV	DEC
	1	10♒44	3♈27	11♈37	1♊01	4♋36	18♌50	20♍31	5♏18	23♐23	0♒42	23♓49	2♉25
☽	3	10♓12	1♉05	9♉37	26♊41	29♋02	12♍28	14♎31	1♐03	21♑30	29♒45	23♈08	0♊33
	5	8♈11	27♉04	5♊53	21♋05	22♌46	6♎29	9♏36	28♐35	21♒08	29♓42	22♉05	27♊46
	7	4♉43	21♊52	0♋43	14♌48	16♍30	1♏34	6♐19	27♑50	21♓30	29♈32	19♊49	23♋40
	9	0♊09	15♋56	24♋40	8♍29	10♎53	28♏08	4♑46	28♒02	21♈24	28♉11	15♋53	18♌16
	11	24♊48	9♌39	18♌18	2♎41	6♏24	26♐11	4♒21	28♓03	19♉51	25♊04	10♌30	12♍03
	13	18♋56	3♍18	12♍03	27♎43	3♐10	25♑05	4♓03	26♈52	16♊31	20♋16	4♍15	5♎42
	15	12♌42	27♍10	6♎15	23♏44	0♑55	24♒03	2♈59	24♉08	11♋38	14♌20	27♍53	29♎56
	17	6♍19	21♎34	1♏09	20♐38	29♑09	22♓29	0♉43	19♊57	5♌45	7♍55	22♎01	25♏18
	19	0♎09	16♏55	26♏54	18♑16	27♒27	20♈12	27♉17	14♋41	29♌23	1♎37	17♏06	22♐01
	21	24♎47	13♐38	23♐43	16♒30	25♓37	17♉09	22♊52	8♌42	22♍59	25♎52	13♐12	19♑51
	23	20♏49	12♑00	21♑42	15♓07	23♈29	13♊19	17♋37	2♍21	16♎53	20♏52	10♑11	18♒14
	25	18♐45	11♒46	20♒43	13♈47	20♉48	8♋39	11♌43	25♍56	11♏20	16♐40	7♒43	16♓39
	27	18♑27	12♓02	20♓17	11♉56	17♊15	3♌07	5♍23	19♎47	6♐37	13♑19	5♓40	14♈49
	29	18♒58		19♈32	8♊58	12♋37	26♌56	28♍58	14♏18	2♑59	10♒50	3♈58	12♉35
	31	18♓59		17♉35		6♌56		22♎57	9♐58		9♓17		9♊49
	1	19♐08	5♒43	25♓35	27♓31	14♈46	12♊27	4♌17	7♌43	26♌24	20♎31	1♐34	19♏51
☿	7	27 15	15 57	3♈56	25R44	23 36	25 22	9 58	4R02	7♍57	29 46	5 22	23 43
	13	5♑55	26 37	8 13	27D09	3♉38	7♋16	13 30	3D23	19 26	8♏32	4R54	0♐34
	19	14 57	7♓40	7R28	1♈12	14 51	17 47	14R25	6 52	0♎23	16 46	28♏52	8 43
	25	24 19	18 42	2 59	7 13	27 11	26 49	12 29	14 18	10 44	24 17	21 36	17 26
	31	4♒04		28♓07		10♊15		8 27	24 32		0♐40		26 27

DATE	☉	♀	♂	♃	♄	⚷	♅	♆	♇	☊	STATIONS
1 1	9♑58	24♏24	14♑43	7♌00	13♍53	5♉08	19♏42	18♐50	19♎06	21♍14	
11	20 10	3♐31	22 27	5R50	13R39	5 03	20 07	19 11	19 11	20 42	☿ 15/3 8♈31
21	0♒21	13 31	0♒14	4 32	13 16	5D04	20 28	19 30	19 13	20 10	☿ 7/4 25♓44
31	10 31	24 07	8 04	3 12	12 43	5 10	20 44	19 47	19R12	19 38	☿ 18/7 14♌28
10 2	20 39	5♑08	15 56	1 56	12 03	5 22	20 54	20 02	19 07	19 06	☿ 11/8 3♌10
20	0♓45	16 28	23 49	0 49	11 18	5 40	20 59	20 14	18 59	18 35	☿ 10/11 5♐49
2 3	10 49	28 00	1♓42	29♋56	10 31	6 03	20R59	20 22	18 48	18 03	☿ 30/11 19♏40
12	20 49	9♒42	9 35	29 20	9 43	6 30	20 53	20 28	18 34	17 31	♃ 26/3 29♋01
22	0♈47	21 31	17 27	29 02	8 58	7 00	20 43	20 30	18 19	16 59	♃ 27/12 10♍15
1 4	10 41	3♓25	25 17	29D04	8 19	7 34	20 27	20R28	18 03	16 28	♄ 10/5 7♍04
11	20 31	15 23	3♈05	29 25	7 46	8 10	20 08	20 24	17 46	15 56	♅ 24/2 21♏00
21	0♉19	27 24	10 49	0♌04	7 22	8 47	19 46	20 16	17 29	15 24	♅ 26/7 16♏55
1 5	10 03	9♈27	18 29	0 58	7 08	9 26	19 22	20 06	17 14	14 52	♆ 23/3 20♐30
11	19 44	21 31	26 06	2 08	7D04	10 04	18 57	19 54	16 59	14 20	♆ 30/8 17♐44
21	29 22	3♉37	3♉37	3 30	7 11	10 41	18 32	19 40	16 47	13 49	♇ 22/1 19♎13
31	8♊59	15 44	11 03	5 04	7 28	11 17	18 08	19 24	16 37	13 17	♇ 27/6 16♎25
10 6	18 33	27 53	18 24	6 47	7 55	11 51	17 46	19 08	16 30	12 45	⚷ 15/1 5♉03
20	28 06	10♊02	25 39	8 38	8 31	12 22	17 27	18 52	16 26	12 13	⚷ 19/8 13♉56
30	7♋38	22 14	2♊47	10 35	9 15	12 49	17 12	18 36	16D25	11 42	
10 7	17 11	4♋27	9 50	12 38	10 07	13 13	17 02	18 22	16 28	11 10	
20	26 43	16 42	16 46	14 45	11 05	13 31	16 56	18 09	16 34	10 38	
30	6♌16	28 59	23 35	16 54	12 08	13 45	16D55	17 59	16 43	10 06	
9 8	15 50	11♌18	0♋18	19 05	13 16	13 53	17 00	17 51	16 56	9 35	
19	25 26	23 39	6 53	21 17	14 27	13 56	17 10	17 46	17 11	9 03	
29	5♍05	6♍03	13 20	23 28	15 41	13R53	17 24	17 44	17 29	8 31	
8 9	14 46	18 27	19 40	25 37	16 56	13 44	17 44	17D45	17 49	7 59	
18	24 30	0♎53	25 50	27 43	18 11	13 30	18 07	17 49	18 10	7 27	
28	4♎17	13 19	1♌52	29 44	19 25	13 11	18 35	17 57	18 33	6 56	
8 10	14 07	25 46	7 42	1♍40	20 38	12 48	19 06	18 08	18 56	6 24	
18	24 01	8♏14	13 20	3 28	21 47	12 21	19 39	18 21	19 20	5 52	
28	3♏59	20 41	18 44	5 07	22 53	11 53	20 15	18 37	19 44	5 20	
7 11	13 59	3♐08	23 52	6 36	23 53	11 23	20 51	18 56	20 07	4 49	
17	24 02	15 35	28 41	7 52	24 46	10 54	21 29	19 16	20 28	4 17	
27	4♐08	28 02	3♍06	8 53	25 32	10 26	22 06	19 38	20 48	3 45	
7 12	14 17	10♑27	7 02	9 39	26 09	10 01	22 42	20 00	21 05	3 13	
17	24 27	22 52	10 23	10 06	26 37	9 40	23 16	20 22	21 20	2 41	
27	4♑38	5♒14	13 00	10R15	26 54	9 24	23 48	20 45	21 32	2 10	

SID M/N 1st JAN 6 h 39 m 14 s 1980 LEAP BST 16/3 to 26/10

	DAY	JAN	FEB	MAR	APR	MAY	JUN	JUL	AUG	SEP	OCT	NOV	DEC
	1	23♊09	10♌10	1♍02	15♎23	18♏28	5♑52	12♒38	5♈29	28♉55	6♋16	23♌44	26♍25
☽	3	19♋05	4♍18	24♍45	9♏21	13♐23	2♒31	10♓40	4♉11	26♊18	2♌07	17♍52	20♎07
	5	13♌59	28♍00	18♎24	3♐49	9♑02	29♒54	9♈00	2♊12	22♋24	26♌48	11♎34	13♏55
	7	8♍02	21♎39	12♏20	29♐05	5♒34	27♓59	7♉22	29♊20	17♌29	20♍50	5♏18	8♐10
	9	1♎39	15♏48	6♐57	25♑27	3♓11	26♈41	5♊29	25♋31	11♍51	14♎34	29♏17	3♑02
	11	25♎29	11♐03	2♑44	23♒18	1♈58	25♉34	2♋57	20♌47	5♎46	8♏17	23♐41	28♑35
	13	20♏13	7♑54	0♒08	22♓40	1♉36	23♊56	29♋26	15♍15	29♎27	2♐11	18♑41	24♒55
	15	16♐23	6♒29	29♒15	22♈56	1♊07	21♋05	24♌45	9♎08	23♏15	26♐35	14♒38	22♓12
	17	14♑09	6♓20	29♓33	22♉53	29♊30	16♌45	19♍06	2♏50	17♐35	21♑53	11♓55	20♈34
	19	13♒07	6♈24	29♈51	21♊23	26♋08	11♍11	12♎53	26♏52	13♑01	18♒37	10♈46	19♉46
	21	12♓30	5♉37	28♉56	17♋57	21♌09	4♎58	6♏42	21♐49	10♒03	17♓09	10♉48	19♊07
	23	11♈27	3♊24	26♊12	12♌53	15♍08	28♎46	1♐11	18♑12	8♓55	17♈15	10♊55	17♋39
	25	9♉30	29♊41	21♋47	6♍49	8♎47	23♏12	26♐50	16♒13	9♈07	17♉53	9♋51	14♌41
	27	6♊33	24♋47	16♌09	0♎25	2♏43	18♐38	23♑52	15♓34	9♉29	17♊34	6♌55	10♍09
	29	2♋39	19♌05	9♍55	24♎11	27♏20	15♑11	22♒06	15♈25	8♊45	15♋24	2♍15	4♎27
	31	27♋51		3♎32		22♐49		21♓00	14♉42		11♌19		28♎13
	1	27♐58	18♒49	20♓17	13♓43	27♈13	0♋09	24♋53	19♋30	13♍56	1♏15	14♏12	22♏48
☿	7	7♑14	29 25	15R02	20 00	9♉08	9 15	22R33	26 42	24 45	8 36	6R49	1♐48
	13	16 45	9♓31	9 39	27 40	21 55	16 31	18 49	6♌44	4♎50	14 45	4D01	11 00
	19	26 31	17 35	7 26	6♈29	4♊58	21 46	15 49	18 24	14 17	18 56	7 23	20 18
	25	6♒38	21 25	8D45	16 20	17 24	24 40	15D28	0♍27	23 06	19R40	14 20	29 42
	31	17 04		12 50		28 28		18 37	12 04		15 22		9♑14

DATE	☉	♀	♂	♃	♄	⚷	♅	♆	♇	☊	STATIONS
1 1	9♑43	11♒25	13♍59	10♍13	26♍59	9♉18	24♏03	20♐56	21♎37	1♍54	
11	19 55	23 43	15 11	9R53	27R00	9 10	24 30	21 17	21 43	1 22	☿ 26/2 21♓30
21	0♒06	5♓56	15R12	9 14	26 50	9D08	24 53	21 37	21 46	0 50	☿ 20/3 7♓25
31	10 16	18 03	13 56	8 19	26 29	9 12	25 11	21 54	21R46	0 19	☿ 28/6 25♋08
10 2	20 24	0♈02	11 23	7 11	26 00	9 22	25 24	22 09	21 42	29♌47	☿ 23/7 15♋13
20	0♓31	11 50	7 51	5 55	25 23	9 38	25 32	22 22	21 34	29 15	☿ 23/10 19♏56
1 3	10 34	23 26	3 54	4 37	24 39	9 59	25R34	22 31	21 24	28 43	☿ 12/11 3♏59
11	20 35	4♉44	0 17	3 21	23 53	10 25	25 31	22 38	21 11	28 11	♀ 25/5 2♋35
21	0♈32	15 41	27♌35	2 13	23 06	10 55	25 23	22 40	20 57	27 40	♀ 7/7 16♊04
31	10 26	26 09	26 07	1 19	22 20	11 28	25 10	22R40	20 41	27 08	♂ 16/1 15♍21
10 4	20 17	6♊00	25D57	0 40	21 39	12 04	24 52	22 36	20 24	26 36	♂ 6/4 25♌52
20	0♉04	14 59	26 57	0 19	21 04	12 42	24 32	22 29	20 07	26 04	♃ 26/4 0♍15
30	9 49	22 44	28 57	0D16	20 37	13 21	24 09	22 20	19 51	25 33	♄ 7/1 27♍01
10 5	19 30	28 44	1♍45	0 32	20 19	13 60	23 44	22 08	19 36	25 01	♄ 23/5 20♍11
20	29 08	2♋08	5 13	1 05	20 12	14 39	23 19	21 54	19 23	24 29	♅ 29/2 25♏34
30	8♊45	2R03	9 14	1 55	20D14	15 16	22 54	21 39	19 12	23 57	♅ 30/7 21♏30
9 6	18 19	28♊08	13 41	2 59	20 27	15 52	22 31	21 23	19 04	23 25	♆ 24/3 22♐41
19	27 52	22 04	18 30	4 16	20 50	16 25	22 11	21 07	19 00	22 54	♆ 1/9 19♐54
29	7♋25	17 18	23 38	5 44	21 22	16 55	21 54	20 51	18D58	22 22	♇ 24/1 21♎46
9 7	16 57	16D09	29 03	7 23	22 03	17 21	21 41	20 36	19 00	21 50	♇ 29/6 18♎58
19	26 29	18 39	4♎41	9 10	22 51	17 43	21 33	20 23	19 05	21 18	⚷ 19/1 9♉08
29	6♌02	23 55	10 32	11 04	23 46	17 59	21 30	20 12	19 13	20 47	⚷ 23/8 18♉17
8 8	15 36	1♋07	16 35	13 03	24 46	18 10	21D32	20 03	19 25	20 15	
18	25 13	9 38	22 49	15 07	25 52	18 16	21 39	19 57	19 40	19 43	
28	4♍51	19 05	29 13	17 14	27 01	18R16	21 51	19 55	19 57	19 11	
7 9	14 32	29 14	5♏46	19 23	28 13	18 10	22 08	19D55	20 16	18 40	
17	24 16	9♌54	12 28	21 33	29 27	17 58	22 30	19 59	20 37	18 08	
27	4♎03	20 58	19 18	23 43	0♎42	17 41	22 55	20 06	21 00	17 36	
7 10	13 53	2♍21	26 17	25 50	1 56	17 19	23 25	20 16	21 23	17 04	
17	23 47	14 01	3♐24	27 55	3 08	16 54	23 57	20 29	21 47	16 32	
27	3♏44	25 53	10 38	29 56	4 18	16 25	24 31	20 44	22 11	16 01	
6 11	13 44	7♎56	17 59	1♎51	5 24	15 56	25 07	21 02	22 34	15 29	
16	23 48	20 07	25 27	3 39	6 25	15 25	25 44	21 22	22 56	14 57	
26	3♐54	2♏24	3♑00	5 17	7 20	14 56	26 22	21 43	23 17	14 25	
6 12	14 02	14 46	10 39	6 45	8 07	14 29	26 58	22 05	23 35	13 54	
16	24 12	27 11	18 22	8 01	8 47	14 06	27 33	22 28	23 50	13 22	
26	4♑23	9♐40	26 10	9 02	9 17	13 47	28 07	22 50	24 03	12 50	

SID M/N 1st JAN 6 h 42 m 13 s — 1981 COMMON — BST 29/3 to 25/10

DAY	JAN	FEB	MAR	APR	MAY	JUN	JUL	AUG	SEP	OCT	NOV	DEC
1	10♏06	24♐26	2♑12	19♒14	25♓46	19♉21	28♊11	19♌22	6♎48	9♏38	23♐43	26♑24
☽ 3	4♐13	20♑05	27♑52	17♓27	25♈33	19♊39	27♋10	15♍56	1♏25	3♐27	17♑28	20♒55
5	29♐06	17♒02	25♒10	17♈17	26♉10	19♋00	24♌46	11♎14	25♏21	27♐07	11♒56	16♓37
7	24♑56	15♓05	23♓58	17♉38	26♊10	16♌38	20♍46	5♏31	19♐06	21♑13	7♓47	14♈03
9	21♒39	13♈44	23♈35	17♊12	24♋31	12♍31	15♎28	29♏19	13♑18	16♒27	5♈34	13♉16
11	19♓07	12♉23	22♉58	15♋11	21♌01	7♎07	9♏25	23♐14	8♒35	13♓24	5♉11	13♊41
13	17♈09	10♊35	21♊20	11♌34	16♍06	1♏02	3♐11	17♑52	5♓23	12♈09	5♊43	13♋59
15	15♉33	8♋06	18♋27	6♍45	10♎19	24♏46	27♐17	13♒34	3♈38	12♉04	5♋46	12♌59
17	14♊02	4♌51	14♌30	1♎11	4♏08	18♐43	22♑04	10♓27	2♉44	11♊55	4♌19	10♍11
19	12♋07	0♍45	9♍43	25♎12	27♏54	13♑05	17♒42	8♈18	1♊48	10♋42	1♍09	5♎45
21	9♌18	25♍48	4♎18	19♏00	21♐48	8♒06	14♓15	6♉41	0♋11	8♌05	26♍36	0♏10
23	5♍17	20♎05	28♎23	12♐45	16♑04	3♓58	11♈41	5♊08	27♋40	4♍14	21♎09	23♏59
25	0♎07	13♏54	22♏10	6♑48	11♒02	0♈58	9♉52	3♋20	24♌17	29♍30	15♏09	17♐38
27	24♎09	7♐44	15♐58	1♒36	7♓10	29♈13	8♊34	1♌02	20♍08	24♎07	8♐52	11♑26
29	17♏55		10♑19	27♒46	4♈53	28♉32	7♋21	28♌02	15♎15	18♏12	2♑31	5♒39
31	12♐03		5♒50		4♉15		5♌36	24♍08		11♐55		0♓31
1	10♑51	0♓19	19♒57	18♓11	14♉28	2♋30	26♊36	28♋28	27♍00	2♏21	20♎06	3♐22
☿ 7	20 36	4 43	20D57	27 42	27 10	4 59	26D50	10♌50	6♎04	3R51	26 31	12 48
13	0♒35	3R10	24 56	8♈06	8♊47	4R46	0♋07	23 06	14 21	1 01	5♏06	22 14
19	10 41	27♒00	0♓54	19 25	18 36	2 16	6 21	4♍41	21 44	24♎17	14 25	1♑43
25	20 33	21 29	8 16	1♉38	26 21	28♊53	15 19	15 27	27 56	18 48	23 54	11 17
31	29 08		16 42		1♋49		26 27	25 25		19D25		20 56

DATE	☉	♀	♂	♃	♄	⚷	♅	♆	♇	☊	STATIONS
1 1	10♑30	17♐09	0♒51	9♎31	9♎30	13♉38	28♏25	23♐04	24♎09	12♌31	
11	20 41	29 39	8 43	10 06	9 44	13 28	28 53	23 25	24 16	11 59	☿ 9/2 4♓56
21	0♒52	12♑10	16 37	10 23	9R46	13 24	29 18	23 45	24 20	11 27	☿ 2/3 19♒51
31	11 02	24 41	24 31	10R20	9 39	13D26	29 38	24 03	24R20	10 56	☿ 9/6 5♋13
10 2	21 10	7♒12	2♓26	9 59	9 20	13 35	29 53	24 18	24 17	10 24	☿ 4/7 26♊21
20	1♓16	19 42	10 20	9 20	8 53	13 49	0♐02	24 31	24 10	9 52	☿ 6/10 3♏52
2 3	11 20	2♓12	18 12	8 25	8 17	14 09	0 07	24 41	24 00	9 20	☿ 27/10 18♎16
12	21 20	14 41	26 02	7 17	7 36	14 34	0R06	24 48	23 48	8 49	♀ 1/1 8♒54
22	1♈17	27 08	3♈49	6 02	6 50	15 03	29♏59	24 51	23 34	8 17	♃ 25/1 10♎24
1 4	11 11	9♈34	11 32	4 45	6 03	15 36	29 48	24R51	23 18	7 45	♃ 28/5 0♎27
11	21 02	21 58	19 12	3 31	5 18	16 12	29 32	24 48	23 01	7 13	♄ 19/1 9♎47
21	0♉49	4♉20	26 47	2 25	4 36	16 51	29 13	24 42	22 44	6 41	♄ 5/6 3♎00
1 5	10 33	16 41	4♉17	1 31	4 00	17 30	28 51	24 32	22 28	6 10	♅ 5/3 0♐07
11	20 14	29 00	11 42	0 52	3 31	18 10	28 27	24 21	22 13	5 38	♅ 4/8 26♏03
21	29 52	11♊18	19 02	0 31	3 11	18 51	28 02	24 07	21 59	5 06	♆ 27/3 24♐52
31	9♊28	23 34	26 16	0D28	3 01	19 30	27 37	23 52	21 48	4 34	♆ 3/9 22♐05
10 6	19 03	5♋48	3♊25	0 43	3D01	20 08	27 13	23 36	21 40	4 03	♇ 26/1 24♎21
20	28 36	18 01	10 28	1 15	3 11	20 43	26 52	23 20	21 34	3 31	♇ 2/7 21♎32
30	8♋08	0♌12	17 26	2 03	3 31	21 15	26 34	23 04	21 32	2 59	⚷ 22/1 13♉24
10 7	17 40	12 22	24 19	3 06	4 00	21 44	26 19	22 49	21D33	2 27	⚷ 28/8 22♉52
20	27 12	24 29	1♋07	4 22	4 38	22 08	26 09	22 36	21 38	1 56	
30	6♌46	6♍33	7 49	5 49	5 24	22 27	26 04	22 25	21 46	1 24	
9 8	16 20	18 34	14 26	7 26	6 17	22 41	26D04	22 15	21 57	0 52	
19	25 56	0♎32	20 58	9 12	7 15	22 49	26 09	22 09	22 11	0 20	
29	5♍35	12 25	27 24	11 06	8 19	22R52	26 19	22 06	22 28	29♋48	
8 9	15 16	24 12	3♌46	13 05	9 27	22 48	26 34	22D06	22 47	29 17	
18	25 00	5♏54	10 01	15 09	10 38	22 38	26 54	22 09	23 08	28 45	
28	4♎47	17 28	16 11	17 16	11 50	22 23	27 18	22 15	23 30	28 13	
8 10	14 38	28 52	22 15	19 25	13 04	22 03	27 46	22 25	23 53	27 41	
18	24 32	10♐04	28 12	21 36	14 17	21 38	28 17	22 38	24 17	27 10	
28	4♏29	21 00	4♍01	23 46	15 30	21 10	28 50	22 53	24 41	26 38	
7 11	14 30	1♑32	9 42	25 54	16 39	20 40	29 26	23 10	25 05	26 06	
17	24 34	11 30	15 13	27 59	17 45	20 09	0♐02	23 30	25 27	25 34	
27	4♐40	20 41	20 33	0♏00	18 47	19 39	0 40	23 51	25 48	25 02	
7 12	14 48	28 41	25 39	1 55	19 42	19 10	1 16	24 13	26 07	24 31	
17	24 58	4♒53	0♎28	3 42	20 30	18 45	1 52	24 36	26 23	23 59	
27	5♑09	8 26	4 58	5 20	21 10	18 24	2 26	24 58	26 36	23 27	

SID M/N 1st JAN 6 h 41 m 16 s — 1982 COMMON — BST 28/3 to 24/10

	DAY	JAN	FEB	MAR	APR	MAY	JUN	JUL	AUG	SEP	OCT	NOV	DEC
	1	13♓18	4♉00	14♉51	8♋08	16♌36	6♎23	10♏43	25♐16	9♒21	12♓31	1♉07	8♊14
☽	3	9♈46	2♊10	13♊02	5♌58	13♍25	1♏26	4♐45	18♑55	4♓05	8♈51	29♉46	8♋06
	5	7♉40	1♋01	11♋17	3♍11	9♎19	25♏44	28♐24	12♒55	29♓47	6♉16	28♊48	7♌38
	7	6♊54	0♌06	9♌26	29♍45	4♏26	19♐34	22♑02	7♓35	26♈22	4♊18	27♋32	6♍05
	9	6♋51	28♌41	7♍11	25♎30	28♏51	13♑10	15♒59	3♈02	23♉40	2♋33	25♌35	3♎13
	11	6♌29	26♍06	4♎06	20♏21	22♐42	6♒53	10♓32	29♈26	21♊34	0♌44	22♍52	29♎10
	13	4♍49	22♎03	29♎51	14♐23	16♑18	1♓10	6♈02	26♉51	19♋59	28♌45	19♎22	24♏09
	15	1♎27	16♏40	24♏27	8♑01	10♒08	26♓32	2♉51	25♊21	18♌41	26♍22	15♏00	18♐25
	17	26♎33	10♐29	18♐17	1♒51	4♓51	23♈29	1♊10	24♋39	17♍10	23♎15	9♐46	12♑13
	19	20♏37	4♑10	11♑58	26♒37	1♈05	22♉13	0♋46	24♌07	14♎46	19♏03	3♑47	5♒47
	21	14♐16	28♑20	6♒12	22♓55	29♈10	22♊15	0♌52	22♍49	11♏00	13♐43	27♑22	29♒32
	23	8♑02	23♒27	1♓37	20♈57	28♉48	22♋33	0♍24	20♎02	5♐50	7♑34	21♒05	23♓57
	25	2♒21	19♓43	28♓29	20♉14	28♊58	21♌57	28♍26	15♏37	29♐44	1♒11	15♓34	19♈36
	27	27♒25	16♈58	26♈37	19♊48	28♋31	19♍44	24♎44	9♐55	23♑22	25♒16	11♈28	16♉57
	29	23♓23		25♉21	18♋44	26♌44	15♎52	19♏34	3♑35	17♒27	20♓28	9♉05	16♊04
	31	20♈14		23♊59		23♍29		13♐28	27♑18		17♈12		16♋20
	1	22♑32	12♒09	13♒21	0♈15	29♉09	11♊26	17♊23	15♌45	4♎43	10♎06	26♎39	14♐44
☿	7	2♒02	5℞31	20 36	11 50	7♊11	8℞17	25 53	27 09	11 00	4℞00	6♏31	24 04
	13	10 44	2 56	28 51	24 09	12 32	6 40	6♋28	7♍38	15 33	2D43	16 18	3♑22
	19	17 03	4D39	7♓56	6♉47	15 01	7D35	18 37	17 12	17 31	7 18	25 54	12 32
	25	18℞21	9 14	17 46	18 48	14℞37	11 13	1♌22	25 51	15℞45	15 27	5♐22	21 14
	31	13 22		28 24		11 59		13 45	3♎33		25 00		28 33

DATE	☉	♀	♂	♃	♄	⚷	♅	♆	♇	☊	STATIONS
1 1	10♑15	8♒54	7♎03	6♏05	21♎27	18♉15	2♐42	25♐09	26♎42	23♋11	
11	20 26	6℞45	10 54	7 26	21 53	18 02	3 12	25 31	26 50	22 40	☿ 23/1 18♒39
21	0♒37	1 18	14 11	8 34	22 09	17 55	3 38	25 51	26 55	22 08	☿ 13/2 2♒56
31	10 47	25♑46	16 46	9 26	22 15	17D54	4 00	26 10	26℞56	21 36	☿ 21/5 15♊11
10 2	20 56	23 23	18 29	10 01	22℞10	18 00	4 17	26 26	26 54	21 04	☿ 14/6 6♊38
20	1♓02	24D58	19 10	10 19	21 54	18 12	4 29	26 39	26 48	20 32	☿ 19/9 17♎32
2 3	11 05	29 43	18℞38	10℞17	21 29	18 30	4 36	26 50	26 39	20 01	☿ 11/10 2♎26
12	21 06	6♒40	16 49	9 57	20 56	18 54	4℞38	26 58	26 27	19 29	♀ 11/2 23♑22
22	1♈03	15 06	13 51	9 19	20 16	19 22	4 34	27 02	26 13	18 57	♂ 21/2 19♎10
1 4	10 57	24 31	10 08	8 26	19 32	19 54	4 25	27℞03	25 58	18 25	♂ 12/5 0♎22
11	20 47	4♓37	6 21	7 20	18 46	20 30	4 11	27 00	25 41	17 54	♃ 24/2 10♏20
21	0♉35	15 11	3 11	6 06	18 01	21 08	3 54	26 55	25 24	17 22	♃ 28/6 0♏27
1 5	10 19	26 06	1 07	4 50	17 18	21 49	3 33	26 46	25 08	16 50	♄ 31/1 22♎15
11	20 00	7♈17	0 22	3 36	16 40	22 30	3 10	26 35	24 52	16 18	♄ 18/6 15♎30
21	29 38	18 39	0D54	2 29	16 09	23 12	2 45	26 22	24 38	15 46	♅ 10/3 4♐38
31	9♊14	0♉09	2 32	1 35	15 47	23 53	2 20	26 07	24 26	15 15	♅ 9/8 0♐35
10 6	18 49	11 47	5 08	0 55	15 34	24 33	1 56	25 52	24 17	14 43	♆ 29/3 27♐03
20	28 22	23 31	8 31	0 32	15D30	25 11	1 33	25 36	24 11	14 11	♆ 6/9 24♐17
30	7♋54	5♊20	12 32	0D27	15 37	25 46	1 14	25 20	24 07	13 39	♇ 29/1 26♎56
10 7	17 26	17 13	17 05	0 40	15 54	26 17	0 57	25 04	24D08	13 08	♇ 5/7 24♎07
20	26 59	29 12	22 05	1 10	16 19	26 45	0 45	24 50	24 11	12 36	⚷ 27/1 17♉54
30	6♌32	11♋15	27 28	1 57	16 54	27 08	0 37	24 38	24 18	12 04	⚷ 2/9 27♉44
9 8	16 06	23 22	3♏11	2 59	17 37	27 25	0 35	24 29	24 28	11 32	
19	25 42	5♌33	9 11	4 14	18 27	27 37	0D37	24 22	24 42	11 01	
29	5♍21	17 49	15 26	5 41	19 23	27 43	0 45	24 18	24 58	10 29	
8 9	15 02	0♍08	21 55	7 18	20 25	27℞43	0 57	24D17	25 16	9 57	
18	24 46	12 31	28 37	9 05	21 31	27 36	1 15	24 19	25 37	9 25	
28	4♎33	24 57	5♐29	10 59	22 40	27 24	1 37	24 25	25 59	8 53	
8 10	14 24	7♎25	12 32	13 00	23 52	27 05	2 03	24 34	26 22	8 22	
18	24 18	19 56	19 44	15 05	25 04	26 42	2 32	24 46	26 46	7 50	
28	4♏15	2♏27	27 04	17 15	26 17	26 15	3 05	25 00	27 10	7 18	
7 11	14 15	15 00	4♑32	19 26	27 29	25 45	3 39	25 17	27 34	6 46	
17	24 19	27 33	12 06	21 38	28 39	25 14	4 15	25 36	27 57	6 15	
27	4♐25	10♐07	19 45	23 51	29 45	24 42	4 52	25 57	28 18	5 43	
7 12	14 33	22 41	27 29	26 01	0♏47	24 12	5 29	26 19	28 37	5 11	
17	24 43	5♑14	5♒16	28 09	1 43	23 44	6 05	26 42	28 54	4 39	
27	4♑54	17 47	13 06	0♐12	2 33	23 20	6 40	27 04	29 09	4 07	

SID M/N 1st JAN 6 h 40 m 19 s — 1983 COMMON — BST 27/3 to 23/10

DAY	JAN	FEB	MAR	APR	MAY	JUN	JUL	AUG	SEP	OCT	NOV	DEC
1	1♌32	24♍10	2♎06	21♏12	24♐22	8♒24	10♓29	26♈00	14♊34	22♋20	15♍51	24♎26
☽ 3	1♍19	21♎58	0♏05	16♐33	18♑33	2♓08	4♈42	21♉47	12♋29	21♌14	14♎39	21♏41
5	29♍34	17♏52	26♏12	10♑43	12♒15	26♓23	29♈57	19♊10	11♌57	20♍54	12♏52	18♐01
7	26♎06	12♐22	20♐47	4♒23	6♓10	21♈44	26♉42	18♋18	12♍16	20♎21	9♐52	13♑19
9	21♏14	6♑06	14♑32	28♒14	0♈54	18♉34	25♊11	18♌39	12♎10	18♏34	5♑28	7♒42
11	15♐25	29♑40	8♒08	22♓50	26♈53	16♊55	25♋01	18♍59	10♏30	15♐02	29♑54	1♓32
13	9♑08	23♒27	2♓07	18♈28	24♉08	16♋14	25♌12	18♎02	6♐54	9♑58	23♒44	25♓21
15	2♒44	17♓44	26♓51	15♉05	22♊22	15♌41	24♍33	15♏12	1♑44	3♒58	17♓34	19♈45
17	26♒29	12♈40	22♈22	12♊28	21♋01	14♍29	22♎23	10♐40	25♑40	27♒40	12♈01	15♉19
19	20♓40	8♉24	18♉38	10♋21	19♌36	12♎11	18♏38	5♑00	19♒21	21♓41	7♉29	12♊21
21	15♈39	5♊11	15♊40	8♌35	17♍45	8♏43	13♐40	28♑48	13♓13	16♈23	4♊04	10♋45
23	11♉51	3♋16	13♋31	6♍59	15♎16	4♐13	7♑55	22♒29	7♈35	11♉54	1♋38	9♌55
25	9♊38	2♌37	12♌12	5♎13	11♏57	28♐54	1♒45	16♓21	2♉31	8♊12	29♋48	9♍01
27	9♋02	2♍36	11♍22	2♏46	7♐41	23♑00	25♒27	10♈35	28♉08	5♋14	28♌12	7♎24
29	9♌25		10♎14	29♏12	2♑29	16♒44	19♓17	5♉25	24♊40	3♌01	26♍30	4♏48
31	9♍34		7♏57		26♑32		13♈33	1♊12		1♍27		1♐13
1	29♑31	17♑39	20♒13	16♈31	25♉32	17♉59	28♊21	29♌20	0♎41	19♍25	8♏51	25♐03
☿ 7	2♒35	22 01	29 43	28 38	24R25	22 04	11♋08	8♍19	29R37	26 56	18 29	3♑29
13	29R16	28 21	9♓53	9♉32	21 12	28 20	24 02	16 12	24 58	6♎39	27 54	10 54
19	21 46	5♒52	20 44	18 03	17 56	6♊35	6♌17	22 50	19 03	16 59	7♐07	15 53
25	16 56	14 15	2♈19	23 29	16 26	16 39	17 32	27 48	16D24	27 14	16 11	15R49
31	17D12		14 28		17D33		27 44	0♎31		7♏13		9 29

DATE	☉	♀	♂	♃	♄	⚷	♅	♆	♇	☊	STATIONS
1 1	10♑00	24♑04	17♒01	1♐11	2♏55	23♉10	6♐57	27♐15	29♎15	3♋52	
11	20 12	6♒36	24 53	3 05	3 32	22 54	7 28	27 37	29 24	3 20	☿ 7/1 2♒35
21	0♒23	19 07	2♓44	4 50	4 00	22 44	7 55	27 58	29 30	2 48	☿ 28/1 16♑29
31	10 33	1♓36	10 34	6 26	4 18	22 40	8 19	28 17	29 32	2 16	☿ 2/5 25♉34
10 2	20 41	14 03	18 23	7 49	4 26	22D43	8 39	28 34	29R31	1 45	☿ 26/5 16♉25
20	0♓47	26 26	26 09	8 59	4R23	22 52	8 53	28 48	29 26	1 13	☿ 2/9 0♎46
2 3	10 51	8♈46	3♈52	9 54	4 10	23 08	9 03	28 59	29 18	0 41	☿ 25/9 16♍24
12	20 51	21 00	11 31	10 32	3 48	23 30	9 07	29 07	29 07	0 09	☿ 22/12 16♑39
22	0♈49	3♉09	19 06	10 53	3 17	23 57	9R05	29 12	28 53	29♊37	♀ 4/8 9♍30
1 4	10 43	15 11	26 36	10R55	2 39	24 28	8 59	29R14	28 38	29 06	♀ 16/9 23♌12
11	20 33	27 05	4♉02	10 38	1 56	25 04	8 48	29 13	28 22	28 34	♃ 28/3 10♐56
21	0♉20	8♊50	11 23	10 03	1 11	25 42	8 32	29 08	28 05	28 02	♃ 29/7 1♐05
1 5	10 05	20 24	18 39	9 12	0 26	26 23	8 13	29 00	27 48	27 30	♄ 12/2 4♏26
11	19 46	1♋45	25 49	8 09	29♎42	27 05	7 50	28 50	27 32	26 59	♄ 2/7 27♎44
21	29 24	12 49	2♊55	6 57	29 04	27 48	7 26	28 37	27 18	26 27	♅ 14/3 9♐07
31	9♊00	23 32	9 56	5 41	28 31	28 31	7 02	28 23	27 05	25 55	♅ 14/8 5♐04
10 6	18 35	3♌48	16 52	4 26	28 06	29 14	6 37	28 07	26 55	25 23	♆ 1/4 29♐14
20	28 08	13 27	23 43	3 18	27 50	29 54	6 14	27 51	26 48	24 51	♆ 8/9 26♐28
30	7♋40	22 15	0♋30	2 21	27 44	0♊32	5 52	27 35	26 44	24 20	♇ 1/2 29♎32
10 7	17 12	29 51	7 13	1 38	27D47	1 07	5 34	27 19	26D43	23 48	♇ 7/7 26♎43
20	26 45	5♍43	13 51	1 12	28 01	1 38	5 20	27 05	26 46	23 16	⚷ 1/2 22♉40
30	6♌18	9 04	20 26	1D05	28 24	2 05	5 10	26 53	26 52	22 44	⚷ 8/9 2♊56
9 8	15 52	8R59	26 58	1 15	28 55	2 27	5 05	26 42	27 01	22 13	
19	25 28	5 06	3♌26	1 43	29 35	2 43	5D05	26 35	27 13	21 41	
29	5♍07	29♌06	9 51	2 29	0♏23	2 52	5 10	26 30	27 29	21 09	
8 9	14 48	24 23	16 12	3 30	1 17	2 56	5 20	26 28	27 47	20 37	
18	24 32	23D18	22 30	4 45	2 17	2R53	5 35	26D30	28 07	20 06	
28	4♎19	25 56	28 46	6 12	3 21	2 44	5 55	26 35	28 28	19 34	
8 10	14 09	1♍24	4♍58	7 51	4 29	2 28	6 19	26 43	28 51	19 02	
18	24 03	8 51	11 07	9 40	5 40	2 07	6 47	26 54	29 15	18 30	
28	4♏00	17 41	17 12	11 37	6 51	1 42	7 18	27 08	29 39	17 58	
7 11	14 01	27 30	23 13	13 40	8 04	1 12	7 51	27 24	0♏03	17 27	
17	24 04	7♎59	29 10	15 48	9 15	0 41	8 27	27 43	0 27	16 55	
27	4♐10	19 00	5♎02	18 01	10 25	0 08	9 03	28 03	0 48	16 23	
7 12	14 19	0♏23	10 48	20 16	11 31	29♉36	9 40	28 25	1 09	15 51	
17	24 28	12 03	16 27	22 32	12 34	29 06	10 17	28 48	1 26	15 20	
27	4♑39	23 55	21 58	24 48	13 31	28 39	10 52	29 10	1 41	14 48	

SID M/N 1st JAN 6 h 39 m 22 s — 1984 LEAP — BST 25/3 to 28/10

	DAY	JAN	FEB	MAR	APR	MAY	JUN	JUL	AUG	SEP	OCT	NOV	DEC
	1	14♐06	0♒24	21♒20	5♈52	9♉00	26♊41	3♌52	27♍31	20♏31	27♐00	13♒53	16♓17
☽	3	9♑17	24♒22	15♓05	0♉02	4♊14	24♋01	2♍44	26♎25	17♐35	22♑42	8♓04	10♈00
	5	3♒47	18♓06	8♈53	24♉43	0♋18	22♌03	1♎30	24♏06	13♑17	17♒18	1♈48	3♉50
	7	27♒44	11♈52	2♉57	20♊11	27♋17	20♍28	29♎43	20♐37	8♒05	11♓16	25♈34	28♉14
	9	21♓27	6♉04	27♉38	16♋45	25♌14	18♎55	27♏09	16♑13	2♓18	5♈01	19♉41	23♊33
	11	15♈23	1♊15	23♊25	14♌44	23♍59	17♏03	23♐48	11♒06	26♓09	28♈46	14♊25	19♋49
	13	10♉09	28♊03	20♋50	14♍05	23♎07	14♐31	19♑38	5♓25	19♈51	22♉47	9♋55	16♌58
	15	6♊20	26♋48	20♌04	14♎04	21♏53	11♑01	14♒39	29♓16	13♉38	17♊22	6♌24	14♍47
	17	4♋18	27♌06	20♍31	13♏34	19♐34	6♒25	8♓56	22♈57	7♊59	12♋55	4♍01	13♎05
	19	3♌51	27♍41	20♎52	11♐38	15♑51	0♓51	2♈45	16♉55	3♋29	9♌55	2♎43	11♏37
	21	4♍00	27♎10	19♏49	7♑57	10♒49	24♓43	26♈33	11♊49	0♌41	8♍33	2♏08	10♐01
	23	3♎33	24♏49	16♐50	2♒49	4♓54	18♈34	20♉59	8♋16	29♌48	8♎28	1♐27	7♑48
	25	1♏40	20♐43	12♑10	26♒49	28♓40	13♉02	16♊40	6♌40	0♎11	8♏40	29♐49	4♒28
	27	28♏16	15♑24	6♒25	20♓32	22♈44	8♊39	14♋03	6♍36	0♏34	7♐57	26♑41	29♒50
	29	23♐40	9♒26	0♓11	14♈30	17♉33	5♋39	13♌00	6♎56	29♏41	5♑33	22♒03	24♓07
	31	18♑17		23♓55		13♊22		12♍43	6♏23		1♒27		17♈51
	1	8♑07	18♑43	4♓00	0♉11	27♈08	18♉54	18♋41	6♍10	2♍34	0♎21	21♏49	29♐39
☿	7	1R39	27 00	15 03	5 24	26D23	28 50	0♌25	10 53	0R02	11 06	0♐44	0R26
	13	0D39	5♒53	26 41	6R38	28 24	10♊15	10 58	13 15	2D33	21 29	9 21	24♐59
	19	4 06	15 18	8♈33	4 20	2♉51	22 52	20 19	12R35	9 42	1♏27	17 27	17 18
	25	10 04	25 15	19 46	0 20	9 17	5♋59	28 27	8 43	19 33	11 02	24 36	14D31
	31	17 24		28 57		17 24		5♍12	3 21		20 18		17 11

DATE	☉	♀	♂	♃	♄	⚷	♅	♆	♇	☊	STATIONS
1 1	9♑45	29♏55	24♎40	25♐56	13♏57	28♉27	11♐09	29♐21	1♏48	14♊32	
11	19 57	12♐00	29 56	28 09	14 44	28 07	11 41	29 43	1 58	14 00	☿ 11/1 0♑23
21	0♒08	24 10	4♏59	0♑18	15 22	27 54	12 10	0♑04	2 05	13 28	☿ 12/4 6♉42
31	10 18	6♑24	9 46	2 23	15 52	27 47	12 36	0 24	2 08	12 57	☿ 6/5 26♈18
10 2	20 26	18 41	14 14	4 21	16 12	27D46	12 58	0 41	2R08	12 25	☿ 15/8 13♍24
20	0♓32	1♒00	18 18	6 11	16 22	27 53	13 14	0 56	2 04	11 53	☿ 7/9 0♍02
1 3	10 36	13 19	21 52	7 51	16R22	28 06	13 26	1 08	1 57	11 21	☿ 5/12 0♑49
11	20 37	25 40	24 48	9 20	16 11	28 26	13 33	1 17	1 47	10 49	☿ 25/12 14♐31
21	0♈34	8♓00	26 57	10 36	15 51	28 51	13R34	1 23	1 34	10 18	♂ 6/4 28♏20
31	10 28	20 20	28 09	11 37	15 22	29 21	13 30	1 26	1 19	9 46	♂ 20/6 11♏41
10 4	20 19	2♈40	28R13	12 22	14 46	29 56	13 21	1R25	1 03	9 14	♃ 30/4 12♑58
20	0♉06	15 00	27 01	12 49	14 04	0♊34	13 07	1 21	0 46	8 42	♃ 30/8 3♑08
30	9 50	27 18	24 37	12R58	13 20	1 16	12 49	1 14	0 29	8 11	♄ 24/2 16♏23
10 5	19 32	9♉36	21 19	12 49	12 35	1 59	12 29	1 04	0 13	7 39	♄ 13/7 9♏42
20	29 10	21 54	17 44	12 20	11 51	2 44	12 06	0 52	29♎58	7 07	♅ 18/3 13♐34
30	8♊47	4♊11	14 35	11 35	11 11	3 29	11 41	0 38	29 45	6 35	♅ 18/8 9♐32
9 6	18 21	16 28	12 28	10 36	10 37	4 13	11 16	0 23	29 34	6 04	♆ 2/4 1♑26
19	27 54	28 45	11 41	9 26	10 11	4 57	10 52	0 07	29 26	5 32	♆ 10/9 28♐40
29	7♋27	11♋02	12D15	8 10	9 52	5 38	10 30	29♐50	29 21	5 00	♇ 4/2 2♏08
9 7	16 59	23 20	14 03	6 54	9 43	6 16	10 10	29 35	29 19	4 28	♇ 9/7 29♎19
19	26 31	5♌38	16 54	5 42	9D44	6 52	9 54	29 20	29D21	3 56	⚷ 5/2 27♉46
29	6♌04	17 56	20 37	4 41	9 55	7 22	9 42	29 07	29 26	3 25	⚷ 14/9 8♊33
8 8	15 38	0♍14	25 03	3 53	10 15	7 48	9 35	28 56	29 34	2 53	
18	25 14	12 33	0♐05	3 21	10 44	8 09	9 32	28 48	29 46	2 21	
28	4♍53	24 50	5 37	3 08	11 21	8 23	9D34	28 42	0♏00	1 49	
7 9	14 34	7♎08	11 33	3D14	12 07	8 31	9 42	28 40	0 18	1 18	
17	24 18	19 24	17 49	3 38	12 59	8R33	9 55	28D40	0 37	0 46	
27	4♎05	1♏39	24 23	4 21	13 57	8 27	10 12	28 44	0 58	0 14	
7 10	13 55	13 52	1♑12	5 20	15 00	8 15	10 34	28 52	1 21	29♉42	
17	23 49	26 04	8 13	6 34	16 06	7 57	11 00	29 02	1 45	29 11	
27	3♏46	8♐14	15 25	8 02	17 16	7 34	11 30	29 16	2 09	28 39	
6 11	13 46	20 22	22 45	9 42	18 27	7 05	12 02	29 32	2 33	28 07	
16	23 50	2♑26	0♒11	11 32	19 39	6 34	12 37	29 50	2 57	27 35	
26	3♐56	14 25	7 42	13 31	20 50	6 01	13 12	0♑10	3 19	27 03	
6 12	14 04	26 18	15 17	15 37	22 00	5 27	13 49	0 31	3 40	26 32	
16	24 14	8♒02	22 55	17 49	23 06	4 54	14 26	0 54	3 58	26 00	
26	4♑25	19 34	0♓33	20 05	24 09	4 25	15 02	1 16	4 14	25 28	

SID M/N 1st JAN 6 h 42 m 21 s — 1985 COMMON — BST 31/3 to 27/10

DAY	JAN	FEB	MAR	APR	MAY	JUN	JUL	AUG	SEP	OCT	NOV	DEC
1	29♈42	13♊57	21♊52	9♌43	16♍57	10♏25	18♐59	9♒53	27♓04	29♈43	13♊49	17♋04
☽ 3	23♉49	9♋57	17♋47	8♍15	16♎34	10♐09	17♑30	6♓08	21♈20	23♉19	7♋48	12♌06
5	18♊58	7♌38	15♌36	8♎17	16♏52	9♑12	14♒53	1♈10	15♉01	16♊58	2♌36	8♍08
7	15♋26	6♍37	15♍04	8♏43	16♐40	6♒49	10♓47	25♈13	8♊41	11♋15	28♌42	5♎29
9	13♌06	5♎59	15♎11	8♐17	15♑01	2♓44	5♈22	18♉51	3♋00	6♌45	26♍29	4♏19
11	11♍28	4♏51	14♏47	6♑17	11♒37	27♓18	29♈08	12♊46	28♋38	3♍59	25♎54	4♐15
13	9♎55	2♐46	13♐05	2♒38	6♓42	21♈04	22♉49	7♋40	25♌57	2♎57	26♏16	4♑20
15	8♏05	29♐44	9♑58	27♒42	0♈47	14♉41	17♊03	3♌57	24♍45	3♏00	26♐22	3♒23
17	5♐51	25♑55	5♒43	21♓54	24♈24	8♊42	12♋17	1♍37	24♎17	3♐02	25♑08	0♓38
19	3♑05	21♒21	0♓35	15♈38	18♉03	3♋28	8♌41	0♎09	23♏35	2♑01	22♒05	26♓06
21	29♑39	16♓03	24♓50	9♉14	12♊03	29♋09	6♍03	28♎53	22♐00	29♑29	17♓25	20♈17
23	25♒17	10♈05	18♈38	2♊59	6♋42	25♌44	3♎59	27♏17	19♑21	25♒32	11♈39	13♉54
25	19♓56	3♉42	12♉13	27♊12	2♌13	23♍08	2♏11	25♐10	15♒40	20♓27	5♉21	7♊33
27	13♈49	27♉24	5♊57	22♋20	28♌48	21♎17	0♐27	22♑26	11♓06	14♈38	28♉57	1♋39
29	7♉27		0♋24	18♌49	26♍37	20♏02	28♐37	18♒58	5♈43	8♉23	22♊46	26♋27
31	1♊31		26♋10		25♎37		26♑20	14♓37		1♊58		22♌00
1	17♐59	29♑30	18♓48	15♈45	13♈50	2♊29	1♌50	24♌39	20♌55	14♎06	0♐24	3♐50
☿ 7	24 07	9♒12	0♈00	11R02	20 22	15 29	10 13	21R18	0♍20	24 01	7 28	28R58
13	1♑38	19 22	9 48	7 30	28 24	28 35	17 05	16 35	11 23	3♏27	12 53	0D20
19	9 56	0♓02	16 27	6D52	7♉47	10♋56	22 08	13 27	22 42	12 28	15R00	5 47
25	18 43	11 12	18R39	9 09	18 28	22 03	24 56	14D16	3♎40	21 03	11 36	13 10
31	27 56		16 26		0♊23		24R57	19 38		29 07		21 28

DATE	☉	♀	♂	♃	♄	⚷	♅	♆	♇	☊	STATIONS
1 1	10♑32	26♒22	5♓08	21♑28	24♏44	4♊09	15♐22	1♑30	4♏22	25♉09	
11	20 43	7♓23	12 46	23 48	25 38	3 46	15 56	1 52	4 33	24 37	☿ 25/3 18♈40
21	0♒54	17 56	20 23	26 09	26 25	3 29	16 26	2 13	4 41	24 05	☿ 17/4 6♈44
31	11 04	27 48	27 57	28 29	27 04	3 19	16 53	2 33	4 45	23 34	☿ 28/7 25♌19
10 2	21 12	6♈43	5♈28	0♒47	27 34	3 15	17 16	2 50	4R45	23 02	☿ 21/8 13♌13
20	1♓18	14 14	12 56	3 01	27 55	3D19	17 34	3 06	4 42	22 30	☿ 19/11 15♐00
2 3	11 22	19 43	20 20	5 11	28 06	3 30	17 48	3 18	4 35	21 58	☿ 8/12 28♏46
12	21 22	22 14	27 40	7 15	28R06	3 48	17 56	3 28	4 25	21 27	♀ 14/3 22♈18
22	1♈19	20R54	4♉56	9 11	27 57	4 11	17 59	3 34	4 13	20 55	♀ 25/4 6♈00
1 4	11 13	15 54	12 07	10 57	27 38	4 41	17R57	3 37	3 59	20 23	♃ 5/6 16♒58
11	21 04	9 52	19 13	12 33	27 10	5 15	17 50	3R37	3 43	19 51	♃ 3/10 7♒07
21	0♉51	6 19	26 15	13 57	26 35	5 53	17 38	3 33	3 26	19 20	♄ 7/3 28♏07
1 5	10 35	6D41	3♊13	15 06	25 55	6 35	17 22	3 26	3 09	18 48	♄ 26/7 21♏28
11	20 16	10 26	10 07	16 00	25 11	7 20	17 02	3 17	2 53	18 16	♅ 23/3 17♐59
21	29 54	16 37	16 56	16 37	24 26	8 06	16 40	3 05	2 38	17 44	♅ 23/8 13♐58
31	9♊30	24 26	23 41	16 56	23 43	8 53	16 16	2 52	2 24	17 12	♆ 5/4 3♑37
10 6	19 05	3♉21	0♋23	16R56	23 02	9 40	15 51	2 36	2 13	16 41	♆ 12/9 0♑51
20	28 38	13 03	7 02	16 37	22 28	10 26	15 27	2 21	2 04	16 09	♇ 6/2 4♏45
30	8♋10	23 18	13 37	15 59	22 00	11 11	15 04	2 04	1 58	15 37	♇ 12/7 1♏56
10 7	17 42	3♊58	20 10	15 06	21 40	11 53	14 43	1 49	1 56	15 05	⚷ 10/2 3♊15
20	27 14	14 56	26 40	13 59	21 30	12 32	14 26	1 34	1D57	14 34	⚷ 21/9 14♊40
30	6♌47	26 10	3♌08	12 45	21D29	13 07	14 12	1 20	2 01	14 02	
9 8	16 22	7♋36	9 34	11 27	21 38	13 37	14 03	1 09	2 09	13 30	
19	25 58	19 14	15 58	10 11	21 57	14 02	13 58	1 00	2 20	12 58	
29	5♍37	1♌01	22 21	9 04	22 24	14 21	13D59	0 54	2 34	12 27	
8 9	15 18	12 57	28 42	8 09	23 00	14 34	14 04	0 51	2 51	11 55	
18	25 02	25 01	5♍03	7 30	23 45	14 39	14 15	0D52	3 10	11 23	
28	4♎49	7♍11	11 22	7 10	24 35	14R38	14 31	0 55	3 31	10 51	
8 10	14 40	19 27	17 40	7D09	25 32	14 30	14 51	1 02	3 53	10 19	
18	24 34	1♎49	23 58	7 29	26 34	14 15	15 15	1 12	4 17	9 48	
28	4♏31	14 15	0♎14	8 07	27 40	13 53	15 44	1 25	4 41	9 16	
7 11	14 32	26 43	6 30	9 03	28 49	13 27	16 15	1 41	5 05	8 44	
17	24 35	9♏15	12 45	10 15	0♐00	12 56	16 48	1 58	5 29	8 12	
27	4♐42	21 48	18 59	11 42	1 11	12 22	17 24	2 18	5 52	7 41	
7 12	14 50	4♐22	25 11	13 22	2 22	11 47	18 00	2 40	6 13	7 09	
17	25 00	16 57	1♏22	15 12	3 31	11 13	18 37	3 02	6 32	6 37	
27	5♑11	29 32	7 31	17 13	4 38	10 40	19 13	3 24	6 48	6 05	

SID M/N 1st JAN 6 h 41 m 24 s — 1986 COMMON — BST 30/3 to 26/10

DAY	JAN	FEB	MAR	APR	MAY	JUN	JUL	AUG	SEP	OCT	NOV	DEC
☽ 1	5♍04	26♎19	7♏02	0♑20	8♒33	27♓32	1♉03	15♊07	29♋24	2♍43	21♎26	28♏39
3	1♎50	24♏22	5♐23	28♑11	5♓09	22♈06	24♉49	8♋57	24♌34	29♍24	20♏31	29♐03
5	29♎33	22♐49	3♑32	25♒02	0♈31	15♉59	18♊26	3♌22	20♍45	27♎17	20♐15	29♑08
7	28♏18	21♑23	1♒18	20♓56	24♈59	9♊37	12♋19	28♌32	17♎49	25♏55	19♑34	27♒48
9	27♐43	19♒26	28♒26	15♈57	18♉55	3♋20	6♌41	24♍27	15♏32	24♐42	17♒47	24♓41
11	26♑59	16♓21	24♓38	10♉14	12♊35	27♋22	1♍40	21♎08	13♐44	23♑07	14♓42	20♈07
13	25♒06	11♈51	19♈47	4♊01	6♋17	21♌58	27♍26	18♏40	12♑10	20♒53	10♈29	14♉37
15	21♓32	6♉10	13♉59	27♊40	0♌22	17♍31	24♎15	17♐06	10♒31	17♓49	5♉26	8♊37
17	16♈23	29♉51	7♊41	21♋43	25♌19	14♎23	22♏24	16♑10	8♓20	13♈52	29♉47	2♋24
19	10♉15	23♊38	1♋28	16♌44	21♍36	12♏54	21♐47	15♒14	5♈11	9♉01	23♊41	26♋09
21	3♊51	18♋09	25♋59	13♍14	19♎37	12♐51	21♑45	13♓25	0♉49	3♊23	17♋24	20♌07
23	27♊50	13♌51	21♌48	11♎27	19♏16	13♑16	21♒07	10♈08	25♉22	27♊13	11♌17	14♍39
25	22♋40	10♍49	19♍09	11♏02	19♐43	12♒51	18♓56	5♉21	19♊15	20♋58	5♍50	10♎15
27	18♌30	8♎42	17♎47	11♐04	19♑42	10♓38	14♈56	29♉30	13♋02	15♌13	1♎40	7♏29
29	15♍10		17♏01	10♑28	18♒10	6♈32	9♉29	23♊14	7♌21	10♍32	29♎16	6♐37
31	12♎29		16♐04		14♓49		3♊17	17♋11		7♎23		7♑06
☿ 1	22♐54	11♒48	28♓11	18♓04	18♈49	20♊56	3♌28	25♋57	3♍41	25♎36	29♏03	18♏27
7	1♑43	22 23	1♈18	20 26	29 04	2♋39	6 07	26D35	15 17	4♏14	27R28	25 50
13	10 50	3♓15	29R10	25 12	10♉26	12 54	6R02	1♌09	26 18	12 16	20 44	4♐18
19	20 15	14 00	23 52	1♈46	22 50	21 32	3 20	9 18	6♎40	19 27	14 11	13 12
25	29 59	23 29	19 20	9 42	5♊55	28 29	29♋16	19 58	16 25	25 20	13D41	22 20
31	10♒05		17D57		18 51		26 12	1♍42		28 50		1♑38

DATE	☉	♀	♂	♃	♄	⚷	♅	♆	♇	☊	STATIONS
1 1	10♑17	5♑49	10♏35	18♒16	5♐10	10♊25	19♐30	3♑36	6♏55	5♉49	
11	20 28	18 24	16 40	20 27	6 10	9 59	20 04	3 58	7 07	5 18	☿ 7/3 1♈19
21	0♒39	0♒59	22 42	22 44	7 05	9 38	20 36	4 20	7 16	4 46	☿ 30/3 17♓56
31	10 49	13 33	28 40	25 04	7 53	9 23	21 04	4 40	7 21	4 14	☿ 10/7 6♌26
10 2	20 57	26 05	4♐33	27 27	8 33	9 15	21 29	4 58	7R22	3 42	☿ 3/8 25♋44
20	1♓04	8♓37	10 20	29 51	9 05	9D15	21 50	5 14	7 20	3 10	☿ 2/11 29♏10
2 3	11 07	21 07	16 00	2♓15	9 27	9 22	22 05	5 27	7 14	2 39	☿ 22/11 13♏06
12	21 08	3♈34	21 31	4 37	9 39	9 37	22 16	5 37	7 05	2 07	♀ 16/10 20♏23
22	1♈05	15 59	26 50	6 57	9R42	9 58	22 22	5 44	6 54	1 35	♀ 26/11 4♏54
1 4	10 59	28 21	1♑56	9 13	9 34	10 25	22R22	5 48	6 40	1 03	♂ 9/6 23♑07
11	20 49	10♉40	6 43	11 23	9 17	10 58	22 17	5R49	6 24	0 32	♂ 12/8 11♑25
21	0♉37	22 56	11 09	13 26	8 51	11 36	22 07	5 46	6 08	0 00	♃ 13/7 22♓52
1 5	10 21	5♊08	15 05	15 22	8 18	12 18	21 53	5 40	5 51	29♈28	♃ 8/11 12♓58
11	20 02	17 16	18 26	17 08	7 39	13 03	21 35	5 31	5 34	28 56	♄ 19/3 9♐42
21	29 40	29 19	21 00	18 42	6 56	13 51	21 14	5 20	5 19	28 25	♄ 7/8 3♐04
31	9♊16	11♋18	22 37	20 04	6 11	14 39	20 51	5 07	5 05	27 53	♅ 27/3 22♐23
10 6	18 51	23 11	23R06	21 11	5 27	15 29	20 26	4 52	4 53	27 21	♅ 28/8 18♐21
20	28 24	4♌57	22 21	22 02	4 46	16 18	20 02	4 36	4 43	26 49	♆ 7/4 5♑49
30	7♋56	16 36	20 27	22 36	4 10	17 07	19 38	4 20	4 36	26 17	♆ 15/9 3♑03
10 7	17 28	28 06	17 45	22 51	3 41	17 53	19 16	4 04	4 33	25 46	♇ 9/2 7♏22
20	27 01	9♍23	14 54	22R47	3 20	18 37	18 57	3 49	4D33	25 14	♇ 15/7 4♏33
30	6♌34	20 27	12 38	22 23	3 07	19 17	18 42	3 35	4 36	24 42	⚷ 15/2 9♊14
9 8	16 08	1♎13	11 30	21 41	3D04	19 53	18 30	3 23	4 43	24 10	⚷ 29/9 21♊23
19	25 44	11 34	11D44	20 43	3 11	20 23	18 23	3 14	4 53	23 39	
29	5♍23	21 24	13 18	19 32	3 27	20 48	18D21	3 07	5 06	23 07	
8 9	15 04	0♏30	16 03	18 15	3 53	21 07	18 25	3 03	5 22	22 35	
18	24 48	8 33	19 47	16 55	4 27	21 18	18 33	3D03	5 41	22 03	
28	4♎35	15 03	24 18	15 40	5 09	21 23	18 46	3 05	6 01	21 31	
8 10	14 26	19 17	29 26	14 35	5 58	21R20	19 04	3 12	6 24	21 00	
18	24 19	20R17	5♒04	13 44	6 54	21 09	19 27	3 21	6 47	20 28	
28	4♏17	17 25	11 05	13 11	7 55	20 52	19 53	3 33	7 11	19 56	
7 11	14 17	11 44	17 23	12 58	9 00	20 28	20 23	3 48	7 35	19 24	
17	24 21	6 36	23 55	13D06	10 08	19 59	20 55	4 05	7 59	18 53	
27	4♐27	4D55	0♓36	13 33	11 18	19 26	21 30	4 25	8 22	18 21	
7 12	14 35	7 08	7 25	14 20	12 29	18 51	22 06	4 46	8 44	17 49	
17	24 45	12 25	14 19	15 25	13 40	18 14	22 42	5 08	9 03	17 17	
27	4♑56	19 49	21 16	16 45	14 49	17 39	23 18	5 30	9 21	16 46	

SID M/N 1st JAN 6 h 40 m 26 s 1987 COMMON BST 29/3 to 25/10

DAY	JAN	FEB	MAR	APR	MAY	JUN	JUL	AUG	SEP	OCT	NOV	DEC
1	22♑26	14♓47	22♓38	10♉56	14♊01	28♋18	0♍42	16♎35	6♐01	14♑36	8♓01	16♈01
☽ 3	22♒24	12♈15	20♈02	6♊02	8♋09	22♌02	24♍54	12♏31	4♑09	13♒18	5♈58	12♉34
5	20♓35	7♉54	15♉51	0♋13	1♌55	16♍15	20♎07	10♐06	3♒29	12♓16	3♉21	8♊24
7	16♈49	2♊18	10♊23	24♋01	25♌53	11♎34	16♏58	9♑24	3♓20	10♈53	29♉51	3♋25
9	11♉38	26♊05	4♋15	18♌01	20♍39	8♏34	15♐47	9♒46	2♈39	8♉31	25♊16	27♋40
11	5♊37	19♋50	28♋03	12♍47	16♎48	7♐26	16♑03	9♓55	0♉35	4♊47	19♋40	21♌23
13	29♊21	13♌55	22♌18	8♎44	14♏33	7♑31	16♒34	8♈42	26♉52	29♊44	13♌27	15♍04
15	23♋08	8♍34	17♍21	5♏56	13♐37	7♒36	15♓57	5♉40	21♊44	23♋47	7♍13	9♎25
17	17♌11	3♎52	13♎20	4♐08	13♑08	6♓33	13♈34	1♊02	15♋45	17♌30	1♎39	5♏07
19	11♍40	29♎57	10♏11	2♑46	12♒08	3♈55	9♉31	25♊21	9♌28	11♍32	27♎21	2♐37
21	6♎49	27♏01	7♐49	1♒19	10♓06	29♈55	4♊18	19♋09	3♍24	6♎24	24♏34	1♑46
23	3♏04	25♐13	6♑01	29♒24	6♈57	24♉55	28♊24	12♌52	27♍56	2♏22	23♐03	1♒39
25	0♐49	24♑22	4♒35	26♓48	2♉51	19♊17	22♋11	6♍49	23♎15	29♏27	22♑02	1♓06
27	0♑10	23♒50	3♓05	23♈25	27♉58	13♋15	15♌54	1♎14	19♏28	27♐19	20♒45	29♓22
29	0♒27		1♈01	19♉10	22♊28	6♌58	9♍46	26♎20	16♐35	25♑35	18♓46	26♈21
31	0♓21		27♈56		16♋26		4♎06	22♏28		23♒55		22♉19
1	3♑12	24♒51	7♓15	13♓33	2♉45	2♋31	13♋35	20♋06	18♍53	2♏37	0♏05	26♏02
☿ 7	12 42	4♓31	1R50	21 22	15 25	9 30	10R00	0♌13	29 04	8 33	27D27	5♐21
13	22 27	11 51	29D57	0♈15	28 25	14 19	7 38	12 00	8♎33	12 26	1♏00	14 43
19	2♒28	14R30	1♓42	10 06	10♊51	16 38	8D01	24 14	17 21	12R52	8 11	24 07
25	12 46	11 21	6 07	20 56	21 53	16R16	11 43	6♍02	25 25	8 27	16 52	3♑37
31	23 08		12 22		1♋09		18 39	17 07		1 07		13 14

DATE	☉	♀	♂	♃	♄	⚷	♅	♆	♇	☊	STATIONS
1 1	10♑02	24♏05	24♓45	17♓31	15♐23	17♊22	23♐36	5♑42	9♏28	16♈30	
11	20 13	3♐28	1♈44	19 12	16 28	16 52	24 11	6 04	9 41	15 58	☿ 19/2 14♓30
21	0♒24	13 38	8 44	21 04	17 29	16 26	24 43	6 26	9 50	15 26	☿ 13/3 29♒57
31	10 34	24 21	15 42	23 05	18 24	16 06	25 13	6 46	9 56	14 54	☿ 21/6 16♋49
10 2	20 43	5♑28	22 39	25 14	19 13	15 54	25 40	7 05	9 59	14 23	☿ 15/7 7♋24
20	0♓49	16 52	29 35	27 30	19 54	15 49	26 02	7 21	9R58	13 51	☿ 17/10 13♏13
2 3	10 52	28 27	6♉28	29 50	20 27	15D52	26 20	7 35	9 53	13 19	☿ 6/11 27♎24
12	20 53	10♒12	13 18	2♈12	20 51	16 02	26 33	7 46	9 45	12 47	♃ 20/8 29♈44
22	0♈50	22 03	20 06	4 37	21 05	16 20	26 41	7 54	9 34	12 15	♃ 15/12 19♈46
1 4	10 44	3♓59	26 51	7 02	21R10	16 45	26 44	7 59	9 21	11 44	♄ 31/3 21♐10
11	20 35	15 58	3♊33	9 27	21 04	17 16	26R41	8R00	9 06	11 12	♄ 19/8 14♐32
21	0♉22	28 00	10 13	11 50	20 48	17 53	26 34	7 58	8 49	10 40	♅ 1/4 26♐44
1 5	10 06	10♈03	16 49	14 09	20 24	18 34	26 21	7 53	8 33	10 08	♅ 2/9 22♐43
11	19 48	22 09	23 24	16 24	19 53	19 19	26 05	7 45	8 16	9 37	♆ 10/4 8♑00
21	29 26	4♉15	29 56	18 34	19 15	20 08	25 46	7 34	8 00	9 05	♆ 17/9 5♑14
31	9♊02	16 23	6♋25	20 36	18 33	20 59	25 23	7 22	7 45	8 33	♇ 11/2 9♏59
10 6	18 37	28 32	12 53	22 30	17 48	21 51	24 59	7 07	7 33	8 01	♇ 18/7 7♏09
20	28 10	10♊42	19 19	24 15	17 05	22 43	24 35	6 52	7 22	7 30	⚷ 21/2 15♊49
30	7♋42	22 53	25 44	25 48	16 23	23 35	24 11	6 35	7 15	6 58	⚷ 8/10 28♊50
10 7	17 14	5♋07	2♌07	27 08	15 46	24 26	23 48	6 19	7 10	6 26	
20	26 47	17 22	8 30	28 13	15 15	25 15	23 27	6 04	7D09	5 54	
30	6♌20	29 40	14 51	29 02	14 52	26 00	23 10	5 50	7 12	5 22	
9 8	15 54	11♌59	21 13	29 32	14 37	26 42	22 57	5 37	7 18	4 51	
19	25 30	24 20	27 35	29 44	14 32	27 19	22 47	5 27	7 27	4 19	
29	5♍09	6♍44	3♍56	29R36	14D37	27 51	22 43	5 20	7 39	3 47	
8 9	14 50	19 08	10 18	29 08	14 51	28 16	22D44	5 15	7 54	3 15	
18	24 34	1♎34	16 41	28 21	15 15	28 35	22 50	5D14	8 12	2 44	
28	4♎21	14 00	23 05	27 19	15 47	28 46	23 01	5 16	8 32	2 12	
8 10	14 11	26 27	29 29	26 05	16 28	28 50	23 17	5 21	8 54	1 40	
18	24 05	8♏54	5♎55	24 45	17 16	28R45	23 37	5 30	9 17	1 08	
28	4♏02	21 21	12 22	23 25	18 10	28 33	24 01	5 41	9 41	0 36	
7 11	14 03	3♐48	18 51	22 11	19 10	28 14	24 30	5 55	10 05	0 05	
17	24 06	16 14	25 21	21 08	20 14	27 48	25 01	6 12	10 29	29♓33	
27	4♐12	28 41	1♏53	20 21	21 22	27 17	25 34	6 31	10 52	29 01	
7 12	14 20	11♑06	8 26	19 53	22 32	26 42	26 10	6 52	11 14	28 29	
17	24 30	23 30	15 01	19D46	23 42	26 05	26 46	7 14	11 35	27 58	
27	4♑41	5♒51	21 37	20 00	24 53	25 27	27 22	7 36	11 53	27 26	

SID M/N 1st JAN 6 h 39 m 29 s   1988 LEAP   BST 27/3 to 23/10

DAY	JAN	FEB	MAR	APR	MAY	JUN	JUL	AUG	SEP	OCT	NOV	DEC
1	5♊00	21♋00	11♌43	25♍55	29♎07	17♐45	25♑24	19♓02	11♉36	17♊41	4♌03	5♍56
☽ 3	29♊51	14♌46	5♍22	20♎23	25♏05	15♑58	24♒47	18♈03	8♊45	13♋22	28♌01	29♍32
5	24♋07	8♍25	29♍13	15♏40	22♐02	14♒33	23♓42	15♉44	4♋22	7♌45	21♍35	23♎27
7	17♌54	2♎11	23♎34	11♐51	19♑43	12♓58	21♈44	12♊04	28♋52	1♍27	15♎24	18♏16
9	11♍30	26♎31	18♏41	8♑57	17♒49	10♈59	18♉50	7♋20	22♌43	25♍02	9♏55	14♐15
11	5♎23	21♏57	14♐55	6♒59	16♓09	8♉31	15♊02	1♌47	16♍18	18♎54	5♐18	11♑18
13	0♏10	19♐00	12♑32	5♓48	14♈31	5♊24	10♋23	25♌40	9♎57	13♏19	1♑32	9♒02
15	26♏34	17♑53	11♒32	4♈59	12♉33	1♋25	4♌57	19♍16	3♏58	8♐29	28♑30	7♓05
17	24♐56	18♒05	11♓26	3♉50	9♊46	26♋27	28♌52	12♎53	28♏43	4♑33	26♒09	5♈14
19	24♑53	18♓28	11♈14	1♊35	5♋48	20♌35	22♍27	7♏01	24♐34	1♒40	24♓29	3♉23
21	25♒19	17♈47	9♉56	27♊50	0♌34	14♍13	16♎12	2♐12	21♑53	0♓00	23♈20	1♊18
23	24♓54	15♉23	6♊57	22♋40	24♌29	8♎00	10♏47	28♐57	20♒47	29♓23	22♉10	28♊33
25	22♈54	11♊18	2♋20	16♌35	18♍08	2♏38	6♐50	27♑29	20♓50	29♈09	20♊12	24♋43
27	19♉20	5♋58	26♋34	10♍13	12♎14	28♏42	4♑41	27♒27	21♈02	28♉16	16♋49	19♌40
29	14♊34	29♋54	20♌15	4♎14	7♏25	26♐26	4♒05	27♓48	20♉13	25♊52	11♌55	13♍41
31	8♋59		13♍56		3♐59		4♓08	27♈22		21♋42		7♎18
1	14♑52	27♒55	14♒39	23♓15	22♉37	26♊47	19♊37	6♌33	1♎39	26♎48	21♎36	8♐48
☿ 7	24 41	26℞02	19 19	3♈45	3♊55	25℞30	23 57	18 54	9 44	23℞00	0♏36	18 14
13	4♒35	19 31	25 45	15 07	13 16	22 27	0♋59	0♍31	16 49	16 09	10 10	27 39
19	14 13	14 02	3♓26	27 19	20 21	19 24	10 30	11 16	22 33	11 47	19 48	7♑07
25	22 35	12D46	12 05	10♉05	24 54	18D09	21 58	21 09	26 16	13D37	29 21	16 36
31	27 36		21 35		26 45		4♌27	0♎13		20 14		25 52

DATE	☉	♀	♂	♃	♄	⚷	♅	♆	♇	☊	STATIONS
1 1	9♑47	12♒01	24♏56	20♈14	25♐28	25♊09	27♐40	7♑48	12♏00	27♓10	
11	19 59	24 18	1♐35	20 58	26 37	24 34	28 15	8 10	12 14	26 38	☿ 2/2 28♒04
21	0♒10	6♓30	8 15	21 59	27 42	24 03	28 49	8 32	12 25	26 06	☿ 24/2 12♒41
31	10 20	18 36	14 56	23 17	28 43	23 38	29 20	8 53	12 32	25 35	☿ 1/6 26♊47
10 2	20 28	0♈33	21 38	24 49	29 39	23 20	29 48	9 12	12 35	25 03	☿ 25/6 18♊09
20	0♓34	12 19	28 22	26 33	0♑29	23 09	0♑12	9 29	12℞35	24 31	☿ 29/9 27♎04
1 3	10 38	23 51	5♑06	28 27	1 12	23D07	0 32	9 44	12 31	23 59	☿ 20/10 11♎39
11	20 39	5♉06	11 51	0♉30	1 46	23 12	0 47	9 55	12 24	23 28	♀ 23/5 0♋26
21	0♈36	15 57	18 36	2 40	2 11	23 26	0 57	10 04	12 14	22 56	♀ 5/7 13♊55
31	10 30	26 19	25 21	4 55	2 27	23 47	1 02	10 10	12 01	22 24	♂ 27/8 11♈29
10 4	20 21	6♊00	2♒05	7 14	2 33	24 15	1℞02	10 12	11 47	21 52	♂ 28/10 29♓54
20	0♉08	14 44	8 47	9 36	2℞29	24 50	0 57	10℞10	11 31	21 20	♃ 25/9 6♊08
30	9 52	22 09	15 26	11 59	2 16	25 31	0 47	10 06	11 14	20 49	♄ 11/4 2♑33
10 5	19 34	27 38	22 02	14 22	1 53	26 16	0 32	9 59	10 57	20 17	♄ 30/8 25♐56
20	29 12	0♋19	28 31	16 44	1 23	27 05	0 14	9 49	10 41	19 45	♅ 5/4 1♑03
30	8♊48	29℞19	4♓52	19 04	0 46	27 57	29♐53	9 36	10 26	19 13	♅ 5/9 27♐02
9 6	18 23	24 39	11 02	21 21	0 05	28 51	29 30	9 22	10 13	18 42	♆ 11/4 10♑12
19	27 56	18 34	16 57	23 33	29♐21	29 47	29 06	9 07	10 02	18 10	♆ 19/9 7♑25
29	7♋28	14 32	22 33	25 39	28 37	0♋43	28 41	8 51	9 53	17 38	♇ 14/2 12♏35
9 7	17 01	14D17	27 42	27 38	27 55	1 38	28 18	8 35	9 48	17 06	♇ 20/7 9♏46
19	26 33	17 31	2♈18	29 29	27 17	2 32	27 56	8 19	9 46	16 35	⚷ 28/ 2 23♊07
29	6♌06	23 18	6 11	1♊10	26 44	3 24	27 37	8 05	9D47	16 03	⚷ 16/10 7♋10
8 8	15 40	0♋50	9 09	2 38	26 19	4 12	27 22	7 52	9 52	15 31	
18	25 16	9 36	10 58	3 54	26 03	4 56	27 11	7 41	10 00	14 59	
28	4♍55	19 14	11℞28	4 54	25 56	5 35	27 04	7 33	10 12	14 27	
7 9	14 36	29 30	10 35	5 37	25D59	6 09	27D02	7 28	10 26	13 56	
17	24 19	10♌15	8 27	6 02	26 11	6 36	27 06	7 25	10 43	13 24	
27	4♎06	21 23	5 36	6℞07	26 33	6 55	27 14	7D26	11 02	12 52	
7 10	13 57	2♍50	2 47	5 52	27 04	7 07	27 28	7 31	11 24	12 20	
17	23 51	14 32	0 45	5 18	27 43	7℞10	27 46	7 39	11 47	11 49	
27	3♏48	26 26	29♓55	4 25	28 30	7 05	28 09	7 49	12 10	11 17	
6 11	13 48	8♎31	0D24	3 18	29 23	6 52	28 35	8 03	12 35	10 45	
16	23 51	20 43	2 06	2 01	0♑22	6 32	29 05	8 19	12 59	10 13	
26	3♐57	3♏01	4 50	0 39	1 26	6 04	29 37	8 38	13 22	9 41	
6 12	14 06	15 24	8 22	29♉20	2 33	5 31	0♑12	8 58	13 45	9 10	
16	24 15	27 50	12 33	28 08	3 43	4 54	0 48	9 20	14 05	8 38	
26	4♑26	10♐18	17 14	27 10	4 53	4 15	1 24	9 42	14 24	8 06	

SID M/N 1st JAN 6 h 42 m 28 s 1989 COMMON BST 26/3 to 29/10

DAY	JAN	FEB	MAR	APR	MAY	JUN	JUL	AUG	SEP	OCT	NOV	DEC
1	19♎11	3♐58	12♐15	0♒42	8♓14	1♉49	10♊33	0♌42	17♍03	19♎41	4♐18	8♑03
☽ 3	13♏32	0♑17	8♑20	29♒00	7♈30	1♊10	8♋24	26♌12	11♎02	13♏23	28♐34	3♒21
5	9♐07	28♑17	6♒10	28♓49	7♉34	29♊49	5♌06	20♍45	4♏44	7♐15	23♑31	29♒33
7	6♑11	27♒36	5♓37	29♈17	7♊17	27♋00	0♍28	14♎39	28♏34	1♑41	19♒35	26♓56
9	4♒27	27♓20	5♈56	29♉04	5♋32	22♌33	24♍46	8♏22	23♐03	27♑12	17♓15	25♈42
11	3♓17	26♈33	5♉53	27♊11	1♌55	16♍52	18♎32	2♐32	18♑47	24♒19	16♈38	25♉28
13	2♈01	24♉39	4♊29	23♋25	26♌43	10♎35	12♏24	27♐41	16♒10	23♓19	17♉05	25♊13
15	0♉13	21♊29	1♋22	18♌09	20♍35	4♏24	7♐00	24♑16	15♓14	23♈40	17♊17	23♋51
17	27♉45	17♋12	26♋47	12♍02	14♎13	28♏51	2♑43	22♒20	15♈19	24♉10	15♋59	20♌43
19	24♊32	12♌02	21♌11	5♎38	8♏07	24♐13	29♑39	21♓26	15♉15	23♊27	12♌41	15♍57
21	20♋29	6♍12	15♍01	29♎23	2♐39	20♑31	27♒34	20♈47	14♊02	20♋51	7♍44	10♎05
23	15♌31	29♍57	8♎40	23♏33	27♐54	17♒35	26♓01	19♉37	11♋13	16♌30	1♎46	3♏48
25	9♍43	23♎35	2♏23	18♐17	23♑55	15♓17	24♈33	17♊28	7♌00	10♍59	25♎27	27♏40
27	3♎25	17♏31	26♏29	13♑47	20♒43	13♈30	22♉51	14♋14	1♍45	4♎51	19♏14	22♐07
29	27♎06		21♐17	10♒20	18♓28	12♉03	20♊36	9♌58	25♍53	28♎33	13♐23	17♑18
31	21♏23		17♑11		17♈11		17♋35	4♍52		22♏20		13♒16
1	27♑22	27♑34	15♒53	7♈33	1♊13	28♉50	20♊56	22♌54	5♎32	26♍31	2♏23	19♐57
☿ 7	5♒34	26D04	24 20	19 48	5 35	28D16	1♋53	3♍18	9 26	26D31	12 15	29 06
13	11 02	28 41	3♓32	2♉17	6R51	0♊21	14 15	12 44	10R29	2♎03	21 54	8♑01
19	11R04	3♒54	13 28	14 01	5 18	4 58	27 06	21 12	7 45	10 46	1♐22	16 20
25	5 01	10 43	24 08	23 54	2 05	11 54	9♌32	28 36	1 45	20 39	10 42	23 01
31	28♑18		5♈35		29♉10		21 04	4♎41		0♏43		25R54

DATE	☉	♀	♂	♃	♄	⚷	♅	♆	♇	☊	STATIONS
1 1	10♑33	17♐48	20♈13	26♉44	5♑36	3♋51	1♑45	9♑56	14♏34	7♓47	
11	20 45	0♑19	25 27	26R14	6 46	3 13	2 21	10 18	14 48	7 15	☿ 16/1 11♒54
21	0♒56	12 50	0♉56	26D06	7 55	2 38	2 55	10 40	14 59	6 44	☿ 6/2 25♑59
31	11 06	25 21	6 36	26 17	9 00	2 08	3 27	11 01	15 07	6 12	☿ 12/5 6♊51
10 2	21 14	7♒52	12 25	26 49	10 02	1 44	3 56	11 21	15 11	5 40	☿ 5/6 28♉10
20	1♓20	20 23	18 20	27 39	10 58	1 27	4 21	11 38	15R11	5 08	☿ 12/9 10♎33
2 3	11 23	2♓52	24 20	28 46	11 48	1 19	4 42	11 53	15 08	4 36	☿ 4/10 25♍44
12	21 24	15 21	0♊24	0♊08	12 31	1D19	4 59	12 05	15 02	4 05	☿ 31/12 25♑54
22	1♈21	27 48	6 30	1 43	13 06	1 28	5 11	12 14	14 52	3 33	♀ 29/12 6♒26
1 4	11 15	10♈14	12 38	3 28	13 32	1 45	5 18	12 20	14 40	3 01	♃ 20/1 26♉06
11	21 05	22 39	18 47	5 23	13 48	2 10	5R20	12 23	14 26	2 29	♃ 29/10 10♋52
21	0♉53	5♉01	24 57	7 25	13 55	2 43	5 16	12R22	14 10	1 58	♄ 23/4 13♑55
1 5	10 36	17 22	1♋08	9 34	13R52	3 21	5 08	12 18	13 54	1 26	♄ 11/9 7♑18
11	20 17	29 41	7 19	11 46	13 40	4 06	4 55	12 11	13 37	0 54	♅ 9/4 5♑20
21	29 56	11♊58	13 30	14 03	13 18	4 56	4 38	12 02	13 20	0 22	♅ 10/9 1♑20
31	9♊32	24 14	19 42	16 21	12 49	5 49	4 18	11 50	13 05	29♒51	♆ 14/4 12♑23
10 6	19 06	6♋28	25 55	18 40	12 13	6 45	3 56	11 36	12 51	29 19	♆ 21/9 9♑37
20	28 40	18 41	2♌08	20 59	11 32	7 44	3 32	11 21	12 40	28 47	♇ 16/2 15♏12
30	8♋12	0♌51	8 21	23 16	10 48	8 43	3 08	11 05	12 31	28 15	♇ 23/7 12♏22
10 7	17 44	13 00	14 36	25 31	10 04	9 43	2 44	10 48	12 25	27 43	⚷ 7/3 1♋18
20	27 16	25 06	20 51	27 42	9 21	10 42	2 21	10 33	12 23	27 12	⚷ 27/10 16♋36
30	6♌49	7♍10	27 08	29 48	8 43	11 40	2 01	10 18	12D23	26 40	
9 8	16 24	19 10	3♍26	1♋48	8 10	12 35	1 45	10 05	12 27	26 08	
19	26 00	1♎06	9 46	3 40	7 44	13 26	1 32	9 54	12 35	25 36	
29	5♍39	12 57	16 08	5 23	7 26	14 14	1 24	9 45	12 46	25 05	
8 9	15 20	24 43	22 32	6 55	7 18	14 55	1 20	9 39	12 59	24 33	
18	25 04	6♏23	28 58	8 15	7D20	15 31	1D22	9 37	13 16	24 01	
28	4♎51	17 54	5♎27	9 20	7 32	15 59	1 28	9D37	13 35	23 29	
8 10	14 42	29 15	11 59	10 09	7 53	16 20	1 40	9 41	13 56	22 57	
18	24 36	10♐23	18 34	10 40	8 23	16 32	1 57	9 49	14 18	22 26	
28	4♏33	21 12	25 11	10 52	9 02	16R36	2 18	9 59	14 42	21 54	
7 11	14 34	1♑36	1♏52	10R44	9 48	16 30	2 43	10 12	15 06	21 22	
17	24 37	11 24	8 37	10 16	10 41	16 16	3 11	10 28	15 30	20 50	
27	4♐43	20 19	15 24	9 30	11 40	15 54	3 43	10 46	15 54	20 19	
7 12	14 52	27 56	22 16	8 28	12 44	15 25	4 16	11 06	16 17	19 47	
17	25 02	3♒35	29 11	7 14	13 51	14 50	4 51	11 28	16 38	19 15	
27	5♑13	6 19	6♐09	5 53	15 01	14 11	5 27	11 50	16 57	18 43	

SID M/N 1st JAN 6 h 41 m 31 s — 1990 COMMON — BST 25/3 to 23/10

DAY	JAN	FEB	MAR	APR	MAY	JUN	JUL	AUG	SEP	OCT	NOV	DEC
1	26♒33	18♈30	28♈57	22♊27	29♋55	17♍54	21♎00	4♐57	19♑07	22♒25	11♈49	19♉35
☽ 3	23♓41	16♉52	27♉50	20♋05	26♌07	12♎22	14♏52	28♐55	14♒31	19♓33	11♉35	20♊10
5	21♈39	15♊09	25♊57	16♌22	21♍06	6♏15	8♐38	23♑32	11♓15	18♈16	11♊54	20♋16
7	20♉19	13♋00	23♋07	11♍38	15♎21	0♐00	2♑42	19♒06	9♈11	17♉49	11♋27	18♌50
9	19♊17	10♌09	19♌24	6♎13	9♏14	23♐53	27♑20	15♓40	7♉49	17♊09	9♌31	15♍36
11	17♋49	6♍19	14♍53	0♏21	3♐00	18♑07	22♒42	13♈07	6♊29	15♋31	6♍04	10♎55
13	15♌13	1♎27	9♎38	24♏10	26♐50	12♒56	18♓58	11♉13	4♋43	12♌45	1♎29	5♏17
15	11♍12	25♎43	3♏47	17♐55	21♑00	8♓43	16♈16	9♊40	2♌21	9♍00	26♎07	29♏08
17	5♎56	19♏32	27♏33	11♑59	15♒59	5♈48	14♉35	8♋09	29♌16	4♎29	20♏14	22♐48
19	29♎52	13♐26	21♐24	6♒57	12♓19	4♉25	13♊40	6♌16	25♍25	29♎17	14♐00	16♑32
21	23♏38	8♑04	15♑56	3♓26	10♈26	4♊13	12♋55	3♍36	20♎42	23♏28	7♑37	10♒35
23	17♐51	3♒56	11♒44	1♈50	10♉15	4♋14	11♌29	29♍51	15♏08	17♐11	1♒27	5♓20
25	12♑58	1♓15	9♓17	1♉52	10♊48	3♌18	8♍45	24♎56	8♐57	10♑50	26♒02	1♈14
27	9♒10	29♓49	8♈29	2♊23	10♋41	0♍43	4♎34	19♏07	2♑41	4♒59	22♓00	28♈43
29	6♓24		8♉28	2♋00	8♌54	26♍28	29♎10	12♐52	26♑57	0♓21	19♈53	27♉51
31	4♈21		8♊05		5♍17		23♏04	6♑51		27♓30		28♊04
1	25♑48	16♑44	25♒28	23♈58	15♉05	15♉50	6♋49	3♍34	21♍31	22♍06	14♏30	28♐44
☿ 7	21R15	23 30	5♓40	4♉26	11R23	22 48	19 46	11 09	16R24	2♎12	23 53	5♑37
13	13 37	1♒18	16 31	12 14	8 33	1♊33	2♌00	17 20	11 07	12 46	3♐02	9 43
19	9 48	9 51	28 02	16 37	8D04	11 59	13 10	21 41	9D46	23 09	11 58	8R24
25	11D06	19 01	10♈04	17R24	10 16	23 55	23 14	23 32	13 53	3♏12	20 38	1 17
31	15 45		22 03		14 52		2♍11	22R06		12 54		24♐51

DATE	☉	♀	♂	♃	♄	⚷	♅	♆	♇	☊	STATIONS
1 1	10♑18	6♒17	9♐40	5♋13	15♑36	13♋51	5♑45	12♑02	17♏05	18♒27	
11	20 30	3R10	16 43	3R54	16 47	13 09	6 21	12 24	17 20	17 56	☿ 20/1 9♑42
21	0♒41	27♑20	23 51	2 45	17 58	12 30	6 56	12 46	17 32	17 24	☿ 23/4 17♉32
31	10 51	22 21	1♑01	1 49	19 07	11 53	7 29	13 08	17 41	16 52	☿ 17/5 7♉55
10 2	20 59	20D59	8 15	1 10	20 13	11 22	7 59	13 28	17 46	16 20	☿ 26/8 23♍33
20	1♓05	23 27	15 33	0 51	21 15	10 58	8 26	13 45	17R48	15 49	☿ 18/9 9♍35
2 3	11 09	28 50	22 53	0D51	22 13	10 42	8 49	14 01	17 45	15 17	☿ 15/12 10♑01
12	21 09	6♒13	0♒15	1 11	23 04	10 34	9 08	14 14	17 40	14 45	♀ 8/2 20♑55
22	1♈07	14 56	7 40	1 50	23 48	10D36	9 22	14 24	17 31	14 13	♂ 21/10 14♊33
1 4	11 01	24 33	15 07	2 46	24 24	10 47	9 31	14 31	17 20	13 41	♃ 25/2 0♋49
11	20 51	4♓48	22 35	3 57	24 52	11 06	9 35	14 34	17 06	13 10	♃ 30/11 13♌35
21	0♉38	15 29	0♓03	5 21	25 11	11 34	9R34	14R34	16 51	12 38	♄ 5/5 25♑20
1 5	10 22	26 29	7 32	6 57	25 19	12 10	9 28	14 31	16 35	12 06	♄ 23/9 18♑42
11	20 03	7♈43	14 59	8 43	25R18	12 52	9 17	14 25	16 18	11 34	♅ 14/4 9♑35
21	29 42	19 07	22 24	10 36	25 08	13 40	9 02	14 16	16 01	11 03	♅ 15/9 5♑36
31	9♊18	0♉40	29 47	12 37	24 48	14 34	8 43	14 04	15 45	10 31	♆ 16/4 14♑34
10 6	18 53	12 20	7♈04	14 43	24 20	15 31	8 22	13 51	15 31	9 59	♆ 24/9 11♑48
20	28 26	24 05	14 15	16 53	23 45	16 32	7 59	13 36	15 19	9 27	♇ 19/2 17♏48
30	7♋58	5♊55	21 19	19 05	23 05	17 35	7 35	13 20	15 10	8 56	♇ 26/7 14♏59
10 7	17 30	17 50	28 13	21 19	22 22	18 39	7 10	13 04	15 03	8 24	⚷ 15/3 10♋34
20	27 02	29 49	4♉55	23 34	21 37	19 43	6 47	12 48	14 59	7 52	⚷ 8 11 27♋20
30	6♌36	11♋53	11 23	25 48	20 54	20 47	6 26	12 33	14D59	7 20	
9 8	16 10	24 01	17 33	28 00	20 14	21 49	6 08	12 19	15 02	6 48	
19	25 46	6♌13	23 22	0♌09	19 40	22 49	5 53	12 08	15 09	6 17	
29	5♍25	18 29	28 44	2 14	19 12	23 45	5 43	11 58	15 18	5 45	
8 9	15 06	0♍49	3♊34	4 13	18 53	24 37	5 37	11 52	15 31	5 13	
18	24 50	13 12	7 44	6 05	18 43	25 23	5D36	11 48	15 47	4 41	
28	4♎37	25 38	11 05	7 49	18D43	26 02	5 40	11D48	16 05	4 10	
8 10	14 27	8♎06	13 24	9 22	18 53	26 35	5 50	11 51	16 26	3 38	
18	24 21	20 37	14 30	10 44	19 12	26 59	6 04	11 58	16 48	3 06	
28	4♏19	3♏08	14R11	11 52	19 41	27 14	6 23	12 07	17 11	2 34	
7 11	14 19	15 41	12 24	12 44	20 19	27 20	6 46	12 20	17 35	2 02	
17	24 23	28 14	9 22	13 18	21 04	27R16	7 13	12 35	17 59	1 31	
27	4♐29	10♐48	5 39	13 34	21 57	27 03	7 43	12 53	18 23	0 59	
7 12	14 37	23 21	2 05	13R31	22 55	26 41	8 16	13 13	18 46	0 27	
17	24 47	5♑55	29♉23	13 08	23 58	26 12	8 50	13 34	19 08	29♑55	
27	4♑58	18 28	27 57	12 26	25 05	25 36	9 26	13 56	19 27	29 24	

SID M/N 1st JAN 6 h 40 m 34 s 1991 COMMON BST

DAY		JAN	FEB	MAR	APR	MAY	JUN	JUL	AUG	SEP	OCT	NOV	DEC
	1	13♋13	4♍52	12♍53	1♏03	4♐11	18♑20	20♒59	7♈49	28♉14	7♋02	0♍07	7♎54
☽	3	12♌51	2♎11	9♎58	25♏57	28♐04	12♒02	15♓28	4♉10	26♊14	5♌19	27♍36	3♏59
	5	10♍55	27♎54	5♏42	19♐58	21♑40	6♓22	11♈03	1♊49	25♋01	3♍41	24♎26	29♏12
	7	7♎11	22♏20	0♐12	13♑37	15♒35	1♈57	8♉09	0♋44	24♌11	1♎43	20♏21	23♐39
	9	2♏02	16♐05	23♐59	7♒33	10♓30	29♈16	6♊54	0♌31	23♍01	28♎53	15♐16	17♑30
	11	26♏00	9♑46	17♑41	2♓30	7♈02	28♉22	6♋54	0♍15	20♎43	24♏47	9♑18	11♒04
	13	19♐38	3♒56	12♒01	28♓57	5♉21	28♊33	7♌08	28♍55	16♏51	19♐26	2♒54	4♓50
	15	13♑23	28♒56	7♓27	26♈57	4♊57	28♋39	6♍28	25♎54	11♐34	13♑14	26♒41	29♓25
	17	7♒34	24♓55	4♈10	25♉55	4♋47	27♌37	4♎10	21♏15	5♑23	6♒53	21♓23	25♈24
	19	2♓25	21♈47	1♉56	25♊00	3♌51	25♍01	0♏10	15♐25	29♑01	1♓05	17♈33	23♉10
	21	28♓06	19♉23	0♊13	23♋31	1♍41	20♎56	24♏50	9♑03	23♒08	26♓25	15♉21	22♊32
	23	24♈50	17♊33	28♊32	21♌14	28♍18	15♏45	18♐43	2♒45	18♓11	23♈09	14♊23	22♋41
	25	22♉45	16♋07	26♋39	18♍08	23♎53	9♐50	12♑19	26♒59	14♈19	21♉02	13♋49	22♌29
	27	21♊46	14♌45	24♌26	14♎17	18♏41	3♑31	6♒03	22♓00	11♉21	19♊31	12♌48	21♍02
	29	21♋21		21♍43	9♏38	12♐50	27♑08	0♓13	17♈51	9♊01	18♋00	10♍51	18♎03
	31	20♌37		18♎11		6♑33		25♓03	14♉34		16♌11		13♏43
	1	24♐19	22♑39	8♓57	28♈11	18♈16	22♉22	24♋07	3♍55	23♌04	5♎11	25♏05	23♐44
☿	7	24D27	1♒39	20 23	28℞45	20 51	3♊46	4♌42	5 52	25 55	15 44	3♐34	18℞13
	13	28 42	11 07	2♈03	25 44	25 45	16 21	14 02	4℞47	3♍12	25 48	11 29	10 34
	19	5♑11	21 05	13 08	21 25	2♉30	29 30	22 03	0 46	13 14	5♏27	18 23	7D56
	25	12 50	1♓37	22 10	18 28	10 50	12♋18	28 35	25♌44	24 14	14 42	23 10	10 50
	31	21 12		27 41		20 36		3♍20	23 04		23 38		16 52

DATE	☉	♀	♂	♃	♄	⚷	♅	♆	♇	☊	STATIONS
1 1	10♑04	24♑44	27♉45	11♌58	25♑40	25♋16	9♑44	14♑07	19♏36	29♑08	
11	20 15	7♒16	28D18	10℞54	26 50	24 34	10 20	14 30	19 52	28 36	☿ 4/1 23♐42
21	0♒26	19 47	29 59	9 38	28 02	23 52	10 55	14 52	20 05	28 04	☿ 5/4 29♈02
31	10 36	2♓15	2♊35	8 19	29 13	23 10	11 28	15 14	20 14	27 32	☿ 28/4 17♈59
10 2	20 45	14 42	5 55	7 00	0♒22	22 32	12 00	15 34	20 20	27 01	☿ 8/8 5♍54
20	0♓51	27 05	9 48	5 49	1 29	21 59	12 28	15 53	20 23	26 29	☿ 1/9 23♌03
2 3	10 54	9♈23	14 08	4 49	2 32	21 34	12 53	16 09	20℞22	25 57	☿ 29/11 24♐11
12	20 55	21 37	18 49	4 06	3 31	21 17	13 13	16 22	20 17	25 25	☿ 18/12 7♐54
22	0♈52	3♉45	23 46	3 40	4 24	21 10	13 30	16 33	20 09	24 54	♀ 1/8 7♍19
1 4	10 46	15 46	28 56	3D33	5 09	21D12	13 41	16 41	19 59	24 22	♀ 13/9 20♌59
11	20 37	27 38	4♋16	3 45	5 47	21 23	13 47	16 45	19 46	23 50	♂ 2/1 27♉45
21	0♉24	9♊21	9 45	4 16	6 17	21 44	13℞49	16℞46	19 31	23 18	♃ 31/3 3♌33
1 5	10 08	20 53	15 20	5 03	6 37	22 14	13 45	16 43	19 15	22 46	♃ 31/12 14♍37
11	19 49	2♋10	21 01	6 06	6 48	22 52	13 36	16 38	18 58	22 15	♄ 17/5 6♒50
21	29 28	13 10	26 47	7 22	6℞49	23 37	13 23	16 30	18 42	21 43	♄ 5/10 0♒11
31	9♊04	23 48	2♌38	8 51	6 41	24 29	13 06	16 19	18 26	21 11	♅ 18/4 13♑49
10 6	18 39	3♌56	8 33	10 29	6 23	25 26	12 46	16 06	18 11	20 39	♅ 19/9 9♑50
20	28 12	13 25	14 31	12 16	5 57	26 27	12 23	15 51	17 58	20 08	♆ 19/4 16♑46
30	7♋44	21 58	20 32	14 11	5 23	27 32	12 00	15 35	17 48	19 36	♆ 26/9 13♑59
10 7	17 16	29 14	26 37	16 11	4 44	28 40	11 35	15 19	17 40	19 04	♇ 22/2 20♏23
20	26 49	4♍35	2♍46	18 16	4 01	29 49	11 12	15 03	17 36	18 32	♇ 29/7 17♏34
30	6♌22	7 12	8 57	20 24	3 17	0♌58	10 50	14 48	17D34	18 01	⚷ 25/3 21♋09
9 8	15 56	6℞12	15 13	22 34	2 33	2 08	10 30	14 34	17 36	17 29	⚷ 22 11 9♌36
19	25 32	1 34	21 32	24 45	1 52	3 16	10 13	14 22	17 42	16 57	
29	5♍11	25♌32	27 54	26 56	1 16	4 21	10 01	14 12	17 51	16 25	
8 9	14 52	21 34	4♎21	29 06	0 47	5 23	9 53	14 05	18 03	15 53	
18	24 36	21D24	10 52	1♍13	0 26	6 20	9 50	14 00	18 18	15 22	
28	4♎23	24 46	17 26	3 16	0 14	7 12	9D52	13D59	18 35	14 50	
8 10	14 13	0♍46	24 06	5 14	0D12	7 58	9 59	14 02	18 55	14 18	
18	24 07	8 35	0♏50	7 06	0 20	8 35	10 11	14 07	19 17	13 46	
28	4♏04	17 39	7 38	8 49	0 38	9 05	10 28	14 16	19 40	13 15	
7 11	14 04	27 38	14 31	10 22	1 05	9 25	10 49	14 28	20 03	12 43	
17	24 08	8♎15	21 29	11 43	1 41	9 35	11 14	14 43	20 28	12 11	
27	4♐14	19 21	28 32	12 51	2 26	9℞35	11 43	15 00	20 52	11 39	
7 12	14 22	0♏48	5♐39	13 43	3 18	9 25	12 14	15 19	21 15	11 07	
17	24 32	12 31	12 51	14 19	4 15	9 05	12 48	15 40	21 37	10 36	
27	4♑43	24 26	20 08	14 36	5 18	8 36	13 23	16 02	21 57	10 04	

SID M/N 1st JAN 6 h 39 m 36 s — 1992 LEAP — BST

DAY		JAN	FEB	MAR	APR	MAY	JUN	JUL	AUG	SEP	OCT	NOV	DEC
	1	26♏09	11♑16	1♒41	16♓00	19♈32	8♊35	16♋10	10♍03	2♏33	7♐58	23♑35	25♒21
☽	3	20♐27	4♒50	25♒24	11♈01	16♉04	7♋15	16♌01	9♎27	29♏33	3♑21	17♒33	19♓06
	5	14♑16	28♒34	19♓38	6♉56	13♊34	6♌17	15♍26	7♏10	24♐50	27♑34	11♓17	13♈15
	7	7♒52	22♓43	14♈33	3♊37	11♋38	5♍04	13♎40	3♐11	19♑02	21♒17	5♈25	8♉21
	9	1♓33	17♈29	10♉11	0♋58	9♌57	3♎08	10♏31	27♐58	12♒45	15♓06	0♉21	4♊41
	11	25♓42	13♉12	6♊40	28♋57	8♍16	0♏18	6♐09	22♑00	6♓28	9♈22	26♉14	2♋16
	13	20♈47	10♊13	4♋10	27♌30	6♎20	26♏31	0♑52	15♒45	0♈29	4♉18	23♊00	0♌43
	15	17♉18	8♋46	2♌49	26♍18	3♏48	21♐50	25♑00	9♓28	24♈56	29♉55	20♋29	29♌26
	17	15♊35	8♌39	2♍20	24♎41	0♐20	16♑20	18♒47	3♈25	20♉01	26♊18	18♌30	27♍54
	19	15♋25	8♍56	1♎52	21♏57	25♐45	10♒15	12♓29	27♈50	16♊00	23♋35	16♍54	25♎47
	21	15♌55	8♎23	0♏23	17♐46	20♑10	3♓57	6♈29	23♉09	13♋14	21♌53	15♎22	22♏56
	23	15♍47	6♏03	27♏11	12♑18	13♒59	27♓56	1♉16	19♊48	11♌57	21♍01	13♏26	19♐15
	25	14♎04	1♐51	22♐20	6♒05	7♓45	22♈47	27♉20	18♋09	11♍49	20♎19	10♐36	14♑41
	27	10♏30	26♐14	16♑21	29♒50	2♈08	19♉01	25♊06	18♌03	11♎52	18♏49	6♑33	9♒16
	29	5♐26	19♑55	9♒57	24♓10	27♈39	16♊54	24♋33	18♍34	10♏49	15♐52	1♒21	3♓14
	31	29♐26		3♓49		24♉36		24♌55	18♎18		11♑20		26♓58
	1	18♐03	3♒27	25♓13	1♈47	14♈59	11♊10	4♌52	12♌11	25♌40	19♎58	2♐22	22♏12
☿	7	25 46	13 31	4♈27	28R58	23 24	24 13	11 12	7R55	7♍01	29 21	7 06	24D40
	13	4♑10	24 02	10 10	29D20	3♉05	6♋27	15 32	5 58	18 31	8♏16	8R11	0♐47
	19	13 01	5♓00	11R02	2♈32	13 57	17 23	17 26	8D03	29 35	16 42	3 41	8 35
	25	22 14	16 12	7 34	7 55	26 01	26 52	16R29	14 20	10♎04	24 30	25♏55	17 08
	31	1♒49		2 31		8♊58		12 56	23 53		1♐22		26 02

DATE	☉	♀	♂	♃	♄	⚷	♅	♆	♇	☊	STATIONS
1 1	9♑49	0♐26	23♐48	14♍37	5♒51	8♌19	13♑41	16♑13	22♏06	9♑48	
11	20 00	12 33	1♑12	14R25	7 00	7 41	14 17	16 36	22 23	9 16	☿ 17/3 11♈18
21	0♒11	24 44	8 39	13 54	8 10	6 58	14 52	16 59	22 36	8 44	☿ 9/4 28♓44
31	10 21	7♑00	16 11	13 06	9 22	6 13	15 26	17 20	22 47	8 13	☿ 20/7 17♌29
10 2	20 30	19 18	23 46	12 04	10 34	5 30	15 58	17 41	22 54	7 41	☿ 13/8 5♌58
20	0♓36	1♒37	1♒24	10 51	11 44	4 49	16 28	18 00	22 57	7 09	☿ 11/11 8♐23
1 3	10 40	13 57	9 05	9 33	12 52	4 14	16 54	18 17	22R57	6 37	☿ 1/12 22♏12
11	20 40	26 18	16 47	8 15	13 56	3 46	17 17	18 31	22 54	6 06	♂ 29/11 27♋36
21	0♈38	8♓39	24 31	7 04	14 56	3 28	17 35	18 42	22 47	5 34	♃ 1/5 4♍38
31	10 32	21 00	2♓16	6 03	15 50	3 18	17 49	18 51	22 37	5 02	♄ 28/5 18♒29
10 4	20 23	3♈20	10 01	5 17	16 38	3D20	17 57	18 56	22 25	4 30	♄ 16/10 11♒49
20	0♉10	15 39	17 46	4 49	17 18	3 31	18 01	18 57	22 10	3 59	♅ 22/4 18♑01
30	9 54	27 58	25 28	4 38	17 49	3 52	17R59	18R56	21 55	3 27	♅ 23/9 14♑02
10 5	19 35	10♉17	3♈09	4D46	18 12	4 23	17 53	18 51	21 38	2 55	♆ 20/4 18♑57
20	29 14	22 34	10 46	5 11	18 25	5 02	17 41	18 43	21 21	2 23	♆ 28/9 16♑11
30	8♊50	4♊51	18 20	5 54	18R29	5 49	17 26	18 33	21 05	1 51	♇ 25/2 22♏58
9 6	18 25	17 09	25 48	6 51	18 22	6 43	17 08	18 21	20 50	1 20	♇ 31/7 20♏09
19	27 58	29 26	3♉12	8 03	18 07	7 43	16 46	18 06	20 37	0 48	⚷ 4/4 3♌18
29	7♋30	11♋43	10 28	9 26	17 42	8 48	16 23	17 51	20 26	0 16	⚷ 6 12 23♌35
9 7	17 02	24 01	17 37	11 00	17 10	9 57	15 59	17 35	20 17	29♐44	
19	26 35	6♌18	24 38	12 43	16 32	11 09	15 35	17 19	20 12	29 13	
29	6♌08	18 37	1♊30	14 34	15 50	12 23	15 12	17 03	20 10	28 41	
8 8	15 42	0♍55	8 11	16 31	15 05	13 38	14 51	16 49	20D11	28 09	
18	25 18	13 13	14 40	18 33	14 20	14 53	14 33	16 36	20 15	27 37	
28	4♍57	25 30	20 56	20 39	13 38	16 07	14 19	16 26	20 23	27 06	
7 9	14 38	7♎47	26 57	22 47	13 01	17 19	14 09	16 18	20 34	26 34	
17	24 21	20 02	2♋40	24 56	12 30	18 28	14 03	16 13	20 48	26 02	
27	4♎08	2♏17	8 02	27 06	12 07	19 32	14D03	16 11	21 05	25 30	
7 10	13 59	14 29	12 59	29 15	11 53	20 32	14 07	16D12	21 24	24 58	
17	23 52	26 40	17 26	1♎21	11D49	21 24	14 17	16 17	21 45	24 27	
27	3♏50	8♐49	21 16	3 24	11 55	22 09	14 32	16 25	22 08	23 55	
6 11	13 50	20 55	24 21	5 21	12 11	22 46	14 51	16 36	22 31	23 23	
16	23 53	2♑58	26 31	7 12	12 37	23 12	15 15	16 50	22 55	22 51	
26	3♐59	14 56	27 32	8 55	13 12	23 29	15 42	17 07	23 19	22 20	
6 12	14 07	26 47	27R16	10 27	13 56	23 35	16 12	17 26	23 43	21 48	
16	24 17	8♒28	25 35	11 48	14 47	23R30	16 45	17 46	24 05	21 16	
26	4♑28	19 56	22 37	12 56	15 44	23 14	17 19	18 08	24 26	20 44	

SID M/N 1st JAN 6 h 42 m 36 s — 1993 COMMON — BST

DAY		JAN	FEB	MAR	APR	MAY	JUN	JUL	AUG	SEP	OCT	NOV	DEC
	1	8♈55	23♉59	2♊41	21♋41	29♌59	23♎47	2♐01	21♑13	7♓24	10♈08	24♉50	28♊47
☽	3	3♉22	20♊16	28♊43	20♌03	29♍10	22♏21	28♐59	16♒19	1♈19	3♉51	19♊21	24♋43
	5	29♉03	18♋26	26♋34	19♍55	28♎47	20♐10	25♑05	10♓44	24♈59	27♉45	14♋39	21♌34
	7	26♊21	18♌16	26♌16	20♎17	27♏52	16♑48	20♒13	4♈37	18♉47	22♊17	11♌07	19♍20
	9	25♋11	18♍42	26♍56	19♏49	25♐37	12♒11	14♓30	28♈19	13♊13	17♋57	8♍59	17♎53
	11	24♌50	18♎25	27♎08	17♐39	21♑45	6♓33	8♈19	22♉24	8♋58	15♌16	8♎11	16♏54
	13	24♍16	16♏31	25♏40	13♑39	16♒32	0♈22	2♉11	17♊32	6♌35	14♍24	8♏07	15♐47
	15	22♎41	12♐56	22♐18	8♒18	10♓30	24♈17	26♉47	14♋17	6♍03	14♎44	7♐42	13♑47
	17	19♏50	8♑05	17♑23	2♓12	4♈16	18♉50	22♊39	12♌52	6♎32	15♏02	6♑00	10♒27
	19	15♐52	2♒28	11♒34	25♓55	28♈20	14♊27	20♋04	12♍43	6♏39	14♐04	2♒37	5♓41
	21	11♑02	26♒25	5♓20	19♈50	23♉05	11♋16	18♌47	12♎40	5♐18	11♑17	27♒43	29♓50
	23	5♒34	20♓11	29♓04	14♉13	18♊42	9♌06	18♍03	11♏37	2♑14	6♒53	21♓50	23♈32
	25	29♒36	13♈56	22♈58	9♊13	15♋13	7♍32	17♎00	9♐09	27♑45	1♓21	15♈32	17♉25
	27	23♓21	7♉57	17♉14	5♋02	12♌37	6♎03	15♏04	5♑23	22♒20	25♓14	9♉21	12♊02
	29	17♈07		12♊08	1♌54	10♍45	4♏18	12♐11	0♒40	16♓22	18♈56	3♊42	7♋44
	31	11♉26		8♋08		9♎23		8♑24	25♒17		12♉47		4♌32
	1	27♐33	18♒07	24♓07	14♓04	24♈34	27♊57	28♋14	20♋03	11♍08	29♎53	19♏48	21♏11
☿	7	6♑45	28 48	20℞39	19 30	6♉03	7♋52	27℞11	25 36	22 13	7♏40	12℞37	29 56
	13	16 11	9♓13	14 52	26 31	18 31	16 04	23 55	4♌24	2♎35	14 30	7 00	9♐02
	19	25 54	18 09	10 56	4♈47	1♊34	22 24	20 10	15 28	12 18	19 48	7D44	18 16
	25	5♒57	23 31	10D34	14 09	14 24	26 34	18 11	27 25	21 24	22 27	13 19	27 36
	31	16 21		13 22		26 09		19D28	9♍14		20℞38		7♑05

DATE		☉	♀	♂	♃	♄	⚷	♅	♆	♇	☊	STATIONS
1	1	10♑35	26♒41	20♋24	13♎29	16♒21	23♌00	17♑40	18♑22	24♏37	20♐25	
11		20 47	7♓36	16℞26	14 11	17 26	22 30	18 16	18 44	24 54	19 53	☿ 28/2 24♓13
21		0♒58	18 01	12 49	14 35	18 35	21 52	18 51	19 07	25 08	19 22	☿ 23/3 10♓17
31		11 08	27 42	10 11	14℞41	19 46	21 09	19 26	19 29	25 19	18 50	☿ 2/7 28♋15
10	2	21 16	6♈20	8 50	14 28	20 58	20 23	19 59	19 50	25 27	18 18	☿ 26/7 18♋09
20		1♓22	13 27	8D48	13 56	22 10	19 37	20 29	20 09	25 31	17 46	☿ 26/10 22♏30
2	3	11 25	18 20	9 55	13 07	23 21	18 54	20 57	20 26	25℞32	17 15	☿ 15/11 6♏31
12		21 26	20℞01	12 01	12 05	24 30	18 17	21 20	20 41	25 29	16 43	♀ 11/3 20♈01
22		1♈23	17 43	14 53	10 53	25 35	17 46	21 40	20 52	25 22	16 11	♀ 23/4 3♈44
1	4	11 17	12 09	18 23	9 36	26 36	17 25	21 55	21 01	25 13	15 39	♂ 15/2 8♋39
11		21 07	6 26	22 22	8 20	27 32	17 13	22 05	21 07	25 01	15 07	♃ 29/1 14♎41
21		0♉54	3 47	26 45	7 10	28 20	17D12	22 11	21 09	24 47	14 36	♃ 1/6 4♎45
1	5	10 38	5D03	1♌26	6 10	29 02	17 22	22℞11	21℞08	24 32	14 04	♄ 10/6 0♓19
11		20 19	9 28	6 24	5 25	29 35	17 42	22 06	21 04	24 15	13 32	♄ 28/10 23♒38
21		29 58	16 06	11 34	4 56	29 59	18 13	21 56	20 56	23 59	13 00	♅ 26/4 22♑11
31		9♊34	24 14	16 56	4 45	0♓14	18 52	21 43	20 47	23 42	12 29	♅ 27/9 18♑13
10	6	19 08	3♉22	22 26	4D53	0 19	19 41	21 25	20 34	23 27	11 57	♆ 23/4 21♑09
20		28 41	13 13	28 06	5 17	0℞15	20 36	21 05	20 20	23 14	11 25	♆ 30/9 18♑23
30		8♋14	23 35	3♍52	5 58	0 00	21 39	20 42	20 05	23 02	10 53	♇ 26/2 25♏32
10	7	17 46	4♊20	9 46	6 55	29♒37	22 47	20 18	19 49	22 53	10 22	♇ 3/8 22♏44
20		27 18	15 22	15 46	8 05	29 06	23 59	19 54	19 33	22 47	9 50	⚷ 17/4 17♌11
30		6♌51	26 39	21 53	9 28	28 28	25 15	19 31	19 17	22 44	9 18	⚷ 23 12 9♍18
9	8	16 26	8♋08	28 05	11 01	27 46	26 34	19 09	19 03	22D45	8 46	
19		26 02	19 47	4♎24	12 44	27 01	27 54	18 50	18 50	22 48	8 14	
29		5♍41	1♌36	10 48	14 34	26 16	29 14	18 34	18 39	22 56	7 43	
8	9	15 22	13 33	17 18	16 31	25 33	0♍34	18 23	18 30	23 06	7 11	
18		25 06	25 38	23 55	18 33	24 55	1 53	18 16	18 25	23 20	6 39	
28		4♎53	7♍49	0♏37	20 39	24 23	3 08	18D13	18 23	23 36	6 07	
8	10	14 44	20 06	7 25	22 48	23 58	4 20	18 16	18D24	23 55	5 36	
18		24 38	2♎28	14 19	24 58	23 43	5 26	18 24	18 28	24 15	5 04	
28		4♏35	14 54	21 19	27 08	23 38	6 26	18 37	18 36	24 38	4 32	
7	11	14 35	27 24	28 25	29 17	23D43	7 19	18 55	18 46	25 01	4 00	
17		24 39	9♏55	5♐36	1♏24	23 58	8 04	19 17	19 00	25 25	3 28	
27		4♐45	22 28	12 53	3 27	24 24	8 38	19 43	19 16	25 49	2 57	
7	12	14 53	5♐02	20 16	5 25	24 58	9 02	20 12	19 35	26 12	2 25	
17		25 03	17 37	27 44	7 16	25 41	9 15	20 44	19 55	26 35	1 53	
27		5♑14	0♑12	5♑17	8 58	26 32	9℞17	21 18	20 17	26 56	1 21	

SID M/N 1st JAN 6 h 41 m 38 s 1994 COMMON BST

DAY	JAN	FEB	MAR	APR	MAY	JUN	JUL	AUG	SEP	OCT	NOV	DEC
1	18♌16	11♎03	20♎58	13♐56	20♑44	8♓21	11♈00	24♉31	8♋47	12♌36	2♎33	10♏19
☽ 3	16♍11	9♏31	20♏02	11♑29	17♒00	2♈44	4♉43	18♊30	4♌37	10♍09	2♏18	10♐38
5	14♎24	7♐19	17♐56	7♒37	11♓54	26♈27	28♉24	13♋28	2♍00	9♎15	2♐39	10♑43
7	12♏39	4♑27	14♑41	2♓38	5♈56	20♉03	22♊37	9♌42	0♎38	9♏06	2♑24	9♒27
9	10♐45	0♒56	10♒31	26♓55	29♈35	14♊00	17♋45	7♍06	29♎44	8♐40	0♒41	6♓19
11	8♑25	26♒38	5♓36	20♈45	23♉12	8♋36	13♌52	5♎14	28♏33	7♑09	27♒16	1♈30
13	5♒16	21♓29	0♈00	14♉21	17♊06	4♌02	10♍53	3♏34	26♐41	4♒21	22♓28	25♈35
15	1♓01	15♈32	23♈52	8♊01	11♋35	0♍24	8♎33	1♐49	24♑00	0♓21	16♈44	19♉12
17	25♓38	9♉10	17♉26	2♋12	7♌00	27♍46	6♏44	29♐49	20♒31	25♓25	10♉29	12♊50
19	19♈29	2♊57	11♊12	27♋25	3♍41	26♎10	5♐16	27♑24	16♓12	19♈44	4♊05	6♋51
21	13♉09	27♊38	5♋47	24♌12	1♎51	25♏22	3♑50	24♒16	11♈00	13♉33	27♊50	1♌26
23	7♊22	23♋51	1♌52	22♍47	1♏20	24♐45	1♒55	20♓07	5♉04	7♊08	22♋00	26♌46
25	2♋45	21♌51	29♌51	22♎49	1♐25	23♑29	28♒56	14♈52	28♉41	0♋52	16♌59	23♍00
27	29♋37	21♍14	29♍30	23♏13	1♑02	20♒50	24♓34	8♉47	22♊22	25♋15	13♍12	20♎24
29	27♌49		29♎50	22♐47	29♑14	16♓35	18♈58	2♊24	16♋48	20♌53	10♎58	19♏05
31	26♍39		29♏34		25♒43		12♉42	26♊25		18♍12		18♐47
1	8♑40	29♒25	23♒39	16♓33	11♉05	3♋16	0♋42	25♋35	24♍54	3♏04	21♎07	1♐17
☿ 7	18 22	5♓57	22D47	25 38	24 00	7 10	29D25	7♌38	4♎18	6 11	25 40	10 42
13	28 18	7℞20	25 26	5♈39	6♊14	8℞25	1♋03	20 00	12 57	5℞35	3♏26	20 07
19	8♒26	2 54	0♓29	16 34	16 56	7 02	5 47	1♍53	20 48	0 19	12 27	29 35
25	18 34	26♒30	7 12	28 26	25 43	3 52	13 29	12 58	27 39	23♎19	21 50	9♑09
31	28 00		15 08		2♋23		23 42	23 15		20D53		18 49

DATE	☉	♀	♂	♃	♄	⚷	♅	♆	♇	☊	STATIONS
1 1	10♑20	6♑30	9♑05	9♏46	27♒00	9♍13	21♑35	20♑28	27♏05	1♐05	
11	20 32	19 05	16 44	11 12	28 00	8 58	22 10	20 51	27 23	0 34	☿ 11/2 7♓35
21	0♒43	1♒40	24 27	12 25	29 06	8 33	22 46	21 13	27 38	0 02	☿ 5/3 22♒38
31	10 53	14 13	2♒13	13 24	0♓14	7 58	23 21	21 35	27 50	29♏30	☿ 13/6 8♋25
10 2	21 01	26 46	10 01	14 07	1 26	7 17	23 54	21 57	27 58	28 58	☿ 7/7 29♊25
20	1♓07	9♓17	17 52	14 32	2 38	6 31	24 26	22 16	28 03	28 27	☿ 9/10 6♏29
2 3	11 11	21 47	25 43	14℞39	3 51	5 44	24 54	22 34	28℞05	27 55	☿ 30/10 20♎49
12	21 11	4♈14	3♓35	14 27	5 03	4 59	25 20	22 49	28 03	27 23	♀ 13/10 18♏00
22	1♈08	16 39	11 27	13 56	6 13	4 17	25 41	23 02	27 58	26 51	♀ 24/11 2♏28
1 4	11 02	29 01	19 17	13 09	7 20	3 41	25 58	23 11	27 49	26 20	♃ 1/3 14♏39
11	20 53	11♉20	27 06	12 09	8 22	3 14	26 11	23 18	27 38	25 48	♃ 2/7 4♏46
21	0♉40	23 35	4♈52	10 58	9 20	2 57	26 18	23 21	27 25	25 16	♄ 23/6 12♓24
1 5	10 24	5♊46	12 35	9 42	10 11	2 51	26℞21	23℞20	27 10	24 44	♄ 9/11 5♓41
11	20 05	17 54	20 14	8 26	10 55	2D56	26 18	23 17	26 53	24 12	♅ 1/5 26♑21
21	29 44	29 56	27 48	7 16	11 31	3 12	26 11	23 10	26 37	23 41	♅ 2/10 22♑23
31	9♊20	11♋54	5♉18	6 16	11 58	3 38	25 59	23 01	26 20	23 09	♆ 25/4 23♑21
10 6	18 55	23 45	12 42	5 30	12 16	4 15	25 43	22 50	26 05	22 37	♆ 3/10 20♑34
20	28 28	5♌30	20 00	4 59	12 24	5 01	25 24	22 36	25 51	22 05	♇ 1/3 28♏05
30	8♋00	17 07	27 12	4 46	12℞22	5 55	25 02	22 21	25 39	21 34	♇ 6/8 25♏17
10 7	17 32	28 34	4♊18	4D52	12 10	6 57	24 39	22 05	25 29	21 02	⚷ 2/ 5 2♍51
20	27 04	9♍48	11 16	5 15	11 49	8 05	24 15	21 49	25 22	20 30	
30	6♌37	20 48	18 08	5 54	11 20	9 19	23 51	21 33	25 18	19 58	
9 8	16 12	1♎28	24 51	6 50	10 44	10 37	23 28	21 18	25D18	19 26	
19	25 48	11 42	1♋26	7 59	10 02	11 58	23 08	21 04	25 21	18 55	
29	5♍27	21 22	7 53	9 22	9 17	13 22	22 51	20 53	25 27	18 23	
8 9	15 08	0♏14	14 10	10 55	8 32	14 47	22 37	20 44	25 36	17 51	
18	24 52	7 57	20 16	12 38	7 48	16 11	22 28	20 38	25 49	17 19	
28	4♎39	13 58	26 11	14 30	7 07	17 35	22 24	20 35	26 04	16 48	
8 10	14 29	17 29	1♌52	16 28	6 33	18 57	22D24	20D35	26 22	16 16	
18	24 23	17℞32	7 18	18 32	6 06	20 16	22 30	20 38	26 42	15 44	
28	4♏20	13 46	12 27	20 40	5 49	21 30	22 40	20 45	27 04	15 12	
7 11	14 21	7 52	17 13	22 51	5 41	22 38	22 56	20 55	27 27	14 41	
17	24 24	3 24	21 34	25 04	5D44	23 40	23 16	21 08	27 51	14 09	
27	4♐30	2D41	25 24	27 16	5 57	24 33	23 40	21 24	28 15	13 37	
7 12	14 39	5 45	28 35	29 28	6 21	25 17	24 08	21 42	28 39	13 05	
17	24 49	11 37	0♍57	1♐38	6 54	25 51	24 39	22 02	29 01	12 33	
27	5♑00	19 26	2 21	3 43	7 36	26 14	25 12	22 23	29 23	12 02	

SID M/N 1st JAN 6 h 40 m 41 s 1995 COMMON BST

DAY	JAN	FEB	MAR	APR	MAY	JUN	JUL	AUG	SEP	OCT	NOV	DEC
1	3♑45	25♒20	3♓48	21♈17	24♉06	8♋24	11♌39	29♍14	20♏08	29♐17	22♒25	29♓32
☽ 3	3♒13	22♓19	0♈16	15♉40	17♊48	2♌22	6♍29	25♎45	18♐15	27♑38	19♓23	24♈59
5	1♓14	17♈43	25♈29	9♊28	11♋30	26♌58	2♎13	23♏22	16♑54	25♒37	15♈25	19♉36
7	27♓24	11♉54	19♉39	3♋08	5♌38	22♍40	29♎14	22♐07	15♒41	22♓55	10♉37	13♊44
9	22♈02	5♊32	13♊20	27♋17	0♍46	19♎53	27♏46	21♑40	13♓55	19♈17	5♊05	7♋33
11	15♉47	29♊21	7♋10	22♌33	27♍24	18♏51	27♐38	21♒07	10♈58	14♉35	29♊02	1♌17
13	9♊22	23♋56	1♌51	19♍20	25♎47	19♐07	27♑54	19♓26	6♉37	8♊58	22♋45	25♌13
15	3♋22	19♌36	27♌49	17♎41	25♏35	19♑31	27♒15	16♈03	1♊06	2♋48	16♌42	19♍51
17	28♋06	16♍19	25♍09	17♏06	25♐51	18♒47	24♓50	11♉05	24♊55	26♋36	11♍28	15♎44
19	23♌40	13♎48	23♎29	16♐41	25♑24	16♓11	20♈33	5♊07	18♋44	21♌00	7♎38	13♏26
21	20♍00	11♏42	22♏14	15♑35	23♒26	11♈49	14♉56	28♊49	13♌09	16♍32	5♏33	12♐58
23	17♎02	9♐51	20♐50	13♒21	19♓49	6♉13	8♊40	22♋46	8♍35	13♎32	5♐01	13♑34
25	14♏50	8♑08	18♑57	9♓54	14♈54	29♉59	2♋20	17♌26	5♎09	11♏52	5♑07	13♒47
27	13♐24	6♒16	16♒24	5♈24	9♉07	23♊36	26♋23	12♍56	2♏42	10♐59	4♒41	12♓27
29	12♑27		13♓02	0♉03	2♊54	17♋25	21♌00	9♎16	0♐52	10♑06	2♓52	9♈13
31	11♒17		8♈46		26♊33		16♍18	6♏20		8♒33		4♉27
1	20♑26	18♒01	12♒55	27♓37	27♉16	16♊22	16♊58	12♌41	3♎46	15♎49	24♎33	12♐39
☿ 7	0♒07	11R00	19 33	8♈52	6♊28	13R08	24 19	24 27	10 42	9R10	4♏19	22 01
13	9 23	6 15	27 20	20 56	13 12	10 28	3♋56	5♍18	16 13	5 06	14 06	1♑23
19	17 09	6D03	6♓02	3♉33	17 13	9D55	15 28	15 16	19 36	7D07	23 45	10 41
25	21 09	9 23	15 32	16 01	18R21	12 06	28 02	24 20	19R48	13 55	3♐15	19 44
31	18R59		25 49		16 49		10♌38	2♎30		22 57		27 57

DATE	☉	♀	♂	♃	♄	⚷	♅	♆	♇	☊	STATIONS
1 1	10♑05	23♏51	2♍38	4♐44	8♓00	26♍21	25♑29	22♑34	29♏32	11♏46	
11	20 17	3♐27	2R13	6 41	8 53	26R27	26 04	22 57	29 51	11 14	☿ 26/1 21♒16
21	0♒28	13 47	0 29	8 31	9 53	26 20	26 39	23 20	0♐06	10 42	☿ 16/2 5♒37
31	10 38	24 37	27♌31	10 11	10 58	26 02	27 14	23 42	0 19	10 10	☿ 24/5 18♊22
10 2	20 46	5♑49	23 44	11 40	12 06	25 34	27 48	24 04	0 29	9 39	☿ 17/6 9♊49
20	0♓52	17 16	19 48	12 56	13 18	24 57	28 21	24 24	0 35	9 07	☿ 22/9 20♎11
2 3	10 56	28 55	16 27	13 58	14 31	24 14	28 51	24 42	0 37	8 35	☿ 14/10 5♎00
12	20 57	10♒42	14 10	14 44	15 45	23 27	29 17	24 58	0R36	8 03	♂ 3/1 2♍39
22	0♈54	22 35	13 12	15 13	16 58	22 40	29 40	25 11	0 32	7 32	♂ 25/3 13♌09
1 4	10 48	4♓32	13D28	15 23	18 09	21 54	29 59	25 21	0 24	7 00	♃ 1/4 15♐23
11	20 39	16 33	14 51	15R14	19 17	21 14	0♒14	25 28	0 14	6 28	♃ 3/8 5♐32
21	0♉26	28 36	17 08	14 48	20 22	20 41	0 23	25 32	0 01	5 56	♄ 6/7 24♓45
1 5	10 10	10♈40	20 10	14 04	21 21	20 16	0 28	25R33	29♏46	5 25	♄ 22/11 18♓00
11	19 51	22 46	23 48	13 06	22 15	20 02	0R28	25 30	29 30	4 53	♅ 5/5 0♒29
21	29 30	4♉53	27 56	11 57	23 02	19D60	0 22	25 24	29 14	4 21	♅ 6/10 26♑32
31	9♊06	17 01	2♍27	10 42	23 41	20 08	0 13	25 16	28 57	3 49	♆ 28/4 25♑33
10 6	18 41	29 11	7 18	9 26	24 11	20 28	29♑58	25 05	28 42	3 17	♆ 5/10 22♑47
20	28 14	11♊21	12 26	8 14	24 32	20 58	29 41	24 52	28 27	2 46	♇ 4/3 0♐37
30	7♋46	23 33	17 49	7 12	24 43	21 39	29 20	24 37	28 14	2 14	♇ 9/8 27♏50
10 7	17 18	5♋47	23 24	6 22	24R45	22 29	28 57	24 21	28 04	1 42	⚷ 10/1 26♍27
20	26 51	18 03	29 11	5 49	24 36	23 27	28 34	24 05	27 56	1 10	⚷ 19/5 19♍59
30	6♌24	0♌20	5♎08	5 33	24 18	24 32	28 10	23 49	27 51	0 39	
9 8	15 58	12 40	11 15	5D35	23 51	25 44	27 47	23 34	27D50	0 07	
19	25 34	25 01	17 31	5 56	23 16	27 01	27 25	23 20	27 52	29♎35	
29	5♍13	7♍25	23 55	6 34	22 35	28 22	27 06	23 08	27 57	29 03	
8 9	14 53	19 49	0♏28	7 28	21 51	29 47	26 51	22 58	28 06	28 31	
18	24 37	2♎14	7 09	8 38	21 05	1♎13	26 40	22 51	28 17	28 00	
28	4♎24	14 41	13 58	10 00	20 19	2 40	26 33	22 47	28 32	27 28	
8 10	14 15	27 07	20 54	11 35	19 37	4 08	26D32	22D47	28 49	26 56	
18	24 09	9♏34	27 57	13 20	19 01	5 33	26 35	22 49	29 09	26 24	
28	4♏06	22 01	5♐08	15 14	18 32	6 57	26 43	22 55	29 30	25 53	
7 11	14 06	4♐27	12 25	17 15	18 12	8 17	26 57	23 05	29 53	25 21	
17	24 10	16 54	19 48	19 22	18 01	9 32	27 15	23 17	0♐16	24 49	
27	4♐16	29 19	27 18	21 33	18D01	10 40	27 37	23 32	0 40	24 17	
7 12	14 24	11♑44	4♑53	23 48	18 12	11 42	28 03	23 50	1 04	23 46	
17	24 34	24 07	12 33	26 04	18 34	12 35	28 33	24 09	1 26	23 14	
27	4♑45	6♒28	20 17	28 21	19 05	13 18	29 05	24 30	1 48	22 42	

SID M/N 1st JAN 6 h 39 m 44 s 1996 LEAP BST

DAY	JAN	FEB	MAR	APR	MAY	JUN	JUL	AUG	SEP	OCT	NOV	DEC
1	16♉41	1♋23	21♋39	6♍03	9♎30	28♏57	7♑04	1♓14	22♈56	27♉48	13♋20	15♌08
☽ 3	10♊42	25♋08	15♌38	1♎22	6♏28	28♐27	7♒31	0♈32	19♉45	23♊12	7♌18	8♍47
5	4♋29	19♌10	10♍12	27♎46	4♐43	28♑17	7♓12	28♈02	15♊01	17♋30	1♍00	2♎51
7	28♋15	13♍38	5♎30	25♏08	3♑41	27♒25	5♈18	23♉50	9♋15	11♌15	25♍08	28♎01
9	22♌12	8♎41	1♏36	23♐12	2♒35	25♓16	1♉45	18♊28	3♌00	5♍05	20♎14	24♏48
11	16♍33	4♏37	28♏32	21♑36	0♓52	21♈49	26♉58	12♋27	26♌46	29♍28	16♏38	23♐10
13	11♎41	1♐44	26♐22	20♒00	28♓18	17♉22	21♊24	6♌10	20♍53	24♎44	14♐15	22♑29
15	8♏09	0♑18	25♑00	18♓04	24♈53	12♊11	15♋22	29♌56	15♎35	20♏58	12♑37	21♒45
17	6♐22	29♑59	24♒03	15♈29	20♉38	6♋27	9♌07	23♍57	11♏04	18♐06	11♒07	20♓12
19	6♑15	29♒54	22♓48	11♉57	15♊37	0♌19	2♍50	18♎31	7♐32	15♑57	9♓21	17♈38
21	6♒50	28♓50	20♈31	7♊21	9♋54	24♌00	26♍50	14♏02	5♑08	14♒18	7♈08	14♉10
23	6♓41	26♈05	16♉50	1♋48	3♌43	17♍56	21♎37	10♐56	3♒50	12♓52	4♉22	9♊57
25	4♈45	21♉39	11♊50	25♋40	27♌30	12♎44	17♏45	9♑28	3♓14	11♈17	0♊54	5♋02
27	0♉54	16♊01	5♋55	19♌31	21♍52	9♏01	15♐45	9♒18	2♈33	9♉02	26♊32	29♋25
29	25♉37	9♋47	29♋41	13♍56	17♎26	7♐13	15♑29	9♓30	0♉55	5♊40	21♋12	23♌14
31	19♊32		23♌45		14♏41		16♒04	8♈51		1♋04		16♍50
1	29♑09	19♑16	19♒54	15♈27	28♉15	20♉19	27♊21	28♌55	3♎00	20♍32	8♏14	24♐47
☿ 7	4♒24	22 12	29 13	27 45	28R15	23 29	9♋54	8♍12	3R06	26 56	17 55	3♑27
13	4R14	27 41	9♓12	9♉10	25 41	28 59	22 50	16 26	29♍29	6♎09	27 23	11 21
19	27♑57	4♒40	19 53	18 30	22 14	6♊35	5♌17	23 30	23 25	16 20	6♐40	17 20
25	21 12	12 39	1♈19	25 00	19 56	16 05	16 47	29 05	19 15	26 35	15 48	19R06
31	19D08		13 23		20D02		27 16	2♎39		6♏35		14 24

DATE	☉	♀	♂	♃	♄	⚷	♅	♆	♇	☊	STATIONS
1 1	9♑51	12♒38	24♑10	29♐29	19♓24	13♎36	29♑21	24♑41	1♐58	22♎26	
11	20 02	24 54	2♒00	1♑44	20 09	14 02	29 56	25 04	2 17	21 54	☿ 10/1 5♒10
21	0♒13	7♓05	9 52	3 56	21 01	14 18	0♒31	25 26	2 33	21 23	☿ 30/1 19♑07
31	10 23	19 09	17 45	6 03	22 00	14R21	1 06	25 49	2 47	20 51	☿ 4/5 28♉38
10 2	20 32	1♈04	25 40	8 05	23 04	14 12	1 41	26 11	2 57	20 19	☿ 28/5 19♉39
20	0♓38	12 47	3♓34	9 59	24 13	13 52	2 14	26 31	3 04	19 47	☿ 4/9 3♎30
1 3	10 41	24 17	11 28	11 45	25 25	13 22	2 45	26 50	3 07	19 15	☿ 27/9 19♍00
11	20 42	5♉27	19 20	13 19	26 38	12 44	3 13	27 06	3R07	18 44	☿ 24/12 19♑13
21	0♈40	16 13	27 10	14 42	27 53	12 00	3 38	27 20	3 04	18 12	♀ 20/5 28♊18
31	10 34	26 26	4♈57	15 50	29 07	11 13	3 58	27 31	2 57	17 40	♀ 2/7 11♊47
10 4	20 24	5♊56	12 41	16 43	0♈20	10 26	4 15	27 39	2 48	17 08	♃ 5/5 17♑39
20	0♉12	14 26	20 21	17 19	1 30	9 42	4 27	27 44	2 35	16 37	♃ 4/9 7♑49
30	9 56	21 28	27 56	17 37	2 36	9 03	4 33	27R45	2 21	16 05	♄ 19/7 7♈24
10 5	19 37	26 23	5♉26	17R36	3 38	8 31	4R35	27 43	2 06	15 33	♄ 4/12 0♈37
20	29 16	28 18	12 51	17 17	4 34	8 09	4 32	27 38	1 50	15 01	♅ 9/5 4♒35
30	8♊52	26R23	20 11	16 40	5 24	7 57	4 24	27 31	1 33	14 30	♅ 10/10 0♒39
9 6	18 27	21 06	27 25	15 47	6 06	7D56	4 12	27 20	1 17	13 58	♆ 29/4 27♑45
19	28 00	15 12	4♊34	14 41	6 40	8 06	3 56	27 07	1 02	13 26	♆ 7/10 24♑59
29	7♋32	11 59	11 37	13 27	7 04	8 28	3 36	26 53	0 49	12 54	♇ 6/3 3♐08
9 7	17 04	12D37	18 34	12 11	7 19	8 60	3 15	26 37	0 38	12 22	♇ 10/8 0♐21
19	26 37	16 31	25 25	10 56	7R24	9 42	2 51	26 21	0 29	11 51	⚷ 29/1 14♎21
29	6♌10	22 46	2♋11	9 49	7 19	10 33	2 27	26 05	0 24	11 19	⚷ 5/6 7♎55
8 8	15 44	0♋38	8 51	8 54	7 04	11 33	2 04	25 50	0 21	10 47	
18	25 20	9 37	15 24	8 15	6 39	12 39	1 41	25 35	0D22	10 15	
28	4♍58	19 24	21 52	7 53	6 07	13 52	1 21	25 23	0 26	9 44	
7 9	14 39	29 47	28 14	7D50	5 28	15 10	1 05	25 13	0 34	9 12	
17	24 23	10♌37	4♌28	8 06	4 44	16 32	0 51	25 05	0 45	8 40	
27	4♎10	21 50	10 36	8 40	3 57	17 56	0 43	25 00	0 59	8 08	
7 10	14 01	3♍20	16 36	9 32	3 11	19 23	0 39	24D59	1 15	7 36	
17	23 54	15 04	22 28	10 40	2 27	20 50	0D40	25 01	1 34	7 05	
27	3♏51	27 00	28 10	12 02	1 48	22 17	0 46	25 06	1 54	6 33	
6 11	13 52	9♎06	3♍41	13 37	1 16	23 42	0 57	25 14	2 17	6 01	
16	23 55	21 19	8 59	15 23	0 53	25 05	1 13	25 26	2 40	5 29	
26	4♐01	3♏38	14 03	17 19	0 40	26 23	1 34	25 40	3 04	4 58	
6 12	14 09	16 02	18 48	19 23	0D37	27 36	1 58	25 57	3 27	4 26	
16	24 19	28 28	23 11	21 33	0 45	28 43	2 26	26 16	3 50	3 54	
26	4♑30	10♐57	27 08	23 48	1 04	29 42	2 57	26 37	4 12	3 22	

SID M/N 1st JAN 6 h 42 m 43 s — 1997 COMMON — BST

	DAY	JAN	FEB	MAR	APR	MAY	JUN	JUL	AUG	SEP	OCT	NOV	DEC
	1	28♍44	14♏17	23♏32	13♑38	22♒22	15♈38	23♉32	12♋15	27♌48	0♎13	15♏11	19♐43
☽	3	23♎09	10♐47	19♐53	11♒56	20♓59	13♉29	19♊59	6♌52	21♍24	24♎00	10♐20	16♑25
	5	18♏59	9♑14	17♑54	11♓14	19♈48	10♊43	15♋36	0♍51	15♎01	18♏16	6♑16	13♒45
	7	16♐43	9♒16	17♒26	10♈54	18♉13	6♋58	10♌19	24♍28	8♏58	13♐16	3♒04	11♓33
	9	16♑10	9♓46	17♓43	9♉57	15♊37	2♌04	4♍16	18♎05	3♐43	9♑19	0♓49	9♈48
	11	16♒21	9♈25	17♈34	7♊38	11♋37	26♌11	27♍51	12♏17	29♐47	6♒42	29♓33	8♉19
	13	16♓01	7♉27	16♉00	3♋40	6♌18	19♍50	21♎42	7♐42	27♑30	5♓30	28♈55	6♊41
	15	14♈20	3♊48	12♊39	28♋18	0♍08	13♎42	16♏29	4♑49	26♒52	5♈23	28♉08	4♋16
	17	11♉13	28♊52	7♋48	22♌07	23♍48	8♏28	12♐48	3♒42	27♓11	5♉25	26♊17	0♌33
	19	6♊55	23♋05	1♌55	15♍45	17♎58	4♐39	10♑51	3♓46	27♈18	4♊28	22♋46	25♌27
	21	1♋48	16♌52	25♌34	9♎46	13♏10	2♑19	10♒11	3♈52	26♉08	1♋47	17♌41	19♍23
	23	26♋04	10♍31	19♍15	4♏32	9♐34	0♒59	9♓51	2♉59	23♊12	27♋20	11♍35	13♎00
	25	19♌55	4♎17	13♎17	0♐15	7♑01	29♒54	8♈57	0♊35	18♋38	21♌35	5♎10	7♏01
	27	13♍32	28♎29	7♏56	26♐52	5♒04	28♓26	6♉57	26♊43	12♌57	15♍13	29♎07	2♐04
	29	7♎16		3♐25	24♑17	3♓21	26♈20	3♊48	21♋42	6♍39	8♎51	23♏55	28♐25
	31	1♏39		29♐56		1♈35		29♊39	15♌53		2♏54		25♑55
	1	13♑06	18♑46	1♓28	29♈12	1♉43	17♉27	15♋29	5♍54	7♍47	27♍48	19♏51	0♑11
☿	7	5R40	26 49	12 18	6♉12	29R36	26 39	27 39	11 34	3R23	8♎34	28 55	3 20
	13	2D58	5♒31	23 45	9 27	0D10	7♊23	8♌43	15 14	3D21	19 04	7♐43	0R47
	19	5 16	14 47	5♈38	8R53	3 23	19 31	18 37	16R10	8 30	29 11	16 08	23♐08
	25	10 33	24 36	17 22	5 33	8 48	2♋31	27 21	13 49	17 20	8♏54	23 53	17 35
	31	17 30		27 42		16 05		4♍48	8 43		18 18		17D57

DATE	☉	♀	♂	♃	♄	⚷	♅	♆	♇	☊	STATIONS
1 1	10♑37	18♐27	29♍14	25♑10	1♈21	0♏13	3♒17	26♑50	4♐25	3♎03	
11	20 48	0♑58	2♎14	27 30	1 56	0 57	3 51	27 13	4 44	2 31	☿ 13/1 2♑58
21	0♒59	13 30	4 26	29 51	2 39	1 31	4 26	27 35	5 00	2 00	☿ 15/4 9♉39
31	11 09	26 01	5 42	2♒12	3 31	1 53	5 01	27 58	5 14	1 28	☿ 9/5 29♈28
10 2	21 18	8♒32	5R49	4 32	4 30	2 04	5 35	28 20	5 25	0 56	☿ 18/8 16♍14
20	1♓24	21 03	4 40	6 49	5 34	2R03	6 09	28 40	5 33	0 24	☿ 10/9 2♍42
2 3	11 27	3♓33	2 15	9 02	6 42	1 51	6 41	28 59	5 37	29♍53	☿ 8/12 3♑22
12	21 27	16 02	28♍49	11 09	7 54	1 28	7 10	29 16	5R37	29 21	☿ 27/12 17♐04
22	1♈25	28 29	24 56	13 09	9 09	0 55	7 35	29 31	5 34	28 49	♀ 27/12 3♒57
1 4	11 19	10♈55	21 18	15 01	10 24	0 16	7 57	29 42	5 28	28 17	♂ 6/2 5♎55
11	21 09	23 19	18 33	16 43	11 39	29♎31	8 15	29 50	5 19	27 46	♂ 28/4 16♍44
21	0♉56	5♉42	17 01	18 13	12 53	28 45	8 29	29 56	5 07	27 14	♃ 10/6 21♒56
1 5	10 40	18 02	16D47	19 30	14 04	27 59	8 37	29 58	4 53	26 42	♃ 8/10 12♒05
11	20 21	0♊21	17 46	20 33	15 12	27 16	8 41	29R56	4 38	26 10	♄ 2/8 20♈22
21	0♊00	12 39	19 45	21 19	16 16	26 39	8R39	29 52	4 22	25 38	♄ 16/12 13♈32
31	9 36	24 54	22 36	21 47	17 15	26 10	8 33	29 44	4 06	25 07	♅ 13/5 8♒41
10 6	19 10	7♋08	26 09	21 56	18 07	25 51	8 22	29 34	3 50	24 35	♅ 14/10 4♒44
20	28 43	19 20	0♎17	21R47	18 52	25 41	8 07	29 22	3 35	24 03	♆ 2/5 29♑58
30	8♋16	1♌30	4 53	21 18	19 28	25D43	7 49	29 08	3 21	23 31	♆ 9/10 27♑11
10 7	17 48	13 38	9 52	20 33	19 56	25 55	7 28	28 52	3 09	23 00	♇ 8/3 5♐37
20	27 20	25 44	15 13	19 32	20 14	26 19	7 05	28 36	3 00	22 28	♇ 13/8 2♐51
30	6♌53	7♍46	20 51	18 21	20 22	26 52	6 41	28 20	2 54	21 56	⚷ 14/2 2♏05
9 8	16 28	19 45	26 45	17 04	20R19	27 35	6 17	28 04	2 51	21 24	⚷ 24/6 25♎41
19	26 04	1♎40	2♏52	15 46	20 07	28 27	5 55	27 50	2D52	20 52	
29	5♍42	13 30	9 13	14 34	19 44	29 27	5 34	27 37	2 55	20 21	
8 9	15 24	25 14	15 45	13 32	19 13	0♏33	5 16	27 26	3 02	19 49	
18	25 08	6♏51	22 28	12 45	18 35	1 46	5 01	27 18	3 12	19 17	
28	4♎55	18 20	29 21	12 15	17 52	3 02	4 51	27 13	3 25	18 45	
8 10	14 45	29 37	6♐24	12 05	17 05	4 23	4 45	27 11	3 41	18 14	
18	24 39	10♐40	13 35	12D15	16 18	5 46	4D45	27D12	4 00	17 42	
28	4♏37	21 23	20 54	12 44	15 33	7 10	4 49	27 17	4 20	17 10	
7 11	14 37	1♑39	28 20	13 31	14 52	8 35	4 59	27 25	4 42	16 38	
17	24 41	11 15	5♑53	14 36	14 18	9 58	5 13	27 36	5 05	16 07	
27	4♐47	19 53	13 31	15 57	13 53	11 20	5 32	27 50	5 28	15 35	
7 12	14 55	27 04	21 14	17 31	13 37	12 38	5 55	28 07	5 52	15 03	
17	25 05	2♒05	29 01	19 17	13D32	13 52	6 22	28 26	6 15	14 31	
27	5♑16	3R57	6♒51	21 14	13 39	14 60	6 52	28 46	6 37	13 59	

SID M/N 1st JAN 6 h 41 m 46 s — 1998 COMMON — BST

DAY	JAN	FEB	MAR	APR	MAY	JUN	JUL	AUG	SEP	OCT	NOV	DEC
1	9♒58	2♈48	12♈03	5♊00	11♋26	28♌17	0♎27	14♏00	28♐44	2♒49	23♓00	1♉19
☽ 3	8♓18	1♉31	11♉30	2♋42	7♌31	22♍26	24♎11	8♐17	24♑44	0♓21	22♈51	1♊34
5	6♈38	29♉20	9♊38	28♋38	2♍07	16♎06	18♏06	3♑36	22♒22	29♓39	23♉31	1♋32
7	4♉43	26♊10	6♋17	23♌16	25♍54	9♏55	12♐45	0♒16	21♓25	0♉01	23♊32	0♌02
9	2♊27	22♋06	1♌40	17♍09	19♎31	4♐20	8♑26	28♒10	21♈10	0♊09	21♋49	26♌36
11	29♊35	17♌10	26♌11	10♎47	13♏23	29♐33	5♒09	26♓52	20♉35	28♊57	18♌09	21♍34
13	25♋51	11♍29	20♍08	4♏30	7♐47	25♑33	2♓40	25♈45	18♊57	25♋58	12♍58	15♎33
15	21♌03	5♎16	13♎48	28♏32	2♑49	22♒19	0♈43	24♉16	15♋58	21♌28	6♎58	9♏14
17	15♍17	28♎54	7♏30	23♐09	28♑37	19♓50	29♈04	22♊05	11♌49	15♍58	0♏39	3♐06
19	8♎58	22♏53	1♐33	18♑38	25♒23	18♈07	27♉27	19♋02	6♍44	9♎55	24♏25	27♐28
21	2♏42	17♐49	26♐25	15♒23	23♓20	17♉01	25♊32	15♌03	1♎01	3♏39	18♐27	22♑26
23	27♏09	14♑15	22♑36	13♓41	22♈30	15♊57	22♋52	10♍10	24♎53	27♏23	12♑56	18♒06
25	22♐56	12♒25	20♒29	13♈27	22♉17	14♋08	19♌07	4♎29	18♏34	21♐21	8♒06	14♓36
27	20♑17	12♓00	20♓01	13♉48	21♊40	10♌56	14♍11	28♎18	12♐26	15♑54	4♓19	12♈09
29	18♒57		20♈26	13♊28	19♋38	6♍15	8♎21	22♏02	7♑00	11♒30	2♈01	10♉48
31	18♓13		20♉29		15♌47		2♏06	16♐16		8♓42		10♊13
1	18♐29	27♑28	16♓02	20♈28	14♈12	29♉19	0♌01	28♌14	20♌13	11♎41	29♏07	10♐07
☿ 7	23 29	6♒59	27 29	16R26	19 49	12♊01	9 04	26R14	28 15	21 47	6♐44	2R59
13	0♑25	16 57	8♈11	12 03	27 07	25 11	16 43	21 50	8♍43	1♏25	13 08	1D34
19	8 21	27 26	16 32	9 52	5♉51	7♋56	22 44	17 25	19 57	10 37	17 07	5 24
25	16 54	8♓27	21 00	10D42	15 56	19 37	26 46	16D02	1♎04	19 25	16R31	12 00
31	25 55		20R53		27 18		28 16	19 14		27 47		19 54

DATE	☉	♀	♂	♃	♄	⚷	♅	♆	♇	☊	STATIONS
1 1	10♑22	3♒24	10♒46	22♒15	13♈46	15♏31	7♒08	28♑57	6♐47	13♍44	
11	20 34	29R23	18 39	24 23	14 08	16 28	7 41	29 19	7 07	13 12	☿ 28/3 21♈30
21	0♒45	23 25	26 33	26 38	14 41	17 17	8 15	29 42	7 24	12 40	☿ 20/4 9♈48
31	10 55	19 11	4♓26	28 57	15 22	17 55	8 50	0♒05	7 39	12 08	☿ 31/7 28♌16
10 2	21 03	18D48	12 18	1♓20	16 12	18 24	9 25	0 27	7 50	11 36	☿ 24/8 15♌58
20	1♓09	22 06	20 08	3 44	17 10	18 41	9 59	0 48	7 59	11 05	☿ 21/11 17♐34
2 3	11 12	28 04	27 56	6 08	18 13	18 47	10 32	1 07	8 04	10 33	☿ 11/12 1♐19
12	21 13	5♒51	5♈40	8 32	19 21	18R41	11 02	1 25	8R05	10 01	♀ 6/2 18♑28
22	1♈10	14 50	13 21	10 53	20 33	18 25	11 29	1 40	8 03	9 29	♃ 18/7 28♓04
1 4	11 04	24 38	20 57	13 12	21 47	17 59	11 53	1 52	7 58	8 58	♃ 13/11 18♓10
11	20 55	5♓01	28 29	15 25	23 03	17 25	12 12	2 01	7 49	8 26	♄ 16/8 3♉38
21	0♉42	15 47	5♉56	17 33	24 19	16 45	12 28	2 07	7 38	7 54	♄ 30/12 26♈46
1 5	10 26	26 52	13 17	19 33	25 34	16 01	12 38	2 10	7 25	7 22	♅ 17/5 12♒45
11	20 07	8♈09	20 34	21 24	26 47	15 15	12 44	2R09	7 11	6 51	♅ 19/10 8♒49
21	29 46	19 37	27 45	23 05	27 57	14 31	12R45	2 06	6 55	6 19	♆ 4/5 2♒10
31	9♊22	1♉12	4♊52	24 34	29 04	13 51	12 40	1 59	6 38	5 47	♆ 12/10 29♑23
10 6	18 56	12 53	11 53	25 49	0♉05	13 16	12 32	1 49	6 22	5 15	♇ 11/3 8♐05
20	28 30	24 40	18 49	26 49	1 00	12 50	12 19	1 37	6 07	4 43	♇ 16/8 5♐19
30	8♋02	6♊31	25 41	27 33	1 49	12 32	12 02	1 24	5 53	4 12	⚷ 2/3 18♏47
10 7	17 34	18 27	2♋27	27 58	2 29	12 25	11 42	1 09	5 41	3 40	⚷ 12/7 12♏25
20	27 06	0♋27	9 10	28R04	3 01	12D28	11 20	0 53	5 31	3 08	
30	6♌39	12 31	15 48	27 50	3 23	12 42	10 56	0 36	5 24	2 36	
9 8	16 14	24 40	22 21	27 17	3 36	13 06	10 32	0 21	5 20	2 05	
19	25 50	6♌52	28 51	26 27	3R37	13 40	10 09	0 06	5D19	1 33	
29	5♍28	19 09	5♌16	25 22	3 29	14 22	9 47	29♑52	5 22	1 01	
8 9	15 09	1♍29	11 38	24 08	3 10	15 14	9 28	29 41	5 28	0 29	
18	24 53	13 53	17 55	22 48	2 42	16 12	9 12	29 32	5 37	29♌57	
28	4♎41	26 19	24 09	21 30	2 06	17 17	8 59	29 26	5 49	29 26	
8 10	14 31	8♎47	0♍18	20 19	1 24	18 27	8 52	29 24	6 05	28 54	
18	24 25	21 18	6 23	19 20	0 37	19 41	8 49	29D24	6 22	28 22	
28	4♏22	3♏49	12 23	18 37	29♈49	20 58	8D51	29 28	6 42	27 50	
7 11	14 23	16 22	18 17	18 14	29 03	22 18	8 58	29 35	7 03	27 19	
17	24 26	28 55	24 05	18D11	28 20	23 38	9 11	29 46	7 26	26 47	
27	4♐32	11♐28	29 46	18 28	27 43	24 58	9 28	29 59	7 49	26 15	
7 12	14 40	24 02	5♎19	19 06	27 14	26 16	9 49	0♒15	8 13	25 43	
17	24 50	6♑35	10 41	20 02	26 55	27 32	10 14	0 33	8 36	25 12	
27	5♑01	19 08	15 53	21 15	26 47	28 44	10 43	0 54	8 58	24 40	

SID M/N 1st JAN 6 h 40 m 48 s   1999 COMMON   BST

DAY	JAN	FEB	MAR	APR	MAY	JUN	JUL	AUG	SEP	OCT	NOV	DEC
1	24♊57	15♌46	24♌31	11♎22	14♏20	28♐57	2♒24	20♓36	12♉34	21♊59	14♌22	20♍41
☽ 3	23♋50	12♍07	20♍16	5♏36	8♐06	23♑04	27♒33	17♈45	10♊59	20♋06	10♍49	15♎54
5	21♌18	7♎15	15♎09	29♏26	1♑53	17♒47	23♓39	15♉45	9♋18	17♌23	6♎20	10♏18
7	17♍08	1♏26	9♏18	23♐11	26♑04	13♓35	20♈58	14♊24	7♌13	13♍53	1♏08	4♐14
9	11♎41	25♏13	3♐05	17♑21	21♒10	10♈57	19♉35	13♋18	4♍31	9♎38	25♏23	27♐55
11	5♏31	19♐12	27♐01	12♒33	17♓48	10♉01	19♊09	11♌50	0♎56	4♏36	19♐11	21♑34
13	29♏18	13♑58	21♑44	9♓22	16♈21	10♊15	18♋48	9♍24	26♎18	28♏51	12♑47	15♒32
15	23♐34	9♒54	17♒47	8♈04	16♉30	10♋26	17♌32	5♎40	20♏44	22♐35	6♒38	10♓17
17	18♑38	7♓05	15♓28	8♉07	17♊04	9♌22	14♍42	0♏40	14♐33	16♑17	1♓24	6♈24
19	14♒37	5♈15	14♈30	8♊19	16♋39	6♍29	10♎19	24♏47	8♑21	10♒37	27♓44	4♉20
21	11♓27	3♉53	14♉04	7♋27	14♌27	1♎58	4♏46	18♐33	2♒47	6♓16	26♈03	3♊59
23	9♈00	2♊25	13♊10	4♌58	10♍32	26♎21	28♏36	12♑36	28♒25	3♈42	26♉01	4♋31
25	7♉08	0♋29	11♋12	1♍01	5♎21	20♏11	22♐25	7♒26	25♓35	2♉49	26♊32	4♌35
27	5♊39	27♋53	8♌04	26♍01	29♎27	13♐56	16♑38	3♓24	24♈03	2♊45	26♋12	3♍08
29	4♋09		3♍56	20♎22	23♏15	7♑56	11♒34	0♈28	23♉07	2♋19	24♌16	29♍52
31	2♌08		29♍03		17♐01		7♓21	28♈25		0♌42		25♎05
1	21♐17	9♒24	27♓44	20♓58	17♈00	17♊43	4♌11	29♋54	0♍44	23♎43	0♐39	18♏17
☿ 7	29 54	19 50	3♈12	21D49	26 43	29 59	8 07	28D38	12 26	2♏36	1R28	24 39
13	8♑52	0♓40	3R34	25 27	7♉35	10♋56	9R30	1♌13	23 41	10 57	26♏53	2♐40
19	18 08	11 38	29♓28	1♈10	19 34	20 21	8 04	7 45	4♎18	18 37	19 12	11 22
25	27 44	21 58	24 12	8 26	2♊26	28 09	4 24	17 24	14 17	25 15	15 38	20 23
31	7♒42		21 09		15 34		0 25	28 46		0♐06		29 35

DATE	☉	♀	♂	♃	♄	⚷	♅	♆	♇	☊	STATIONS
1 1	10♑07	25♑24	18♎23	21♓57	26♈47	29♏18	10♒58	1♒04	9♐09	24♌24	
11	20 19	7♒56	23 12	23 31	26 55	0♐22	11 30	1 26	9 28	23 52	☿ 10/3 4♈04
21	0♒30	20 26	27 41	25 18	27 14	1 20	12 04	1 49	9 46	23 20	☿ 2/4 20♓53
31	10 40	2♓55	1♏47	27 15	27 44	2 09	12 39	2 12	10 02	22 49	☿ 13/7 9♌30
10 2	20 48	15 20	5 24	29 21	28 23	2 50	13 14	2 34	10 14	22 17	☿ 6/8 28♋35
20	0♓54	27 43	8 23	1♈33	29 11	3 21	13 48	2 55	10 23	21 45	☿ 5/11 1♐44
2 3	10 58	10♈01	10 37	3 51	0♉06	3 42	14 21	3 15	10 29	21 13	☿ 25/11 15♏38
12	20 58	22 14	11 55	6 12	1 08	3 52	14 53	3 33	10 31	20 41	♀ 30/7 5♍08
22	0♈56	4♉21	12R06	8 36	2 15	3R51	15 21	3 49	10R30	20 10	♀ 11/9 18♌47
1 4	10 50	16 20	11 03	11 02	3 26	3 40	15 46	4 02	10 26	19 38	♂ 19/3 12♏11
11	20 41	28 11	8 44	13 27	4 40	3 20	16 07	4 11	10 18	19 06	♂ 4/6 24♎25
21	0♉28	9♊52	5 27	15 50	5 56	2 50	16 25	4 18	10 08	18 34	♃ 25/8 5♉00
1 5	10 12	21 21	1 43	18 12	7 13	2 14	16 37	4 22	9 55	18 03	♃ 21/12 25♈01
11	19 53	2♋35	28♎18	20 29	8 29	1 33	16 45	4R22	9 41	17 31	♄ 30/8 17♉11
21	29 32	13 30	25 47	22 42	9 44	0 50	16 48	4 19	9 25	16 59	♅ 22/5 16♒48
31	9♊08	24 02	24 32	24 48	10 57	0 06	16R46	4 13	9 09	16 27	♅ 23/10 12♒52
10 6	18 43	4♌02	24D38	26 47	12 05	29♏24	16 39	4 04	8 53	15 56	♆ 7/5 4♒22
20	28 16	13 20	25 59	28 37	13 10	28 47	16 28	3 53	8 37	15 24	♆ 14/10 1♒36
30	7♋48	21 38	28 23	0♉16	14 08	28 16	16 13	3 40	8 23	14 52	♇ 14/3 10♐31
10 7	17 20	28 30	1♏41	1 43	15 00	27 53	15 54	3 25	8 10	14 20	♇ 19/8 7♐46
20	26 52	3♍18	5 43	2 56	15 45	27 40	15 33	3 09	8 00	13 48	⚷ 16/3 3♐53
30	6♌26	5 08	10 21	3 54	16 21	27D36	15 10	2 53	7 52	13 17	⚷ 29/7 27♏35
9 8	16 00	3R12	15 30	4 34	16 48	27 41	14 46	2 37	7 48	12 45	
19	25 36	27♌57	21 05	4 56	17 05	27 57	14 22	2 22	7 46	12 13	
29	5♍14	22 07	27 01	4R58	17 11	28 23	14 00	2 08	7D48	11 41	
8 9	14 55	18 58	3♐17	4 40	17R07	28 57	13 39	1 56	7 53	11 10	
18	24 39	19D42	9 48	4 03	16 52	29 40	13 22	1 47	8 01	10 38	
28	4♎26	23 45	16 34	3 09	16 28	0♐31	13 08	1 40	8 12	10 06	
8 10	14 17	0♍14	23 32	2 00	15 54	1 28	12 58	1 36	8 27	9 34	
18	24 11	8 22	0♑41	0 43	15 14	2 31	12 53	1D36	8 43	9 02	
28	4♏08	17 40	7 58	29♈22	14 28	3 39	12D53	1 39	9 02	8 31	
7 11	14 08	27 48	15 24	28 03	13 40	4 50	12 58	1 45	9 23	7 59	
17	24 11	8♎32	22 56	26 54	12 52	6 03	13 08	1 55	9 45	7 27	
27	4♐17	19 43	0♒33	25 58	12 07	7 18	13 23	2 08	10 08	6 55	
7 12	14 26	1♏14	8 14	25 20	11 27	8 33	13 42	2 23	10 32	6 24	
17	24 36	13 00	15 58	25 02	10 55	9 47	14 06	2 41	10 55	5 52	
27	4♑47	24 57	23 43	25D05	10 32	10 59	14 33	3 01	11 17	5 20	

SID M/N 1st JAN 6 h 39 m 51 s 2000 LEAP BST

DAY	JAN	FEB	MAR	APR	MAY	JUN	JUL	AUG	SEP	OCT	NOV	DEC
1	7♏17	21♐33	11♑27	25♒41	29♓29	19♉47	28♊00	21♌40	13♎06	17♏51	2♑59	4♒41
☽ 3	1♐13	15♑14	5♒26	21♓26	27♈05	19♊37	28♋20	20♍53	9♏53	13♐01	26♑43	28♒19
5	24♐52	9♒21	0♓15	18♈37	26♉04	19♋40	27♌59	18♎27	5♐03	7♑05	20♒23	22♓34
7	18♑35	4♓10	26♓10	16♉52	25♊33	18♌50	26♍09	14♏18	29♐07	0♒43	14♓42	18♈04
9	12♒38	29♓50	23♈07	15♊32	24♋37	16♍38	22♎39	8♐49	22♑44	24♒37	10♈16	15♉15
11	7♓16	26♈24	20♉48	14♋01	22♌44	13♎03	17♏46	2♑35	16♒32	19♓24	7♉21	14♊03
13	2♈48	23♉55	18♊53	12♌01	19♍49	8♏22	11♐57	26♑11	11♓02	15♈22	5♊41	13♋46
15	29♈37	22♊19	17♋10	9♍28	16♎00	2♐52	5♑40	20♒03	6♈26	12♉28	4♋36	13♌24
17	27♉55	21♋21	15♌27	6♎18	11♏23	26♐49	29♑17	14♓29	2♉43	10♊18	3♌22	12♍06
19	27♊29	20♌28	13♍27	2♏21	6♐00	20♑27	23♒06	9♈41	29♉47	8♋26	1♍35	9♎33
21	27♋31	18♍53	10♎41	27♏27	29♐59	14♒05	17♓26	5♉46	27♊30	6♌37	29♍05	5♏48
23	26♌56	15♎59	6♏47	21♐41	23♑36	8♓10	12♈39	2♊55	25♋49	4♍44	25♎51	1♐03
25	24♍52	11♏34	1♐40	15♑22	17♒20	3♈14	9♉08	1♋11	24♌34	2♎35	21♏47	25♐32
27	21♎04	5♐55	25♐38	9♒06	11♓47	29♈49	7♊07	0♌26	23♍16	29♎46	16♐49	19♑26
29	15♏51	29♐37	19♑17	3♓35	7♈38	28♉10	6♋31	0♍02	21♎14	25♏56	11♑01	13♒03
31	9♐44		13♒19		5♉18		6♌39	29♍04		20♐53		6♓42
1	1♑08	22♒34	12♓00	14♓02	1♉42	2♋42	17♋55	20♋12	18♍06	2♏58	4♏34	25♏38
☿ 7	10 33	2♓46	6℞05	21 26	14 11	10 22	14℞23	29 36	28 28	9 23	0℞04	4♐53
13	20 12	11 30	2 58	0♈00	27 12	15 59	11 16	11♌00	8♎08	14 05	1D58	14 12
19	0♒08	16 39	3D36	9 34	9♊54	19 15	10D29	23 09	17 08	15℞48	8 18	23 35
25	10 22	16℞12	7 13	20 08	21 25	19℞52	13 00	5♍04	25 27	12 54	16 37	3♑03
31	20 49		12 55		1♋15		18 55	16 18		5 48		12 40

DATE	☉	♀	♂	♃	♄	⚷	♅	♆	♇	☊	STATIONS
1 1	9♑52	0♐59	27♒35	25♈14	10♉25	11♐34	14♒48	3♒11	11♐28	5♌04	
11	20 04	13 07	5♓21	25 48	10℞18	12 41	15 19	3 33	11 48	4 32	☿ 22/2 17♓11
21	0♒15	25 19	13 05	26 40	10D22	13 42	15 52	3 56	12 07	4 01	☿ 15/3 2♓47
31	10 25	7♑36	20 47	27 50	10 37	14 38	16 27	4 18	12 22	3 29	☿ 23/6 19♋58
10 2	20 33	19 54	28 27	29 14	11 04	15 26	17 02	4 41	12 35	2 57	☿ 18/7 10♋24
20	0♓40	2♒14	6♈04	0♉52	11 40	16 07	17 36	5 02	12 45	2 25	☿ 19/10 15♏49
1 3	10 43	14 35	13 37	2 41	12 25	16 38	18 10	5 23	12 52	1 54	☿ 8/11 29♎57
11	20 44	26 57	21 06	4 39	13 18	16 60	18 42	5 41	12 55	1 22	♃ 29/9 11♊14
21	0♈41	9♓18	28 30	6 46	14 18	17 12	19 11	5 57	12℞55	0 50	♄ 12/1 10♉18
31	10 36	21 39	5♉50	8 58	15 24	17℞14	19 38	6 11	12 52	0 18	♄ 12/9 0♊59
10 4	20 26	4♈00	13 05	11 15	16 34	17 06	20 01	6 22	12 45	29♋46	♅ 25/5 20♒50
20	0♉14	16 19	20 15	13 35	17 48	16 48	20 20	6 29	12 35	29 15	♅ 27/10 16♒54
30	9 58	28 38	27 20	15 57	19 04	16 23	20 34	6 34	12 23	28 43	♆ 8/5 6♒35
10 5	19 39	10♉57	4♊21	18 20	20 21	15 50	20 44	6℞35	12 10	28 11	♆ 15/10 3♒48
20	29 18	23 15	11 17	20 42	21 38	15 12	20 49	6 33	11 54	27 39	♇ 15/3 12♐56
30	8♊54	5♊32	18 09	23 03	22 54	14 31	20℞49	6 27	11 38	27 08	♇ 21/8 10♐11
9 6	18 29	17 49	24 57	25 21	24 08	13 48	20 45	6 19	11 22	26 36	⚷ 28/ 3 17♐14
19	28 02	0♋06	1♋41	27 35	25 20	13 07	20 35	6 08	11 06	26 04	⚷ 13/ 8 11♐03
29	7♋34	12 24	8 21	29 44	26 27	12 29	20 22	5 56	10 52	25 32	
9 7	17 06	24 41	14 58	1♊47	27 28	11 56	20 05	5 41	10 39	25 01	
19	26 39	6♌59	21 31	3 42	28 24	11 31	19 44	5 25	10 28	24 29	
29	6♌12	19 17	28 02	5 28	29 13	11 13	19 22	5 09	10 19	23 57	
8 8	15 46	1♍35	4♌30	7 03	29 53	11 04	18 59	4 53	10 14	23 25	
18	25 22	13 52	10 56	8 25	0♊25	11D04	18 35	4 38	10 11	22 53	
28	5♍00	26 09	17 19	9 33	0 46	11 14	18 11	4 23	10D12	22 22	
7 9	14 41	8♎25	23 41	10 25	0 58	11 33	17 50	4 11	10 16	21 50	
17	24 25	20 40	0♍01	10 59	0℞58	12 01	17 31	4 01	10 23	21 18	
27	4♎12	2♏54	6 18	11 14	0 48	12 37	17 15	3 53	10 34	20 46	
7 10	14 02	15 06	12 34	11℞09	0 27	13 22	17 03	3 49	10 47	20 15	
17	23 56	27 16	18 49	10 44	29♉57	14 12	16 56	3D48	11 03	19 43	
27	3♏53	9♐24	25 01	10 00	29 19	15 09	16D54	3 50	11 22	19 11	
6 11	13 54	21 29	1♎12	8 59	28 35	16 10	16 57	3 56	11 42	18 39	
16	23 57	3♑30	7 20	7 47	27 47	17 15	17 05	4 05	12 04	18 07	
26	4♐03	15 26	13. 26	6 26	26 58	18 23	17 18	4 17	12 26	17 36	
6 12	14 11	27 14	19 30	5 05	26 11	19 33	17 35	4 31	12 49	17 04	
16	24 21	8♒53	25 29	3 49	25 29	20 42	17 57	4 49	13 13	16 32	
26	4♑32	20 17	1♏26	2 44	24 53	21 52	18 23	5 08	13 35	16 00	

SID M/N 1st JAN 6 h 42 m 50 s 2001 COMMON BST

DAY	JAN	FEB	MAR	APR	MAY	JUN	JUL	AUG	SEP	OCT	NOV	DEC
1	18♓42	5♉09	14♉54	5♋30	14♌27	7♎42	15♏15	2♑55	17♒53	20♓25	5♉52	10♊29
☽ 3	13♈23	1♊44	11♊23	3♌36	12♍53	5♏06	11♐02	27♑03	11♓36	14♈36	1♊30	7♋44
5	9♉27	29♊59	9♋10	2♍33	11♎18	1♐38	5♑58	20♒52	5♈31	9♉20	27♊54	5♌42
7	7♊17	29♋46	8♌18	1♎50	9♏11	27♐11	0♒13	14♓34	29♈50	4♊42	25♋04	4♍01
9	6♋46	0♍15	8♍19	0♏34	5♐58	21♑48	24♒02	8♈27	24♉50	0♋55	23♌00	2♎22
11	7♌07	0♎08	8♎06	27♏54	1♑28	15♒44	17♓44	2♉54	20♊54	28♋17	21♍37	0♏28
13	7♍07	28♎22	6♏31	23♐37	25♑51	9♓27	11♈48	28♉22	18♋27	26♌57	20♎33	28♏01
15	5♎46	24♏42	3♐03	18♑00	19♒37	3♈31	6♉46	25♊22	17♌39	26♍36	19♏04	24♐40
17	2♏42	19♐29	27♐57	11♒43	13♓25	28♈34	3♊08	24♋09	17♍57	26♎18	16♐28	20♑17
19	28♏08	13♑21	21♑50	5♓28	7♈55	25♉02	1♋14	24♌20	18♎07	24♏56	12♑26	14♒54
21	22♐32	6♒55	15♒25	29♓50	3♉33	23♊00	0♌48	24♍47	16♏53	21♐50	7♒08	8♓50
23	16♑21	0♓37	9♓16	25♈10	0♊27	22♋04	0♍57	24♎11	13♐42	17♑06	1♓03	2♈36
25	9♒57	24♓44	3♈45	21♉29	28♊23	21♌29	0♎31	21♏46	8♑50	11♒15	24♓49	26♈48
27	3♓38	19♈26	29♈00	18♊36	26♋53	20♍26	28♎41	17♐34	2♒56	4♓58	19♈04	22♉01
29	27♓40		25♉01	16♋18	25♌28	18♎24	25♏18	12♑08	26♒37	28♓52	14♉13	18♊39
31	22♈24		21♊48		23♍45		20♐36	6♒02		23♈20		16♋41
1	14♑17	29♒51	16♒00	21♓07	19♉32	29♊34	21♊35	3♌18	29♍58	29♎39	20♎27	6♐42
☿ 7	24 07	29℞55	19 28	1♈15	1♊32	29℞41	24 23	15 47	8♎28	28℞00	28 46	16 07
13	4♒05	24 23	25 06	12 14	11 52	27 26	0♋04	27 43	16 04	22 05	8♏06	25 33
19	13 56	18 04	2♓13	24 07	20 05	24 07	8 26	8♍48	22 32	15 42	17 40	5♑02
25	22 54	15 26	10 24	6♉44	25 58	21 40	19 04	19 03	27 23	14D34	27 13	14 34
31	29 14		19 31		29 17		1♌12	28 29		19 17		24 03

DATE	☉	♀	♂	♃	♄	⚷	♅	♆	♇	☊	STATIONS
1 1	10♑39	26♒59	4♏57	2♊12	24♉36	22♐32	18♒40	5♒21	13♐48	15♋41	
11	20 50	7♓48	10 45	1℞33	24℞15	23 38	19 10	5 42	14 08	15 10	☿ 4/2 0♓42
21	1♒01	18 04	16 27	1 14	24 05	24 40	19 43	6 05	14 27	14 38	☿ 26/2 15♒25
31	11 11	27 32	22 02	1D15	24D06	25 38	20 17	6 27	14 43	14 06	☿ 4/6 29♊58
10 2	21 19	5♈52	27 27	1 37	24 18	26 30	20 51	6 50	14 57	13 34	☿ 28/6 21♊16
20	1♓25	12 32	2♐41	2 17	24 42	27 15	21 26	7 12	15 07	13 02	☿ 2/10 29♎41
2 3	11 29	16 46	7 41	3 16	25 15	27 53	22 00	7 32	15 14	12 31	☿ 23/10 14♎12
12	21 29	17℞34	12 24	4 30	25 58	28 22	22 32	7 51	15 18	11 59	♀ 9/3 17♈44
22	1♈27	14 21	16 45	5 58	26 49	28 42	23 03	8 07	15℞18	11 27	♀ 20/4 1♈28
1 4	11 20	8 24	20 40	7 38	27 48	28 53	23 30	8 21	15 15	10 55	♂ 12/5 29♐01
11	21 11	3 11	24 00	9 27	28 52	28℞55	23 54	8 33	15 09	10 24	♂ 20/7 15♐04
21	0♉58	1D29	26 37	11 25	0♊02	28 47	24 15	8 41	15 00	9 52	♃ 25/1 1♊12
1 5	10 42	3 35	28 21	13 30	1 15	28 31	24 31	8 45	14 48	9 20	♃ 3/11 15♋42
11	20 23	8 38	29 01	15 40	2 30	28 07	24 42	8℞47	14 35	8 48	♄ 25/1 24♉04
21	0♊02	15 41	28℞27	17 54	3 48	27 36	24 49	8 45	14 20	8 16	♄ 27/9 14♊59
31	9 38	24 06	26 40	20 11	5 05	26 60	24℞51	8 41	14 04	7 45	♅ 30/5 24♒51
10 6	19 12	3♉26	23 54	22 29	6 22	26 20	24 47	8 33	13 48	7 13	♅ 31/10 20♒55
20	28 45	13 26	20 41	24 47	7 38	25 40	24 40	8 22	13 32	6 41	♆ 11/5 8♒47
30	8♋18	23 53	17 45	27 05	8 51	24 60	24 27	8 10	13 17	6 09	♆ 18/10 6♒00
10 7	17 50	4♊43	15 45	29 21	10 00	24 23	24 12	7 56	13 04	5 38	♇ 18/3 15♐18
20	27 22	15 49	15D04	1♋33	11 04	23 50	23 52	7 40	12 53	5 06	♇ 24/8 12♐34
30	6♌55	27 08	15 46	3 41	12 03	23 24	23 31	7 24	12 44	4 34	⚷ 8/4 28♐55
9 8	16 30	8♋39	17 46	5 44	12 55	23 05	23 07	7 08	12 38	4 02	⚷ 26/8 22♐51
19	26 06	20 21	20 51	7 40	13 39	22 54	22 44	6 52	12 35	3 31	
29	5♍44	2♌11	24 51	9 27	14 14	22D52	22 20	6 38	12D35	2 59	
8 9	15 25	14 09	29 36	11 04	14 39	22 58	21 58	6 25	12 38	2 27	
18	25 09	26 15	4♑56	12 30	14 54	23 14	21 38	6 14	12 45	1 55	
28	4♎57	8♍27	10 44	13 42	14℞59	23 38	21 21	6 07	12 55	1 23	
8 10	14 47	20 45	16 56	14 38	14 52	24 11	21 08	6 02	13 08	0 52	
18	24 41	3♎08	23 26	15 18	14 35	24 51	20 59	6D00	13 23	0 20	
28	4♏39	15 34	0♒10	15 39	14 08	25 37	20 55	6 02	13 41	29♊48	
7 11	14 39	28 04	7 06	15℞40	13 32	26 29	20D56	6 07	14 01	29 16	
17	24 43	10♏36	14 10	15 21	12 49	27 25	21 03	6 15	14 22	28 45	
27	4♐49	23 09	21 21	14 43	12 02	28 26	21 14	6 27	14 45	28 13	
7 12	14 57	5♐43	28 36	13 48	11 12	29 29	21 30	6 41	15 08	27 41	
17	25 07	18 18	5♓54	12 39	10 24	0♑33	21 50	6 58	15 31	27 09	
27	5♑18	0♑53	13 13	11 21	9 40	1 38	22 15	7 17	15 53	26 38	

SID M/N 1st JAN 6 h 41 m 53 s — 2002 COMMON — BST

	DAY	JAN	FEB	MAR	APR	MAY	JUN	JUL	AUG	SEP	OCT	NOV	DEC
☽	1	1♌06	24♍35	3♎18	25♏59	1♑38	17♒58	20♓09	3♉50	18♊41	23♋15	14♍21	23♎05
	3	0♍15	23♎45	3♏06	23♐26	27♑31	12♓13	13♈57	28♉03	14♋44	21♌00	14♎05	22♏38
	5	29♍09	21♏27	1♐10	19♑07	22♒06	6♈00	7♉54	23♊24	12♌41	20♍35	14♏23	21♐52
	7	27♎17	17♐43	27♐27	13♒35	15♓59	29♈56	2♊37	20♋21	12♍20	21♎07	14♐00	19♑56
	9	24♏28	12♑57	22♑24	7♓26	9♈43	24♉31	28♊33	18♌56	12♎39	21♏15	12♑03	16♒24
	11	20♐44	7♒28	16♒35	1♈08	3♉46	20♊01	25♋50	18♍29	12♏20	19♐52	8♒20	11♓26
	13	16♑10	1♓33	10♓25	25♈01	28♉24	16♋33	24♌12	17♎57	10♐32	16♑42	3♓12	5♈28
	15	10♒52	25♓20	4♈10	19♉15	23♊45	14♌00	23♍00	16♏30	7♑11	12♒04	27♓13	29♈09
	17	4♓58	19♈04	27♈59	14♊03	19♋59	12♍07	21♎37	13♐51	2♒39	6♓29	20♈54	23♉03
	19	28♓43	13♉06	22♉09	9♋44	17♌11	10♎34	19♏39	10♑09	27♒18	0♈23	14♉43	17♊38
	21	22♈33	7♊59	17♊02	6♌39	15♍22	9♏02	16♐57	5♒37	21♓27	24♈06	8♊56	13♋08
	23	17♉03	4♋21	13♋12	5♍05	14♎22	7♐08	13♑28	0♓25	15♈15	17♉52	3♋46	9♌34
	25	12♊50	2♌40	11♌09	4♎46	13♏34	4♑28	9♒11	24♓37	8♉55	11♊57	29♋27	6♍50
	27	10♋22	2♍40	10♍51	4♏49	12♐12	0♒44	4♓03	18♈24	2♊47	6♋42	26♌10	4♎45
	29	9♌33		11♎26	4♐02	9♑35	25♒54	28♓11	12♉06	27♊21	2♌34	24♍05	3♏08
	31	9♍36		11♏31		5♒30		21♈56	6♊14		0♍00		1♐46
☿	1	25♑36	2♒39	14♒40	4♈36	0♊53	3♊20	19♊07	20♌13	5♎31	1♎09	0♏06	17♐57
	7	4♒29	28R50	22 43	16 37	6 46	1R28	29 12	1♍02	10 28	28D20	10 01	27 11
	13	11 35	29D39	1♓35	29 08	9 41	2D05	11♋00	10 54	13 05	1♎30	19 44	6♑18
	19	14R29	3♒45	11 11	11♉23	9R36	5 22	23 44	19 49	12R17	9 01	29 16	15 03
	25	10 59	9 51	21 32	22 16	7 07	11 07	6♌24	27 45	7 31	18 28	8♐39	22 45
	31	3 44		2♈40		3 49		18 20	4♎32		28 26		27 48

DATE	☉	♀	♂	♃	♄	⚷	♅	♆	♇	☊	STATIONS
1 1	10♑24	7♑11	16♓52	10♋40	9♊20	2♑10	22♒28	7♒28	16♐04	26♊22	
11	20 35	19 46	24 12	9R20	8R46	3 14	22 57	7 49	16 25	25 50	☿ 19/1 14♒29
21	0♒46	2♒20	1♈29	8 06	8 21	4 15	23 29	8 11	16 44	25 18	☿ 9/2 28♑38
31	10 56	14 54	8 45	7 03	8 06	5 13	24 03	8 34	17 01	24 46	☿ 16/5 10♊00
10 2	21 05	27 27	15 59	6 16	8D03	6 07	24 37	8 57	17 15	24 15	☿ 9/6 1♊22
20	1♓11	9♓58	23 09	5 47	8 10	6 55	25 12	9 19	17 26	23 43	☿ 15/9 13♎15
2 3	11 14	22 27	0♉16	5D38	8 30	7 37	25 46	9 39	17 34	23 11	☿ 7/10 28♍19
12	21 15	4♈55	7 20	5 49	8 59	8 12	26 19	9 59	17 38	22 39	♀ 11/10 15♏36
22	1♈12	17 19	14 20	6 18	9 38	8 39	26 50	10 16	17R39	22 07	♀ 21/11 0♏03
1 4	11 06	29 41	21 16	7 06	10 26	8 57	27 19	10 30	17 37	21 36	♃ 2/3 5♋38
11	20 57	11♉59	28 09	8 09	11 22	9 07	27 44	10 42	17 32	21 04	♃ 4/12 18♌07
21	0♉44	24 14	4♊58	9 27	12 24	9R08	28 06	10 51	17 24	20 32	♄ 8/2 8♊02
1 5	10 28	6♊24	11 43	10 56	13 31	9 01	28 24	10 57	17 13	20 00	♄ 11/10 29♊06
11	20 09	18 31	18 25	12 37	14 43	8 45	28 38	10 59	17 00	19 29	♅ 3/6 28♒50
21	29 48	0♋33	25 04	14 27	15 58	8 22	28 46	10R58	16 45	18 57	♅ 4/11 24♒55
31	9♊24	12 29	1♋40	16 23	17 15	7 52	28 50	10 54	16 30	18 25	♆ 13/5 10♒59
10 6	18 58	24 19	8 14	18 26	18 32	7 18	28R49	10 47	16 14	17 53	♆ 20/10 8♒12
20	28 31	6♌02	14 45	20 33	19 50	6 40	28 43	10 38	15 58	17 21	♇ 20/3 17♐39
30	8♋04	17 37	21 13	22 44	21 07	6 01	28 33	10 26	15 43	16 50	♇ 26/8 14♐56
10 7	17 36	29 01	27 40	24 57	22 21	5 23	28 19	10 12	15 29	16 18	⚷ 17/4 9♑09
20	27 08	10♍12	4♌06	27 11	23 33	4 47	28 01	9 56	15 17	15 46	⚷ 7/9 3♑13
30	6♌41	21 07	10 30	29 25	24 40	4 15	27 40	9 40	15 08	15 14	
9 8	16 16	1♎42	16 53	1♌37	25 42	3 49	27 18	9 24	15 01	14 43	
19	25 52	11 48	23 16	3 47	26 37	3 29	26 54	9 08	14 57	14 11	
29	5♍30	21 17	29 38	5 54	27 25	3 17	26 30	8 53	14D56	13 39	
8 9	15 11	29 54	6♍00	7 55	28 05	3D13	26 07	8 40	14 59	13 07	
18	24 55	7♏15	12 21	9 50	28 35	3 18	25 46	8 29	15 04	12 36	
28	4♎42	12 43	18 43	11 38	28 56	3 31	25 28	8 20	15 13	12 04	
8 10	14 33	15 28	25 05	13 16	29 05	3 52	25 13	8 15	15 25	11 32	
18	24 27	14R33	1♎28	14 42	29R03	4 22	25 02	8 12	15 40	11 00	
28	4♏24	10 00	7 51	15 56	28 51	4 58	24 56	8D13	15 57	10 28	
7 11	14 25	4 06	14 15	16 55	28 27	5 40	24D55	8 18	16 17	9 57	
17	24 28	0 26	20 39	17 37	27 55	6 28	24 59	8 25	16 38	9 25	
27	4♐34	0D42	27 04	18 01	27 15	7 21	25 08	8 36	17 00	8 53	
7 12	14 42	4 32	3♏30	18R06	26 29	8 17	25 22	8 50	17 23	8 21	
17	24 52	10 57	9 56	17 51	25 40	9 15	25 41	9 06	17 45	7 50	
27	5♑03	19 07	16 22	17 17	24 51	10 15	26 04	9 25	18 08	7 18	

SID M/N 1st JAN 6 h 40 m 56 s — 2003 COMMON — BST

DAY	JAN	FEB	MAR	APR	MAY	JUN	JUL	AUG	SEP	OCT	NOV	DEC
1	16♐01	6♒13	15♒26	1♈58	4♉42	19♊10	22♋58	12♍15	4♏45	13♐50	5♒50	11♓41
☽ 3	14♑06	2♓10	10♓45	25♈53	28♉18	13♋35	18♌48	9♎59	3♐12	11♑57	2♓12	6♈41
5	11♒08	27♓05	5♈18	19♉29	22♊06	8♌49	15♍32	8♏05	1♑14	9♒02	27♓24	0♉44
7	6♓51	21♈07	29♈12	13♊08	16♋30	5♍06	13♎06	6♐22	28♑43	5♓11	21♈46	24♉23
9	1♈23	14♉46	22♉47	7♋21	11♌56	2♎37	11♏28	4♑40	25♒32	0♈27	15♉36	18♊00
11	25♈10	8♊40	16♊38	2♌46	8♍51	1♏25	10♐24	2♒39	21♓29	24♈56	9♊13	11♋54
13	18♉54	3♋32	11♋25	29♌55	7♎28	1♐06	9♑25	29♒49	16♈27	18♉49	2♋53	6♌20
15	13♊13	29♋57	7♌49	28♍56	7♏25	0♑49	7♒46	25♓47	10♉32	12♊23	27♋01	1♍32
17	8♋39	27♌58	6♍06	29♎11	7♐43	29♑35	4♓49	20♈32	4♊09	6♋08	22♌06	27♍52
19	5♌23	27♍03	5♎47	29♏27	7♑11	26♒45	0♈21	14♉25	27♊55	0♌41	18♍36	25♎37
21	3♍12	26♎16	5♏48	28♐36	5♒04	22♓15	24♈38	8♊03	22♋32	26♌37	16♎52	24♏50
23	1♎33	24♏52	5♐02	26♑08	1♓13	16♈32	18♉19	2♋10	18♌36	24♍19	16♏39	25♐00
25	29♎54	22♐32	2♑56	22♒07	25♓59	10♉11	12♊04	27♋23	16♍19	23♎39	17♐05	24♑58
27	27♏59	19♑22	29♑32	16♓56	19♈53	3♊51	6♋31	24♌01	15♎20	23♏46	16♑55	23♒36
29	25♐42		25♒05	11♈01	13♉29	28♊01	2♌01	21♍53	14♏48	23♐33	15♒12	20♓21
31	22♑53		19♓50		7♊10		28♌36	20♎26		22♑07		15♈25
1	28♑11	16♑37	23♒19	21♈11	19♉41	16♉06	3♋24	2♍06	25♍45	20♍30	12♏20	27♐28
☿ 7	26R43	22 38	3♓15	2♉30	16R32	22 03	16 25	10 16	21R55	29 55	21 49	5♑07
13	19 38	29 57	13 50	11 41	13 02	29 55	29 00	17 11	16 05	10♎18	1♐05	10 51
19	13 30	8♒10	25 06	17 49	11 12	9♊33	10♌37	22 32	12 22	20 44	10 09	12R24
25	12D33	17 03	7♈00	20 27	11D58	20 50	21 10	25 45	13D56	0♏54	19 00	7 35
31	15 48		19 11		15 19		0♍38	26R02		10 43		29♐49

DATE	☉	♀	♂	♃	♄	⚷	♅	♆	♇	☊	STATIONS
1 1	10♑09	23♏41	19♏36	16♌54	24♊27	10♑46	26♒16	9♒35	18♐19	7♊02	
11	20 20	3♐29	26 02	15R55	23R43	11 46	26 44	9 56	18 40	6 30	☿ 3/1 28♑28
21	0♒31	13 57	2♐29	14 44	23 05	12 45	27 15	10 18	18 59	5 58	☿ 23/1 12♑18
31	10 41	24 54	8 56	13 26	22 36	13 42	27 48	10 41	19 16	5 27	☿ 26/4 20♉34
10 2	20 50	6♑11	15 22	12 06	22 17	14 36	28 22	11 03	19 31	4 55	☿ 20/5 11♉08
20	0♓56	17 42	21 47	10 51	22 09	15 25	28 56	11 26	19 43	4 23	☿ 29/8 26♍20
2 3	11 00	29 23	28 11	9 46	22D12	16 10	29 31	11 47	19 51	3 51	☿ 20/9 12♍13
12	21 00	11♒13	4♑33	8 55	22 26	16 48	0♓04	12 06	19 57	3 20	☿ 18/12 12♑34
22	0♈58	23 07	10 52	8 21	22 51	17 20	0 36	12 24	19 59	2 48	♂ 29/7 10♓08
1 4	10 52	5♓06	17 09	8 05	23 26	17 44	1 06	12 39	19R57	2 16	♂ 27/9 0♓07
11	20 42	17 08	23 20	8D09	24 10	17 60	1 33	12 52	19 53	1 44	♃ 4/4 8♌04
21	0♉30	29 12	29 26	8 31	25 03	18 08	1 57	13 02	19 45	1 12	♄ 22/2 22♊08
1 5	10 14	11♈17	5♒23	9 11	26 02	18R08	2 16	13 08	19 35	0 41	♄ 26/10 13♋15
11	19 55	23 24	11 10	10 06	27 07	17 59	2 32	13 11	19 23	0 09	♅ 7/6 2♓49
21	29 34	5♉32	16 44	11 16	28 17	17 43	2 42	13R11	19 09	29♉37	♅ 8/11 28♒54
31	9♊10	17 40	22 00	12 39	29 30	17 20	2 48	13 08	18 54	29 05	♆ 16/5 13♒12
10 6	18 44	29 50	26 52	14 12	0♋46	16 52	2R49	13 02	18 38	28 34	♆ 23/10 10♒25
20	28 18	12♊01	1♓13	15 55	2 04	16 18	2 46	12 53	18 22	28 02	♇ 23/3 19♐59
30	7♋50	24 13	4 55	17 46	3 22	15 42	2 37	12 41	18 07	27 30	♇ 29/8 17♐16
10 7	17 22	6♋28	7 46	19 43	4 39	15 05	2 25	12 27	17 52	26 58	⚷ 26/4 18♑09
20	26 54	18 43	9 34	21 46	5 55	14 28	2 08	12 12	17 40	26 26	⚷ 18/9 12♑22
30	6♌27	1♌01	10R08	23 52	7 08	13 53	1 49	11 57	17 30	25 55	
9 8	16 02	13 21	9 24	26 01	8 18	13 23	1 27	11 40	17 22	25 23	
19	25 38	25 42	7 31	28 11	9 22	12 57	1 03	11 24	17 18	24 51	
29	5♍16	8♍06	4 57	0♍22	10 21	12 38	0 39	11 09	17 16	24 19	
8 9	14 57	20 30	2 27	2 32	11 13	12 26	0 16	10 55	17D18	23 48	
18	24 41	2♎55	0 41	4 40	11 57	12 22	29♒54	10 44	17 23	23 16	
28	4♎28	15 21	0D07	6 45	12 32	12D26	29 34	10 35	17 31	22 44	
8 10	14 19	27 48	0 52	8 45	12 57	12 38	29 18	10 28	17 42	22 12	
18	24 12	10♏14	2 51	10 39	13 11	12 58	29 05	10 25	17 56	21 41	
28	4♏10	22 40	5 51	12 26	13R14	13 25	28 57	10D25	18 12	21 09	
7 11	14 10	5♐07	9 42	14 03	13 06	13 59	28 54	10 28	18 31	20 37	
17	24 13	17 32	14 11	15 29	12 48	14 38	28D56	10 35	18 52	20 05	
27	4♐19	29 58	19 11	16 43	12 19	15 24	29 03	10 45	19 13	19 33	
7 12	14 27	12♑22	24 34	17 41	11 42	16 13	29 15	10 58	19 36	19 02	
17	24 37	24 44	0♈15	18 24	10 58	17 06	29 32	11 14	19 58	18 30	
27	4♑48	7♒05	6 09	18 49	10 10	18 01	29 53	11 32	20 21	17 58	

SID M/N 1st JAN 6 h 39 m 59 s 2004 LEAP BST

DAY	JAN	FEB	MAR	APR	MAY	JUN	JUL	AUG	SEP	OCT	NOV	DEC
1	27♈29	11♊09	0♋53	15♌35	19♍44	10♏12	18♐34	12♒30	3♈32	7♉46	22♊36	24♋39
☽ 3	21♉11	4♋59	25♋10	11♍46	17♎32	10♐10	19♑02	11♓34	29♈51	2♊34	16♋22	18♌26
5	14♊46	29♋33	20♌32	9♎26	16♏49	10♑36	18♒55	8♈54	24♉44	26♊35	10♌12	12♍46
7	8♋43	25♌05	17♍08	8♏12	16♐46	10♒12	17♓08	4♉26	18♊43	20♋20	4♍39	8♎14
9	3♌17	21♍28	14♎45	7♐22	16♑20	8♓09	13♈26	28♉44	12♋26	14♌28	0♎20	5♏23
11	28♌35	18♎33	12♏54	6♑12	14♒44	4♈21	8♉12	22♊26	6♌32	9♍31	27♎35	4♐23
13	24♍39	16♏12	11♐14	4♒17	11♓41	29♈11	2♊06	16♋11	1♍26	5♎50	26♏21	4♑37
15	21♎37	14♐23	9♑28	1♓26	7♈21	23♉12	25♊43	10♌25	27♍18	3♏23	25♐56	4♒52
17	19♏37	12♑59	7♒25	27♓38	2♉03	16♊53	19♋30	5♍20	24♎04	1♐48	25♑22	3♓53
19	18♐40	11♒35	4♓50	22♈56	26♉08	10♋33	13♌42	0♎59	21♏34	0♑31	23♒51	1♈10
21	18♑14	9♓29	1♈22	17♉25	19♊52	4♌28	8♍27	27♎24	19♐36	29♑01	21♓05	26♈55
23	17♒22	6♈06	26♈48	11♊19	13♋31	28♌52	3♎57	24♏41	18♑00	26♒59	17♈10	21♉38
25	15♓07	1♉16	21♉14	4♋58	7♌28	24♍08	0♏28	22♐55	16♒29	24♓12	12♉21	15♊45
27	11♈06	25♉22	15♊01	28♋52	2♍10	20♎40	28♏19	21♑58	14♓35	20♈33	6♊52	9♋36
29	5♉38	19♊01	8♋44	23♌36	28♍06	18♏50	27♐32	21♒13	11♈47	15♉59	0♋54	3♌21
31	29♉21		3♌01		25♎44		27♑33	19♓46		10♊34		27♌13
1	28♐49	21♑00	8♓05	29♈56	21♈08	21♉50	23♋17	5♍31	25♌55	4♎23	24♏46	26♐44
☿ 7	26D17	29 45	19 27	1℞56	22 45	2♊50	4♌12	8 24	27D10	15 00	3♐24	22℞59
13	28 52	9♒00	1♈11	0 02	26 52	15 08	13 54	8℞23	3♍15	25 10	11 35	15 05
19	4♑25	18 45	12 37	25♈57	3♉00	28 12	22 21	5 12	12 38	4♏54	18 56	10 35
25	11 33	29 04	22 27	22 21	10 49	11♋10	29 24	0 04	23 26	14 16	24 35	12D03
31	19 35		29 12		20 08		4♍49	26♌11		23 18		17 19

DATE	☉	♀	♂	♃	♄	⚷	♅	♆	♇	☊	STATIONS
1 1	9♑54	13♒14	9♈10	18♍54	9♋45	18♑29	0♓05	11♒42	20♐32	17♉42	
11	20 06	25 29	15 17	18℞50	8℞56	19 25	0 31	12 03	20 53	17 10	☿ 7/1 26♐17
21	0♒17	7♓38	21 31	18 27	8 10	20 22	1 01	12 25	21 13	16 39	☿ 7/4 1♉56
31	10 27	19 41	27 49	17 46	7 29	21 17	1 33	12 47	21 30	16 07	☿ 1/5 21♈07
10 2	20 35	1♈34	4♉11	16 49	6 56	22 10	2 06	13 10	21 46	15 35	☿ 10/8 8♍47
20	0♓41	13 15	10 34	15 40	6 33	22 59	2 41	13 33	21 58	15 03	☿ 3/9 25♌45
1 3	10 45	24 41	16 58	14 23	6 20	23 45	3 15	13 54	22 07	14 32	☿ 1/12 26♐45
11	20 46	5♉46	23 23	13 05	6D18	24 25	3 49	14 [illegible]	22 14	14 00	☿ 20/12 10♐27
21	0♈43	16 26	29 48	11 51	6 27	24 60	4 22	14 32	22 16	13 28	♀ 18/5 26♊09
31	10 37	26 32	6♊12	10 45	6 47	25 28	4 52	14 48	22℞16	12 56	♀ 30/6 9♊38
10 4	20 28	5♊50	12 35	9 53	7 18	25 49	5 20	15 01	22 12	12 25	♃ 4/1 18♍55
20	0♉16	14 02	18 58	9 17	7 58	26 02	5 45	15 12	22 05	11 53	♃ 5/5 8♍56
30	10 00	20 40	25 20	8 58	8 46	26 08	6 07	15 19	21 56	11 21	♄ 8/3 6♋17
10 5	19 41	24 59	1♋41	8D58	9 42	26℞06	6 24	15 23	21 44	10 49	♄ 8/11 27♋21
20	29 20	26℞04	8 01	9 16	10 44	25 56	6 37	15℞24	21 31	10 17	♅ 11/6 6♓48
30	8♊56	23 15	14 20	9 51	11 52	25 39	6 45	15 21	21 16	9 46	♅ 12/11 2♓53
9 6	18 31	17 30	20 38	10 42	13 04	25 16	6 48	15 16	21 00	9 14	♆ 17/5 15♒24
19	28 04	11 59	26 57	11 47	14 18	24 47	6℞46	15 07	20 44	8 42	♆ 24/10 12♒37
29	7♋36	9 39	3♌14	13 05	15 35	24 15	6 40	14 56	20 29	8 10	♇ 24/3 22♐17
9 7	17 08	11D07	9 32	14 35	16 53	23 40	6 29	14 43	20 14	7 39	♇ 31/8 19♐35
19	26 41	15 39	15 51	16 14	18 10	23 04	6 14	14 29	20 02	7 07	⚷ 2/5 26♑08
29	6♌14	22 20	22 09	18 01	19 27	22 29	5 56	14 13	19 51	6 35	⚷ 27/9 20♑30
8 8	15 48	0♋29	28 29	19 55	20 42	21 56	5 35	13 57	19 43	6 03	
18	25 24	9 40	4♍49	21 55	21 53	21 27	5 12	13 41	19 37	5 31	
28	5♍02	19 36	11 10	23 59	23 00	21 03	4 48	13 25	19 35	5 00	
7 9	14 43	0♌05	17 33	26 06	24 02	20 45	4 25	13 11	19D36	4 28	
17	24 27	11 01	23 58	28 15	24 57	20 34	4 02	12 59	19 40	3 56	
27	4♎14	22 17	0♎25	0♎25	25 45	20 30	3 41	12 49	19 47	3 24	
7 10	14 04	3♍50	6 53	2 34	26 24	20D34	3 23	12 42	19 57	2 53	
17	23 58	15 36	13 24	4 41	26 53	20 46	3 09	12 38	20 10	2 21	
27	3♏55	27 34	19 57	6 46	27 12	21 05	2 59	12D37	20 26	1 49	
6 11	13 55	9♎41	26 33	8 45	27 20	21 31	2 53	12 40	20 44	1 17	
16	23 59	21 55	3♏12	10 39	27℞17	22 04	2D53	12 46	21 04	0 46	
26	4♐05	4♏16	9 53	12 25	27 03	22 42	2 58	12 55	21 25	0 14	
6 12	14 13	16 40	16 37	14 02	26 38	23 25	3 08	13 07	21 47	29♈42	
16	24 22	29 07	23 25	15 28	26 04	24 12	3 22	13 22	22 10	29 10	
26	4♑33	11♐36	0♐15	16 41	25 23	25 02	3 42	13 40	22 32	28 38	

SID M/N 1st JAN 6 h 42 m 58 s 2005 COMMON BST

DAY	JAN	FEB	MAR	APR	MAY	JUN	JUL	AUG	SEP	OCT	NOV	DEC
1	9♍17	26♎17	6♏20	27♐46	7♒10	29♓55	6♉35	23♊31	8♌16	10♍35	25♎59	0♐50
☽ 3	4♎01	22♏53	3♐07	26♑06	5♓25	26♈33	1♊51	17♋31	2♍00	4♎55	22♏11	28♐58
5	29♎59	21♐07	1♑03	24♒45	3♈04	22♉19	26♊24	11♌17	26♍01	29♎58	19♐25	27♑49
7	27♏45	20♑52	0♒05	23♓16	29♈59	17♊20	20♋28	5♍00	20♎31	25♏52	17♑20	26♒35
9	27♐21	21♒13	29♒39	21♈04	26♉01	11♋43	14♌14	28♍[illegible]	15♏49	22♐43	15♒36	24♓46
11	28♑00	20♓51	28♓46	17♉43	21♊08	5♌36	7♍55	23♎25	12♐14	20♑29	13♓54	22♈14
13	28♒14	18♈46	26♈35	13♊07	15♋26	29♌19	1♎57	19♏00	10♑02	19♒04	12♈02	19♉02
15	26♓52	14♉49	22♉46	7♋30	9♌15	23♍21	26♎52	16♐11	9♒12	18♓06	9♉41	15♊07
17	23♈32	9♊28	17♊35	1♌20	3♍07	18♎22	23♏19	15♑10	9♓06	16♈59	6♊31	10♋25
19	18♉38	3♋21	11♋33	25♌14	27♍38	14♏57	21♐43	15♒27	8♈42	14♉58	2♋15	4♌52
21	12♊48	27♋04	5♌18	19♍46	23♎25	13♐24	21♑45	15♓48	7♉03	11♊37	26♋54	28♌41
23	6♋34	21♌01	29♌24	15♎22	20♏45	13♑14	22♒19	14♈58	3♊43	6♋52	20♌47	22♍19
25	0♌19	15♍28	24♍11	12♏12	19♐29	13♒21	22♓00	12♉20	28♊53	1♌05	14♍29	16♎26
27	24♌15	10♎32	19♎52	10♐06	18♑53	12♓34	20♈00	8♊01	23♋02	24♌49	8♎41	11♏45
29	18♍34		16♏26	8♑36	18♒00	10♈17	16♉18	2♋32	16♌46	18♍42	4♏01	8♐48
31	13♎28		13♐48		16♓13		11♊19	26♋25		13♎18		7♑34
1	18♐25	2♒52	22♓52	7♈06	14♈10	7♊41	3♌57	17♌20	23♌23	17♎45	1♐52	25♏38
☿ 7	25 45	12 50	3♈07	3R01	21 55	20 51	11 09	12R51	4♍14	27 21	7 43	25D25
13	3♑57	23 16	10 44	1D46	1♉00	3♋32	16 34	9 20	15 43	6♏29	10 49	0♐07
19	12 39	4♓10	14 02	3 36	11 19	15 04	19 47	9D15	26 56	15 10	9R04	7 15
25	21 46	15 25	12R33	7 55	22 52	25 13	20R20	13 34	7♎38	23 19	1 59	15 27
31	1♒15		7 57		5♊30		17 58	21 45		0♐44		24 11

DATE	☉	♀	♂	♃	♄	⚷	♅	♆	♇	☊	STATIONS
1 1	10♑40	19♐07	4♐22	17♎18	24♋55	25♑33	3♓55	13♒52	22♐46	28♈19	
11	20 52	1♑38	11 17	18 07	24R07	26 26	4 21	14 12	23 07	27 48	☿ 20/3 14♈06
21	1♒03	14 10	18 14	18 38	23 18	27 19	4 49	14 34	23 27	27 16	☿ 12/4 1♈45
31	11 13	26 41	25 15	18 52	22 30	28 12	5 21	14 57	23 44	26 44	☿ 23/7 20♌29
10 2	21 21	9♒13	2♑18	18R46	21 48	29 03	5 54	15 19	24 00	26 12	☿ 16/8 8♌46
20	1♓27	21 43	9 24	18 22	21 12	29 52	6 28	15 42	24 13	25 41	☿ 14/11 10♐56
2 3	11 31	4♓13	16 32	17 40	20 46	0♒38	7 02	16 03	24 22	25 09	☿ 4/12 24♏44
12	21 31	16 42	23 43	16 43	20 29	1 19	7 36	16 24	24 29	24 37	♀ 24/12 1♒28
22	1♈28	29 10	0♒56	15 34	20 23	1 55	8 09	16 42	24 32	24 05	♂ 2/10 23♉24
1 4	11 22	11♈36	8 10	14 19	20D29	2 25	8 41	16 58	24R32	23 33	♂ 10/12 8♉16
11	21 13	24 00	15 25	13 02	20 45	2 49	9 10	17 12	24 29	23 02	♃ 2/2 18♎52
21	1♉00	6♉22	22 41	11 49	21 12	3 05	9 36	17 23	24 23	22 30	♃ 5/6 8♎56
1 5	10 44	18 43	29 56	10 45	21 48	3 15	9 58	17 31	24 14	21 58	♄ 22/3 20♋23
11	20 25	1♊02	7♓11	9 53	22 34	3R17	10 17	17 35	24 03	21 26	♄ 22/11 11♌18
21	0♊03	13 19	14 23	9 17	23 27	3 12	10 31	17R36	23 49	20 55	♅ 15/6 10♓46
31	9 40	25 34	21 31	8 59	24 26	2 60	10 41	17 34	23 35	20 23	♅ 16/11 6♓51
10 6	19 14	7♋48	28 34	8D58	25 31	2 41	10 45	17 29	23 19	19 51	♆ 20/5 17♒36
20	28 47	19 59	5♈29	9 16	26 41	2 17	10R45	17 21	23 03	19 19	♆ 27/10 14♒49
30	8♋20	2♌09	12 15	9 50	27 54	1 48	10 41	17 11	22 48	18 47	♇ 27/3 24♐33
10 7	17 52	14 16	18 48	10 40	29 10	1 16	10 31	16 58	22 33	18 16	♇ 2/9 21♐52
20	27 24	26 21	25 06	11 45	0♌27	0 42	10 18	16 44	22 20	17 44	⚷ 9/5 3♒17
30	6♌57	8♍23	1♉04	13 02	1 45	0 07	10 00	16 28	22 09	17 12	⚷ 5 10 27♑48
9 8	16 32	20 20	6 36	14 31	3 02	29♑34	9 40	16 12	22 01	16 40	
19	26 08	2♎14	11 37	16 10	4 17	29 03	9 18	15 55	21 55	16 09	
29	5♍46	14 02	15 59	17 58	5 29	28 36	8 54	15 40	21 52	15 37	
8 9	15 27	25 44	19 31	19 52	6 37	28 14	8 30	15 26	21D52	15 05	
18	25 11	7♏19	22 01	21 52	7 41	27 59	8 07	15 13	21 56	14 33	
28	4♎59	18 44	23 17	23 57	8 38	27 50	7 46	15 03	22 02	14 02	
8 10	14 49	29 58	23R08	26 05	9 29	27D48	7 27	14 55	22 12	13 30	
18	24 43	10♐55	21 30	28 15	10 10	27 54	7 11	14 51	22 25	12 58	
28	4♏40	21 32	18 39	0♏25	10 43	28 07	7 00	14D49	22 40	12 26	
7 11	14 41	1♑38	15 10	2 35	11 05	28 27	6 53	14 51	22 58	11 54	
17	24 44	11 01	11 52	4 44	11 17	28 54	6D51	14 57	23 17	11 23	
27	4♐51	19 21	9 27	6 48	11R17	29 26	6 54	15 06	23 38	10 51	
7 12	14 59	26 04	8 20	8 49	11 06	0♒04	7 02	15 18	24 00	10 19	
17	25 09	0♒24	8D33	10 43	10 45	0 46	7 15	15 33	24 22	9 47	
27	5♑20	1R20	9 59	12 29	10 14	1 32	7 33	15 50	24 45	9 16	

SID M/N 1st JAN 6 h 42 m 0 s   2006 COMMON   BST

DAY	JAN	FEB	MAR	APR	MAY	JUN	JUL	AUG	SEP	OCT	NOV	DEC
1	22♑23	15♓58	24♓08	16♉09	21♊35	7♌46	9♍47	23♎26	8♐57	14♑21	5♓50	14♈38
☽ 3	22♒10	15♈08	23♈47	13♊35	17♋27	1♍50	3♎24	17♏46	5♑18	12♒06	5♈04	13♉39
5	21♓17	12♉42	21♉48	9♋20	11♌58	25♍29	27♎20	13♐27	3♒28	11♓25	4♉55	12♊27
7	19♈12	8♊48	18♊06	3♌48	5♍44	19♎25	22♏19	10♑5[illegible]	3♓10	11♈40	4♊21	10♋14
9	15♉55	3♋49	13♋02	27♌33	29♍25	14♏18	18♐49	9♒5[illegible]	3♈32	11♉44	2♋24	6♌28
11	11♊44	28♋07	7♌06	21♍11	23♎36	10♐28	16♑53	9♓53	3♉21	10♊31	28♋38	1♍15
13	6♋48	21♌59	0♍47	15♎08	18♏42	7♑55	15♒57	9♈34	1♊43	7♋28	23♌20	25♍05
15	1♌15	15♍38	24♍26	9♏45	14♐52	6♒11	15♓10	8♉12	28♊26	2♌45	17♍07	18♎42
17	25♌09	9♎20	18♎22	5♐11	11♑57	4♓40	13♈49	5♊30	23♋43	26♌54	10♎42	12♏47
19	18♍45	3♏28	12♏50	1♑33	9♒41	2♈59	11♉36	1♋34	18♌01	20♍31	4♏39	7♐52
21	12♎30	28♏34	8♐11	28♑52	7♓51	0♉56	8♊31	26♋38	11♍46	14♎07	29♏20	4♑05
23	7♏01	25♐13	4♑44	27♒09	6♈17	28♉24	4♋34	20♌57	5♎21	8♏05	24♐53	1♒15
25	2♐59	23♑41	2♒46	26♓12	4♉42	25♊10	29♋47	14♍46	29♎03	2♐38	21♑13	28♒59
27	0♑53	23♒41	2♓08	25♈28	2♊41	21♋01	24♌12	8♎19	23♏11	27♐57	18♒18	27♓01
29	0♒31		2♈10	24♉11	29♊41	15♌49	18♍00	2♏01	18♐09	24♑13	16♓06	25♈12
31	0♓55		1♉48		25♋24		11♎34	26♏21		21♒39		23♉23
1	25♐40	15♒38	26♓39	15♓01	22♈08	25♊25	0♌48	21♋31	8♍15	28♎20	24♏20	19♏48
☿ 7	4♑44	26 19	25℞38	19 24	3♉09	6♋06	1℞11	25 15	19 35	6♏29	18℞49	28 11
13	14 04	7♓02	20 31	25 40	15 13	15 08	28♋55	2♌35	0♎13	13 51	11 28	7♐07
19	23 40	16 55	15 21	3♈21	28 07	22 26	25 04	12 45	10 12	20 02	9D09	16 15
25	3♒35	24 16	13 12	12 12	11♊11	27 46	21 49	24 24	19 33	24 11	12 49	25 32
31	13 53		14D30		23 29		21D15	6♍18		24℞44		4♑56

DATE	☉	♀	♂	♃	♄	⚷	♅	♆	♇	☊	STATIONS
1 1	10♑26	0♒16	11♉06	13♏18	9♌55	1♒56	7♓44	15♒59	24♐56	9♈00	
11	20 37	25℞29	13 57	14 50	9℞12	2 45	8 08	16 19	25 17	8 28	☿ 3/3 26♓56
21	0♒48	19 37	17 31	16 09	8 25	3 35	8 35	16 41	25 37	7 56	☿ 26/3 13♓11
31	10 58	16 15	21 37	17 14	7 36	4 25	9 05	17 04	25 55	7 24	☿ 5/7 1♌22
10 2	21 06	16D52	26 10	18 04	6 48	5 15	9 38	17 26	26 11	6 53	☿ 29/7 21♋03
20	1♓13	20 55	1♊02	18 36	6 04	6 03	10 11	17 49	26 24	6 21	☿ 29/10 25♏05
2 3	11 16	27 25	6 09	18 51	5 25	6 48	10 46	18 11	26 35	5 49	☿ 18/11 9♏04
12	21 17	5♒33	11 28	18℞47	4 55	7 29	11 20	18 31	26 42	5 17	♀ 3/2 16♑01
22	1♈14	14 47	16 57	18 24	4 34	8 07	11 53	18 50	26 46	4 46	♃ 5/3 18♏52
1 4	11 08	24 45	22 33	17 44	4 23	8 39	12 26	19 07	26℞47	4 14	♃ 6/7 8♏59
11	20 59	5♓15	28 15	16 48	4D24	9 05	12 56	19 22	26 45	3 42	♄ 6/4 4♌22
21	0♉46	16 07	4♋02	15 41	4 35	9 25	13 23	19 33	26 39	3 10	♄ 6/12 25♌04
1 5	10 30	27 16	9 53	14 27	4 57	9 39	13 47	19 42	26 31	2 38	♅ 19/6 14♓44
11	20 11	8♈36	15 47	13 11	5 29	9 45	14 07	19 47	26 20	2 07	♅ 20/11 10♓49
21	29 50	20 06	21 44	11 58	6 10	9℞45	14 23	19 49	26 07	1 35	♆ 22/5 19♒49
31	9♊26	1♉43	27 44	10 53	6 59	9 37	14 35	19℞48	25 53	1 03	♆ 29/10 17♒02
10 6	19 00	13 26	3♌46	10 00	7 55	9 23	14 42	19 44	25 38	0 31	♇ 29/3 26♐47
20	28 33	25 14	9 50	9 23	8 57	9 04	14℞44	19 36	25 22	0 00	♇ 5/9 24♐07
30	8♋06	7♊07	15 56	9 03	10 04	8 39	14 41	19 26	25 07	29♓28	⚷ 15/5 9♒46
10 7	17 38	19 04	22 05	9D00	11 16	8 09	14 34	19 14	24 52	28 56	⚷ 13 10 4♒25
20	27 10	1♋05	28 16	9 16	12 30	7 38	14 22	19 00	24 39	28 24	
30	6♌43	13 10	4♍30	9 49	13 46	7 04	14 06	18 45	24 27	27 52	
9 8	16 18	25 19	10 47	10 38	15 03	6 31	13 47	18 28	24 18	27 21	
19	25 54	7♌32	17 06	11 42	16 19	5 59	13 26	18 12	24 11	26 49	
29	5♍32	19 49	23 28	12 59	17 35	5 30	13 03	17 56	24 07	26 17	
8 9	15 13	2♍10	29 53	14 28	18 48	5 06	12 39	17 42	24D07	25 45	
18	24 57	14 33	6♎22	16 08	19 58	4 46	12 15	17 29	24 09	25 14	
28	4♎44	27 00	12 55	17 56	21 04	4 33	11 53	17 18	24 15	24 42	
8 10	14 35	9♎28	19 31	19 53	22 03	4 26	11 32	17 09	24 24	24 10	
18	24 29	21 59	26 11	21 55	22 56	4D26	11 15	17 04	24 36	23 38	
28	4♏26	4♏30	2♏55	24 02	23 41	4 33	11 02	17 02	24 51	23 07	
7 11	14 26	17 03	9 43	26 12	24 17	4 47	10 53	17D03	25 08	22 35	
17	24 30	29 36	16 36	28 25	24 44	5 08	10 49	17 08	25 26	22 03	
27	4♐36	12♐09	23 33	0♐38	24 59	5 35	10D50	17 16	25 47	21 31	
7 12	14 44	24 42	0♐34	2 51	25℞04	6 07	10 56	17 27	26 09	20 59	
17	24 54	7♑15	7 40	5 02	24 57	6 44	11 07	17 41	26 31	20 28	
27	5♑05	19 48	14 50	7 10	24 40	7 25	11 23	17 58	26 53	19 56	

SID M/N 1st JAN 6 h 41 m 3 s 2007 COMMON BST

DAY	JAN	FEB	MAR	APR	MAY	JUN	JUL	AUG	SEP	OCT	NOV	DEC
1	7♊24	27♋11	6♌33	22♍13	24♎43	9♐39	13♑54	3♓40	26♈35	5♊44	27♋19	2♍15
☽ 3	4♋57	22♌29	1♍15	15♎54	18♏32	4♑39	10♒19	1♈56	25♉32	4♋03	23♌20	26♍58
5	1♌29	16♍55	25♍19	9♏35	12♐48	0♒24	7♓29	0♉25	23♊37	0♌50	18♍03	20♎52
7	26♌46	10♎43	19♎02	3♐33	7♑40	26♒56	5♈16	28♉48	20♋40	26♌20	12♎03	14♏32
9	20♍58	4♏22	12♏42	28♐07	3♒22	24♓27	3♉37	26♊46	16♌42	20♍56	5♏46	8♐23
11	14♎37	28♏27	6♐47	23♑43	0♓15	23♈01	2♊17	24♋02	11♍51	15♎00	29♏31	2♑37
13	8♏25	23♐38	1♑49	20♒47	28♓35	22♉22	0♋46	20♌22	6♎17	8♏47	23♐27	27♑22
15	3♐02	20♑22	28♑21	19♓34	28♈13	21♊43	28♋27	15♍39	0♏11	2♐29	17♑48	22♒48
17	28♐59	18♒43	26♒38	19♈42	28♉23	20♋05	24♌51	10♎01	23♏53	26♐26	12♒58	19♓14
19	26♑20	18♓10	26♓24	20♉07	27♊49	16♌50	19♍55	3♏50	17♐49	21♑04	9♓24	17♈00
21	24♒43	17♈47	26♈41	19♊30	25♋35	12♍00	14♎02	27♏37	12♑35	16♒58	7♈33	16♉09
23	23♓29	16♉42	26♉19	17♋06	21♌29	6♎05	7♏46	21♐59	8♒43	14♓36	7♉22	16♊06
25	22♈03	14♊28	24♊27	12♌52	15♍58	29♎47	1♐46	17♑30	6♓34	14♈03	7♊57	15♋44
27	20♉06	11♋02	20♋55	7♍20	9♎43	23♏43	26♐37	14♒27	5♈58	14♉36	7♋52	13♌58
29	17♊31		16♌03	1♎06	3♏22	18♐21	22♑37	12♓47	6♉05	14♊52	6♌03	10♍23
31	14♋10		10♍18		27♏24		19♒45	11♈56		13♋39		5♎16
1	6♑31	27♒54	28♒19	15♓09	7♉44	3♋23	5♋24	23♋03	22♍39	3♏14	23♎27	29♏12
☿ 7	16 09	6♓01	25R29	23 47	20 40	8 34	2R52	4♌33	2♎22	7 38	25D32	8♐36
13	26 01	10 06	26D32	3♈22	3♊20	11 16	2D50	16 51	11 22	9R02	2♏04	18 01
19	6♒07	8R16	0♓30	13 53	14 50	11R15	5 57	28 57	19 37	5 56	10 36	27 27
25	16 22	2 12	6 27	25 22	24 34	8 52	12 13	10♍21	27 01	28♎57	19 49	7♑00
31	26 20		13 49		2♋18		21 18	20 58		23 44		16 40

DATE	☉	♀	♂	♃	♄	⚷	♅	♆	♇	☊	STATIONS
1 1	10♑11	26♑04	18♐26	8♐12	24♌27	7♒47	11♓33	18♒07	27♐04	19♓40	
11	20 22	8♒36	25 43	10 12	23R55	8 33	11 55	18 27	27 25	19 08	☿ 14/2 10♓14
21	0♒33	21 06	3♑03	12 06	23 15	9 20	12 21	18 48	27 46	18 36	☿ 8/3 25♒25
31	10 43	3♓34	10 27	13 50	22 30	10 08	12 50	19 11	28 04	18 05	☿ 16/6 11♋36
10 2	20 52	15 59	17 55	15 25	21 42	10 55	13 22	19 33	28 20	17 33	☿ 10/7 2♋28
20	0♓58	28 21	25 26	16 47	20 53	11 42	13 55	19 56	28 34	17 01	☿ 12/10 9♏05
2 3	11 01	10♈38	3♒00	17 56	20 07	12 27	14 29	20 18	28 45	16 29	☿ 2/11 23♎22
12	21 02	22 50	10 36	18 49	19 26	13 08	15 03	20 39	28 53	15 58	♀ 28/7 2♍57
22	0♈59	4♉56	18 14	19 26	18 53	13 46	15 37	20 59	28 58	15 26	♀ 9/9 16♌35
1 4	10 54	16 54	25 54	19 44	18 28	14 20	16 10	21 16	29R00	14 54	♂ 15/11 12♋28
11	20 44	28 43	3♓34	19R44	18 13	14 49	16 41	21 31	28 58	14 22	♃ 6/4 19♐47
21	0♉32	10♊22	11 14	19 26	18D09	15 11	17 09	21 43	28 54	13 51	♃ 7/8 9♐56
1 5	10 16	21 48	18 54	18 49	18 16	15 28	17 35	21 53	28 46	13 19	♄ 20/4 18♌09
11	19 57	2♋59	26 32	17 57	18 33	15 38	17 57	21 59	28 36	12 47	♄ 20/12 8♍34
21	29 36	13 50	4♈07	16 53	19 00	15 41	18 15	22 02	28 24	12 15	♅ 24/6 18♓42
31	9♊12	24 15	11 39	15 40	19 37	15R38	18 28	22R01	28 10	11 43	♅ 24/11 14♓47
10 6	18 46	4♌07	19 06	14 24	20 21	15 28	18 37	21 58	27 55	11 12	♆ 25/5 22♒02
20	28 20	13 12	26 27	13 10	21 14	15 12	18 41	21 51	27 39	10 40	♆ 1/11 19♒15
30	7♋52	21 13	3♉42	12 02	22 13	14 51	18R41	21 42	27 24	10 08	♇ 1/4 29♐00
10 7	17 24	27 40	10 49	11 07	23 17	14 25	18 35	21 30	27 09	9 36	♇ 8/9 26♐20
20	26 56	1♍51	17 47	10 26	24 26	13 56	18 25	21 17	26 55	9 05	⚷ 21/5 15♒41
30	6♌29	2R51	24 34	10 02	25 38	13 24	18 11	21 02	26 43	8 33	⚷ 20 10 10♒28
9 8	16 04	0 01	1♊09	9D56	26 53	12 52	17 54	20 46	26 33	8 01	
19	25 40	24♌18	7 30	10 09	28 09	12 20	17 33	20 29	26 26	7 29	
29	5♍18	18 51	13 34	10 40	29 25	11 50	17 10	20 13	26 22	6 57	
8 9	14 59	16 36	19 19	11 28	0♍41	11 23	16 47	19 58	26D20	6 26	
18	24 43	18D11	24 40	12 31	1 55	11 01	16 23	19 45	26 22	5 54	
28	4♎30	22 52	29 34	13 48	3 06	10 43	16 00	19 33	26 27	5 22	
8 10	14 20	29 47	3♋53	15 19	4 12	10 32	15 39	19 24	26 35	4 50	
18	24 14	8♍13	7 31	17 00	5 14	10 28	15 20	19 18	26 46	4 19	
28	4♏11	17 44	10 17	18 50	6 09	10D30	15 05	19 15	27 00	3 47	
7 11	14 12	28 00	12 00	20 49	6 57	10 39	14 54	19D16	27 16	3 15	
17	24 15	8♎51	12R27	22 54	7 36	10 55	14 48	19 20	27 34	2 43	
27	4♐21	20 07	11 30	25 05	8 06	11 16	14D47	19 27	27 54	2 12	
7 12	14 29	1♏41	9 10	27 19	8 25	11 44	14 51	19 37	28 16	1 40	
17	24 39	13 30	5 43	29 35	8 34	12 17	15 00	19 51	28 38	1 08	
27	4♑50	25 29	1 47	1♑53	8R31	12 53	15 14	20 07	29 00	0 36	

SID M/N 1st JAN 6 h 40 m 6 s 2008 LEAP BST

DAY	JAN	FEB	MAR	APR	MAY	JUN	JUL	AUG	SEP	OCT	NOV	DEC
1	17♎20	0♐55	20♐40	5♒29	9♓52	1♉01	9♊57	3♌23	23♍31	27♎41	12♐37	14♑51
☽ 3	11♏05	24♐58	15♑04	1♓43	7♈50	1♊12	10♋05	1♍44	19♎30	22♏20	6♑17	8♒34
5	4♐52	19♑48	10♒34	29♓43	7♉34	1♋42	9♌29	28♍39	14♏20	16♐17	29♑59	2♓53
7	29♐07	15♒40	7♓29	29♈10	8♊03	1♌11	7♍19	24♎06	8♐21	9♑58	24♒23	28♓29
9	24♑03	12♓34	5♈43	29♉05	7♋55	28♌52	3♎25	18♏28	2♑06	4♒02	20♓10	25♈54
11	19♒45	10♈17	4♉42	28♊22	6♌13	24♍48	28♎11	12♐17	26♑14	29♒10	17♈50	25♉14
13	16♓13	8♉30	3♊38	26♋19	2♍47	19♎30	22♏10	6♑08	21♒19	25♓53	17♉17	25♊44
15	13♈32	6♊53	1♋57	22♌55	28♍03	13♏30	15♐54	0♒33	17♓40	24♈13	17♊32	26♋02
17	11♉42	5♋08	29♋23	18♍28	22♎28	7♐15	9♑51	25♒48	15♈17	23♉34	17♋18	25♌00
19	10♊34	2♌56	25♌58	13♎15	16♏27	1♑04	4♒17	22♓03	13♉42	22♊57	15♌42	22♍10
21	9♋35	29♌56	21♍43	7♏32	10♐14	25♑09	29♒23	19♈14	12♊20	21♋31	12♍35	17♎48
23	7♌58	25♍54	16♎42	1♐25	4♑00	19♒45	25♓21	17♉08	10♋40	19♌01	8♎16	12♏23
25	5♍04	20♎50	11♏01	25♐09	28♑02	15♓13	22♈21	15♊31	8♌29	15♍32	3♏07	6♐20
27	0♎44	14♏57	4♐51	19♑05	22♒46	11♈59	20♉27	14♋05	5♍40	11♎16	27♏23	0♑02
29	25♎12	8♐43	28♐38	13♒47	18♓44	10♉17	19♊28	12♌25	2♎07	6♏18	21♐14	23♑42
31	19♏03		22♑57		16♈28		18♋50	10♍05		0♐39		17♒37
1	18♑17	22♒57	13♒46	26♓54	26♉46	20♊31	18♊01	11♌34	3♎53	20♎09	24♎10	12♐08
☿ 7	28 04	17R02	19 55	7♈56	6♊39	17R36	24 32	23 31	11 12	13R49	3♏47	21 31
13	7♒41	10 40	27 22	19 50	14 13	14 29	3♋29	4♍36	17 14	8 18	13 32	0♑55
19	16 25	8 19	5♓47	2♉23	19 13	13 00	14 30	14 47	21 26	8D28	23 11	10 17
25	22 33	10D06	15 03	15 02	21 26	14D07	26 51	24 07	22R49	14 05	2♐42	19 32
31	23R26		25 08		20R51		9♌30	2♎34		22 37		28 10

DATE	☉	♀	♂	♃	♄	⚷	♅	♆	♇	☊	STATIONS
1 1	9♑56	1♐31	29♊54	3♑01	8♍25	13♒13	15♓22	20♒16	29♐11	0♓20	
11	20 07	13 41	26R44	5 18	8R06	13 55	15 43	20 35	29 32	29♒49	☿ 29/1 23♒53
21	0♒18	25 55	24 44	7 32	7 38	14 39	16 08	20 56	29 52	29 17	☿ 19/2 8♒19
31	10 28	8♑12	24D06	9 42	7 01	15 25	16 35	21 18	0♑11	28 45	☿ 27/5 21♊32
10 2	20 37	20 31	24 42	11 48	6 17	16 11	17 06	21 41	0 28	28 13	☿ 20/6 12♊59
20	0♓43	2♒52	26 24	13 46	5 30	16 56	17 38	22 04	0 42	27 41	☿ 24/9 22♎50
1 3	10 47	15 14	28 58	15 36	4 42	17 40	18 12	22 26	0 54	27 10	☿ 16/10 7♎34
11	20 48	27 35	2♋14	17 16	3 55	18 21	18 46	22 47	1 03	26 38	♂ 31/1 24♊06
21	0♈45	9♓57	6 02	18 45	3 13	18 60	19 21	23 07	1 08	26 06	♃ 9/5 22♑22
31	10 39	22 19	10 17	20 01	2 36	19 34	19 54	23 25	1 11	25 34	♃ 8/9 12♑32
10 4	20 30	4♈39	14 52	21 02	2 08	20 04	20 26	23 41	1R10	25 03	♄ 3/5 1♍40
20	0♉17	16 59	19 44	21 47	1 49	20 29	20 55	23 54	1 06	24 31	♄ 1/1 21♍46
30	10 02	29 19	24 49	22 14	1 41	20 48	21 22	24 04	0 59	23 59	♅ 27/6 22♓39
10 5	19 43	11♉37	0♌05	22R22	1D43	21 01	21 46	24 11	0 50	23 27	♅ 28/11 18♓44
20	29 22	23 55	5 31	22 12	1 56	21 08	22 05	24 15	0 38	22 56	♆ 26/5 24♒15
30	8♊58	6♊13	11 04	21 43	2 18	21R08	22 21	24R15	0 24	22 24	♆ 2/11 21♒28
9 6	18 33	18 30	16 45	20 57	2 50	21 02	22 32	24 12	0 10	21 52	♇ 2/4 1♑11
19	28 06	0♋47	22 32	19 57	3 31	20 50	22 38	24 06	29♐54	21 20	♇ 9/9 28♐32
29	7♋38	13 05	28 25	18 47	4 20	20 32	22R39	23 58	29 39	20 48	⚷ 25/ 5 21♒09
9 7	17 10	25 22	4♍23	17 31	5 16	20 09	22 36	23 47	29 24	20 17	⚷ 25 10 16♒02
19	26 42	7♌40	10 26	16 14	6 17	19 43	22 28	23 33	29 10	19 45	
29	6♌15	19 57	16 35	15 03	7 24	19 13	22 16	23 19	28 58	19 13	
8 8	15 50	2♍15	22 48	14 02	8 34	18 42	21 59	23 03	28 47	18 41	
18	25 26	14 32	29 06	13 14	9 47	18 11	21 40	22 46	28 39	18 10	
28	5♍04	26 48	5♎30	12 44	11 02	17 40	21 18	22 30	28 34	17 38	
7 9	14 45	9♎04	11 58	12 32	12 17	17 12	20 55	22 15	28 32	17 06	
17	24 29	21 18	18 32	12D40	13 33	16 47	20 31	22 01	28D33	16 34	
27	4♎16	3♏31	25 10	13 06	14 46	16 27	20 07	21 49	28 37	16 02	
7 10	14 06	15 42	1♏55	13 50	15 58	16 13	19 45	21 39	28 44	15 31	
17	24 00	27 52	8 44	14 51	17 06	16 04	19 25	21 32	28 54	14 59	
27	3♏57	9♐58	15 39	16 07	18 09	16D02	19 09	21 29	29 07	14 27	
6 11	13 57	22 02	22 40	17 37	19 06	16 07	18 56	21D28	29 23	13 55	
16	24 00	4♑01	29 46	19 19	19 55	16 18	18 48	21 31	29 41	13 24	
26	4♐06	15 55	6♐57	21 11	20 37	16 35	18 44	21 38	0♑00	12 52	
6 12	14 14	27 41	14 13	23 12	21 10	16 58	18D46	21 47	0 21	12 20	
16	24 24	9♒16	21 35	25 20	21 32	17 27	18 53	22 00	0 43	11 48	
26	4♑35	20 37	29 02	27 34	21 44	17 60	19 05	22 16	1 05	11 17	

SID M/N 1st JAN 6 h 43 m 5 s — 2009 COMMON — BST

	DAY	JAN	FEB	MAR	APR	MAY	JUN	JUL	AUG	SEP	OCT	NOV	DEC
	1	29♒46	17♈41	27♈59	20♊15	29♋26	21♍29	27♎42	14♐02	28♑10	0♓17	16♈13	21♉29
☽	3	24♓44	14♉41	25♉22	18♋31	27♌21	17♎51	22♏46	7♑48	21♒58	25♓03	13♉14	20♊13
	5	21♈00	12♊56	23♊24	16♌37	24♍30	13♏16	17♐01	1♒24	16♓20	20♈52	11♊14	19♋33
	7	18♉57	12♋13	21♋57	14♍23	20♎56	7♐56	10♑47	25♒12	11♈30	17♉37	9♋39	18♌38
	9	18♊30	11♌54	20♌42	11♎35	16♏33	1♑59	4♒24	19♓28	7♉30	15♊03	8♌01	16♍54
	11	18♋51	11♍00	19♍07	7♏53	11♐21	25♑38	28♒08	14♈29	4♊22	12♋56	6♍06	14♎12
	13	18♌47	8♎45	16♎34	3♐05	5♑23	19♒16	22♓24	10♉32	2♋09	11♌10	3♎47	10♏35
	15	17♍16	4♏51	12♏40	27♐17	29♑00	13♓24	17♈40	7♊51	0♌48	9♍37	0♏53	6♐04
	17	13♎57	29♏33	7♐26	20♑58	22♒47	8♈39	14♉24	6♋33	0♍02	7♎54	27♏07	0♑44
	19	9♏06	23♐23	1♑19	14♒46	17♓25	5♉33	12♊48	6♌16	29♍08	5♏25	22♐19	24♑44
	21	3♐13	17♑01	24♑59	9♓25	13♈32	4♊17	12♋38	6♍10	27♎13	1♐42	16♑34	18♒21
	23	26♐54	11♒00	19♒05	5♈28	11♉26	4♋17	12♌56	5♎12	23♏46	26♐38	10♒13	12♓01
	25	20♑34	5♓44	14♓11	3♉04	10♊45	4♌27	12♍34	2♏37	18♐46	20♑35	3♓55	6♈21
	27	14♒35	1♈24	10♈33	1♊47	10♋32	3♍42	10♎39	28♏18	12♑44	14♒12	28♓20	1♉57
	29	9♓12		8♉00	0♋48	9♌47	1♎27	7♏00	22♐40	6♒21	8♓12	24♈06	29♉16
	31	4♈36		6♊06		7♍53		1♐56	16♑22		3♈13		28♊17
	1	29♑29	21♑45	18♒11	12♈19	0♊02	22♉54	24♊32	26♌43	4♎28	21♍47	5♏58	22♐58
☿	7	5♒51	23D34	27 11	24 42	1 44	24 40	6♋35	6♍27	6 13	26 02	15 44	1♑52
	13	7R35	28 20	6♓53	6♉42	0R27	28 57	19 27	15 11	4R25	4♎12	25 17	10 17
	19	2 50	4♒54	17 16	17 10	27♉16	5♊29	2♌10	22 50	29♍06	14 02	4♐38	17 26
	25	25♑29	12 35	28 25	25 06	24 09	14 04	14 05	29 13	23 18	24 14	13 52	21 34
	31	21 51		10♈16		22 52		24 59	3♎54		4♏18		19R56

DATE	☉	♀	♂	♃	♄	⚷	♅	♆	♇	☊	STATIONS
1 1	10♑42	27♒15	3♑32	28♑56	21♍46	18♒21	19♓14	22♒26	1♑18	10♒57	
11	20 54	7♓57	11 05	1♒15	21R40	19 00	19 34	22 45	1 39	10 26	☿ 12/1 7♒45
21	1♒05	18 04	18 43	3 37	21 24	19 42	19 57	23 06	1 59	9 54	☿ 1/2 21♑45
31	11 15	27 19	26 24	5 59	20 57	20 25	20 24	23 28	2 18	9 22	☿ 7/5 1♊44
10 2	21 23	5♈19	4♒08	8 20	20 22	21 09	20 54	23 51	2 35	8 50	☿ 31/5 22♉52
20	1♓29	11 30	11 55	10 39	19 41	21 53	21 26	24 14	2 50	8 19	☿ 7/9 6♎13
2 3	11 32	15 00	19 43	12 54	18 55	22 35	21 59	24 36	3 02	7 47	☿ 30/9 21♍36
12	21 33	14R52	27 33	15 05	18 07	23 16	22 33	24 57	3 11	7 15	☿ 27/12 21♑48
22	1♈30	10 47	5♓23	17 10	17 20	23 55	23 07	25 17	3 17	6 43	♀ 7/3 15♈27
1 4	11 24	4 40	13 12	19 06	16 37	24 29	23 41	25 36	3 20	6 11	♀ 18/4 29♓12
11	21 15	0 08	21 01	20 54	15 59	25 00	24 13	25 52	3R19	5 40	♂ 21/12 19♌42
21	1♉02	29D24	28 47	22 31	15 29	25 26	24 44	26 05	3 16	5 08	♃ 15/6 27♒01
1 5	10 46	2♈18	6♈31	23 55	15 08	25 47	25 11	26 16	3 09	4 36	♃ 13/10 17♒10
11	20 27	7 54	14 12	25 06	14 56	26 02	25 36	26 23	3 00	4 04	♄ 17/5 14♍54
21	0♊05	15 20	21 48	26 01	14D55	26 11	25 57	26 27	2 49	3 33	♅ 1/7 26♓37
31	9 42	24 01	29 20	26 39	15 04	26R14	26 14	26R28	2 36	3 01	♅ 2/12 22♓42
10 6	19 16	3♉32	6♉47	26 58	15 24	26 10	26 26	26 26	2 21	2 29	♆ 29/5 26♒29
20	28 49	13 39	14 08	26R59	15 53	26 01	26 34	26 21	2 06	1 57	♆ 5/11 23♒41
30	8♋21	24 13	21 23	26 40	16 31	25 46	26 37	26 13	1 51	1 26	♇ 4/4 3♑20
10 7	17 54	5♊06	28 30	26 03	17 17	25 26	26R36	26 02	1 36	0 54	♇ 12/9 0♑42
20	27 26	16 16	5♊31	25 10	18 10	25 01	26 29	25 49	1 22	0 22	⚷ 30/5 26♒14
30	6♌59	27 38	12 23	24 04	19 09	24 33	26 18	25 34	1 09	29♑50	⚷ 31 10 21♒13
9 8	16 33	9♋12	19 07	22 49	20 13	24 04	26 03	25 19	0 58	29 18	
19	26 10	20 55	25 41	21 31	21 21	23 33	25 45	25 02	0 50	28 47	
29	5♍48	2♌46	2♋05	20 15	22 33	23 03	25 24	24 46	0 44	28 15	
8 9	15 29	14 46	8 18	19 07	23 47	22 34	25 01	24 30	0 42	27 43	
18	25 13	26 53	14 18	18 12	25 01	22 08	24 37	24 16	0D42	27 11	
28	5♎00	9♍06	20 03	17 33	26 16	21 47	24 13	24 04	0 46	26 40	
8 10	14 51	21 24	25 32	17 13	27 30	21 30	23 50	23 54	0 53	26 08	
18	24 45	3♎47	0♌41	17D12	28 41	21 18	23 29	23 47	1 02	25 36	
28	4♏42	16 14	5 26	17 32	29 49	21 13	23 12	23 42	1 15	25 04	
7 11	14 43	28 44	9 44	18 11	0♎52	21D15	22 58	23D41	1 30	24 33	
17	24 46	11♏16	13 26	19 08	1 50	21 22	22 48	23 44	1 47	24 01	
27	4♐52	23 49	16 26	20 21	2 41	21 36	22 43	23 50	2 06	23 29	
7 12	15 01	6♐24	18 33	21 49	3 24	21 56	22D43	23 59	2 27	22 57	
17	25 11	18 59	19 37	23 30	3 58	22 21	22 48	24 11	2 48	22 25	
27	5♑22	1♑34	19R25	25 22	4 22	22 51	22 59	24 27	3 10	21 54	

SID M/N 1st JAN 6 h 41 m 11 s 2010 COMMON BST

DAY	JAN	FEB	MAR	APR	MAY	JUN	JUL	AUG	SEP	OCT	NOV	DEC
1	29♏14	17♑53	27♑19	12♓34	15♈03	0♊02	4♋16	24♌45	18♎25	27♏10	17♑51	22♒15
☽ 3	25♐50	12♒37	21♒36	6♈17	9♉03	25♊21	1♌18	23♍52	17♏36	25♐19	13♒47	17♓02
5	21♑33	6♓48	15♓31	0♉06	3♊31	21♋34	29♌15	22♎52	15♐26	21♑50	8♓29	10♈58
7	16♒23	0♈36	9♈16	24♉13	28♊39	18♌42	27♍40	21♏08	11♑58	17♒04	2♈27	4♉39
9	10♓30	24♈20	3♉02	18♊54	24♋39	16♍39	26♎08	18♐30	7♒30	11♓31	26♈10	28♉33
11	4♈15	18♉28	27♉10	14♋34	21♌50	15♎14	24♏18	15♑00	2♓19	5♈29	19♉56	23♊01
13	28♈10	13♊36	22♊10	11♌43	20♍17	14♏04	21♐56	10♒44	26♓35	29♈13	14♊00	18♋15
15	22♉53	10♋21	18♋39	10♍36	19♎45	12♐36	18♑48	5♓42	20♈26	22♉55	8♋38	14♌21
17	18♊57	8♌59	17♌03	10♎46	19♏24	10♑13	14♒43	29♓59	14♉05	16♊55	4♌10	11♍23
19	16♋38	9♍04	17♍09	11♏05	18♐15	6♒34	9♓38	23♈47	7♊58	11♋39	0♍57	9♎21
21	15♌42	9♎23	17♎50	10♐13	15♑35	1♓40	3♈46	17♉31	2♋41	7♌42	29♍13	8♏06
23	15♍18	8♏41	17♏38	7♑32	11♒20	25♓49	27♈32	11♊48	28♋54	5♍33	28♎45	7♐14
25	14♎28	6♐18	15♐38	3♒07	5♓50	19♈37	21♉32	7♋19	27♌03	5♎08	28♏46	6♑03
27	12♏33	2♑22	11♑48	27♒31	29♓42	13♉37	16♊25	4♌35	26♍55	5♏37	28♐09	3♒49
29	9♐25		6♒37	21♓20	23♈29	8♊24	12♋39	3♍33	27♎24	5♐41	26♑03	0♓07
31	5♑16		0♓40		17♉41		10♌25	3♎29		4♑15		25♓02
1	19♐50	25♑31	13♓14	24♈17	15♈10	26♉23	27♋54	1♍00	20♌26	9♎11	27♏40	16♐13
☿ 7	23 19	4♒50	24 46	21R40	19 44	8♊38	7♌35	0R33	26 43	19 29	5♐41	8R21
13	29 27	14 37	6♈02	17 10	26 12	21 42	15 55	27♌08	6♍15	29 17	12 48	3 57
19	6♑56	24 54	15 43	13 42	4♉14	4♋44	22 47	22 13	17 14	8♏40	18 11	5D39
25	15 12	5♓44	22 12	12D59	13 40	16 55	27 54	18 56	28 24	17 40	20R05	11 10
31	24 00		24R21		24 27		0♍47	19D49		26 16		18 31

DATE	☉	♀	♂	♃	♄	⚷	♅	♆	♇	☊	STATIONS
1 1	10♑12	23♏34	18♑23	26♓33	16♎40	23♒07	26♓58	26♒44	5♑22	2♑18	
11	20 24	3♐33	26 09	28 01	17 01	23 43	27 13	27 02	5 43	1 46	☿ 31/3 24♈21
21	0♒35	14 10	3♒58	29 42	17 12	24 22	27 33	27 22	6 04	1 15	☿ 23/4 12♈53
31	10 45	25 13	11 49	1♈34	17R12	25 02	27 57	27 44	6 23	0 43	☿ 3/8 1♍12
10 2	20 53	6♑34	19 43	3 35	17 02	25 44	28 25	28 06	6 41	0 11	☿ 27/8 18♌42
20	1♓00	18 08	27 36	5 44	16 41	26 27	28 55	28 29	6 56	29♐39	☿ 24/11 20♐07
2 3	11 03	29 52	5♓30	7 59	16 12	27 09	29 27	28 52	7 10	29 07	☿ 14/12 3♐51
12	21 04	11♒44	13 23	10 19	15 35	27 49	0♈00	29 14	7 20	28 36	♃ 30/8 10♉21
22	1♈01	23 40	21 15	12 42	14 52	28 27	0 35	29 35	7 27	28 04	♃ 26/12 0♉22
1 4	10 55	5♓40	29 04	15 06	14 06	29 03	1 09	29 54	7 31	27 32	♄ 26/1 17♎13
11	20 46	17 43	6♈51	17 31	13 20	29 35	1 42	0♓11	7R32	27 00	♄ 13/6 10♎26
21	0♉33	29 48	14 34	19 56	12 35	0♓02	2 14	0 26	7 30	26 29	♅ 10/7 4♈34
1 5	10 18	11♈54	22 13	22 18	11 54	0 25	2 44	0 38	7 25	25 57	♅ 10/12 0♈39
11	19 59	24 02	29 47	24 38	11 20	0 42	3 11	0 47	7 17	25 25	♆ 3/6 0♓55
21	29 37	6♉10	7♉17	26 53	10 53	0 53	3 36	0 53	7 07	24 53	♆ 10/11 28♒08
31	9♊14	18 19	14 41	29 03	10 35	0 59	3 56	0 55	6 55	24 21	♇ 9/4 7♑32
10 6	18 48	0♊29	21 59	1♉06	10 27	0 58	4 12	0R55	6 41	23 50	♇ 17/9 4♑55
20	28 21	12 41	29 12	3 01	10D28	0 52	4 24	0 51	6 26	23 18	⚷ 4/6 0R59
30	7♋54	24 54	6♊19	4 46	10 40	0 40	4 31	0 44	6 11	22 46	⚷ 6 11 26D04
10 7	17 26	7♋08	13 20	6 19	11 02	0 23	4R34	0 35	5 56	22 14	
20	26 58	19 24	20 15	7 40	11 33	0 01	4 31	0 23	5 42	21 43	
30	6♌31	1♌42	27 03	8 46	12 12	29♒35	4 24	0 09	5 28	21 11	
9 8	16 06	14 02	3♋45	9 36	12 59	29 07	4 13	29♒54	5 17	20 39	
19	25 42	26 23	10 20	10 08	13 53	28 37	3 57	29 37	5 07	20 07	
29	5♍20	8♍47	16 48	10 21	14 52	28 07	3 38	29 21	5 01	19 36	
8 9	15 01	21 11	23 08	10R14	15 56	27 38	3 17	29 05	4 56	19 04	
18	24 45	3♎36	29 21	9 47	17 05	27 11	2 54	28 50	4D55	18 32	
28	4♎32	16 02	5♌25	9 01	18 15	26 48	2 30	28 37	4 57	18 00	
8 10	14 22	28 28	11 19	7 59	19 28	26 29	2 06	28 25	5 02	17 28	
18	24 16	10♏54	17 03	6 46	20 41	26 15	1 43	28 17	5 11	16 57	
28	4♏13	23 20	22 35	5 26	21 54	26 06	1 23	28 11	5 22	16 25	
7 11	14 14	5♐46	27 52	4 05	23 05	26 04	1 06	28 08	5 35	15 53	
17	24 17	18 11	2♍53	2 50	24 14	26 08	0 52	28D09	5 51	15 21	
27	4♐23	0♑36	7 34	1 46	25 19	26 18	0 43	28 13	6 09	14 50	
7 12	14 31	13 00	11 51	0 59	26 18	26 34	0 39	28 21	6 29	14 18	
17	24 41	25 22	15 38	0 30	27 11	26 56	0D40	28 32	6 50	13 46	
27	4♑52	7♒41	18 48	0D22	27 58	27 22	0 46	28 46	7 11	13 14	

(f) The Stellar Zodiac

The 'tropical' or 'moving' or 'equinox' zodiac is the one that now, as for centuries past, is almost unanimously used for astrology, except in India. It begins at the vernal equinox, so that positions given in an ephemeris or table of houses (which use the tropical zodiac) correspond exactly to geocentric celestial longitude as understood by astronomers.

But the vernal equinox moves round a circle among the fixed, or remote, stars in about 26,000 years, in reverse direction of the signs. Thus, after a sufficient length of time, a different sign of this zodiac will cover any given group of stars.

A very few leading European astrologers in modern times prefer to use the stellar, or fixed, or sidereal, zodiac, the traditional zodiac in Hindu astrology. This begins at a particular point among the fixed stars, so that each sign of this stellar zodiac will always cover the same part of the 'remote star-pattern'. The two zodiacs, of course, coincided at some past date. Exactly when is much disputed. The difference between the two zodiacs increases at the rate of (roughly) $1°$ every 72 years. The rate – that is, the precession of the equinoxes – is not in dispute. But the distance from (for example) $0°$ of Aries in the tropical zodiac to $0°$ of Aries in the stellar zodiac, at a given date, depends on an extremely controversial estimate of the date when both zodiacs in reality were the same. The difference between them at any given date is called the 'ayanamsa' for that date. Various authorities differ by some four or five degrees on the amount of this ayanamsa. About the greatest value assigned to it is that which is the result of considering the star *Spica Virginis* as $0 \triangleq 0$. This is the majority view among Hindu authorities. Dr V. B. Raman, the Hindu writer, adopted an 'average' ayanamsa of about $3°$ less. Mr Cyril Fagan, a leading European authority on the subject in his time, as a result of much scholarly, and original, research in astronomical archaeology, regarded *Spica Virginis* as corresponding to 29° ♍ 0.

The ayanamsa for each year from 1900 to 2010 inclusive, given in the table opposite, is based on Mr Fagan's reckoning. It ignores the small amount of precession during a single year, but, for any reader wishing to experiment with the stellar zodiac, will give a result as close as consistent with the use of condensed ephemeris and tables of houses. After casting the horoscope, simply deduct the ayanamsa from every zodiacal longitude: cusps of houses, and positions of planets etc., alike. For Dr Raman's ayanamsa, take 2°28′ from the ayanamsa given in the table below, for any date.

(g) Table of Ayanamsa

year	ayan		year	ayan		year	ayan		year	ayan		year	ayan		year	ayan		year	ayan	
	°	′		°	′		°	′		°	′		°	′		°	′		°	′
1900	23	27	1916	23	40	1932	23	54	1948	24	7	1964	24	20	1980	24	33	1996	24	46
1901	23	28	1917	23	41	1933	23	54	1949	24	8	1965	24	21	1981	24	34	1997	24	47
1902	23	29	1918	23	42	1934	23	55	1950	24	9	1966	24	22	1982	24	35	1998	24	47
1903	23	29	1919	23	43	1935	23	56	1951	24	9	1967	24	23	1983	24	36	1999	24	48
1904	23	30	1920	23	44	1936	23	57	1952	24	10	1968	24	23	1984	24	37	2000	24	49
1905	23	31	1921	23	44	1937	23	58	1953	24	11	1969	24	24	1985	24	37	2001	24	50
1906	23	32	1922	23	45	1938	23	59	1954	24	12	1970	24	25	1986	24	38	2002	24	51
1907	23	33	1923	23	46	1939	23	59	1955	24	13	1971	24	26	1987	24	39	2003	24	52
1908	23	33	1924	23	47	1940	24	0	1956	24	14	1972	24	27	1988	24	40	2004	24	52
1909	23	34	1925	23	48	1941	24	1	1957	24	14	1973	24	27	1989	24	41	2005	24	53
1910	23	35	1926	23	49	1942	24	2	1958	24	15	1974	24	28	1990	24	41	2006	24	54
1911	23	36	1927	23	49	1943	24	3	1959	24	16	1975	24	29	1991	24	42	2007	24	55
1912	23	37	1928	23	50	1944	24	4	1960	24	17	1976	24	30	1992	24	43	2008	24	56
1913	23	38	1929	23	51	1945	24	4	1961	24	18	1977	24	31	1993	24	43	2009	24	57
1914	23	38	1930	23	52	1946	24	5	1962	24	18	1978	24	32	1994	24	44	2010	24	58
1915	23	39	1931	23	53	1947	24	6	1963	24	19	1979	24	32	1995	24	45			
1916	23	40	1932	23	54	1948	24	7	1964	24	20	1980	24	33	1996	24	46			

XII
Universal Tables of Houses

According to all current systems of house division for all geographical latitudes from 0° to 60° north. Ascendant and MC in degrees and minutes, for all systems; intermediate cusps for the Regiomontanus, Campanus, Placidus and Koch systems and for Natural Graduation, in whole degrees (not needed for using the Porphyry and Equal House systems).

NB: When the sign changes in a column, the new sign is given, for Ascendant or MC, between the degrees and the minutes, as: 4♌23 – but in the case of an intermediate cusp (11, 12, 2 or 3) the new sign is given before the degrees, as: ♌4 (the same as 4♌0), which may not so readily catch the eye. Therefore great care must be taken always to cast the eye up the column to be sure where the sign last changed before the entry wanted.

(h) Zero Latitude

THE MC: this, being the same at all latitudes, may be taken from a table for any other latitude.

THE ASCENDANT: at latitude 0° is always the same as the MC at sidereal time 6h later, or 18h earlier.

INTERMEDIATE CUSPS (11, 12, 2, 3): in the systems of Regiomontanus, Campanus and Placidus, which are all alike at latitude 0°, cusps 11, 12, 2 and 3, respectively, are the same as the MC at sidereal times later by 2h, 4h, 8h, 10h, respectively, or earlier by 22h, 20h, 16h, 14h, respectively. In the Natural Graduation system they are as shown opposite.

0° Latitude

Sid. Time		Houses			
h	m	11 ♉	12 ♊	2 ♌	3 ♍
0	0	0	0	0	0
0	24	6	6	6	6
0	48	13	12	12	13
1	12	19	17	17	19
1	36	25	23	23	25
2	0	♊1	29	29	♎1
2	24	7	♋5	♍5	7
2	48	13	11	11	13
3	12	19	17	17	19
3	36	24	24	24	24
4	0	♎♋1	29	29	♏1
4	24	7	♌5	♎5	7
4	48	13	11	11	13
5	12	19	17	17	19
5	36	24	24	24	24
6	0	♌0	♍0	♏0	♐0
6	24	6	6	6	6
6	48	12	13	13	12
7	12	17	19	19	17
7	36	23	25	25	23
8	0	29	♎1	♐1	29

Natural Graduation Intermediate Cusps

Sid. Time		Houses			
h	m	11 ♌	12 ♎	2 ♐	3 ♐
8	0	29	1	1	29
8	24	♍5	7	7	♑5
8	48	11	13	13	11
9	12	17	19	19	17
9	36	23	25	25	23
10	0	29	♏1	♑1	29
10	24	♎5	7	7	♒5
10	48	11	13	13	11
11	12	17	19	19	17
11	36	25	23	23	25
12	0	♏0	♐0	♒0	♓0
12	24	6	6	6	6
12	48	13	12	12	13
13	12	19	17	17	19
13	36	25	23	23	25
14	0	♐1	29	29	♈1
14	24	7	♑5	♓5	7
14	48	13	11	11	13
15	12	19	17	17	19
15	36	25	23	23	25
16	0	♑1	29	29	♉1

Sid. Time		Houses			
h	m	11 ♑	12 ♑	2 ♓	3 ♉
16	0	1	29	29	1
16	24	7	♒5	♈5	7
16	48	13	11	11	13
17	12	19	17	17	19
17	36	24	24	24	24
18	0	♒0	♓0	♉0	♊0
18	24	6	6	6	6
18	48	12	13	13	12
19	12	17	19	19	17
19	36	23	25	25	23
20	0	29	♈1	♊1	29
20	24	♓5	7	7	♋5
20	48	11	13	13	11
21	12	17	19	19	17
21	36	23	25	25	23
22	0	29	♉1	♋1	29
22	24	♈5	7	7	♌5
22	48	11	13	13	11
23	12	17	19	19	17
23	36	24	24	24	24
24	0	♉0	♊0	♌0	♍0

SID TIME	MC LONG	ASC	REGIOMONT				CAMPANUS				PLACIDUS				NAT. GRAD.				KOCH			
			11	12	2	3	11	12	2	3	11	12	2	3	11	12	2	3	11	12	2	3
h m	♈	♋	♉	Ⅱ	♌		♉	Ⅱ	♌		♉	Ⅱ	♌		♉	Ⅱ	♌	♍	♉	Ⅱ	♌	♍
0 0	0♈00	4♋01	3	5	♌1	29	3	5	♌1	29	3	5	♌0	29	♉1	3	3	♍1	5	6	♌1	♍0
12	3♈16	6 45	7	8	4	♍2	6	8	4	♍2	6	7	3	♍2	4	6	6	4	8	9	4	3
24	6 32	9 29	10	11	7	5	9	11	7	5	9	10	6	5	7	9	9	7	11	12	7	6
36	9 48	12 12	13	14	9	8	12	14	10	8	12	13	9	8	10	12	12	10	14	14	10	9
48	13 03	14 56	16	17	12	11	16	16	13	12	15	16	12	11	13	15	15	13	17	17	13	12
1 0	16 17	17 40	19	20	15	14	19	19	15	15	19	19	15	14	17	17	17	17	20	20	16	16
12	19 30	20 24	22	22	18	17	22	22	18	18	22	22	17	17	20	20	20	20	23	23	19	19
24	22 42	23 08	25	25	21	21	25	25	21	21	25	24	20	20	23	23	23	23	26	25	22	22
36	25 53	25 53	28	28	24	24	28	28	24	24	27	27	23	24	26	26	26	26	29	28	25	25
48	29 03	28 39	Ⅱ1	♋1	27	27	Ⅱ1	♋0	27	27	Ⅱ0	♋0	26	27	29	29	29	29	Ⅱ2	♋1	28	28
2 0	2♉11	1♌25	4	3	♍0	♎0	4	3	♍0	♎0	3	3	29	♎0	Ⅱ2	♋2	♍2	♎2	4	3	♍1	♎1
12	5 18	4 12	7	6	3	3	6	6	3	4	6	5	♍2	3	5	4	4	5	7	6	4	5
24	8 23	6 59	9	9	6	6	9	9	6	7	8	8	5	6	8	7	7	8	10	9	7	8
36	11 26	9 48	13	12	9	9	12	11	9	10	12	11	8	10	11	10	10	11	13	11	10	11
48	14 28	12 38	15	14	12	13	15	14	12	13	15	14	11	13	14	13	13	14	16	14	13	14
3 0	17 28	15 28	18	17	15	16	18	17	15	16	18	16	14	16	17	16	16	17	18	17	16	17
12	20 26	18 20	21	20	18	19	21	20	18	19	20	19	18	19	20	19	19	20	21	19	19	20
24	23 23	21 13	24	23	21	22	23	22	21	22	23	22	21	22	23	22	22	23	24	22	22	23
36	26 19	24 07	27	25	24	25	26	25	24	25	26	25	24	25	26	25	25	26	26	25	25	26
48	29 13	27 02	29	28	27	28	29	28	27	28	29	27	27	28	29	28	28	29	29	28	28	♏0
4 0	2♊05	29 58	♋2	♌1	♎0	♏1	♋2	♌1	♎0	♏1	♋1	♌0	♎0	♏1	♋2	♌0	♎0	♏2	♋2	♌0	♎1	3
12	4 57	2♍55	5	4	3	4	4	3	3	4	4	3	3	4	4	3	3	4	3	3	4	6
24	7 47	5 53	8	7	6	7	7	6	7	7	7	6	6	8	7	6	6	7	7	6	7	8
36	10 36	8 51	10	9	9	10	10	9	10	10	10	9	9	11	10	9	9	10	10	9	10	10
48	13 24	11 51	13	12	12	13	13	12	13	13	12	12	12	13	13	12	12	13	12	11	14	14
5 0	16 11	14 51	16	15	15	16	15	15	16	16	15	15	16	16	16	15	15	16	15	14	17	17
12	18 58	17 52	19	18	18	19	18	18	19	19	18	17	19	19	19	18	18	19	18	17	20	20
24	21 44	20 54	21	21	21	22	21	20	22	22	21	20	22	22	22	21	21	22	21	20	23	23
36	24 30	23 56	24	24	24	25	24	23	25	25	23	23	25	25	24	24	24	25	23	23	26	26
48	27 15	26 58	27	27	27	27	27	26	28	28	26	26	28	28	27	27	27	27	26	26	29	29
6 0	0♋00	0♎00	♌0	♍0	♏0	♐0	29	29	♏1	♐1	29	29	♏1	♐1	♌0	♍0	♏0	♐0	29	29	♏1	♐1
12	2 45	3 02	3	3	3	3	♌2	♍2	4	3	♌2	♍2	4	4	3	3	3	3	♌1	♍1	4	4
24	5 30	6 04	5	6	6	6	5	5	7	5	5	5	7	7	6	6	6	6	4	4	7	7
36	8 16	9 06	8	9	9	9	8	8	10	9	8	8	10	9	8	9	9	8	7	7	10	9
48	11 02	12 08	11	12	12	11	11	11	12	12	11	11	13	12	11	12	12	11	10	10	13	12
7 0	13 49	15 09	14	15	15	14	14	14	15	15	14	14	15	15	14	15	15	14	13	13	16	15
12	16 36	18 09	17	18	18	17	17	17	18	17	17	18	18	18	17	18	18	17	16	16	19	18
24	19 24	21 09	20	21	21	20	20	20	21	20	19	21	21	20	20	21	21	20	19	20	21	20
36	22 13	24 07	23	24	23	22	23	23	24	23	22	24	24	23	23	24	24	23	22	23	24	23
48	25 03	27 05	26	27	26	25	26	27	27	26	26	27	27	26	26	27	27	26	24	26	27	26
8 0	27 55	0♏02	29	♎0	29	28	29	♎0	29	28	29	♎0	29	29	28	♎0	♐0	28	27	29	♐0	28
12	0♌47	2 58	♍2	3	♐2	♑1	♍2	3	♐2	♑1	♍2	3	3	♑1	♍1	2	2	♑1	♍0	♎2	2	♑1
24	3 41	5 53	5	6	5	3	5	6	5	4	5	6	5	4	4	5	5	4	4	5	5	4
36	6 37	8 47	8	9	7	6	8	9	8	7	8	9	8	7	7	8	8	7	7	8	8	6
48	9 34	11 40	11	12	10	9	11	12	11	9	11	12	11	10	10	11	11	10	10	11	11	9
9 0	12 32	14 32	14	15	13	12	14	15	13	12	14	16	14	12	13	14	13	12	13	14	13	12
12	15 32	17 22	17	18	16	15	17	18	16	15	17	19	16	15	16	17	17	16	16	17	16	14
24	18 34	20 12	21	21	18	17	20	21	19	18	20	22	19	18	19	20	20	19	19	20	19	17
36	21 37	23 01	24	24	21	20	23	24	21	20	24	25	22	21	22	23	23	22	22	23	21	20
48	24 42	25 48	27	27	24	23	26	27	24	23	27	28	25	24	25	26	26	25	25	26	24	23
10 0	27 49	28 35	♎0	♏0	27	26	♎0	♏0	27	26	♎0	♏1	27	27	28	28	28	28	29	29	27	26
12	0♍57	1♐21	3	3	29	29	3	3	♐0	29	3	4	♑0	♒0	♎1	♏1	♑1	♒1	♎2	♏2	29	28
24	4 07	4 07	6	6	♐2	♒2	6	6	2	♒2	6	7	3	3	4	4	4	3	5	5	♑2	♒1
36	7 18	6 52	9	9	5	5	9	9	5	5	10	10	6	5	7	7	7	7	8	8	5	4
48	10 30	9 36	13	12	8	8	12	12	8	8	13	13	8	8	10	10	10	10	11	11	7	7
11 0	13 43	12 20	16	15	10	11	15	15	11	11	16	15	11	11	13	13	13	13	14	14	10	10
12	16 57	15 04	19	18	13	14	18	17	14	14	19	18	14	15	17	15	15	17	18	17	13	13
24	20 12	17 48	22	21	16	17	22	20	16	18	22	21	17	18	20	18	18	20	21	20	16	16
36	23 28	20 31	25	23	19	20	25	23	19	21	25	24	20	21	23	21	21	23	24	23	18	19
48	26 44	23 15	28	26	22	23	28	26	22	24	28	27	23	24	26	24	24	26	27	26	21	22
12 0	0♎00	25 59	♏1	29	25	27	♏1	29	25	27	♏1	♐0	25	27	29	27	27	29	♏0	29	24	25

SID TIME	MC	ASC	REGIOMONT.				CAMPANUS				PLACIDUS				NAT. GRAD.				KOCH			
TIME	LONG	1	11	12	2	3	11	12	2	3	11	12	2	3	11	12	2	3	11	12	2	3
h m	♎	♐	♏	♏	♑	≈	♏	♏	♑	≈	♏	♐	♑	≈	♎	♏	♑	≈	♏	♏	♑	≈
12 0	0≏00	25♐59	♏1	29	25	27	♏1	29	25	27	♏1	♐0	25	27	29	27	27	29	♏0	29	24	25
12	3 16	28 44	4	♐2	28	♓0	4	♐1	28	♓0	4	3	28	♓0	♏2	♐0	≈0	♓2	3	♐1	27	29
24	6 32	1♑29	7	5	≈1	3	7	4	≈1	4	8	5	≈1	3	5	3	3	5	6	4	≈0	♓2
36	9 48	4 15	10	7	4	6	10	7	4	7	11	8	4	7	9	6	5	9	9	7	3	5
48	13 03	7 02	13	10	7	10	13	10	7	10	13	11	7	10	12	8	8	12	12	10	6	8
13 0	16 17	9 50	16	13	10	13	16	13	10	14	16	14	10	13	15	11	11	15	15	13	9	12
12	19 30	12 39	19	16	13	16	19	15	13	17	19	16	14	17	18	14	14	18	18	15	12	15
24	22 42	15 29	22	18	16	20	21	18	16	20	22	19	17	20	21	17	17	21	21	18	15	18
36	25 53	18 21	25	21	19	23	24	21	20	24	25	22	20	23	24	20	20	24	24	21	18	22
48	29 03	21 15	27	24	22	27	27	23	23	27	28	25	23	27	27	23	23	27	27	24	21	25
14 0	2♏11	24 10	♐0	27	26	♈0	♐0	26	26	♈0	♐1	27	26	♈0	♐0	26	26	♈0	♐0	27	25	28
12	5 18	27 07	3	29	29	3	3	29	29	4	4	♈0	29	3	3	29	29	4	3	29	28	♈2
24	8 23	0≈06	6	♑2	♓2	7	6	♑2	♓3	7	7	3	♓3	7	6	♑2	♓2	7	6	♑2	♓1	5
36	11 26	3 08	9	5	6	10	8	4	6	11	9	6	6	10	9	5	5	10	9	5	4	8
48	14 28	6 11	11	8	9	14	11	7	10	14	12	8	9	13	11	8	8	13	11	8	8	12
15 0	17 28	9 17	14	10	13	17	14	10	13	17	15	11	13	17	16	11	11	16	14	11	11	15
12	20 26	12 26	17	13	16	20	17	13	16	21	18	14	16	20	19	14	14	19	17	14	15	19
24	23 23	15 37	20	16	20	24	19	16	20	24	20	17	20	23	22	17	17	22	20	17	18	22
36	26 19	18 50	22	19	23	27	22	19	23	27	23	20	23	27	25	21	20	25	23	19	22	25
48	29 13	22 05	25	22	26	♉0	25	21	27	♉1	26	23	27	♉0	28	24	24	28	25	22	25	29
16 0	2♐05	25 23	28	25	♈0	3	28	24	♈0	4	29	25	♈0	3	♉1	27	27	♉1	28	25	29	♉2
12	4 57	28 43	♉1	28	4	7	♉0	27	4	7	♉1	28	3	6	4	≈0	♈0	4	♉1	28	♈2	5
24	7 47	2♓06	3	≈1	7	10	3	≈0	7	10	4	≈1	7	9	6	3	3	7	4	≈1	6	8
36	10 36	5 30	6	4	10	13	6	3	11	13	7	4	10	12	9	7	7	10	7	5	9	11
48	13 24	8 56	9	7	14	16	9	6	14	16	10	7	14	15	12	10	10	12	10	8	12	15
17 0	16 11	12 24	12	10	17	19	12	9	18	19	12	10	17	19	15	13	13	15	12	11	16	18
12	18 58	15 54	15	13	21	22	14	12	21	22	15	14	21	22	18	17	17	18	15	14	19	21
24	21 44	19 24	17	16	24	25	17	16	25	25	18	17	24	25	21	20	20	21	18	17	23	24
36	24 30	22 56	20	19	28	28	20	19	28	28	21	20	27	27	24	23	23	24	21	20	26	27
48	27 15	26 28	23	22	♉1	♊1	23	22	♉1	♊1	24	23	♉1	♊0	27	27	27	27	24	24	♉0	♊0
18 0	0♑00	0♈00	26	26	4	4	26	25	5	4	27	26	4	3	≈0	♓0	♉0	♊0	27	27	3	3
12	2 45	3 32	29	29	8	7	29	29	8	7	≈0	29	7	6	3	3	3	3	≈0	♈0	6	6
24	5 30	7 04	≈2	♓2	11	10	≈2	♓2	11	10	3	♓3	10	9	6	7	7	6	3	4	10	9
36	8 16	10 36	5	6	14	13	5	5	14	13	5	6	13	12	9	10	10	9	6	7	13	12
48	11 02	14 06	8	9	17	15	8	9	18	16	8	9	16	15	12	13	13	12	9	11	16	15
19 0	13 49	17 36	11	13	20	18	11	12	21	18	11	13	20	18	15	17	17	15	12	14	19	18
12	16 36	21 04	14	16	23	21	14	16	24	21	15	16	23	20	18	20	20	18	15	18	22	20
24	19 24	24 30	17	20	26	24	17	19	27	24	18	20	26	23	20	23	23	21	19	21	25	23
36	22 13	27 54	20	23	29	27	20	23	♊0	27	21	23	29	26	23	27	27	24	22	24	29	26
48	25 03	1♉17	23	26	♊2	29	23	26	3	♋0	24	27	♊2	29	26	♈0	♊0	26	25	28	♊2	29
20 0	27 55	4 37	27	♈0	5	♋2	26	♈0	6	2	27	♈0	5	♋1	29	3	3	29	28	♈1	5	♋2
12	0≈47	7 55	♈0	4	8	5	29	3	9	5	♈0	3	7	4	♈2	6	6	♋2	♈1	5	8	5
24	3 41	11 10	3	7	11	8	♈3	7	11	8	3	7	10	7	5	10	9	5	5	8	11	7
36	6 37	14 23	6	10	14	10	6	10	14	11	7	10	13	10	8	13	13	8	8	12	13	10
48	9 34	17 34	10	14	17	13	9	14	17	13	10	14	16	12	11	16	16	11	11	15	16	13
21 0	12 32	20 43	13	17	20	16	13	17	20	16	13	17	19	15	14	19	19	14	15	19	19	16
12	15 32	23 49	16	21	22	19	16	20	23	19	17	21	22	18	17	22	22	17	18	22	22	19
24	18 34	26 52	20	24	25	21	19	24	26	22	20	24	24	21	20	25	25	21	22	26	25	21
36	21 37	29 54	23	28	28	24	23	27	28	24	24	27	28	24	23	28	28	24	25	29	28	24
48	24 42	2♉53	27	♉1	♋1	27	26	♉1	♋1	27	27	♉1	♋0	26	26	♉1	♋1	27	28	♉2	♋1	27
22 0	27 49	5 50	♈0	4	3	♌0	♈0	4	4	♌0	♈0	4	3	29	♈0	4	4	♌0	♈2	5	3	♌0
12	0♓57	8 45	3	8	6	3	3	7	7	3	3	7	5	♌2	3	7	7	3	5	9	6	3
24	4 07	11 39	7	11	9	5	6	10	9	6	7	10	8	5	6	10	10	6	8	12	9	6
36	7 18	14 31	10	14	12	8	10	14	12	9	10	13	11	8	9	13	13	9	12	15	12	9
48	10 30	17 21	14	17	14	11	13	17	15	11	13	16	14	11	12	16	16	12	15	18	15	12
23 0	13 43	20 10	17	20	17	14	16	20	17	14	17	20	16	14	15	19	19	15	18	21	17	15
12	16 57	22 58	20	23	20	17	20	23	20	17	20	23	19	17	18	22	22	18	22	24	20	18
24	20 12	25 45	24	26	23	20	23	26	23	20	23	26	22	19	21	25	24	21	25	27	23	21
36	23 28	28 31	27	29	25	23	26	29	26	23	27	29	25	22	25	27	27	25	28	♊0	26	24
48	26 44	1♊16	♉0	♊2	28	26	♉0	♊2	29	26	♉0	♊2	27	26	28	♊0	♌0	28	♊1	3	29	27
24 0	0♓00	4 01	3	5	♌1	29	3	5	♌1	29	3	5	♌0	29	♊1	3	3	♍1	5	6	♌1	♍0

LAT 20°N **CUSPS OF HOUSES** **SID TIME 0h–12h**

SID TIME h m	MC LONG ♈	ASC ♋	REGIOMONT. 11 ♉	12 ♊	2 ♌	3 ♍	CAMPANUS 11 ♉	12 ♊	2 ♌	3 ♍	PLACIDUS 11 ♉	12 ♊	2 ♌	3 ♌	NAT. GRAD. 11 ♉	12 ♊	2 ♌	3 ♍	KOCH 11 ♉	12 ♊	2 ♌	3 ♍
0 0	0♈00	8♋14	5	9	4	♍0	3	7	5	♍1	4	7	3	29	♉2	7	6	♍2	8	10	5	♍2
12	3♈16	10 56	8	12	7	3	6	10	8	4	7	10	5	♍2	5	9	9	5	11	13	8	5
24	6 32	13 36	11	15	9	6	9	13	11	7	10	13	8	5	8	12	12	8	14	16	10	8
36	9 48	16 16	14	18	12	9	13	16	13	10	13	16	11	8	11	15	15	11	17	18	13	11
48	13 03	18 56	18	21	15	12	16	19	16	13	17	19	14	11	14	18	18	14	20	21	16	14
1 0	16 17	21 35	21	23	18	15	19	22	19	16	20	22	17	15	17	20	20	17	23	24	19	17
12	19 30	24 15	24	26	20	18	22	25	22	19	23	25	19	18	21	23	23	21	26	26	22	20
24	22 42	26 54	27	29	23	21	25	27	24	22	26	27	22	21	24	26	26	24	29	29	25	24
36	25 53	29 33	♊0	♋2	26	24	28	♋0	27	25	29	♋0	25	24	27	29	29	27	♊1	♋2	28	27
48	29 03	2♌13	3	4	29	27	♊1	3	♍0	28	♊2	3	28	27	♊0	♋2	♍1	♎0	4	4	♍0	♎0
2 0	2♉11	4 52	6	7	♍1	♎0	4	6	3	♎2	5	6	♏1	♎0	3	4	4	3	7	7	3	3
12	5 18	7 32	9	10	4	3	7	8	6	5	8	8	4	3	6	7	7	6	10	9	6	6
24	8 23	10 13	12	13	7	6	10	11	9	8	10	11	6	6	9	10	10	9	13	12	9	9
36	11 26	12 54	15	15	10	9	13	14	11	11	13	14	9	9	12	13	13	12	15	15	12	12
48	14 28	15 36	18	18	13	12	16	16	14	14	16	16	12	12	15	15	15	15	18	17	15	15
3 0	17 28	18 18	20	21	16	15	19	19	17	17	19	19	15	15	18	18	18	18	20	20	18	18
12	20 26	21 01	23	23	19	18	21	22	20	20	22	22	18	19	21	21	21	21	23	22	21	21
24	23 23	23 44	26	26	21	21	24	24	23	23	25	25	21	22	23	24	24	23	26	25	24	24
36	26 19	26 28	29	29	24	24	27	27	26	26	27	27	24	25	26	26	26	26	28	27	27	27
48	29 13	29 13	♋1	♌1	27	27	♋0	♌0	29	29	♋0	♌0	27	28	29	29	29	29	♋1	♌0	♎0	♏0
4 0	2♊05	1♍58	4	4	♎0	♏0	3	2	♎2	♏2	3	3	♎0	♏1	♋2	♋2	♎2	♏2	4	3	2	3
12	4 57	4 45	7	7	3	3	5	5	4	4	6	5	3	4	5	5	5	5	6	5	5	6
24	7 47	7 31	10	9	6	6	8	8	7	7	8	8	6	7	8	8	8	8	9	8	8	9
36	10 36	10 18	12	12	9	9	11	11	10	10	11	11	9	10	11	10	10	10	11	10	11	11
48	13 24	13 06	15	15	11	12	13	13	13	13	14	14	12	13	13	13	13	13	14	13	14	14
5 0	16 11	15 54	18	18	14	14	16	16	16	16	16	17	15	15	16	16	16	16	16	16	17	17
12	18 58	18 43	21	20	17	17	19	19	19	19	19	19	18	18	19	19	19	19	19	18	20	20
24	21 44	21 32	23	23	20	20	22	22	22	22	22	22	21	21	22	22	22	22	22	21	22	22
36	24 30	24 21	26	26	23	23	24	24	24	24	25	25	24	24	24	24	24	24	24	24	25	25
48	27 15	27 11	29	29	26	26	27	27	27	27	28	28	26	27	27	27	27	27	27	26	28	28
6 0	0♋00	0♎00	♌2	♍1	29	28	♌0	♍0	♏0	♐0	♌0	♍1	29	♐0	♌0	♍0	♏0	♐0	♌0	29	♏0	♐0
12	2 45	2 49	4	4	♏1	♐1	3	3	3	3	3	4	♏2	2	3	3	3	3	2	♍2	4	3
24	5 30	5 39	7	7	4	4	6	6	6	6	6	6	5	5	6	6	6	6	5	5	6	6
36	8 16	8 28	10	10	7	7	8	8	8	8	9	9	8	8	8	8	8	8	8	8	9	8
48	11 02	11 17	13	13	10	9	11	11	11	11	12	12	11	11	11	11	11	11	10	10	12	11
7 0	13 49	14 06	16	16	12	12	14	14	14	14	15	15	13	14	14	14	14	14	13	13	14	14
12	16 36	16 54	18	19	15	15	17	17	17	17	18	18	16	16	17	17	17	17	16	16	17	16
24	19 24	19 42	21	21	18	18	20	20	19	19	20	21	19	19	19	20	20	19	19	19	20	19
36	22 13	22 29	24	24	21	20	23	23	22	22	23	24	22	22	22	22	22	22	21	22	22	21
48	25 03	25 15	27	27	23	23	26	26	25	25	26	27	25	24	25	25	25	25	24	25	25	24
8 0	27 55	28 02	♍0	♎0	26	26	28	28	28	27	29	♎0	27	27	28	28	28	28	27	28	27	26
12	0♌47	0♏47	3	3	29	29	♍1	≏1	♐0	♑0	♍2	3	♐0	♑0	♍1	≏1	♐1	♑1	♍0	≏0	♐0	29
24	3 41	3 32	6	6	♐1	♑1	4	4	3	3	5	6	3	3	4	4	4	4	3	3	3	♑2
36	6 37	6 16	9	9	4	4	7	7	6	6	8	9	5	5	7	6	6	7	6	6	5	4
48	9 34	8 59	12	11	7	7	10	10	8	9	11	12	8	8	9	9	9	9	9	9	8	7
9 0	12 32	11 42	15	14	9	10	13	13	11	11	15	15	11	11	12	12	12	12	12	12	10	10
12	15 32	14 24	18	17	12	13	16	16	14	14	18	18	14	14	15	15	15	15	15	15	13	12
24	18 34	17 06	21	20	15	15	19	19	16	17	21	21	16	17	18	17	17	18	18	18	15	15
36	21 37	19 47	24	23	17	18	22	21	19	20	24	24	19	20	21	20	20	21	21	21	18	17
48	24 42	22 28	27	26	20	21	25	24	22	23	27	26	22	22	24	23	23	24	24	24	21	20
10 0	27 49	25 08	≏0	29	23	24	28	27	24	26	≏0	29	24	25	27	26	26	27	27	27	23	23
12	0♍57	27 47	3	♏1	26	27	≏2	♏0	27	29	3	♏2	27	28	≏0	29	28	♒0	≏0	♏0	26	26
24	4 07	0♐27	6	4	28	♒0	5	3	♑0	♒2	6	5	♑0	♒1	3	♏1	♑1	♒1	3	2	28	29
36	7 18	3 06	9	7	♑1	3	8	6	3	5	9	8	3	4	6	5	♑1	3	6	5	♑1	♒1
48	10 30	5 45	12	10	4	6	11	8	5	8	12	11	5	7	9	7	7	9	10	8	4	4
11 0	13 43	8 25	15	12	7	9	14	11	8	11	15	13	8	10	13	10	10	13	13	11	6	7
12	16 57	11 04	18	15	9	12	17	14	11	14	19	16	11	13	16	12	12	16	16	14	9	10
24	20 12	13 44	21	18	12	16	20	17	14	17	22	19	14	17	19	15	15	19	19	17	12	13
36	23 28	16 24	24	21	15	19	23	19	17	21	25	22	17	20	22	18	18	22	22	20	14	16
48	26 44	19 04	27	23	18	22	26	22	20	24	28	25	20	23	25	21	21	25	25	22	17	19
12 0	0♎00	21 46	♏0	26	21	25	29	25	23	27	♏1	27	23	26	28	24	23	28	28	25	20	22

SID TIME (h m)	MC LONG (♎)	ASC (♐)	REG. 11	12	2	3	CAMP. 11	12	2	3	PLAC. 11	12	2	3	NAT.GRAD. 11	12	2	3	KOCH 11	12	2	3
12 0	0♎00	21♐46	♏0	26	21	25	29	25	23	27	♏1	27	23	26	28	24	23	28	28	25	20	22
12	3 16	24 28	3	29	24	29	♏2	27	26	♑0	4	♐0	26	29	♏1	27	26	♓1	♏1	28	23	26
24	6 32	27 11	6	♐1	27	♓2	4	♐0	29	4	7	3	29	♓3	4	29	29	5	4	♐1	26	29
36	9 48	29 55	9	4	≈0	5	7	3	≈2	7	10	5	≈2	6	7	♐2	≈2	8	7	4	29	♓2
48	13 03	2♑41	12	7	3	9	10	5	5	11	13	8	5	9	11	5	5	11	10	6	≈2	5
13 0	16 17	5 29	14	9	7	12	13	8	8	14	15	11	8	13	14	8	8	14	13	9	5	9
12	19 30	8 18	17	12	10	16	16	11	12	18	18	14	11	16	17	11	11	17	16	12	8	12
24	22 42	11 09	20	15	13	19	19	13	15	21	21	16	14	20	20	14	14	20	19	15	11	16
36	25 53	14 02	23	17	16	23	22	16	18	25	24	19	18	23	23	17	16	23	22	17	14	19
48	29 03	16 57	26	20	20	26	24	19	22	28	27	22	21	27	26	20	19	27	25	20	17	23
14 0	2♏11	19 55	28	23	23	♈0	27	22	25	♈2	♐0	24	24	♈0	29	23	22	♈0	28	23	21	26
12	5 18	22 56	♐1	26	27	4	♐0	24	29	5	2	27	28	3	♐2	26	25	3	♐1	26	24	♈0
24	8 23	26 00	4	28	♑0	7	3	27	♑2	9	5	♑0	♑1	7	5	29	26	4	4	29	27	3
36	11 26	29 06	7	♑1	4	11	6	♑0	6	12	8	3	5	10	8	♑2	♑2	7	6	♑2	♑1	7
48	14 28	2≈16	9	4	8	14	8	2	9	16	11	5	8	14	12	5	5	12	9	5	4	10
15 0	17 28	5 29	12	7	11	18	11	5	13	19	14	8	12	17	15	8	8	15	12	7	8	14
12	20 26	8 45	15	9	15	21	14	8	17	23	16	11	15	21	18	12	11	18	15	10	12	17
24	23 23	12 05	18	12	19	25	16	11	21	26	19	14	19	24	21	15	14	21	18	13	15	21
36	26 19	15 28	20	15	22	28	19	14	24	♉0	22	17	23	27	24	18	18	24	21	16	19	24
48	29 13	18 55	23	18	26	♉1	22	17	28	3	24	20	26	♉1	27	21	21	27	24	19	23	28
16 0	2♐05	22 25	26	21	♈0	5	25	20	♈2	6	27	23	♈0	4	♈0	25	24	♉0	26	23	27	♉1
12	4 57	25 59	29	24	4	8	27	23	6	10	♈0	26	4	7	3	28	28	3	29	26	♈0	5
24	7 47	29 36	♉1	27	8	11	♑0	26	10	13	3	29	7	10	6	≈2	♈1	6	♉2	29	4	8
36	10 36	3♓10	4	♈0	11	14	3	29	13	16	5	≈2	11	13	9	5	5	9	5	≈2	8	11
48	13 24	7 00	7	3	15	18	6	≈2	17	19	8	5	15	17	12	8	8	12	8	5	12	15
17 0	16 11	10 45	10	7	19	21	8	5	21	22	11	8	18	20	15	12	12	15	11	9	16	18
12	18 58	14 33	13	10	22	24	11	8	24	25	14	11	22	23	18	16	16	18	14	12	19	21
24	21 44	18 23	15	13	26	27	14	11	28	28	17	14	25	26	21	19	19	21	17	15	23	25
36	24 30	22 15	18	16	♉0	♊0	17	15	♉2	♊1	20	18	29	29	24	23	23	24	20	19	27	28
48	27 15	26 07	21	20	3	3	20	18	5	4	22	21	♉2	♊2	27	26	26	27	23	22	♉0	♊1
18 0	0♑00	0♈00	24	23	7	6	23	22	8	7	25	24	6	5	≈0	♈0	♉0	♊0	26	26	4	4
12	2 45	3 53	27	27	10	9	26	25	12	10	28	28	9	8	3	4	4	3	29	♈0	8	7
24	5 30	7 45	≈0	♈0	14	12	29	28	15	13	≈1	♈1	12	10	6	7	7	6	≈2	3	11	10
36	8 16	11 37	3	4	17	15	≈2	♈2	19	16	4	5	16	13	9	11	11	9	5	7	15	13
48	11 02	15 27	6	8	20	17	5	6	22	19	7	8	19	16	12	14	14	12	9	11	18	16
19 0	13 49	19 15	9	11	23	20	8	9	25	22	10	12	22	19	15	18	18	15	12	14	21	19
12	16 36	23 00	12	15	27	23	11	13	28	24	13	15	25	22	18	22	22	18	15	18	25	22
24	19 24	26 44	16	19	♊0	26	14	17	♊1	26	17	19	28	25	21	25	25	21	19	22	28	25
36	22 13	0♉24	19	22	3	29	17	20	4	♋0	20	23	♊1	27	24	29	28	24	22	26	♊1	28
48	25 03	4 01	22	26	6	♋1	20	24	7	3	23	26	4	♋0	27	♈2	♊2	27	25	♈0	4	♋1
20 0	27 55	7 35	25	♈0	9	4	24	28	10	5	26	♈0	7	3	♈0	6	5	♋0	29	3	7	4
12	0≈47	11 05	29	4	12	7	27	♈2	13	8	29	4	10	6	3	9	9	3	♈2	7	11	6
24	3 41	14 32	♓2	8	15	10	♈0	6	16	11	♈3	7	13	8	6	12	12	6	6	11	14	9
36	6 37	17 55	5	11	18	12	4	9	19	14	6	11	16	11	9	16	15	9	9	15	17	12
48	9 34	21 15	9	15	21	15	7	13	22	16	9	15	19	12	12	19	18	12	13	18	20	15
21 0	12 32	24 31	12	19	23	18	11	17	25	19	13	18	22	16	15	22	22	15	16	22	23	18
12	15 32	27 44	16	22	26	21	14	21	28	22	16	22	25	19	18	25	25	18	20	26	25	21
24	18 34	0♊54	19	26	29	23	18	24	♋0	24	20	25	27	22	21	28	28	22	23	29	28	24
36	21 33	4 00	23	♉0	♋2	26	21	28	3	27	23	29	♋0	25	24	♉1	♋1	25	27	♉3	♋1	26
48	24 42	7 04	26	3	4	29	25	♉1	5	♌0	27	♉2	3	28	27	5	4	28	♈0	6	4	29
22 0	27 49	10 05	♈0	7	7	♌2	28	5	8	3	♈0	6	6	♌0	♈0	8	7	♌1	4	9	7	♌2
12	0♓57	13 03	4	10	10	4	♈2	8	11	6	3	9	8	3	3	11	10	4	7	13	10	5
24	4 07	15 58	7	14	13	7	5	12	14	8	7	12	11	6	7	14	13	7	11	16	13	8
36	7 18	18 51	11	17	15	10	9	15	17	11	10	16	14	9	10	16	16	9	14	19	15	11
48	10 30	21 42	14	20	18	13	12	18	19	14	14	19	16	12	13	19	19	13	18	22	18	14
23 0	13 43	24 31	18	23	21	16	16	22	22	17	17	22	19	15	16	22	22	16	21	25	21	17
12	16 57	27 19	21	27	23	18	19	25	25	20	21	25	22	17	19	25	25	19	25	28	24	20
24	20 12	0♋05	25	♊0	26	21	23	28	27	23	24	28	25	20	22	28	28	22	♋1	♉0	26	23
36	23 28	2 49	28	3	29	24	26	♊1	♌0	26	27	♊1	27	23	25	♊1	♋1	26	♉1	4	29	26
48	26 44	5 32	♉1	6	♌1	27	♉0	4	3	28	♉1	4	♌0	26	29	4	3	29	4	7	♌2	29
24 0	0♈00	8 14	5	9	4	♍0	3	7	5	♍1	4	7	3	29	♉2	7	6	♍2	8	10	5	♍2

SID TIME	M C LONG	ASC 1	REGIOMONT. 11	12	2	3	CAMPANUS 11	12	2	3	PLACIDUS 11	12	2	3	NAT. GRAD. 11	12	2	3	KOCH 11	12	2	3
h m	♈	♋	♉	♊	♌	♍	♉	♊	♌	♍	♉	♊	♌	♍	♉	♊	♌	♍	♉	♊	♌	♍
0 0	0♈00	10♋31	5	11	6	♍1	♉3	8	8	3	4	9	4	♍0	♉2	8	8	♍2	9	12	7	3
12	3♈16	13 10	9	14	8	3	6	11	10	6	8	12	7	3	5	11	11	6	13	15	9	6
24	6 32	15 48	12	17	11	6	9	14	13	9	11	15	9	6	8	14	14	9	16	18	12	9
36	9 48	18 26	15	20	14	9	13	17	16	12	14	18	12	9	12	17	16	12	19	21	15	12
48	13 03	21 02	19	23	16	12	16	20	18	14	17	20	15	12	15	19	19	15	22	23	18	15
1 0	16 17	23 39	22	25	19	15	19	23	21	17	20	23	18	15	18	22	22	18	25	26	21	18
12	19 30	26 15	25	28	22	18	22	26	24	20	23	26	20	18	21	25	25	21	27	29	23	21
24	22 42	28 51	28	♋1	24	21	25	28	26	23	26	29	23	21	24	28	27	24	Ⅱ0	♋1	26	24
36	25 53	1♋27	Ⅱ1	4	27	24	28	♋1	29	26	29	♋2	26	24	27	♋0	♍0	27	3	4	29	27
48	29 03	4 03	4	6	♍0	27	Ⅱ1	4	♍2	29	Ⅱ2	4	29	27	Ⅱ0	3	3	♍0	6	6	♍2	♍0
2 0	2♋11	6 39	7	9	2	♍0	4	7	5	♍2	5	7	♍1	♍0	3	6	6	3	9	9	5	4
12	5 18	9 15	10	12	5	3	7	9	7	5	8	10	4	3	6	8	8	6	11	11	8	7
24	8 23	11 51	13	14	8	6	10	12	10	8	11	12	7	6	9	11	11	9	14	14	10	10
36	11 26	14 28	16	17	11	9	13	15	13	11	14	15	10	9	12	14	14	12	17	16	13	13
48	14 28	17 05	19	20	13	12	16	17	16	14	17	18	13	12	15	17	16	15	19	19	16	16
3 0	17 28	19 43	21	22	16	15	19	20	18	17	20	21	16	15	18	19	19	18	22	21	19	19
12	20 26	22 21	24	25	19	18	22	23	21	20	23	23	18	18	21	22	22	21	24	24	22	21
24	23 23	25 00	27	28	22	21	24	25	24	23	26	26	21	21	24	25	25	24	27	26	25	24
36	26 19	27 39	♋0	♌0	24	24	27	28	27	26	28	29	24	24	27	27	27	27	29	29	27	27
48	29 13	0♍18	3	3	27	27	♋0	♌1	♎0	29	♋1	♌1	27	27	29	♌0	♎0	29	♋2	♌1	♎0	♍0
4 0	2♊05	2 58	5	6	♎0	29	3	3	2	♍2	4	4	♎0	♍0	♌2	3	3	♍2	4	4	3	3
12	4 57	5 39	8	8	3	♏2	5	6	5	5	6	7	3	3	5	5	5	5	7	6	6	6
24	7 47	8 20	11	11	6	5	8	8	8	8	9	9	6	6	8	8	8	8	10	9	9	9
36	10 36	11 01	13	14	8	8	11	11	11	10	12	12	9	9	11	11	11	11	12	11	11	11
48	13 24	13 43	16	16	11	11	14	14	13	13	14	15	12	12	13	14	14	13	15	14	14	14
5 0	16 11	16 25	19	19	14	14	16	16	16	16	17	18	14	15	16	16	16	16	17	16	17	17
12	18 58	19 08	22	22	17	16	19	19	19	19	20	20	17	18	19	19	19	19	20	19	20	20
24	21 44	21 51	24	24	19	19	22	22	22	22	23	23	20	21	22	22	22	22	22	22	22	22
36	24 30	24 34	27	27	22	22	25	25	25	24	25	26	23	23	25	25	25	25	25	24	25	25
48	27 15	27 17	♌0	♍0	25	25	27	27	27	27	28	29	26	26	27	27	27	27	27	27	28	27
6 0	0♋00	0♎00	2	2	28	28	♌0	♍0	♏0	♐0	♌1	♍1	29	29	♌0	♍0	♏0	♐0	♌0	♍0	♏0	♐0
12	2 45	2 43	5	5	♏0	♐0	3	3	3	3	3	4	♏1	♐2	3	3	3	3	3	2	3	3
24	5 30	5 26	8	8	3	3	6	5	5	5	7	7	4	5	5	5	5	5	5	5	6	5
36	8 16	8 09	11	11	6	6	8	8	8	8	9	10	7	7	8	8	8	8	8	8	8	8
48	11 02	10 52	14	13	8	8	11	11	11	11	12	13	10	10	11	11	11	11	10	10	11	10
7 0	13 49	13 35	16	16	11	11	14	14	14	14	15	16	12	13	14	14	14	14	13	13	14	13
12	16 36	16 17	19	19	14	14	17	17	16	16	18	18	15	16	17	16	16	17	16	16	16	15
24	19 24	18 59	22	22	16	17	20	19	19	19	21	21	18	18	19	19	19	19	19	19	19	18
36	22 13	21 40	25	24	19	19	22	22	22	22	24	24	21	21	22	22	22	22	21	21	21	20
48	25 03	24 21	28	27	22	22	25	25	24	24	27	27	23	24	25	25	25	24	24	24	24	23
8 0	27 55	27 02	♍1	♎0	24	24	28	28	27	27	♍0	♎0	26	26	28	27	27	28	27	27	26	26
12	0♌47	29 42	3	3	27	27	♍1	♎0	29	♑0	3	3	29	29	♍1	♎0	♐0	♑1	♍0	♎0	29	28
24	3 41	2♏21	6	♍0	♐0	♑0	4	3	♐2	3	6	6	♐1	♑2	3	3	3	3	3	3	♐1	♑1
36	6 37	5 00	9	8	2	3	7	6	5	6	9	9	4	5	6	5	5	6	6	5	4	3
48	9 34	7 39	12	11	5	6	10	9	8	8	12	12	7	7	9	8	8	9	9	8	6	6
9 0	12 32	10 17	15	14	8	9	13	12	10	11	15	14	9	10	12	11	11	12	11	11	9	8
12	15 32	12 55	18	17	10	11	16	14	13	14	18	17	12	13	15	14	13	15	14	14	11	11
24	18 34	15 32	21	19	13	14	19	17	15	17	21	20	15	16	18	16	16	18	17	17	14	13
36	21 37	18 09	24	22	16	17	22	20	18	20	24	23	18	19	21	19	19	21	20	20	16	16
48	24 42	20 45	27	25	18	20	25	23	21	23	27	26	20	22	24	22	22	24	23	22	19	19
10 0	27 49	23 21	♎0	28	21	23	28	25	23	26	♎0	29	23	25	♎0	24	24	27	26	25	21	21
12	0♍57	25 57	3	♍0	24	26	♎1	28	26	29	3	♍0	26	28	♎0	27	27	♏0	♎0	28	24	24
24	4 07	28 33	6	3	26	29	4	♏1	29	♒2	6	4	28	♏1	3	♏0	♑0	3	3	♏1	26	27
36	7 18	1♐09	9	6	29	♒2	7	4	♒2	5	9	7	♏1	4	6	3	2	6	6	4	29	♏0
48	10 30	3 45	12	8	♒2	5	10	6	4	8	12	10	4	7	9	5	5	9	9	7	♏1	3
11 0	13 43	6 21	15	11	5	8	13	9	7	11	15	12	7	10	12	8	8	12	12	9	4	5
12	16 57	8 58	18	14	7	11	16	12	10	14	18	15	10	13	15	11	11	15	15	12	7	8
24	20 12	11 34	21	16	10	15	18	14	13	17	21	18	12	16	18	14	13	18	18	15	9	11
36	23 28	14 12	24	19	13	18	21	17	16	21	24	21	15	19	21	16	16	22	21	18	12	14
48	26 44	16 50	27	22	16	21	24	20	19	24	27	23	18	22	24	19	19	25	24	21	15	17
12 0	0♎00	19 29	29	24	19	25	27	22	22	27	♏0	26	21	26	28	22	22	28	27	23	18	21

286

SID TIME (h m)	MC LONG (♎)	ASC 1 (⚹)	REGIOMONT. 11	12	2	3	CAMPANUS 11	12	2	3	PLACIDUS 11	12	2	3	NAT. GRAD. 11	12	2	3	KOCH 11	12	2	3
			≏	♏	♑	≈	≏	♏	♑	≈	♏	♏	♑	≈	≏	♏	♑	≈	≏	♏	♑	≈
12 0	0≏00	19⚹29	29	24	19	25	27	22	22	27	♏0	26	21	26	28	22	22	28	27	23	18	21
12	3 16	22 10	♏2	27	22	28	♏0	25	25	♈1	3	29	24	29	♏1	25	24	♈1	♏0	26	20	24
24	6 32	24 51	5	⚹0	25	♈1	3	28	28	4	6	⚹1	27	♈2	4	28	27	4	3	29	23	27
36	9 48	27 34	8	2	28	5	6	⚹0	≈1	8	9	4	≈0	6	7	⚹0	≈0	7	6	⚹2	26	♈0
48	13 03	0♑18	11	5	≈1	8	9	3	4	11	12	7	3	9	10	3	3	10	9	4	29	4
13 0	16 17	3 05	14	8	5	12	12	6	8	15	15	9	7	13	13	6	6	14	12	7	≈2	7
12	19 30	5 53	16	10	8	16	14	8	11	18	18	12	10	16	16	9	9	17	15	10	5	11
24	22 42	8 43	19	13	11	19	17	11	14	22	21	15	13	20	19	12	12	20	18	13	8	14
36	25 53	11 36	22	16	15	23	20	14	18	26	23	18	16	23	22	15	14	23	21	16	12	18
48	29 03	14 32	25	18	18	26	23	16	21	29	26	20	20	26	26	18	17	26	24	18	15	21
14 0	2♏11	17 30	28	21	22	♈0	26	19	25	♈3	29	23	23	♈0	29	21	20	29	27	21	18	25
12	5 11	20 32	⚹0	24	25	4	28	22	29	6	⚹2	26	27	4	⚹2	24	23	♈2	⚹0	24	22	28
24	8 23	23 37	3	26	29	7	⚹1	24	♈2	10	5	28	♈0	7	5	27	27	5	2	27	25	♈2
36	11 26	26 45	6	29	♈3	11	4	27	6	14	7	♈1	4	10	8	♈0	♈0	8	5	♈0	29	6
48	14 28	29 58	8	♑2	7	14	7	♑0	10	17	10	4	8	14	11	3	3	12	8	3	♈2	9
15 0	17 28	3≈14	11	5	10	18	9	2	14	21	13	7	11	17	14	7	6	15	11	6	6	13
12	20 26	6 34	14	7	14	22	12	5	18	24	16	10	15	21	17	10	9	18	14	9	10	17
24	23 23	9 58	17	10	18	25	15	8	21	28	18	12	19	24	20	13	13	21	17	12	14	20
36	26 19	13 27	19	13	22	29	17	11	25	♉1	21	15	22	28	23	17	16	24	20	15	18	24
48	29 13	17 00	22	16	26	♉2	20	14	29	5	24	18	26	♉1	26	20	19	27	23	18	21	27
16 0	2⚹05	20 37	25	19	♈0	5	23	17	♈3	8	26	21	♈0	4	29	23	23	♉0	26	21	25	♉1
12	4 57	24 18	27	22	4	9	26	20	7	11	29	24	4	8	♑2	27	27	3	28	24	29	5
24	7 47	28 04	28	♑0	8	12	28	23	11	14	♑2	27	8	11	5	≈0	♈0	6	♑1	27	♈3	8
36	10 36	1♓54	3	28	12	15	♑1	26	15	18	5	≈0	11	14	9	4	4	9	4	≈1	7	12
48	13 24	5 47	6	≈1	16	19	4	29	19	21	7	3	15	17	12	8	7	12	7	4	11	15
17 0	16 11	9 44	9	5	20	22	7	≈2	23	24	10	7	19	20	15	11	11	15	10	7	15	18
12	18 58	13 43	11	8	23	25	9	5	26	27	13	10	22	23	18	15	15	18	13	11	19	22
24	21 44	17 45	14	11	27	28	12	9	♉0	♊0	16	13	26	26	21	19	19	21	16	14	23	25
36	24 30	21 49	17	15	♉1	♊1	15	12	4	3	19	16	♉0	29	24	22	22	24	19	18	27	28
48	27 15	25 54	20	18	5	4	18	15	7	6	22	20	3	♊2	27	26	26	27	22	22	♉1	♊1
18 0	0♑00	0♈00	23	22	8	7	21	19	11	9	25	23	7	5	≈0	♈0	♉0	♊0	25	25	5	5
12	2 45	4 06	26	25	12	10	24	23	15	12	28	27	10	8	3	4	4	3	29	29	8	8
24	5 30	8 11	29	29	15	13	27	26	18	15	≈1	♈0	14	11	6	8	8	6	≈2	♈3	12	11
36	8 16	12 15	≈2	♈3	19	16	≈0	♈0	21	18	4	4	17	14	9	11	11	9	5	7	16	14
48	11 02	16 17	5	7	22	19	3	4	25	21	7	8	20	17	12	15	15	12	8	11	19	17
19 0	13 49	20 16	8	10	25	21	6	7	28	23	10	11	23	20	15	19	19	15	12	15	23	20
12	16 36	24 13	11	14	29	24	9	11	♊1	26	13	15	27	23	18	23	22	18	15	19	26	23
24	19 24	28 06	15	18	♊2	27	12	15	4	29	16	19	♊0	25	21	26	26	21	18	23	29	26
36	22 13	1♋56	18	22	5	♋0	16	19	7	♋2	19	22	3	28	24	♈0	♊0	25	22	27	♊3	29
48	25 03	5 42	21	26	8	3	19	23	10	4	22	26	6	♋1	27	3	3	28	25	♈1	6	♋2
20 0	27 55	9 23	25	♈0	11	5	22	27	13	7	26	♈0	9	4	♈0	7	7	♋1	29	5	9	4
12	0≈47	13 00	28	4	14	8	25	♈1	16	10	29	4	12	6	3	11	10	4	♈3	9	12	7
24	3 41	16 33	♈1	8	17	11	29	5	19	13	♈2	8	15	9	6	14	13	7	6	12	15	10
36	6 37	20 02	5	12	20	13	♈2	9	22	15	6	11	18	12	9	17	17	10	10	16	18	13
48	9 34	23 26	8	16	23	16	6	12	25	18	9	15	20	14	12	21	20	13	13	20	21	16
21 0	12 32	26 46	12	20	25	19	9	16	28	21	13	19	23	17	15	24	23	16	17	24	24	19
12	15 32	0♊02	16	23	28	22	13	20	♋0	25	16	22	26	20	18	27	26	19	21	28	27	22
24	18 34	3 15	19	27	♋1	24	16	24	3	26	20	26	29	23	22	♉0	♋0	22	24	♉1	♋0	25
36	21 37	6 23	23	♉1	4	27	20	28	6	29	23	♉0	♋2	25	25	3	3	25	28	5	3	28
48	24 42	9 28	26	5	6	♌0	24	♋1	8	♌2	26	3	4	28	28	7	6	28	♈2	8	6	♌0
22 0	27 49	12 30	♈0	8	9	2	27	5	11	4	♈0	7	7	♌1	♈1	10	9	♌1	5	12	9	3
12	0♓57	15 28	4	12	12	5	♈1	9	14	7	4	10	10	4	4	13	12	4	9	15	12	6
24	4 07	18 24	7	15	14	8	4	12	16	10	7	14	12	7	7	16	15	8	12	18	14	9
36	7 18	21 17	11	19	17	11	8	16	19	13	10	17	15	9	10	18	18	11	16	22	17	12
48	10 30	24 07	14	22	20	14	12	19	22	16	14	20	18	12	13	21	21	14	19	25	20	15
23 0	13 43	26 55	18	25	22	16	15	22	24	18	17	23	21	15	16	24	24	17	23	28	23	18
12	16 57	29 42	22	29	25	19	19	26	27	21	21	27	23	18	20	27	27	20	26	♊1	26	21
24	20 12	2♋26	25	♊2	28	22	22	29	♌0	24	24	♊0	26	21	23	♊0	♌0	23	♉0	4	28	24
36	23 28	5 09	29	5	♌0	25	26	♊2	2	27	28	3	29	24	26	3	2	26	3	7	♌1	27
48	26 44	7 50	♉2	8	3	28	29	5	5	♍0	♉1	6	♌1	27	29	6	5	29	6	10	4	♍0
24 0	0♈00	10 31	5	11	6	♍1	♉3	8	8	3	4	9	4	♍0	♉2	8	8	♍2	9	12	7	3

SID TIME	MC LONG	ASC 1	REGIOMONT. 11 12 2 3				CAMPANUS 11 12 2 3				PLACIDUS 11 12 2 3				NAT. GRAD. 11 12 2 3				KOCH 11 12 2 3			
h m	♈	♋	♉	♊	♌	♍	♉	♊	♌	♍	♉	♊	♌	♍	♉	♊	♌	♍	♉	♊	♌	♍
0 0	0♈00	12♋56	6	13	7	♍1	♋2	9	10	4	5	11	5	♍0	♋3	10	10	3	12	15	8	4
12	3♈16	15 33	10	16	10	4	5	12	13	7	8	14	8	3	6	13	13	6	15	18	11	7
24	6 32	18 08	13	19	12	7	9	15	15	10	11	17	11	6	9	16	15	9	18	21	14	10
36	9 48	20 42	16	22	15	10	12	18	18	13	15	19	13	9	12	18	18	12	21	23	17	13
48	13 03	23 16	20	25	18	13	15	21	21	16	18	22	16	12	15	21	21	15	24	26	19	16
1 0	16 17	25 49	23	28	20	16	19	24	23	19	21	25	19	15	18	24	24	19	27	28	22	19
12	19 30	28 21	26	♋0	23	18	22	27	26	22	24	28	21	18	21	26	26	22	29	♋1	25	22
24	22 42	0♌53	29	3	25	21	25	29	28	25	27	♋1	24	21	24	29	29	25	♊2	3	28	25
36	25 53	3 25	♊2	6	28	24	28	♋2	♍1	27	♌0	3	27	24	27	♋2	♍2	28	5	6	♍1	28
48	29 03	5 57	5	9	♍1	27	♊1	5	4	♎0	3	6	29	27	♊1	4	4	♎1	8	8	3	♎1
2 0	2♉11	8 29	8	11	3	♎0	4	8	6	3	6	9	♍2	♎0	4	7	7	4	10	11	6	4
12	5 18	11 01	11	14	6	3	7	10	9	6	9	11	5	3	7	10	10	7	13	13	9	7
24	8 23	13 33	14	17	9	6	10	13	12	9	12	14	8	6	9	12	12	10	16	16	12	10
36	11 26	16 05	17	19	11	9	13	15	14	12	15	17	10	9	12	15	15	12	18	18	14	13
48	14 28	18 37	20	22	14	12	16	18	17	15	18	19	13	12	15	18	18	15	21	21	17	16
3 0	17 28	21 10	23	24	17	14	19	21	20	18	21	22	16	15	18	20	20	18	23	23	20	19
12	20 26	23 43	26	27	19	17	22	23	23	21	23	25	19	18	21	23	23	21	26	25	23	22
24	23 23	26 16	28	29	22	20	24	26	25	24	26	27	22	21	24	26	26	24	28	28	25	25
36	26 19	28 50	♋1	♌2	25	23	27	29	28	27	29	♌0	24	24	27	28	28	27	♋1	♌0	28	28
48	29 13	1♍24	4	5	27	26	♋0	♌1	♎1	♏0	♋2	3	27	27	♋0	♌1	♎1	♏0	3	3	♎1	♏0
4 0	2♊05	3 59	7	7	♎0	29	3	4	3	2	4	5	♎0	♏0	3	4	4	3	6	5	4	3
12	4 57	6 34	9	10	3	♏2	5	6	6	5	7	8	3	3	5	6	6	5	8	7	6	6
24	7 47	9 09	12	12	5	4	8	9	9	8	10	11	6	6	8	9	9	8	10	10	9	9
36	10 36	11 44	15	15	8	7	11	11	11	11	13	13	8	9	11	11	11	11	13	12	11	11
48	13 24	14 20	17	18	11	10	14	14	14	14	15	16	11	11	14	14	14	14	15	15	14	14
5 0	16 11	16 57	20	20	13	13	16	17	17	16	18	19	14	14	16	17	17	16	18	17	17	17
12	18 58	19 33	23	23	16	16	19	19	20	19	21	21	17	17	19	19	19	19	20	20	20	19
24	21 44	22 09	25	25	19	18	22	22	22	22	24	24	20	20	22	22	22	22	23	22	22	22
36	24 30	24 46	28	28	21	21	24	25	25	25	26	27	22	23	25	25	25	25	25	25	25	25
48	27 15	27 23	♌1	♍1	24	24	27	27	28	27	29	29	25	25	27	27	27	27	28	27	28	27
6 0	0♋00	0♌00	4	3	27	26	♌0	♍0	♏0	♐0	♌2	♍2	28	28	♌0	♍0	♏0	♐0	♌0	♍0	♏0	♐0
12	2 45	2 37	6	6	29	29	3	2	3	2	5	5	♏1	♐1	3	3	3	3	3	2	3	2
24	5 30	5 14	9	9	♏2	♐2	5	5	5	6	7	8	3	4	5	5	5	5	5	5	5	5
36	8 16	7 50	12	11	5	5	8	8	8	8	10	10	6	6	8	8	8	8	8	8	8	7
48	11 02	10 27	14	14	7	7	11	10	11	11	13	13	9	9	11	11	11	11	11	10	10	10
7 0	13 49	13 03	17	17	10	10	14	13	13	14	16	16	11	12	14	13	13	14	13	13	13	12
12	16 36	15 40	20	19	12	13	16	16	16	16	19	19	14	15	16	16	16	16	16	16	15	15
24	19 24	18 16	23	22	15	15	19	19	19	19	21	22	17	17	19	19	19	19	19	19	18	17
36	22 13	20 51	26	25	18	18	22	21	21	22	24	24	19	20	22	21	21	22	21	21	20	20
48	25 03	23 26	28	27	20	21	25	24	24	25	27	27	22	23	25	24	24	25	24	24	23	22
8 0	27 55	26 01	♍1	♎0	23	23	28	27	26	27	♍0	♎0	25	26	27	26	26	27	27	26	25	24
12	0♌47	28 36	4	3	25	26	♍0	29	29	♑0	3	3	27	28	♍0	29	29	♑0	♍0	29	27	27
24	3 41	1♏10	7	5	28	♐0	3	♎2	♐1	3	6	6	♐0	29	3	♎2	♐2	3	2	♎2	♐0	29
36	6 37	3 44	10	8	♐1	♑2	6	5	4	6	9	8	3	4	6	4	4	6	5	5	2	♑2
48	9 34	6 17	13	11	3	4	9	7	7	8	12	11	5	7	9	7	7	9	8	7	5	4
9 0	12 32	8 50	16	13	6	7	12	10	9	11	15	14	8	9	12	10	10	12	11	10	7	7
12	15 32	11 23	18	16	8	10	15	13	12	14	18	17	11	12	15	12	12	14	14	13	9	9
24	18 34	13 55	21	19	11	13	18	16	15	17	21	20	13	15	18	15	15	16	17	16	12	12
36	21 37	16 27	24	21	13	16	21	18	17	20	24	22	16	18	20	18	18	21	20	18	14	14
48	24 42	18 59	27	24	16	19	24	21	20	23	27	25	19	21	23	20	20	23	23	21	17	17
10 0	27 49	21 31	♎0	27	19	22	27	24	22	26	♎0	28	21	24	26	23	23	26	26	24	19	20
12	0♍57	24 03	3	29	21	25	♎0	26	25	29	3	♏1	24	27	29	26	26	29	29	27	22	22
24	4 07	26 35	6	♏2	24	28	3	29	28	♒2	6	3	27	♒0	♎2	28	28	♒3	♎2	29	24	25
36	7 18	29 07	9	5	27	♒1	5	♏2	♑1	5	9	6	29	3	5	♏1	♑1	6	5	♏2	27	28
48	10 30	1♐39	12	7	♑0	4	8	4	3	8	12	9	♑2	6	8	4	4	9	8	5	29	♒1
11 0	13 43	4 11	14	10	2	7	11	7	6	11	15	11	5	9	11	6	6	12	11	8	♒2	3
12	16 57	6 44	17	12	5	10	14	9	9	15	18	14	8	12	15	9	9	15	14	11	4	6
24	20 12	9 18	20	15	8	14	17	12	12	18	21	17	11	15	18	12	12	18	17	13	7	9
36	23 28	11 52	23	18	11	17	20	15	15	21	24	19	13	19	21	15	14	21	20	16	9	12
48	26 44	14 27	26	20	14	20	23	17	18	25	27	22	16	22	24	17	17	24	23	19	12	15
12 0	0♎00	17 04	29	23	17	24	26	20	21	28	♏0	25	19	25	27	20	20	27	26	22	15	18

288

SID TIME	MC	ASC	REGIOMONT.				CAMPANUS				PLACIDUS				NAT. GRAD.				KOCH			
h m	LONG	1	11	12	2	3	11	12	2	3	11	12	2	3	11	12	2	3	11	12	2	3
	♎	♐	♎	♏	♐	≈	♎	♏	♐	≈	♏	♏	♐	≈	♎	♏	♐	≈	♎	♏	♐	≈
12 0	0♎00	17♐04	29	23	17	24	26	20	21	28	♏0	25	19	25	27	20	20	27	26	22	15	18
12	3 16	19♏41	♏2	25	20	27	29	23	24	♓2	3	27	22	28	♏0	23	22	♓1	29	24	18	22
24	6 32	22 20	4	28	23	♓1	♏2	25	27	5	6	♐0	25	♓2	3	26	25	4	♏2	27	20	25
36	9 48	25 01	7	♐1	26	4	4	28	≈0	9	9	3	29	5	6	29	28	7	5	♐0	23	28
48	13 03	27 43	10	3	29	8	7	♐0	4	12	11	5	≈2	9	9	♐1	≈1	10	8	2	26	♓2
13 0	16 17	0♑28	13	6	≈2	11	10	3	7	16	14	8	5	12	12	4	4	13	11	5	29	5
12	19 30	3 14	16	8	6	15	13	5	10	20	17	11	8	16	16	7	6	16	14	8	≈2	9
24	22 42	6 03	18	11	9	19	16	8	14	23	20	13	12	19	19	10	9	19	17	11	6	12
36	25 53	8 55	21	13	13	23	18	11	18	27	23	16	15	23	22	13	12	23	20	14	9	16
48	29 03	11 50	24	16	16	26	21	13	21	♈1	25	19	19	26	25	16	15	26	23	16	12	19
14 0	2♏11	14 49	26	19	20	♈0	24	16	25	4	28	21	22	♈0	28	19	18	29	26	19	15	23
12	5 18	17 51	29	21	24	4	27	19	29	8	♐1	24	26	4	♐1	22	21	♈2	28	22	19	27
24	8 23	20 56	♐2	24	28	7	29	21	♈3	12	4	27	29	7	4	25	24	5	♐1	25	23	♈1
36	11 26	24 06	5	27	♓1	11	♐2	24	7	15	6	29	♈3	11	7	28	28	8	4	28	26	4
48	14 28	27 20	7	♑0	5	15	5	27	10	19	9	♑2	7	14	10	♑2	♓1	11	7	♈1	♓0	8
15 0	17 28	0≈39	10	2	9	19	8	29	15	22	12	5	11	18	13	5	4	14	10	4	4	12
12	20 26	4 03	13	5	13	22	10	♑2	19	26	15	8	14	21	16	8	7	17	13	7	8	16
24	23 23	7 31	15	8	18	26	13	5	23	29	17	11	18	25	20	11	11	20	16	10	12	19
36	26 19	11 05	18	11	22	29	16	8	27	♉3	20	13	22	28	23	15	14	23	19	13	16	23
48	29 13	14 44	21	14	26	♉3	18	11	♈1	6	23	16	26	♉2	26	18	18	26	22	16	20	27
16 0	2♐05	18 29	23	17	♈0	6	21	14	5	10	26	19	♈0	5	29	22	21	29	24	19	24	♉1
12	4 57	22 19	26	20	4	10	24	16	9	13	28	22	4	8	♑2	25	25	♉2	27	22	28	4
24	7 47	26 14	29	23	8	13	26	19	13	16	♑1	25	8	11	5	29	29	5	♑0	26	♈2	8
36	10 36	0♓14	♑2	26	12	16	29	23	17	20	4	29	12	15	8	≈3	♈2	8	3	29	7	12
48	13 24	4 20	4	29	17	20	♑2	26	21	23	7	≈2	16	18	11	6	6	12	6	≈2	11	15
17 0	16 11	8 29	7	≈2	21	23	5	29	25	26	9	5	19	21	14	10	10	15	9	6	15	19
12	18 58	12 42	10	6	25	26	8	≈2	29	29	12	8	23	24	18	14	14	18	12	10	19	22
24	21 44	16 59	13	9	29	29	10	5	♉3	♊2	15	12	27	27	21	18	18	21	15	13	23	25
36	24 30	21 18	16	13	♉2	♊2	13	9	7	5	18	15	♉1	♊0	24	22	22	24	18	17	27	29
48	27 15	25 38	19	16	6	5	16	12	10	8	21	19	4	3	27	26	26	27	22	21	♉1	♊2
18 0	0♓00	0♈00	22	20	10	8	19	16	14	11	24	22	8	6	≈0	♓0	♉0	♊0	25	25	5	5
12	2 45	4 22	25	24	14	11	22	20	18	14	27	26	11	9	3	4	4	3	28	29	9	8
24	5 30	8 42	28	28	17	14	25	23	21	17	≈0	29	15	12	6	8	8	6	≈1	♓3	13	12
36	8 16	13 01	≈1	♓1	21	17	28	27	25	20	3	♓3	18	15	9	12	12	9	5	7	17	15
48	11 02	17 18	4	5	24	20	≈1	♓1	28	22	6	7	22	18	12	16	16	12	8	11	20	18
19 0	13 49	21 31	7	9	28	23	4	5	♊1	25	9	11	25	21	15	20	20	16	11	15	24	21
12	16 36	25 40	10	13	♊1	26	7	9	4	28	12	14	28	23	18	24	24	19	15	19	28	24
24	19 24	29 46	14	18	4	28	10	13	7	♋1	15	18	♊1	26	22	28	27	22	18	23	♊1	27
36	22 13	3♉46	17	22	7	♋1	14	17	11	4	19	22	5	29	25	♈1	♊1	25	22	28	4	♋0
48	25 03	7 41	20	26	10	4	17	21	14	6	22	26	8	♋2	28	5	5	28	26	♈2	8	3
20 0	27 55	11 31	24	♈0	13	7	20	25	16	9	25	♈0	11	4	♓1	9	8	♋1	29	6	11	6
12	0≈47	15 16	27	4	16	9	24	29	19	12	28	4	14	7	4	12	12	4	♓3	10	14	8
24	3 41	18 55	♈1	8	19	12	27	♈3	22	14	♓2	8	17	10	7	16	15	7	7	14	17	11
36	6 37	22 29	4	12	22	15	♈1	7	25	17	5	12	19	13	10	19	19	10	11	18	20	14
48	9 34	25 57	8	17	25	17	4	11	28	20	9	16	22	15	13	23	22	14	14	22	23	17
21 0	12 32	29 21	11	21	28	20	8	15	♋1	22	12	19	25	18	16	26	25	17	18	26	26	20
12	15 32	2♊40	15	25	♋0	23	11	20	3	25	16	23	28	21	19	29	28	20	22	♉0	29	23
24	18 34	5 54	19	29	3	25	15	23	6	28	19	27	♋1	24	22	♉2	♋2	23	26	4	♋2	26
36	21 37	9 04	23	♉2	6	28	18	27	9	♋1	23	♉1	3	26	26	5	5	26	29	7	5	29
48	24 42	12 09	26	6	9	♋1	22	♉1	11	3	26	4	6	29	28	9	8	29	♈3	11	8	♋2
22 0	27 49	15 11	♈0	10	11	4	26	5	14	6	♈0	8	9	♋2	♈1	12	11	♋2	7	15	11	4
12	0♓57	18 10	4	14	14	6	29	9	17	9	4	11	11	5	4	15	14	5	11	18	14	7
24	4 07	21 05	7	17	17	9	♈3	12	19	12	7	15	14	7	7	18	17	8	14	21	16	10
36	7 18	23 57	11	21	19	12	7	16	22	14	11	18	17	10	11	21	20	11	18	24	19	13
48	10 30	26 46	15	24	22	14	10	20	25	17	14	22	19	13	14	24	23	14	21	28	22	16
23 0	13 43	29 32	19	28	24	17	14	23	27	20	18	25	22	16	17	26	26	18	25	♊1	25	19
12	16 57	2♊17	22	♊1	27	20	18	26	♋0	23	21	28	25	19	20	29	29	21	29	4	28	22
24	20 12	4 59	26	4	29	23	21	♊0	2	26	25	♊1	27	21	23	♊2	♋1	24	♉2	7	♊0	25
36	23 28	7 40	29	7	♊2	26	25	3	5	28	28	5	♊0	24	26	5	4	27	5	10	3	28
48	26 44	10 19	♊3	10	5	28	28	6	7	♍1	♉2	8	3	27	29	8	7	♍0	8	12	6	♍1
24 0	0♈00	12 56	6	13	7	♍1	♉2	9	10	4	5	11	5	♍0	♉3	10	10	3	12	15	8	4

SID TIME (h m)	M C LONG ♈	ASC 1 ♋	REGIOMONT. 11 ♉	12 ♊	2 ♌	3 ♍	CAMPANUS 11 ♉	12 ♊	2 ♌	3 ♍	PLACIDUS 11 ♉	12 ♊	2 ♌	3 ♍	NAT.GRAD. 11 ♉	12 ♊	2 ♌	3 ♍	KOCH 11 ♉	12 ♊	2 ♌	3 ♍
0 0	0♈00	15♋01	7	15	9	♍2	♉1	10	12	5	5	12	6	♍1	3	12	11	4	14	18	10	5
12	3♈16	17 35	11	18	11	4	5	13	15	8	9	15	9	3	6	15	14	7	17	20	13	8
24	6 32	20 07	14	21	14	7	8	16	17	11	12	18	12	6	9	17	17	10	20	23	15	11
36	9 48	22 38	17	24	16	10	12	19	20	14	15	21	14	9	12	20	20	13	23	25	18	14
48	13 03	25 09	21	27	19	13	15	22	22	17	19	24	17	12	16	23	22	16	26	28	21	17
1 0	16 17	27 38	24	♋0	21	16	18	24	25	20	22	27	20	15	19	25	25	19	28	♋1	24	20
12	19 30	0♌08	27	2	24	19	21	27	28	23	25	29	22	18	22	28	28	22	♊1	3	26	23
24	22 42	2 36	♊0	5	26	21	25	♋0	♌0	26	28	♋2	25	21	25	♋1	♌0	25	4	5	29	26
36	25 53	5 05	3	8	29	24	28	3	3	28	♊1	5	27	24	28	3	3	28	7	8	♍2	29
48	29 03	7 33	6	10	♍1	27	♊1	5	5	♎1	4	8	♍0	27	♊1	6	6	♎1	9	10	4	♍2
2 0	2♉11	10 01	9	13	4	♎0	4	8	8	4	7	10	3	♎0	4	8	8	4	12	13	7	5
12	5 18	12 29	12	16	7	3	7	11	11	7	10	13	6	3	7	11	11	7	14	15	10	8
24	8 23	14 57	15	18	9	6	10	13	13	10	13	16	9	6	10	14	13	10	17	17	13	11
36	11 26	17 25	18	21	12	9	13	16	16	13	16	18	11	9	13	16	16	13	20	20	15	14
48	14 28	19 54	21	23	14	11	16	19	18	16	19	21	14	12	16	19	19	16	22	22	18	16
3 0	17 28	22 22	24	26	17	14	19	21	21	19	21	23	16	15	19	21	21	21	24	24	21	19
12	20 26	24 51	27	28	20	17	21	24	24	22	24	26	19	18	21	24	24	21	27	27	23	22
24	23 23	27 20	29	♌1	22	20	24	26	26	24	27	29	22	21	24	26	26	24	29	29	26	25
36	26 19	29 49	♋2	4	25	23	27	29	29	27	29	♎2	24	24	27	29	29	27	♌2	♍1	29	28
48	29 13	2♍19	5	6	27	26	♋0	♌1	♎2	♏0	2	4	27	27	♋0	♌2	♎2	♏0	4	4	♎1	♏1
4 0	2♊05	4 48	8	9	♎0	28	3	4	4	3	5	6	♎0	29	3	4	4	3	7	6	4	3
12	4 57	7 19	10	11	3	♏1	5	7	7	5	8	9	3	♏2	5	7	7	5	9	8	7	6
24	7 47	9 49	13	14	5	4	8	9	10	9	11	12	5	5	8	9	9	8	11	11	9	9
36	10 36	12 20	16	16	8	7	11	12	12	11	13	14	8	8	11	12	12	11	14	13	12	11
48	13 24	14 51	18	19	10	9	13	14	15	14	16	17	11	11	14	15	15	14	16	15	15	14
5 0	16 11	17 22	21	21	13	12	16	17	17	17	19	20	14	14	16	17	17	16	18	18	17	17
12	18 58	19 53	24	24	16	15	19	19	20	20	21	22	16	17	19	20	20	19	21	20	20	19
24	21 44	22 25	26	26	18	18	22	22	22	22	24	25	19	19	22	22	22	22	23	23	22	22
36	24 30	24 56	29	29	21	20	24	24	25	25	27	27	22	22	25	25	25	25	26	25	25	24
48	27 15	27 28	♌2	♍1	23	23	27	27	27	27	♌0	♍0	24	25	27	27	27	27	28	28	27	27
6 0	0♋00	0♎00	4	4	26	26	♌0	♍0	♏0	♐0	2	3	27	28	♌0	♍0	♏0	♐0	♌1	♍0	♏0	29
12	2 45	2 32	7	7	29	28	2	2	3	3	5	6	♏0	♐0	3	3	3	3	3	3	2	♐2
24	5 30	5 04	10	9	♏1	♐1	5	5	6	6	8	8	3	3	5	5	5	5	5	5	5	4
36	8 16	7 35	12	12	4	♑1	8	7	8	7	11	11	5	6	8	8	8	8	8	8	7	7
48	11 02	10 07	15	14	6	6	10	10	11	11	13	14	8	9	11	10	10	11	11	10	10	9
7 0	13 49	12 38	18	17	9	9	13	13	13	14	16	16	10	11	14	13	13	14	13	13	12	12
12	16 36	15 09	21	20	11	12	16	15	16	17	19	19	13	14	16	15	15	16	16	15	15	14
24	19 24	17 40	23	22	14	14	19	18	18	19	22	22	16	16	19	18	18	19	18	18	17	16
36	22 13	20 11	26	25	16	17	21	20	21	22	25	25	18	19	22	21	21	22	21	21	19	19
48	25 03	22 41	29	27	19	20	24	23	23	25	28	27	21	22	25	23	23	25	24	23	22	21
8 0	27 55	25 12	♍2	♎0	24	27	♍1	26	26	27	♍1	♎0	24	25	♍1	26	26	27	26	26	24	23
12	0♌47	27 41	4	3	24	25	♍0	28	29	♑0	3	3	26	28	♍0	28	28	♑0	29	29	26	26
24	3 41	0♏11	7	5	26	28	3	♎1	♐1	3	6	5	29	♑0	3	♎1	♐1	3	♍2	♎1	29	28
36	6 37	2 40	10	8	29	♑1	6	4	4	6	9	8	♐1	3	6	4	4	6	5	4	♐1	♑1
48	9 34	5 09	13	10	♐2	3	8	6	6	8	12	11	4	6	9	6	6	9	8	7	3	3
9 0	12 32	7 38	16	13	4	6	11	9	9	11	15	14	7	9	11	9	9	11	11	9	6	6
12	15 32	10 06	19	16	7	9	14	12	11	14	18	16	9	11	14	11	11	14	14	12	8	8
24	18 34	12 35	21	18	9	12	17	14	14	17	21	19	12	14	17	14	14	17	16	15	10	10
36	21 37	15 03	24	21	12	15	20	17	17	20	24	22	14	17	20	17	16	19	19	17	13	13
48	24 42	17 31	27	23	14	18	23	19	19	23	27	24	17	20	23	19	19	23	22	20	15	16
10 0	27 49	19 59	♎0	26	17	21	26	22	22	26	♎0	27	20	23	26	22	22	26	25	23	17	18
12	0♍57	22 27	3	29	20	24	3	♐0	25	29	3	♐0	23	26	3	♐0	27	2♒	28	26	20	23
24	4 07	24 55	6	♏1	22	27	♏2	27	27	♒2	6	3	25	29	♎2	27	27	♒2	♎1	28	22	23
36	7 18	27 24	9	4	25	♒0	4	♏0	♑0	5	9	5	28	♒2	5	♏0	29	5	4	♏1	25	26
48	10 30	29 52	11	6	28	3	7	2	♒2	8	12	8	♑1	8	7	2	♑2	8	7	4	27	29
11 0	13 43	2♐22	14	9	♑0	6	10	5	6	12	15	10	3	8	11	5	5	11	10	6	29	♒2
12	16 57	4 51	17	11	3	9	13	8	8	15	18	13	6	11	14	8	7	14	13	9	♓2	4
24	20 12	7 22	20	14	6	13	16	10	11	18	21	16	9	15	17	10	10	18	16	12	5	7
36	23 28	9 53	23	16	9	16	19	13	14	22	24	18	12	18	20	13	13	21	19	15	7	10
48	26 44	12 25	26	19	12	19	22	15	17	25	27	21	15	21	23	16	15	24	22	17	10	13
12 0	0♎00	14 59	28	21	15	23	25	18	20	29	29	24	18	25	26	19	18	27	25	20	12	16

SID TIME	MC LONG	ASC 1	REGIOMONT. 11	12	2	3	CAMPANUS 11	12	2	3	PLACIDUS 11	12	2	3	NAT. GRAD. 11	12	2	3	KOCH 11	12	2	3
h m	♎	♐	♎	♏	♑	≈	♎	♏	♑	≈	♎	♏	♑	≈	♎	♏	♑	≈	♎	♏	♑	≈
12 0	0♎00	14♐59	28	21	15	23	25	18	20	29	29	24	18	25	26	19	18	27	25	20	12	16
12	3 16	17 33	♏1	24	18	26	27	20	23	♑2	♏2	26	21	28	29	21	21	♑0	28	23	15	20
24	6 32	20 10	4	26	21	♑0	♏0	23	27	6	5	29	24	♑1	♏3	24	23	3	♏1	25	18	23
36	9 48	22 48	7	29	24	4	3	25	≈0	10	8	♐1	27	5	6	27	26	6	4	28	21	26
48	13 03	25 28	9	♐2	27	7	6	28	3	13	11	4	≈0	8	9	♐0	29	10	7	♐1	24	♑0
13 0	16 17	28 10	12	4	≈0	11	9	♐1	7	17	14	7	4	12	12	3	≈2	13	10	4	27	3
12	19 30	0♑55	15	7	4	15	11	3	10	21	17	9	7	16	15	5	5	16	13	6	≈0	7
24	22 42	3 42	18	9	7	19	14	6	14	24	19	12	10	19	18	8	7	19	16	9	3	10
36	25 53	6 33	20	12	11	22	17	8	18	28	22	14	14	23	21	11	10	22	19	12	6	14
48	29 03	9 26	23	14	15	26	20	11	21	♈2	25	17	17	26	24	14	13	25	22	15	9	18
14 0	2♏11	12 24	26	17	18	♈0	22	13	25	6	28	20	21	♈0	27	17	16	28	25	17	13	21
12	5 18	15 25	28	20	22	4	25	16	29	9	♐0	22	25	4	♐0	20	19	♈1	27	20	16	25
24	8 23	18 31	♐1	22	26	8	28	19	♈3	13	3	25	28	7	3	23	22	5	♐0	23	20	29
36	11 26	21 41	4	25	♈0	11	♐1	21	7	17	6	28	♈2	11	7	27	25	8	3	26	24	♈3
48	14 28	24 56	6	28	4	15	3	24	11	20	9	♈1	6	14	10	♈0	29	11	6	29	28	7
15 0	17 28	28 17	9	♈0	8	19	6	27	16	24	11	3	10	18	13	3	♈2	14	9	♈2	♈2	11
12	20 26	1≈43	12	3	13	23	9	29	20	28	14	6	14	22	16	6	5	17	12	5	6	15
24	23 23	5 14	14	6	17	26	11	♈2	24	♉1	17	9	18	25	19	10	9	20	15	8	10	19
36	26 19	8 52	17	9	21	♉0	14	5	28	5	19	12	22	29	22	13	12	23	18	11	14	23
48	29 13	12 37	20	12	26	4	17	8	♈3	8	22	15	26	♉2	25	17	16	26	21	14	18	26
16 0	2♐05	16 28	22	15	♈0	7	19	11	7	11	25	18	♈0	5	28	20	20	29	23	17	22	♉0
12	4 57	20 25	25	18	4	11	22	14	11	15	28	21	4	9	♉1	24	23	♉2	26	21	27	4
24	7 47	24 29	28	21	9	14	25	17	15	18	♉0	24	8	12	5	28	27	5	29	24	♈1	8
36	10 36	28 39	♉1	24	13	17	28	20	20	21	3	27	12	15	8	≈1	♈1	8	♉2	27	6	11
48	13 24	2♈55	3	27	17	21	♉0	23	24	25	6	≈0	16	19	11	5	5	11	5	≈1	10	15
17 0	16 11	7 16	6	≈0	22	24	3	26	28	28	9	4	20	22	14	9	9	14	8	5	15	19
12	18 58	11 43	9	4	26	27	6	29	♉2	♊1	11	7	24	25	17	13	13	17	11	8	19	22
24	21 44	16 13	12	7	♉0	♊0	9	≈2	6	4	14	10	28	28	20	17	17	21	15	12	23	26
36	24 30	20 47	15	11	4	3	11	6	10	7	17	14	♉2	♊1	24	22	22	24	18	16	28	29
48	27 15	25 23	18	15	8	6	14	9	13	10	20	17	5	4	27	26	26	27	21	20	♉2	♊2
18 0	0♑00	0♈00	21	18	12	9	17	13	17	13	23	21	9	7	≈0	♈0	♉0	♊0	24	24	6	6
12	2 45	4 37	24	22	15	12	20	17	21	16	26	25	13	10	3	4	4	3	28	28	10	9
24	5 30	9 13	27	26	19	15	23	20	24	19	29	28	16	13	6	8	8	6	≈1	♈2	14	12
36	8 16	13 47	≈0	♈0	23	18	26	24	28	21	≈2	♈2	20	16	9	13	13	10	4	7	18	15
48	11 02	18 17	3	4	26	21	29	28	♊1	24	5	6	23	19	13	17	17	13	8	11	22	19
19 0	13 49	22 44	6	8	♊0	24	≈2	♈2	4	27	8	10	26	21	16	21	21	16	11	15	25	22
12	16 36	27 05	9	13	3	27	5	6	7	♋0	11	14	♊0	24	19	25	25	19	15	20	29	25
24	19 24	1♉21	13	17	6	29	9	10	10	2	15	18	3	27	22	29	29	22	19	24	♊3	28
36	22 13	5 31	16	21	9	♋2	12	15	13	5	18	22	6	♋0	25	♈3	♊2	25	22	29	6	♋1
48	25 03	9 35	19	26	12	5	15	19	16	8	21	26	9	2	28	7	6	29	26	♈3	9	4
20 0	27 55	13 32	23	♈0	15	8	19	23	19	11	25	♈0	12	5	♈1	10	10	♋2	♈0	8	13	7
12	0≈57	17 23	26	4	18	10	22	27	22	13	28	4	15	8	4	14	13	5	4	12	16	9
24	3 41	21 08	♈0	9	21	13	25	♈2	25	16	♈1	8	18	11	7	18	17	8	7	16	19	12
36	6 37	24 46	4	13	24	16	29	6	28	19	5	12	21	13	10	21	20	11	11	20	22	15
48	9 34	28 17	7	17	27	18	♈2	10	♋1	21	8	16	24	16	13	25	24	14	15	24	25	18
21 0	12 32	1♊43	11	22	♋0	21	6	14	3	24	12	20	27	19	16	28	27	17	19	28	28	21
12	15 32	5 04	15	26	2	24	10	19	6	27	16	24	29	21	19	♊1	♋0	20	23	♋2	♋1	24
24	18 34	8 19	19	♋0	5	26	13	23	9	29	19	28	♋2	24	22	5	3	23	27	6	4	27
36	21 37	11 29	22	4	8	29	17	27	11	♌2	23	♋2	5	27	25	8	7	27	♈1	10	7	♌0
48	24 42	14 35	26	8	10	♌2	21	♋1	14	5	26	5	8	♌0	29	11	10	♌0	5	14	10	3
22 0	27 49	17 36	♋0	12	13	4	24	5	17	8	♋0	9	10	2	♊2	14	13	3	9	17	13	5
12	0♓57	20 34	4	15	16	7	28	9	19	10	4	13	13	5	5	17	16	6	12	21	15	8
24	4 07	23 27	8	19	18	10	♌2	12	22	13	7	16	16	8	8	20	19	9	16	24	18	11
36	7 18	26 18	11	23	21	12	6	16	24	16	11	20	18	11	11	23	22	12	20	27	21	14
48	10 30	29 05	15	26	23	15	9	20	27	19	14	23	21	13	14	25	25	15	23	♊0	24	17
23 0	13 43	1♋50	19	♊0	26	18	13	23	29	21	18	26	23	16	17	28	27	18	27	3	26	20
12	16 57	4 32	23	3	28	21	17	27	♌2	24	22	♊0	26	19	20	♊1	♌0	21	♋0	6	29	23
24	20 12	7 12	26	6	♌1	23	20	♌0	5	27	25	3	29	22	24	4	3	24	4	9	♌2	26
36	23 28	9 50	♊0	9	4	26	24	3	7	♍0	29	6	♌1	25	27	7	6	27	7	12	5	29
48	26 44	12 27	4	12	6	29	28	7	10	3	♌2	9	4	28	♊0	9	9	♍1	10	15	7	♍2
24 0	0♈00	15 01	7	15	9	♍2	♉1	10	12	5	5	12	6	♍1	3	12	11	4	14	18	10	5

SID TIME h m	MC LONG ♈	ASC ♋	REGIOMONT 11 ♉	12 ♊	2 ♌	3 ♍	CAMPANUS 11 ♉	12 ♊	2 ♌	3 ♍	PLACIDUS 11 ♉	12 ♊	2 ♌	3 ♍	NAT. GRAD. 11 ♉	12 ♊	2 ♌	3 ♍	KOCH 11 ♉	12 ♊	2 ♌	3 ♍
0 0	0♈00	17♋16	8	18	10	2	♉0	10	15	7	6	14	8	♍1	3	14	13	4	16	20	12	6
12	3♈16	19 46	12	21	13	5	4	13	17	10	9	17	10	4	7	17	16	7	19	23	14	9
24	6 32	22 15	15	24	15	8	7	16	20	12	13	20	13	7	10	19	18	10	22	25	17	12
36	9 48	24 42	18	26	17	10	11	19	22	15	16	23	15	10	13	22	21	13	25	28	20	15
48	13 03	27 09	22	29	20	13	14	22	25	18	19	26	18	12	16	24	24	16	28	♋0	22	18
1 0	16 17	29 35	25	♋2	22	16	18	25	27	21	22	28	20	15	19	27	26	19	♊1	3	25	21
12	19 30	2♌00	28	5	25	19	21	28	♍0	24	26	♋1	23	18	22	29	29	22	3	5	28	23
24	22 42	4 25	♊2	7	27	22	24	♋1	2	27	29	4	26	21	25	♋2	♍2	25	6	8	♍0	26
36	25 53	6 49	5	10	♍0	24	27	3	5	♎0	♊2	7	28	24	28	5	4	28	9	10	3	29
48	29 03	9 14	8	12	2	27	♍0	6	7	2	5	9	♍1	27	♊1	7	7	♎1	11	12	6	♎2
2 0	2♉11	11 38	11	15	5	♎0	4	9	10	5	8	12	3	♎0	4	10	9	4	14	15	8	5
12	5 18	14 01	14	18	7	3	7	11	12	8	11	14	6	3	7	12	12	7	16	17	11	8
24	8 23	16 25	17	20	10	6	10	14	15	11	14	17	9	6	10	15	15	11	19	19	14	11
36	11 26	18 49	19	23	12	8	13	16	17	14	17	20	11	9	13	17	17	13	21	21	16	14
48	14 28	21 13	22	25	15	11	15	19	20	17	19	22	14	12	16	20	20	16	23	24	19	17
3 0	17 28	23 37	25	28	17	14	18	22	22	20	22	25	17	15	19	22	22	19	26	26	22	20
12	20 26	26 01	28	♌0	20	17	21	24	25	22	25	27	19	18	22	25	25	22	28	28	24	23
24	23 23	28 25	♋1	3	22	20	24	27	28	25	28	♌0	22	20	24	27	27	25	♋1	♌0	27	25
36	26 19	0♍50	3	5	25	22	27	29	♎0	28	♋1	2	25	23	27	♌0	♎0	27	3	3	29	28
48	29 13	3 15	6	8	27	25	♋0	♌2	3	♏1	3	5	27	26	♋0	2	2	♏0	5	5	♎2	♏1
4 0	2♊05	5 40	9	10	♎0	28	2	4	5	4	6	8	♎0	29	3	5	5	3	8	7	5	3
12	4 57	8 05	12	13	3	♏0	5	7	8	6	9	10	3	♏2	6	7	7	6	10	9	7	6
24	7 47	10 30	14	15	5	3	8	9	10	9	11	13	5	5	8	10	10	8	12	12	10	9
36	10 36	12 56	17	17	8	6	10	12	13	12	14	15	8	8	11	12	12	11	14	14	12	11
48	13 24	15 22	19	20	10	9	13	14	16	15	17	18	11	10	14	15	15	14	17	16	15	14
5 0	16 11	17 48	22	22	13	11	16	17	18	17	20	20	13	13	17	17	17	17	19	19	17	17
12	18 58	20 14	25	25	15	14	19	19	21	20	22	23	16	16	19	20	20	19	22	21	20	19
24	21 44	22 41	27	27	18	17	21	22	23	23	25	26	19	19	22	22	22	22	24	23	22	22
36	24 30	25 07	♌0	♍0	20	19	24	24	26	25	28	28	21	21	25	25	25	25	26	26	25	24
48	27 15	27 33	3	2	23	22	27	27	28	28	♌0	♍1	24	24	27	27	27	27	29	28	27	27
6 0	0♋00	0♎00	5	5	25	25	29	29	♏1	♐1	3	3	27	27	♌0	♍0	♏0	♐0	♋1	♍0	♏0	29
12	2 45	2 27	8	7	28	27	♌2	♍2	3	3	6	6	29	♐0	3	3	3	3	3	3	2	♐1
24	5 30	4 53	11	10	♏0	♐0	5	4	6	6	9	9	♏2	2	5	5	5	5	6	5	4	4
36	8 16	7 19	13	12	3	3	7	7	8	9	11	11	4	5	8	8	8	8	8	8	7	6
48	11 02	9 46	16	15	5	5	10	9	11	11	14	14	7	8	11	10	10	11	11	10	9	8
7 0	13 49	12 12	19	17	8	8	13	12	13	14	17	17	10	10	13	13	13	13	13	13	11	11
12	16 36	14 38	21	20	10	11	15	14	16	17	20	19	12	13	16	15	15	16	16	15	14	13
24	19 24	17 04	24	22	13	13	18	17	18	20	22	22	15	16	19	18	18	19	19	18	16	16
36	22 13	19 30	27	25	15	16	21	20	21	22	25	25	17	19	22	20	20	22	21	20	18	18
48	25 03	21 55	♍0	27	17	18	24	22	23	25	28	27	20	21	24	23	23	24	24	23	21	20
8 0	27 55	24 20	2	♎0	20	21	26	25	26	28	♍1	♎0	22	24	27	25	25	27	27	25	23	22
12	0♌47	26 45	5	3	22	24	29	27	28	♐0	4	3	25	27	♍0	28	28	♐0	29	28	25	25
24	3 41	29 10	8	5	25	27	♏2	♎0	♐1	3	7	5	28	29	3	♎0	♐0	3	♍2	♎1	27	27
36	6 37	1♏35	10	8	27	29	5	2	3	6	10	8	♐0	♐2	5	3	3	6	5	3	♐0	29
48	9 34	3 59	13	10	♐0	♐2	8	5	6	9	12	11	3	5	8	5	5	8	7	6	2	♐2
9 0	12 32	6 23	16	13	2	5	10	8	8	12	15	13	5	8	11	8	8	11	10	8	4	4
12	15 32	8 47	19	15	5	8	13	10	11	15	18	16	8	11	14	10	10	14	13	11	6	7
24	18 34	11 11	22	18	7	11	16	13	14	17	21	19	10	13	17	13	13	17	16	14	9	9
36	21 37	13 35	24	20	10	13	19	15	16	20	24	21	13	16	20	15	15	20	19	16	11	11
48	24 42	15 59	27	23	12	16	22	18	19	23	27	24	16	19	23	18	18	23	22	19	13	14
10 0	27 49	18 22	♎0	25	15	19	25	20	21	26	♎0	27	18	22	26	21	20	26	25	22	15	16
12	0♍57	20 46	3	28	18	22	28	23	24	♑0	3	29	21	25	29	23	23	29	28	24	18	19
24	4 07	23 11	6	♏0	20	25	♎0	25	27	3	6	♏2	23	28	♎2	26	25	♑2	♎1	27	20	21
36	7 18	25 35	8	3	23	28	3	28	29	6	9	4	26	♒1	5	28	28	5	4	♏0	22	24
48	10 30	28 00	11	5	25	♒2	6	♏0	♑2	9	12	7	29	4	8	♏1	♑1	8	7	2	25	27
11 0	13 43	0♐25	14	8	28	5	9	3	5	12	15	10	♒2	8	11	4	3	11	9	5	27	29
12	16 57	2 51	17	10	♑1	8	12	5	8	16	18	12	4	11	14	6	6	14	12	8	♑0	♒2
24	20 12	5 18	20	13	4	12	15	8	11	19	20	15	7	14	17	9	8	17	15	10	2	5
36	23 28	7 45	22	15	6	15	18	10	14	23	23	17	10	17	20	12	11	20	18	13	5	8
48	26 44	10 14	25	17	9	18	20	13	17	26	26	20	13	21	23	14	13	23	21	16	7	11
12 0	0♎00	12 44	28	20	12	22	23	15	20	♓0	29	22	16	24	26	17	16	27	24	18	10	14

292

SID TIME	MC LONG	ASC	REGIOMONT				CAMPANUS				PLACIDUS				NAT. GRAD.				KOCH			
		1	11	12	2	3	11	12	2	3	11	12	2	3	11	12	2	3	11	12	2	3
h m	♎	♐	♎	♏	♐	♒	♎	♏	♐	♓	♎	♏	♐	♒	♎	♏	♐	♒	♎	♏	♐	♒
12 0	0♎00	12♐44	28	20	12	22	23	15	20	♓0	29	22	16	24	26	17	16	27	24	18	10	14
12	3 16	15 15	♏0	22	15	26	26	18	23	3	♏2	25	19	28	29	20	19	♓0	27	21	12	17
24	6 32	17 48	3	25	18	29	29	20	26	7	5	28	22	♓1	♏2	22	21	3	♏0	24	15	20
36	9 48	20 23	6	27	22	♓3	♏2	23	♒0	11	8	♐0	25	5	5	25	24	6	3	26	18	24
48	13 03	23 00	9	♐0	25	7	4	25	3	14	10	3	29	8	8	28	27	9	6	29	21	27
13 0	16 17	25 39	11	2	28	10	7	28	7	18	13	5	♒2	12	11	♐1	♒0	12	9	♐2	24	♓1
12	19 30	28 21	14	5	♒2	14	10	♐0	10	22	16	8	5	15	14	4	2	15	12	4	27	4
24	22 42	1♑06	17	7	5	18	13	3	14	26	19	10	9	19	17	6	5	19	15	7	♒0	8
36	25 53	3 54	19	10	9	22	15	6	18	29	21	13	12	23	20	9	8	22	18	10	3	12
48	29 03	6 46	22	12	13	26	18	8	22	♈3	24	16	16	26	23	12	11	25	21	13	6	15
14 0	2♏11	9 41	25	15	16	♈0	21	11	26	7	27	18	20	♈0	27	15	14	28	24	15	10	19
12	5 18	12 41	27	18	20	4	24	13	♓0	11	♐0	21	23	4	♐0	18	17	♈1	26	18	13	23
24	8 23	15 46	♐0	20	24	8	26	16	4	15	2	23	27	7	3	21	20	4	29	21	17	27
36	11 26	18 56	3	23	29	12	29	18	8	18	5	26	♈1	11	6	25	23	7	♐2	24	21	♈1
48	14 28	22 11	5	25	♈3	16	♐2	21	13	22	8	29	5	15	9	28	26	10	5	27	25	5
15 0	17 28	25 32	8	28	7	20	4	24	17	26	10	♏2	9	18	12	♑1	♈0	13	8	♑0	29	9
12	20 26	29 00	11	♏1	12	23	7	26	21	29	13	4	13	22	15	4	3	16	11	3	♈3	14
24	23 23	2♏35	13	4	16	27	10	29	26	♉3	16	7	17	25	18	8	7	19	14	6	7	18
36	26 19	6 16	16	6	21	♉1	12	♏2	♈0	6	19	10	22	29	21	11	10	22	17	9	12	22
48	29 13	10 06	18	9	25	4	15	5	5	10	21	13	26	♉2	24	15	14	26	20	12	16	26
16 0	2♐05	14 03	21	12	♈0	8	18	7	9	13	24	16	♈0	6	28	18	18	29	22	15	21	♉0
12	4 57	18 08	24	15	5	12	20	10	14	17	27	19	4	9	♑1	22	21	♉2	25	19	25	4
24	7 47	22 21	27	18	9	15	23	13	18	20	29	22	8	13	4	26	25	5	28	22	♈0	7
36	10 36	26 42	29	22	14	18	26	16	22	23	♑2	25	13	16	7	♒0	♈0	8	♑1	26	5	11
48	13 24	1♐11	♑2	25	18	22	29	19	27	26	5	29	17	19	10	4	4	11	4	29	9	15
17 0	16 11	5 47	5	28	23	25	♑1	23	♉1	♊0	8	♒2	21	22	14	8	8	14	7	♒3	14	19
12	18 58	10 29	8	♒2	27	28	4	26	5	3	11	5	25	26	17	12	12	17	11	7	19	23
24	21 44	15 17	11	5	♉1	♊2	7	29	9	6	13	9	29	29	20	17	17	20	14	11	23	26
36	24 30	20 09	13	9	6	5	10	♒3	13	9	16	12	♊3	♊2	24	21	21	24	17	15	28	♊0
48	27 15	25 04	16	13	10	8	13	6	17	12	19	16	7	5	27	26	26	27	20	19	♉2	3
18 0	0♑00	0♒00	19	16	14	11	15	10	20	15	22	20	10	8	♒0	♓0	♉0	♊0	24	23	7	6
12	2 45	4 56	22	20	17	14	18	13	24	17	25	23	14	11	3	4	4	3	27	28	11	10
24	5 30	9 51	25	24	21	17	21	17	27	20	28	27	18	14	6	9	9	6	♒0	♓2	15	13
36	8 16	14 43	28	29	25	19	24	21	♊1	23	♒1	♓1	21	17	10	13	13	10	4	7	19	16
48	11 02	19 31	♒2	♓3	28	22	27	25	4	26	4	5	25	19	13	18	18	13	7	11	23	19
19 0	13 49	24 13	5	7	♊2	25	♒0	29	7	29	8	9	28	22	16	22	22	16	11	16	27	23
12	16 36	28 49	8	12	5	28	4	♓3	11	♋1	11	13	♊1	25	19	26	26	20	15	21	♊1	26
24	19 24	3♉18	12	16	8	♋1	7	8	14	4	14	17	5	28	22	♈0	♊0	23	19	25	4	29
36	22 13	7 39	15	21	12	3	10	12	17	7	17	22	8	♋1	25	5	4	26	22	♈0	8	♋2
48	25 03	11 52	18	25	15	6	13	16	20	10	21	26	11	3	28	9	8	29	26	5	11	5
20 0	27 55	15 57	22	♈0	18	9	17	21	23	12	24	♈0	14	6	♓1	12	12	♋2	♓0	9	15	8
12	0♒00	19 54	26	5	21	12	20	25	25	15	28	4	17	9	4	16	15	6	4	14	18	10
24	3 41	23 44	29	9	24	14	24	♈0	28	18	♓1	8	20	11	8	20	19	9	8	18	21	13
36	6 37	27 25	♈3	14	26	17	27	4	♋1	20	5	13	23	14	11	23	22	12	12	23	24	16
48	9 34	1♊00	7	18	29	19	♈1	9	4	23	8	17	26	17	14	27	26	15	16	27	27	19
21 0	12 32	4 28	10	23	♋2	22	4	13	6	26	12	21	28	20	17	♉0	29	18	21	♉1	♋0	22
12	15 32	7 49	14	27	5	25	8	17	9	28	15	25	♋1	22	20	4	♊2	21	25	5	3	25
24	18 34	11 04	18	♉1	7	27	12	22	12	♋1	19	29	4	25	23	♉3	7	28	29	9	6	28
36	21 37	14 14	22	6	10	♋0	15	26	14	4	23	♉3	7	28	26	10	9	27	♈3	13	9	♋1
48	24 42	17 19	26	10	12	3	19	♉0	17	6	26	7	9	♋0	29	13	12	♋0	7	17	12	4
22 0	27 49	20 19	♈0	14	15	5	23	4	19	9	♈0	10	12	3	♉2	16	15	3	11	20	15	6
12	0♓57	23 14	4	17	18	8	27	8	22	12	4	14	14	6	5	19	18	7	15	24	17	9
24	4 07	26 06	8	21	20	11	♈1	12	24	15	7	18	17	9	8	22	21	10	18	27	20	12
36	7 18	28 54	12	25	23	13	4	16	27	17	11	21	20	11	11	25	24	13	22	♊0	23	15
48	10 30	1♋39	16	28	25	16	8	20	♌0	20	15	25	22	14	15	28	26	16	26	3	26	18
23 0	13 43	4 21	20	♊2	28	19	12	23	2	23	18	28	25	17	18	♊0	29	19	29	6	28	21
12	16 57	7 00	23	5	♌0	21	16	27	5	26	22	♊1	27	20	21	3	♌2	22	♋3	9	♌1	24
24	20 12	9 37	27	8	3	24	19	♊0	7	28	25	5	♌0	22	24	6	5	25	6	12	4	27
36	23 28	12 12	♊1	12	5	27	23	4	10	♍1	29	8	2	25	27	9	8	28	10	15	6	♍0
48	26 44	14 45	4	15	8	♍0	27	7	12	4	♊2	11	5	28	♊0	11	10	♍1	13	18	9	3
24 0	0♈00	17 16	8	18	10	2	♉0	10	15	7	6	14	8	♍1	3	14	13	4	16	20	12	6

SID TIME h m	MC LONG ♈	ASC ♋	REG 11 ♉	12 Ⅱ	2 ♌	3 ♍	CAM 11 ♈	12 Ⅱ	2 ♌	3 ♍	PLA 11 ♉	12 Ⅱ	2 ♌	3 ♍	NAT 11 ♉	12 Ⅱ	2 ♌	3 ♍	KOC 11 ♉	12 Ⅱ	2 ♌	3 ♍
0 0	0♈00	19♋43	9	20	12	3	29	10	17	8	7	16	9	♍1	4	16	15	5	19	23	13	7
0 12	3♈16	22 08	13	23	14	6	♋3	14	19	11	10	19	11	4	7	18	17	8	22	26	16	9
0 24	6 32	24 33	16	26	16	8	7	17	22	14	13	22	14	7	10	21	20	11	25	28	19	12
0 36	9 48	26 56	20	29	19	11	10	20	24	17	17	25	16	10	13	24	23	14	28	♋1	21	15
0 48	13 03	29 18	23	♋2	21	14	13	23	27	19	20	28	19	13	16	26	25	17	Ⅱ0	3	24	18
1 0	16 17	1♌40	26	4	24	16	17	25	29	22	23	♋0	21	16	19	29	28	20	3	5	26	21
1 12	19 30	4 01	Ⅱ0	7	26	19	20	28	♍2	25	26	3	24	18	22	♋1	♍1	23	6	8	29	24
1 24	22 42	6 21	3	10	28	22	23	♋1	4	28	Ⅱ0	6	27	21	25	4	3	26	8	10	♍2	27
1 36	25 53	8 41	6	12	♍1	25	27	4	7	♎1	3	8	29	24	28	6	6	29	11	12	4	♎0
1 48	29 03	11 00	9	15	3	27	Ⅱ0	6	9	4	6	11	♍2	27	Ⅱ1	9	8	♎2	13	14	7	3
2 0	2♉11	13♌20	12	17	6	≏0	3	9	12	6	9	14	4	≏0	4	11	11	5	16	17	9	6
2 12	5 18	15 39	15	20	8	3	6	12	14	9	12	16	7	3	7	14	13	8	18	19	12	9
2 24	8 23	17 58	18	22	10	5	9	14	17	12	15	19	9	6	10	16	16	11	21	21	15	12
2 36	11 26	20 17	21	25	13	8	12	17	19	15	18	21	12	9	13	18	18	14	23	23	17	14
2 48	14 28	22 36	24	27	15	11	15	19	22	18	20	24	14	12	16	21	21	16	25	25	20	17
3 0	17 28	24 55	27	♍0	18	14	18	22	24	20	23	26	17	14	19	23	23	19	27	27	22	20
3 12	20 26	27 15	29	2	20	16	21	24	27	23	26	29	20	17	22	26	26	22	♋0	♌0	25	23
3 24	23 23	29 34	♌2	4	23	19	24	27	29	26	29	♋1	22	20	25	28	28	25	2	2	28	26
3 36	26 19	1♍54	5	7	25	22	26	29	≏2	29	♋2	4	25	23	28	♋1	≏1	28	4	4	≏0	28
3 48	29 13	4 13	7	9	28	24	29	♌2	4	♏2	4	6	27	26	♋0	3	3	♏0	6	6	3	♏1
4 0	2Ⅱ05	6 33	10	12	≏0	27	♋2	4	7	4	7	9	≏0	29	3	6	6	3	9	8	5	4
4 12	4 57	8 53	13	14	2	♏0	5	7	9	7	10	11	3	♏1	6	8	8	6	11	10	8	6
4 24	7 47	11 13	15	16	5	3	7	9	12	10	12	14	5	4	9	10	10	9	13	13	10	9
4 36	10 36	13 34	18	19	7	5	10	12	14	13	15	16	8	7	11	13	13	11	15	15	13	11
4 48	13 24	15 54	21	21	10	8	13	14	17	15	18	19	10	10	14	15	15	14	18	17	15	14
5 0	16 11	18 15	23	24	12	11	15	16	19	18	20	21	13	13	17	18	18	17	20	19	18	16
5 12	18 58	20 36	26	26	15	13	18	19	21	21	23	24	16	15	19	20	20	19	22	21	20	19
5 24	21 44	22 57	29	28	17	16	21	21	24	23	26	27	18	18	22	23	23	22	24	24	22	21
5 36	24 30	25 18	♌1	♍1	20	18	23	24	26	26	28	29	21	21	25	25	25	25	27	26	25	24
5 48	27 15	27 39	4	3	22	21	26	26	29	29	♌1	♍2	23	23	27	28	28	27	29	28	27	26
6 0	0♋00	0≏00	6	6	24	24	29	29	♏1	♐1	4	4	26	26	♌0	♍0	♏0	♐0	♌1	♍1	29	29
6 12	2 45	2 21	9	8	27	26	♌1	♍1	4	4	7	7	28	29	3	2	2	3	4	3	♏2	♐1
6 24	5 30	4 42	12	10	29	29	4	4	6	7	9	9	♏1	♐2	5	5	5	5	6	5	4	3
6 36	8 16	7 03	14	13	♏2	♐1	7	6	9	9	12	12	3	4	8	7	7	8	9	8	6	6
6 48	11 02	9 24	17	15	4	4	9	9	11	12	15	14	6	7	11	10	10	9	11	10	9	8
7 0	13 49	11 45	19	18	6	7	12	11	14	15	17	17	9	10	13	12	12	13	14	12	11	10
7 12	16 36	14 06	22	20	9	9	15	13	16	17	20	20	11	12	16	15	15	16	16	15	13	12
7 24	19 24	16 26	25	23	11	12	17	16	18	20	23	22	14	15	19	17	17	19	19	17	15	15
7 36	22 13	18 47	27	25	14	15	20	18	21	23	26	25	16	18	21	20	20	21	21	20	17	17
7 48	25 03	21 07	♍0	28	16	17	23	21	23	25	29	27	19	20	24	22	22	24	24	22	20	19
8 0	27 55	23 27	3	≏0	18	20	26	23	26	28	♍1	≏0	21	23	27	24	24	27	26	25	22	21
8 12	0♌47	25 47	6	2	21	23	28	26	28	♑1	4	3	24	26	♍0	27	27	♑0	29	27	24	24
8 24	3 41	28 06	8	5	23	25	♍1	28	♐1	4	7	5	26	28	2	29	29	2	♍2	≏0	26	26
8 36	6 37	0♏26	11	7	26	28	4	≏1	3	6	10	8	29	♑1	5	≏2	♐2	5	4	2	28	28
8 48	9 34	2 45	14	10	28	♑1	7	3	6	9	13	10	♐1	4	8	4	4	8	7	5	♐0	♑0
9 0	12 32	5 05	16	12	♐0	3	10	6	8	12	16	13	4	7	11	7	7	11	10	8	3	3
9 12	15 32	7 24	19	15	3	6	12	8	11	15	18	16	6	10	14	9	9	14	13	10	5	5
9 24	18 34	9 43	22	17	5	9	15	11	13	18	21	18	9	12	16	12	12	17	16	13	7	7
9 36	21 37	12 02	25	20	8	12	18	13	16	21	24	21	11	15	19	14	14	20	18	15	9	9
9 48	24 42	14 21	27	22	10	15	21	16	18	24	27	23	14	18	22	17	16	23	21	18	11	12
10 0	27 49	16 40	≏0	24	13	18	24	18	21	27	≏0	26	16	21	25	19	19	26	24	21	13	14
10 12	0♍57	19 00	3	27	15	21	26	21	24	≏0	3	28	19	24	28	22	21	29	27	23	16	17
10 24	4 07	21 19	5	29	18	24	29	23	26	3	6	♏1	22	27	≏1	24	24	≏2	≏0	26	18	19
10 36	7 18	23 39	8	♏2	20	27	≏2	26	29	7	9	3	24	≏0	4	27	26	5	3	28	20	22
10 48	10 30	25 59	11	4	23	≏0	5	28	♏2	10	12	6	27	4	7	29	29	8	6	♏1	22	24
11 0	13 43	28 20	14	6	26	4	8	♏1	5	13	14	9	♑0	7	10	♏2	♑1	11	9	4	25	27
11 12	16 57	0♐42	16	9	28	7	11	3	7	17	17	11	2	10	13	5	4	14	12	6	♑0	≏0
11 24	20 12	3 04	19	11	♑1	10	13	6	10	20	20	14	5	13	16	7	6	17	15	9	29	2
11 36	23 28	5 27	22	14	4	14	16	8	13	23	23	16	8	17	19	10	9	20	18	11	♑2	5
11 48	26 44	7 52	25	16	7	17	19	11	16	27	26	19	11	20	22	13	12	23	21	14	4	8
12 0	0≏00	10 17	27	18	10	21	22	13	20	♒1	29	21	14	23	25	15	14	26	23	17	7	11

SID TIME	MC LONG	ASC	REGIOMONT				CAMPANUS				PLACIDUS				NAT. GRAD.				KOCH			
h m	♎	♐	11	12	2	3	11	12	2	3	11	12	2	3	11	12	2	3	11	12	2	3
12 0	0♎00	10♐17	27	18	10	21	22	13	20	♓1	29	21	14	23	25	15	14	26	23	17	7	11
12	3 16	12 45	♏0	21	13	25	25	15	23	4	♏1	24	17	27	28	18	17	29	26	19	9	14
24	6 32	15 13	3	23	16	28	27	18	26	8	4	26	20	♒0	♏1	21	19	♓2	29	22	12	17
36	9 48	17 44	5	26	19	♒2	♏0	20	29	12	7	29	23	4	4	23	22	6	♏2	25	15	21
48	13 03	20 17	8	28	22	6	3	23	♒3	16	10	♐1	27	8	7	26	25	9	5	27	17	24
13 0	16 17	22 52	11	♐0	26	10	6	25	7	19	13	4	♒0	11	10	29	27	12	8	♐0	20	28
12	19 30	25 30	13	3	29	14	8	28	10	23	15	6	3	15	13	♐2	♒0	15	11	3	23	♓1
24	22 42	28 12	16	5	♒3	18	11	♐0	14	27	18	9	7	19	16	4	3	18	14	5	26	5
36	25 53	0♏56	18	8	6	22	14	3	18	♈1	21	11	10	22	20	7	6	21	17	8	29	9
48	29 03	3 44	21	10	10	26	17	5	22	5	23	14	14	26	23	10	8	24	20	11	♒3	13
14 0	2♏11	6 37	24	13	14	♈0	19	8	26	9	26	16	18	♈0	26	13	11	28	22	13	6	17
12	5 18	9 34	26	15	18	4	22	10	♈1	13	29	19	22	4	29	16	14	♈1	25	16	10	21
24	8 23	12 37	29	18	22	8	25	13	5	16	♐2	22	26	8	♐2	19	17	4	28	19	13	25
36	11 26	15 45	♐1	20	27	12	27	15	10	20	4	24	♈0	11	5	22	20	7	♐1	22	17	29
48	14 59	18 59	4	23	♈1	16	♐0	18	14	24	7	27	4	15	8	25	24	10	4	25	21	♈3
15 0	17 28	22 20	7	26	6	20	3	20	19	28	10	♑0	8	19	11	29	27	13	7	28	25	8
12	20 26	25 48	9	28	11	24	5	23	23	♉1	12	2	12	22	14	♑2	♈0	16	10	♑1	♈0	12
24	23 23	29 25	12	♑1	15	28	8	26	28	5	15	5	17	26	17	5	4	19	13	4	4	16
36	26 19	3♒09	15	4	20	♉2	11	28	♈3	8	18	8	21	♉0	20	9	7	22	15	7	9	21
48	29 13	7 03	17	7	25	5	13	♑1	8	12	20	11	26	3	24	13	11	25	18	10	13	25
16 0	2♐05	11 06	20	10	♈0	9	16	4	12	15	23	14	♈0	7	27	16	15	28	21	13	18	29
12	4 57	15 20	23	13	5	13	19	7	17	19	26	17	4	10	♑0	20	19	♉1	24	17	23	♉3
24	7 47	19 43	25	16	10	16	21	10	21	22	28	20	9	13	3	24	23	4	27	20	28	7
36	10 36	24 16	28	19	15	20	24	13	26	25	♑1	23	13	17	7	28	28	7	♑0	24	♈3	11
48	13 24	29 00	♑1	22	19	23	27	16	♉0	28	4	27	18	20	10	♒2	♈2	11	3	27	8	15
17 0	16 11	3♒53	3	26	24	26	29	19	5	♊2	7	♒0	22	23	13	7	6	14	6	♒1	14	19
12	18 58	8 55	6	29	29	♊0	♒2	22	9	5	10	3	26	26	17	11	11	17	10	5	19	23
24	21 44	14 04	9	♒3	♉3	3	5	25	13	8	12	7	♉0	♊0	20	16	16	20	13	9	24	27
36	24 30	19 19	12	6	8	6	8	29	17	11	15	10	4	3	23	21	20	23	16	13	28	♊0
48	27 15	24 38	15	10	12	9	11	♒2	21	14	18	14	8	6	27	25	25	27	19	18	♉3	4
18 0	0♒00	0♈00	18	14	16	12	13	6	24	17	21	18	12	9	♒0	♈0	♉0	♊0	23	22	8	7
12	2 45	5 22	21	18	20	15	16	9	28	19	24	22	16	12	3	5	5	3	26	27	12	11
24	5 30	10 41	24	22	24	18	19	13	♊1	22	27	26	20	15	7	10	9	7	♒0	♈2	17	14
36	8 16	15 56	27	27	27	21	22	17	5	25	♒0	♈0	23	18	10	14	14	10	3	6	21	17
48	11 02	21 05	♒0	♈1	♊1	24	25	21	8	28	4	4	27	20	13	19	19	13	7	11	25	20
19 0	13 49	26 07	4	6	4	27	28	25	11	♋1	7	8	♊0	23	16	24	23	17	11	16	29	24
12	16 36	1♉00	7	11	8	29	♒2	♈0	14	3	10	12	3	26	19	28	28	20	15	22	♊3	27
24	19 24	5 44	10	15	11	♋2	5	4	17	6	13	17	7	29	23	♈2	♊2	23	19	27	6	♋0
36	22 13	10 17	14	20	14	5	8	9	20	9	17	21	10	♋2	26	7	6	27	23	♈2	10	3
48	25 03	14 40	17	25	17	7	11	13	23	11	20	26	13	4	29	11	10	♋0	27	7	13	6
20 0	27 55	18 54	21	♈0	20	10	15	18	26	14	23	♈0	16	7	♈2	15	14	3	♈1	12	17	9
12	0♈47	22 57	25	5	23	13	18	22	29	17	27	4	19	10	5	19	17	6	5	17	20	12
24	3 41	26 51	28	10	26	16	22	27	♋2	19	♈0	9	22	12	8	23	21	10	9	21	23	15
36	6 37	0♊35	♈2	15	29	18	25	♈2	4	22	4	13	25	15	11	26	25	13	14	26	26	18
48	9 34	4 12	6	19	♋2	21	29	7	7	25	8	18	28	18	14	♉0	28	16	18	♉0	29	20
21 0	12 32	7 40	10	24	4	23	♈2	11	10	27	11	22	♋0	20	17	3	♋1	19	22	5	♋2	23
12	15 32	11 01	14	29	7	26	6	16	12	♌0	15	26	3	23	20	6	5	22	27	9	5	26
24	18 34	14 15	18	♉3	10	29	10	20	15	3	19	♉0	6	26	23	10	8	25	♈1	13	8	29
36	21 37	17 23	22	8	12	♌1	14	25	17	5	22	4	8	28	26	13	11	28	5	17	11	♌2
48	24 42	20 26	26	12	15	4	17	29	20	8	26	8	11	♌1	29	16	14	♌1	9	20	14	5
22 0	27 49	23 23	♈0	16	17	6	21	♉4	22	11	♈0	12	14	4	♈2	19	17	4	13	24	17	8
12	0♓57	26 16	4	20	20	9	25	8	25	13	4	16	16	7	6	22	20	7	17	27	19	10
24	4 07	29 04	8	24	22	12	29	12	27	16	8	20	19	9	9	24	23	10	21	♊1	22	13
36	7 18	1♋48	12	27	25	14	♈3	16	♌0	19	11	23	21	12	12	27	26	14	25	4	25	16
48	10 30	4 30	16	♊1	27	17	7	20	2	22	15	27	24	15	15	♊0	28	17	29	7	27	19
23 0	13 43	7 08	20	4	♌0	19	11	23	5	24	19	♊0	26	17	18	3	♋1	20	♉2	10	♌0	22
12	16 57	9 43	24	8	2	22	14	27	7	27	23	3	29	20	21	5	4	23	6	13	3	25
24	20 12	12 16	28	11	4	25	18	♊1	10	♍0	26	7	♋1	23	24	8	7	26	9	15	5	28
36	23 28	14 47	♉2	14	7	27	22	4	12	3	♊0	10	4	26	28	11	9	29	13	18	8	♍1
48	26 44	17 15	5	17	9	♍0	26	7	15	5	3	13	6	29	♊1	13	12	♍2	16	21	11	4
24 0	0♈00	19 43	9	20	12	3	29	10	17	8	7	16	9	♍1	4	16	15	5	19	23	13	7

SID TIME (h m)	MC LONG	ASC 1	REGIOMONT 11	12	2	3	CAMPANUS 11	12	2	3	PLACIDUS 11	12	2	3	NAT. GRAD. 11	12	2	3	KOCH 11	12	2	3
	♈	♋	♉	♊	♌	♍	♈	♊	♌	♍	♉	♊	♌	♍	♉	♊	♌	♍	♉	♊	♌	♍
0 0	0♈00	21♋42	10	22	13	3	28	11	19	9	7	18	10	♍2	4	18	16	5	22	26	15	7
12	3♈16	24 04	14	25	15	6	♉2	14	21	12	11	21	12	4	7	20	19	8	25	28	17	10
24	6 32	26 24	17	28	18	9	6	17	24	15	14	24	15	7	10	23	21	11	27	♋1	20	13
36	9 48	28 44	21	♋1	20	11	9	20	26	18	17	26	17	10	13	25	24	14	♊0	3	22	16
48	13 03	1♋02	24	4	22	14	13	23	29	20	21	29	20	13	17	28	27	17	3	5	25	19
1 0	16 17	3 20	28	6	25	17	16	26	♍1	23	24	♋2	22	1♍	20	♋0	29	20	5	8	28	22
12	19 30	5 37	♊1	9	27	19	20	29	3	26	27	5	25	19	23	2	♍2	23	8	10	♍0	25
24	22 42	7 54	4	12	29	22	23	♋1	6	29	♊0	7	27	21	26	5	4	26	11	12	3	28
36	25 53	10 10	7	14	♍2	25	26	4	8	≏2	3	10	♍0	24	29	7	7	29	13	14	5	≏1
48	29 03	12 26	10	17	4	27	29	7	11	4	7	13	2	27	♊2	10	9	≏2	15	16	8	3
2 0	2♉11	14 41	13	19	6	≏0	♊2	9	13	7	10	15	5	≏0	5	12	12	5	18	18	10	6
12	5 18	16 57	16	21	9	3	6	12	16	10	13	18	7	3	8	15	14	8	20	20	13	9
24	8 23	19 12	19	24	11	5	9	14	18	13	15	20	10	6	11	17	17	11	22	23	16	12
36	11 26	21 27	22	26	13	8	12	17	20	16	18	23	12	9	14	19	19	14	24	25	18	15
48	14 28	23 42	25	29	16	11	15	19	23	18	21	25	15	11	16	22	22	17	27	27	21	18
3 0	17 28	25 57	28	♋1	18	13	17	22	25	21	24	28	17	14	19	24	24	19	29	29	23	20
12	20 26	28 13	♋0	3	20	16	20	24	28	24	27	♌0	20	17	22	27	26	22	♋1	♌1	26	23
24	23 23	0♍28	3	6	23	19	23	27	≏0	27	♋0	3	22	20	25	29	29	25	3	3	28	26
36	26 19	2 44	6	8	25	21	26	29	3	♍0	2	5	25	23	28	♌1	≏1	28	5	5	≏1	29
48	29 13	4 59	9	11	28	24	29	♌2	5	2	5	8	27	26	♋0	4	4	♏1	8	7	3	♏1
4 0	2♊05	7 15	11	13	≏0	27	♋2	4	8	5	8	10	≏0	28	3	6	6	3	10	9	6	4
12	4 57	9 31	14	15	2	29	4	7	10	8	10	12	3	♏1	6	9	8	6	12	11	8	6
24	7 47	11 47	17	18	5	♏2	7	9	12	10	13	15	5	4	9	11	11	9	14	13	10	9
36	10 36	14 03	19	20	7	5	10	12	15	13	16	17	8	7	11	13	13	11	16	15	13	11
48	13 24	16 20	22	22	10	7	12	14	17	16	18	20	10	9	14	16	16	14	18	18	15	14
5 0	16 11	18 36	24	25	12	10	15	16	20	18	21	22	13	12	17	18	18	17	20	20	18	16
12	18 58	20 53	27	27	14	12	18	19	22	21	24	25	15	15	19	20	20	19	23	22	20	19
24	21 44	23 10	29	29	17	15	20	21	25	24	26	27	18	18	22	23	23	22	25	24	22	21
36	24 30	25 26	♌2	♍2	19	18	23	23	27	26	29	♍0	20	20	25	25	25	25	27	26	25	24
48	27 15	27 43	5	4	21	20	26	26	29	29	♌2	2	23	23	27	28	28	27	29	29	27	26
6 0	0♋00	0≏00	7	6	24	23	28	28	♏2	↗2	4	5	25	26	♌0	♍0	♏0	↗0	♌2	♍1	29	28
12	2 45	2 17	10	9	26	25	♌1	♍1	4	4	7	7	28	28	3	2	2	3	4	3	♏1	↗1
24	5 30	4 34	12	11	28	28	4	3	7	7	10	10	♏0	↗1	5	5	5	5	6	5	4	3
36	8 16	6 50	15	13	♏1	↗1	6	5	9	10	12	12	3	4	8	7	7	8	9	8	6	5
48	11 02	9 07	18	16	3	3	9	8	11	12	15	15	5	6	11	10	10	11	11	10	8	7
7 0	13 49	11 24	20	18	5	6	12	10	14	15	18	17	8	9	13	12	12	13	14	12	10	10
12	16 36	13 40	23	20	8	8	14	13	16	18	21	20	10	12	16	14	14	16	16	15	12	12
24	19 24	15 57	25	23	10	11	17	15	19	20	23	22	13	14	19	17	17	19	19	17	15	14
36	22 13	18 13	28	25	12	13	20	18	21	23	26	25	15	17	21	19	19	21	21	20	17	16
48	25 03	20 29	♍1	28	15	16	22	20	23	26	29	27	18	20	24	22	21	24	24	22	19	18
8 0	27 55	22 45	3	≏0	17	19	25	22	26	28	♍2	≏0	20	22	27	24	24	27	26	24	21	20
12	0♌47	25 01	6	2	19	21	28	25	28	♑1	4	3	22	25	29	26	26	♑0	29	27	23	22
24	3 41	27 16	9	5	22	24	♍0	27	↗1	4	7	5	25	28	♍2	29	29	2	♍1	29	25	25
36	6 37	29 32	11	7	24	27	3	≏0	3	7	10	8	27	♑0	5	≏1	↗1	5	4	≏2	27	27
48	9 34	1♍47	14	10	27	♑0	6	2	6	10	13	10	↗0	3	8	4	3	8	7	4	29	29
9 0	12 32	4 03	17	12	29	2	9	5	8	13	16	13	2	6	11	6	6	11	10	7	↗1	♑1
12	15 32	6 18	19	14	↗1	5	12	7	11	15	19	15	5	9	13	8	8	14	12	9	3	3
24	18 34	8 33	22	17	4	8	14	10	13	18	21	18	7	12	16	11	11	16	15	12	5	6
36	21 37	10 48	25	19	6	11	17	12	16	21	24	20	10	15	18	13	13	19	18	14	7	8
48	24 42	13 03	27	21	9	14	20	14	18	24	27	23	12	17	22	16	15	22	21	17	10	10
10 0	27 49	15 19	≏0	24	11	17	23	17	21	28	≏0	25	15	20	25	18	18	25	24	20	12	12
12	0♍57	17 34	3	26	13	20	26	19	23	≈1	3	28	18	23	28	21	20	28	27	22	14	15
24	4 07	19 50	5	28	16	23	28	22	26	4	6	♏0	20	27	≏1	23	23	≈1	29	25	16	17
36	7 18	22 06	8	♏1	18	26	≏1	24	29	7	9	3	23	≈0	4	26	25	4	≏2	27	18	19
48	10 30	24 23	11	3	21	29	4	27	♑1	11	11	5	25	3	7	28	28	7	5	♏0	20	22
11 0	13 43	26 40	13	5	24	≈2	7	29	4	14	14	8	28	6	10	♏1	♑0	10	8	2	22	25
12	16 57	28 58	16	8	26	6	10	♏1	7	17	17	10	♑1	9	13	3	2	13	11	5	25	27
24	20 12	1↗16	19	10	29	9	12	4	10	21	20	13	4	13	16	6	5	17	14	8	27	≈0
36	23 28	3 36	21	12	♑2	13	15	6	13	24	23	15	6	16	19	9	7	20	17	10	29	3
48	26 44	5 56	24	15	5	16	18	9	16	28	26	18	9	19	22	11	10	23	20	13	♑2	5
12 0	0≏00	8 18	27	17	8	20	21	11	19	♓2	28	20	12	23	25	14	12	26	23	15	4	8

SID TIME h m	MC LONG	ASC 1	REGIOMONT 11	12	2	3	CAMPANUS 11	12	2	3	PLACIDUS 11	12	2	3	NAT. GRAD. 11	12	2	3	KOCH 11	12	2	3
	≏	♐	≏	♏	♑	♒	≏	♏		♓	≏	♏	♑	♒	≏	♏	♑	♒	≏	♏	♑	♒
12 0	0≏00	8♐18	27	17	8	20	21	11	19	♓2	28	20	12	23	25	14	12	26	23	15	4	8
12	3 16	10 42	29	19	10	24	23	13	23	5	♏1	22	15	26	28	16	15	29	26	18	6	11
24	6 32	13 07	♏2	22	14	28	26	16	26	9	4	25	18	♓0	♏1	19	17	♓2	29	20	9	15
36	9 48	15 34	5	24	17	♓1	29	18	29	13	7	27	22	4	4	22	20	5	♏1	23	12	18
48	13 03	18 03	7	27	20	5	♏2	21	♒3	17	9	♐0	25	7	7	24	23	8	4	26	14	21
13 0	16 17	20 34	10	29	23	9	4	23	7	21	12	2	28	11	10	27	25	12	7	28	17	25
12	19 30	23 09	12	♐1	27	13	7	26	11	25	15	5	♒2	15	13	♐0	28	15	10	♐1	20	28
24	22 42	25 46	15	4	♒0	18	10	28	15	28	18	7	5	19	16	3	♒1	18	13	4	23	♓2
36	25 53	28 27	18	6	4	22	13	♐0	19	♈2	20	10	9	22	19	5	3	21	16	6	26	6
48	29 03	1♑12	20	9	8	26	15	3	23	6	23	12	13	26	22	8	6	24	19	9	29	10
14 0	2♏11	4 01	23	11	12	♈0	18	5	27	10	26	15	17	♈0	25	11	9	27	22	12	♒3	14
12	5 18	6 55	25	13	16	4	21	8	♈2	14	28	17	20	4	28	14	12	♈0	24	14	6	18
24	8 23	9 55	28	16	21	8	23	10	6	18	♐1	20	25	8	♐1	17	15	3	27	17	10	23
36	11 26	13 00	♐1	18	25	12	26	13	11	22	4	23	29	11	4	20	18	6	♐0	20	14	27
48	14 28	16 12	3	21	♑0	17	29	15	16	25	6	25	♑3	15	7	23	21	9	3	23	18	♈1
15 0	17 28	19 32	6	24	4	21	♐1	18	21	29	9	28	7	19	10	27	25	12	6	26	22	6
12	20 26	23 00	8	26	9	25	4	20	25	♉3	12	♑1	12	23	13	♑0	28	16	9	29	26	10
24	23 23	26 36	11	29	14	29	7	23	♈0	6	14	4	16	26	16	3	♑1	19	12	♑2	♈1	15
36	26 19	0♒22	13	♑2	20	♉2	9	26	5	10	17	6	21	♑0	20	7	5	22	14	5	6	20
48	29 13	4 18	16	5	25	6	12	28	10	13	20	9	25	4	23	11	9	25	17	8	11	24
16 0	2♐05	8 26	19	8	♈0	10	14	♑1	15	17	22	12	♈0	♐0	26	14	13	28	20	11	16	28
12	4 57	12 45	21	10	5	14	17	4	20	20	25	15	5	11	29	18	17	♉1	23	15	21	♉3
24	7 47	17 16	24	14	10	17	20	7	24	24	28	18	9	14	♑3	22	14	17	26	18	27	7
36	10 36	22 00	27	17	16	21	23	10	29	27	♑0	22	14	17	6	27	26	7	29	22	♈2	11
48	13 24	26 56	♑0	20	21	24	25	13	♉4	♊0	3	25	18	21	9	♒1	♈0	10	♑2	26	7	15
17 0	16 11	2♒04	2	23	26	28	28	16	8	3	6	28	23	24	13	5	5	13	5	29	13	19
12	18 58	7 14	5	27	♉0	♊1	♑1	19	12	6	9	♒2	27	27	16	10	10	17	9	♒3	18	23
24	21 44	12 54	8	♒0	5	4	3	22	16	9	12	5	♉1	♊0	20	15	15	20	12	8	24	27
36	24 30	18 31	11	4	9	7	6	25	20	12	15	9	5	3	23	20	20	23	15	12	29	♊1
48	27 15	24 14	14	8	14	10	9	29	24	15	17	13	10	7	27	25	25	27	19	17	♉4	4
18 0	0♑00	0♈00	17	12	18	13	12	♒2	28	18	20	17	13	10	♒0	♈0	♉0	♊0	22	21	9	8
12	2 45	5 46	20	16	22	16	15	6	♊1	21	23	20	17	13	3	5	5	3	26	26	13	11
24	5 30	11 29	23	21	26	19	18	10	5	24	27	25	21	15	7	10	10	7	29	♈1	18	15
36	8 16	17 06	26	25	♊0	22	21	14	8	27	♒0	29	25	18	10	15	15	10	♒3	6	22	18
48	11 02	22 36	29	♈0	3	25	24	18	11	29	3	♈3	28	21	13	20	20	14	7	12	27	21
19 0	13 49	27 56	♈2	4	7	28	27	22	14	♋2	6	7	♊2	24	17	25	25	17	11	17	♊1	25
12	16 36	3♉04	4	10	10	♋0	♈0	26	17	5	9	12	5	27	20	♈0	29	21	15	23	4	28
24	19 24	8 00	9	14	13	3	3	♈1	20	7	13	16	8	♋0	23	4	♊3	24	19	28	8	♋1
36	22 13	12 44	13	20	16	6	6	6	23	10	16	21	12	2	26	9	8	27	23	♈3	12	4
48	25 03	17 15	16	25	20	9	10	10	26	13	19	25	15	5	29	13	12	♋1	27	9	15	7
20 0	27 55	21 34	20	♈0	22	11	13	15	29	16	23	♈0	18	8	♈2	17	16	4	♈2	14	19	10
12	0♒47	25 42	24	5	25	14	17	20	♋2	18	26	5	21	10	5	21	19	7	6	19	22	13
24	3 41	29 38	28	10	28	17	20	25	4	21	♈0	9	24	13	8	25	22	10	10	24	25	16
36	6 37	3♊24	♈1	16	♋1	19	24	♈0	7	23	4	14	26	16	11	29	27	13	15	29	28	18
48	9 34	7 00	5	21	4	22	27	5	10	26	7	18	29	18	14	♉2	♋0	17	20	♉4	♋1	21
21 0	12 32	10 28	9	26	6	24	♈1	9	12	28	11	23	♋2	21	18	5	3	20	24	8	4	24
12	15 32	13 48	13	♉0	9	27	5	14	15	♌1	15	27	5	24	21	9	7	23	29	12	7	27
24	18 34	17 00	18	5	12	29	8	19	17	4	19	♉1	7	26	24	12	10	26	♈3	16	10	♌0
36	21 37	20 05	22	9	14	♌2	12	24	20	7	22	5	10	29	27	15	13	29	7	20	13	3
48	24 42	23 05	26	14	17	5	16	28	22	9	26	10	13	♌2	♈0	18	16	♌2	12	24	16	6
22 0	27 49	25 59	♉0	18	19	7	20	♉3	25	12	♈0	13	15	4	3	21	19	5	16	27	18	8
12	0♓57	28 48	4	22	21	10	24	7	27	15	4	17	18	7	6	24	22	8	20	♊1	21	11
24	4 07	1♋33	8	26	24	12	28	11	♌0	17	8	21	20	10	9	27	25	11	24	4	24	14
36	7 18	4 14	12	♊0	26	15	♉2	15	2	20	11	25	22	13	12	29	27	14	28	7	26	17
48	10 30	6 51	17	3	29	18	5	19	4	23	15	28	25	15	15	♊2	♌0	17	♊1	10	29	20
23 0	13 43	9 26	21	7	♌1	20	9	23	7	26	19	♊2	28	18	18	5	3	20	5	13	♌2	23
12	16 57	11 57	25	10	3	23	13	27	9	29	23	5	♌0	21	22	7	6	23	9	16	4	26
24	20 12	14 26	29	13	6	25	17	♊1	12	♍1	26	8	3	23	25	10	8	26	12	18	7	29
36	23 28	16 53	♊2	16	8	28	21	4	14	4	♉0	12	5	26	28	13	11	29	15	21	10	♍1
48	26 44	19 18	6	20	11	♍1	25	7	17	7	4	15	8	29	♉1	15	14	♍2	19	24	12	4
24 0	0♈00	21 42	10	22	13	3	28	11	19	9	7	18	10	♍2	4	18	16	5	22	26	15	7

SID TIME	MC	ASC	REGIOMONTAN 11	12	2	3	CAMPANUS 11	12	2	3	PLACIDUS 11	12	2	3	NAT. GRAD. 11	12	2	3	KOCH 11	12	2	3
h m	♈ LONG	♋	♉	♊	♌	♍	♈	♊	♌	♍	♉	♊	♌	♍	♉	♊	♌	♍	♉	♊	♌	♍
0 0	0♈00	23♋50	11	25	14	4	27	11	21	10	8	20	11	♍2	4	19	18	6	25	29	16	8
12	3♈16	26 08	15	28	16	6	♉1	14	23	13	11	23	14	5	8	22	20	9	28	♋1	19	11
24	6 32	28 24	18	♋1	19	9	5	17	26	16	15	26	16	8	11	24	23	12	♊0	3	21	14
36	9 48	0♌39	22	3	21	12	8	20	28	19	18	28	18	10	14	27	25	15	3	6	24	17
48	13 03	2 54	25	6	23	14	12	23	♍0	22	22	♋1	21	13	17	29	28	18	6	8	26	20
1 0	16 17	5 07	29	9	26	17	15	26	3	24	25	4	23	16	20	♋1	♍0	21	8	10	29	22
12	19 30	7 20	♊2	11	28	19	19	29	5	27	28	6	26	19	23	4	3	24	11	12	♍1	25
24	22 42	9 32	5	14	♍0	22	22	♋1	8	≏0	♊1	9	28	22	26	6	5	27	13	14	4	28
36	25 53	11 44	9	16	2	25	25	4	10	3	4	12	♍0	24	29	9	8	≏0	15	16	6	≏1
48	29 03	13 56	12	19	5	27	29	7	12	5	7	14	3	27	♊2	11	10	3	18	18	9	4
2 0	2♉11	16 07	15	21	7	≏0	♊2	9	15	8	11	17	5	≏0	5	13	13	6	20	20	11	7
12	5 18	18 18	18	23	9	3	5	12	17	11	13	19	8	3	8	16	15	8	22	22	14	10
24	8 23	20 30	21	26	12	5	8	15	19	14	16	22	10	6	11	18	18	11	24	24	16	12
36	11 26	22 41	23	28	14	8	11	17	22	17	19	24	13	8	14	20	20	14	26	26	19	15
48	14 28	24 52	26	♌0	16	11	14	19	24	19	22	27	15	11	17	23	22	17	28	28	21	18
3 0	17 28	27 03	29	3	18	13	17	22	27	22	25	29	18	14	19	25	25	20	♋0	♌0	24	21
12	20 26	29 14	♋2	5	21	16	20	24	29	25	28	♌1	20	17	22	27	27	22	3	2	26	23
24	23 23	1♍25	4	7	23	18	23	27	≏1	28	♋1	4	23	20	25	♌0	≏0	25	5	4	29	26
36	26 19	3 36	7	10	25	21	25	29	4	♏0	3	6	25	22	28	2	2	28	7	6	≏1	29
48	29 13	5 47	10	12	28	24	28	♌2	6	3	6	9	28	25	♋1	4	4	♏1	9	8	4	♏1
4 0	2♊05	7 59	12	14	≏0	26	♋1	4	9	6	9	11	≏0	28	3	7	7	3	11	10	6	4
12	4 57	10 11	15	16	2	29	4	6	11	8	11	14	2	♏1	6	9	9	6	13	12	8	7
24	7 47	12 22	18	19	5	♏1	6	9	13	11	14	16	5	3	9	11	11	9	15	14	11	9
36	10 36	14 34	20	21	7	4	9	11	16	14	17	18	7	6	11	14	14	12	17	16	13	12
48	13 24	16 46	23	23	9	7	12	13	18	16	19	21	10	9	14	16	16	14	19	18	15	14
5 0	16 11	18 58	26	26	12	9	14	16	21	19	22	23	12	12	17	18	18	17	21	20	18	16
12	18 58	21 11	28	28	14	12	17	18	23	22	25	26	15	14	19	21	21	19	23	22	20	19
24	21 44	23 23	♌0	♍0	16	14	20	21	25	24	27	28	17	17	22	23	23	22	25	25	22	21
36	24 30	25 35	3	2	18	17	22	23	28	27	♌0	♍0	20	20	25	25	25	25	28	27	25	23
48	27 15	27 48	6	5	21	19	25	25	♏0	✗0	2	3	22	22	27	28	28	27	♋0	29	27	26
6 0	0♋00	0≏00	8	7	23	22	28	28	2	2	5	5	25	25	♋0	♍0	♏0	✗0	2	♍1	29	28
12	2 45	2 13	11	9	25	24	♋0	♍0	5	5	8	8	27	28	3	2	2	3	4	3	♏1	✗0
24	5 30	4 25	13	12	28	27	3	2	7	8	10	10	♏0	✗0	5	5	5	5	7	5	3	2
36	8 16	6 37	16	14	♏0	✗0	6	5	9	10	13	13	2	3	8	7	7	8	9	8	5	5
48	11 02	8 49	18	16	2	2	8	7	12	13	16	15	4	5	11	9	9	11	11	10	8	7
7 0	13 49	11 02	21	18	4	5	11	9	14	16	18	18	7	8	13	12	12	13	14	12	10	9
12	16 36	13 14	23	21	7	7	14	12	17	18	21	20	9	11	16	14	14	16	16	15	12	11
24	19 24	15 26	26	23	9	10	16	14	19	21	24	23	12	13	18	16	16	19	18	17	14	13
36	22 13	17 38	29	25	11	12	19	17	21	24	27	25	14	16	21	19	19	21	21	19	16	15
48	25 03	19 49	♍1	28	14	15	22	19	24	26	29	28	16	19	24	21	21	24	23	22	18	17
8 0	27 55	22 01	4	≏0	16	18	24	21	26	29	♍2	≏0	19	21	27	23	23	27	26	24	20	19
12	0♌47	24 13	6	2	18	20	27	24	28	♏2	5	2	21	24	29	26	26	29	29	26	22	21
24	3 41	26 24	9	5	20	23	♍0	26	✗1	5	8	5	24	27	♍2	28	28	♏2	♍1	29	24	23
36	6 37	28 35	12	7	23	26	2	29	3	7	10	7	26	29	5	≏0	✗0	5	4	≏1	26	25
48	9 34	0♍46	14	9	25	28	5	≏1	6	10	13	10	29	♏2	8	3	3	8	7	4	28	27
9 0	12 32	2 57	17	12	27	♏1	8	3	8	13	16	12	✗1	5	10	5	5	11	9	6	✗0	♏0
12	15 32	5 08	19	14	✗0	4	11	6	11	16	19	15	3	8	13	8	7	13	12	9	2	2
24	18 34	7 19	22	16	2	7	13	8	13	19	22	17	6	11	16	10	10	16	15	11	4	4
36	21 37	9 30	25	18	4	9	16	11	15	22	24	20	8	14	19	12	12	19	18	14	6	6
48	24 42	11 42	27	21	7	12	19	13	18	25	27	22	11	17	22	15	14	22	20	16	8	8
10 0	27 49	13 53	≏0	23	9	15	22	15	21	28	≏0	25	13	19	24	17	17	25	23	19	10	10
12	0♍57	16 04	3	25	11	18	25	18	23	♋1	3	27	16	23	27	20	19	28	26	21	12	12
24	4 07	18 16	5	28	14	21	27	20	26	5	6	♏0	18	26	≏0	22	21	♋1	29	24	14	15
36	7 18	20 28	8	♏0	16	25	≏0	22	29	8	8	2	21	29	3	25	24	4	≏2	26	16	17
48	10 30	22 40	11	2	19	28	3	25	♋1	11	11	4	24	♋2	6	27	26	7	5	29	18	19
11 0	13 43	24 53	13	4	21	♋1	6	27	4	15	14	7	26	5	9	♏0	29	10	8	♏1	20	22
12	16 57	27 06	16	7	24	5	8	♏0	7	18	17	9	29	8	12	2	✗1	13	10	4	22	24
24	20 12	29 21	18	9	27	8	11	2	10	22	20	12	✗2	12	15	5	3	16	13	6	24	27
36	23 28	1✗36	21	11	29	12	14	4	13	25	22	14	4	15	18	7	6	19	16	9	27	♋0
48	26 44	3 52	24	14	♋2	15	17	7	16	29	25	16	7	19	21	10	8	22	19	11	29	2
12 0	0≏00	6 10	26	16	5	19	20	9	19	♋3	28	19	10	22	24	12	11	26	22	14	♋1	5

298

SID TIME (h m)	MC LONG	ASC 1	REGIOMONT 11	12	2	3	CAMPANUS 11	12	2	3	PLACIDUS 11	12	2	3	NAT. GRAD. 11	12	2	3	KOCH 11	12	2	3
12 0	0≏00	6♐10	26	16	5	19	20	9	19	♓3	28	19	10	22	24	12	11	26	22	14	♑1	5
12	3 16	8 29	29	18	8	23	22	11	23	6	♏1	21	13	26	27	15	13	29	25	16	3	8
24	6 32	10 49	♏1	20	11	27	25	14	26	10	3	24	16	29	♏0	17	16	♓2	28	19	6	11
36	9 48	13 11	4	23	14	♓1	28	16	≈0	14	6	26	20	♓3	3	20	18	5	♏1	22	8	14
48	13 03	15 36	7	25	17	5	♏1	18	3	18	9	29	23	7	6	23	21	8	4	24	11	18
13 0	16 17	18 03	9	27	21	9	3	21	7	22	12	♐1	26	11	9	25	23	11	6	27	14	21
12	19 30	20 33	12	♐0	24	13	6	23	11	26	14	3	≈0	15	12	28	26	14	9	29	16	25
24	22 42	23 06	14	2	28	17	9	26	15	♈0	17	6	3	18	15	♐1	28	18	12	♐2	19	29
36	25 53	25 42	17	4	≈1	21	11	28	19	4	20	8	7	22	18	4	≈1	21	15	4	22	♓3
48	29 03	28 22	19	7	5	26	14	♐0	24	8	22	11	11	26	21	6	4	24	18	7	26	7
14 0	2♏11	1♐07	22	9	9	♈0	17	3	28	12	25	13	15	♈0	24	9	6	27	21	10	29	11
12	5 18	3 57	24	11	14	4	19	5	♓3	16	28	16	19	4	27	12	9	♈0	24	12	≈2	15
24	8 23	6 52	27	14	18	9	22	8	8	19	♐0	18	23	8	♐0	15	12	3	26	15	6	20
36	11 26	9 53	♐0	16	23	13	25	10	13	23	3	21	27	12	3	18	15	6	29	18	10	24
48	14 28	13 02	2	19	28	17	27	13	18	27	5	24	♓2	15	6	21	18	9	♐2	21	14	29
15 0	17 28	16 18	5	21	♓3	21	♐0	15	23	♉1	8	26	6	19	9	24	22	12	5	24	18	♈4
12	20 26	19 43	7	24	8	25	3	18	28	4	11	29	11	23	12	28	25	15	8	27	23	8
24	23 23	23 18	10	27	13	29	5	20	♈3	8	13	♉2	16	27	16	♏1	29	18	11	♏0	27	13
36	26 19	27 04	12	29	19	♉3	8	23	8	12	16	4	20	♉1	19	5	♓2	21	13	3	♓2	18
48	29 13	1≈01	15	♉2	24	7	10	25	13	15	19	7	25	4	22	8	6	24	16	6	8	23
16 0	2♐05	5 12	18	5	♈0	11	13	28	18	19	21	10	♈0	8	25	12	10	27	19	9	13	28
12	4 57	9 36	20	8	6	15	16	♉1	23	22	24	13	5	11	28	16	14	♉0	22	12	19	♉2
24	7 47	14 15	23	11	11	18	18	4	28	25	27	16	10	15	♉2	20	19	3	25	16	24	7
36	10 36	19 10	26	14	17	22	21	6	♉3	28	29	20	14	18	5	25	23	7	28	20	♈0	11
48	13 24	24 20	28	17	22	25	24	9	7	♊2	♉2	23	19	22	9	29	28	10	♉1	23	6	15
17 0	16 11	29 47	♉1	21	27	29	26	12	12	5	5	26	24	25	12	≈4	♈3	13	4	27	12	20
12	18 58	5♓28	4	24	♉2	♊2	29	15	16	8	8	≈0	28	28	16	9	8	16	8	≈2	18	24
24	21 44	11 23	7	28	7	5	♉2	19	20	11	11	3	♉3	♊1	19	14	14	20	11	6	24	28
36	24 30	17 29	9	≈1	12	9	5	22	24	14	14	7	7	4	23	19	19	23	14	10	29	♊2
48	27 15	23 42	12	5	16	12	8	25	27	17	17	11	11	7	26	25	24	26	18	15	♉5	5
18 0	0♑00	0♈00	15	9	21	15	10	29	♊1	20	19	15	15	11	≈0	♈0	♉0	♊0	21	20	10	9
12	2 45	6 18	18	14	25	18	13	≈3	5	22	23	19	19	13	4	6	5	4	25	25	15	12
24	5 30	12 31	21	18	29	21	16	6	8	25	26	23	23	16	7	11	11	7	28	♓1	20	16
36	8 16	18 37	25	23	♊2	23	19	10	11	28	29	27	27	19	10	16	16	11	≈2	6	24	19
48	11 02	24 32	28	28	6	26	22	14	15	♊1	≈2	♈2	♊0	22	14	22	21	14	6	12	28	22
19 0	13 49	0♉13	≈1	♓3	9	29	25	18	18	4	5	6	4	25	17	27	26	18	10	18	♊3	26
12	16 36	5 40	5	8	13	♋2	28	23	21	6	8	11	7	28	20	♈2	♊1	21	15	24	7	29
24	19 24	10 50	8	13	16	4	≈2	27	24	9	12	16	10	♋1	23	7	5	25	19	♈0	10	♋2
36	22 13	15 45	12	19	19	7	5	♓2	26	12	15	20	14	3	27	11	10	28	23	6	14	5
48	25 03	20 24	15	24	22	10	8	7	29	14	19	25	17	6	♓0	16	14	♋2	28	11	18	8
20 0	27 55	24 48	19	♈0	25	12	11	12	♋2	17	22	♈0	20	9	3	20	18	5	♓2	17	21	11
12	0≈47	28 59	23	6	28	15	15	17	5	20	26	5	23	11	6	24	22	8	7	22	24	14
24	3 41	2♊56	27	11	♋1	18	18	22	7	22	29	10	26	14	9	28	25	11	12	28	27	17
36	6 37	6 42	♓1	17	3	20	22	27	10	25	♓3	14	28	17	12	♉1	29	14	17	♉3	♋0	19
48	9 34	10 17	5	22	6	23	26	♈2	12	27	7	19	♋1	19	15	5	♋2	18	22	7	3	22
21 0	12 32	13 42	9	27	9	25	29	7	15	♋0	11	24	4	22	18	8	6	21	26	12	6	25
12	15 32	16 58	13	♉2	11	28	♓3	12	17	3	15	28	6	25	21	12	9	24	♈1	16	9	28
24	18 34	20 07	17	7	14	♌0	7	17	20	5	18	♉3	9	27	24	15	12	27	6	20	12	♌1
36	21 37	23 08	21	12	16	3	11	22	22	8	22	7	12	♌0	27	18	15	♌0	10	24	15	4
48	24 42	26 03	26	16	19	6	14	27	25	11	26	11	14	2	♈0	21	18	3	15	28	18	6
22 0	27 49	28 53	♈0	21	21	8	18	♉2	27	13	♈0	15	17	5	3	24	21	6	19	♊1	20	9
12	0♓57	1♋38	4	25	23	11	22	6	♌0	16	4	19	19	8	6	26	24	9	23	4	23	12
24	4 07	4 18	9	29	26	13	26	11	2	19	8	23	22	10	9	29	26	12	27	8	26	15
36	7 18	6 54	13	♊2	28	16	♈0	15	4	21	12	27	24	13	12	♊2	29	15	♉1	11	28	18
48	10 30	9 27	17	6	♌0	18	4	19	7	24	15	♊0	27	16	16	4	♌2	18	5	14	♌1	21
23 0	13 43	11 57	21	9	3	21	8	23	9	27	19	4	29	18	19	7	5	21	9	16	3	24
12	16 57	14 24	25	13	5	23	12	27	12	29	23	7	♌1	21	22	9	7	24	12	19	6	26
24	20 12	16 49	29	16	7	26	16	♊0	14	♍2	27	10	4	24	25	12	10	27	16	22	8	29
36	23 28	19 11	♌3	19	10	29	20	4	16	5	♌1	14	6	27	28	14	13	♍0	19	24	11	♍2
48	26 44	21 31	7	22	12	♍1	24	7	19	8	4	17	9	29	♌1	17	15	3	22	27	14	5
24 0	0♈00	23 50	11	25	14	4	27	11	21	10	8	20	11	♍2	4	19	18	6	25	29	16	8

299

SID TIME	MC	ASC	REGIOMONT				CAMPANUS				PLACIDUS				NAT. GRAD.				KOCH			
h m	LONG ♈	1 ♋	11 ♉	12 ♊	2 ♌	3 ♍	11 ♈	12 ♊	2 ♌	3 ♍	11 ♉	12 ♊	2 ♌	3 ♍	11 ♉	12 ♊	2 ♌	3 ♍	11 ♉	12 ♋	2 ♌	3 ♍
0 0	0♈00	25♋22	12	27	15	4	27	11	22	11	8	21	12	2	5	21	19	6	27	♋1	17	8
12	3♈16	27 36	16	♋0	17	7	♉0	14	25	14	12	24	14	5	8	23	21	9	♊0	3	20	11
24	6 32	29 49	19	2	20	9	4	17	27	17	15	27	17	8	11	25	24	12	3	5	22	14
36	9 48	2♌01	23	5	22	12	8	20	29	20	19	♋0	19	11	14	28	26	15	5	8	25	17
48	13 03	4 12	26	8	24	14	11	23	♍2	22	22	2	21	13	17	♋0	29	18	8	10	27	20
1 0	16 17	6 23	♊0	10	26	17	15	26	4	25	25	5	24	16	20	3	♍1	21	10	12	♍0	23
12	19 30	8 33	3	13	29	20	18	29	6	28	29	8	26	19	23	5	4	24	13	14	2	26
24	22 42	10 42	6	15	♍1	22	22	♋2	9	♎1	♊2	10	29	22	26	7	6	27	15	16	5	29
36	25 53	12 51	10	18	3	25	25	4	11	3	5	13	♍1	24	29	10	9	♎0	17	18	7	♎2
48	29 03	14 59	13	20	5	27	28	7	13	6	8	15	3	27	♊2	12	11	3	19	20	10	4
2 0	2♉11	17 08	16	22	7	♎0	♊1	9	16	9	11	18	6	♎0	5	14	14	6	21	22	12	7
12	5 18	19 16	19	25	10	3	5	12	18	12	14	20	8	3	8	16	16	9	24	24	15	10
24	8 23	21 24	22	27	12	5	8	15	21	14	17	23	11	6	11	19	18	11	26	25	17	13
36	11 26	23 32	24	29	14	8	11	17	23	17	20	25	13	8	14	21	21	14	28	27	19	16
48	14 28	25 40	27	♌2	16	10	14	19	25	20	23	28	15	11	17	23	23	17	♋0	29	22	18
3 0	17 28	27 48	♋0	4	19	13	17	22	28	23	26	♌0	18	14	20	26	25	20	2	♌1	24	21
12	20 26	29 56	3	6	21	16	19	24	♎0	25	29	2	20	17	22	28	28	23	4	3	27	24
24	23 23	2♍04	5	8	23	18	22	27	2	28	♋1	5	23	19	25	♌0	♎0	25	6	5	29	26
36	26 19	4 13	8	11	25	21	25	29	5	♏1	4	7	25	22	28	3	2	28	8	7	♎2	29
48	29 13	6 21	11	13	28	23	28	♌1	7	4	7	10	28	25	♋1	5	5	♏1	10	9	4	♏2
4 0	2♊05	8 29	13	15	♎0	26	♋1	4	9	6	9	12	♎0	28	3	7	7	4	12	11	6	4
12	4 57	10 38	16	17	2	28	3	6	12	9	12	14	2	♏0	6	9	9	6	14	13	9	7
24	7 47	12 47	19	20	5	♏1	6	9	14	12	15	17	5	3	9	12	12	9	16	15	11	9
36	10 36	14 56	21	22	7	4	9	11	16	14	17	19	7	6	12	14	14	12	18	17	13	12
48	13 24	17 05	24	24	9	6	11	13	19	17	20	21	10	8	14	16	16	14	20	19	16	14
5 0	16 11	19 14	26	26	11	9	14	16	21	20	23	24	12	11	17	19	19	17	22	21	18	16
12	18 58	21 23	29	29	14	11	17	18	23	22	25	26	15	14	19	21	21	20	24	23	20	19
24	21 44	23 32	♌1	♍1	16	14	19	20	26	25	28	29	17	16	22	23	23	22	26	25	22	21
36	24 30	25 41	4	3	18	16	22	23	28	27	♌0	♍1	19	19	25	25	25	25	♌0	27	24	24
48	27 15	27 51	6	5	20	19	25	25	♏1	♐0	3	3	22	22	27	28	28	27	♌0	29	27	26
6 0	0♋00	0♎00	9	7	23	21	27	27	3	3	6	6	24	24	♌0	♍0	♏0	♐0	2	♍1	29	28
12	2 45	2 09	11	10	25	24	♌0	29	5	5	8	8	27	27	3	2	2	3	4	3	♏1	♐0
24	5 30	4 19	14	12	27	26	3	♍2	7	8	11	11	29	♐0	5	5	5	5	7	5	3	2
36	8 16	6 28	16	14	29	29	5	4	10	11	14	13	♏1	2	8	7	7	8	9	8	5	4
48	11 02	8 37	19	16	♏1	♐1	8	7	12	13	16	15	4	5	10	9	9	11	11	10	7	6
7 0	13 49	10 46	21	19	4	4	10	9	14	16	19	18	6	7	13	11	11	13	14	12	9	8
12	16 36	12 55	24	21	6	6	13	11	17	19	22	20	9	10	16	14	14	16	16	14	11	10
24	19 24	15 04	26	23	8	9	16	14	19	21	24	23	11	13	18	16	16	18	18	17	13	12
36	22 13	17 13	29	25	10	11	18	16	21	24	27	25	13	15	21	18	18	21	21	19	15	14
48	25 03	19 22	♍2	28	13	14	21	18	24	27	♍0	28	16	18	24	21	21	24	24	21	18	16
8 0	27 55	21 31	4	♎0	15	17	24	21	26	29	2	♎0	18	21	26	23	23	27	26	24	19	18
12	0♌47	23 39	7	2	17	19	26	23	29	♏2	5	2	20	23	29	25	25	29	28	26	21	20
24	3 41	25 47	9	5	19	22	29	25	♐1	5	8	5	23	26	♍2	28	28	♐2	♍1	28	23	22
36	6 37	27 56	12	7	22	25	♍2	28	3	8	11	7	25	29	5	♎0	♐0	5	4	♎1	25	24
48	9 34	0♏04	14	9	24	27	5	♎0	6	11	13	10	28	♑1	7	2	2	8	6	3	27	26
9 0	12 32	2 12	17	11	26	♐0	7	2	8	13	16	12	♐0	4	10	5	4	10	9	6	29	28
12	15 32	4 20	20	14	28	3	10	5	11	16	19	15	2	7	13	7	7	13	12	8	♐1	♑0
24	18 34	6 28	22	16	♐1	6	13	7	13	19	22	17	5	10	16	10	10	16	14	11	3	2
36	21 37	8 36	25	18	3	8	16	9	15	22	24	19	7	13	19	12	11	19	17	13	5	4
48	24 42	10 44	27	20	5	11	18	12	18	25	27	22	10	16	21	14	14	22	20	15	6	6
10 0	27 49	12 52	♎0	23	8	14	21	14	21	29	♎0	24	12	19	24	16	16	25	23	18	8	9
12	0♍57	15 01	3	25	10	17	24	17	23	♑2	3	27	15	22	27	19	18	28	26	20	10	11
24	4 07	17 09	5	27	12	20	27	19	26	5	6	29	17	25	♎0	21	20	♑1	28	23	12	13
36	7 18	19 18	8	29	15	24	29	21	28	8	8	♏1	20	28	3	24	23	4	♎1	25	14	15
48	10 30	21 27	10	♏1	17	27	♎2	24	♑1	12	11	4	22	♑1	6	26	25	7	4	28	16	17
11 0	13 43	23 37	13	4	20	♑0	5	26	4	15	14	6	25	5	9	29	27	10	7	♏0	18	20
12	16 57	25 48	16	6	22	4	8	28	7	19	17	9	28	8	12	♏1	♑0	13	10	3	20	22
24	20 12	27 59	18	8	25	7	10	♏1	10	22	19	11	♑0	11	15	4	2	16	13	5	22	25
36	23 28	0♐11	21	10	28	11	13	3	13	26	22	13	3	15	18	6	5	19	16	8	25	27
48	26 44	2 24	23	13	♑0	14	16	5	16	♑0	25	16	6	18	21	9	7	22	19	10	27	♑0
12 0	0♎00	4 38	26	15	3	18	19	8	19	3	28	18	9	22	24	11	9	25	22	13	29	3

SID TIME	MC	ASC	REGIOMONT				CAMPANUS				PLACIDUS				NAT. GRAD.				KOCH			
TIME	LONG	1	11	12	2	3	11	12	2	3	11	12	2	3	11	12	2	3	11	12	2	3
h m	♎	♐	♎	♏	♍	♒	♎	♏	♍	♓	♎	♏	♍	♒	♎	♏	♍	♒	♎	♏	♐	♒
12 0	0♎00	4♐38	26	15	3	18	19	8	19	3	28	18	9	22	24	11	9	25	22	13	29	3
12	3 16	6 53	28	17	6	22	21	10	23	7	♏0	20	12	25	27	14	12	28	24	15	♈1	6
24	6 32	9 11	♏1	19	9	26	24	12	26	11	3	23	15	29	♏0	16	14	♓2	27	18	4	9
36	9 48	11 29	4	22	12	♈0	27	15	♒0	15	6	25	18	♓3	2	19	17	5	♏0	20	6	12
48	13 03	13 50	6	24	15	4	♏0	17	3	19	8	28	21	7	5	21	19	8	3	23	9	15
13 0	16 17	16 14	9	26	19	8	2	19	7	23	11	♐0	25	10	8	24	21	11	6	25	11	18
12	19 30	18 40	11	28	22	13	5	22	11	27	14	2	28	14	11	27	24	14	9	28	14	22
24	22 42	21 09	14	♐1	26	17	8	24	16	♈1	16	5	♒2	18	14	29	27	17	12	♐1	17	26
36	25 53	23 41	16	3	29	21	10	26	20	5	19	7	6	22	17	♐2	29	20	14	3	20	♓0
48	29 03	26 18	19	5	♒3	26	13	29	24	9	22	10	9	26	20	5	♒2	23	17	6	23	4
14 0	2♏11	28 59	21	8	8	♈0	16	♐1	29	13	24	12	13	♈0	23	8	5	27	20	8	26	8
12	5 18	1♐45	24	10	12	4	18	3	♓4	17	27	15	18	4	26	11	7	♈0	23	11	29	12
24	8 23	4 36	26	12	16	9	21	6	9	21	♐0	17	22	8	29	14	10	3	26	14	♒3	17
36	11 26	7 34	29	15	21	13	24	8	14	24	2	20	26	12	♐2	17	13	6	28	16	7	22
48	14 28	10 39	♐1	17	26	17	26	11	19	28	5	22	♈1	16	6	20	16	9	♐1	19	11	27
15 0	17 28	13 52	4	20	♓1	22	29	13	25	♉2	7	25	6	20	9	23	20	12	4	22	15	♈2
12	20 26	17 14	6	22	7	26	♐2	16	♈0	6	10	28	10	23	12	26	23	15	7	25	19	7
24	23 23	20 47	9	25	12	♉0	4	18	5	9	13	♈0	15	27	15	29	27	18	10	28	24	12
36	26 19	24 31	11	28	18	4	7	21	10	13	15	3	20	♉1	18	♈3	♈0	21	13	♈1	29	17
48	29 13	28 28	14	♈0	24	8	9	23	16	16	18	6	25	5	21	6	4	24	16	4	♈5	22
16 0	2♐05	2♒39	17	3	♈0	12	12	26	21	20	21	9	♈0	8	24	10	8	27	18	7	10	27
12	4 57	7 06	19	6	6	16	15	29	26	23	23	12	5	12	28	14	12	♉0	21	11	16	♉2
24	7 47	11 49	22	9	12	19	17	♈1	♈1	26	26	15	10	15	♈1	18	17	3	24	14	22	6
36	10 36	16 51	25	12	18	23	20	4	5	♉0	29	18	15	19	5	23	21	6	27	18	29	11
48	13 24	22 12	27	15	23	26	23	7	10	3	♈1	21	20	22	8	27	26	9	♈0	22	♈5	15
17 0	16 11	27 52	♈0	18	29	♈0	25	10	14	6	4	25	24	25	12	♈2	♈1	13	4	26	11	20
12	18 58	3♓50	3	22	♉4	3	28	13	18	9	7	28	29	29	15	7	7	16	7	♈0	18	24
24	21 44	10 06	6	26	9	6	♈1	16	22	12	10	♈2	♉4	♈2	19	13	12	19	10	4	24	28
36	24 30	16 35	8	29	14	10	4	19	26	15	13	6	8	5	23	18	18	23	13	9	♉0	♈2
48	27 15	23 15	11	♈3	18	13	7	23	♈0	19	16	9	12	8	26	24	24	26	17	14	5	6
18 0	0♐00	0♈00	14	8	22	16	9	26	4	21	19	13	17	11	♈0	♈0	♉0	♈0	20	19	11	10
12	2 45	6 45	17	12	27	19	12	♈0	7	23	22	18	21	14	4	6	6	4	24	25	16	13
24	5 30	13 25	20	16	♈1	22	15	4	11	26	25	22	24	17	7	12	12	7	28	♈0	21	17
36	8 16	19 54	24	21	4	24	18	8	14	29	28	26	28	20	11	18	17	11	♈2	6	26	20
48	11 02	26 10	27	26	8	27	21	12	17	♈2	♈1	♈1	♈2	23	14	23	23	15	6	12	♈0	23
19 0	13 49	2♉08	♈0	♈1	11	♈0	24	16	20	5	5	6	5	26	17	29	28	18	10	19	4	26
12	16 36	7 48	4	7	15	3	27	20	23	7	8	10	9	29	21	♈4	♈3	22	15	25	8	♉0
24	19 24	13 09	7	12	18	5	♈0	25	26	10	11	15	12	♈1	24	9	7	25	19	♈1	12	5
36	22 13	18 11	11	18	21	8	4	29	29	13	15	20	15	4	27	13	12	29	24	8	16	6
48	25 03	22 54	14	24	24	11	7	♈4	♈1	15	18	25	18	7	♈0	18	16	♉2	♈0	26	19	9
20 0	27 55	27 21	18	♈0	27	13	10	9	4	18	22	♈0	21	9	3	22	20	6	♉3	20	29	12
12	0♒47	1♈32	22	6	♈0	16	14	14	7	21	25	5	24	12	6	26	24	9	8	25	26	14
24	3 41	5 29	26	12	2	19	17	20	9	23	29	10	27	15	9	♉0	27	12	13	♉1	29	17
36	6 37	9 13	♈0	18	5	21	21	25	12	26	♈3	15	♉0	17	12	4	♉1	15	18	6	♉2	20
48	9 34	12 46	4	23	8	24	24	♈0	14	28	7	20	2	20	15	7	4	18	23	11	5	23
21 0	12 32	16 08	8	29	10	26	28	5	17	♉1	10	24	5	23	18	10	7	21	28	15	8	26
12	15 32	19 21	13	♉4	13	29	♈2	11	19	4	14	29	8	25	21	14	10	24	♈3	19	11	29
24	18 34	22 26	17	9	15	♈1	6	16	22	6	18	♉4	10	28	24	17	13	28	8	23	14	♈2
36	21 37	25 24	21	14	18	4	9	21	24	9	22	8	13	♈0	27	20	16	♉1	13	27	16	4
48	24 42	28 15	26	18	20	6	13	26	27	12	26	12	15	3	♈0	23	19	4	18	♈1	19	7
22 0	27 49	1♉01	♈0	22	22	9	17	♉1	29	14	♈0	17	18	6	3	25	22	7	22	4	22	10
12	0♓57	3 42	4	27	25	11	21	6	♉1	17	4	21	20	8	7	28	25	10	26	7	24	13
24	4 07	6 19	9	♉1	27	14	25	10	4	20	8	24	23	11	10	♉1	28	13	♉0	10	27	16
36	7 18	8 51	13	4	29	16	29	14	6	22	12	28	25	14	13	3	♉1	16	4	13	29	18
48	10 30	11 20	17	8	♉2	19	♈3	19	8	25	16	♉2	28	16	16	6	3	19	8	16	♉2	21
23 0	13 43	13 46	22	11	4	21	7	23	11	28	20	5	♉0	19	19	9	6	22	12	19	5	24
12	16 10	16 10	26	15	6	24	11	27	13	♍0	23	9	2	22	22	♈0	9	25	15	21	7	26
24	20 12	18 31	♉0	18	8	26	15	♉0	15	3	27	12	5	24	25	13	11	28	18	24	10	♍0
36	23 28	20 49	4	21	11	29	19	4	18	6	♉1	15	7	27	28	16	14	♍0	21	26	12	3
48	26 44	23 07	8	24	13	♍2	23	7	20	9	5	18	10	♍0	♉2	18	16	3	24	29	15	6
24 0	0♈00	25 22	12	27	15	4	27	11	22	11	8	21	12	2	5	21	19	6	27	♋1	17	8

301

SID TIME	MC LONG	ASC	REGIOMONT				CAMPANUS				PLACIDUS				NAT. GRAD.				KOCH			
h m	♈	1 ♋	11 ♉	12 ♊	2 ♌	3 ♍	11 ♈	12 ♊	2 ♌	3 ♍	11 ♉	12 ♊	2 ♌	3 ♍	11 ♉	12 ♊	2 ♌	3 ♍	11 ♉	12 ♋	2 ♌	3 ♍
0 0	0♈00	26♋10	12	28	16	4	26	11	23	12	9	22	12	2	5	21	19	7	29	2	18	9
12	3♈16	28 22	16	♋1	18	7	♉0	14	25	14	12	25	15	5	8	24	22	10	♊1	4	20	12
24	6 32	0♌34	20	3	20	9	4	17	28	17	16	28	17	8	11	26	24	13	4	6	23	15
36	9 48	2 44	23	6	22	12	7	20	♍0	20	19	♋1	19	11	14	28	27	16	7	9	25	17
48	13 03	4 53	27	8	24	15	11	23	2	23	22	3	22	13	17	♋1	29	19	9	11	28	20
1 0	16 17	7 02	♊0	11	27	17	14	26	5	25	26	6	24	16	20	3	♍2	21	11	13	♍0	23
12	19 30	9 10	4	13	29	20	18	29	7	28	29	9	27	19	23	5	4	24	14	15	3	26
24	22 42	11 18	7	16	♍1	22	21	♋2	9	♎1	♊2	11	29	22	26	8	7	27	16	17	5	29
36	25 53	13 25	10	18	3	25	25	4	12	4	5	14	♍1	24	29	10	9	♎0	18	18	7	♎2
48	29 03	15 32	13	21	5	27	28	7	14	6	9	16	4	27	♊2	12	12	3	20	20	10	5
2 0	2♉11	17 39	16	23	8	♎0	♊1	9	16	9	12	19	6	♎0	5	15	14	6	22	22	12	7
12	5 18	19 46	19	25	10	3	4	12	19	12	15	21	8	3	8	17	16	9	24	24	15	10
24	8 23	21 52	22	28	12	5	7	15	21	15	18	23	11	6	11	19	19	11	26	26	17	13
36	11 26	23 59	25	♌0	14	8	10	17	23	17	20	26	13	8	14	21	21	14	28	28	20	16
48	14 28	26 05	28	2	17	10	13	19	26	20	23	28	16	11	17	24	23	17	♋0	♌0	22	18
3 0	17 28	28 11	♌0	4	19	13	16	22	28	23	26	♋1	18	14	20	26	26	20	2	2	25	21
12	20 26	0♍18	3	7	21	15	19	24	♎0	26	29	3	20	17	22	28	28	23	4	4	27	24
24	23 23	2 25	6	9	23	18	22	27	3	28	♋2	5	23	19	25	♌1	♎0	26	6	5	29	26
36	26 19	4 31	9	11	26	21	25	29	5	♏1	4	8	25	22	28	3	3	28	8	7	♎2	29
48	29 13	6 38	11	13	28	23	28	♌1	7	4	7	10	28	25	♋1	5	5	♏1	10	9	4	♏2
4 0	2♊05	8 45	14	16	♎0	26	♋0	4	10	6	10	12	♎0	28	4	7	7	4	12	11	7	4
12	4 57	10 52	16	18	2	28	3	6	12	9	12	15	2	♏0	6	10	10	6	14	13	9	7
24	7 47	12 59	19	20	4	♏1	6	8	14	12	15	17	5	3	9	12	12	9	16	15	11	9
36	10 36	15 07	22	22	7	3	9	11	17	14	18	19	7	6	12	14	14	12	18	17	13	12
48	13 24	17 14	24	24	9	6	11	13	19	17	20	22	10	8	14	16	16	14	20	19	16	14
5 0	16 11	19 22	27	27	11	8	14	15	21	20	23	24	12	11	17	19	19	17	22	21	18	16
12	18 58	21 29	29	29	13	11	17	18	24	22	25	27	14	14	20	21	21	20	24	23	20	19
24	21 44	23 37	♌2	♍1	16	13	19	20	26	25	28	29	17	16	22	23	23	22	26	25	22	21
36	24 30	25 44	4	3	18	16	22	23	28	28	♌1	♍1	19	19	25	25	25	25	28	27	25	23
48	27 15	27 52	7	5	20	18	24	25	♏1	♐0	3	4	22	21	27	28	28	27	♌0	29	27	26
6 0	0♋00	0♎00	9	8	22	21	27	27	3	3	6	6	24	24	♌0	♍0	♏0	♐0	2	♍1	29	28
12	2 45	2 08	12	10	25	23	♌0	29	5	6	9	8	26	27	3	2	2	3	4	3	♏1	♐0
24	5 30	4 16	14	12	27	26	2	♍2	8	8	11	11	29	29	5	5	5	5	7	5	3	2
36	8 16	6 23	17	14	29	28	5	4	10	11	14	13	♏1	♐2	8	7	7	8	9	8	5	4
48	11 02	8 31	19	17	♏1	♐1	8	6	13	13	16	16	3	5	10	9	9	10	11	10	7	6
7 0	13 49	10 38	22	19	3	3	10	9	15	16	19	18	6	7	13	11	11	13	14	12	9	8
12	16 36	12 46	24	21	6	6	13	11	17	19	22	20	8	10	16	14	14	16	16	14	11	10
24	19 24	14 53	27	23	8	8	16	13	19	21	24	23	11	12	18	16	16	18	18	17	13	12
36	22 13	17 01	29	26	10	11	18	16	22	24	27	25	13	15	21	18	18	21	21	19	15	14
48	25 03	19 08	♍2	28	12	14	21	18	24	27	♍0	28	15	18	24	20	20	24	23	21	17	16
8 0	27 55	21 15	4	♎0	14	16	24	20	26	♑0	2	♎0	18	20	26	23	23	26	26	23	19	18
12	0♌47	23 22	7	2	17	19	26	23	29	2	5	2	20	23	29	25	25	29	28	26	21	20
24	3 41	25 29	9	4	19	21	29	25	♐1	5	8	5	23	25	♍2	27	27	♑2	♍1	28	23	22
36	6 37	27 35	12	7	21	24	♎2	27	4	7	11	7	25	28	4	♎0	29	5	4	♎1	25	24
48	9 34	29 42	15	9	23	27	4	♎0	6	11	13	10	27	♑1	7	2	♐2	8	6	3	26	26
9 0	12 32	1♏49	17	11	26	♑0	7	2	8	14	16	12	♐0	4	10	4	4	10	9	5	28	28
12	15 32	3 55	20	13	28	2	10	4	11	17	19	14	♐2	6	13	7	6	13	12	8	♐0	♑0
24	18 34	6 01	22	16	♐0	5	13	7	13	20	22	17	4	10	16	9	9	16	14	10	2	2
36	21 37	8 08	25	18	2	8	15	9	15	22	24	19	7	12	18	11	11	19	17	13	4	4
48	24 42	10 14	27	20	5	11	18	11	18	26	27	22	9	15	21	14	13	22	20	15	6	6
10 0	27 49	12 21	♎0	22	7	14	21	14	21	29	♎0	24	11	18	24	16	15	25	23	18	8	8
12	0♍57	14 28	3	25	9	17	24	16	23	♒2	3	26	14	20	27	18	18	28	25	20	10	10
24	4 07	16 35	5	27	12	20	26	18	26	5	6	29	16	25	♎0	21	20	♒1	28	23	12	12
36	7 18	18 42	8	29	14	23	29	21	28	9	8	♏1	19	28	3	23	22	4	♎1	25	13	14
48	10 30	20 50	10	♏1	17	26	♎2	23	♑1	12	11	3	21	♒1	6	26	25	7	4	27	15	16
11 0	13 43	22 58	13	3	19	♒0	5	25	4	16	14	6	24	4	9	28	27	10	7	♏0	17	19
12	16 57	25 07	15	6	22	3	7	28	7	19	17	8	27	8	11	♏1	29	13	10	2	19	21
24	20 12	27 16	17	8	24	7	10	♏0	10	23	19	11	29	11	14	3	♑2	16	13	5	21	23
36	23 28	29 26	21	10	27	10	13	2	13	26	22	13	♒2	14	17	6	4	19	15	7	24	26
48	26 44	1♐38	23	12	29	14	16	5	16	♓0	25	15	5	18	20	8	6	22	18	10	26	29
12 0	0♎00	3 50	26	14	♑2	18	18	7	19	4	28	18	8	21	23	11	9	25	21	12	28	♒1

SID TIME	MC LONG	ASC 1	REG 11	REG 12	REG 2	REG 3	CAM 11	CAM 12	CAM 2	CAM 3	PLA 11	PLA 12	PLA 2	PLA 3	NAT 11	NAT 12	NAT 2	NAT 3	KOC 11	KOC 12	KOC 2	KOC 3
h m	♎	♐	♎	♏	♌	≈	♎	♏	♌	♓	♎	♏	♌	≈	♎	♏	♌	≈	♎	♏	♐	≈
12 0	0♎00	3♐50	26	14	♉2	18	18	7	19	4	28	18	8	21	23	11	9	25	21	12	28	≈1
12	3 16	6 04	28	17	5	22	21	9	23	8	♏0	20	11	25	26	13	11	28	24	15	♉0	4
24	6 32	8 19	♏1	19	8	26	24	11	26	12	3	22	14	29	29	16	13	♓2	27	17	2	7
36	9 48	10 36	3	21	11	♐0	27	14	≈0	15	6	25	17	♓3	♏2	18	16	5	♏0	20	5	10
48	13 03	12 55	6	23	14	4	29	16	4	19	8	27	21	6	5	21	18	8	3	22	7	13
13 0	16 17	15 16	8	26	18	8	♏2	18	8	23	11	29	24	10	8	23	21	11	6	25	10	17
12	19 30	17 40	11	28	21	12	5	21	12	27	14	♐2	27	14	11	26	23	14	8	27	12	20
24	22 42	20 07	13	♐0	25	17	7	23	16	♈1	16	4	≈1	18	14	29	26	17	11	♐0	15	24
36	25 53	22 38	16	2	28	21	10	25	20	5	19	7	5	22	17	♐1	28	20	14	3	18	28
48	29 03	25 12	18	5	≈2	26	13	28	25	9	21	9	9	26	20	4	≈1	23	17	5	21	♓2
14 0	2♏11	27 51	21	7	6	♈0	15	♐0	♈0	13	24	11	13	♈0	23	7	4	26	20	8	24	6
12	5 18	0♉34	23	9	11	4	18	2	5	17	27	14	17	4	26	10	6	♈0	22	10	28	11
24	8 23	3 23	26	12	15	9	21	5	10	21	29	16	21	8	29	13	9	3	25	13	≈1	16
36	11 26	6 19	28	14	20	13	23	7	15	25	♐2	19	26	12	♐2	16	12	6	28	16	5	20
48	14 28	9 22	♐1	17	25	18	26	10	20	29	5	21	♈0	16	5	19	15	9	♐1	18	9	25
15 0	17 28	12 33	3	19	♈1	22	28	12	26	♉3	7	24	5	20	8	22	18	12	4	21	13	♈0
12	20 26	15 53	6	22	6	26	♈1	15	♈1	6	10	27	10	24	11	25	22	15	7	24	18	6
24	23 23	19 24	8	24	12	♉0	4	17	6	10	12	29	15	27	14	28	25	18	9	27	22	11
36	26 19	23 07	11	27	18	4	6	20	12	13	15	♉2	20	♉1	18	♉2	29	21	12	♉0	28	16
48	29 13	27 03	14	29	24	8	9	22	17	17	18	5	25	5	21	5	♈3	24	15	3	♈3	21
16 0	2♐05	1≈14	16	♉2	♈0	12	12	25	22	20	20	8	♈0	9	24	9	7	27	18	7	9	26
12	4 57	5 41	19	5	6	16	14	27	27	24	23	11	5	12	27	13	11	♉0	21	10	15	♉1
24	7 47	10 27	21	8	12	20	17	♉0	♉2	27	26	14	10	16	♉1	17	15	3	24	13	21	6
36	10 36	15 32	24	11	18	23	20	3	7	♈0	28	17	15	19	4	22	20	6	27	17	28	11
48	13 24	20 58	27	14	24	27	22	6	11	3	♉1	21	20	22	8	27	25	9	♉0	21	♈4	15
17 0	16 11	26 45	♉0	18	29	♊0	25	9	16	6	4	24	25	26	11	≈2	♈1	12	3	25	11	20
12	18 58	2≈33	2	21	♉5	4	28	12	20	9	7	27	♉0	29	15	7	6	16	6	29	17	24
24	21 44	9 20	5	25	10	7	♉0	15	24	12	10	≈1	4	♊2	19	12	12	19	10	≈4	24	28
36	24 30	16 04	8	28	15	10	3	18	28	15	12	5	9	5	23	18	18	23	13	8	♉0	♊2
48	27 15	22 59	11	≈2	19	13	6	21	♊2	18	15	9	13	9	26	24	24	26	17	13	6	6
18 0	0♐00	0♈00	14	6	24	16	9	25	5	21	18	13	17	12	≈0	♈0	♉0	♊0	20	19	11	10
12	2 45	7 01	17	11	28	19	12	28	9	24	21	17	21	15	4	6	6	4	24	24	17	13
24	5 30	13 56	20	15	♊2	22	15	≈2	12	27	25	21	25	18	7	12	12	7	28	♈0	22	17
36	8 16	20 40	23	20	5	25	18	6	15	♋0	28	26	29	20	11	18	18	11	≈2	6	26	20
48	11 02	27 07	26	25	9	28	21	10	18	2	≈1	♈0	♊3	23	14	24	23	15	6	13	♊1	24
19 0	13 49	3♈15	≈0	♈1	12	♋0	24	14	21	5	4	5	6	26	18	29	28	19	10	19	5	27
12	16 36	9 02	3	6	16	3	27	19	24	8	8	10	9	29	21	♈5	♊3	22	15	26	9	♋0
24	19 24	14 28	7	12	19	6	≈0	23	27	10	11	15	13	♋2	24	10	8	26	19	♈2	13	3
36	22 13	19 33	10	18	22	9	3	28	♋0	13	14	20	16	4	27	15	13	29	24	9	17	6
48	25 03	24 19	14	24	25	11	6	♈3	3	16	18	25	19	7	♈0	19	17	♋3	29	15	20	9
20 0	27 55	28 46	18	♈0	28	14	10	8	5	18	21	♈0	22	10	3	23	21	6	♈4	21	23	12
12	0≈47	2♉57	22	6	♋1	16	13	13	8	21	25	5	25	12	6	27	25	9	9	27	27	15
24	3 41	6 53	26	12	3	19	17	18	10	24	29	10	28	15	9	♉1	28	12	14	♉2	♋0	18
36	6 37	10 36	♈0	18	6	22	20	24	13	26	♈3	15	♋1	18	12	5	♋2	16	19	8	3	21
48	9 34	14 07	4	24	8	24	24	29	15	29	6	20	3	20	15	8	5	19	24	12	6	23
21 0	12 32	17 27	8	29	11	27	27	♉4	18	♌2	10	25	6	23	18	12	8	22	♉0	17	9	26
12	15 32	20 38	12	♉5	13	29	♈1	10	20	4	14	♉0	9	25	21	15	11	25	5	21	12	29
24	18 34	23 41	17	10	16	♌2	5	15	23	7	18	4	11	28	24	18	14	28	10	25	14	♌2
36	21 37	26 37	21	15	18	4	9	20	25	9	22	9	14	♌1	27	21	17	♌1	14	29	17	5
48	24 42	29 26	26	19	21	7	13	25	28	12	26	13	16	3	♉0	24	20	4	19	♉2	20	8
22 0	27 49	2♊09	♈0	24	23	9	17	♉0	♌0	15	♈0	17	19	6	4	26	23	7	24	6	22	10
12	0♓57	4 48	4	28	25	12	21	5	2	17	4	21	21	9	7	29	26	10	28	9	25	13
24	4 07	7 22	9	♊2	28	14	25	10	5	20	8	25	23	11	10	♊2	29	13	♉2	12	27	16
36	7 18	9 53	13	5	♌0	17	29	14	7	23	12	29	26	14	13	4	♌1	16	6	15	♌0	19
48	10 30	12 20	18	9	2	19	♊3	18	9	25	16	♊3	28	16	16	7	4	19	10	18	3	22
23 0	13 43	14 44	22	12	4	22	7	22	12	28	20	6	♌1	19	19	9	7	22	13	20	5	24
12	16 57	17 05	26	16	7	24	11	26	14	♍1	24	9	3	22	22	12	9	25	17	23	8	27
24	20 12	19 24	♊0	19	9	27	15	♊0	16	3	27	13	5	24	25	14	12	28	20	25	10	♍0
36	23 28	21 41	4	22	11	29	18	4	19	6	♊1	16	8	27	28	17	14	♍1	23	28	13	3
48	26 44	23 56	8	25	13	♍2	22	7	21	9	5	19	10	♍0	♊2	19	17	4	26	♊0	15	6
24 0	0♈00	26 10	12	28	16	4	26	11	23	12	9	22	12	2	5	21	19	7	29	2	18	9

Legend — each house system has columns **11, 12, 2, 3**.
Sign glyphs in header: MC = ♈ · ASC = ♋ · REGIOMONT = ♉ ♊ ♌ ♍ · CAMPANUS = ♈ ♊ ♌ ♍ · PLACIDUS = ♉ ♊ ♌ ♍ · NAT. GRAD. = ♉ ♊ ♌ ♍ · KOCH = ♊ ♋ ♌ ♍

SID TIME h m	MC LONG	ASC 1	REG 11	REG 12	REG 2	REG 3	CAM 11	CAM 12	CAM 2	CAM 3	PLA 11	PLA 12	PLA 2	PLA 3	NAT 11	NAT 12	NAT 2	NAT 3	KOCH 11	KOCH 12	KOCH 2	KOCH 3
0 0	0♈00	26♋34	13	28	16	4	26	11	23	12	9	22	13	3	5	22	20	7	♊0	3	18	9
0 12	3♈16	28 46	16	♋1	18	7	♉0	14	26	15	12	25	15	5	8	24	22	10	2	5	20	12
0 24	6 32	0♌56	20	4	20	10	3	17	28	17	16	28	17	8	11	26	25	13	5	7	23	15
0 36	9 48	3 06	24	6	22	12	7	20	♍0	20	19	♋1	20	11	14	29	27	16	7	9	25	17
0 48	13 03	5 14	27	9	25	15	11	23	3	23	23	4	22	13	17	♋1	♍0	19	10	11	28	20
1 0	16 17	7 22	♊1	11	27	17	14	26	5	26	26	6	24	16	20	3	2	22	12	13	♍0	23
1 12	19 30	9 29	4	14	29	20	18	29	7	28	29	9	27	19	23	6	5	24	14	15	3	26
1 24	22 42	11 36	7	16	♍1	22	21	♋2	10	♎1	♊3	11	29	22	26	8	7	27	16	17	5	29
1 36	25 53	13 43	10	19	3	25	25	4	12	4	6	14	♍1	24	29	10	9	♎0	19	19	8	♎2
1 48	29 03	15 49	13	21	6	27	28	7	14	7	9	16	4	27	♊2	13	12	3	21	21	10	5
2 0	2♉11	17 55	16	23	8	♎0	♊1	9	17	9	12	19	6	♎0	5	15	14	6	23	23	13	7
2 12	5 18	20 01	19	26	10	3	4	12	19	12	15	21	8	3	8	17	16	9	25	25	15	10
2 24	8 23	22 06	22	28	12	5	7	15	21	15	18	24	11	6	11	19	19	12	27	26	17	13
2 36	11 26	24 12	25	♌0	14	8	10	17	24	18	21	26	13	8	14	22	21	14	29	28	20	16
2 48	14 28	26 18	28	3	17	10	13	19	26	20	23	29	16	11	17	24	23	17	♋1	♌0	22	18
3 0	17 28	28 23	♋1	5	19	13	16	22	28	23	26	♌1	18	14	20	26	26	20	3	2	25	21
3 12	20 26	0♍29	3	7	21	15	19	24	♎1	26	29	3	20	17	23	28	28	23	5	4	27	24
3 24	23 23	2 35	6	9	23	18	22	27	3	29	♋2	6	23	19	25	♋1	♎0	26	6	6	♎0	27
3 36	26 19	4 41	9	11	26	20	25	29	5	♏1	5	8	25	22	28	3	3	28	8	8	2	29
3 48	29 13	6 47	11	14	28	23	28	♌1	8	4	7	10	28	25	♋1	5	5	♏1	10	9	4	♏2
4 0	2♊05	8 53	14	16	♎0	26	♌0	4	10	7	10	13	♎0	27	4	7	7	4	12	11	7	4
4 12	4 57	10 59	17	18	2	28	3	6	12	9	13	15	2	♏0	6	10	10	6	14	13	9	7
4 24	7 47	13 06	19	20	4	♏1	6	8	15	12	15	17	5	3	9	12	14	12	16	15	11	9
4 36	10 36	15 12	22	22	7	3	9	11	17	15	18	20	7	6	12	14	14	12	18	17	14	12
4 48	13 24	17 19	24	25	9	6	11	13	19	17	20	22	10	8	14	16	16	14	20	19	16	14
5 0	16 11	19 26	27	27	11	8	14	15	22	20	23	24	12	11	17	19	19	17	22	21	18	16
5 12	18 58	21 32	29	29	13	11	16	18	24	23	26	27	14	13	20	21	21	20	24	23	20	19
5 24	21 44	23 39	♌2	♍1	16	13	19	20	26	25	28	29	17	16	22	23	23	22	26	25	22	21
5 36	24 30	25 46	4	3	18	16	22	22	29	28	♌1	♍1	19	19	25	25	25	25	28	27	25	23
5 48	27 15	27 53	7	6	20	18	24	25	♏1	♐0	3	4	22	21	27	28	28	27	♌0	29	27	25
6 0	0♋00	0♎00	9	8	22	21	27	27	3	3	6	6	24	24	♌0	♍0	♏0	♐0	2	♍1	29	28
6 12	2 45	2 07	12	10	24	23	♎0	29	5	6	9	8	26	27	3	2	2	3	5	3	♏1	♐0
6 24	5 30	4 14	14	12	27	26	2	♏1	8	8	11	11	29	29	5	5	5	5	7	5	3	2
6 36	8 16	6 21	17	14	29	28	5	4	10	11	14	13	♏1	♐2	8	7	7	8	9	8	5	4
6 48	11 02	8 28	19	17	♏1	♐1	7	6	12	14	17	16	3	4	9	9	9	10	11	10	7	6
7 0	13 49	10 34	22	19	3	3	10	8	15	16	19	18	6	7	13	11	11	13	14	12	9	8
7 12	16 36	12 41	24	21	5	6	13	11	17	19	22	20	8	10	16	14	14	16	16	14	11	10
7 24	19 24	14 48	27	23	8	8	15	13	19	21	24	23	10	12	18	16	16	18	18	16	13	12
7 36	22 13	16 54	29	26	10	11	18	15	22	24	27	25	13	15	21	18	18	21	21	19	15	14
7 48	25 03	19 01	♍2	28	12	13	21	18	24	27	♍0	28	15	17	24	20	20	24	23	21	17	16
8 0	27 55	21 07	4	♎0	14	16	23	20	26	♑0	3	♎0	17	20	26	23	23	26	26	23	19	18
8 12	0♌47	23 13	7	2	16	19	26	22	29	2	5	2	20	23	29	25	25	29	28	26	21	20
8 24	3 41	25 19	10	4	19	21	29	25	♐1	5	8	5	22	25	♍2	27	27	♑2	♍1	28	22	22
8 36	6 37	27 25	12	7	21	24	♏1	27	3	8	11	7	24	28	7	♎0	♐0	7	3	♎0	24	24
8 48	9 34	29 31	15	9	23	27	4	29	6	11	13	10	27	♑1	7	2	2	7	6	3	26	25
9 0	12 32	1♏32	17	11	25	29	7	♏2	8	14	16	12	29	4	10	4	4	10	9	5	28	27
9 12	15 32	3 42	20	13	27	♑2	10	4	11	17	19	14	♐1	7	13	6	6	13	12	8	♐0	29
9 24	18 34	5 48	22	16	♐0	5	12	6	13	20	22	17	4	9	16	9	8	16	14	10	2	♑1
9 36	21 37	7 54	25	18	2	8	15	9	15	23	24	19	6	12	18	11	11	19	17	13	4	3
9 48	24 42	9 59	27	20	4	11	18	11	18	26	27	22	9	15	21	14	13	22	20	15	5	5
10 0	27 49	12 05	♎0	22	7	14	21	13	21	29	♎0	24	11	18	24	16	15	25	23	17	7	7
10 12	0♍57	14 11	3	24	9	17	23	16	23	♒2	3	26	14	21	27	18	17	28	25	20	9	9
10 24	4 07	16 17	5	27	11	20	26	18	26	5	6	29	16	24	♎0	21	20	♒1	28	22	11	11
10 36	7 18	18 24	8	29	14	23	29	20	28	9	8	♏1	19	27	3	23	22	4	♎1	25	13	14
10 48	10 30	20 31	10	♏1	16	26	♎2	23	♑1	12	11	3	21	♒0	6	25	24	7	4	27	15	16
11 0	13 43	22 38	13	3	19	29	4	25	4	16	14	6	24	4	8	28	27	10	7	♏0	17	18
11 12	16 57	24 46	15	5	21	♒2	7	27	7	19	17	8	26	7	11	♏0	29	13	10	2	19	20
11 24	20 12	26 54	18	8	24	6	10	♏0	10	23	19	10	29	11	14	3	♑1	16	13	5	21	23
11 36	23 28	29 04	20	10	26	10	13	2	13	27	22	13	♑2	14	17	5	4	19	15	7	23	25
11 48	26 44	1♐14	23	12	29	14	15	4	16	♓0	25	15	5	18	20	8	6	22	18	10	25	28
12 0	0♎00	3 26	26	14	♑2	17	18	7	19	4	27	17	8	21	23	10	8	25	21	12	27	♓0

LAT 51°N 30' CUSPS OF HOUSES SID TIME 12h - 24h

SID TIME	M C LONG	ASC 1	REGIOMONT 11	12	2	3	CAMPANUS 11	12	2	3	PLACIDUS 11	12	2	3	NAT. GRAD. 11	12	2	3	KOCH 11	12	2	3
h m	♎	♐	♎	♏	♑	♒	♎	♏	♑	♓	♎	♏	♑	♒	♎	♏	♑	♒	♎	♏	♐	♒
12 0	0♎00	3♐26	26	14	♑2	17	18	7	19	4	27	17	8	21	23	10	8	25	21	12	27	♎0
12	3 16	5 38	28	16	5	21	21	9	23	8	m0	20	11	25	26	13	11	28	24	15	29	3
24	6 32	7 53	m1	19	7	25	24	11	26	12	3	22	14	29	29	15	13	♓1	27	17	♑2	6
36	9 48	10 09	3	21	11	29	26	13	♎0	16	6	24	17	♓2	m2	18	15	5	m0	20	4	9
48	13 03	12 27	6	23	14	♓4	29	16	4	20	8	27	20	6	5	20	18	8	3	22	6	13
13 0	16 17	14 47	8	25	17	8	m2	18	8	24	11	29	23	10	8	23	20	11	5	25	9	16
12	19 30	17 10	11	27	20	12	4	20	12	28	13	♐1	27	14	11	26	23	14	8	27	12	19
24	22 42	19 36	13	♐0	24	17	7	23	16	♈2	16	4	♒1	18	14	28	25	17	11	♐0	14	23
36	25 53	22 05	16	2	28	21	10	25	20	6	19	6	4	22	17	♐1	28	20	14	2	17	27
48	29 03	24 38	18	4	♒2	26	12	27	25	10	21	9	8	26	20	4	♒0	23	17	5	20	♓1
14 0	2♏11	27 15	21	7	6	♈0	15	♐0	♓0	14	24	11	12	♈0	23	7	3	26	19	7	23	6
12	5 18	29 58	23	9	10	4	18	2	5	18	27	14	17	4	26	9	6	29	22	10	27	10
24	8 23	2♏46	26	11	15	9	20	4	10	21	29	16	21	8	29	12	9	♈3	25	13	♒0	15
36	11 26	5 40	28	14	20	13	23	7	15	25	♐2	19	25	12	♈2	15	12	6	28	15	4	20
48	14 28	8 42	♐1	16	25	18	26	9	21	29	4	21	♑0	16	5	18	15	9	♈1	18	8	25
15 0	17 28	11 52	3	19	♑0	22	28	12	26	♉3	7	24	5	20	8	21	18	12	4	21	12	♈0
12	20 26	15 11	6	21	6	26	♐1	14	♈2	7	10	26	10	24	11	25	21	15	6	24	17	5
24	23 23	18 41	8	24	12	♉1	3	17	7	10	12	29	15	28	14	28	24	18	9	27	22	10
36	26 19	22 23	11	26	18	5	6	19	12	14	15	♑2	20	♉1	17	♐1	28	21	12	♑0	27	16
48	29 13	26 18	13	29	24	9	9	22	18	17	17	5	25	5	21	5	♈2	24	15	3	♈2	21
16 0	2♐05	0♏29	16	♑2	♈0	13	11	24	23	21	20	8	♈0	9	24	9	6	27	18	6	8	26
12	4 57	4 57	19	5	6	16	14	27	28	24	23	11	5	12	27	13	10	♑0	21	9	14	♑1
24	7 47	9 43	21	7	12	20	17	♑0	♉3	27	25	14	10	16	♑1	17	15	3	24	13	21	6
36	10 36	14 50	24	11	18	24	19	2	♉8	♊0	28	17	15	19	4	21	20	6	27	17	27	11
48	13 24	20 09	27	14	24	27	22	5	12	4	♑1	20	20	23	8	26	25	9	♑0	20	♈4	15
17 0	16 11	26 09	29	17	♉0	♊1	25	8	16	7	4	23	25	26	11	♒1	♈0	12	3	24	11	20
12	18 58	2♒22	♑2	20	5	4	27	11	21	10	7	27	♉0	29	15	6	6	16	6	29	17	24
24	21 44	8 56	5	24	10	7	♑0	14	25	13	9	♒1	5	♊3	19	12	12	19	9	♒3	24	28
36	24 30	15 46	8	28	15	10	3	17	29	16	12	4	9	6	22	18	18	23	13	8	♉0	♊2
48	27 15	22 50	11	♒2	20	13	6	21	♊2	19	15	8	13	9	26	24	24	26	16	13	6	6
18 0	0♐00	0♈00	14	6	24	16	9	24	6	21	18	12	18	12	♒0	♈0	♉0	♊0	20	18	12	10
12	2 45	7 10	17	10	28	19	11	28	9	24	21	17	22	15	4	6	6	4	24	24	17	14
24	5 30	14 14	20	15	♊2	22	14	♒1	13	27	24	21	26	18	7	12	12	8	28	♈0	22	17
36	8 16	21 04	23	20	6	25	17	5	16	♋0	27	25	29	21	11	18	18	11	♒2	6	27	21
48	11 02	27 38	26	25	10	28	20	9	19	3	♒1	♈0	♊3	24	14	24	24	15	6	13	♊1	24
19 0	13 49	3♉51	29	♈0	13	♋1	23	14	22	5	4	5	7	26	18	♈0	29	19	10	19	6	27
12	16 36	9 41	♈3	6	16	3	26	18	25	8	7	10	10	29	21	5	♊4	22	15	26	10	♋0
24	19 24	15 10	6	12	19	6	♒0	22	28	11	11	15	13	♋2	24	10	9	26	19	♈3	13	3
36	22 13	20 17	10	18	23	9	3	27	♋0	13	14	20	16	5	27	15	13	29	24	9	17	6
48	25 03	25 03	14	24	25	11	6	♈2	3	16	18	25	19	7	♈0	20	17	♋3	29	16	21	9
20 0	27 55	29 31	17	♈0	28	14	9	7	6	19	21	♈0	22	10	3	24	21	6	♋4	22	24	12
12	0♒47	3♊42	21	6	♋1	17	13	12	8	21	25	5	25	13	6	28	25	9	9	28	27	15
24	3 41	7 37	25	12	4	19	16	18	11	24	29	10	28	15	9	♉2	29	13	14	♉3	♋0	18
36	6 37	11 19	29	18	6	22	20	23	13	27	♈2	15	♋1	18	12	6	♋2	16	20	8	3	21
48	9 34	14 49	♈4	24	9	24	23	28	16	29	6	20	4	20	15	9	5	19	25	13	6	24
21 0	12 32	18 08	8	♉0	11	27	27	♈4	♌2	♋2	10	25	6	23	18	12	9	22	♈0	18	9	26
12	15 32	21 18	12	5	14	29	♈1	9	21	4	14	♋0	9	26	21	15	12	25	5	22	12	29
24	18 34	24 20	17	10	16	♌2	5	15	23	7	18	5	11	28	24	18	15	28	10	26	15	♌2
36	21 37	27 14	21	15	19	4	9	20	26	10	22	9	14	♌1	27	21	18	♌1	15	♍0	17	5
48	24 42	0♋02	26	20	21	7	12	25	28	12	26	13	16	3	♈1	24	21	4	20	3	20	8
22 0	27 49	2 45	♈0	24	23	9	16	♉0	♌0	15	♈0	18	19	6	4	27	23	7	24	7	23	11
12	0♓57	5 22	4	28	26	12	20	5	3	18	4	22	21	9	7	♉0	26	10	29	10	25	13
24	4 07	7 55	9	♊2	28	14	24	10	5	20	8	26	24	11	10	2	29	13	♉3	13	28	16
36	7 18	10 24	13	6	♌0	17	28	14	7	23	12	29	26	14	13	5	♌2	16	7	16	♌0	19
48	10 30	12 50	18	10	3	19	♈2	18	10	26	16	♊3	29	17	16	7	4	19	11	18	3	22
23 0	13 43	15 13	22	13	5	22	6	22	12	28	20	7	♌1	19	19	10	7	22	14	21	5	25
12	16 57	17 33	26	16	7	24	10	26	14	♍1	24	10	3	22	22	12	10	25	17	24	8	27
24	20 12	19 51	♊1	19	9	27	14	♊0	17	4	28	13	6	24	25	15	12	28	21	26	10	♍0
36	23 28	22 07	5	23	11	29	18	4	19	6	♊1	16	8	27	29	17	15	♍1	24	28	13	3
48	26 44	24 22	9	25	14	♍2	22	7	21	9	5	19	10	♍0	♉2	19	17	4	27	♋1	15	6
24 0	0♈00	26 34	13	28	16	4	26	11	23	12	9	22	13	3	5	22	20	7	♊0	3	18	9

SID TIME	MC LONG	ASC 1	REGIOMONT 11	12	2	3	CAMPANUS 11	12	2	3	PLACIDUS 11	12	2	3	NAT. GRAD. 11	12	2	3	KOCH 11	12	2	3
h m	♈	♋	♉	♊	♌	♍	♈	♊	♌	♍	♉	♊	♌	♍	♉	♊	♌	♍	♊	♋	♌	♍
0 0	0♈00	26♋59	13	29	16	5	26	11	24	12	9	23	13	3	5	22	20	7	♊0	3	18	9
12	3♈16	29 10	17	♋2	18	7	♉0	14	26	15	12	26	15	5	8	24	23	10	3	5	21	12
24	6 32	1♌19	20	4	20	10	3	17	28	18	16	29	18	8	11	27	25	13	6	8	23	15
36	9 48	3 28	24	7	23	12	7	20	♍1	20	19	♋1	20	11	14	29	27	16	8	10	26	18
48	13 03	5 35	27	9	25	15	11	23	3	23	23	4	22	13	17	♋1	♍0	19	10	12	28	20
1 0	16 17	7 42	♊1	12	27	17	14	26	5	26	26	7	24	16	20	4	2	22	13	14	♍1	23
12	19 30	9 49	4	14	29	20	18	29	8	29	29	9	27	19	23	6	5	25	15	15	3	26
24	22 42	11 55	7	17	♍1	22	21	♋2	10	♎1	♊3	12	29	22	26	8	7	27	17	17	5	29
36	25 53	14 00	11	19	4	25	24	4	12	4	6	14	♍2	24	29	10	10	♎0	19	19	8	♎2
48	29 03	16 06	14	21	6	27	28	7	15	7	9	17	4	27	♊2	13	12	3	21	21	10	5
2 0	2♉11	18 11	17	24	8	♎0	♊1	9	17	10	12	19	6	♎0	5	15	14	6	23	23	13	8
12	5 18	20 16	20	26	10	3	4	12	19	12	15	22	9	3	8	17	17	9	25	25	15	10
24	8 23	22 21	23	28	12	5	7	15	22	15	18	24	11	6	11	20	19	12	27	27	18	13
36	11 26	24 26	25	♌1	15	8	10	17	24	18	21	26	13	8	14	22	21	15	29	29	20	16
48	14 28	26 31	28	3	17	10	13	19	26	21	24	29	16	11	17	24	24	17	♋1	♌0	22	19
3 0	17 28	28 35	♋1	5	19	13	16	22	29	23	27	♌1	18	14	20	26	26	20	3	2	25	21
12	20 26	0♍40	4	7	21	15	19	24	♎1	26	29	4	20	17	23	29	28	23	5	4	27	24
24	23 23	2 45	6	10	23	18	22	27	3	29	♋2	6	23	19	25	♌1	♎1	26	7	6	♎0	27
36	26 19	4 51	9	12	26	20	25	29	6	♏1	5	8	25	22	28	3	3	28	9	8	2	29
48	29 13	6 56	12	14	28	23	27	♌1	8	4	7	11	28	25	♋1	5	5	♏1	11	10	4	♏2
4 0	2♊05	9 01	14	16	♎0	25	♋0	4	10	7	10	13	♎0	27	4	8	7	4	12	12	7	4
12	4 57	11 07	17	18	2	28	3	6	13	9	13	15	2	♏0	6	10	10	6	14	13	9	7
24	7 47	13 12	19	20	4	♏1	6	8	15	12	15	18	5	3	9	12	12	9	16	15	11	9
36	10 36	15 18	22	23	7	3	8	11	17	15	18	20	7	5	12	14	14	12	18	17	14	12
48	13 24	17 24	24	25	9	6	11	13	19	17	21	22	10	8	14	17	16	14	20	19	16	14
5 0	16 11	19 30	27	27	11	8	14	15	22	20	23	24	12	11	17	19	19	17	22	21	18	16
12	18 58	21 36	♌0	29	13	11	16	17	24	23	26	27	14	13	20	21	21	20	24	23	20	19
24	21 44	23 42	2	♍1	15	13	19	20	26	25	28	29	17	16	22	23	23	22	26	25	22	21
36	24 30	25 48	4	4	18	16	22	22	29	28	♌1	♍2	19	19	25	26	26	25	28	27	25	23
48	27 15	27 54	7	6	20	18	24	24	♏1	♐0	4	4	21	21	27	28	28	27	♋0	29	27	25
6 0	0♋00	0♎00	9	8	22	21	27	27	3	3	6	6	24	24	♌0	♍0	♏0	♐0	2	♍1	29	28
12	2 45	2 06	12	10	24	23	♌0	29	6	6	9	9	26	26	3	2	2	3	5	3	♏1	♐0
24	5 30	4 12	14	12	26	26	2	♍1	8	8	11	11	28	29	5	4	4	5	7	5	3	2
36	8 16	6 18	17	15	29	28	5	4	10	11	14	13	♏1	♐2	8	7	7	8	9	8	5	4
48	11 02	8 24	19	17	♏1	♐0	7	6	13	14	17	16	3	4	10	9	10	10	11	10	7	6
7 0	13 49	10 30	22	19	3	3	10	8	15	16	19	18	6	7	13	11	11	13	14	12	9	8
12	16 36	12 36	24	21	5	6	13	11	17	19	22	20	8	9	16	14	13	16	16	14	11	10
24	19 24	14 42	27	23	7	8	15	13	19	22	25	23	10	12	18	16	16	18	18	16	13	12
36	22 13	16 48	29	26	10	11	18	15	22	24	27	25	12	15	21	18	18	21	21	19	15	14
48	25 03	18 53	♍2	28	12	13	21	17	24	27	♍0	28	15	17	24	20	20	24	23	21	17	16
8 0	27 55	20 59	5	♎0	14	16	23	20	26	♑0	3	♎0	17	20	26	23	22	26	26	23	18	18
12	0♌47	23 04	7	2	16	18	26	22	29	3	5	2	19	23	29	25	25	29	28	26	20	19
24	3 41	25 09	10	4	18	21	29	24	♐1	5	8	5	22	25	♍2	27	27	♑2	♍1	28	22	21
36	6 37	27 15	12	7	20	24	♍1	27	3	8	11	7	24	27	4	29	29	5	3	♎0	24	23
48	9 34	29 20	15	9	23	26	4	29	6	11	13	10	26	♑1	7	♎2	♐1	7	6	3	26	25
9 0	12 32	1♏25	17	11	25	29	7	♎1	8	14	16	12	29	3	10	4	4	10	9	5	28	27
12	15 32	3 29	20	13	27	♑2	9	4	11	17	19	14	♐1	6	13	6	6	13	11	8	♐0	29
24	18 34	5 34	22	15	29	5	12	6	13	20	22	17	4	9	15	9	8	16	14	10	1	♑1
36	21 37	7 39	25	18	♐2	7	15	8	15	23	24	19	6	12	18	11	10	19	17	12	3	3
48	24 42	9 44	27	20	4	10	18	11	18	26	27	21	8	15	21	13	13	22	20	15	5	5
10 0	27 49	11 49	♎0	22	6	13	20	13	21	29	♎0	24	11	18	24	16	15	25	22	17	7	7
12	0♍58	13 54	3	24	9	16	23	15	23	≈2	3	26	13	21	27	18	17	28	25	20	9	9
24	4 07	16 00	5	26	11	19	26	18	26	6	6	28	16	24	♎0	20	20	≈1	28	22	11	11
36	7 18	18 05	8	29	13	23	29	20	28	9	8	♏1	18	27	3	23	22	4	♎1	25	13	13
48	10 30	20 11	10	♏1	16	26	♎1	23	♐1	12	11	3	21	≈1	5	25	24	7	4	27	15	15
11 0	13 43	22 18	13	3	18	29	4	25	4	16	14	6	23	4	8	28	26	10	7	29	16	17
12	16 57	24 25	15	5	21	≈3	7	27	7	19	17	8	26	7	11	♏0	29	13	10	♏2	18	20
24	20 12	26 32	18	7	23	6	10	29	10	23	19	10	♑1	11	14	3	♑1	16	12	4	20	22
36	23 28	28 41	20	10	26	10	12	♏2	13	27	22	12	♑1	14	17	5	3	19	15	7	22	24
48	26 44	0♐50	23	12	28	13	15	4	16	♓0	25	15	4	18	20	7	6	22	18	9	24	27
12 0	0♏00	3 01	25	14	♑1	17	18	6	19	4	27	17	7	21	23	10	8	25	21	12	27	≈0

SID TIME	MC	ASC	REGIOMONT				CAMPANUS				PLACIDUS				NAT. GRAD.				KOCH			
h m	LONG	1	11	12	2	3	11	12	2	3	11	12	2	3	11	12	2	3	11	12	2	3
	♎	♐	♎	♏	♑		♎	♏	♑	♓	♎	♏	♑	♒	♎	♏	♑	♒	♎	♏	♐	♒
12 0	0♎00	3♐01	25	14	♑01	17	18	6	19	4	27	17	7	21	23	10	8	25	21	12	27	♒0
12	3 16	5 13	28	16	4	21	21	8	23	8	♏0	19	10	25	26	12	10	28	24	14	29	2
24	6 32	7 26	♏1	18	7	25	23	11	26	12	3	22	13	29	29	15	13	♓1	27	17	♑1	5
36	9 48	9 41	3	20	10	29	26	13	♒0	16	5	24	16	♓2	♏2	18	15	5	♏0	19	3	8
48	13 03	11 58	6	23	13	♓3	29	15	4	20	8	26	20	6	5	20	17	8	2	22	6	12
13 0	16 17	14 17	8	25	16	8	♏1	18	8	24	11	29	23	10	8	23	20	11	5	24	8	15
12	19 30	16 39	11	27	20	12	4	20	12	28	13	♐1	27	14	11	25	22	14	8	27	11	19
24	22 42	19 04	13	29	23	16	7	22	16	♈2	16	4	♒0	18	14	28	25	17	11	29	14	22
36	25 53	21 32	16	♐2	27	21	10	25	21	6	19	6	4	22	17	♐1	27	20	14	♐2	16	26
48	29 03	24 03	18	4	♒1	25	12	27	25	10	21	8	8	26	20	3	♒0	23	17	4	19	♓0
14 0	2♏11	26 40	21	6	5	♈0	15	29	♓0	14	24	11	12	♈0	23	6	2	26	19	7	22	5
12	5 18	29 21	23	9	10	5	17	♐2	5	18	26	13	16	4	26	9	5	29	22	10	26	9
24	8 23	2♈07	26	11	14	9	20	4	10	22	29	16	21	8	29	12	8	♈2	25	12	29	14
36	11 26	5 01	28	13	19	14	23	6	16	26	♐2	18	25	12	♐2	15	11	6	28	15	♒3	19
48	14 28	8 01	♐0	16	24	18	25	9	21	29	4	21	♓0	16	5	18	14	9	♐1	18	7	24
15 0	17 28	11 09	3	18	♓0	22	28	11	27	♉3	7	23	5	20	8	21	17	12	3	20	11	29
12	20 26	14 28	6	21	6	27	♐1	14	♈2	7	9	26	10	24	11	24	20	15	6	23	16	♈4
24	23 23	17 56	8	23	11	♉1	3	16	8	10	12	29	15	28	14	27	24	18	9	26	21	10
36	26 19	21 37	11	26	17	5	6	19	13	14	15	♉1	20	♉1	17	♉1	27	21	12	29	26	15
48	29 13	25 32	13	28	24	9	8	21	18	17	17	4	25	5	20	4	♓1	24	15	♉2	♈1	20
16 0	2♐05	29 42	16	♉1	♈0	13	11	24	24	21	20	7	♈0	9	24	8	5	27	18	6	7	26
12	4 57	4♒10	18	4	6	17	14	26	29	24	23	10	5	12	27	12	10	♉0	21	9	13	♉1
24	7 47	8 57	21	7	13	20	16	29	♉4	27	25	13	10	16	♉0	16	14	3	23	12	20	6
36	10 36	14 06	24	10	19	24	19	♉2	8	♊1	28	16	15	19	4	21	19	6	26	16	27	11
48	13 24	19 37	26	13	24	27	22	5	13	4	♉1	20	20	23	7	26	24	9	♉0	20	♈3	15
17 0	16 11	25 31	29	16	♉0	13	24	8	17	7	3	23	25	26	11	♒1	29	12	3	24	10	20
12	18 58	1♈49	♉2	20	6	4	27	11	21	10	6	27	♉0	29	15	6	♈5	16	6	28	17	24
24	21 44	8 29	5	23	11	7	♉0	14	25	13	9	♒0	5	♊3	19	12	11	19	9	♒3	24	29
36	24 30	15 28	7	27	16	11	3	17	29	16	12	4	9	6	22	18	17	23	13	8	♉0	♊3
48	27 15	22 40	10	♒1	20	14	5	20	♊3	19	15	8	14	9	26	24	24	26	16	13	6	7
18 0	0♉00	0♈00	13	5	25	17	8	24	6	22	18	12	18	12	♒0	♓0	♉0	♊0	20	18	12	10
12	2 45	7 20	16	10	29	20	11	27	10	25	21	16	22	15	4	6	6	4	23	24	17	14
24	5 30	14 32	19	14	♊3	23	14	♒1	13	27	24	21	26	18	7	13	12	8	27	♓0	22	17
36	8 16	21 31	23	19	7	25	17	5	16	♋0	27	25	♊0	21	11	19	18	11	♒1	6	27	21
48	11 02	28 11	26	24	10	28	20	9	19	3	♒1	♓0	3	24	14	25	24	15	6	13	♊2	24
19 0	13 49	4♉29	29	♓0	14	♋1	23	13	22	6	4	5	7	27	18	♈1	29	19	10	20	6	27
12	16 36	10 23	♒3	6	17	4	26	17	25	8	7	10	10	29	21	6	♊4	23	15	27	10	♋0
24	19 24	15 54	6	11	20	6	29	22	28	11	11	15	14	♋2	24	11	9	♋0	19	♈3	14	4
36	22 13	21 03	10	17	23	9	♒3	26	♋1	14	14	20	17	5	27	16	14	♋0	24	10	18	7
48	25 03	25 50	13	24	26	12	6	♋1	4	16	18	25	21	7	♋0	20	18	3	29	17	21	9
20 0	27 55	0♒18	17	♈0	29	14	9	6	6	19	21	♈0	23	10	3	25	22	6	♋4	23	24	12
12	0♒47	4 28	21	6	♋2	17	13	12	9	22	25	5	26	13	6	29	26	10	10	29	28	15
24	3 41	8 23	25	13	4	19	16	17	11	24	29	10	29	15	9	♓3	29	13	15	♋4	♋1	18
36	6 37	12 04	29	19	7	22	20	22	14	27	♓2	15	♋1	18	12	6	♋3	16	20	9	4	21
48	9 34	15 32	♓3	24	9	24	23	28	16	29	6	20	4	21	15	10	6	19	26	14	7	24
21 0	12 32	18 51	8	♋0	12	27	27	♈3	19	♋2	10	25	7	23	18	13	9	22	♈1	19	10	27
12	15 32	21 59	12	6	14	♌0	♓1	9	21	5	14	♋0	9	26	21	16	12	25	6	23	12	29
24	18 34	24 59	16	11	17	2	4	14	24	7	18	5	12	28	24	19	15	28	11	27	15	♌2
36	21 37	27 53	21	16	19	4	8	20	26	10	22	9	14	♌1	28	22	18	♌1	16	♋1	18	5
48	24 42	0♋39	25	20	21	7	12	25	28	13	26	14	17	4	♈1	25	21	4	21	4	20	8
22 0	27 49	3 20	♈0	25	24	10	16	♉0	♌1	15	♈0	18	19	6	4	28	24	7	25	8	23	11
12	0♓57	5 57	5	29	26	12	20	5	3	18	4	22	22	9	7	♊0	27	10	♉0	11	26	13
24	4 07	8 28	9	♊3	28	14	24	9	5	20	8	26	24	11	10	3	29	13	4	14	28	16
36	7 18	10 56	14	7	♌1	17	28	14	8	23	12	♊0	26	14	13	5	♌2	16	8	16	♌1	19
48	10 30	13 21	18	10	3	19	♈2	18	10	26	16	3	29	17	16	8	5	19	11	19	3	22
23 0	13 43	15 43	22	14	5	22	6	22	12	29	20	7	♌1	19	19	10	7	22	15	22	6	25
12	16 57	18 02	27	17	7	24	10	26	15	♍1	24	10	4	22	22	13	10	25	18	24	8	28
24	20 12	20 19	♌1	20	10	27	14	♊0	17	4	28	14	6	25	25	15	12	28	22	27	11	♍0
36	23 28	22 34	5	23	12	29	18	4	19	7	♌1	17	8	27	29	17	15	♍1	25	29	13	3
48	26 44	24 47	9	26	14	♍2	22	7	22	9	5	20	11	♍0	♉2	20	18	4	28	♋1	16	6
24 0	0♈00	26 59	13	29	16	5	26	11	24	12	9	23	13	3	5	22	20	7	♊0	3	18	9

SID TIME (h m)	MC LONG	ASC 1	REGIOMONT 11	12	2	3	CAMPANUS 11	12	2	3	PLACIDUS 11	12	2	3	NAT. GRAD. 11	12	2	3	KOCH 11	12	2	3
0 0	0♈00	27♋50	13	♋0	17	5	25	11	25	12	9	24	13	3	5	23	21	7	♊12	5	19	9
12	3♈16	29♋59	11	3	19	7	29	14	27	15	13	27	16	5	8	25	23	10	5	7	21	12
24	6 32	2♌06	21	5	21	10	♋3	17	29	18	16	29	18	8	11	27	26	13	7	9	24	15
36	9 48	4 13	24	8	23	12	7	20	♍1	21	20	♋2	20	11	14	♋0	28	16	9	11	26	18
48	13 03	6 19	28	10	25	15	10	23	4	23	23	5	23	14	17	2	♍0	19	12	13	29	21
1 0	16 17	8 24	♊11	13	27	17	14	26	6	26	27	7	25	16	20	4	3	22	14	15	♍1	24
12	19 30	10 28	5	15	♍0	20	17	29	8	29	♊0	10	27	19	24	6	5	25	16	16	3	26
24	22 42	12 33	8	18	2	22	21	♋2	11	♎2	3	13	29	22	27	9	8	28	18	18	6	29
36	25 53	14 37	11	20	4	25	24	4	13	4	6	15	♍2	25	♊0	11	10	♎1	20	20	8	♎2
48	29 03	16 40	14	22	6	27	27	7	15	7	9	18	4	27	3	13	12	3	22	22	11	5
2 0	2♉11	18 44	17	25	8	♎0	♊1	9	18	10	12	20	6	♎0	5	15	15	6	24	24	13	8
12	5 18	20 47	20	27	10	3	4	12	20	13	15	22	9	3	8	18	17	9	26	26	16	10
24	8 23	22 50	23	29	13	5	7	15	22	15	18	25	11	5	11	20	19	12	28	27	18	13
36	11 26	24 53	26	♌1	15	8	10	17	24	18	21	27	13	8	14	22	22	15	♋0	29	20	16
48	14 28	26 57	29	4	17	10	13	19	27	21	24	29	16	11	17	24	24	17	2	♌1	23	19
3 0	17 28	29 00	♋2	6	19	13	16	22	29	24	27	♌2	18	14	20	27	26	20	4	3	25	21
12	20 26	1♍03	4	8	21	15	19	24	♎1	26	♋0	4	21	16	23	29	29	23	6	5	28	24
24	23 23	3 07	7	10	23	18	22	27	4	29	2	6	23	19	25	♌1	♎1	26	7	6	♎0	27
36	26 19	5 10	10	12	26	20	24	29	6	♏2	5	9	25	22	28	3	3	28	9	8	2	29
48	29 13	7 14	12	14	28	23	27	♌1	8	4	8	11	28	25	♋1	6	5	♏1	11	10	5	♏2
4 0	2♊05	9 17	15	17	♎0	25	♌0	4	11	7	11	13	♎0	27	4	8	8	4	13	12	7	4
12	4 57	11 21	17	19	2	28	3	6	13	10	13	16	2	♏0	6	10	10	6	15	14	9	7
24	7 47	13 25	20	21	4	♏0	5	8	15	12	16	18	5	3	9	12	12	9	17	16	11	9
36	10 36	15 29	22	23	7	3	8	10	18	15	18	20	7	5	12	14	14	12	19	17	14	12
48	13 24	17 33	25	25	9	5	11	13	20	18	21	23	9	8	14	17	17	14	20	19	16	14
5 0	16 11	19 38	27	27	11	8	14	15	22	20	24	25	12	10	17	19	19	17	22	21	18	16
12	18 58	21 42	♌0	♍0	13	10	16	17	24	23	26	27	14	13	20	21	21	20	24	23	20	19
24	21 44	23 46	2	2	15	13	19	20	27	25	29	29	17	16	22	23	23	22	26	25	22	21
36	24 30	25 51	5	4	17	15	21	22	29	28	♌1	♍2	19	18	25	26	26	25	28	27	25	23
48	27 15	27 55	7	6	20	18	24	24	♏1	♐1	4	4	21	21	27	28	28	27	♌0	29	27	25
6 0	0♋00	0♌00	10	8	22	20	27	26	4	3	6	6	24	24	♌0	♍0	♏0	♐0	3	♍1	29	27
12	2 45	2 05	12	10	24	23	29	29	6	6	9	9	26	26	3	2	2	3	5	3	♏1	♐0
24	5 30	4 09	15	13	26	25	♌2	♍1	9	8	12	11	28	29	5	4	4	5	7	5	3	2
36	8 16	6 14	17	15	28	28	5	3	10	11	14	13	♏1	♐1	8	7	7	8	9	8	5	4
48	11 02	8 18	20	17	♏0	♐0	7	6	13	14	17	16	3	4	10	9	9	10	11	10	7	6
7 0	13 49	10 22	22	19	3	3	10	8	15	16	20	18	5	6	13	11	11	13	14	12	9	8
12	16 36	12 27	25	21	5	5	12	10	17	19	22	21	7	9	16	13	13	16	16	14	11	10
24	19 24	14 31	27	23	7	8	15	12	20	22	25	23	10	12	18	16	16	18	18	16	13	11
36	22 13	16 35	♍0	26	9	10	18	15	22	25	27	25	12	14	21	18	18	21	21	19	14	13
48	25 03	18 39	2	28	11	13	20	17	24	27	♍0	28	14	17	24	20	20	24	23	21	16	15
8 0	27 55	20 43	5	♎0	13	15	23	19	26	♐0	3	♍0	17	19	26	22	22	26	26	23	18	17
12	0♌47	22 46	7	2	16	18	26	22	29	3	5	2	19	22	29	25	24	29	28	25	20	19
24	3 41	24 50	10	4	18	20	28	24	♐1	6	8	5	21	25	♍2	27	27	♐2	♍1	28	22	21
36	6 37	26 53	12	7	20	23	♍1	26	3	8	11	7	24	28	4	29	29	5	3	♎0	24	23
48	9 34	28 57	15	9	22	26	4	29	6	11	14	9	26	♐0	7	♎1	♐1	7	6	2	25	24
9 0	12 32	1♍00	17	11	24	28	6	♎1	8	14	16	12	28	3	10	4	3	10	9	5	27	26
12	15 32	3 03	20	13	26	♐1	9	3	11	17	19	14	♐1	6	13	6	6	13	11	7	29	28
24	18 34	5 07	22	15	29	4	12	6	13	20	22	17	3	9	15	8	8	16	14	10	♐1	♑0
36	21 37	7 10	25	17	♐1	7	15	8	15	23	25	19	5	12	18	11	10	19	17	12	3	2
48	24 42	9 13	27	20	3	10	17	10	18	26	27	21	8	15	21	13	12	22	20	14	4	4
10 0	27 49	11 16	♎0	22	5	13	20	12	21	29	♎0	24	10	18	24	15	15	25	22	17	6	6
12	0♍57	13 20	3	24	8	16	23	15	23	♑3	3	26	12	21	27	18	17	27	25	19	8	8
24	4 07	15 23	5	26	10	19	26	17	26	6	5	28	15	24	29	20	19	♑0	28	22	10	10
36	7 18	17 27	8	28	12	22	28	19	28	9	8	♏1	17	27	♎2	22	21	3	♎1	24	12	12
48	10 30	19 32	10	♏0	15	25	♎1	22	♐1	13	11	3	20	♑0	5	25	24	6	4	27	14	14
11 0	13 43	21 36	13	3	17	29	4	24	4	16	14	5	23	3	8	27	26	10	6	29	15	16
12	16 57	23 41	15	5	20	♒2	7	26	7	20	16	7	25	7	11	♏0	28	13	9	♏1	17	18
24	20 12	25 47	18	7	22	6	9	29	10	23	19	10	♐0	11	14	2	♑0	16	12	4	19	21
36	23 28	27 54	20	9	25	9	12	♏1	13	27	22	12	♑1	14	17	4	3	19	15	6	21	23
48	26 44	0♎01	23	11	27	13	15	3	16	♓1	25	14	3	17	20	7	5	22	18	9	23	25
12 0	0♎00	2 10	25	13	♑0	17	18	5	19	5	27	17	6	21	23	9	7	25	21	11	25	28

LAT 53°N — CUSPS OF HOUSES — SID TIME 12h-24h

SID TIME	MC LONG	ASC	REGIOMONT 11	12	2	3	CAMPANUS 11	12	2	3	PLACIDUS 11	12	2	3	NAT. GRAD. 11	12	2	3	KOCH 11	12	2	3
h m	♎	♐	♎	♏	♑	♒	♎	♏	♑	♓	♎	♏	♑	♒	♎	♏	♑	♒	♎	♏	♐	♑
12 0	0♎00	2♐10	25	13	♑50	10	18	5	19	5	27	17	6	21	23	9	7	25	21	11	25	28
12	3 16	4 20	28	16	3	21	20	8	23	9	♏0	19	9	25	26	12	9	28	24	14	28	♒1
24	6 32	6 31	♏0	18	6	25	23	10	26	12	3	21	12	28	29	14	12	♓1	26	16	♑50	4
36	9 48	8 44	3	20	9	29	26	12	♒0	16	5	24	15	♓2	♏2	17	14	4	29	19	2	7
48	13 03	10 59	5	22	12	♓3	28	15	4	20	8	26	19	6	5	19	16	8	♏2	21	4	10
13 0	16 17	13 16	8	24	15	7	♏1	17	8	24	10	28	22	10	8	22	19	11	5	24	7	13
12	19 30	15 35	10	26	19	12	4	19	12	28	13	♐1	26	14	11	25	21	14	8	26	9	17
24	22 42	17 57	13	29	22	16	6	21	17	♈2	16	3	29	18	13	27	24	17	11	29	12	20
36	25 53	20 23	15	♐1	26	21	9	24	21	6	18	5	♒3	22	16	♐0	26	20	13	♐1	15	24
48	29 03	22 52	18	3	♒0	25	12	26	26	11	21	8	7	26	19	3	29	23	16	4	18	28
14 0	2♏11	25 26	20	5	4	♈0	14	28	♓1	14	24	10	11	♈0	22	5	♒1	26	19	6	21	♓3
12	5 18	28 04	23	8	8	5	17	♐1	6	18	26	12	15	4	25	8	4	29	22	9	24	7
24	8 23	0♑48	25	10	13	9	20	3	11	22	29	15	20	8	28	11	7	♈2	25	11	27	12
36	11 26	3 38	28	12	18	14	22	5	17	26	♐1	17	24	12	♐1	14	10	5	27	14	♒1	17
48	14 28	6 36	♐0	15	23	18	25	8	22	♈0	4	20	29	16	4	17	13	8	♐0	17	5	22
15 0	17 28	9 41	3	17	29	23	28	10	28	4	6	23	♓4	20	7	20	16	11	3	20	9	27
12	20 26	12 57	5	20	♓5	27	♐0	13	♈3	7	9	25	9	24	10	23	19	14	6	22	14	♈3
24	23 23	16 23	8	22	11	♈1	3	15	9	11	12	28	14	28	13	26	22	17	9	25	18	8
36	26 19	20 02	10	25	17	5	5	17	14	15	14	♑1	19	♉2	17	♑0	26	20	11	28	24	14
48	29 13	23 54	13	27	23	9	8	20	18	18	17	3	25	5	20	3	♓0	23	14	♑1	29	20
16 0	2♐05	28 04	15	♑0	♈0	13	11	23	25	21	19	6	♈0	9	23	7	4	26	17	5	♓5	25
12	4 57	2♒31	18	3	7	17	13	25	♉0	25	22	9	5	13	26	11	8	29	20	8	12	♉0
24	7 47	7 19	20	6	13	21	16	28	5	28	25	12	11	16	♑0	15	13	♉2	23	11	18	6
36	10 38	12 31	23	9	19	24	19	♑1	10	♊1	28	15	16	20	3	20	18	4	26	15	25	11
48	13 24	18 07	26	12	25	28	21	3	14	4	♑0	19	21	23	7	25	23	9	29	19	♈2	15
17 0	16 11	24 09	28	15	♉1	♊1	24	6	19	8	3	22	26	27	11	♑0	28	12	♉2	23	10	20
12	18 58	0♓38	♑1	19	7	5	27	9	23	11	6	26	♉1	♊0	14	5	♈4	15	5	27	17	25
24	21 44	7 32	4	22	12	8	29	12	27	14	9	29	6	3	18	11	10	19	9	♒2	24	29
36	24 30	14 47	7	26	17	11	♓2	15	♊1	17	12	♈3	10	6	22	17	17	22	12	7	♉0	♊3
48	27 15	22 19	10	♒0	22	14	5	19	4	19	15	7	15	9	26	23	23	26	16	12	6	7
18 0	0♑00	0♈00	13	4	26	17	8	22	8	22	18	11	19	12	♒0	♓0	♉0	♊0	19	18	12	11
12	2 45	7 41	16	8	♊0	20	11	26	11	25	21	15	23	15	4	7	4	4	23	25	18	15
24	5 30	15 13	19	13	4	23	13	29	15	28	24	20	27	18	8	13	13	8	27	♓0	23	18
36	8 16	22 28	22	18	8	26	16	♒3	18	♋1	27	24	♊1	21	11	20	19	12	♒1	6	28	21
48	11 02	29 22	25	23	11	29	19	7	21	3	♒0	29	4	24	15	26	25	15	5	13	♊3	25
19 0	13 49	5♉51	29	29	15	♋2	22	11	24	6	3	♈4	8	27	18	♈2	♊0	19	10	20	7	28
12	16 36	11 53	♒2	♉5	18	4	26	16	♋0	9	7	9	11	♋0	21	7	5	23	15	28	11	♋1
24	19 24	17 29	6	11	21	7	29	20	29	11	10	14	15	2	24	12	10	27	19	♈5	15	4
36	22 13	22 41	9	17	24	10	♒2	25	♋2	14	14	19	18	5	28	17	15	♋0	24	12	19	7
48	25 03	27 31	13	23	27	12	5	♈0	5	17	17	25	21	8	♈1	22	19	4	♋0	18	22	10
20 0	27 55	1♊56	17	♈0	♋0	15	9	5	7	19	21	♈0	24	11	4	26	23	7	5	25	25	13
12	0♒47	6 06	21	7	3	17	12	10	10	22	25	5	27	13	7	♉0	27	10	10	♉1	29	16
24	3 41	9 58	25	13	5	20	15	16	13	25	28	11	♋0	16	10	4	♋0	13	16	6	♋2	19
36	6 37	13 37	29	19	8	22	19	21	15	27	♈2	16	♋2	18	13	8	4	17	22	12	5	21
48	9 34	17 03	♈3	25	10	25	23	27	17	♌0	6	21	5	21	16	11	7	20	27	16	8	24
21 0	12 32	20 19	7	♉1	13	27	26	♈2	20	2	10	26	7	24	19	14	10	23	♈3	21	10	27
12	15 32	23 24	12	7	15	♌0	♈0	8	22	5	14	♉1	10	26	22	17	13	26	8	25	13	♌0
24	18 34	26 22	16	12	18	2	4	13	25	8	18	6	13	29	25	20	16	29	13	29	16	3
36	21 37	29 12	21	17	20	5	8	19	27	10	22	10	15	♌1	28	23	19	♌2	18	♊3	19	5
48	24 42	1♋56	25	22	22	7	12	24	29	13	26	15	18	4	♈1	26	22	5	23	6	21	8
22 0	27 49	4 34	♈0	26	25	10	16	29	♌2	16	♈0	19	20	6	4	29	25	8	27	9	24	11
12	0♓57	7 08	5	♊0	27	12	19	♉4	4	18	4	23	22	9	7	♉1	27	11	♉2	12	26	14
24	4 07	9 37	9	4	29	15	24	9	6	21	8	27	25	12	10	4	♌0	14	6	15	29	17
36	7 18	12 03	13	8	♌1	17	28	13	8	23	12	♊1	27	14	13	6	3	17	10	18	♌1	19
48	10 30	14 25	18	11	4	20	♈2	18	11	26	16	4	29	17	16	9	5	19	13	21	4	22
23 0	13 43	16 44	23	15	6	22	6	22	13	29	20	8	♌2	20	19	11	8	22	17	23	6	25
12	16 57	19 01	27	18	8	25	10	26	15	♍2	24	11	4	22	22	14	11	25	20	26	9	28
24	20 12	21 16	♉1	21	10	27	14	♊0	18	4	28	15	6	25	26	16	13	28	23	28	11	♍1
36	23 28	23 29	5	24	12	♍0	18	4	20	7	♉2	18	9	27	29	18	16	♍1	26	♋0	14	4
48	26 44	25 40	9	27	14	2	21	7	22	10	5	21	11	♍0	♉2	21	18	4	29	2	16	6
24 0	0♈00	27 50	13	♋0	17	5	25	11	25	12	9	24	13	3	5	23	21	7	♊2	5	19	9

309

SID TIME	MC LONG	ASC 1	REGIOMONT 11	12	2	3	CAMPANUS 11	12	2	3	PLACIDUS 11	12	2	3	NAT. GRAD. 11	12	2	3	KOCH 11	12	2	3
h m	♈	♉	♉	♊	♌	♍	♈	♊	♌	♍	♉	♊	♌	♍	♉	♊	♌	♍	♊	♊	♌	♍
0 0	0♈00	28♋42	14	♋1	17	5	25	11	25	13	9	25	14	3	5	24	21	7	4	6	19	10
12	3♈16	0♌49	18	4	19	7	29	14	28	16	13	28	16	6	8	26	24	10	6	8	22	12
24	6 32	2 54	21	6	21	10	♉2	17	♍0	18	17	♋0	18	8	11	28	26	13	9	10	24	15
36	9 48	4 59	25	9	24	12	6	20	2	21	20	3	21	11	14	♋0	29	16	11	12	27	18
48	13 03	7 03	29	11	26	15	10	23	4	24	24	6	23	14	17	3	♍1	19	13	14	29	21
1 0	16 17	9 06	♊2	14	28	17	13	26	7	27	27	8	25	16	21	5	3	22	15	16	♍1	24
12	19 30	11 09	5	16	♍0	20	17	29	9	29	♊0	11	27	19	24	7	6	25	17	17	4	27
24	22 42	13 11	9	19	2	22	20	♋2	11	♎2	4	13	♍0	22	27	9	8	28	19	19	6	29
36	25 53	15 14	12	21	4	25	24	4	14	5	7	16	2	25	♊0	11	10	♎1	21	21	9	♎2
48	29 03	17 15	15	23	6	27	27	7	16	8	10	18	4	27	3	14	13	4	23	23	11	5
2 0	2♉11	19 17	18	25	8	♎0	♊0	9	18	10	13	21	7	♎0	6	16	15	6	25	25	13	8
12	5 18	21 19	21	28	11	3	3	12	20	13	16	23	9	3	8	18	17	9	27	26	16	11
24	8 23	23 20	24	♌0	13	5	7	14	23	16	19	25	11	5	11	20	20	12	29	28	18	13
36	11 26	25 22	27	2	15	8	10	17	25	18	22	28	14	8	14	22	22	15	♋1	♌0	21	16
48	14 28	27 23	29	4	17	10	13	19	27	21	25	♌0	16	11	17	25	24	18	3	2	23	19
3 0	17 28	29 25	♋2	6	19	13	16	22	♎0	24	27	2	18	14	20	27	27	20	4	3	25	22
12	20 26	1♍27	5	9	21	15	19	24	2	27	♋0	5	21	16	23	29	29	23	6	5	28	24
24	23 23	3 28	8	11	24	18	21	26	4	29	3	7	23	19	25	♌1	♎1	26	8	7	♎0	27
36	26 19	5 30	10	13	26	20	24	29	6	♏2	6	9	25	22	28	4	3	28	10	9	2	29
48	29 13	7 32	13	15	28	23	27	♎1	9	5	8	12	28	24	♋1	6	6	♏1	12	10	5	♏2
4 0	2♊05	9 34	15	17	♎0	25	♋0	3	11	7	11	14	♎0	27	4	8	8	4	13	12	7	4
12	4 57	11 36	18	19	2	28	3	6	13	10	14	16	2	♏0	6	10	10	6	15	14	9	7
24	7 47	13 39	20	21	4	♏0	5	8	16	13	16	18	5	2	9	12	12	9	17	16	12	9
36	10 36	15 41	23	24	6	3	8	10	18	15	19	21	7	5	12	15	15	12	19	18	14	12
48	13 24	17 43	25	26	9	5	11	13	20	18	21	23	9	8	14	17	17	14	21	20	16	14
5 0	16 11	19 46	28	28	11	7	13	15	22	20	24	25	12	10	17	19	19	17	23	21	18	16
12	18 58	21 49	♌0	♍0	13	10	16	17	25	23	27	27	14	13	20	21	21	20	25	23	20	19
24	21 44	23 51	3	2	15	12	19	19	27	26	29	♍0	16	15	22	23	23	22	27	25	23	21
36	24 30	25 54	5	4	17	15	21	22	29	28	♌2	2	19	18	25	26	26	25	29	27	25	23
48	27 15	27 57	8	6	19	17	24	24	♏2	♐1	4	4	21	21	27	28	28	27	♌1	29	27	25
6 0	0♋00	0♍00	10	8	22	20	26	26	4	4	7	7	23	23	♌0	♍0	♏0	♐0	3	♍1	29	27
12	2 45	2 03	13	11	24	22	29	28	6	6	9	9	26	26	3	2	2	3	5	3	♏1	29
24	5 30	4 06	15	13	26	25	♌2	♍1	8	9	12	11	28	28	5	4	4	5	7	5	3	♐1
36	8 16	6 09	18	15	28	27	4	3	11	11	15	14	♏0	♐1	8	7	7	8	9	8	5	3
48	11 02	8 11	20	17	♏0	♐0	7	5	13	14	17	16	3	3	10	9	9	10	11	10	7	5
7 0	13 49	10 14	23	19	2	2	10	8	15	17	20	18	5	6	13	11	11	13	14	12	9	7
12	16 36	12 17	25	21	4	5	12	10	17	19	22	21	7	9	16	13	13	16	16	14	10	9
24	19 24	14 19	27	24	6	7	15	12	20	22	25	23	9	11	18	15	15	18	18	16	12	11
36	22 13	16 21	♍0	26	9	10	17	14	22	25	28	25	12	14	21	18	18	21	21	18	14	13
48	25 03	18 24	2	28	11	12	20	17	24	27	♍0	28	14	16	24	20	20	24	23	21	16	15
8 0	27 55	20 26	5	♎0	13	15	23	19	27	♐0	3	♎0	16	19	26	22	22	26	26	23	18	17
12	0♌47	22 28	7	2	15	17	25	21	29	3	6	2	18	22	29	24	24	29	28	25	20	18
24	3 41	24 30	10	4	17	20	28	24	♐1	6	8	5	21	24	♍2	27	26	♐2	♍1	28	21	20
36	6 37	26 32	12	6	19	22	♍1	26	4	9	11	7	23	27	4	29	29	5	3	♎0	23	22
48	9 34	28 33	15	9	21	25	3	28	6	11	14	9	25	♐0	7	♎1	♐1	7	6	2	25	24
9 0	12 32	0♎35	17	11	24	28	6	♎0	8	14	16	12	28	3	10	3	3	10	8	5	27	26
12	15 32	2 37	20	13	26	♐1	9	3	11	17	19	14	♐0	5	12	6	5	13	11	7	28	27
24	18 34	4 38	22	15	28	3	12	5	13	20	22	16	2	8	15	8	7	16	14	9	♐0	29
36	21 37	6 40	25	17	♐0	6	14	7	16	23	25	19	5	11	18	10	10	19	17	12	2	♐1
48	24 42	8 41	27	19	2	9	17	10	18	27	27	21	7	14	21	13	12	22	19	14	4	3
10 0	27 49	10 43	♎0	22	5	12	20	12	21	♐0	♎0	23	9	17	24	15	14	24	22	17	5	5
12	0♍57	12 45	3	24	7	15	22	14	23	3	3	26	12	20	26	17	16	27	25	19	7	7
24	4 07	14 46	5	26	9	18	25	16	26	8	5	28	14	23	29	20	19	♐0	28	21	9	9
36	7 18	16 49	8	28	11	21	28	19	28	10	8	♏0	17	26	♎2	22	21	3	♎1	24	11	11
48	10 30	18 51	10	♏0	14	25	♎1	21	♐1	13	11	3	19	♏0	5	24	23	6	3	26	13	13
11 0	13 43	20 54	13	2	16	28	3	23	4	17	14	5	22	3	8	27	25	9	6	29	14	15
12	16 57	22 57	15	4	19	♐1	6	26	7	20	16	7	24	6	11	29	27	13	9	♏1	16	17
24	20 12	25 01	18	6	21	5	9	28	10	24	19	9	27	10	14	♏1	♐0	16	12	3	18	19
36	23 28	27 06	20	9	24	9	12	♏0	13	28	22	12	♐0	13	17	4	2	19	15	6	20	21
48	26 44	29 11	23	11	26	12	14	2	16	♑1	24	14	2	17	20	6	4	22	18	8	22	24
12 0	0♎00	1♐18	25	13	29	16	17	5	19	5	27	16	5	21	23	9	6	25	20	11	24	26

SID TIME (h m)	MC LONG	ASC	REGIOMONT 11	12	2	3	CAMPANUS 11	12	2	3	PLACIDUS 11	12	2	3	NAT. GRAD. 11	12	2	3	KOCH 11	12	2	3
12 0	0≏00	1♐18	25	13	29	16	17	5	19	5	27	16	5	21	23	9	6	25	20	11	24	26
12	3 16	3 25	28	15	♏2	20	20	7	23	9	♏0	18	8	24	26	11	9	28	23	13	26	29
24	6 32	5 34	♏0	17	5	24	23	9	26	13	2	21	11	28	28	14	11	♓1	26	16	28	≈2
36	9 48	7 45	3	19	8	28	25	11	≈0	17	5	23	14	♓2	♏1	16	13	4	29	18	♈1	5
48	13 03	9 57	5	21	11	♓3	28	14	4	21	8	25	18	6	4	19	16	7	♏2	20	3	8
13 0	16 17	12 12	7	24	14	7	♏1	16	8	25	10	28	21	10	7	21	18	11	5	23	5	11
12	19 30	14 29	10	26	17	12	3	18	12	29	13	♐0	25	14	10	24	20	14	7	25	8	14
24	22 42	16 48	12	28	21	16	6	20	17	♈3	15	2	28	18	13	26	23	17	10	28	10	18
36	25 53	19 11	15	♐0	25	21	9	23	22	7	18	5	≈2	22	16	29	25	20	13	♐0	13	22
48	29 03	21 38	17	2	28	25	11	25	26	11	21	7	6	26	19	♐2	28	23	16	3	16	26
14 0	2♏11	24 08	20	5	≈3	♈0	14	27	♓2	15	23	9	10	♈0	22	4	≈0	26	19	5	19	♓0
12	5 18	26 44	22	7	7	5	17	♐0	7	19	26	12	15	4	25	7	3	29	21	8	22	5
24	8 23	29 24	25	9	12	9	19	2	12	23	28	14	19	8	28	10	6	♈2	24	11	25	10
36	11 26	2♏11	27	11	17	14	22	4	18	27	♐1	17	24	12	♐1	13	8	5	27	13	29	15
48	14 28	5 06	♐0	14	22	18	24	7	23	♉1	3	19	29	16	4	16	11	8	♐0	16	≈3	20
15 0	17 28	8 08	2	16	28	23	27	9	29	4	6	22	♓3	20	7	19	14	11	2	19	7	26
12	20 26	11 20	5	19	♓4	27	♐0	11	♈5	8	9	24	9	24	10	22	17	14	5	21	11	♈1
24	23 23	14 43	7	21	10	♉2	2	14	10	12	11	27	14	28	13	25	21	17	8	24	16	7
36	26 19	18 19	10	24	17	6	5	16	16	15	14	♈0	19	♉2	16	29	24	20	11	27	21	13
48	29 13	22 10	12	26	23	10	7	19	21	19	16	2	25	6	19	♈2	28	23	14	♈0	27	18
16 0	2♐05	26 17	15	29	♈0	14	10	21	27	22	19	5	♈0	9	23	6	♈2	26	17	4	♓3	24
12	4 57	0≈43	17	♈2	7	18	13	24	♉2	25	22	8	5	13	26	10	6	29	20	7	10	♉0
24	7 47	5 32	20	5	13	21	15	27	7	29	24	11	11	17	29	14	11	♉2	22	10	17	5
36	10 36	10 45	22	8	20	25	18	29	11	Ⅱ2	27	14	16	20	♈3	19	16	5	25	14	24	10
48	13 24	16 26	25	11	26	29	21	♈2	16	5	♉0	18	21	24	6	23	21	9	29	18	♈1	15
17 0	16 11	22 36	28	14	♉2	Ⅱ2	23	5	20	8	3	21	27	27	10	29	27	12	♉2	22	9	20
12	18 58	29 16	♈1	17	8	5	26	8	24	11	5	25	♉1	Ⅱ0	14	≈4	♈3	15	5	26	16	25
24	21 44	6♓26	3	21	13	9	29	11	28	14	8	28	6	4	18	10	9	19	8	≈1	23	29
36	24 30	14 01	6	25	18	12	♉2	14	Ⅱ2	17	11	≈2	11	7	22	16	16	22	12	6	♉0	Ⅱ3
48	27 15	21 55	9	28	23	15	4	17	6	20	14	6	15	10	26	23	23	26	15	11	7	7
18 0	0♑00	0♈00	12	≈3	27	18	7	21	9	23	17	10	20	13	≈0	♓0	♉0	Ⅱ0	19	17	13	11
12	2 45	8 05	15	7	Ⅱ2	21	10	24	13	26	20	15	24	16	4	7	7	4	23	19	15
24	5 30	15 59	18	12	5	24	13	28	16	28	23	19	28	19	8	14	14	8	27	♓0	24	18
36	8 16	23 34	21	17	9	27	16	≈2	19	♋1	26	24	Ⅱ2	22	11	21	20	12	≈1	7	29	22
48	11 02	0♉44	25	22	13	29	19	6	22	4	≈0	29	5	25	15	27	26	16	5	14	Ⅱ4	25
19 0	13 49	7 24	28	28	16	♋2	22	10	25	7	3	♓3	9	27	18	♈3	Ⅱ1	20	10	21	8	28
12	16 36	13 34	≈1	♓4	19	5	25	14	28	9	6	9	12	♋0	21	9	7	24	15	29	12	♋1
24	19 24	19 15	5	10	22	8	28	19	♋1	12	10	14	16	3	25	14	11	27	20	♈6	16	5
36	22 13	24 28	9	17	25	10	≈1	23	3	15	13	19	19	6	28	19	16	♋1	25	13	20	8
48	25 03	29 17	12	23	28	13	5	28	6	17	17	25	22	8	♈1	24	20	4	♈0	20	23	10
20 0	27 55	3Ⅱ48	16	♈0	♋1	15	8	♓3	9	20	21	♈0	25	11	4	28	24	7	6	27	26	13
12	0≈47	7 50	20	7	4	18	11	9	11	23	24	5	28	14	7	♉2	28	11	12	♉3	♋0	16
24	3 41	11 41	24	13	6	20	15	14	14	25	28	11	♋0	16	10	6	♋1	14	17	9	3	19
36	6 37	15 17	28	20	9	23	18	20	16	28	♓2	16	3	19	13	9	5	17	23	14	6	22
48	9 34	18 40	♓3	26	11	25	22	25	19	♌0	6	21	6	21	16	13	8	20	29	19	9	25
21 0	12 32	21 52	7	♉2	14	28	26	♈1	21	3	10	27	8	24	19	16	11	23	♈4	23	11	28
12	15 32	24 54	12	8	16	♌0	29	7	23	6	14	♉1	11	27	22	19	14	26	10	27	14	♌0
24	18 34	27 49	16	13	19	3	♓3	12	26	8	18	6	13	29	25	22	17	29	15	Ⅱ1	17	3
36	21 37	0♋36	21	18	21	5	7	18	28	11	22	11	16	♌2	28	26	20	♌2	20	5	19	6
48	24 42	3 16	25	23	23	8	11	23	♌0	13	26	15	18	4	♈1	27	23	5	25	8	22	9
22 0	27 49	5 52	♈0	27	25	10	15	28	3	16	♈0	20	21	7	4	Ⅱ0	26	8	♉0	11	25	11
12	0♓57	8 22	5	Ⅱ2	28	13	19	♉4	5	19	4	24	23	9	7	2	28	11	4	14	27	14
24	4 07	10 49	9	5	♌0	15	23	8	7	21	8	28	25	12	10	5	♌1	14	8	17	♌0	17
36	7 18	13 12	14	9	2	18	27	13	10	24	12	Ⅱ2	28	15	13	7	4	17	12	20	2	20
48	10 30	15 31	18	13	4	20	♈1	18	12	27	15	5	♌0	17	16	10	6	20	16	22	5	23
23 0	13 43	17 48	23	16	6	23	5	22	14	29	20	9	2	20	19	12	9	23	19	25	7	25
12	16 57	20 03	27	19	9	25	9	26	16	♍2	24	12	5	22	23	14	11	26	22	27	10	28
24	20 12	22 15	♉2	22	11	27	13	Ⅱ0	19	5	28	16	7	25	26	17	14	29	25	29	12	♍1
36	23 28	24 26	6	25	13	♍0	17	4	21	7	♉2	19	9	28	29	19	16	♍2	28	♋2	14	4
48	26 44	26 35	10	28	15	2	21	7	23	10	6	22	12	♍0	♉2	21	19	4	Ⅱ1	4	17	7
24 0	0♈00	0♋00	14	♋1	17	5	25	11	25	13	9	25	14	3	5	24	21	7	4	6	19	10

SID TIME (h m)	M C LONG	ASC 1	REGIOMONT 11	12	2	3	CAMPANUS 11	12	2	3	PLACIDUS 11	12	2	3	NAT. GRAD. 11	12	2	3	KOCH 11	12	2	3
	♈	♋	♉	♋	♌	♍	♈	♊	♌	♍	♉	♊	♌	♍	♉	♊	♌	♍	♊	♋	♌	♍
0 0	0♈00	29♋36	14	♋6	18	5	24	10	26	13	10	26	14	3	5	24	22	8	6	7	20	10
12	3♈16	1♌41	18	5	20	8	28	14	28	16	13	29	17	6	8	27	24	11	8	9	22	13
24	6 32	3 44	22	7	22	10	♉2	17	♍1	19	17	♋1	19	8	11	29	27	14	10	11	25	16
36	9 48	5 47	26	10	24	13	6	20	3	22	21	4	21	11	15	♋1	29	16	13	13	27	18
48	13 03	7 49	29	12	26	15	9	23	5	24	24	7	23	14	18	3	♍2	19	15	15	29	21
1 0	16 17	9 50	♊3	15	28	18	13	26	7	27	27	9	26	16	21	5	4	22	17	17	♍2	24
12	19 30	11 51	6	17	♍0	20	17	29	10	≏0	♊1	12	28	19	24	8	6	25	19	18	4	27
24	22 42	13 51	9	19	2	23	20	♋2	12	2	4	14	♍0	22	27	10	9	28	21	20	7	≏0
36	25 53	15 52	12	22	5	25	23	4	14	5	7	17	2	25	♋0	12	11	≏1	23	22	9	3
48	29 03	17 52	16	24	7	28	27	7	16	8	10	19	5	27	3	14	13	4	25	24	11	5
2 0	2♉11	19 52	19	26	9	≏0	♊0	9	19	11	13	21	7	≏0	6	16	16	7	26	25	14	8
12	5 18	21 51	22	28	11	2	3	12	21	13	16	24	9	3	9	19	18	9	28	27	16	11
24	8 23	23 51	24	♌1	13	5	6	14	23	16	19	26	12	5	11	21	20	12	♋0	29	19	14
36	11 26	25 51	27	3	15	7	9	17	26	19	22	28	14	8	14	23	22	15	2	♌1	21	16
48	14 28	27 51	♋0	5	17	10	12	19	28	22	25	♋1	16	11	17	25	25	18	4	2	23	19
3 0	17 28	29 50	3	7	19	12	15	22	≏0	24	28	3	18	14	20	27	27	20	5	4	26	22
12	20 26	1♍50	5	9	21	15	18	24	2	27	♋1	5	21	16	23	29	29	23	7	6	28	24
24	23 23	3 50	8	11	24	17	21	26	5	♏0	3	8	23	19	26	♋2	≏1	26	9	7	≏0	27
36	26 19	5 51	11	13	26	20	24	29	7	2	6	10	25	22	28	4	4	29	10	9	3	♏0
48	29 13	7 51	13	16	28	22	27	♌1	9	5	9	12	28	24	♋1	6	6	♏1	12	11	5	2
4 0	2♊05	9 51	16	18	≏0	25	♋0	3	12	8	11	14	≏0	27	4	8	8	4	14	13	7	5
12	4 57	11 52	18	20	2	27	2	6	14	10	14	17	2	♏0	6	10	10	7	16	14	10	7
24	7 47	13 52	21	22	4	♏0	5	8	16	13	17	19	5	2	9	13	12	9	17	16	12	9
36	10 36	15 53	23	24	6	2	8	10	18	16	19	21	7	5	12	15	15	12	19	18	14	12
48	13 24	17 54	26	26	8	5	10	12	21	18	22	23	9	7	14	17	17	14	21	20	16	14
5 0	16 11	19 55	28	28	11	7	13	15	23	21	24	26	12	10	17	19	19	17	23	22	18	16
12	18 58	21 56	♌1	♏0	13	10	16	17	25	23	27	28	14	13	20	21	21	20	25	24	20	19
24	21 44	23 57	3	2	15	12	18	19	27	26	29	♏0	16	15	22	23	23	22	27	25	23	21
36	24 30	25 58	6	5	17	14	21	21	♏0	♐0	♌2	2	18	18	25	26	26	25	29	27	25	23
48	27 15	27 59	8	7	19	17	24	24	2	♐1	5	5	21	20	27	28	28	27	♌1	29	27	25
6 0	0♋00	0♎00	11	9	21	19	26	26	4	4	7	7	23	23	♌0	♍0	♏0	♐0	3	♍1	29	27
12	2 45	2 01	13	11	23	22	29	28	6	6	10	9	25	25	3	2	3	3	5	3	♏1	29
24	5 30	4 02	16	13	25	24	♌1	♍0	9	9	12	12	28	28	5	4	4	5	7	5	3	♐1
36	8 16	6 03	18	15	28	27	4	3	11	12	15	14	♏0	♐1	8	7	7	8	9	7	5	3
48	11 02	8 04	20	17	♏0	29	7	5	13	14	17	16	2	3	10	9	9	10	11	10	6	5
7 0	13 49	10 05	23	19	2	♐2	9	7	15	17	20	18	4	6	13	11	11	13	14	12	8	7
12	16 36	12 06	25	21	4	4	12	9	18	20	23	21	7	8	16	13	13	16	16	14	10	9
24	19 24	14 07	28	24	6	7	14	12	20	22	25	23	9	11	18	15	15	18	18	16	12	11
36	22 13	16 08	♍0	26	8	9	17	14	22	25	28	25	11	13	21	18	17	21	21	18	14	13
48	25 03	18 08	3	28	10	12	20	16	24	28	♍0	28	13	16	23	20	20	24	23	20	16	14
8 0	27 55	20 09	5	≏0	12	14	22	18	27	♑0	3	≏0	16	19	26	22	22	26	25	23	17	16
12	0♌47	22 09	8	2	14	17	25	21	29	3	6	2	18	21	29	24	24	29	28	25	19	18
24	3 41	24 09	10	4	17	19	28	23	♐1	6	8	5	20	24	♍1	26	26	♑2	♍0	27	21	20
36	6 37	26 10	13	6	19	22	♍0	25	4	9	11	7	22	27	4	29	28	4	3	≏0	23	21
48	9 34	28 10	15	9	21	25	3	28	6	12	14	9	25	29	7	≏1	♐1	7	6	2	24	23
9 0	12 32	0♏11	18	11	23	27	6	≏0	8	15	16	12	27	♑2	10	3	3	10	8	4	26	25
12	15 32	2 09	20	13	25	♑0	8	2	11	18	19	14	29	5	12	5	5	13	11	7	28	26
24	18 34	4 09	23	15	27	3	11	4	13	21	22	16	♐2	8	15	8	7	16	14	9	29	28
36	21 37	6 09	25	17	29	6	14	7	16	24	25	18	4	11	18	10	10	♑1	16	11	♐1	♑0
48	24 42	8 09	28	19	♐2	9	17	9	18	27	27	21	6	14	21	12	11	21	19	14	3	2
10 0	27 49	10 08	≏0	21	4	11	19	11	21	♒0	≏0	23	9	17	23	14	14	24	22	16	5	4
12	0♍57	12 08	2	23	6	14	22	14	23	3	3	25	11	20	26	17	16	27	25	19	6	6
24	4 07	14 08	5	25	8	18	25	16	26	7	5	28	13	23	29	19	18	♒0	27	21	8	7
36	7 18	16 09	7	28	11	21	28	18	28	10	8	♏0	16	26	≏2	21	20	3	≏0	23	10	9
48	10 30	18 09	10	♏0	13	24	≏0	20	♑1	13	11	2	18	29	5	24	22	6	3	26	12	11
11 0	13 43	20 10	12	2	15	27	3	23	4	17	14	4	21	♒3	8	26	25	9	6	28	13	13
12	16 57	22 11	15	4	18	♒1	6	25	7	21	16	7	23	6	11	29	♐1	15	9	♏1	15	15
24	20 12	24 13	17	6	20	4	8	27	10	24	19	9	26	9	14	♏1	29	15	12	3	17	17
36	23 28	26 16	20	8	23	8	11	29	13	28	22	11	29	13	16	3	♑1	19	14	5	19	20
48	26 44	28 19	22	10	25	12	14	♏2	16	♓2	24	13	♑1	17	19	6	3	22	17	8	21	22
12 0	0♎00	0♏24	25	12	28	16	17	4	20	6	27	16	4	20	22	8	6	25	20	10	23	24

LAT 55°N — CUSPS OF HOUSES — SID TIME 12h - 24h

SID	MC	ASC	REGIOMONT				CAMPANUS				PLACIDUS				NAT. GRAD.				KOCH			
TIME	LONG	1	11	12	2	3	11	12	2	3	11	12	2	3	11	12	2	3	11	12	2	3
h m	♎	♐	♎	♏	♐	♒	♎	♏	♑	♓	♎	♏	♑	♒	♎	♏	♑	♒	♎	♏	♐	♑
12 0	0♎00	0♐24	25	12	28	16	17	4	20	6	27	16	4	20	22	8	6	25	20	10	23	24
12	3 16	2 29	27	14	♑1	20	19	6	23	9	♏0	18	7	24	25	11	8	28	23	13	25	27
24	6 32	4 36	♏0	17	3	24	22	8	27	13	2	20	10	28	28	13	10	♓1	26	15	27	♒0
36	9 48	6 44	2	19	6	28	25	11	♒0	17	5	22	13	♓2	♏1	15	12	4	29	17	29	2
48	13 03	8 54	5	21	9	♓2	27	13	4	21	7	25	17	6	4	18	15	7	♏1	20	♑1	5
13 0	16 17	11 06	7	23	12	7	♏0	15	9	26	10	27	20	10	7	20	17	10	4	22	3	9
12	19 30	13 20	10	25	16	11	3	17	13	♈0	13	29	23	14	10	23	19	14	7	25	6	12
24	22 42	15 37	12	27	19	16	6	20	17	4	15	♐2	27	18	13	26	22	17	10	27	8	15
36	25 53	17 57	14	29	23	21	8	22	22	8	18	4	♒1	22	16	28	24	20	13	♐0	11	19
48	29 03	20 20	17	♐2	27	25	11	24	27	12	20	6	5	26	19	♐1	26	23	15	2	14	23
14 0	2♏11	22 48	19	4	♒1	♈0	13	26	♓2	16	23	9	9	♈0	22	3	29	26	18	5	16	28
12	5 18	25 20	22	6	6	5	16	29	8	20	25	11	14	4	24	6	♒2	29	21	7	20	♓2
24	8 23	27 57	24	8	10	9	19	♐1	13	24	28	13	18	8	27	9	4	♈2	24	10	23	7
36	11 26	0♑40	27	11	15	14	21	3	19	27	♐1	16	23	12	♐0	12	7	5	26	12	26	12
48	14 28	3 31	29	13	21	19	24	6	25	♉1	3	18	28	16	3	15	10	8	29	15	♒0	18
15 0	17 28	6 30	♐2	15	27	23	27	8	♈0	5	6	21	♓3	20	6	18	13	11	♐2	18	4	23
12	20 26	9 38	4	18	♓3	28	29	10	6	9	8	23	8	24	9	21	16	14	5	20	9	29
24	23 23	12 57	7	20	9	♉2	♐2	13	12	12	11	26	13	28	12	24	19	17	8	23	13	♈5
36	26 19	16 29	9	23	16	6	4	15	18	16	13	29	19	♉2	16	27	23	20	10	26	19	11
48	29 13	20 17	12	25	23	10	7	18	23	19	16	♑1	24	6	19	♑1	26	23	13	29	24	17
16 0	2♐05	24 21	14	28	♈0	14	10	20	28	23	19	4	♈0	10	22	5	♓0	26	16	♑2	♓1	23
12	4 57	28 46	17	♑1	7	18	12	23	♉4	26	21	7	6	13	25	8	5	29	19	6	7	29
24	7 47	3♒34	19	3	14	22	15	25	8	29	24	10	11	17	29	13	9	♉2	22	9	15	♉5
36	10 36	8 49	22	6	21	26	17	28	13	♊2	27	13	17	21	♑2	17	14	5	25	13	22	10
48	13 24	14 34	25	9	27	29	20	♑1	18	6	29	17	22	24	6	22	20	8	28	17	♈0	15
17 0	16 11	20 51	27	12	♉3	♊3	23	4	22	9	♑2	20	27	27	10	27	25	12	♑1	21	8	20
12	18 58	27 43	♑0	16	9	6	26	7	26	12	5	23	♉2	♊1	14	♒3	♈2	15	4	25	16	25
24	21 44	5♓10	3	19	15	9	28	10	♊0	15	8	27	7	4	18	9	8	18	8	♒0	23	29
36	24 30	13 06	6	23	20	12	♑1	13	4	18	11	♒1	12	7	22	16	15	22	11	5	♉1	♊4
48	27 15	21 27	8	27	24	16	4	16	7	21	14	5	16	10	26	23	23	26	15	10	8	8
18 0	0♑00	0♈00	11	♒1	29	19	7	19	11	23	17	9	21	13	♒0	♓0	♉0	♊0	18	16	14	12
12	2 45	8 33	14	6	♊3	22	9	23	14	26	20	14	25	16	4	7	7	4	22	22	20	15
24	5 30	16 54	18	10	7	24	12	26	17	29	23	18	29	19	8	15	14	8	26	29	25	19
36	8 16	24 50	21	15	11	27	15	♒0	20	♋2	26	23	♊3	22	12	22	21	12	♒1	♓7	♊0	22
48	11 02	2♉17	24	21	14	♋0	18	4	23	4	29	28	7	25	15	28	27	16	5	14	5	26
19 0	13 49	9 09	27	27	18	3	21	8	26	7	♒3	♓3	10	28	18	♈5	♊3	20	10	22	9	29
12	16 36	15 26	♒1	♓3	21	5	24	12	29	10	6	8	13	♋1	22	10	8	24	15	♈0	13	♋2
24	19 24	21 11	4	9	24	8	28	17	♋2	13	9	13	17	3	25	16	13	28	20	8	17	5
36	22 13	26 26	8	16	27	11	♒1	22	5	15	13	19	20	6	28	21	17	♋1	25	15	21	8
48	25 03	1♊14	12	23	29	13	4	26	7	18	17	24	23	9	♓1	25	22	5	♓1	23	24	11
20 0	27 55	5 39	16	♈0	♋2	16	7	♓2	10	20	20	♈0	26	11	4	♉0	25	8	7	29	28	14
12	0♒47	9 43	20	7	5	18	11	7	12	23	24	6	29	14	7	4	29	11	13	♉6	♋1	17
24	3 41	13 31	24	14	7	21	14	12	15	26	28	11	♋1	17	10	7	♋3	14	19	11	4	20
36	6 37	17 03	28	21	10	23	18	18	17	28	♓2	17	4	19	13	11	6	18	25	17	7	22
48	9 34	20 22	♓2	27	12	26	21	24	20	♌1	6	22	7	22	16	14	9	21	♈1	21	10	25
21 0	12 32	23 30	7	♉3	15	28	25	♈0	22	3	10	27	9	24	19	17	12	24	7	26	12	28
12	15 32	26 29	11	9	17	♌1	29	5	24	6	14	♉2	12	27	22	20	15	27	12	♊0	15	♌1
24	18 34	29 20	16	15	19	3	♓3	11	27	9	18	7	14	29	25	23	18	♌0	18	4	18	4
36	21 37	2♋03	21	20	22	6	6	17	29	11	22	12	17	♌2	28	26	21	3	23	7	20	6
48	24 42	4 40	25	24	24	8	10	22	♌1	14	26	16	19	5	♈1	28	24	6	28	10	23	9
22 0	27 49	7 12	♈0	29	26	11	14	28	4	17	♈0	21	21	7	4	♊1	27	8	♉2	14	25	12
12	0♓57	9 40	5	♊3	28	13	18	♉3	6	19	4	25	24	10	7	4	29	11	7	16	28	15
24	4 07	12 03	9	7	♌1	16	22	8	8	22	8	29	26	12	10	6	♌2	14	11	19	♌0	17
36	7 18	14 23	14	11	3	18	26	13	10	24	12	♊3	28	15	13	8	4	17	15	22	3	20
48	10 30	16 40	19	14	5	20	♈0	17	13	27	16	7	♌1	17	16	11	7	20	18	24	5	23
23 0	13 43	18 54	23	18	7	23	4	21	15	♍0	20	10	3	20	20	13	10	23	21	27	8	26
12	16 57	21 06	28	21	9	25	9	26	17	3	24	13	5	23	23	15	12	26	25	29	10	29
24	20 12	23 16	♉2	24	11	28	13	♊0	19	5	28	17	8	25	26	18	15	29	28	♋1	13	♍1
36	23 28	25 24	6	27	13	♍0	17	3	22	8	♉2	20	10	28	29	20	17	♍2	♊0	3	15	4
48	26 44	27 31	10	29	16	3	21	7	24	11	6	23	12	♍0	♉2	22	19	5	3	5	17	7
24 0	0♈00	29 36	14	♋2	18	5	24	10	26	13	10	26	14	3	5	24	22	8	6	7	20	10

SID TIME h m	MC LONG ♈	ASC 1 ♌	REGIOMONT 11 ♉	12 ♊	2 ♌	3 ♍	CAMPANUS 11 ♈	12 ♊	2 ♌	3 ♍	PLACIDUS 11 ♉	12 ♊	2 ♌	3 ♍	NAT. GRAD. 11 ♉	12 ♊	2 ♌	3 ♍	KOCH 11 ♊	12 ♋	2 ♌	3 ♍
0 0	0♈00	0♌32	15	3	18	5	24	10	27	14	10	27	15	3	5	25	23	8	8	9	20	10
12	3♈16	2 34	19	6	20	8	28	14	29	16	14	♋00	17	6	8	27	25	11	10	11	23	13
24	6 32	4 35	23	9	22	10	2♉	17	♈01	19	17	2	19	9	12	♋00	27	14	12	12	25	16
36	9 48	6 36	26	11	24	13	5	20	4	22	21	5	21	11	15	2	♍00	17	14	14	28	19
48	13 03	8 36	II0	13	27	15	9	23	6	25	25	8	24	14	18	4	2	20	17	16	♍00	21
1 0	16 17	10 35	3	16	29	18	13	26	8	27	28	10	26	17	21	6	4	22	18	18	2	24
12	19 30	12 34	7	18	♍01	20	16	29	10	♎00	II1	13	28	19	24	8	7	25	20	19	5	27
24	22 42	14 32	10	20	3	23	20	♋02	13	3	5	15	♍00	22	27	10	9	28	22	21	7	♎00
36	25 53	16 31	13	23	5	25	23	4	15	6	8	17	3	25	II0	13	11	♎1	24	23	10	3
48	29 03	18 29	16	25	7	28	26	7	17	8	11	20	5	27	3	15	14	4	26	25	12	6
2 0	2♉11	20 27	19	27	9	♎0	II0	9	19	11	14	22	7	♎0	6	17	16	7	28	26	14	8
12	5 18	22 25	22	29	11	2	3	12	22	14	17	25	9	3	9	19	18	9	29	28	17	11
24	8 23	24 23	25	♌1	13	5	6	14	24	16	20	27	12	5	12	21	20	12	♋1	♌0	19	14
36	11 26	26 21	28	4	15	7	9	17	26	19	23	29	14	8	14	23	23	15	3	1	21	17
48	14 28	28 19	♋1	6	17	10	12	19	28	22	26	♌1	16	11	17	26	25	18	4	3	24	19
3 0	17 28	0♍17	3	8	20	12	15	22	♎1	25	28	4	19	13	20	28	27	21	6	5	26	22
12	20 26	2 15	6	10	22	15	18	24	3	27	♋1	6	21	16	23	♌0	29	23	8	6	28	24
24	23 23	4 13	9	12	24	17	21	26	5	♏0	4	8	23	19	26	2	♎2	26	9	8	♎1	27
36	26 19	6 11	11	14	26	20	24	29	7	3	7	10	25	21	28	4	4	29	11	10	3	♏0
48	29 13	8 10	14	16	28	22	27	♌1	10	5	9	13	28	24	♋1	6	6	♏1	13	11	5	2
4 0	2II05	10 09	16	18	♎0	25	29	3	12	8	12	15	♎0	27	4	8	8	4	14	13	7	5
12	4 57	12 07	19	20	2	27	♋2	5	14	11	15	17	2	29	6	11	10	7	16	15	10	7
24	7 47	14 06	21	22	4	♏0	5	8	16	13	17	19	5	♏2	9	13	13	9	18	17	12	10
36	10 36	16 05	24	24	6	2	8	10	19	16	20	21	7	5	12	15	15	12	20	18	14	12
48	13 24	18 04	26	27	8	4	10	12	21	18	22	24	9	7	14	17	17	14	21	20	16	14
5 0	16 11	20 03	29	29	10	7	13	14	23	21	25	26	11	10	17	19	19	17	23	22	18	17
12	18 58	22 03	♌1	♍1	13	9	15	17	25	24	27	28	14	12	20	21	21	20	25	24	21	19
24	21 44	24 02	4	3	15	12	18	19	28	26	♌0	♍0	16	15	22	24	24	22	27	26	23	21
36	24 30	26 01	6	5	17	14	21	21	♏0	29	2	3	18	17	25	26	26	25	29	27	25	23
48	27 15	28 01	9	7	19	17	23	23	2	✗1	5	5	21	20	27	28	28	27	♌1	29	27	25
6 0	0♋00	0♎00	11	9	21	19	26	26	4	4	7	7	23	23	♌0	♍0	♏0	✗0	3	♍1	29	27
12	2 45	1 59	13	11	23	21	29	28	7	7	10	9	25	25	3	2	2	3	5	3	♏1	29
24	5 30	3 59	16	13	25	24	♌1	♍0	9	9	13	12	27	28	5	4	4	5	7	5	3	✗1
36	8 16	5 58	18	15	27	26	4	2	11	12	15	14	♏0	✗0	8	6	6	8	9	7	4	3
48	11 02	7 57	21	17	29	29	6	5	13	15	18	16	2	3	10	9	9	10	11	9	6	5
7 0	13 49	9 57	23	20	♏1	✗1	9	7	16	17	20	19	4	5	13	11	11	13	13	12	8	7
12	16 36	11 56	26	22	3	4	12	9	18	20	23	21	6	8	16	13	13	16	16	14	10	9
24	19 24	13 55	28	24	6	6	14	11	20	22	25	23	9	10	18	15	15	18	18	16	12	10
36	22 13	15 54	♍0	26	8	9	17	14	22	25	28	25	11	13	21	17	17	21	20	18	13	12
48	25 03	17 53	3	28	10	11	19	16	25	28	♍1	28	13	15	23	20	19	24	23	20	15	14
8 0	27 55	19 51	5	♎0	12	14	22	18	27	♏1	3	♎0	16	17	26	22	22	26	25	23	17	16
12	0♌47	21 50	8	2	14	16	25	20	29	3	6	2	17	21	29	24	24	29	28	25	19	17
24	3 41	23 49	10	4	16	19	27	23	✗1	6	9	5	20	23	♍1	26	26	♏2	♍0	27	20	19
36	6 37	25 47	13	6	18	21	♍0	25	4	9	11	7	22	26	4	28	28	4	3	29	22	21
48	9 34	27 45	15	8	20	24	3	27	6	12	14	9	24	29	7	♎1	✗0	7	6	♎2	24	22
9 0	12 32	29 43	18	10	22	27	5	29	8	15	17	11	26	♏2	9	3	2	10	8	4	25	24
12	15 32	1♏41	20	13	24	29	8	♎2	11	18	19	14	29	4	12	5	4	13	11	6	27	26
24	18 34	3 39	23	15	26	♏2	11	4	13	21	22	16	✗1	7	15	7	7	16	13	9	29	27
36	21 37	5 37	25	17	29	5	14	6	16	24	25	18	3	10	18	10	9	18	16	11	✗0	29
48	24 42	7 35	28	19	✗1	8	16	8	18	27	27	21	5	13	21	12	11	21	19	13	2	♏1
10 0	27 49	9 33	♎0	21	3	11	19	11	21	≈0	♎0	23	8	16	23	14	13	24	22	16	4	2
12	0♍57	11 31	2	23	5	14	22	13	23	4	3	25	10	19	26	16	15	27	24	18	5	4
24	4 07	13 29	5	25	7	17	24	15	26	7	5	27	13	22	29	19	17	≈0	27	20	7	6
36	7 18	15 28	7	27	10	20	27	17	28	10	8	♏0	15	25	≈2	21	20	3	≈0	23	9	8
48	10 30	17 26	10	29	12	23	≈0	20	♏1	14	11	2	17	29	5	23	22	6	3	25	11	10
11 0	13 43	19 25	12	♏1	14	27	3	22	4	17	13	4	20	≈2	8	26	24	9	6	28	12	12
12	16 57	21 24	15	3	17	≈0	5	24	7	21	16	6	22	5	10	28	26	12	9	♏0	14	13
24	20 12	23 24	17	6	19	4	8	26	10	25	19	9	25	9	13	♏0	♍0	18	11	2	16	16
36	23 28	25 25	20	8	21	7	11	29	13	28	21	11	28	13	16	3	♍0	18	14	5	18	18
48	26 44	27 26	22	10	24	11	14	♏1	16	✗2	24	13	♍0	16	19	5	3	22	17	7	19	20
12 0	0♎00	29 28	25	12	27	15	16	3	20	6	27	15	3	20	22	7	5	25	20	10	21	22

LAT 56°N — CUSPS OF HOUSES — SID TIME 12h - 24h

SID	MC	ASC	REGIOMONT				CAMPANUS				PLACIDUS				NAT. GRAD.				KOCH			
TIME	LONG	1	11	12	2	3	11	12	2	3	11	12	2	3	11	12	2	3	11	12	2	3
h m	♎	♏	♎	♏	♐	♒	♎	♏	♑	♓	♎	♏	♑	♒	♎	♏	♑	♒	♎	♏	♐	♑
12 0	0♎00	29♏28	25	12	27	15	16	3	20	6	27	15	3	20	22	7	5	25	20	10	21	22
12	3 16	1♐31	27	14	29	19	19	5	23	10	29	17	6	24	25	10	7	28	23	12	23	25
24	6 32	3 35	♏0	16	♑2	23	22	8	27	14	♏2	20	9	27	28	12	9	♓1	25	14	25	27
36	9 48	5 41	2	18	5	27	24	10	♒1	18	5	22	12	♓1	♏1	15	11	4	28	17	27	♒0
48	13 03	7 48	4	20	8	♓2	27	12	5	22	7	24	15	5	4	17	14	7	♏1	19	29	3
13 0	16 17	9 57	7	22	11	6	♏0	14	9	26	10	26	19	9	7	20	16	10	4	22	♑2	6
12	19 30	12 09	9	24	14	11	2	16	13	♈0	12	29	22	13	9	22	18	14	7	24	4	9
24	22 42	14 23	12	26	18	16	5	19	18	4	15	♐1	26	18	12	25	20	17	9	26	6	13
36	25 53	16 39	14	29	21	20	8	21	23	8	17	3	♒0	22	15	27	23	20	12	29	9	16
48	29 03	18 59	17	♐1	25	25	10	23	28	12	20	5	4	26	18	♐0	25	23	15	♐1	11	20
14 0	2♏11	21 23	19	3	♒0	♈0	13	25	♓3	16	23	8	8	♈0	21	3	28	26	18	4	14	25
12	5 18	23 52	21	5	4	5	16	28	9	20	25	10	12	4	24	5	♒0	29	21	6	17	29
24	8 23	26 25	24	7	9	10	18	♐0	14	24	28	13	17	8	27	8	3	♈2	23	9	20	♓4
36	11 26	29 05	26	10	14	14	21	2	20	28	♐0	15	22	12	♐0	11	5	5	26	11	24	9
48	14 28	1♑51	29	12	19	19	23	5	26	♉2	3	17	27	17	3	14	8	8	29	14	27	15
15 0	17 28	4 45	♐1	14	25	24	26	7	♈2	6	5	20	♓2	21	6	16	11	11	♐2	17	♒1	21
12	20 26	7 49	4	17	♓2	28	29	9	8	9	8	22	8	25	9	20	14	14	4	19	6	27
24	23 23	11 04	6	19	8	♉3	♐1	12	14	13	10	25	13	29	12	23	17	17	7	22	10	♈3
36	26 19	14 32	9	21	15	7	4	14	19	16	13	28	19	♉3	15	26	21	20	10	25	16	9
48	29 13	18 15	11	24	23	11	6	17	25	20	15	♑0	24	6	18	29	24	23	13	28	21	16
16 0	2♐05	22 16	14	27	♈0	15	9	19	♉0	23	18	3	♈0	10	21	♑3	28	26	16	♑1	28	22
12	4 57	26 37	16	29	7	19	12	22	5	27	21	6	6	14	25	7	♓3	29	18	4	♓5	28
24	7 47	1♒24	19	♑2	15	23	14	24	10	♊0	23	9	11	17	28	11	7	♉2	21	8	12	♉4
36	10 36	6 39	21	5	22	26	17	27	15	3	26	12	17	21	♑2	16	12	5	24	11	20	10
48	13 24	12 27	24	8	28	♊0	20	♑0	19	6	29	15	22	25	5	21	18	8	27	15	28	15
17 0	16 11	18 52	27	11	♉5	3	22	2	24	9	♑2	19	28	28	9	26	24	11	♑1	19	♈7	20
12	18 58	25 56	29	14	11	7	25	5	28	12	4	22	♉3	♊1	13	♒2	♈0	15	4	24	15	25
24	21 44	3♓41	♑2	18	16	10	28	8	♊2	15	7	26	8	5	17	8	7	18	7	28	23	♊0
36	24 30	12 03	5	21	21	13	♑0	11	5	18	10	♒0	13	8	22	15	15	22	11	♒4	♉1	4
48	27 15	20 53	8	25	26	16	3	14	9	21	13	4	18	11	26	22	22	26	14	9	8	8
18 0	0♑00	0♈00	11	♒0	♊0	19	6	18	12	24	16	8	22	14	♒0	♓0	♉0	♊0	18	15	15	12
12	2 45	9 07	14	4	5	22	9	21	16	27	19	12	26	17	4	8	8	4	22	22	21	16
24	5 30	17 57	17	9	9	25	12	25	19	♋0	22	17	♊0	20	8	15	15	8	26	29	26	19
36	8 16	26 19	20	14	12	28	15	28	22	2	25	22	4	23	12	23	22	13	♒0	♓7	♊2	23
48	11 02	4♉04	23	19	16	♋1	18	♒2	25	5	29	27	8	26	15	♈0	28	17	5	15	6	26
19 0	13 49	11 08	27	25	19	3	21	6	28	8	♒2	♓2	11	28	19	6	♊4	21	10	23	11	29
12	16 36	17 33	♒0	♓2	22	6	24	11	♋0	10	5	8	15	♋1	22	12	9	25	15	♈2	15	♋3
24	19 24	23 21	4	8	25	9	27	15	3	13	9	13	18	4	25	18	14	28	20	10	19	6
36	22 13	28 36	7	15	28	11	♒0	20	6	16	13	19	21	7	28	23	19	♋2	26	18	22	9
48	25 03	3♊23	11	23	♋1	14	3	25	8	18	16	24	24	9	♓1	27	23	5	♓2	25	26	12
20 0	27 55	7 44	15	♈0	3	16	7	♓0	11	21	20	♈0	27	12	4	♉2	27	9	8	♉2	29	14
12	0♒47	11 45	19	7	6	19	10	5	13	24	24	6	♋0	15	7	6	♋1	12	14	9	♋2	17
24	3 41	15 28	23	15	9	21	14	11	16	26	27	11	2	17	10	9	4	15	21	14	5	20
36	6 37	18 56	27	22	11	24	17	16	18	29	♓1	17	5	20	13	13	7	18	27	20	8	23
48	9 34	22 11	♓2	28	13	26	21	22	21	♌1	5	22	8	22	16	16	10	21	♈3	24	11	26
21 0	12 32	25 15	6	♉5	16	29	24	28	23	4	9	28	10	25	19	19	14	24	9	29	13	28
12	15 32	28 09	11	11	18	♌1	28	♈4	25	7	13	♉3	13	27	22	22	16	27	15	♊3	16	♌1
24	18 34	0♋55	16	16	20	4	♓2	10	28	9	18	8	15	♌0	25	25	19	♌0	21	6	19	4
36	21 37	3 35	20	21	23	6	6	16	♌0	12	22	13	17	2	28	27	22	3	26	10	21	7
48	24 42	6 08	25	26	25	9	10	21	2	14	26	18	20	5	♈1	♊0	25	6	♉1	13	24	9
22 0	27 49	8 37	♈0	♊0	27	11	14	27	5	17	♈0	22	22	7	4	2	27	9	5	16	26	12
12	0♓57	11 01	5	5	29	13	18	♉2	7	20	4	26	25	10	7	5	♌0	12	10	19	29	15
24	4 07	13 21	10	9	♌1	16	22	7	9	22	8	♊0	27	13	10	7	3	15	14	21	♌1	18
36	7 18	15 37	14	12	4	18	26	12	11	25	12	4	29	15	13	10	5	18	17	24	4	21
48	10 30	17 51	19	16	6	21	♈0	17	14	28	17	8	♌1	18	16	12	8	21	21	26	6	23
23 0	13 43	20 03	24	19	8	23	4	21	16	♍0	21	11	4	20	20	14	10	23	24	28	8	26
12	16 57	22 12	28	22	10	26	8	25	18	3	25	15	6	23	23	16	13	26	27	♋1	11	29
24	20 12	24 19	♉3	25	12	28	12	29	20	6	29	18	8	25	26	19	15	29	♊0	3	13	♍2
36	23 28	26 25	7	28	14	♍0	16	♊3	22	8	♉3	21	10	28	29	21	18	♍2	3	5	16	5
48	26 44	28 29	11	♋1	16	3	20	7	25	11	6	24	13	♍1	♉2	23	20	5	5	7	18	7
24 0	0♈00	0♌32	15	3	18	5	24	10	27	14	10	27	15	3	5	25	23	8	8	9	20	10

LAT 57°N — CUSPS OF HOUSES — SID TIME 0h - 12h

SID TIME	MC LONG	ASC	REGIOMONT 11	12	2	3	CAMPANUS 11	12	2	3	PLACIDUS 11	12	2	3	NAT.GRAD. 11	12	2	3	KOCH 11	12	2	3
h m	♈	♌	♉	♋	♌	♍	♈	♈	♌	♍	♉	♈	♌	♍	♉	♈	♌	♍	♊	♋	♌	♍
0 0	0♈00	1♌30	16	5	19	6	23	10	28	14	11	28	15	3	5	26	23	8	10	10	21	10
12	3♈16	3 29	20	7	21	8	27	14	♏0	17	14	♋1	18	6	9	28	26	11	12	12	23	13
24	6 32	5 28	23	10	23	10	♉1	17	2	20	18	4	20	9	12	♋0	28	14	14	14	26	16
36	9 48	7 26	27	12	25	13	5	20	4	22	22	6	22	11	15	2	♏0	17	16	15	28	19
48	13 03	9 24	♊1	15	27	15	9	23	7	25	25	9	24	14	18	5	3	20	18	17	♍1	22
1 0	16 17	11 21	4	17	29	18	12	26	9	28	28	11	26	17	21	7	5	23	20	19	3	25
12	19 30	13 18	8	19	♏1	20	16	29	11	♎0	♊2	14	29	19	24	9	7	26	22	21	5	27
24	22 42	15 14	11	21	3	23	19	♋1	13	3	5	16	♏1	22	27	11	10	28	24	22	8	♎0
36	25 53	17 11	14	24	5	25	23	4	16	6	8	18	3	25	♊0	13	12	♎1	26	24	10	3
48	29 03	19 07	17	26	7	28	26	7	18	9	11	21	5	27	3	15	14	4	27	25	12	6
2 0	2♉11	21 03	20	28	9	♎0	29	9	20	11	15	23	7	♎0	6	17	16	7	29	27	15	8
12	5 18	22 59	23	♌0	11	2	♊3	12	22	14	18	25	10	3	9	20	19	10	♋1	29	17	11
24	8 23	24 55	26	2	13	5	6	14	25	17	21	28	12	5	12	22	21	12	2	♌0	19	14
36	11 26	26 51	29	4	16	7	9	17	27	19	23	♌0	14	8	15	24	23	15	4	2	22	17
48	14 28	28 47	♋1	6	18	10	12	19	29	22	26	2	16	11	17	26	25	18	5	4	24	19
3 0	17 28	0♍44	4	8	20	12	15	21	♎1	25	29	4	19	13	20	28	28	21	7	5	26	22
12	20 26	2 40	7	11	22	15	18	24	3	28	♋2	6	21	16	23	♌0	♎0	23	9	7	29	25
24	23 23	4 36	9	13	24	17	21	26	6	♏0	5	9	23	19	26	2	2	26	10	8	♎1	27
36	26 19	6 33	12	15	26	20	24	28	8	3	7	11	25	21	28	4	4	29	12	10	3	♏0
48	29 13	8 30	15	17	28	22	26	♌1	10	4	10	13	28	24	♋1	7	6	♏1	13	12	5	2
4 0	2♊05	10 26	17	19	♎0	24	29	3	12	8	12	15	♎0	27	4	9	8	4	15	13	8	5
12	4 57	12 23	20	21	2	27	♋2	5	15	11	15	18	2	29	7	11	11	7	17	15	10	7
24	7 47	14 20	22	23	4	29	5	8	17	13	18	20	5	♏2	9	13	13	9	18	17	12	10
36	10 36	16 18	24	25	6	♏2	7	10	19	16	20	22	7	4	12	15	15	12	20	19	14	12
48	13 24	18 15	27	27	8	4	10	12	21	19	23	24	9	7	14	17	17	15	22	20	16	14
5 0	16 11	20 12	29	29	10	7	13	14	24	21	25	26	11	9	17	19	19	17	23	22	19	17
12	18 58	22 10	♌2	♏1	12	9	15	16	26	24	28	29	14	12	20	21	21	20	25	24	21	19
24	21 44	24 07	4	3	14	11	18	19	28	27	♌0	♏1	16	15	22	24	24	22	27	26	23	21
36	24 30	26 05	7	5	17	14	20	21	♏0	29	3	3	18	17	25	26	26	25	29	28	25	23
48	27 15	28 02	9	7	19	16	23	23	2	✗2	5	5	20	20	27	28	28	27	♌1	29	27	25
6 0	0♋00	0♎00	11	9	21	19	26	25	5	4	8	7	23	22	♌0	♏0	♏0	✗0	3	♏1	29	27
12	2 45	1 58	14	11	23	21	28	28	7	7	10	10	25	25	3	2	2	3	5	3	♏1	29
24	5 30	3 55	16	13	25	23	♎1	♏0	9	10	13	12	27	27	5	4	4	5	7	5	2	✗1
36	8 16	5 53	19	16	27	26	3	2	11	12	15	14	29	✗0	8	6	6	8	9	7	4	3
48	11 02	7 50	21	18	29	28	6	4	14	15	18	16	♏1	2	10	9	9	10	11	9	6	5
7 0	13 49	9 48	23	20	♏1	✗1	9	6	16	17	21	19	4	5	13	11	11	13	13	11	8	7
12	16 36	11 45	26	22	3	3	11	9	18	20	23	21	6	7	15	13	13	16	16	14	10	8
24	19 24	13 42	28	24	5	6	14	11	20	23	26	23	8	10	18	15	15	18	18	16	11	10
36	22 13	15 40	♍1	26	7	8	17	13	22	25	28	25	10	12	21	17	17	21	20	18	13	12
48	25 03	17 37	3	28	9	10	19	15	25	28	♍1	28	12	15	23	19	19	23	23	20	15	13
8 0	27 55	19 34	6	♎0	11	13	22	18	27	♑1	3	♎0	15	18	26	22	21	26	25	22	17	15
12	0♌47	21 30	8	2	13	15	24	20	29	4	6	2	17	20	29	24	23	29	28	25	18	17
24	3 41	23 27	10	4	15	18	27	22	✗2	6	9	5	19	23	♏1	26	26	♑2	♏0	27	20	18
36	6 37	25 24	13	6	17	21	♏0	24	4	9	11	7	21	25	4	28	28	4	3	29	22	20
48	9 34	27 20	15	8	19	23	2	27	6	12	14	9	24	28	7	♎0	✗0	7	5	♎1	23	21
9 0	12 32	29 16	18	10	22	26	5	29	9	15	17	11	26	♑1	9	2	2	10	8	4	25	23
12	15 32	1♏13	20	12	24	29	8	♎1	11	18	19	14	28	4	12	5	4	13	11	6	26	25
24	18 34	3 09	23	14	26	♑1	11	3	13	21	22	16	✗0	7	15	7	6	15	13	8	28	26
36	21 37	5 05	25	17	28	4	13	5	16	24	25	18	2	9	18	9	8	18	16	11	✗0	28
48	24 42	7 01	28	19	✗0	7	16	8	18	27	27	20	5	12	20	11	10	21	19	13	1	29
10 0	27 49	8 57	♎0	21	2	10	19	10	21	≈1	♎0	23	7	15	23	14	13	24	22	15	3	♑1
12	0♍57	10 53	2	23	4	13	21	12	23	4	3	25	9	19	26	16	15	27	24	18	5	3
24	4 07	12 49	5	25	6	16	24	14	26	7	5	27	12	22	29	18	17	≈0	27	20	6	4
36	7 18	14 46	7	27	9	19	27	17	29	11	8	29	14	25	≈2	20	19	3	≈0	22	8	6
48	10 30	16 42	10	29	11	22	≈0	19	♑1	14	11	♏1	16	28	4	23	21	6	3	25	9	8
11 0	13 43	18 39	12	♏1	13	26	2	21	4	18	13	4	19	≈2	7	25	23	9	5	27	11	10
12	16 57	20 36	15	3	15	29	5	23	7	21	16	6	21	5	10	27	25	12	8	29	13	12
24	20 12	22 34	17	5	18	≈3	8	26	10	25	19	8	24	8	13	♏0	28	15	11	♏2	15	14
36	23 28	24 32	20	7	20	7	10	28	13	29	21	10	26	12	16	2	♑0	18	14	4	16	16
48	26 44	26 31	22	9	23	10	13	♏0	16	✗3	24	12	29	16	19	4	2	21	17	7	18	18
12 0	0♎00	28 30	24	11	25	14	16	2	20	7	27	15	♑2	19	22	7	4	25	20	9	20	20

316

SID TIME	MC	ASC	REGIOMONT				CAMPANUS				PLACIDUS				NAT. GRAD.				KOCH			
h m	LONG ♎	1 ♏	11 ♎	12 ♏	2 ♐	3 ♒	11 ♎	12 ♏	2 ♑	3 ♓	11 ♎	12 ♏	2 ♑	3 ♒	11 ♎	12 ♏	2 ♑	3 ♒	11 ♎	12 ♏	2 ♐	3 ♑
12 0	0♎00	28♏30	24	11	25	14	16	2	20	7	27	15	♑2	19	22	7	4	25	20	9	20	20
12	3 16	0♐31	27	13	28	18	19	4	23	10	29	17	5	23	25	9	6	28	22	11	22	22
24	6 32	2 33	29	15	♑1	23	21	7	27	14	♏2	19	8	27	28	12	8	♓1	25	14	24	25
36	9 48	4 36	♏2	17	3	27	24	9	≈1	19	4	21	11	♓1	♏0	14	10	4	28	16	26	27
48	13 03	6 40	4	19	6	♓1	27	11	5	23	7	24	14	5	3	16	13	7	♏1	18	28	≈0
13 0	16 17	8 46	7	22	9	6	29	13	9	27	9	26	17	9	6	19	15	10	4	21	♑0	3
12	19 30	10 55	9	24	13	11	♏2	16	14	♈1	12	28	21	13	9	21	17	13	6	23	2	6
24	22 42	13 05	11	26	16	15	5	18	18	5	15	♐0	25	17	12	24	19	17	9	26	4	10
36	25 53	15 19	14	28	20	20	7	20	23	9	17	2	28	22	15	26	22	20	12	28	7	13
48	29 03	17 35	16	♐0	24	25	10	22	29	13	20	5	♒3	26	18	29	24	23	15	♐0	9	17
14 0	2♏11	19 55	19	2	28	♈0	12	24	♓4	17	22	7	7	♈0	21	♐2	26	26	17	3	12	21
12	5 18	22 20	21	4	♒2	5	15	27	10	21	25	9	11	4	23	4	29	29	20	5	15	26
24	8 23	24 49	23	6	7	10	18	29	15	25	27	12	16	8	26	7	♒1	♈2	23	8	18	♓1
36	11 26	27 24	26	9	12	15	20	♐1	21	29	♐0	14	21	13	29	10	4	5	26	10	21	6
48	14 28	0♑06	28	11	18	19	23	4	27	♉3	2	16	26	17	♐2	12	7	8	28	13	25	12
15 0	17 28	2 55	♐1	13	24	24	26	6	♈3	6	5	19	♓1	21	5	15	9	11	♐1	16	29	18
12	20 26	5 54	3	15	♈0	29	28	8	9	10	7	21	7	25	8	18	12	14	4	18	♒3	24
24	23 23	9 03	6	18	7	♉3	♈1	11	15	14	10	24	13	29	11	21	15	17	7	21	7	♈1
36	26 19	12 26	8	20	15	7	3	13	21	17	12	26	18	♉3	14	25	19	20	9	24	12	7
48	29 13	16 03	10	23	22	12	6	15	27	21	15	29	24	7	17	28	22	23	12	27	18	14
16 0	2♐05	19 59	13	25	♈0	16	9	18	♉2	24	18	♑2	♈0	11	21	♏2	26	26	15	♑0	24	21
12	4 57	24 17	15	28	8	20	11	20	7	27	20	5	6	14	24	5	♓1	29	18	3	♓1	27
24	7 47	29 00	18	♏1	15	23	14	23	12	♊1	23	8	12	18	27	9	5	♉2	21	6	9	♉3
36	10 36	4≈14	21	3	23	27	16	26	17	4	25	11	17	22	♏1	14	10	5	24	10	17	9
48	13 24	10 04	23	6	♉0	♊1	19	28	21	7	28	14	23	25	5	19	16	8	27	14	26	15
17 0	16 11	16 35	26	9	6	4	22	♏1	26	10	♏1	17	29	28	9	24	22	11	♑0	18	♈5	20
12	18 58	23 52	29	13	12	8	24	4	♊0	13	4	21	♉4	♊2	13	≈0	28	14	3	22	14	25
24	21 44	1♓56	♑1	16	18	11	27	7	3	16	7	25	9	5	17	7	♈6	18	6	27	23	♊0
36	24 30	10 46	4	20	23	14	♑0	10	7	19	9	28	14	8	21	14	14	22	10	≈2	♉1	5
48	27 15	20 13	7	24	28	17	3	13	11	22	12	♒3	19	11	26	22	22	26	13	8	9	9
18 0	0♑00	0♈00	10	28	♊2	20	5	16	14	25	15	7	23	15	≈0	♈0	♉0	♊0	17	14	16	13
12	2 45	9 47	13	♒2	6	23	8	19	17	27	19	11	27	18	4	8	8	4	21	21	22	17
24	5 30	19 14	16	7	10	26	11	23	20	♋0	22	16	♊2	21	8	16	16	9	25	29	28	20
36	8 16	28 04	19	12	14	29	14	27	23	3	25	21	5	23	12	24	23	13	≈0	♈7	♊3	24
48	11 02	6♉08	22	18	17	♋1	17	≈0	26	6	28	26	9	26	16	♈2	♊0	17	5	16	8	27
19 0	13 49	13 25	26	24	21	4	20	4	29	8	≈2	♓1	13	29	19	8	6	21	10	25	12	♋0
12	16 36	19 56	29	♈0	24	7	23	9	♋2	11	5	7	16	♋2	22	14	11	25	15	♈4	16	3
24	19 24	25 46	≈3	7	27	9	26	13	4	14	8	13	19	5	25	20	16	29	21	13	20	6
36	22 13	1♊00	7	15	29	12	29	18	7	16	12	18	22	7	28	25	21	♋3	27	21	24	9
48	25 03	5 43	10	22	♋2	15	≈3	23	10	19	16	24	25	10	♈1	29	25	6	♋3	29	27	12
20 0	27 55	10 01	14	♈0	5	17	6	28	12	21	19	♈0	28	12	4	♉4	28	9	9	♉6	♋0	15
12	0≈47	13 57	18	8	7	20	9	♓3	15	24	23	6	♋1	15	7	8	♋2	13	16	12	3	18
24	3 41	17 34	23	15	10	22	13	9	17	27	27	12	4	18	10	11	5	16	23	18	6	21
36	6 37	20 57	27	23	12	24	16	15	19	29	♓1	17	6	20	13	15	9	19	29	23	9	23
48	9 34	24 06	♓1	♉0	15	27	20	21	22	♌2	5	23	9	23	16	18	12	22	♈6	27	12	26
21 0	12 32	27 05	6	6	17	29	24	27	24	4	9	29	11	25	19	21	15	25	12	♊2	14	29
12	15 32	29 54	11	12	19	♌2	27	♈3	26	7	13	♉4	14	28	22	23	18	28	18	5	17	♌2
24	18 34	2♋36	15	18	21	4	♈1	9	29	10	17	9	16	♌0	25	26	20	♌1	24	9	20	4
36	21 37	5 11	20	23	24	7	5	15	♌1	12	22	14	18	3	28	29	23	4	29	12	22	7
48	24 42	7 40	25	28	26	9	9	20	3	15	26	19	21	5	♈1	♊1	26	7	♉4	15	25	10
22 0	27 49	10 05	♈0	♊2	28	11	13	26	6	18	♈0	23	23	8	4	4	28	9	9	18	27	13
12	0♓57	12 25	5	6	♌0	14	17	♉1	8	20	4	27	25	10	7	6	♌1	12	13	21	♌0	15
24	4 07	14 41	10	10	2	16	21	7	10	23	8	♊2	28	13	10	8	4	15	17	23	2	18
36	7 18	16 56	15	14	4	19	25	12	12	25	13	5	♌0	15	13	11	6	18	20	26	4	21
48	10 30	19 05	19	17	6	21	29	16	14	28	17	9	2	18	17	13	9	21	24	28	7	24
23 0	13 43	21 14	24	21	8	23	♈3	21	17	♍1	21	13	4	21	20	15	11	24	27	♋0	9	26
12	16 52	23 20	29	24	11	26	7	25	19	3	25	16	6	23	23	17	14	27	♊0	2	12	29
24	20 12	25 24	♉3	27	13	28	11	29	21	6	29	19	9	26	26	20	16	♍0	3	4	14	♍2
36	23 28	27 27	7	29	15	♍1	16	♊3	23	9	♉3	22	11	28	29	22	18	2	5	6	16	5
48	26 44	29 29	12	♋2	17	3	20	7	26	11	7	25	13	♍1	♉2	24	21	5	8	8	19	8
24 0	0♈00	1♌30	16	5	19	6	23	10	28	14	11	28	15	3	5	26	23	8	10	10	21	10

SID TIME	MC	ASC	REGIOMONT				CAMPANUS				PLACIDUS				NAT. GRAD.				KOCH			
TIME	LONG	1	11	12	2	3	11	12	2	3	11	12	2	3	11	12	2	3	11	12	2	3
h m	♈	♌	♉	♋	♌	♍	♈	♊	♌	♍	♉	♊	♌	♍	♉	♊	♌	♍	♊	♋	♌	♍
0 0	0♈00	2♌29	16	6	19	6	23	10	29	15	11	29	16	4	6	27	24	9	12	12	22	11
12	3♈16	4 26	20	9	21	8	27	13	♍1	17	15	♋2	18	6	9	29	26	11	15	13	24	14
24	6 32	6 23	24	11	23	11	♉1	17	3	20	18	5	20	9	12	♋1	29	14	17	15	26	16
36	9 48	8 18	28	13	25	13	4	20	5	23	22	7	22	11	15	3	♍1	17	19	17	29	19
48	13 03	10 14	♊1	16	27	15	8	23	7	25	26	10	25	14	18	5	3	20	20	18	♍1	22
1 0	16 17	12 09	5	18	29	18	12	26	10	28	29	12	27	17	21	7	6	23	22	20	3	25
12	19 30	14 03	8	20	♍2	20	15	29	12	♎1	♊2	15	29	19	24	10	8	26	24	22	6	28
24	22 42	15 58	12	22	4	23	19	♋1	14	4	6	17	♍1	22	27	12	10	29	26	23	8	♎0
36	25 53	17 52	15	25	6	25	22	4	16	6	9	19	3	25	♊0	14	12	♎1	27	25	10	3
48	29 03	19 46	18	27	8	28	26	7	18	9	12	22	6	27	3	16	15	4	29	26	13	6
2 0	2♉11	21 40	21	29	10	♎0	29	9	21	12	15	24	8	♎0	6	18	17	7	♋0	28	15	9
12	5 18	23 34	24	♌1	12	2	♉2	12	23	14	18	26	10	3	9	20	19	10	2	♌0	17	11
24	8 23	25 28	27	3	14	5	5	14	25	17	21	28	12	5	12	22	21	13	3	1	20	14
36	11 26	27 23	29	5	16	7	9	17	27	20	24	♌1	14	8	15	24	24	15	5	3	22	17
48	14 28	29 17	♋2	7	18	10	12	19	♎0	23	27	3	17	11	17	26	26	18	7	4	24	20
3 0	17 28	1♍11	5	9	20	12	15	21	2	25	♋0	5	19	13	20	28	28	21	8	6	27	22
12	20 26	3 06	7	11	22	15	17	24	4	28	2	7	21	16	23	♌1	♎0	23	10	7	29	25
24	23 23	5 00	10	13	24	17	20	26	6	♏1	5	9	23	19	25	3	2	26	11	9	♎1	27
36	26 19	6 55	13	15	26	19	23	28	8	3	8	12	26	21	29	5	4	29	13	11	3	♏0
48	29 13	8 50	15	17	28	22	26	♌1	11	6	10	14	28	24	♋1	7	7	♏1	14	12	6	2
4 0	2♊05	10 45	18	19	♎0	24	29	3	13	8	13	16	♎0	26	4	9	9	4	16	14	8	5
12	4 57	12 40	20	21	2	27	♋2	5	15	11	16	18	2	29	7	11	11	7	17	15	10	7
24	7 47	14 35	23	23	4	29	4	7	17	14	18	20	4	♏2	9	13	13	9	19	17	12	10
36	10 36	16 30	25	25	6	♏1	7	10	20	16	21	22	7	4	12	15	15	12	20	19	14	12
48	13 24	18 26	27	27	8	4	10	12	22	19	23	25	9	7	14	17	17	15	22	21	17	14
5 0	16 11	20 21	♌0	29	10	6	12	14	24	22	26	27	11	9	17	19	19	17	24	22	19	17
12	18 58	22 17	2	♍2	12	9	15	16	26	24	28	29	13	12	20	22	22	20	26	24	21	19
24	21 44	24 13	5	4	14	11	18	18	28	27	♌1	♍1	16	14	22	24	24	22	27	26	23	21
36	24 30	26 08	7	6	16	13	20	21	♏1	29	3	3	18	17	25	26	26	25	29	28	25	23
48	27 15	28 04	10	8	18	16	23	23	3	♐2	6	6	20	19	27	28	28	27	♌1	♍0	27	25
6 0	0♋00	0♎00	12	10	20	18	25	25	5	5	8	8	22	22	♌0	♍0	♏0	♐0	3	1	29	27
12	2 45	1 56	14	12	22	20	28	27	7	7	11	10	24	24	3	2	2	3	5	3	♏0	29
24	5 30	3 52	17	14	24	23	♎1	29	9	10	13	12	27	27	5	4	4	5	7	5	2	♐1
36	8 16	5 47	19	16	26	25	3	♏2	11	12	16	14	29	29	8	6	6	6	9	7	4	3
48	11 02	7 43	21	18	28	28	6	4	14	15	18	17	♏1	♐2	10	8	8	10	11	9	6	4
7 0	13 49	9 39	24	20	♏1	♐0	8	6	16	18	21	19	3	4	13	11	11	13	13	11	8	6
12	16 36	11 34	26	22	3	3	11	8	18	20	23	21	5	7	15	13	13	16	16	13	9	8
24	19 24	13 30	29	24	5	5	14	10	20	23	26	23	8	9	18	15	15	18	18	15	11	10
36	22 13	15 25	♍1	26	7	7	16	13	23	26	28	26	10	12	21	17	17	21	20	18	13	11
48	25 03	17 21	3	28	9	10	19	15	25	28	♍1	28	12	14	23.	19	19	23	23	20	15	13
8 0	27 55	19 15	6	♎0	11	12	22	17	27	♑1	4	♎0	14	17	26	21	21	26	25	22	16	14
12	0♌47	21 10	8	2	13	15	24	19	29	4	6	2	16	20	29	23	23	29	28	24	18	16
24	3 41	23 05	11	4	15	17	27	22	♐2	7	9	4	18	22	♍1	26	25	♑1	♍0	27	19	17
36	6 37	25 00	13	6	17	20	29	24	4	10	11	7	21	25	4	28	27	4	3	29	21	19
48	9 34	26 54	15	8	19	23	♍2	26	6	13	14	9	23	28	7	♎0	29	7	5	♎1	23	20
9 0	12 32	28 49	18	10	21	25	5	28	9	15	17	11	25	♑0	9	2	♐2	10	8	3	24	22
12	15 32	0♏43	20	12	23	28	7	♎0	11	18	19	13	27	3	12	4	4	13	10	6	26	23
24	18 34	2 37	23	14	25	♑1	10	3	13	21	22	16	29	6	15	6	6	15	13	8	27	25
36	21 37	4 32	25	16	27	3	13	5	16	25	25	18	♐2	9	17	9	8	18	16	10	29	27
48	24 42	6 26	28	18	29	6	16	7	18	28	27	20	4	12	20	11	10	21	19	13	♐0	28
10 0	27 49	8 20	♎0	20	♐1	9	18	9	21	≈1	≈0	22	6	15	23	13	12	24	21	15	2	♑0
12	0♍57	10 14	2	22	3	12	21	12	23	4	3	24	8	18	26	15	14	27	24	17	4	1
24	4 07	12 08	5	24	5	15	24	14	26	8	5	27	11	21	29	18	16	≈0	27	20	5	3
36	7 18	14 02	7	26	8	18	26	16	29	11	8	29	13	24	≈1	20	18	3	≈0	22	7	4
48	10 30	15 57	10	28	10	22	29	18	♑1	15	11	♏1	15	28	4	22	20	6	2	24	8	6
11 0	13 43	17 51	12	♏1	12	25	≈2	20	4	18	13	3	18	≈1	7	24	23	9	5	27	10	8
12	16 57	19 46	15	3	14	29	5	23	7	22	16	5	20	4	10	27	25	12	8	29	12	10
24	20 12	21 42	17	5	17	≈2	7	25	10	26	19	8	23	8	13	29	27	15	11	♏1	13	11
36	23 28	23 37	19	7	19	6	10	27	13	29	22	10	25	11	16	♏1	29	18	14	4	15	13
48	26 44	25 34	22	9	21	10	13	29	17	♓3	24	12	28	15	19	4	♑1	21	16	6	17	15
12 0	0♎00	27 31	24	11	24	14	15	♏1	20	7	26	14	♑1	19	21	6	3	24	19	8	18	18

SID TIME	M C	ASC	REGIOMONT				CAMPANUS				PLACIDUS				NAT. GRAD.				KOCH			
	LONG	1	11	12	2	3	11	12	2	3	11	12	2	3	11	12	2	3	11	12	2	3
h m	≏	♏	≏	♏	♐	♑	≏	♏	♐	♑	≏	♏	♑	♒	≏	♏	♑	♒	≏	♏	♑	♑
12 0	0≏00	27♏31	24	11	24	14	15♏1	20	7		26	14♑51	19		21	6	3	24	19	8	18	18
12	3 16	29 29	27	13	26	18	18	4	24	11	29	16	3	23	24	8	5	28	22	11	20	20
24	6 32	1♐28	29	15	29	22	21	6	27	15	♏2	18	6	27	27	11	7♑1		25	13	22	22
36	9 48	3 28	♏1	17♑52	26		23	8	≏1	19	4	21	9♑1		♏0	13	9	4	28	15	24	24
48	13 03	5 29	4	19	5♑1		26	10	5	23	7	23	13	5	3	16	11	7	♏0	18	26	27
13 0	16 17	7 32	6	21	8	5	29	12	10	27	9	25	16	9	6	18	14	10	3	20	28	≏0
12	19 30	9 37	9	23	11	10	♏1	15	14♈1		12	27	19	13	9	20	16	13	6	22♑50		3
24	22 42	11 45	11	25	14	15	4	17	19	5	14	29	23	17	12	23	18	16	9	25	2	6
36	25 53	13 54	13	27	18	20	7	19	24	10	17♐2	27	22		14	25	20	20	11	27	4	10
48	29 03	16 07	16	29	22	25	9	21	29	14	19	4≏1	26		17	28	22	23	14♐0		7	13
14 0	2♏11	18 23	18♐1	26♈0			12	24♅5	18		22	6	5♈0		20♐0	25	26		17	2	9	17
12	5 18	20 43	20	3≏0	5		15	26	11	22	24	8	10	4	23	3	27	29	20	4	12	22
24	8 23	23 08	23	5	5	10	17	28	17	26	27	11	15	8	26	6≏0	♈2		22	7	15	27
36	11 26	25 38	25	8	10	15	20♐0	23	29		29	13	20	13	29	8	2	5	25	9	18♅2	
48	14 28	28 14	28	10	16	20	22	3	29♊3		♐2	15	25	17	♐2	11	5	8	28	12	21	8
15 0	17 28	0♑58	♐0	12	22	25	25	5♑5	7		4	18♅1	21		4	14	7	11	♐1	14	25	14
12	20 26	3 51	3	14	29	29	28	7	11	11	7	20	6	25	7	17	10	14	3	17	29	20
24	23 23	6 55	5	17♅6	♉4		♐0	9	17	14	9	23	12	29	10	20	13	17	6	20	≏4	27
36	26 19	10 10	7	19	14	8	3	12	23	18	12	25	18♉3		13	23	17	20	9	23	9♈4	
48	29 13	13 42	10	21	22	12	5	14	29	21	14	28	24	7	17	26	20	23	12	26	14	12
16 0	2♐05	17 31	12	24♈0	16		8	17♉4	25		17♑51	♈0	11		20♑50	24	26		14	29	21	19
12	4 57	21 42	15	26	8	20	11	19	9	28	20	3	6	15	23	4	28	29	17♑52	28	26	
24	7 47	26 21	17	29	16	24	13	22	14♊1		22	6	12	18	26	8♅3	♉2		20	5♅6	♉2	
36	10 36	1≏31	20♑52	24	28		16	24	19	4	25	9	18	22	♑50	12	8	4	23	8	14	9
48	13 24	7 21	23	5♉1	♊1		19	27	23	7	28	13	24	26	4	17	13	8	26	12	24	15
17 0	16 11	13 57	25	8	8	5	21♑50	27	11		♑50	16	29	29	8	22	19	11	29	16♈3		20
12	18 58	21 25	28	11	14	8	24	2♊1	14		3	19♉5	♊2		12	29	26	14	♑52	21	13	26
24	21 44	29 52	♑51	14	20	12	27	5	5	16	6	23	10	6	16≏5	♈4	18		6	25	23♊1	
36	24 30	9♅14	3	18	25	15	29	8	9	19	9	27	15	9	21	13	12	21	9≏1	♉1	5	
48	27 15	19 24	6	22♊0	18		♑52	11	12	22	12≏1	20	12		25	21	21	26	13	7	10	9
18 0	0♑00	0♈00	9	26	4	21	5	14	16	25	15	5	25	15	≏0♅0	♉0	♊0		17	13	17	13
12	2 45	10 36	12≏0	8	24		8	18	19	28	18	10	29	18	4	9	9	5	21	20	23	17
24	5 30	20 46	15	5	12	27	11	21	22♊1		21	15♊3	21		9	18	19	11	25	29	29	21
36	8 16	0♉08	18	10	16	29	14	25	25	3	24	20	7	24	12	26	25	14	29♈7	♊5	24	
48	11 02	8 35	22	16	19♊2		16	29	28	6	28	25	11	27	16♈4	♉1	18		≏4	17	9	28
19 0	13 49	16 03	25	22	22	5	19≏3	♊0	9		≏1♈1	14♊0			19	11	8	22	10	27	14♊1	
12	16 36	22 39	29	29	25	7	23	7	3	11	4	6	17	2	22	17	13	26	15♈6		18	4
24	19 24	28 29	♉2♊6	28	10		26	11	6	14	8	12	21	5	26	22	18♊0		21	16	22	7
36	22 13	3♊39	6	14♊1	13		29	16	8	17	12	18	24	8	28	27	22	4	28	24	25	10
48	25 03	8 18	10	22	4	15	≏2	21	11	19	15	24	27	10	♈1♉2	26	7		♈4♉2	28	13	
20 0	27 55	12 29	14♈0	6	18		5	26	13	22	19♈0	29	13		4	6♊0	10		11	9♊1	16	
12	0≏47	16 18	18	8	9	20	9♈1	16	25		23	6♉2	16		7	10	4	13	18	16	4	18
24	3 41	19 50	22	16	11	23	12	7	18	27	27	12	5	18	10	13	7	17	26	21	7	21
36	6 37	23 05	26	24	13	25	16	13	21♌0		♈1	18	7	21	13	17	10	20	♈3	26	10	24
48	9 34	26 09	♈1♉1	16	27		19	19	23	2	5	24	10	23	16	20	13	23	10♊1		13	27
21 0	12 32	29 02	5	8	18♌0		23	25	25	5	9	29	12	26	19	23	16	26	16	5	16	29
12	15 32	1♊46	10	14	20	2	27♈1	27	8		13♉5	15	28		22	25	19	28	22	9	18♌2	
24	18 34	4 22	15	20	22	5	♈1	7♌0	10		17	10	17	♉1	25	28	22♉1		28	12	21	5
36	21 37	6 52	20	25	25	7	4	13	2	13	22	15	19	3	28♊0	24	4		♉3	15	23	8
48	24 42	9 17	25♊0	27	10		8	19	4	15	26	20	22	6	♈1	3	27	7	8	18	26	10
22 0	27 49	11 37	♈0	4	29	12	12	25	6	18	♈0	25	24	8	4	5♉0	10		13	21	28	13
12	0♏57	13 53	5	8♌1	14		16♉1	9	21		4	29	26	11	7	8	2	13	17	23♌0		16
24	4 07	16 06	10	12	3	17	20	6	11	23	8♊3	28	13		10	10	5	16	20	26	3	19
36	7 18	18 15	15	16	5	19	25	11	13	26	13	7♌1	16		14	12	7	18	24	28	5	21
48	10 30	20 23	20	19	7	21	29	16	15	29	17	11	3	18	17	14	10	21	27♊0		8	24
23 0	13 43	22 28	25	22	9	24	♈3	20	18♍1		21	14	5	21	20	16	12	24	♉0	2	10	27
12	16 57	24 31	29	25	11	26	7	25	20	4	25	17	7	23	23	19	14	27	3	4	12♍0	
24	20 12	26 32	♉4	28	13	29	11	29	22	7	29	21	9	26	26	21	17♍0		6	6	15	2
36	23 28	28 32	8♊1	15♍1			15♊3	24	9		♌3	24	12	28	29	23	19	3	8	8	17	5
48	26 44	0♌31	12	4	17	3	19	6	26	12	7	27	14♍1		♉2	25	22	6	10	10	19	8
24 0	0♈00	2 29	16	6	19	6	23	10	29	15	11	29	16	4	6	27	24	9	12	12	22	11

SID TIME h m	MC LONG ♈	ASC ♌	REG 11 ♉	REG 12 ♋	REG 2 ♌	REG 3 ♍	CAM 11 ♈	CAM 12 ♊	CAM 2 ♌	CAM 3 ♍	PLA 11 ♉	PLA 12 ♋	PLA 2 ♌	PLA 3 ♍	NAT 11 ♉	NAT 12 ♋	NAT 2 ♌	NAT 3 ♍	KOC 11 ♊	KOC 12 ♌	KOC 2 ♌	KOC 3 ♍
0 0	0♈00	4♌34	18	9	21	6	22	10♏	♏0	16	12	2	17	4	6	29	25	9	18	15	23	11
0 12	3♈16	6 26	22	11	23	9	26	13	2	18	16	5	19	7	9	♋1	28	12	20	16	25	14
0 24	6 32	8 17	26	14	25	11	♋0	16	5	21	20	7	21	9	12	3	♏0	15	22	18	28	17
0 36	9 48	10 08	♊0	16	27	13	4	20	7	24	23	10	23	12	15	5	2	18	23	20	♏0	20
0 48	13 03	11 58	3	18	28	16	7	23	9	26	27	12	25	14	18	7	4	21	25	21	2	23
1 0	16♈17	13 49	7	20	♏0	18	11	26	11	29	♊0	15	28	17	21	9	7	23	26	23	4	25
1 12	19 30	15 39	10	23	2	20	15	28	13	♎2	4	17	♏0	20	24	11	9	26	28	24	7	28
1 24	22 42	17 28	13	25	4	23	18	♋1	15	4	7	19	2	22	27	13	11	29	29	26	9	♎1
1 36	25 53	19 18	16	27	6	25	22	4	18	7	10	21	4	25	♊0	15	14	♎2	♋1	27	11	4
1 48	29 03	21 08	20	29	8	28	25	7	20	10	14	24	6	27	3	17	16	5	2	29	14	6
2 0	2♉11	22 58	22	♋1	10	♎0	28	9	22	13	17	26	8	♎0	6	19	18	7	4	♌0	16	9
2 12	5 18	24 48	25	3	12	2	♊2	12	24	15	20	28	10	3	9	21	20	10	5	1	18	12
2 24	8 23	26 38	28	5	14	5	5	14	26	18	23	♌0	13	5	12	23	22	13	6	3	21	15
2 36	11 26	28 28	♋1	7	16	7	8	16	29	21	26	2	15	8	15	25	24	16	8	4	23	17
2 48	14 28	0♍18	4	9	18	10	11	19	♎1	23	28	4	17	10	18	27	26	18	9	6	25	20
3 0	17 28	2 09	6	11	20	12	14	21	3	26	♋1	6	19	13	20	29	29	21	10	7	27	23
3 12	20 26	3 59	9	13	22	14	17	23	5	29	4	9	21	16	23	♋1	♎1	24	12	9	♎0	25
3 24	23 23	5 50	12	15	24	17	20	26	7	♏1	6	11	23	18	26	3	3	26	13	10	2	28
3 36	26 19	7 40	14	17	26	19	23	28	10	4	9	13	26	21	29	5	5	29	14	12	4	♏0
3 48	29 13	9 31	17	19	28	21	25	♌0	12	7	12	15	28	23	♋1	7	7	♏2	16	13	6	3
4 0	2♊05	11 23	19	21	♎0	24	28	2	14	9	14	17	♎0	26	4	9	9	4	17	15	8	5
4 12	4 57	14 21	21	23	2	26	♋1	5	16	12	17	19	2	28	7	11	11	7	18	16	11	8
4 24	7 47	15 05	24	25	4	28	4	7	18	14	19	21	4	♏1	9	14	13	9	20	18	13	10
4 36	10 36	16 57	26	27	6	♏1	6	9	20	17	22	23	7	4	12	16	15	12	21	19	15	12
4 48	13 24	18 48	28	29	8	3	9	11	23	20	24	25	9	6	15	18	18	15	23	21	17	15
5 0	16 11	20 40	♌1	♍0	10	5	12	13	25	22	27	28	11	9	17	20	20	17	24	23	19	17
5 12	18 58	22 32	3	2	12	8	14	16	27	25	29	♍0	13	11	20	22	22	20	26	24	21	19
5 24	21 44	24 24	6	4	14	10	17	18	29	27	♌2	2	15	14	22	24	24	22	28	26	23	21
5 36	24 30	26 16	8	6	16	12	20	20	♏1	♐0	4	4	17	16	25	26	26	25	29	28	25	23
5 48	27 15	28 08	11	8	18	15	22	22	4	3	7	6	20	19	27	28	28	27	♌1	♍0	27	25
6 0	0♋00	0♎00	13	10	20	17	25	24	6	5	9	8	22	21	♌0	♍0	♏0	♐0	3	1	29	27
6 12	2 45	1 52	15	12	22	19	27	26	8	8	11	10	24	23	3	2	2	3	5	3	♏0	29
6 24	5 30	3 44	18	14	24	22	♌0	29	10	10	14	13	26	26	5	4	4	5	7	5	2	♐1
6 36	8 16	5 36	20	16	26	24	3	♏1	12	13	16	15	28	28	8	6	6	8	9	7	4	2
6 48	11 02	7 28	22	18	28	27	5	3	14	16	19	17	♏0	♐1	10	8	8	10	11	9	6	4
7 0	13 49	9 20	25	20	♏0	29	8	5	17	18	21	19	2	3	13	10	10	13	13	11	7	6
7 12	16 36	11 12	27	22	2	♐1	10	7	19	21	24	21	5	6	15	12	12	15	15	13	9	7
7 24	19 24	13 03	29	24	3	4	13	10	21	24	26	23	7	8	18	15	14	18	18	15	11	9
7 36	22 13	14 55	♍2	26	5	6	16	12	23	26	29	26	9	11	21	17	16	21	20	17	12	10
7 48	25 03	16 46	4	28	7	9	18	14	25	29	♍2	28	11	13	23	19	19	23	22	19	14	12
8 0	27 55	18 37	6	♎0	9	11	21	16	28	♑2	4	♎0	13	16	26	21	21	26	25	22	15	13
8 12	0♌47	20 29	9	2	11	13	23	18	♐0	5	7	2	15	18	29	24	23	29	27	24	17	14
8 24	3 41	22 20	11	4	13	16	26	20	2	7	9	4	17	21	♍1	25	25	♎1	♍0	26	18	16
8 36	6 37	24 10	13	6	15	18	29	23	4	10	12	7	19	24	4	27	27	4	2	28	20	17
8 48	9 34	26 01	16	8	17	21	♍1	25	6	12	14	9	21	26	7	29	29	7	5	♎0	21	18
9 0	12 32	27 51	18	10	19	24	4	27	9	16	17	11	24	29	9	♎1	♐1	10	7	3	23	20
9 12	15 32	29 42	20	12	21	26	7	29	11	19	20	13	26	♑2	12	4	3	12	10	5	24	22
9 24	18 34	1♍32	23	14	23	29	9	♎1	14	22	22	15	28	4	14	6	5	15	13	7	26	22
9 36	21 37	3 22	25	16	25	♑2	12	4	16	25	25	17	♐0	7	17	8	7	18	15	9	27	24
9 48	24 42	5 12	28	18	27	5	15	6	18	27	27	20	2	10	20	10	9	21	18	12	29	25
10 0	27 49	7 02	♎0	20	29	8	17	8	21	♒2	♎0	22	4	13	23	12	11	24	21	14	♐0	26
10 12	0♍57	8 52	2	22	♐1	10	20	10	23	5	3	24	6	16	25	14	13	27	24	16	1	28
10 24	4 07	10 42	5	24	3	14	23	12	26	8	5	26	9	20	28	17	15	♒0	26	19	3	29
10 36	7 18	12 32	7	26	5	17	26	15	29	12	8	28	11	23	♎1	19	17	3	29	21	4	♑1
10 48	10 30	14 21	10	28	7	20	28	17	♒2	15	10	♏0	13	26	4	21	19	6	♎2	23	6	2
11 0	13 43	16 11	12	♏0	10	23	♎1	19	4	19	13	2	15	♒0	7	23	21	9	5	26	9	5
11 12	16 57	18 02	14	2	12	27	4	21	7	23	16	5	18	3	10	25	23	12	7	28	9	5
11 24	20 12	19 52	17	3	14	♒0	6	23	10	26	18	7	20	7	12	28	25	15	10	♏0	10	7
11 36	23 28	21 43	19	5	16	4	9	25	14	♈0	21	9	23	10	15	♏0	27	18	12	2	11	8
11 48	26 44	23 34	21	7	19	8	12	28	17	4	23	11	25	14	18	2	29	21	16	5	14	10
12 0	0♎00	25 26	24	9	21	12	14	♏0	20	8	26	13	28	18	21	5	♑1	24	19	7	15	12

SID TIME (h m)	MC LONG ♎	ASC 1 ♏	REGIOMONT 11	12	2	3	CAMPANUS 11	12	2	3	PLACIDUS 11	12	2	3	NAT.GRAD. 11	12	2	3	KOCH 11	12	2	3
12 0	0♎00	25♏26	24	9	21	12	14	♏0	20	8	26	13	28	18	21	5	♑1	24	19	7	15	12
12	3 16	27 18	26	11	23	16	17	2	24	12	28	15	♑0	22	24	7	3	27	21	9	17	14
24	6 32	29 11	28	13	26	21	20	4	28	16	♏1	17	3	26	27	9	5	♓1	24	12	18	16
36	9 48	1♐05	♏1	15	29	25	23	6	♒2	20	4	19	6	♓0	29	12	7	4	27	14	20	18
48	13 03	3 00	3	17	♑1	♓0	25	8	6	24	6	21	9	4	♏2	14	9	7	♏0	16	22	20
13 0	16 17	4 56	5	19	4	4	28	11	11	28	9	24	13	8	5	16	11	10	2	18	24	23
12	19 30	6 54	8	21	7	9	♏1	13	15	♈3	11	26	16	13	8	19	13	13	5	21	25	25
24	22 42	8 54	10	23	10	14	3	15	20	7	14	28	20	17	11	21	15	16	8	23	27	28
36	25 53	10 55	12	25	14	20	6	17	26	11	16	♐0	24	21	13	23	17	19	11	25	29	♒1
48	29 03	12 59	15	27	18	25	8	19	♓1	15	19	2	28	26	16	26	19	23	13	28	♑2	4
14 0	2♏11	15 06	17	29	22	♈0	11	22	7	19	21	4	♒2	♈0	19	28	22	26	16	♐0	4	8
12	5 18	17 16	19	♐1	26	5	14	24	13	23	23	6	7	4	22	♐1	24	29	19	2	6	12
24	8 23	19 30	22	3	♒1	10	16	26	20	27	26	9	12	9	25	3	26	♈2	21	5	9	17
36	11 26	21 49	24	5	6	16	19	28	26	♑1	28	11	17	13	27	6	28	5	24	7	11	22
48	14 28	24 13	27	7	12	21	21	♐0	♈2	5	♐1	13	23	17	♐0	8	♒1	8	27	10	14	27
15 0	17 28	26 44	29	10	18	26	24	3	9	8	3	15	28	22	3	11	3	11	29	12	18	♓3
12	20 26	29 22	♐1	12	25	♉0	27	5	15	12	6	18	♈4	26	6	14	6	14	♐2	15	21	10
24	23 23	2♐10	4	14	♓3	5	29	7	21	16	8	20	11	♉0	9	17	9	17	5	17	25	18
36	26 19	5 10	6	16	12	9	♐2	9	27	19	11	23	17	4	12	20	12	20	8	20	♒0	26
48	29 13	8 23	9	19	21	14	4	12	♉3	23	13	25	23	8	15	23	15	23	10	23	5	♈4
16 0	2♐05	11 54	11	21	♈0	18	7	14	8	26	16	28	♈0	12	18	26	18	26	13	25	11	13
12	4 57	15 47	13	23	9	22	10	17	13	29	18	♑0	7	16	21	♑0	22	28	16	28	18	21
24	7 47	20 07	16	26	18	26	12	19	18	♊2	21	3	13	20	24	3	27	♉1	19	♑2	26	29
36	10 36	25 02	18	29	27	♊0	15	22	23	6	24	6	19	23	28	8	♓2	4	22	5	♓6	♉7
48	13 24	0♐41	21	♑1	♉5	3	18	24	27	9	26	9	26	27	♑2	12	7	7	25	9	16	14
17 0	16 11	7 17	24	4	12	7	20	27	♊1	12	29	13	♉2	♊0	6	18	13	10	28	13	28	20
12	18 58	15 03	26	7	18	10	23	29	5	15	♑2	16	7	4	10	24	21	13	♑1	17	♈0	26
24	21 44	24 13	29	10	24	13	26	♑2	9	18	4	20	13	7	15	♒1	29	17	4	22	21	♉1
36	24 30	4♓55	♑2	14	29	16	28	5	12	21	7	24	18	10	20	10	♈9	21	8	27	♉2	6
48	27 15	17 01	5	18	♊4	20	♑1	8	16	23	10	28	23	14	25	19	19	25	11	♒3	11	11
18 0	0♑00	0♈00	8	22	8	22	4	11	19	26	13	♒2	28	17	♒0	♈0	♉0	♊0	15	10	20	15
12	2 45	12 59	10	26	12	25	7	14	22	29	16	7	♊2	20	5	11	11	5	19	19	20	19
24	5 30	25 05	14	♒1	16	28	9	18	25	♋2	20	12	6	23	9	21	20	10	24	28	♊3	22
36	8 16	5♉47	17	6	20	♋1	12	21	28	4	23	17	10	26	13	♈1	29	15	29	♈9	8	26
48	11 02	14 57	20	12	23	4	15	25	♋1	7	26	23	14	28	17	9	♊6	20	♒4	20	13	29
19 0	13 49	22 43	23	18	26	6	18	29	4	9	♒0	28	17	♋1	20	17	12	24	10	♈2	17	♋2
12	16 36	29 19	27	25	29	9	21	♒3	6	12	3	♈4	21	4	23	23	18	28	16	14	21	5
24	19 24	4♊58	♒0	♈3	♋1	12	24	7	8	15	7	11	24	6	26	28	22	♋2	23	24	25	8
36	22 13	9 53	4	12	4	14	28	12	11	18	10	17	27	9	29	♋3	27	6	♈1	♉4	28	11
48	25 03	14 13	8	21	7	17	♒1	17	13	20	14	23	♋0	9	♈2	8	♋0	9	9	12	♋2	14
20 0	27 55	18 06	12	♈0	9	19	4	22	16	23	18	♈0	2	14	4	12	4	12	17	19	5	17
12	0♒47	21 37	16	9	11	21	7	27	18	26	22	7	5	17	7	15	7	15	26	25	7	20
24	3 41	24 50	21	18	14	24	11	♈3	21	28	26	13	7	19	10	18	10	18	♈4	♊0	10	22
36	6 37	27 50	25	27	16	26	14	9	23	♌1	♈0	19	10	22	12	21	13	21	12	5	13	25
48	9 34	0♊38	♈0	♉5	18	29	18	15	25	3	4	26	12	24	16	24	16	24	20	9	15	28
21 0	12 32	3 16	4	12	20	♌1	22	21	27	6	8	♉2	15	27	19	27	19	27	27	12	18	♌1
12	15 32	5 47	9	18	23	3	25	28	♌0	9	13	7	17	29	22	29	♌2	♌0	♌3	16	20	3
24	18 34	8 11	14	24	25	6	29	♈4	2	11	17	13	19	♌2	25	♊2	24	3	8	19	23	6
36	21 37	10 30	20	29	27	8	♈3	10	4	14	21	18	21	4	28	4	27	5	13	21	25	9
48	24 42	12 44	25	♊4	29	11	7	17	6	16	26	23	24	7	♈1	6	29	8	18	24	28	12
22 0	27 49	14 54	♈0	8	♌1	13	11	23	8	19	♈0	28	26	9	4	8	♌2	11	22	26	♌0	14
12	0♓57	17 01	5	12	3	15	15	29	11	22	4	♊2	28	11	7	11	4	14	26	28	2	17
24	4 07	19 05	10	16	5	18	19	♉4	13	24	9	6	♌0	14	11	13	7	17	♊0	♋1	5	19
36	7 18	21 06	16	20	7	20	23	10	15	27	13	10	2	16	14	15	9	19	♊2	3	7	22
48	10 30	23 06	21	23	9	22	27	15	17	29	17	14	4	19	17	17	11	22	5	5	9	25
23 0	13 43	25 04	26	26	11	25	♈2	19	19	♍2	22	17	6	21	20	19	14	25	7	6	12	28
12	16 57	27 00	♉0	29	13	27	6	24	22	5	26	21	9	24	23	21	16	28	10	8	14	♍0
24	20 12	28 55	5	♋1	15	29	10	28	24	7	♉0	24	11	26	26	23	18	♍1	12	10	16	3
36	23 28	0♋49	9	4	17	♍2	14	♋2	26	10	4	27	13	29	29	25	21	3	14	12	18	6
48	26 44	2 42	14	7	19	4	18	6	28	13	8	♋0	15	♍2	♋3	27	23	6	16	13	21	9
24 0	0♈00	4 34	18	9	21	6	22	10	♍0	16	12	2	17	4	6	29	25	9	18	15	23	11

(i) Closer Precision

Tables for finding approximate minutes on minor cusps and for finding Campanus and Natural Graduation midcusps.

REGIOMONTANUS, CAMPANUS, PLACIDUS, CUSPS 11, 12, 2, 3, AND CAMPANUS MIDCUSPS: same as Ascendants at fictitious latitudes and at time (sidereal) diminished (for cusps etc. between 10 and 1), or (below Ascendant) increased, by time differences. Tables below give fictitious latitudes and (for Campanus) time differences. For Regiomontanus and Placidus, time differences are: 4h for cusps 11 and 3; 2h for 12 and 2.

MIDCUSPS DENOTED THUS: 10/11 = midcusp between cusps 10 and 11.

NATURAL GRADUATION: Q is degrees of zodiac from MC to Ascendant.

Table below gives values of A,B,a,b, for different values of Q. When Q exceeds 90°, take columns as named at FOOT; otherwise, as named at TOP. Then MC + A = cusp 11; Asc. − A = 12; Asc. + B = 2; cusp 4 − B = 3.

Midcusps 11/12 and 2/3: halve degrees between cusps.

MC + a = midcusp 10/11; Asc. − a = 12/1; Asc. + b = 1/2, cusp 4 − b = 3/4.

FICTITIOUS LATITIUDES FOR REGIOMONTANUS AND PLACIDUS

real	REGIOMONTANUS				PLACIDUS				real	REGIOMONTANUS				PLACIDUS			
Lat.	11 &3		12 &2		11 &3		12 &2		Lat.	11 &3		12 &2		11 &3		12 &2	
10°	5°	2'	8°	41'	3°	23'	6°	43'	50°	30°	47'	45°	54'	22°	31'	39°	12'
20	10	19	17	30	6	57	13	41	52	32	37	47	56	24	10	41	22
30	16	6	26	34	10	59	21	9	54	34	31	50	0	26	0	43	37
35	19	18	31	14	13	17	25	10	56	36	33	52	5	27	59	45	58
40	22	40	36	0	15	56	29	32	58	38	40	58	11	30	14	48	26
45	26	34	40	54	18	57	34	10	60	40	54	56	18	32	47	51	3

FICT.LATS, (° ') and TIME DIFFS, (h m s), CAMPANUS

real	10/11 and 3/4.					11 and 3.					11/12 and 2/3.					12 and 2.					12/1 and 1/2.				
Lat.	°	'	h	m	s	°	'	h	m	s	°	'	h	m	s	°	'	h	m	s	°	'	h	m	s
10	2	35	5	0	52	4	59	4	1	31	7	3	3	1	45	8	39	2	1	32	9	39	1	0	53
20	5	5	5	1	40	9	51	4	6	4	14	0	3	7	7	17	14	2	6	16	19	26	1	0	56
30	7	27	5	7	45	14	29	4	13	44	20	42	3	12	26	25	40	2	14	45	28	53	1	8	42
35	8	32	5	10	29	16	40	4	18	45	23	56	3	18	43	29	47	2	20	37	33	39	1	12	27
40	9	27	5	13	36	18	45	4	24	34	27	2	3	30	11	33	59	2	28	2	38	4	1	17	7
45	10	33	5	17	5	20	42	4	31	9	30	0	3	38	56	37	46	2	39	0	43	5	1	23	22
50	11	26	5	20	56	22	31	4	38	34	32	33	3	48	4	41	34	2	47	39	47	44	1	30	31
52	11	46	5	22	32	23	13	4	41	44	33	52	3	53	31	43	3	2	52	39	49	34	1	33	5
54	12	51	5	24	12	23	52	4	45	1	34	54	3	58	9	44	29	2	57	59	51	24	1	38	1
56	12	23	5	27	38	24	56	4	48	26	35	53	4	3	13	45	54	3	3	40	53	13	1	42	25
58	12	41	5	29	29	25	7	4	5	57	36	51	4	8	21	47	17	3	9	49	55	0	1	47	12
60	12	57	5	29	29	25	40	4	55	35	37	46	4	13	51	48	35	3	17	44	56	47	1	52	45

NATURAL GRADUATION

Q	A		B		a		b		..	Q	A		B		a		b		..
°	°	'	°	'	°	'	°	'	°	°	°	'	°	'	°	'	°	'	°
38	15	10	36	22	9	13	14	19	142	64	23	22	34	44	12	50	15	39	116
40	15	51	36	33	9	33	14	31	140	66	23	56	34	27	13	3	15	40	114
42	16	12	36	33	9	33	14	42	138	68	24	30	34	9	13	16	15	40	112
44	17	12	36	29	10	12	14	51	136	70	25	3	33	51	13	28	15	39	110
46	17	51	36	25	10	30	15	0	134	72	25	35	33	31	13	39	15	38	108
48	18	30	36	19	10	48	15	7	132	74	26	7	33	11	13	50	15	36	106
50	19	8	36	11	11	5	15	14	130	76	26	38	32	50	14	1	15	33	104
52	19	46	36	2	11	21	15	20	128	78	27	9	32	28	14	11	15	30	102
54	20	24	35	52	11	38	15	25	126	80	27	39	32	5	14	20	15	27	100
56	21	0	35	41	11	53	15	30	124	82	28	8	31	41	14	29	15	22	98
58	21	36	35	28	12	8	15	33	122	84	28	37	31	17	14	38	15	18	96
60	22	12	35	15	12	23	15	36	120	86	29	5	30	52	14	45	15	12	94
62	22	48	35	0	12	37	15	38	118	88	29	33	30	26	14	55	15	6	92
64	23	22	34	44	12	50	15	39	116	90	30	0	30	0	15	0	15	0	90
..	B		A		b		a		Q	..	B		A		b		a		Q

XIII
Geographical and Time Data

Latitudes and longitude equivalents for nearly 1,000 places. Zone and Standard Times of most countries and states and dates of many changes in these between 1870 and 1990. Dates of calendar change in countries using old style after 1870 and foreign summer time or daylight saving details from 1916 to 1951.

(j) Explanations

PLACES LISTED The lists on pp. 326–32 date from the 1953 edition and have been reproduced almost unchanged for purposes of historical accuracy and because they are familiar to long-time users of the book and have served them so well.

LATITUDE: 51n30 = 51°30′ north, 51s30 = 51°30′ south.

LONGITUDE EQUIVALENT: Geographical longitude expressed as time ($+$1h $=$ 15° east; $-$1h $=$ 15° west); amount by which local differs from Greenwich Mean or sidereal time.

ZONE TIMES (whole or half hours only) given in column headed 'h'; date of adoption (where known) in column headed 'from'; but other standard times (involving minutes and/or seconds) thus: 1h23m35s, or (to nearest minute) 1h35m – farther to the left, with no attention to width of column.

PRESENT STANDARD TIME (early 1952) given *first*; standard times for past years, if different and known, given after, in *backward* order of date of adoption or use.

Plus ($+$) means fast on Greenwich; subtract to get GMT.

Minus ($-$) means slow on Greenwich; add to get GMT.

‡ means 'except for some part(s) of this' (country etc.).

NAME UNDERLINED means 'has used some variation, summer time or the like, in certain years of 1916–51'.

SUMMER OR DAYLIGHT-SAVING TIME. Began on date given before the / or ∤ or ∦ or ✶, and ended on date following that sign;

the sign / means single summer time (1h advance);

the sign ∤ means only a half-hour advance;

the sign // means double summer time – total advance of 2 h;

the sign ∦ means semi-double – total advance of 1½h;

the sign ✶ means twenty minutes advance only.

THE TIME WHEN CLOCKS CHANGED (by law), if known, shown thus:

a = 1 a.m.; b = 2 a.m.; c = 3 a.m.; x = 10 p.m.; y = 11 p.m.; z = 12 p.m. (not o a.m.); so that y24Ap/a23Se would mean: 1h summer time from 11 p.m. on the 24 April till 1 a.m. on the 23 September. Times thus shown are intended as expressed in standard time, but sometimes are doubtful, especially for the *ending* of summer time, etc.

DATES ABBREVIATED FOR WIDTH OF COL., thus: 12Ja32 = 12 January 1932; but 12Ja92 = 12 January *1*892 (all years between 1870 and 1952). Months: first two letters, but note: Ja, Je, JL (not Jl) are used for January, June, July; Mh, My for March, May; Oc used for October.

IN SOUTH LATITUDES 'summer' is from a late month one civil year to an early month the next year; so, under 1920, Oc/Mh means 'to Mh 1921'.

CONT. (INSTEAD OF A DATE) = continuous from preceding, or into following, year.

LATITUDES AND LONGITUDE EQUIVALENTS OF PLACES IN THE BRITISH ISLES

PLACE	LAT.	m s	PLACE	LAT.	m s	PLACE	LAT.	m s
Aberdare	51n32	-13 40	Chesterfield	53n14	- 5 40	Greenock	55n57	-19 0
Aberdeen	57n 9	- 8 24	Chorley	53n39	- 9 32	Grimsby	53n54	- 0 16
Abertillery	51n45	-12 40	Clackman'n	56n 6	-14 56	Guildford	51n14	- 2 16
Aberystwyth	52n25	-20 20	Clonmel	52n21	-30 52	Haddington	55n57	-11 8
Accrington	53n45	- 9 28	Clydebank	55n55	-17 36	Halesowen	52n27	- 8 12
Acton, Middx	51n31	- 1 4	Coatbridge	55n52	-16 4	Halifax	53n42	- 7 28
Airdrie	55n52	-15 48	Colchester	51n53	+ 3 32	Hamilton	55n47	-16 8
Aldershot	51n15	- 3 8	Cork	52n54	+33 52	Hanley	53n 2	- 8 44
Appleby	54n35	-10 0	Coulsdon	51n19	- 0 28	Harrowgate	53n59	- 6 12
Arbroath	56n34	-10 20	Coventry	52n25	- 6 0	Hartlepool	54n42	- 4 40
Armagh	54n21	-26 20	Cowes, IOW	50n45	- 5 12	Hastings	50n51	+ 2 16
Ashton	53n30	- 8 28	Crewe	53n 5	- 9 52	Haverford W.	51n47	-17 52
Aylesbury	51n49	- 3 16	Crosby, Gt	53n28	-12 8	Hendon	51n36	- 0 52
Ayr	55n26	-18 28	Croydon	51n22	- 0 24	Hereford	52n10	-11 0
Ballymena	54n52	-25 4	Cupar	56n19	-12 0	Heston	51n29	- 0 23
Banff	51n40	-10 8	Dagenham	51n33	+ 0 40	Hornsea	51n37	- 0 28
Bangor	53n14	-16 28	Darlington	54n32	- 6 8	Hove	50n50	- 0 48
Barking	51n33	+ 0 20	Darwen	53n45	- 5 52	Huddersfield	53n39	- 7 8
Barnes	51n28	- 0 56	Derby	52n56	- 5 52	Hull	53n45	- 1 20
Barnsley	53n33	- 5 56	Dewsbury	53n42	- 6 28	Huntingdon	52n21	- 0 44
Barrow in F	54n 7	-12 52	Dolgelly	52n45	-15 32	Hyde	53n27	- 8 20
Barry, Glam	56n30	-11 4	Doncaster	53n31	- 4 32	Ilford	51n34	+ 0 20
Bath	51n21	- 9 20	Dorchester	50n43	- 9 40	Ilkeston	52n59	- 5 16
Batley	53n43	- 6 32	Douglas	54n 9	-17 56	Inverary	56n14	-20 20
Beckenham	51n24	- 0 8	Dover	51n 7	+ 5 16	Inverness	57n29	-16 52
Bedford	52n 9	- 0 56	Downpatrick	54n20	-22 56	Ipswich	52n 4	+ 4 40
Belfast	54n27	-23 40	Drogheda	53n45	-25 8	Jarrow	54n58	- 6 0
Bexley	51n26	+ 0 36	Dublin	53n24	-25 0	Jedburgh	55n29	-10 16
Bilston	52n33	- 8 12	Dudley	52n31	- 8 20	Keighley	53n52	- 7 36
Birkenhead	53n23	-12 8	Dumbarton	56n 5	-18 40	Kidderminster	52n24	- 8 52
Birmingham	52n29	- 7 28	Dumfries	55n 4	-14 32	Kildare	53n10	-27 40
Blackburn	53n45	- 8 56	Dundalk	54n 0	-25 24	Kilkenny	52n35	-29 0
Blackpool	53n49	-12 12	Dundee	56n28	-11 52	Kingston	51n25	- 1 12
Blaydon	54n58	- 7 48	Dunfermline	56n 6	-13 48	Kingstown	53n17	-24 36
Blyth	55n 8	- 6 0	Durham	54n47	- 6 16	Kinross	56n12	-13 40
Bodmin	50n29	-18 52	Ealing	51n33	- 0 32	Kirkcaldy	57n 7	-12 36
Bolton	53n36	- 9 56	Eastbourne	50n46	+ 5 8	Kirkcudb't	54n50	-12 12
Bootle	53n27	-11 56	East Ham	51n32	+ 0 12	Kirkwall	58n59	-11 48
Bournemouth	50n44	- 7 28	Ebbw Vale	51n47	-12 40	Lanark	55n44	-15 8
Bradford	53n48	- 7 0	Eccles	53n28	- 9 24	Lancaster	54n 3	-11 12
Brecon	51n57	-13 32	Edinburgh	55n57	-12 48	Leeds	53n48	- 6 12
Brentford	51n29	- 1 16	Edmonton	51n37	- 0 12	Leicester	52n39	- 4 32
Brighton	50n49	- 0 36	Elgin	57n39	-13 12	Leigh, Lancs	53n29	- 6 8
Bristol	51n27	-10 12	Enfield	51n40	- 0 20	Lerwick	60n10	- 4 40
Bromley, Kent	51n25	+ 0 4	Ennis	52n51	-35 56	Lewis	50n52	+ 0 4
Burnley	53n47	- 9 0	Enniskillen	54n20	-30 36	Leyton	51n34	- 0 4
Burton-on-Tr	52n48	- 6 42	Epsom	51n20	- 1 8	Lifford	54n50	-30 40
Bury	53n27	- 0 28	Erith	51n28	+ 0 48	Limerick	52n30	-35 0
Caerphilly	51n35	-12 0	Eston	54n34	- 4 28	Lincoln	53n15	- 2 8
Cambridge	52n13	+ 0 28	Exeter	50n44	-14 8	Linlithgow	55n58	-14 28
Cannock	52n43	- 8 4	Falkirk	56n 0	-14 32	Lisburn	54n31	-24 12
Canterbury	51n17	+ 4 20	Falmouth	50n10	-20 20	Liverpool	53n24	-11 56
Cardiff	51n28	-12 40	Finchley	51n36	- 0 40	Llandudno	53n20	-15 40
Carlisle	54n54	-11 40	Folkestone	51n 5	+ 4 44	Llanelly	51n41	-16 36
Carlow	52n50	-27 40	Forfar	56n39	-11 32	Llangefni	53n16	-17 6
Carmarthen	51n55	-17 12	Galway	53n17	-36 16	LONDON: City	51n31	- 0 24
Cernarvon	53n 8	-17 0	Gellygaer	51n41	-13 4	Battersea	51n28	- 0 40
Carrick	53n57	-32 20	Gateshead	54n58	- 6 24	Bermondsey	51n30	- 0 16
Castlebar	53n52	-37 12	Gillingham	51n24	+ 2 12	Bethnal Gr.	51n31	- 0 12
Cavan	53n29	-23 28	Glasgow	53n52	-17 0	Camberwell	51n28	- 0 16
Chatham	51n23	+ 2 8	Gloucester	51n52	- 8 56	Chelsea	51n29	- 0 44
Chelmsford	51n42	+ 1 52	Gosport	50n48	- 8 32	Deptford	51n29	- 0 8
Cheltenham	51n53	+ 8 20	Gravesend	51n27	+ 1 28	Finsbury	51n34	- 0 24
Chester	53n12	-11 36				Fulham	51n28	- 0 52

PLACE	LAT.	m s	PLACE	LAT.	m s	PLACE	LAT.	m s
LONDON (cont)			Oakham	52n41	- 2 56	Spenboro'	53n44	- 6 44
Greenwich	51n31	0 0	Oldbury	52n59	- 8 0	Stafford	52n43	- 8 24
Hackney	51n33	- 0 12	Oldham	53n33	- 8 32	Stirling	56n 7	-15 44
Hammers'th	51n30	- 0 56	Omagh	54n36	-29 16	Stockton-on-T	54n34	- 5 20
Holborn	51n31	- 0 28	Orpington	51n23	- 0 24	Stoke-on-T	53n 1	- 8 44
Islington	51n32	- 0 24	Oxford	51n45	- 5 4	Stonehaven	56n58	- 8 52
Kensington	51n30	- 0 38	Paisley	55n51	-17 44	Stornaway	58n13	-25 28
Lambeth	51n30	- 0 28	Peebles	55n39	-12 44	Streatham	51n26	- 0 32
Lewisham	51n28	- 0 4	Pembroke	51n40	-17 36	Sunderland	54n55	- 5 28
Marylebone	51n31	- 0 40	Perth	56n23	-13 44	Sutton, Sur.	51n22	- 0 48
Paddington	51n31	- 0 40	Peterborough	52n36	- 0 56	Swansea	51n37	-15 40
Poplar	51n31	- 0 4	Plymouth	50n23	-16 32	Swindon	51n33	- 7 0
St. Pancras	51n32	- 0 28	Pontypool	51n42	-12 8	Swinton	53n29	- 5 20
Shoreditch	51n32	- 0 20	Pontypridd	51n35	-13 16	Taunton	51n 1	-12 24
Southwark	51n31	- 0 16	Poole	50n43	- 7 56	Tralee	53n16	-38 48
Stepney	51n31	- 0 8	Portadown	54n25	-25 48	Trim	53n34	-27 8
Stoke N'n	51n34	- 0 16	Portsmouth	50n48	- 4 24	Tullamore	53n16	-30 0
Wandsworth	51n27	- 0 48	Port Talbot	51n35	-15 4	Tunbridge W	51n 8	+ 1 4
Westminster	51n31	- 0 28	Presteign	52n17	-12 0	Twickenham	51n27	- 1 20
Woolwich	51n29	+ 0 16	Preston	52n44	- 9 52	Tynemouth	55n 1	- 5 40
Londonderry	55n 0	-29 24	Ramsgate	51n20	+ 5 40	Uxbridge	51n33	- 1 56
Longford	53n44	-31 12	Reading	51n27	- 3 52	Wakefield	53n41	- 6 0
Lowestoft	52n29	+7 0	Reigate	51n14	- 0 52	Wallasey	53n25	-12 20
Lurgan	55n48	-25 20	Renfrew	55n23	-17 40	Wallsend	54n59	- 6 8
Macclesford	53n16	- 8 32	Rhondda	51n39	-13 56	Walsall	52n34	- 7 52
Maidstone	51n17	- 2 4	Richmond	51n27	- 1 12	Walthamstow	51n38	- 0 16
Manchester	53n29	- 9 4	Rochdale	53n37	- 8 44	Warrington	53n25	-10 32
Mansfield	53n 8	- 4 48	Rochester	51n24	+2 4	Warwick	52n17	- 6 20
Margate	51n23	- 5 32	Romford	51n35	+ 0 40	Wednesbury	52n33	- 8 0
Maryboro'	53n 2	-29 16	Roscommon	53n39	-32 48	Welshpool	52n40	-12 36
Middlesboro'	54n35	- 4 56	Rutherglen	55n49	-16 48	Wembley	51n33	- 1 16
Mitcham	51n24	- 0 40	Ryde, IOW	50n44	- 4 44	W. Bromwich	52n31	- 8 0
Mold	53n10	-12 36	St. Helens	53n21	-11 0	West Ham	51n33	+ 0 8
Monaghan	54n10	-28 0	St. Helier	49n11	-33 36	Wexford	52n20	-25 52
Monmouth	51n44	-12 0	Salford	53n30	- 9 8	Wicklow	52n58	-24 12
Motherwell	55n47	-15 56	Salisbury	51n 4	- 7 12	Widnes	53n22	-11 0
Mulingar	53n32	-29 24	Scarboro'	54n17	- 1 40	Wigan	53n33	-10 32
Nairn	57n30	-15 20	Scunthorpe	53n36	- 2 20	Wigtown	54n45	-17 0
Neath	51n32	-15 12	Selkirk	53n32	-11 24	Willesden	51n32	- 0 56
Nelson	53n52	- 8 56	Shepley	53n36	- 6 48	Wimbledon	51n26	- 0 52
Newcastle/T	54n59	- 6 24	Shrewsbury	52n43	-11 0	Winchester	51n 4	- 5 12
Newcastle/L	53n 1	- 8 56	Skye	57n20	-25 20	Windsor	51n29	- 2 28
Newmarket	52n15	+1 40	Sligo	54n17	-34 20	Wolverham'n	52n35	- 8 24
Newport, IOW	50n43	- 5 12	Slough	51n30	- 2 20	Wolverton	52n 5	- 3 12
Newport, Mon	51n35	-12 0	Southall	51n31	- 1 32	Wood Green	51n36	- 0 28
Newry	54n11	-25 40	Southampton	50n55	- 5 36	Worcester	52n11	- 8 52
Newtonards	54n36	-22 44	Southend/S	51n33	+ 2 48	Worthing	50n49	- 1 32
Northampton	52n15	- 3 46	Southgate	51n38	- 0 28	Yarmouth	50n43	- 6 52
Nottingham	52n57	- 4 32	Southport	53n39	-11 56	Yeovil	50n57	-10 28
Norwich	52n38	+5 12	Southsea	50n47	- 4 16	York	53n58	- 4 16
Nuneaton	52n32	- 5 52	South Shields	55n 0	- 5 40	LONG. EQUIVS to the nearest 4 secs.		

Notes: Longitude equivalents above are given to the nearest 4 seconds.

In the table below after each degree of longitude are given hours (h) and minutes (m) of equivalent time (for minutes of longitude, read ° as ′, and h m as m s of time). For longitude exceeding 90°, use 6h plus equivalent of excess.

(k) Longitude Equivalent

°	h	m	°	h	m	°	h	m	°	h	m	°	h	m	°	h	m	°	h	m	°	h	m
1	0	4	13	0	52	25	1	40	37	2	28	49	3	16	61	4	4	73	4	52	85	5	40
2	0	8	14	0	56	26	1	44	38	2	32	50	3	20	62	4	8	74	4	56	86	5	44
3	0	12	15	1	0	27	1	48	39	2	36	51	3	24	63	4	12	75	5	0	87	5	48
4	0	16	16	1	4	28	1	52	40	2	40	52	3	28	64	4	16	76	5	4	88	5	52
5	0	20	17	1	8	29	1	56	41	2	44	53	3	32	65	4	20	77	5	8	89	5	56
6	0	24	18	1	12	30	2	0	42	2	48	54	3	36	66	4	24	78	5	12	90	6	0
7	0	28	19	1	16	31	2	4	43	2	52	55	3	40	67	4	28	79	5	16	EXAMPLE		
8	0	32	20	1	20	32	2	8	44	2	56	56	3	44	68	4	32	80	5	20	106°32′		
9	0	36	21	1	24	33	2	12	45	3	0	57	3	48	69	4	36	81	5	24	= 6h0m0s		
10	0	40	22	1	28	34	2	16	46	3	4	58	3	52	70	4	40	82	5	28	+ 1h4m0s		
11	0	44	23	1	32	35	2	20	47	3	8	59	3	56	71	4	44	83	5	32	+ 0h2m8s		
12	0	48	24	1	36	36	2	24	48	3	12	60	4	0	72	4	48	84	5	36	= 7h6m8s		

Greater London births are about a quarter of those in all England. So improving their accuracy goes a long way to improving English astrology. For whole-degree approximate charts 51° 30′ N., 0° longitude is perhaps near enough for them all. Using this, as (alas) too often is done, when the Ascendant is professedly correct to the nearest minute, is an utter absurdity, however, for the *whole* of Greater London's 700 or so square miles! So, above, London suburban towns are treated as any of the other towns of Britain, and boroughs are given under London.

LATITUDES AND LONGITUDE EQUIVALENTS OF PLACES IN OTHER COUNTRIES

PLACE	Country	LAT	h	m	s	PLACE	Country	LAT	h	m	s
AACHEN	Germ.	50n46	+ 0	24	20	BOGOTA	Colombia	4n30	- 4	58	0
AARAU	Switz.	47n23	+ 0	32	16	BOLOGNA	Italy	44n29	+ 0	45	24
ABERCORN	Zambia	8s47	+ 2	5	20	BOMBAY	India	19n 0	+ 4	51	40
ACCRA	Ghana	5n38	- 0	0	48	BONN	Germ.	50n43	+ 0	28	16
ADDIS ABABA	Ethiopia	9n 2	+ 2	34	52	BORDEAUX	France	44n50	- 0	2	4
ADELAIDE	S. Aus.	34s54	+ 9	14	24	BOSTON, MASS	USA	42n25	- 4	44	20
ADEN	S. Yemen	12n58	+ 3	4	0	BOULOGNE	France	50n43	+ 0	6	32
AGRA	India	27n 7	+ 5	12	20	BOURGES	France	47n 5	+ 0	9	24
AHMADABAD	India	23n 3	+ 4	50	32	BRATISLAVA	Czech.	48n10	+ 1	8	24
AJACCIO	Corsica	41n55	+ 0	34	48	BREMEN	Germ.	53n 6	+ 0	35	4
AJMER	India	26n22	+ 4	58	40	BRESCIA	Italy	45n36	+ 0	40	48
AKRON, OHIO	USA	41n 8	- 5	26	0	BRESLAU	Germ.	51n 8	+ 1	8	0
ALBANY, NY	USA	42n38	- 4	56	0	BREST	France	48n26	- 0	18	0
ALEPPO	Syria	36n14	+ 2	29	4	BRIDGEPORT	USA	41n14	- 4	53	20
ALESSANDRIA	Italy	44n55	+ 0	34	28	BRIDGETOWN	Barbados	13n 0	- 4	0	0
ALEXANDRIA	Egypt	31n 9	+ 1	59	32	BRISBANE	Aus.	27s30	+ 10	12	0
ALGIERS	Alger.	36n50	+ 0	11	40	BRNO	Czech.	49n11	+ 1	6	32
ALICE SPR	Aus.	23s36	+ 8	55	32	BRUGES	Belgium	51n13	+ 0	12	48
ALLAHABAD	India	25n22	+ 5	27	30	BRUNSWICK	Germ.	52n15	+ 0	42	0
ALMA-ATA	USSR	43n28	+ 5	7	52	BRUSSELS	Belgium	50n51	+ 0	17	24
ALTDORF	Switz.	46n53	+ 0	34	32	BUCHAREST	Rom.	44n25	+ 1	44	20
AMIENS	France	49n53	+ 0	9	12	BUCKEBURG	Germ.	52n17	+ 0	36	8
AMRITSAR	India	31n35	+ 4	59	12	BUDAPEST	Hung.	47n29	+ 1	16	20
AMSTERDAM	Neth.	52n21	+ 0	19	40	BUENOS AIRES	Arg.	34s40	- 3	54	0
ANDORRA	Andorra	42n30	+ 0	5	56	BUFFALO, N.Y.	USA	42n55	- 5	15	52
ANGERS	France	47n29	- 0	2	20	BYDGOSZCZ	Poland	53n 8	+ 1	12	0
ANGRA DO H.	Azores	19s 0	- 1	48	20	CAGLIARI	Italy	39n15	+ 0	36	32
ANKARA	Turkey	39n52	+ 2	11	56	CAIRO	Egypt	30n 1	+ 2	4	52
ANTANANARIVO	Madag.	19s 0	+ 3	9	20	CALCUTTA	India	22n32	+ 5	56	0
ANTIOCH	Syria	36n 4	+ 2	24	40	CAMAGUEY	Cuba	21n22	- 5	11	56
ANTOFAGASTA	Chile	23s30	- 4	41	40	CAMDEN, NJ	USA	40n 0	- 5	0	0
ANTWERP	Belgium	51n14	+ 0	17	32	CANBERRA	Aus.	35s15	+ 9	56	40
ARNHEM	Neth.	51n58	+ 0	23	36	CANDIA	Crete	35n15	+ 1	40	0
ASTRAKHAN	Ukraine	46n13	+ 3	12	0	CANEA	Crete	35n32	+ 1	36	4
ASUNCION	Paraguay	25s15	- 3	50	20	CANTON	China	23n15	+ 7	33	20
ATHENS	Greece	37n59	+ 1	35	8	CANTON, OHIO	USA	40n53	- 5	25	20
ATLANTA, GA	USA	33n45	- 5	37	20	CAPE TOWN	S. Africa	33s58	+ 1	13	44
ATLANTIC C, NJ	USA	39n26	- 4	58	0	CARACAS	Venez.	10n31	- 4	27	56
AUCKLAND	N.Z.	36s54	+ 11	47	4	CARTAGENA	Spain	37n37	- 0	3	48
AUGSBURG	Germ.	48n23	+ 0	43	40	CASABLANCA	Moroc.	33n30	- 0	32	0
BAGHDAD	Iraq	33n18	+ 2	58	0	CASSEL	Germ.	51n18	+ 0	37	40
BAHIA BLANCA	Arg.	38s30	- 4	9	20	CATANIA	Sicily	37n29	+ 1	0	24
BAKU	USSR	40n22	+ 3	19	4	CAWNPORE	India	26n24	+ 5	21	36
BALTA	USSR	47n59	+ 1	58	0	CERNAVODA	Rom.	48n18	+ 1	43	44
BALTIMORE	USA	39n23	- 5	6	20	CETINJE	Yugos.	42n25	+ 1	15	52
BANGALORE	India	12n59	+ 5	10	32	CHATTANOOGA	USA	35n 3	- 5	40	28
BANJUL	Gambia	13n23	+ 9	58	20	CHICAGO	USA	41n50	- 5	51	0
BANGKOK	Thailand	13n45	+ 6	42	20	CHISINAU	Rom.	47n 4	+ 1	54	44
BARCELONA	Spain	41n22	+ 0	8	40	CHRISTCHURCH	N.Z.	43s31	+ 11	30	28
BAREILLY	India	23n20	+ 5	12	20	CHUNGKING	China	29n35	+ 7	6	32
BARI	Italy	41n 8	+ 1	7	28	CINCINNATI	USA	39n 3	- 5	38	0
BARHILA	Brazil	10s40	- 2	25	48	CIUDAD	Venez.	8n 7	- 4	15	28
BASLE	Switz.	47n33	+ 0	30	16	CLEVELAND	USA	41n30	- 5	26	0
BASRA	Iraq	30n34	+ 3	11	20	COLOMBO	Sri Lanka	6n58	+ 5	19	52
BATHURST	Australia	33s22	+ 1	6	33	COLUMBUS	USA	39n57	- 5	32	0
BEIRUT	Lebanon	33n54	+ 2	22	8	CONSTANTA	Rom.	44n12	+ 1	54	44
BELGRADE	Yugos.	44n50	+ 1	22	4	CONSTANTINE	Alger.	36n30	+ 0	26	0
BELIZE	Belize	17n30	- 5	52	8	COPENHAGEN	Denmark	55n43	+ 0	50	32
BELLINZONA	Switz.	46n12	+ 0	36	8	CORDOBA	Arg.	31s1C	- 4	17	40
BELO HORIZ.	Brazil	19s50	- 2	57	40	CORDOVA	Spain	37n52	- 0	19	12
BERGEN	Norway	60n 2	+ 0	21	20	CRACOW	Pol.	50n 5	+ 1	19	56
BERLIN	Germ.	52n34	+ 0	53	0	DACCA	Bangladesh	23n46	+ 6	2	0
BERNE	Switz.	46n58	+ 0	29	52	DAIREN	China	39n 0	+ 8	6	20
BIELSK	Poland	49n50	+ 1	16	4	DAKAR	Senegal	14n40	- 1	9	52
BLOEMFONT'N	S. Africa	29s12	+ 1	44	52	DALLAS	USA	32n50	- 6	27	20
BOCHUM	Germ.	51n28	+ 0	29	8	DAMASCUS	Syria	33n30	+ 2	25	20

329

PLACE	Country	LAT		h	m	s	PLACE	Country	LAT		h	m	s
DARMSTADT	Germ.	49n54	+	0	34	32	HELSINKI	Finland	60n13	+	1	39	52
DAYTON, OHIO	USA	39n42	-	5	56	48	HONG KONG	HK	22n20	+	7	35	40
DELHI	India	28n35	+	5	9	12	HONOLULU	Hawaii	21n25	-	10	31	40
DENVER, COL	USA	39n43	-	6	59	56	HOUSTON	USA	29n49	-	6	21	20
DES MOINES	USA	41n33	-	6	14	20	HOWRAH	India	22n37	+	5	53	8
DESSAU	Germ.	51n50	+	0	49	4	HSINKING	China	44n 0	+	8	20	0
DETMOLD	Germ.	51n56	+	0	35	20	HYDERABAD	India	17n25	+	5	14	20
DETROIT	USA	42n20	-	5	32	20	INDIANAPOLIS	USA	39n45	-	5	45	8
DIJON	France	47n19	+	0	20	16	ISTANBUL	Turkey	41n 1	+	1	55	52
DORTMUND	Germ.	51n32	+	0	29	44	IVANOVO VOZ	USSR	57n 3	+	2	43	52
DRESDEN	Germ.	51n 5	+	0	54	40	JACKSONVILLE	USA	30n20	-	5	26	40
DUISBURG	Germ.	51n26	+	0	27	0	JAKARTA	Indonesia	6s10	+	7	7	20
DULUTH, MINN	USA	46n47	-	6	8	40	JASSY	Rom.	47n15	+	1	49	40
DUSSELDORF	Germ.	51n15	+	0	27	4	JERUSALEM	Israel	31n48	+	2	20	48
EDMONTON	Canada	53n35	-	7	33	36	JOHOR BAHARU	Malaysia	1n35	+	6	55	40
EL PASO	USA	31n52	-	7	5	56	JOGYAKARTA	Java	7n57	+	7	21	20
ELBERFELD	Germ.	51n15	+	0	29	0	KABUL	Afgan.	34n33	+	4	36	40
ELIZABETH, NJ	USA	40n40	-	4	57	8	KANSAS,KAN	USA	38n30	-	6	36	0
ERFURT	Germ.	51n 0	+	0	44	0	KANSAS,MO	USA	39n 0	-	6	18	0
ERIE, PENN	USA	42n 8	-	4	40	8	KARACHI	Pak.	24n52	+	4	28	0
ERIVAN	Armenia	40n10	+	2	58	4	KARLSRUHE	Germ.	49n 3	+	0	33	20
ESSEN	Germ.	51n26	+	0	27	0	KATOWICE	Poland	50n17	+	1	16	12
EVANSVILLE	USA	37n 0	-	5	50	12	KAUNAS	USSR	55n17	+	1	35	40
EVORA	Portugal	38n34	-	0	31	40	KAZAN	USSR	55n42	+	3	16	24
FALL RIVER	USA	41n45	-	5	44	0	KHARKOV	USSR	49n50	+	2	25	0
FEZ	Moroc.	44n 0	+	0	20	0	KHARTOUM	Sudan	15n37	+	2	11	28
FLORENCE	Italy	43n46	+	0	45	8	KIEL	Germ.	54n20	+	0	40	40
FORTALEZA	Brazil	3s50	-	2	34	40	KIEV	USSR	50n26	+	2	1	52
FT. DE FRANCE	Mart.	14n36	-	4	4	8	KINGSTON	Jamaica	18n 0	-	5	7	8
FT. WAYNE	USA	41n 0	-	5	40	8	KINSHASA	Zaire	4s22	+	1	1	20
FT. WORTH	USA	32n45	-	6	29	20	KLAGENFURT	Austria	46n37	+	0	57	16
FRANKFURT	Germ.	50n 7	+	0	34	40	KNOXVILLE	USA	35n50	-	5	36	0
FREETOWN	S. Leone	8n30	-	0	52	48	KOBE	Japan	34n41	+	9	0	48
FUNCHAL	Madeira	32n45	-	1	8	0	KOLN	Germ.	51n 0	+	0	28	0
GALATI	Rum.	45n28	+	1	52	8	KORITZA	Albania	40n38	+	1	23	12
GARY, IND	USA	41n35	-	5	49	20	KREFELD	Germ.	51n20	+	0	26	16
GDANSK	Poland	54n20	+	1	19	40	KUALA LUMPUR	Malaysia	3n 5	+	6	46	40
GELSENKIR'N	Germ.	51n32	+	0	28	32	KURSK	USSR	51n47	+	2	24	20
GENEVA	Switz.	46n12	+	0	24	36	KYOTO	Japan	34n57	+	9	3	44
GENOVA	Italy	44n24	+	0	36	0	LA PAZ	Bol.	16s30	-	4	33	0
GEORGETOWN	Guyana	6n46	-	3	52	32	LA PLATA	Arg.	34s55	-	3	52	0
GEORGE TOWN	Malaya	5n30	+	6	40	24	LAGOS	Nigeria	6n27	+	0	13	40
GHENT	Belgium	51n 4	+	0	14	52	LAHORE	Pak.	31n31	+	4	57	28
GIBRALTAR	Gib.	36n10	-	0	21	28	LAUSANNE	Switz.	46n32	+	0	26	28
GODTHAAB	Greenland	64n15	-	3	24	40	LEIPZIG	Germ.	51n20	+	0	49	20
GOTEBORG	Sweden	57n40	+	0	48	0	LEMBERG	Poland	49n50	+	1	36	4
GRANADA	Spain	37n10	-	0	14	20	LENINGRAD	USSR	60n 0	+	2	1	20
GRAZ	Austria	47n 4	+	1	1	44	LHASA	Tibet	29n50	+	6	4	40
GRENADA	W. Indies	12n 5	-	4	7	0	LIEGE	Belg.	50n39	+	0	22	16
GRONINGEN	Neth.	53n10	+	0	26	20	LILLE	France	50n37	+	0	12	16
GUATEMALA	Guat.	14n41	-	6	2	20	LIMA	Peru	12s15	-	5	7	20
GUAYAQUIL	Ecuador	2s13	-	5	19	36	LINZ	Austria	48n 1	+	0	57	12
HAARLEM	Neth.	52n21	+	0	18	36	LISBON	Port.	38n32	-	0	36	40
HALIFAX	Canada	44n38	-	4	14	12	LIVORNO	Italy	43n33	+	0	41	20
HAMBURG	Germ.	53n34	+	0	40	8	LODZ	Poland	51n46	+	1	17	4
HAMILTON	Bermuda	32n18	-	4	18	48	LONG BEACH	USA	33n45	-	7	51	20
HAMILTON,ONT	Canada	43n16	-	5	19	36	LOS ANGELES	USA	34n 1	-	7	53	20
HAMMERFEST	Norway	70n40	+	1	34	40	LOUISVILLE	USA	38n15	-	5	43	0
HANGCHOW	China	30n10	+	8	0	20	LOUVAIN	Belg.	50n53	+	0	18	44
HANKOW	China	30n50	+	7	37	0	LOWELL	USA	42n43	-	4	45	20
HANOI	Vietnam	21n 0	+	7	3	0	LUANDA	Angola	8s48	+	0	52	4
HANOVER	Germ.	52n23	+	0	39	32	LUBECK	Germ.	53n52	+	0	42	40
HARTFORD	USA	41n49	-	4	51	8	LUBLIN	Poland	51n13	+	1	30	16
HAVANA	Cuba	23n 0	-	5	30	0	LUCERNE	Switz.	47n 3	+	0	33	4
LE HARVRE	France	49n30	+	0	0	28	LUCKNOW	India	26n47	+	5	23	56

PLACE	Country	LAT		h	m	s	PLACE	Country	LAT		h	m	s
LUDWIGSHAFN	Germ.	49n30	+	0	33	28	ODESSA	USSR	46n29	+	2	2	24
LUXEMBOURG	Belg.	49n37	+	0	24	28	OKLAHOMA	USA	35n28	-	6	30	0
LYNN	USA	42n30	-	4	44	0	OLDENBURG	Germ.	53n 8	+	0	32	48
LYON	France	45n44	+	0	19	24	OMAHA	USA	41n15	-	6	24	0
MACAU	Brazil	5s 0	-	3	6	0	OMSK	USSR	55n 0	+	4	54	32
MADRAS	India	13n 7	+	5	21	0	OPORTO	Port.	41n 8	-	0	33	0
MADRID	Spain	40n25	-	0	15	0	ORAN	Algeria	35n40	-	0	3	10
MADURA	India	9n50	+	5	12	40	ORENBURG	USSR	51n48	+	3	40	40
MAGDEBURG	Germ.	52n 8	+	0	46	40	ORLEANS	France	47n53	+	0	7	28
MAINZ	Germ.	50n 0	+	0	32	52	OSLO	Norway	59n54	-	0	43	20
MALACCA	Malaysia	2n15	+	6	49	0	OSTEND	Belg.	51n13	+	0	12	0
MALMO	Sweden	55n38	+	0	51	48	OTTAWA	Canada	45n26	-	5	2	44
MANAGUA	Nicarag.	12n 0	-	5	45	0	PANAMA	Panama	8n59	-	5	18	8
MANDALAY	Burma	22n 3	+	6	24	8	PARA	Brazil	1s10	-	3	13	0
MANILA	Philip.	14n10	+	8	4	0	PARAMARIBO	Indon.	5n45	-	3	41	40
MANNHEIM	Germ.	49n30	+	0	33	44	PARIS	France	48n52	+	0	9	20
MARRAKESH	Moroc.	31n38	-	0	31	56	PATERSON, NJ	USA	41n 0	-	4	49	40
MARSEILLE	France	43n18	+	0	21	40	PERNAMBUCO	Brazil	8s 0	-	2	36	0
MEDELLIN	Colom.	6n10	-	5	3	20	PERTH	Aus.	31s52	+	7	43	20
MEERUT	India	29n 1	+	5	11	12	PERUGIA	Italy	43n 8	+	0	49	24
MELBOURNE	Aus.	37s50	+	9	39	52	PESHAWAR	Pak.	34n 8	+	4	46	8
MEMEL	Lith.	55n42	+	1	24	40	PHILADELPHIA	USA	40n 0	-	5	1	0
MEMPHIS	USA	35n 9	-	6	0	0	PILSEN	Czech.	49n45	+	0	53	32
MESSINA	Italy	38n11	+	1	2	12	PITTSBURGH	USA	40n30	-	5	19	40
MEXICO CITY	Mexico	19n25	-	6	37	8	PHNOM-PENH	Cam.	11n30	+	6	59	40
MIAMI	USA	25n45	-	5	21	0	PONDICHERRY	India	12n 0	+	5	19	40
MIDDLEBURG	Neth.	51n30	+	0	14	40	PT. AU PRINCE	Haiti	18n40	-	4	49	40
MILAN	Italy	45n28	+	0	36	40	PT. OF SPAIN	Trin.	10n36	-	4	5	56
MILWAUKEE	USA	43n 0	-	5	52	0	PORTO NOVO	Benin	6n30	+	0	10	40
MINNEAPOLIS	USA	45n 3	-	6	13	20	P'TOFERRAJO	Italy	42n50	+	0	41	20
MINSK	USSR	54n 0	+	1	50	8	PORTLAND	USA	45n30	-	8	10	4
MONACO	Monaco	43n43	+	0	29	48	POZNAN	Poland	52n22	+	1	8	0
MONROVIA	Liberia	6n20	-	0	43	20	PRETORIA	S. Africa	25s36	+	1	53	0
MONS	Belg.	50n28	+	0	15	48	PRAGUE	Czech.	50n 6	+	0	57	44
MONTERREY	Mexico	25n39	-	6	41	40	PROVIDENCE	USA	41n55	-	4	46	0
MONTEVIDEO	Urug.	34s40	-	3	44	40	PUEBLO	USA	38n17	-	6	58	36
MONTREAL	Canada	45n30	-	5	54	24	QUEBEC	Canada	46n52	-	4	45	4
MOSCOW	USSR	55n45	+	2	30	24	QUITO	Ecuador	0s15	-	5	15	0
MUKDEN	China	41n51	+	8	13	40	RABAT	Moroc.	34n 0	-	0	28	0
MULHOUSE	France	47n45	+	0	28	48	RANGOON	Burma	16n47	+	6	25	0
MULLHEIM	Germ.	47n48	+	0	30	32	READING,PA	USA	40n26	-	5	3	20
MUNICH	Germ.	48n10	+	0	46	24	REICHENBURG	Czech.	50n42	+	1	0	28
MUNSTER	Germ.	51n58	+	0	30	24	REIMS	France	49n17	+	0	16	8
MURCIA	Spain	38n 0	-	0	4	28	RHODOS	Greece	36n25	+	1	53	8
NAGASAKI	Japan	32n43	+	8	39	48	RICHMOND,VA	USA	37n30	-	5	10	0
NAIROBI	Kenya	1s18	+	2	27	12	RIGA	Latvia	57n30	+	1	34	0
NAMUR	Belg.	50n29	+	0	19	24	RIO DE JAN.	Brazil	22s 5	-	2	54	0
NANCY	France	48n41	-	0	24	48	RIYADH	Saudi A.	24n50	+	3	5	12
NANKING	China	32n10	+	7	55	20	ROSTOV ON D	USSR	47n15	+	2	38	8
NANTES	France	47n14	-	0	6	16	ROTTERDAM	Neth.	51n55	+	0	17	56
NAPLES	Italy	40n50	+	0	55	8	ROUEN	France	49n28	+	0	4	16
NASHVILLE	USA	36n 8	-	5	47	20	SAARBRUCKEN	Germ.	49n17	+	0	28	0
NASSAU	Germ.	50n18	+	0	31	4	SAIGON	Viet.	10n45	+	7	7	0
NEW BEDFORD	USA	41n40	-	4	44	0	ST. ETIENNE	France	43n12	+	0	6	0
NEW HAVEN	USA	41n18	-	4	51	48	ST. JOHN	Nfdld	47n37	-	3	31	20
NEW ORLEANS	USA	30n 0	-	6	0	0	ST. LOUIS	USA	38n39	-	6	0	52
NEWARK	USA	40n48	-	4	57	0	ST. PAUL	USA	45n 0	-	6	8	12
NEWCASTLE	Aus.	32s56	+	10	6	48	SALEM	India	11n35	+	5	12	48
NIAGARA F	Canada	43n 7	-	5	16	0	SALONIKA	Greece	40n40	+	1	32	0
NICE	France	43n44	+	0	28	56	SALT LAKE C.	USA	40n44	-	7	32	20
NICOSIA	Italy	37n48	+	0	57	28	SAMARA	USSR	53n14	+	3	20	16
NITEROI	Brazil	23s 0	-	2	52	0	SAMARKAND	USSR	39n40	+	4	27	40
NORFOLK,VA	USA	36n55	-	5	5	0	SAN ANTONIO	USA	29n27	-	6	34	8
OAKLAND	USA	37n47	-	8	8	20	SAN DIEGO	USA	32n45	-	7	8	28
OBERHAUSEN	Germ.	51n28	+	0	27	20	S. FRANCISCO	USA	37n45	-	8	10	0

PLACE	Country	LAT		h	m	s	PLACE	Country	LAT		h	m	s
SAN JOSE	C. Rica	9n59	-	5	36	8	TOKYO	Japan	35n43	+	9	19	0
SAN JUAN	P. Rico	18n29	-	4	24	8	TOLEDO	Spain	39n50	-	0	16	20
SAN MARINO	San M.	45n57	+	0	50	0	TORONTO	Canada	43n40	-	5	17	40
SAN SALVADOR	El Salv	13n45	-	5	59	12	TOULON	France	43n 7	+	0	23	44
SANTA CRUZ	Bol.	17s50	-	4	13	0	TOULOUSE	France	43n36	+	0	5	32
SANTA FE	Arg.	31s30	-	4	3	56	TOURS	France	47n23	+	0	2	48
SANTIAGO	Chile	33s25	-	4	42	0	TRENTON,NJ	USA	40n17	-	4	58	36
SANTIAGO	Cuba	20n 0	-	5	3	20	TRICHINOPOLY	India	10n50	+	5	15	0
S'TO DOMINGO	Dom.	18n30	-	4	39	56	TRIESTE	Italy	45n40	+	0	54	48
SANTOS	Brazil	24s 0	-	3	6	0	TRIPOLI	Lebanon	34n40	+	2	24	0
SAO PAULO	Brazil	23s40	-	3	6	20	TROYES	France	48n17	+	0	16	16
SARAGOSSA	Spain	41n40	-	0	3	24	TULA	USSR	54n15	+	2	30	8
SARATOV	USSR	51n33	+	3	3	56	TULSA,OK	USA	36n 6	-	6	23	52
SCRANTON,PA	USA	41n26	-	5	2	40	TUNIS	Tunisia	36n45	+	0	41	0
SCHWERIN	Germ.	48n 4	+	0	35	44	TURIN	Italy	45n 5	+	0	30	32
SCUTARI	Turkey	41n 0	+	1	56	4	TVER	USSR	56n52	+	2	22	40
SEATTLE	USA	47n31	-	8	9	0	UPPSALA	Sweden	59n55	+	1	10	0
SEOUL	Korea	37n26	+	8	27	52	UTICA,NY	USA	43n 0	-	5	0	48
SEVILLE	Spain	37n25	-	0	24	0	UTRECHT	Neth.	52n 5	+	0	20	32
SHANGHAI	China	31n25	+	8	6	0	VADUZ	Liech.	47n10	+	0	38	8
SHOLAPUR	India	17n40	+	5	3	44	VALENCIA	Spain	39n28	-	0	1	24
SINGAPORE	Malay.	1n20	+	6	55	20	VALETTA	Malta	35n52	+	0	58	0
SION	Switz.	46n13	+	0	29	28	VALLADOLID	Spain	41n38	-	0	18	44
SMYRNA	Turkey	38n25	+	1	48	36	VANCOUVER	Canada	49n 7	-	8	11	8
SOPHIA	Bulg.	42n41	+	1	33	20	VENICE	Italy	45n23	+	0	49	20
SOMERVILLE	USA	42n25	-	4	44	16	VERONA	Italy	45n27	+	0	44	4
S. BEND,IND	USA	41n40	-	5	45	28	VICTORIA	Canada	48n20	-	8	12	8
SPEZIA	Italy	44n 5	+	0	39	16	VICTORIA	Hong Kong	22n20	+	7	45	40
SPOKANE	USA	47n33	-	7	49	52	VIENNA	Austria	48n12	+	1	5	32
SPRINGFIELD	USA	42n 6	-	4	50	20	VILNIUS	Lith.	54n42	+	1	41	0
STETTIN	Germ.	53n26	+	0	58	0	VLADIVOSTOK	USSR	43n10	+	8	48	0
STOCKHOLM	Sweden	59n17	+	1	12	12	VOLGOGRAD	USSR	48n40	+	2	57	28
STRASBOURG	France	48n37	+	0	30	48	VORONEZH	USSR	51n42	+	2	36	40
STUTTGART	Germ.	48n50	+	0	37	0	WARSAW	Poland	52n15	+	1	24	4
SVERDLOVSK	USSR	56n52	+	4	0	48	WASHINGTON	USA	38n58	-	5	8	0
SYDNEY	Aus.	33n55	+	10	4	48	WEIMAR	Germ.	51n 0	+	0	45	20
SYRACUSE,NY	USA	43n 0	-	5	4	40	WELLINGTON	NZ	41s15	+	11	47	4
SZEGED	Hung.	46n16	+	1	4	40	WICHITA	USA	37n48	-	6	29	0
TABRIZ	Iran	37n59	+	3	5	28	WIESBADEN	Germ.	50n 5	+	0	33	0
TACOMA	USA	47n14	-	8	9	52	WILMINGTON	USA	39n48	-	4	54	20
TALCA	Chile	35s20	-	4	47	4	WINNIPEG	Canada	49n57	-	6	29	8
TALLIN	Estonia	59n20	+	1	39	20	WORCESTER	USA	42n18	-	4	47	20
TANGIER	Morocco	35n40	-	0	23	20	WUPPERTAL	Germ.	51n17	+	0	28	52
TARANTO	Italy	40n29	+	1	9	0	XIANNEN	China	24n30	+	7	52	40
TASHKENT	USSR	41n 7	+	4	37	0	YAROSLAVL	USSR	57n40	+	2	39	0
TEGUCIGALPA	Hond.	14n13	-	5	48	0	YOKOHAMA	Japan	35n30	+	9	18	32
TEHRAN	Iran	35n57	+	3	25	48	YONKERS,NY	USA	40n57	-	4	55	20
THORSHAVN	Denmark	52n 0	-	0	27	0	ZAGREB	Yugos.	45n51	+	1	4	0
TIENTSIN	China	39n 5	+	7	49	0	ZANZIBAR	Tanzania	6s 9	+	2	36	48
TIFLIS	USSR	41n45	+	2	59	48	ZURICH	Switz.	47n23	+	0	34	8
TIRANA	Albania	41n19	+	1	19	12	Above Long. Equivs to the nearest four secs.						

Table to estimate latitude and longitude equivalent of any place by its distance and direction (roughly known) from a place in either of the preceding lists.

Miles north or south change latitude equivalent; miles east or west change longitude equivalent; miles north-east, north-west, south-east and south-west change both by the amounts shown below for number of miles and for near latitude.

Lat near	Miles N or S						Miles E or W						Miles N-E, N-W, S-E or S-W												
	1 0		3 0		5 0		1 0		3 0		5 0		1 0				3 0				5 0			
°	°	'	°	'	°	'	m	s	m	s	m	s	°	'	m	s	°	'	m	s	°	'	m	s
0	0	9	0	26	0	44	0	35	1	44	2	53	0	6	0	25	0	19	1	13	0	31	2	3
15	0	9	0	26	0	44	0	36	1	48	3	0	0	6	0	25	0	19	1	14	0	31	2	7
30	0	9	0	26	0	44	0	40	2	0	3	20	0	6	0	28	0	18	1	25	0	31	2	22
45	0	9	0	26	0	43	0	49	2	27	4	5	0	6	0	36	0	18	1	49	0	31	3	2
60	0	9	0	26	0	43	1	11	3	34	5	56	0	6	0	50	0	18	2	31	0	31	4	12

(l) Difficulties With Time in Foreign Horoscopes

'We have great difficulty in collecting information for the lists of standard times, and often find that the legal time is not the time in general use in the country concerned.' *Remark by a spokesman of the Nautical Almanac Office of the Royal Observatory (Greenwich), at Herstmonceux Castle, Sussex, replying to telephone call from author* [Evans] *in London regarding suspected errors in the Nautical Almanac.*

Whenever at all possible, family inquiries are advisable in every case in which the exact kind of time used in recording a birth is not unambiguously specified.

Despite every possible care, and systematic inquiries in official quarters of a large number of nationalities, and the expenditure, for these few pages, of an amount of time, relatively to the space to be filled, over 1,000 per cent more than for any other part of the book – some of the details that follow, both for standard time and about the use of summer time etc., remain subject to doubt or amendment.

Just one example from a very large number.

Sierra Leone. Koppenstätter's valuable book, *Zonen und Sommerzeiten* (preface dated 1937), gives standard time as 1 hour slow on GMT, with date of adoption unknown, and gives use of summer time as apparently confined to a single year, 1935, namely, clocks advanced, on standard time, by *40 minutes*, from (an unknown day of) June to (an unknown day of) September, and then discontinued ('*beendet*').

Irene Hume Taylor's Supplement (covering years from 1936 to 1942, inclusive) to the completely unobtainable, else probably equally valuable work, Curran and Taylor's *World Summer Time* (1935), says clocks advanced 40 minutes from (unknown day of) June to (unknown day of) September in the years 1936–42 inclusive.

The *Nautical Almanac*, 1951 (and some other recent years), published under the aegis of the Astronomer Royal by HM Stationery Office annually, gives standard time as oh (= GMT), with an asterisk denoting a place where 'Variations of this time have been used in recent years for summer time or other purposes.'

Prolonged efforts to discover, first, at what date the standard or zone time was changed from − 1h to oh, and, secondly, for how many years after 1942 the '40 minutes' summer-time advance was used, finally resulted thus:

The British Colonial Office, responsible for Sierra Leone affairs and legislation, after looking into the matter, reported that, by a fortunate coincidence, the author's inquiry was made on the very day on which that office had received from the BBC a note ('Correction of World Time, no. 2') stating that the standard time was 'now' oh and was the only clock time all round the year, no variation for the purpose of summer time being 'now' used. Asked as from what date this applied, they did not know, but referred the author to the BBC, as the Colonial Office's own source of information.

The BBC (Overseas Information Dept) kindly communicated their own information − the text of a Public Relations Officer's report, in which an ordinance of 1932 was quoted, making the legal time: − 1h, 1 June to 31 August each year, and − oh 40m (a *20* minutes advance), from 1 September to 31 May; with the further information that this remained in operation till 1939, when it was superseded by standard time oh, with no summer time.

On further inquiries being pressed at the Colonial Office, their legal department eventually reported that they had found the ordinance (same as quoted by BBC), but that it was republished in 1946

334

and was still (1952) in force, and had this year (1952) at last been 'accepted' by Greenwich, after much correspondence.

Some caution must evidently be used, and some uncertainty admitted, in following even the most authoritative works of reference, and in regard to exact house cusps in some foreign charts.

ZONE AND STANDARD TIMES OF MOST COUNTRIES FROM 1870

STATE etc.	from	h	
ADEN		+	3
formerly	+ 2h59m54s		
ALASKA	20Au00		
Central zone		-	10
inc. Valdez,			
Seward, Anchorage			
Ketchikan zone,		-	8
including S.E. coast, ✓			
Cross Sd.,			
Douglas, Juneau,			
Kimsham Cove,			
Petersburg, S.E. coast			
north of above		-	9
West coast, Nome			
zone, and the			
Aleutians		-	11
ALBANIA	1914	+	1
ALGERIA	2Mh11		0
15Mh91 + 0h9m5s			
ANGOLA	1Ja12	+	1
ANTIGUA	1Ja11	-	4
ARGENTINE	5Oc69	-	3
	1My20	-	4
1No94 - 4h17m			
AUSTRALIA			
Broken Hill	1My99	+	9.5
	25Ja96	+	9
	1Fe95	+	10
Capital Ter.		+	10
New South Wales,			
exc. Brok. H.	1945	+	10
	1My95	+	9.5
	25Ja96	+	9
	1Fe95	+	10
North. Ter.	1Fe95	+	9.5
Queensld.	1Fe95	+	10
South Aus.	1My95	+	9.5
Victoria	1Fe95	+	10
West Aus.	1Fe95	+	8
AUSTRIA	1Oc91	+	1
AZORES	1Ja12	-	1
BAHAMAS		-	5
BARBADOS	1932	-	4
BELGIUM	3Se44		0
(Germ)	17My40	+	1
(Indep)	11No18		0
(Germ) ✓	- ?Au14	+	1
(Indep)	1My92		0
BELIZE	1Ap12	-	6
BENIN	1Ja12		0
BERMUDA	1Ja30	-	4
formerly	- 4h19m		
BOLIVIA	21Mh32	-	4
formerly	- 4h32m		
BORNEO, Br. N.	1Oc04	+	8
BORNEO, Du	194-?	+	8
formerly		+	7.5
BOTSWANA		+	2
BRAZIL	1Ja14		
Central zone		-	4
East zone, coast		-	3
West zone		-	5
BULGARIA	30No94	+	2
BURMA	1920	+	6

STATE etc.	from	h	
CAMEROONS	1Ja20	+	1
CANADA	✓ 18No91		
Alberta	1Se06	-	7
B. Colombia		-	8
Manitoba		-	8
N. Brunswick	15Je02	-	4
	9De83	-	5
Nova Scotia	18Je84	-	4
Ontario	1895		
E. of 90°		-	5
W. of 90°		-	6
P. Edward I.	15Je02	-	4
Quebec			
E. of 68°		-	5
W. of 68°		-	6
Saskatchewan	1920	-	7
Yukon	20Au00	-	9
CEYLON	1Ja06	+	5.5
CHILE	1Se32	-	4
	1Ja10	-	5
CHINA			
Coast	1Je03	+	8
Canton	1904	+	8
Interior	1928	+	8
Shanghai	1904	+	8
Pakhoi, Hainan,			
and from Chungking			
up river			
to Shahsze		+	7
COLUMBIA	23No14	-	5
CORSICA	11Mh19		0
COSTA RICA	15Ja21	-	5
CRETE		+	2
CUBA	19JL25	-	5
formerly	- 5h29m		
CYPRUS		+	2
CZECHOSLOV.	1Ja91	+	1
DENMARK	1Ap94	+	1
DOMINICA	194-?	-	5
	1Ap33 - 4h40m		
ECUADOR	194-?	-	5
Quito, etc.	- 5h14m		
Guayaquil, etc.	- 5h19m		
EGYPT	1Oc00	+	2
ERITREA		+	3
ESTONIA	1My21	+	2
FAROES	1No08		0
FERNANDO PO			0
FIJI			12
FINLAND	1My21	+	2
FLORES		+	8
FRANCE	2Mh11		0
15Mh91 + 0h9m5s			
GAMBIA	194-?		0
	1918	-	1
GDANSK	1Ap93	+	1
GERMANY	✓ 1Ap93	+	1
Baden	1Ap92	+	1
15Mh91 + 0h34m			
Brandenbg.	1Ap92	+	1
formerly	+ 0h54m		
Saar (Fr)	1945?		0

STATE etc.	from	h	
GERMANY	(continued)		
(Germ)	1Mh35	+	1
(Fr)	31No18		0
(Germ)	1Ap93	+	1
Wurtembg.	1Ap92	+	1
15Mh91 + 0h37m			
GHANA	1918 -0h20m		
GIBRALTAR			0
GILBERT IS.		+	12
GT. BRITAIN	1Oc80		0
inc. Channel Is.			
NOT inc. Ireland			
GREECE	28JL16	+	2
GREENLAND	✓	-	3
GRENADA	1JL11	-	4
GUADELOUPE	8JL11	-	4
GUATEMALA	5Oc18	-	6
GUIANA, Du	194-?	-	3.5
formerly	- 3h41m	-	4
GUIANA, Fr.	194-?	-	3.5
	1JL11	-	4
GUINEA, Fr	1Ja12	-	1
GUINEA, Port	1Ja12	-	1
GUINEA, Span.			0
GUYANA	194-? -3h45m		
	1JL11	-	4
HAITI		-	5
HAWAII	194-?	-	10
formerly		-	10.5
HOLLAND	see Netherlds		
HONDURAS, Rep	1Ap12	-	6
HUNGARY	1Oc91	+	1
ICELAND	✓ 1Ja08	-	1
INDIA	✓ 1Ja06	+	5.5
Fr. India	18JL11	+	5.5
Port. India	1911?	+	5.5
Calcutta	1911?	+	5.5
formerly	+ 5h53m		
INDO-CHINA	1My31	+	7
IRAN		+	3
IRAQ	1917	+	3
IRELAND	1Oc16		0
	1880 - 0h25m21s		
ISRAEL	1917	+	2
ITALY	1No93	+	1
IVORY COAST			0
JAMAICA	1Fe12	-	5
JAPAN	1Ja88	+	9
JAVA	194-?	+	8
	1No32	+	7.5
JORDAN		+	2
KENYA	194-?	+	3
	1Ja32	+	2.5
	1JL28	+	3
KOREA	1932	+	9
	1928	+	8.5
	1De04	+	9
LABRADOR		-	3.5
LABUAN	1Oc04	+	8
LATVIA	1920	+	2
LESOTHO	1895	+	2
LITHUANIA	1920	+	1
formerly		+	2
(Luxembourg: next page)			

336

STATE etc.	from	h
LUXEMBOURG	1De18	0
	1Ap92	+ 1
LIBYA		
Cyrenaica		+ 2
Tripolitania		+ 1
MADAGASCAR	1JL11	+ 3
MADEIRA	1Ja12	- 1
MALAWI		+ 2
MALAYSIA	194-?	+ 7.5
	1Ja33 + 7h33m	
	JL05	+ 7
MALTA		+ 1
MANCHURIA	194-?	+ 9
	1Mh32	+ 8
	1928	+ 8.5
	1De04	+ 9
MARIANA IS. ✗		+ 9
Guam		+ 10
MARQUESAS		- 10
MARSHALL Is		+ 10
MARTINIQUE	1My11	- 4
MAURETANIA	26Fe34	- 1
MAURITIUS	1Ja07	+ 4
formerly	+ 3h50m	
MEXICO ✗	1Ap32	- 6
Lower California,		
Narayat, Sonora		
and Sinalos	194-?	- 7
Lower California		
	1Ap32	- 8
	1Ja22	- 7
MONACO		0
MOROCCO		0
MOZAMBIQUE	1Mh03	+ 2
NAMIBIA		+ 2
NETHERLANDS	14My40	+ 1
	1JL37 + 0h20m	
	7No08 + 0h19m28s	
NEW CALED.	13Ja12	+ 11
NEW GUINEA, Du		+ 9
NEW ZEALAND	1945	+ 12
	1886	+ 11.5
NEWFOUNDLAND		- 3
NICARAGUA ✗	23Je34	- 6
formerly	- 5h40m	
Bluefield always	- 5h35m	
NIGERIA	1Se19	+ 1
NORWAY	1Ja95	+ 1
NOVAYA ZEMLYA	1930	+ 4
PAKISTAN	1Ja06	+ 5.5
PALESTINE	1917	+ 2
PANAMA	2Ap18	- 5
PAPUA NEW GUINEA		+ 10
PARAGUAY	10Oc31	- 4
PERU	28JL08	- 5
PHILIPPINES	2My99	+ 8
POLAND	1My16	+ 1
PUERTO RICO	26Mh99	- 4
PORTUGAL	1Ja12	0
RIO DE ORO		+ 1
ROMANIA	24JL31	+ 2
RUSSIA	1930	
W. of 40°E		+ 2
40°E to 52.5°E		+ 3
E. of 52.5°E		+ 4

STATE etc.	from	h
SALVADOR		- 6
SAMOA	194-?	+ 11
	1911	+ 11.5
SANTA CRUZ		+ 11
SAO TOME		0
SARAWAK		+ 7.5
SARDINIA	1No93	+ 1
SENEGAL	1Ja12	- 1
SEYCHELLES	Je06	- 4
SIBERIA	1930	
W. of 67.5°E		+ 4
67.5°E to 82.5°E		+ 5
82.5°E to 97.5°E		+ 6
97.5°E to 112.5°E		+ 7
112.5°E to 127.5°E		+ 8
127.5°E to 142.5°E		+ 9
142.5°E to 157.5°E		+ 10
157.5°E to 172.5°E		+ 11
E. of 172.5°E		+ 12
SICILY	1No93	+ 1
SIERRA LEONE	1939?	0?
	1Ja32	- 1
SOMALILAND	1JL11	+ 3
SOUTH AFRICA		
Cape	1No03	+ 2
	8Fe92	+ 1.5
Natal	1Se94	+ 2
Orange F. S.	1Mh30	+ 2
	8Fe92	+ 1.5
Transvaal	1Mh03	+ 2
	8Fe92	+ 1.5
SPAIN	1Ja01	0
SUDAN		+ 2
SUMATRA	194-?	+ 7
Northern	1No32	+ 6.5
Southern	1No32	+ 7
SWEDEN	1Ja00	+ 1
SWITZERLAND	1Je94	+ 1
SYRIA		+ 2
TAIWAN	194-?	+ 9
	1Ja96	+ 8
TANZANIA		+ 3
TASMANIA	1Fe95	+ 10
THAILAND	1Ap20	+ 7
TOGOLAND		0
TRINIDAD	1JL11	- 4
TUNIS	9Mh11	+ 1
	15Mh91 + 0h9m5s	
TURKEY	1Ja16	+ 2
UGANDA	194-?	+ 3
	1Ja30	+ 2.5
	1My28	+ 3
formerly		+ 2.5
URUGUAY	194-?	- 3
	1My20	- 3.5
U.S.A	✗ 18No83	
Note: brackets () mean		
that what is enclosed		
within them, (✗), or		
(towns, different zone)		
could not be verified		
for years after 1940,		
Alabama		- 6
Arizona (✗)		- 7
(Seligman and W.		- 8)

STATE etc.	from	h
U.S.A	(continued)	
Arkansas		- 7
California		- 8
Colorado (✗)		- 7
(Springfield		- 6)
Connecticut		- 5
Delaware		- 5
D.C.	13Mh84	- 5
Florida ✗	30My89	- 5
W. of 85°W		- 6
Georgia ✗		- 5
(Albany, Macon,		
Atlanta and w.		- 6)
Idaho (✗)	31Mh18	- 7
(Grangeville, Cottonwood,		
Stites, Burke		
and west		- 8)
Formerly, without		
the exceptions		- 7
Illinois		- 6
Indiana		- 6
Iowa		- 6
Kansas ✗		- 6
(Syracuse, Cimarron,		
Scott City, Ellis, Colby		- 7)
Kentucky (✗)		- 6
(Covington, Newpt.		- 5)
Louisiana		- 6
Maine	1887	- 5
Maryland		- 5
Massachusetts		- 5
Michigan	26Ap31	- 5
	8Se85	- 6
Minnesota		- 6
Mississippi		- 6
Missouri		- 6
Montana		- 7
Nebraska ✗		- 6
(inc. N. Platte,		
Stapleton, Valentine		
-west of these		- 7)
Nevada (✗)		- 8
(Minto, Acoma,		
Crestlin		- 7)
New Hampshire		- 5
New Jersey		- 5
New Mexico		- 7
New York State		- 5
N. Carolina ✗		- 5
(Ashville and W.		- 6)
N. Dakota	1919	- 6
formerly,		- 6
Portal, Flaxman,		
Minot, and W.		- 7
Ohio	1Ap96-6	- 5
Oklahoma		- 6
Oregon (✗)		- 8
(Becker, Seneca		- 7)
Pennsylvania		- 5
Rhode Island		- 5
S. Carolina ✗	1Ja84	- 5
Tennessee ✗		- 6
(Bristol		- 5)
Texas (✗)	1Ja84	- 6
(El Paso, Pecos		- 7)

STATE etc.	from	h	STATE etc.	from	h	STATE etc.	from	h
U.S.A			**USSR**			**ZAIRE**		
Utah ✗		- 7	see Novaya Zemlya, Russia,			Eastern	1Ja35	+ 2
(Salt Lake City,			Siberia and Wrangel			inc. Lusambo, Stanleyville,		
Garfield and west		- 8)	Island			Costermansville,		
Vermont		- 5	**VANATU**	13Ja12	+ 11	Elisabethsville		
Virginia (✗)		- 5	**VENEZUELA**	194-?	- 4.5	Western	1Ja12	+ 1
(Norton and west		- 6)	**WRANGEL ISLAND**	1930	+ 12	inc. Leopoldville,		
Washington State		- 8	**YUGOSLAVIA**		+ 1	Coquilhatville		
W. Virginia	1Ja87	- 5	Bosnia	1No91		**ZAMBIA**	1Mh03	+ 2
Wisconsin		- 6	Croatia	1No91		**ZANZIBAR**		+ 3
Wyoming		- 7	Serbia	1884		**ZIMBABWE**	1Mh08	+ 2

(m) 'Permanent Summer Time' or 'New Standard Time'?

The distinction is not always very clear. For example, France is (and apparently permanently, but it *might* be discontinued at any moment) now (1952) using time that is one hour ahead of Greenwich, and therefore the same as Germany (Central European Time). This, however, is simply because for a number of years France has continued to use summer time all the year round, the country's standard time being in theory the same as Greenwich. It becomes a moot point whether we are to say the standard or zone time is oh and summer time (1 hour fast on standard time) is used continuously, or to say that (at some date difficult to fix) the standard time of France changed from oh to +1h and so became the same as standard time of Germany, which is not using summer time at all. The Argentine, similarly, of which the zone time is 4h behind Greenwich, is using continuous daylight-saving or 'permanent summer' time of 1 hour, making its clocks only 3 hours behind Greenwich. In both these cases the *Nautical Almanac* will, so the author has learned privately, in future issues give the clock time – 1 hour fast on Greenwich, and 3 hours slow on Greenwich, respectively – in its list of standard times, but with a distinguishing symbol to show that these times result from the combination of permanent or continuous 'summer time' with an older standard time. Up to now, however, it has given the Argentine as 3 hours behind Greenwich, while giving France as using Greenwich (standard) time, marking *both* with a note that variations of *this* standard time have been used in recent – unspecified – years for summer time or other purposes. This is a correct statement for France, incorrect for the Argentine.

The same error seems to have occurred in other cases, but in some of these the author has been unable to verify the true position. One or two cases where present standard time (supposed) is marked as from '194–?' in the above list, and is in advance of that given in the next line for the same country, *may* be examples of 'permanent summer time' *mistaken* for change of standard time. (*C. Evans*)

(n) Calendar Changes in Countries Using Old-Style Dates After 1870

New Style (Gregorian) calendar replaced Old Style (Julian) in most countries long before 1870, and is that in which all dates are now given. To convert OS dates to NS, add 12 days to dates *before* 1 March (Old Style) in 1900, and to dates before 1900; add 13 days to dates since 1900 and after 20 February in 1900, 1900 was a leap year by OS, not by NS. Calendar changes since 1870:

Bulgaria 18 September 1920, OS
China 30 January 1912, OS
Greece 16 July 1916, OS
Japan 1872
Romania 18 March 1920, OS
Russia 18 March 1918, OS
Yugoslavia (Serbia, Croatia, Bosnia) 17 February 1920, OS

But the Orthodox Greek, Romanian, Russian, Serbian Churches would not recognize the change till May 1923 in their countries.

(o) Initials Used for Some Zone Times

E(astern) S(tandard) T(ime): − 5h; C(entral) ST: − 6; M(ountain) ST: − 7; P(acific) ST: − 8; in continental USA also A(tlantic) ST: − 4 (American possessions and Canada). W (War) for S in the above means all-the-year-round daylight-saving time (1 hour advance). W(est) E(uropean) Time = Greenwich time (0h); C(entral) ET: + 1 and EET (East European Time): + 2. DST: Daylight-Saving Time, but in ephemeris here Double Summer Time.

339

(*p*) **British Summer Time** (BST) was initiated in 1916, although until 1920 it was used only in England and Scotland. Wales and Northern Ireland remained on GMT.

From 25 February 1940 until 7 October 1945, BST was used (GMT plus one hour), and Double Summer Time (DST) was introduced. DST is given in the tables, where appropriate, during these years. For births in this period, one hour should be deducted from the local time of birth unless DST was in effect, in which case two hours should be subtracted. From 7 October 1945, GMT was re-adopted, and BST used, until 1968.

From 18 February 1968 to 31 October 1971, Central European Time was adopted. This amounted to adding one hour to GMT, and *not* using BST. At the time of writing it seems likely that the whole system may change, so no dates for BST are given in the tables after 1990.

From 1 January 1880 until 21 May 1916, Northern Ireland used Belfast Time, which is 23m 40s behind GMT (requiring, therefore, an addition of that sum to find GMT). On 21 May 1916, Northern Ireland transferred to GMT. A permanent summer time (1 hour ahead of GMT) was also adopted in Northern Ireland from 16 April 1939 to 24 July 1945.

Time changes before 1981 were made at 2.00 a.m. GMT. During 1941–5 and in 1947 and after 1981, time changes were made at 1.00 a.m. GMT.

(*q*) *Summer or Daylight-Saving Time, 1916 to 1970*

Austria, Gdansk: as Germany.

Azores, Madeira: as Portugal.

British Isles, including all Ireland, and Channel Is.: same as Great Britain (see ephemeris pages and above) except: Eire, *no Double Summer Time*.

Hungary: as Germany to 1940.

Labrador: as Newfoundland.

Monaco: as France.

San Marino, Sardinia, Sicily: as Italy.

USA, Canada: local rules varying from town to town yearly: so no useful information possible in space available.

USSR (including Russia, Siberia, Novaya Zemlya, Wrangel I.): 'permanent' summer time (1 hour advance) in all zones since 1930.

Important: unless otherwise indicated, Double Summer Time (//) or $1\frac{1}{2}$ hour (#), also implies single summer time, 1h, (/), throughout that year.

Country	1916	1917	1918	1919	1920
ALASKA	none?	none?	b31Mh/b27Oc	b30Mh/b26Oc	none
AUSTRALIA	b1Oc/b25Mh	(NS.b28Oc/b25Mhb27Oc/b2Mh)		none	none
BELGIUM	z30Ap/z30Se	b16Ap/b17Se	b15Ap/16Se	y1Mh/z4Oc	y15Mh/z23Oc
BELIZE	none	none	z25Oc‡z15Fe	z24Oc‡z14Fe	z22Oc‡z21Fe
BULGARIA	none	none	none?	date?/date?	date?/date?
CHILE	none	none	z31Au/z1Jl		
DENMARK	a15My/a30Sep	none?	none	none	none
FRANCE	y14Je/a1Oc	y24Mh/a7Oc	y9Mh/a6Oc	y1Mh/a5Oc	y15Mh/a24Oc
GERMANY	z30Ap/z30Se	b16Ap/b17Se	b15Ap/b16Se	none	none
HAWAII	none?	none?	b31Mh/b27Oc	b30Mh/b26Oc	none
HONDURAS	none	none	10c?/15Fe	as in 1918?	as in 1918?
ICELAND	none	20Fe/25Oc	20Fe/15Oc	19Fe/15Oc	none
ITALY	z3Je/z30Sep	z31Mh/z30Se	z9Mh/z6Oc	z1Mh/z4Oc	z20Mh/z1Oc
LUXEMBURG	y10My/z30Se	y30Ap/z30Se	b15Ap/b16Se	y1Mh/z4Oc	y14Fe/a23Oc
MOROC,Tan	none	none	6My/7Oc	none?	none?
NETHERLS	z30Ap/z30Se	b16Ap/b17Se	b14Ap/b31Oc	b7Ap/b29Se	b5Ap/b27Se
N'FOUNDL	none	b8Ap/b17Se	b14Ap/b31Oc	y5Ap/y12Au	y2Ap/y31Oc
NORWAY	y21my/y21Oc	none	none	none	none·
POLAND	z30Ap/z30Se	c16Ap/c17Se	c15Ap/16Se	none	none
PORTUGAL	y17Je/z31Oc	y28Fe/z14Oc	y1Mh/z14Oc	y28Fe/z14Oc	y29Fe/z14Oc
RUSSIA N.S.	none	y13My/z13Se	y29Je/z31Au	none?	none
SPAIN	none	y7Ap/z6Oc	y6Ap/z5Oc	y5Ap/z4Oc	none
TURKEY	none?	none?	none?	none	b28Mh/b25Oc

1921-1930,PLACES OMITTED,If named above-(believed)none,1921-30

Country	1921	1922	1923	1924	1925
BELGIUM	y14Mh/z25Oc	y25Mh/z7Oc	y31Mh/z6Oc	y29Mh/z4Oc	y4Ap/z3Oc
BELIZE	z1Oc‡z11Fe	z7Oc‡z10Fe	z6Oc‡z9Fe	z4Oc‡z14Fe	z3Oc‡z13Fe
FRANCE	y14Mh/z25Oc	y25Mh/z7Oc	y31Mh/z6Oc	y29Mh/z4Oc	y4Ap/z3Oc
HONDURAS	(Koppenstatter says: 1Oc/Fe every year,not verified)				
ICELAND	19Mh/22Je	none	none	none	none
LUXEMBG.	y14Mh/z25Oc	y25Mh/z7Oc	y31Mh/z6Oc	y29Mh/z4Oc	y4Ap/z3Oc
MOROCCO	Span & Tang zones none till			y16Ap/y4Oc	none?
NETHERLS	b4Ap/b28Se	b26Mh/b8Oc	b1Je/b7Oc	b30Mh/b5Oc	b5Ap/c4Oc
N'FOUNDL	y1My/y30Oc	y7My/y29Oc	y6My/y28Oc	y4My/y26Oc	y3My/y25Oc
PORTUGAL	y28Fe/z14Oc	none	none	y16Ap/z14Oc	none
SPAIN	y28Fe/z14Oc	none	none	y16Ap/z14Oc	none
TURKEY	b3Ap/b3Oc	b26Mh/b8Oc	b28Ap/b16Se	none?	none?
URUGUAY	(Montevideo only) none till....		z1Oc‡z31Mh	z1Oc‡z31Mh	z1Oc‡z31Mh

Country	1926	1927	1928	1929	1930
ARGENTINE	?none till....				z30No/z31Mh
BELIZE	z2Oc‡z12Fe	z1Oc‡z11Fe	z6Oc‡z9Fe	z5Oc‡z8Fe	z4Oc‡z14Fe
CHILE	none	z31Au/z31Mh	z31Au/z31Mh	z31Au/z31Mh	z31Au/z31Mh
CUBA	?none till...		z9Je/z9Oc	none?	none?
FRANCE	y17Ap/z2Oc	y9Ap/z1Oc	y14Ap/z6Oc	y14Ap/z5Oc	y12Ap/z4Oc
HONDURAS	(see 1921-1925, same source, unchecked, same for 1926-1930)				
MEXICO	?none till...				date?/z14No
MOR,SpanTan	y17Ap/y2Oc	y9Ap/y1Oc	y14Ap/y6Oc	none	none
NETHERLS	b15Ap/b3Oc	b15Ap/b2Oc	b15Ap/b7Oc	b15Ap/b6Oc	b5Ap/b5Oc
N.ZEALAND	none	z6No/z4Mh	z4No/z31De z31De/z3Mh	z13Oc/z16Mh	z12Oc/z15Mh
N'FOUNDL	y2My/y31Oc	y1My/y30Oc	y6My/y28Oc	y5My/y27Oc	y4My/y26Oc
PORTUGAL	y17Ap/z2Oc	y9Ap/z1Oc	y14Ap/z6Oc	y20Ap/z5Oc	none
SPAIN	y17Ap/z2Oc	y9Ap/z1Oc	y14Ap/z6Oc	none	none

Country	1931	1932	1933	1934	1935
ARGENTINE	z31Se/z31Mh	z31Oc/z28Fe	z31Oc/z28Fe	z31Oc/z28Fe	z31Oc/z29Fe
BELGIUM	y18Ap/z3Oc	y2Ap/z1Oc	y25Mh/z7Oc	y7Ap/z6Oc	y30Mh/z5Oc
BRAZIL	y3Oc/z31Mh	(z2Oc/z31Mh exc. Maranh.) none.Ap1933-1948inclus.			
BELIZE	z2Oc≠z13Fe	z7Oc≠z11Fe	z6Oc≠z10Fe	z5Oc≠z9Fe	z4Oc≠z8Fe
CHILE	z31Au/z31Mh	none till 1942, but new Zone Time 1932.			
FRANCE	y18Ap/z3Oc	y21Fe/z7Oc	y25Mh/z7Oc	y7Ap/z6Oc	y30Mh/z5Oc
GHANA	z31Au*z31De	z31Au*z31De	z31Au*z31De	z31Au*z31De	z31Au*z31De
GREECE	none?	z5Jl/b1No	none?	none?	none?
HONDURAS,Rep.	as before, ending 31De32?				
LUXEMBG	apparently the same as Belgium each year				
MEXICO	z30Ap/z29Se	z31Mh/z30Se	z31Mh/z30Se	z31Mh/z30Se	z31Mh/z30Se
NETHERLS	b15My/b4Oc	b22My/b2Oc	b15My/b8Oc	b15My/b7Oc	b15My/b6Oc
N.ZEALAND	z11Oc≠z20Mh	z9Oc≠b19Mh	b8Oc≠b29Ap	b30Se≠b28Ap	b29Se≠b26Ap
N'FOUNDL	y3Ap/y20Oc	y1Ap/y30Oc	y7Ap/y29Oc	y6Ap/y28Oc	y5Ap/y27Oc
PORTUGAL	y18Ap/z8Oc	y2Ap/z1Oc	none	y7Ap/z5Oc	y30Mh/z5Oc
ROMANIA	none?	none?	z21My/a2Oc	z1AP/a1Oc	z6Ap/a6Oc
SARAWAK	none until ?...				z13Se*z13De
SIERRA LEONE	z31Mh*z31Au	z31Mh*z31Au	z31Mh*z31Au	z31Mh*z31Au	z31Mh*z31Au
URUGUAY	none?	none?	z28Oc≠z31Mh	z27Oc≠z30Mh	z26Oc≠z28Mh

Country	1936	1937	1938	1939	1940
ARGENTINE	z31Oc/z28Fe	z31Oc/z28Fe	z31Oc/z28Fe	z31Oc/z29Fe	z30Oc/z29Fe
BELGIUM	y18Ap/z3Oc	y3Ap/z1Oc	y26Mh/z1Oc	y15Ap/z19No	b26Fe/c20My
	using German zone and summer time from 20My 1940				
BELIZE	z3Oc≠z13Fe	z2Oc≠z12Fe	z1Oc≠z11Fe	z27Oc≠z10Fe	z5Oc≠z9Fe
CUBA	none until?...				z1Je/z31Au
DENMARK	none until ?....1940 b30Ap, then as Germany, includ.				b30Ap/cont.
FALKL.ISL.	z27Se/27Ma	z26Se/z19Mh	z24Se/z18MH	z30Se/z23Mh	z27Se/z22Mh
FRANCE	y18Ap/z3Oc	y3Ap/z2Oc	y26Mh/z1Oc	y15Ap/z19No	y24Fe/cont.
	and in occupied areas (including Paris)				y15Je/date?
GERMANY	none until...				c1Ap/cont.
GHANA	z31Au*z31De	z31Au*z31De	z31Au*z31De	z31Au*z31De	z31Au*z31De
HONDURAS,Rep.	apparently every year (?),-?Oc/about middle of Fe				
ITALY	none until...				15Je/cont.
LUXEMBG	same as Belgium, unless for few days diff.1940, beg. Germ. t.				
MEXICO	z31Mh/z30Se	z31Mh/z30Se	z31Mh/z30Se	z31Mh/z30Se	z31Mh/cont.
NETHERLS	b15My/b4Oc	b23My/b3Oc	b15My/b2Oc	b15Ap/b1Oc	b19Ap/cont.
	but note that from 26My 1940, new zone time must be taken.				
N.ZEALAND	b27Se≠b25Ap	b25Se≠b24Ap	b25Se≠b30Ap	b24Se≠b29Ap	b29Se≠b27Ap
N'FOUNDL	z10My /z4Oc	z9My/z3Oc	z8My/z2Oc	z14My/z1Oc	z12My/z6Oc
NORWAY	none until..				b11Au
PALESTINE	none till TWO periods in 1940, 30My/30Se AND 17No/cont.				
PERU	?	23Se?/31Mh	24Se/25Mh	23Se/24Mh	26Se/29Mh
POLAND	none until...				23Je/cont.
PORTUGAL	y18Ap/z3Oc	y2Ap/z2Oc	y26Mh/z1Oc	y15Ap/z7Oc	y24Fe/z5Oc
SARAWAK	z13Se*z13De	z13Se*z13De	z13Se*z13De	z13Se*z13De	z13Se*z13De
SIERRA LEONE	z31Mh*z31Au	z31Mh*z31Au	z31Mh*z31Au	z31Mh*z31Au	z31Mh*z31Au
SPAIN	none	y16Je/z2Oc	y16Ap/z1Oc	y15Ap/z7Oc	y13Ap/cont.
SWITZERLAND	none until...				2No/date?
TURKEY	none until TWO periods in 1940; z30Je/z5Oc AND z30No/cont.				
URUGUAY	z31Oc/z26Mh	z3Oc/z25Mh	z28Oc/z24Mh*	z28Oc/z29Mh	z26Oc/z28Mh

Country	1941	1942	1943	1944	1945
ARGENTINE	z30Je40/z14Je	z14Oc41/z31JL43	z14Oc/cont.	cont./cont.	to z28Fe46
AUSTRALIA	1942: b1Ja/b29Mh 42 AND b27Se/b28Mh 43: 1943 exc. W.A.				b3Oc/b26Mh
BELGIUM	German zone and summer time until....			b3Ap//c17Se	b2Ap//c16Se
BELIZE	z4Oc/z8Fe	z3Oc/z14Fe	z2Oc/z13Fe	z10Oc/z11Fe	z7Oc/z10Fe
BULGARIA	no summer time: temporary new zone (+1h only) 4Ap43/3Ap44				
CZECHOSLOV.	none	none	b29Mh/b4Oc	b3Ap/b2Oc	b2Ap/b1Oc
DENMARK	as Germany except....				
FALKL.ISL.	z27Se/z20Mh?	apparently none after 1941...			
FRANCE	b25Fe//x5Oc	y8Mh//a2No	a29Mh//b4Oc	a3Ap//y7Oc	
GERMANY	b25Fe?/b5Oc?	cont./a2No	b29Mh/b4Oc	a3Au/y7Oc	
GHANA	z31Au/z31De	z31Au/z31De	z31Au/z31De	z31Au/z31De	z31Au/z31De
GREECE	25Ap/date? (zone +1H only? Fe42-29Mh43 4Oc43-3Ap44, 2Oc-31Oc44)				
HONDURAS,Rep.	apparently every year (?),-?Oc ‡ about middle of Fe.				
HUNGARY	7Ap/2No	29Mh/4Oc	3Ap/4Oc	3Ap/2No	y1My/y1No
ICELAND	2Fe/24Oc?	8Mh/25Oc	7Mh/23Oc	5Mh/22Oc	4Mh/22Oc
ITALY	cont./cont.	cont./b2No	z29Mh/b4Oc	z1Ap/z16Se	z31Mh/z15Se
	(but in 1943, Brit. and allied-occupied areas....				z29Mh/z26Se
NETHERLS	cont./cont.	cont./b2No	b29Mh/b7Oc	b3Ap/b4Oc	b3Ap/c16Se
N.ZEALAND	b28Se‡b26Ap	b27Se‡b25Ap	b26Se‡b30Ap	b24Se‡b29Ap	(new zone T)
N'FOUNDL	z11My/z1No	z1My/cont.	z30My/z25Se	z10Jy/z2Se	cont./z7Oc
NORWAY	cont./cont.	cont./x1No	b29Mh/b4Oc	b3Ap/b2Oc	z1Ap/c1Oc
PALESTINE	cont./date!	date!/date!	date!/date!	date!/date!	date!/date!
POLAND	cont./cont.	cont./b2No	b29Mh/b4Oc	b3Ap/z31No	z28Ap/z31Oc
PORTUGAL	y6Ap/z5Oc	y14Mh/z25Oc	y13Mh/z31Oc	y11Mh/z29Oc	y10Mh/z28Oc
SIERRA LEONE	z31Mh*z31De	z31Mh*z31De	z31Mh*z31De	z31Mh*z31De	z31Mh*z31De
SPAIN	cont.//cont.	y2My//z15Se	y17Ap//a1Oc	y15Ap//a1Oc	y14Ap//a30Se
SWITZERLAND	z4My/z5Oc	z3My/z4Oc	none	none	none
TURKEY	cont./z20Se	z31Mh/cont.	cont./date!	date!/date!	date!/date!
URUGUAY	24Oc‡27Mh	14De‡13Ap43	13Ap‡cont.	cont.‡cont.	cont.‡15Mh46

Country	1946	1947	1948	1949	1950
ARGENTINE	z30Se/cont.	cont./cont.	cont./cont.	cont./cont.	cont./cont.
BELGIUM	b19My//c7Oc	cont./cont.	cont./cont.	cont./cont.	cont./cont.
BELIZE	z6Oc/z9Fe	z5Oc/z8Fe	z3Oc/z14Fe	z2Oc/z12Fe	z1Oc/z11Fe
BRAZIL	none	none	none	z30No/z30Ap	z30No/z31Mh
CHILE	y25Se/y21My	none after 21My47	none	none	none
CZECHOSLOV.	z6My/(8Oc)?	z19Ap/z4Oc	z17Ap/z2Oc	z9Ap/z1Oc	none
	(Note: 1946. clocks 1 hour SLOW on standard time				1De-26Fe)
DENMARK	z30Ap/z31Au	z3Ap/z9Au	z7My/z7Au	z9Ap/z1Oc	none
FRANCE	cont./cont.	cont./cont.	cont./cont.	cont./cont.	none
GERMANY	b14Ap/b7Oc	b6Ap/b5Oc	b18Ap/b31Oc	b10Ap/b1Oc	none
		and in 1947. b11My//b29Je			
GHANA	z31Au*z31De	z31Au*z31De	z31Au*z31De	z31Au*z31De	z31Au*z31De
HONDURAS,Rep.	every year (!),-Oc/about middle of Fe.				
HUNGARY	z31Mh/z6Oc	25Ap/24Oc	23Ap/3Oc	29Ap/2Oc	none
ICELAND	z3Mh/z27Oc	z5Ap/z26Oc	z3Ap/z23Oc	z2Ap/z30Oc	z1Ap/z22Oc
ISRAEL	(Palestine 1946-1947(!)		none	27Ap/31Oc	15Au/14Se
MEXICO	(Mexico - CITY ONLY) none till 1950:				14Mh/-1Mh51
N'FOUNDL	z5My/z10Oc	z4My/z5Oc	z9My/z3Oc	z1My/z2Oc	z30Ap/z24Se
POLAND	z13Ap/z6Se	z3My/z4Oc	z17Ap/z2Oc	z9Ap/z1Oc	none
PORTUGAL	y6Ap/z5Oc	y5Ap/z4Oc	b4Ap/c3Oc	b3Ap/c2Oc	none
SIERRA LEONE	z31Mh*z31Au	z31Mh*z31Au	z31Mh*z31Au	z31Mh*z31Au	z31Mh*z31Au
SPAIN	y13Ap//a29Se	cont./cont.	cont./cont.	y23Ap//a1Oc	cont./cont.
TURKEY	z1Je/z30Se	z19Ap/z4Oc	z17Ap/z2Oc	z9Ap/z1Oc	z21Ap/z7Oc
URUGUAY	cont.‡cont.	cont.‡cont.	cont.‡cont.	cont.‡cont.	cont.‡cont.

Country	1951	1952	1953	1954	1955
ARGENTINE	cont./cont.	cont./cont.	cont./cont.	cont./cont.	cont./cont.
BELGIUM	cont./cont.	cont./cont.	cont./cont.	cont./cont.	cont./cont.
BELIZE	z7Oc/z10Fe	z5Oc/z15Fe	z4Oc/z14Fe	b3Oc/z12Fe	z5Oc/z11Fe
BRAZIL	z30No/z3Mh	z1De/z1Mh	none	none	none
FRANCE	cont./cont.	cont./cont.	cont./cont.	cont./cont.	cont./cont.
GHANA	z31Au/z31De	z1Se/1Ja	z1Se/1Ja	z1Se/1Ja	z1Se/1Ja
GREECE	none	1Jl/31Oc	none	none	none
ICELAND	1Ap/28Oc	6Ap/26Oc	5Ap/25Oc	4Ap/24Oc	3Ap/23Oc
ISRAEL	31Mh/10No	19Ap/18Oc	12Ap/12Se	12Je/12Se	11Je/10Se
N'FOUNDL	z30Ap/z24Se	z27Ap/z28Se	z26Ap/z27Se	z25Ap/z26Se	z24Ap/z25Se
PORTUGAL	b1Ap/c7Oc	b6Ap/c5Oc	b5Ap/c25Oc	4Ap/3Oc	3Ap/2Oc
SIERRA LEONE	z31Mh≠z31De	none	none	none	none
SPAIN	cont./cont.	cont./cont.	cont./cont.	cont./cont.	cont./cont.
TURKEY	z21Ap/z6Oc	none	none	none	none
URUGUAY	cont.≠cont.	cont.≠cont.	cont.≠cont.	cont.≠cont.	cont.≠cont.

Country	1956	1957	1958	1959	1960
ARGENTINE	cont./cont.	cont./cont.	cont./cont.	cont./cont.	cont./cont.
BELIZE	6Oc/9Fe	5Oc/8Fe	4Oc/14Fe	3Oc/13Fe	2Oc/11Fe
EGYPT	none	30Ap/1Oc	30Ap/30Se	30Ap/30Se	30Ap/1Oc
ICELAND	1Ap/28Oc	7Ap/1Oc	30Ap/26Oc	5Ap/25Oc	3Ap/23Oc
ISRAEL	2Je/29Se	27Ap/21Se	none	none	none
N'FOUNDL	29Ap/30Se	29Ap/29Se	28Ap/28Se	26Ap/27Se	24Ap/30Oc
PORTUGAL	1Ap/7Oc	7Ap/10Oc	6Ap/5Oc	5Ap/4Oc	3Ap/2Oc
URUGUAY	cont.≠cont.	cont.≠cont.	cont.≠cont.	cont.≠z24My	z14No59/z16Ja

Country	1961	1962	1963	1964	1965
ARGENTINE	cont./cont.	cont./cont.	cont/z30Se	z14De63/z29Fe	z14Oc64/z28Fe
BELIZE	7Oc61/10Fe	6Oc62/9Fe	5Oc63/8Fe	3Oc64/13Fe	3Oc65/12Fe
BRAZIL	none	none	23Oc63/1Mh	none	31Ja/31Mh
CANADA) N'FOUNDL) NEW YORK)	30Ap/29Oc	29Ap/28Oc	28Ap/27Oc	26Ap/25Oc	25Ap/31Oc
CUBA	none	none	1Je/1Oc	31My/1Oc	23My/3Oc
EGYPT	30Ap/30Se	30Ap/30Se	30Ap/30Se	30Ap/30Se	30Ap/1Oc
ICELAND	2Ap/22Oc	1Ap/28Oc	7Ap/27Oc	5Ap/25Oc	4Ap/24Oc
PORTUGAL	2Ap/1Oc	1Ap/7Oc	7Ap/6Oc	5Ap/4Oc	4Ap/3Oc
TURKEY	none	15Jl/cont.	cont./29Oc	15My/1Oc	none
URUGUAY	none	none	none	none	3Ap/25Se

Country	1966	1967	1968	1969	1970
ARGENTINE	z14Oc65/z28Fe	z14Oc66/z1Ap	z30Se69/z6Ap	z5Oc68/z5Ap	None
BELGIUM	none	none	none	none	none
BELIZE	1Oc66/11Fe	Oc67/Fe68	Oc68/Fe69	Oc69/Fe70	Oc70/Fe71
BRAZIL	1De65/Fe67	No67/Mh68	none	none	none
CANADA	Ap/Oc	Ap/Oc	Ap/Oc	Ap/Oc	Ap/Oc
CUBA	7My/4Se	Ap/Oc	Ap68/...		.../Se70
EGYPT	1My/1Oc	My/Oc	My/Oc	My/Oc	My/Oc
ICELAND	Ap/Oc	Ap/Oc	Ap? Standard Time changed to G.M.T.		
ITALY	21My/25Se	My/Se	My/Se	June/Se	June/Se
PORTUGAL	Ap/Permanent Summer Time throughout Year 1 hour				
URUGUAY	none	?/De	?/?		Ap 1 ?
USA	Each Year	Last sunday in April/Last Sunday in Oct. (1 Hour)			

NOTES

NOTES

NOTES